This book offers a valuable focus on the role of ordinary African people as agents and architects of meaning in their interface with the global economy, rather than adopting the conventional perspective on Africans as victims, lumpen elements or criminals. This allows a consideration of the positive potential of African engagement with the global economy, and reflects on the creative tensions that emerge from the struggles of creating livelihoods on the margins.

**Kate Meagher, Lecturer in Development Studies,
London School of Economics, UK**

This wide-ranging and stimulating collection is a wonderful tribute to the work of Jane Guyer – one of the most original and provocative thinkers in African studies and economic anthropology of the last half century. Building on the theme of the 'political economy of everyday life' the contributors engage us with questions of livelihood and life, economic values and transactions, and processes of social composition and recomposition. In doing so, they highlight some of the important ways in which 'everyday life' on the continent has challenged the wider scholarly community to rethink orthodoxies and think more creatively across disciplinary divides.

**Megan Vaughan, Professor of African History and Health,
University College, London, UK**

It is no easy task to decide quite how to pay tribute to the wide-ranging fertility and suggestibility of Jane Guyer's writings as an anthropologist about African political economy. Adebanwi and the contributors have responded to the challenge in the most appropriate of ways, by offering a set of essays, addressing her most fundamental concerns, that look themselves set to be future classics. The contributors demonstrate how people at the margins keep on keeping on, not just through fortitude, though there is plenty of that, but by trusting their imagination and creativity to forge the connections in life that at least get them by and at best bring them success.

**Richard Fardon, Professor of West African Anthropology,
School of Oriental and African Studies, London, UK**

The Political Economy of Everyday Life in Africa

Beyond the Margins

Edited by
Wale Adebanwi

Foreword by James Ferguson

JAMES CURREY

James Currey
an imprint of
Boydell & Brewer Ltd
PO Box 9, Woodbridge
Suffolk IP12 3DF (GB)
www.jamescurrey.com

and of

Boydell & Brewer Inc.
668 Mt Hope Avenue
Rochester, NY 14620-2731 (US)
www.boydellandbrewer.com

First published in 2017
© Contributors 2017

All Rights Reserved. Except as permitted under current legislation no part of this work may be photocopied, stored in a retrieval system, published, performed in public, adapted, broadcast, transmitted, recorded or reproduced in any form or by any means, without the prior permission of the copyright owner.

The publisher has no responsibility for the continued existence or accuracy of URLs for external or third-party internet websites referred to in this book, and does not guarantee that any content on such websites is, or will remain, accurate or appropriate.

British Library Cataloguing in Publication Data
available on request

ISBN 978-1-84701-165-7 James Currey (Cloth)
ISBN 978-1-84701-166-4 (James Currey Africa only paperback)

This publication is printed on acid-free paper

Typeset in 10 on 12pt Photina MT
by Avocet Typeset, Somerton, Somerset TA11 6RT

Printed and bound in Great Britain by
TJ International Ltd, Padstow, Cornwall

For Jane I. Guyer

Contents

Maps, Illustrations & Tables ... ix
Notes on Contributors ... x
Foreword by James Ferguson ... xvii
Acknowledgements ... xix

Approaching the Political Economy of Everyday Life
An Introduction
Wale Adebanwi ... 1

Part I — MONEY MATTERS: CURRENCY & FISCAL LIFE STRUGGLES ... 33

1 Cattle, Currencies & the Politics of Commensuration on a Colonial Frontier
Jean & John L. Comaroff ... 35

2 Currency & Conflict in Colonial Nigeria
David Pratten ... 72

3 Coercion or Trade? Multiple Self-realization during the Rubber Boom in German Kamerun (1899–1913)
Peter Geschiere & Tristan Oestermann ... 92

4 The Macroeconomics of Marginal Gains
Africa's Lessons to Social Theorists
Célestin Monga ... 115

Part II — LABOUR, SOCIAL LIVES & PRECARITY ... 133

5 From Enslavement to Precarity? The Labour Question in African History
Frederick Cooper ... 135

6 Navigating Formality in a Migrant Labour Force
Maxim Bolt ... 157

Part III — MARGINALITY, DISAFFECTION & BIO-ECONOMIC DISTRESS — 177

7 Precarious Life
Violence & Poverty under Boko Haram & MEND
Michael J. Watts — 179

8 The Debt Imperium
Relations of Owing after Apartheid
Anne-Maria Makhulu — 216

9 Marginal Men & Urban Social Conflicts
Okada *Riders in Lagos*
Gbemisola Animasawun — 239

10 Sopona, Social Relations & the Political Economy of Colonial Smallpox Control in Ekiti, Nigeria
Elisha P. Renne — 266

Part IV — HISTORICITY, TEMPORALITY, AGENCY & DEMOCRATIC LIFE — 285

11 History as Value Added? Valuing the Past in Africa
Sara Berry — 287

12 Cultural Mediation, Colonialism & Politics
Colonial 'Truchement', Postcolonial Translator
Souleymane Bachir Diagne — 308

13 *'Kos'ona Miran?'* Patronage, Prebendalism & Democratic Life in Contemporary Nigeria
Adigun Agbaje — 318

AFTERWORD

The Landscapes Beyond the Margins
Agency, Optimization & the Power of the Empirical
Jane I. Guyer — 335

Index — 353

Maps, Illustrations & Tables

Maps
1.1 Map of South Africa in the early nineteenth century   37
10.1 Map of Ekiti, 1952   272

Illustrations
1.1 Examples of Griqua Town coins   57
1.2 Cattle being herded in Mochudi   64
2.1 Line drawing of Manilla currency   87
6.1 The Grootplaas packshed and office   159
6.2 New arrivals at Grootplaas struggle to get their identity cards and papers into the hands of a senior worker   168
7.1 Mothers of some of the 276 girls adopted by Boko Haram participating in the #BringBackOurGirls campaign   183
7.2 Movement for the Emancipation of the Niger Delta (MEND) militants on a canoe   185
7.3 Conflict events and reported fatalities, Nigeria, 1997 – March 2013   186
8.1 Women participating in South Africa's SaveAct initiative   217
8.2 Participants in SaveAct's programme, which 'facilitates the formation of savings and credit groups in rural communities as a simple but effective tool to fight poverty'   217
8.3 Men seeking loans wait for a money lender   223
9.1 A crowd of *okada* riders in Lagos   241
9.2 'Mass transit': *okada* rider with seven passengers   245
9.3 Joint Action Front (JAF) in the forefront of the protests in support of the *okada* riders   257
9.4 Several *okada* riders accompanying Governor Fashola during his re-election campaign in 2007   259
10.1 Chief G.O. Kupolati (in white), with companions, in his traditional medicine shop, Iye-Ekiti   275
10.2 'SMALLPOX made me BLIND', poster by Ernest Hough   278

Tables
2.1 Manilla exchange rate and palm oil price, 1900–1948   78
2.2 Index of manilla exchange rates and palm oil prices, 1931–1947   81
2.3 Motives of the 'man-leopard murders', 1947   85
4.1 The search for a theoretical strategy   125

Notes on Contributors

Wale Adebanwi is the Rhodes Professor of Race Relations, African Studies Centre, School of Interdisciplinary Area Studies, Oxford University. He was until recently a Professor in the Department of African American and African Studies, University of California, Davis, USA. He was educated at the University of Ibadan, Nigeria and the University of Cambridge, UK, where he earned doctorates in political science and social anthropology, respectively. A visiting Professor at Rhodes University, Grahamstown, South Africa, Adebanwi is the author of *Nation as Grand Narrative: The Nigerian Press and the Politics of Meaning* (University of Rochester Press, 2016); *Yoruba Elites and Ethnic Politics in Nigeria: Obafemi Awolowo and Corporate Agency* (Cambridge University Press, 2014) and *Authority Stealing: Anti-corruption War and Democratic Politics in Post-military Nigeria* (Carolina Academic Press, 2012). He has edited or co-edited six books on democracy, democratization, politics, the state and public intellectuals.

Adigun Agbaje is a Professor of Political Science at the University of Ibadan where he was for a few years the Dean, Faculty of Social Sciences and later, Deputy Vice Chancellor. He is the author of *The Nigerian Press; Hegemony and the Social Construction of Legitimacy, 1960–1983* (1992) and co-editor of *African Traditional Political Thought and Institutions* (1989); *Federalism and Political Restructuring in Nigeria* (1998); *Nigeria: Politics of Transition and Governance* (1999); *Money Struggles and City Life: Devaluation in Ibadan and Other Urban Centers in Southern Nigeria, 1986–1996* (2002); and *Nigeria's Struggle for Democracy and Good Governance* (2004). His articles have appeared in leading peer-reviewed journals such as *The Journal of Commonwealth and Comparative Studies; African Affairs; Journal of Modern African Studies and Media; Culture and Society*. Agbaje was Director, Centre for Social Science Research and Development, Lagos, Nigeria, and the first Director-General, Obafemi Awolowo Institute of Government and Public Policy (OAIPP), Lekki, Lagos, Nigeria.

Gbemisola Animasawun, a 2014 post-doctoral grantee of the Social Science Research Council (SSRC) African Peace-Building Network (APN), teaches at the Centre for Peace & Strategic Studies University of Ilorin. He has published in peer-reviewed journals such as the *African Security Review*, and *Canadian Journal of Peace and Conflict Studies* and contributed chapters and entries to edited books and encyclopaedia. His research interests include

Notes on Contributors

peace processes; autochthony and fault-line conflicts; human security; neo-patrimonialism; inter-faith relations and radical Islamism.

Sara Berry recently retired as Professor of History at Johns Hopkins University, Baltimore, USA. She has researched land, development, agrarian change and socio-economic history in sub-Saharan Africa, with primary emphasis on Ghana and Nigeria. Her publications include *No Condition is Permanent: The Social Dynamics of Agrarian Change in Sub-Saharan Africa* (1993); *Chiefs Know their Boundaries: Essays on Property, Power and the Past in Asante, 1896–1996* (2001); and 'Property, authority and citizenship: Land claims, politics and the dynamics of social division in West Africa', *Development and Change*, 40 (1): 23–45 (2009).

Maxim Bolt is a Reader in Anthropology and African Studies in the Department of African Studies and Anthropology, University of Birmingham, and Research Associate at the Wits Institute of Social and Economic Research (WISER), University of the Witwatersrand. His first monograph, *Zimbabwe's Migrants and South Africa's Border Farms: The Roots of Impermanence*, was published in 2015 by Cambridge University Press. Bolt is an anthropologist of Southern Africa specializing in labour, migration, borders, development, the social dynamics of money and – most recently will-making and inheritance. He is currently an editor of the *Journal of Southern African Studies*.

Jean Comaroff, Alfred North Whitehead Professor of African and African American Studies and of Anthropology, and Oppenheimer Fellow in African Studies at Harvard University, was educated at the University of Cape Town and the London School of Economics. After a spell as research fellow in Medical Anthropology at the University of Manchester, she moved to the University of Chicago, where she remained until 2012 as the Bernard E. and Ellen C. Sunny Distinguished Service Professor of Anthropology, and Director of the Chicago Center for Contemporary Theory. She is also Honorary Professor at the University of Cape Town. Her writing has covered a range of topics, from religion, medicine and body politics to state formation, crime, democracy and difference. Her publications include *Body of Power, Spirit of Resistance: The Culture and History of a South African People* (1985); 'Beyond the Politics of Bare Life: AIDS and the Global Order' (2007); and, with John L. Comaroff, *Of Revelation and Revolution*, vols. I (1991) and II (1997); *Ethnography and the Historical Imagination* (1992); *Millennial Capitalism and the Culture of Neoliberalism* (2000); *Law and Disorder in the Postcolony* (2006); *Ethnicity, Inc.* (2009); and *Theory from the South, or How Euro-America is Evolving Toward Africa* (2011).

John L. Comaroff is Hugh K. Foster Professor of African and African American Studies and Anthropology and Oppenheimer Research Scholar at Harvard University. Before joining the Department of African and African American Studies, John Comaroff was the Harold H. Swift Distinguished

Professor of Anthropology at the University of Chicago, Honorary Professor of Anthropology at the University of Cape Town and Research Professor at the American Bar Foundation. His current research in South Africa is on crime, policing and the workings of the state, on democracy and difference, and on postcolonial politics. His authored and edited books include, with Jean Comaroff, *Of Revelation and Revolution* (2 vols); *Ethnography and the Historical Imagination*; *Modernity and its Malcontents*; *Civil Society and the Political Imagination in Africa*; *Millennial Capitalism and the Culture of Neoliberalism*; *Law and Disorder in the Postcolony*; *Ethnicity, Inc.*; *Zombies et Frontières à l'Ère Néolibérale* and *Theory from the South: Or, how Euro-America is evolving toward Africa*.

Frederick Cooper is Professor of History at New York University and a specialist in the history of Africa, empires and decolonization. He is the author most recently of *Colonialism in Question: Theory, Knowledge, History* (California, 2005); *Empires in World History: Power and the Politics of Difference* (with Jane Burbank, Princeton, 2010); *Citizenship between Empire and Nation: Remaking France and French Africa, 1945–1960* (Princeton, 2014); and *Africa in the World: Capitalism, Empire, Nation-State* (Harvard, 2014).

Souleymane Bachir Diagne, a Professor at Columbia University in the departments of French and Philosophy, holds an *agrégation* in Philosophy and a PhD from the Sorbonne in the same discipline. An alumnus of École Normale Supérieure, he studied with Althusser and Derrida. His areas of research and publication include History of Philosophy, History of Logic and Mathematics, Islamic Philosophy, African Philosophy and Francophone Literature. His latest publications are *Islam and the open society: Fidelity and movement in Muhammad Iqbal's thought* (Codesria, 2010); *African Art as philosophy: Senghor, Bergson, and the idea of Negritude* (Seagull, 2011); *Bergson postcolonial: L'élan vital dans la pensée de L.S. Senghor et de Mohamed Iqbal* (CNRS Editions, 2011); *Comment philosopher en Islam?* (Philippe Rey, 2013); *L'encre des savants: Réflexions sur la philosophie en Afrique* (Présence africaine, 2013).

James Ferguson is the Susan S. and William H. Hindle Professor in the School of Humanities and Sciences, and Professor in the Department of Anthropology at Stanford University, USA. He previously taught for many years at the University of California, Irvine. His major publications include *The Anti-politics Machine: 'Development', Depoliticization, and Bureaucratic Power in Lesotho* (Cambridge University Press, 1990); *Expectations of Modernity: Myths and Meanings of Urban Life on the Zambian Copperbelt* (University of California Press, 1999); *Global Shadows: Africa in the Neoliberal World Order* (Duke University Press, 2006); and *Give a Man a Fish: Reflections on the New Politics of Distribution* (Duke University Press, 2015).

Peter Geschiere is Professor of African Anthropology at the University of Amsterdam and co-editor of *Ethnography* (Sage). Since 1971 he undertook historical–anthropological fieldwork in various parts of Cameroon and else-

Notes on Contributors

where in West Africa. His publications include *The Modernity of Witchcraft: Politics and the Occult in Post-colonial Africa* (University of Virginia Press, 1997); *Perils of Belonging: Autochthony, Citizenship and Exclusion in Africa and Europe* (University of Chicago Press, 2009); and *Witchcraft, Intimacy and Trust: Africa in Comparison* (University of Chicago Press, 2013).

Jane I. Guyer is a Professor Emerita at The Johns Hopkins University, Baltimore, USA. Before she retired, she was the George Armstrong Kelly Professor in the Department of Anthropology at Johns Hopkins. She had served previously on the faculties of Harvard, Boston and Northwestern Universities. Her research career has been devoted to economic transformations in West Africa, particularly the productive economy, the division of labour and the management of money. Theoretically she focuses on the interface between formal and informal economies, and particularly the instabilities to which that interface gives rise. She is the author and editor of numerous books including *Family and Farm in Southern Africa* (1984); *Feeding African Cities: Essays in Regional Social History* (1987); *An African Niche Economy* (1997); *Money Matters: Instability, Values and Social Payments in the Modern History of West African Communities* (1995); *Marginal Gains: Monetary Transactions in Atlantic Africa* (2004); *Money Struggles and City Life: Devaluation in Ibadan and Other Urban Centres in Southern Nigeria, 1986–1996* (2002, co-edited with LaRay Denzer and Adigun Agbaje); *Marginal Gains: Monetary Transactions in Atlantic Africa* (2004); and *Legacies, Logics, Logistics: Essays in the Anthropology of the Platform Economy* (2016). In 2008 she was elected to the National Academy of Sciences (Anthropology Section).

Anne-Maria Makhulu is an Associate Professor of Cultural Anthropology and African and African American Studies at Duke University, Durham, USA. Her research interests cover: Africa and more specifically South Africa, cities, space, globalization, political economy, neoliberalism, the anthropology of finance, as well as questions of aesthetics, including the literature of South Africa. Makhulu is co-editor of *Hard Work, Hard Times: Global Volatility and African Subjectivities* (2010). She is a contributor to *Producing African Futures: Ritual and Reproduction in a Neoliberal Age* (2004); *New Ethnographies of Neoliberalism* (2010); and the author of *Making Freedom: Apartheid, Squatter Politics and the Struggle for Home* (2015) as well as articles in *Anthropological Quarterly* and *PMLA*. A new project, 'Black and Bourgeois: Defining Race and Class After Apartheid', examines the relationship between race and mobility in post-apartheid South Africa.

Célestin Monga is Vice President and Chief Economist of the African Development Bank (AfDB), based in Abidjan (Côte d'Ivoire). Before he joined AfDB, be was with the United Nations Industrial Development Organization (UNIDO) as the Managing Director of the Programme Support and General Management Division. He has wide-ranging experience as an economist, author, academic and scholar. Monga was the economics editor for the widely-acclaimed five-volume *New Encyclopedia of Africa* (Charles Scribner, 2007) and director of the two-volume *Oxford Handbook of Africa and Economics* (2015). He has also co-authored academic articles and policy reports with many of the world's leading economists, including Ernest Aryeetey, Robert Barro, Olivier Blanchard, Justin Yifu Lin, Robert Solow, Joseph Stiglitz and the late John Kenneth Galbraith. Monga has also written several books on the challenges of African modernity, translated into several languages. Before joining UNIDO, Monga was Senior Advisor for Structural Economic Transformation at the World Bank. He has also held various board and senior positions in academia, financial services and international development, including as a pro-bono member of the advisory boards of the Sloan Fellows Program at the Massachusetts Institute of Technology's (MIT)'s Sloan School of Management, the Quantum Global Group and the Official Monetary and Financial Institutions Forum (OMFIF). He taught economics at Boston University and the University of Bordeaux. Monga holds graduate degrees from MIT's Sloan School of Management, the Universities of Paris 1, Panthéon Sorbonne, Bordeaux and Pau (France).

Tristan Oestermann is a PhD student in history at Humboldt Universität, Berlin, Germany. His research interests focus on the history of colonial and postcolonial African-European interaction in Central and West Africa, featuring e.g. resource exploitation, development aid or humanitarian interventions. He currently is working on a PhD thesis about the relation between labour and violence in the rubber trade of colonial Cameroon during the German period, combining cultural, economic and environmental history.

David Pratten is an Associate Professor at the African Studies Centre and Institute of Social and Cultural Anthropology, Oxford University, UK. He is author of *The Man-Leopard Murders: History and Society in Colonial Nigeria* (2007). Until recently, he co-edited *AFRICA: The Journal of the International African Institute*. His research focuses on youth, vigilantism and masking.

Elisha P. Renne is a Professor in the Department of Anthropology and the Department of Afroamerican and African Studies, University of Michigan, Ann Arbor, USA. Her ongoing research includes a study of the historical, cultural and political context of the polio eradication initiative in northern Nigeria, discussed in her book, *The Politics of Polio in Northern Nigeria* (2010), and in articles published in *Social Science & Medicine* (2006); Post-Polio *International* (2008); and *History Compass* (2012).

Michael J. Watts is Class of 1963 Professor of Geography, and Director of Development Studies at the University of California, Berkeley where he has taught for 30 years. He served as the Director of the Institute of International Studies at Berkeley from 1994–2004. His research has addressed a number of development issues especially food security, resource development and land reform in Africa, South Asia and Vietnam. Over the last 20 years he has

Notes on Contributors

written extensively on the oil industry, especially in Nigeria and the Gulf of Guinea; his most recent book is *The Curse of the Black Gold: Fifty Years of Oil in the Niger Delta* with photographer Ed Kashi (2008). Watts was a Guggenheim fellow in 2003 and was awarded the Victoria Medal by the Royal Geographical Society in 2004. He has consulted for a number of development organizations including the United Nations and has provided expert testimony for governmental and other agencies. He was educated at University College London and the University of Michigan and has held visiting appointments at the Smithsonian Institution and the Universities of Bergen, Bologna and London. He serves on the Board of Advisors of a number of non-profits including Food First and the Pacific Institute (both UK) and is Chair of the Board of Trustees of the Social Science Research Council (USA).

Foreword by James Ferguson

This volume presents an exciting collection of recent scholarship addressing some of the most important and intellectually consequential issues in contemporary African studies. It is inspired by, and achieves its thematic coherence in relation to, the extraordinarily profound and extensive contributions to that field by Jane I. Guyer over the last four decades. Guyer's insights have extended widely across a range of foundational issues in African studies, but they have largely clustered around a set of themes and questions that animate the contributions to this volume. These include gender and household economy; wealth, knowledge and personhood; currencies, money and value; labour and informality; and the intersections of debt, social obligation and temporality. One way of characterizing this volume, then, would be to say that it is a collection of outstanding recent contributions to scholarship that are united by their focus on a set of linked topics associated with Guyer's most important work.

To put matters this way would be accurate enough, but I do not feel that it would really get at the real core either of this volume or of Jane Guyer's scholarly contributions over the years. Instead, it seems to me that it is perhaps less a unity of topical focus than a shared intellectual sensibility that is the real common thread here. Central to this sensibility is what I regard as an extremely valuable, and perhaps not always fully appreciated, approach to the relation of the theoretical and the empirical. While we have long ago learned to mistrust the old separation of empirical descriptions from the theories that would account for them, there are few scholars who have so completely worked through the full implications of treating empirical accounts as always-already theoretical. Guyer's most profound theoretical contributions have never involved 'applying' a theoretical framework to a body of 'raw' data; instead, they have always worked from a careful and imaginative interpretation of the mundane realities that lie right before our eyes. Engaging ordinary practices – of work, of trade, of coordinating and 'composing' social relationships – in all their concreteness, she has enabled us, again and again, to see how taken-for-granted analytical frames have misled us. Sometimes this has involved revealing the way that abstract accounts of systemic 'logics' blind us to the heterogeneities and differentials that in fact drive sophisticated regimes of practice, as in her now-classic account of monetary transactions in 'Atlantic Africa' (2004). At other times, it has involved exposing the way that what seem like the dullest of 'empirical facts' in fact embed unacknowledged theoretical premises – like all those surveys of African 'households' that beg the question of what a household is, and whether or not it makes sense to treat it as an economic atom (Guyer 1981). Here, the contributions to this volume follow Guyer's lead in conceiving the empirical in a richly theoretical way, recognizing that the most formidable challenges to our theoretical habits of mind are often found in those not-so-plain empirical realities that lie right in front of us.

One of the key reasons, I think, that Guyer has been able to see so deeply into the mundane doings of ordinary people is her profound appreciation that African societies have long been sites of enormous conceptual and social innovation, and that African social life has for centuries been, as she once put it, 'far more inventive from day to day than we can now easily imagine' (1996: 1). Indeed, what I think of as her own most-characteristic intellectual virtue (a questioning of the idea of social life as governed by seamless holistic systems, and a relentless insistence on the importance – indeed, the productivity – of the messy differences within, and frontiers between, 'systems') is one she herself credits to the Equatorial African societies that she has studied. These societies' 'traditions of invention' have long enabled their members to 'live a life on the edge,' making their way through the world not via a mechanical enactment of a social structure, but instead as 'a constant and volatile engagement on its boundless frontiers' (1996: 4,1).

Those who have tried, over the years, to follow some of the pathways that Jane Guyer's work has opened up (and here I speak of myself as well as the contributors to this volume) have found her distinctive intellectual sensibility both enabling and energizing. And perhaps this volume, with its extraordinary range of insightful and conceptually challenging contributions, is the most convincing sort of proof of that. Indeed, the quality and intellectual scope of recent Africanist work inspired by Guyer suggests that her approach is yielding, in the academic domain, something of the same sort of spur to innovation that she long ago described for Equatorial African practices of sociality and knowledge – what she termed 'the regular creation of effectivity and novelty' (1996: 2).

Palo Alto, California

References

Guyer, Jane I. (1981). 'Household and Community in African Studies'. *African Studies Review* 24(2): 87–137.
—. (1996). 'Traditions of Invention in Equatorial Africa'. *African Studies Review* 39(3): 1–28.
—. (2004). *Marginal Gains: Monetary Transactions in Atlantic Africa*. Chicago, IL: University of Chicago Press.

Acknowledgements

Beyond the necessary pain and temporary frustrations of the process of editing a volume is its sheer joy. Between the singular thrill of being the first to read and comment on one or another excellent contribution and the special pleasure of *studying* the intellectual landscape by bringing together diverse expertise in different areas of specialization – and in this case, also different disciplines – the delight of editing a volume can totally submerge the pain of the tortuous process. It has been so with this volume, which brings together some of the most accomplished scholars, some mid-career and other emerging scholars working and researching in and on Africa in various disciplines. It is particularly pleasurable to *survive* the arduous process of bringing together these fascinating analyses of the process of life in a continent in which, to use Judith Butler's phrase, millions are 'obdurately living'. The contributors to this volume *came together* to examine the political economy of everyday life in Africa using, as a departure point, the impressive oeuvre of a most distinguished Africanist (economic) anthropologist, Jane Isabel Guyer.

I am indebted to those who helped not only make to this happen, but also to lighten my burden. First, I am grateful to Jane Guyer. When I eventually informed her about this project, she encouraged me and later gave an inspiring response to the contributions. I am particularly gratified that this book represents four generations of Africanist scholars across three continents – Africa, Europe and North America. I thank all the contributors for their very engaging contributions and also for suffering through my 'harassments' with much equanimity and grace. My especial appreciation goes to Michael Watts, Sara Berry, Adigun Agbaje, Peter Geschiere, David Pratten and Moradewun Adejunmobi – the last, my colleague at UC Davis, for encouraging me in various ways to pursue this project.

The operators of the Starbucks coffee shops in Davis, California, particularly the one at West Covell Boulevard, deserve my gratitude for the countless hours I spent 'monopolizing' particular tables, usually the biggest, in their shops, as I fled from the 'distractions' of my office and other spots on campus. The workers in the newest Starbucks in the city on Mace Boulevard, where I spent the most time in the final stage of editing of this book, were remarkably pleasant. I hope I get more free drinks as I remain a faithful customer – except that I will now have to claim the drinks in Oxford, UK! Finally, I thank the anonymous reviewers and my editors at James Currey, Jaqueline Mitchell and Lynn Taylor and those who worked with them on this book.

Approaching the Political Economy of Everyday Life
An Introduction

Wale Adebanwi

It is widely agreed that the two social mechanisms available for the generation and distribution of well-being are markets and politics.
(Benjamin Radcliff 2001: 941)

Africa is often encountered as a continent in which all manners of extremities converge. Abundant natural resources coexist with extreme poverty;[1] excessive wealth and conspicuous consumption are exhibited in the context of widespread immiseration. In the global imagination, life in Africa is characterized by excess and abjection: the excess of natural wealth and the abjection of pervasive poverty. In recent decades, due to a myriad of economic crises, political instability and social paralysis, the extremities of wealth and poverty have produced a progressive eradication of the middle ground between human happiness and human misery. Thus, much of the scholarship on Africa tends 'toward a deterministically pessimistic view of development [in the continent] with the logic of neopatrimonialism unavoidably pushing the analysis towards ontological despair, hence its association with Afro-pessimism' (Mkandawire 2015a: 602). Against this backdrop, Africa is often presented in 'urgent and troubled tones' (Ferguson 2006: 2).

Jane I. Guyer (2014: 13–14) recently summarized the implication of the conclusion reached by global neoliberal institutions regarding the current metrics of economic growth thus: 'All the worst values of every indicator meet in Africa.' Africa is, therefore, a very good template for examining the political-economic dynamics, structures, agencies and processes that define and determine human wellbeing, that is, how or whether people are able to live and live well – including the questions of 'the vulnerability of human life and ... what makes for a livable life' (Butler and Athanasiou 2013: viii). Even though what we describe in this volume as the political economy of everyday life is not a culturally or regionally specific model, in practice, it is experienced in culturally or regionally specific ways.[2]

---

[1] In his strongly Marxian reading of this binary, the late Nigerian Marxist economist, Bade Onimode (1988: 3), describes the 'paradox of continental wealth and mass poverty' as 'cynical asymmetry'.
[2] Ghassan Hage (2004) makes this point regarding the capacity to 'die for' (something). I think it is true for his larger argument about the political economy of everyday life.

Given the fact that 'the "market principle" could never be understood shorn of its larger social and political history' (Guyer 1997a: 5), this volume examines how African economies and economic institutions, processes and practices – in relation to the political and the social in the longue durée – enhance or weaken the possibilities of human viability and expand or limit the 'vistas of human possibility' (Guyer 2002a), that is, the capacity to live a good life. The capacity for a liveable life implies that such capacity can be enhanced and expanded or weakened and destroyed. This is especially true in a continent where, to use Lauren Berlant's (2007: 754) fitting words, 'life building and the attrition of human life are indistinguishable'. Therefore, the conditions determining the process of letting live or letting die are already implicated, or in fact, imbricated, in the process of examining the capacity to live – including the living of a good life. In a continent that is ignored or dismissed – as 'the hopeless continent', as *The Economist*[3] regrettably concluded at the start of the twenty-first century – because of what Manuel Castells (1996: 134–6) describes as its 'structural irrelevance', how do we capture the 'practice of everyday life' (de Certeau 1984) and the political economy of that practice that 'encompasses systems of employments, provisioning, and meaning making of impressive magnitude and relentless resilience' (Guyer 2002a: ix)? If indeed, 'the systematic logic of the new global economy does not have much of a role for the majority of the African population', as Castells (1996: 135) concluded, how do those who constitute this population react to, subvert – or, even invert – this 'systematic logic', rendering it logical in some instances, and illogical in others? How have they made sense of the global economy and participated in it in the context of both the logic internal to the ('global') system and their own locally- and historically-developed logics? How do we 'offer intellectual and political traction on the state-people-economy relationship[s]' (Guyer 2016: 67–8) that is useful even if at first it might seem unintelligible within formal economic theories and structures, particularly in a continent with a huge informal sector that is 'recalcitrant to regulation and taxation' (ibid.: 68)? In all, how do we understand 'the different modalities through which power has been implemented in economic life'? (Guyer 2004a: 12)

These are the kind of questions that form the bases of the intellectual exploration of the subject of everyday life in modern Africa to which this volume addresses itself.

There have been many scholarly endeavours in the last four decades that bring together various perspectives and experiences in different countries – within one volume or in one significant article – on the larger or macro issues

---

[3] *The Economist* cover story, 11 May 2000. The magazine concluded that the 'new millennium has brought more disaster than hope to Africa. Worse, the few candles of hope are flickering weakly'. However, apologizing for this apocalyptic prognosis 11 years later, *The Economist* (3 December 2011) sang a different tune, announcing on its cover: 'Africa rising', and stating: 'Since *The Economist* regrettably labelled Africa "the hopeless continent" a decade ago, a profound change has taken hold ... The politics of the continent's Mediterranean shore may have dominated headlines this year, but the new boom south of the Sahara will affect more lives.' In another cover story ('Aspiring Africa') and special report, *The Economist* (22 March 2013) declares Africa 'A Hopeful Continent', commenting that 'African lives have already greatly improved over the past decade' and that 'the next ten years will be even better'.

of the political economy in Africa (see, Ake 1976; Cohen and Daniel 1996; Bates 1983; Shaw 1985; Onimode 1988; Hope 1997; Ndulu et al. 2008a, 2008b; Padayachee 2010; Mkandawire 2015b). There are also some interesting recent works that focus on everyday life in the context of governance, development and public services (Bierschenk and Olivier de Sardan 2014; De Herdt and Olivier de Sardan 2015). The recent examination of everyday life in Africa builds on the earlier anthropological literature that uses the perspective of the everyday life typified by Ronald Cohen's 'Everyday Life in Africa' in which he concludes rather simplistically that '(g)iven the basically non-industrial background of African societies, the nature of everyday life on that continent is such that it binds an individual into the network of his social relationships so that these predominate over other possible sources of felt responsibility' (Cohen 1961/62: 34). No doubt, anthropological scholarship of everydayness in Africa has become far more nuanced and more informed since Cohen published his article. This book uses the political economy perspective – focusing on the micro level in relation to the macro level – to examine everyday life in Africa, not only from the disciplinary traditions of anthropology, but also from the traditions of history, political science, economics, geography, philosophy and literature. We examine everyday life in modern Africa within the context of the popular economy in the areas of, or in relation to, labour (local, transnational and migrant), trade, debt, currency, natural resources, religion, urban life, health, history, language and democratic life.

Political Economy & Everydayness

In two of his published courses, Michel Foucault (2007, 2008) reflects on the relations between political economy, bio-politics, 'market' and 'life' and alerts us to 'the objectives and strategies within which political economy is inscribed ... with reference to the modes of political action that it suggests' (Terranova 2009: 235). Against the backdrop of these lectures scholars are able to think in creative ways about the process by which 'the economic-institutional reality of capitalism ... has not only subsumed life in its economic processes of production, but actually drawn on life as a means of redefining a whole new political rationality where economic and vital processes are from the beginning deeply intertwined' (ibid.). While what Foucault calls *the reality of capitalism*, in its expansion across the world – particularly the margins of the world – has attempted not only to 'subsume' but also to soak up *life* within the economic processes of production – and consumption – the African experience has been markedly different. The nature of economic transactions in the continent, since contact with the Europeans in the fifteenth century (which constitutes the *modern* era in the continent), has creatively challenged the bid to entirely subsume or soak up life in the processes of production and consumption. Indeed, the political economy of everyday life in modern Africa provides a limitation to Foucault's totalizing conception of the 'economic-institutional reality of capitalism'. In Africa, capitalism has not been successful in becoming the 'universal form of economic life' (Roitman 2007: 156), as people invent 'diverse modes of getting by' (Ferguson 2008: 8). In the light of this, we might ask: what kinds of profound implications can originate (Guyer 2004a: 6) at the interface of global and local logics in which Africans respond to 'the dangers of extraction and [Africa's] marginality in the global economy' with 'flexibility, negotiability, resilience, innovation and entrepreneurship' (ibid.)?

This book sets out to explain how the political economy of everyday life has been shaped and reshaped in modern Africa, particularly with a focus on how this affects individual lives of the population. Here it is apposite to note Jane Guyer's important perspective, which urges Africanists to move away from 'conventional systematic approaches' given their inadequacy, since they explain satisfactorily 'only a certain modicum of the reality' (ibid.: 7). The 'persistent elements and relationships by which people individually and collectively create economies' (ibid.: 6–7) in modern Africa[4] do not submit themselves to the totalizing conception of the 'economic-institutional reality of (Western) capitalism'. Accordingly, the economic anthropologist offers important insights into how we can capture contemporary forms of capitalism in Africa beyond the limitations of the binary logics of 'the universalization of capitalist relations and arrangements versus the specificity of local forms of economic arrangement' (Roitman 2007: 156).

Specifically, this volume is provoked by what we assume to be a crucial matter: how to understand the fundamental issues, processes, structures, agencies and dynamics that shape the political economy of everyday life in Africa. In grappling with this question, in this introductory chapter, I reflect, and reflect on, why and how the *political economy of everyday life* approach is critical in understanding and analysing the social process in modern Africa.

What is the political economy of everyday life? As stated earlier, this is not a perspective that is specific to Africa; however, it is experienced or encountered in specific ways in Africa. Ghassan Hage (2004: 8) has argued that the political economy of life, as a heuristic model, involves 'an examination of the different ways in which life acquires a value in different social and cultural settings and the many variables that affect such process of valorization'. Even though it can be argued that Hage's 'many variables' can include the economic, this sphere is too central to the determination of the political economy of everyday life to remain merely implied, because *living* through economic *striving, struggling* or *surviving* is pervasive in Africa.[5] Therefore, the economic ought to be clearly expressed in the articulation of what constitutes the everydayness of life. In this volume, we use the political economy of everyday life to capture the ways in which global and local economic policies, institutions, activities and processes of valuation produce cultural meanings with which people engage

---

[4] Based on an 'interface' between on the one hand, the 'centre' of the financial world (West) and its 'margins' (Africa), and on the other hand, 'formal' and 'informal' economy – which 'coexist, interrelate, and reconstitute one another'. Guyer 2004a, p. 7.

[5] For interesting perspectives on 'the politics of striving ... surviving ... struggling', see chapters 5, 6 and 7 of Chabal 2009.

in and with forms of everyday transaction. The cultural meanings produced by and deduced from economic policies, institutions, activities, policies and processes of valuation in turn generate pragmatic attitudes that render economic conditions, policies, philosophies, activities, etc. intelligible while determining the ways in which people live their lives. Deploying a pragmatic attitude towards the economy results in people actively (re)constructing the overarching conditions of life while using their agency to re-determine these conditions, thus creating meanings that give value to their lives and make life liveable even under the most stressful economic – as well as political and social – conditions. This is what is captured in the idea of '*kos'ona miran'* ('no other way'), a powerful pragmatic approach to life which Guyer encountered during fieldwork and embraced as a useful heuristic tool. This question of having no other way is taken up in a different way by Judith Butler (2015: 193) recently in asking 'how does one lead a good life in a bad life?' It is evident in what Michael Jackson (2011: 61) found among the Kuranko of Sierra Leone where wellbeing is defined by 'how one endures the situation in which one finds oneself thrown', a process by which one learns 'how to live within limits ... [t]o withstand disappointment and go on in the face of adversity [that] imparts quality of life'. Thus, life acquires value within, but also despite, the prevailing economic systems of valuation.

From the prism of the political economy of everyday life in Africa, *no other way* is a discourse that encapsulates the practical ways and the creative means by which people invent or initiate alternatives – alternative economy, alternative means of livelihood, alternative means of transportation, even alternative means of exchange, etc. – in order to 'generate life' and 'gain existential potency' (Jackson 2011: 93, 99). Thus, the political economy of everyday life is about a system of adaptation and circumvention through which life, despite the odds, is lived. It is about how a certain, often difficult and challenging political economy is encountered, domesticated and made sensible; how people attempt to impose some measure of order and stability on their lives, even in the context of acute precarity, poverty and various forms of fiscal, social or political instability. This unending attempt to impose some order and stability and place value on human life, even if only at the level of meaning, could manifest whether one is caught in the web of the 'debt imperium' in post-apartheid South Africa (Chapter 8), fighting against environmental devastation while living with precarity in the Niger Delta region of Nigeria (Chapter 7), struggling to find work and survive as a migrant in contemporary South Africa (Chapter 6), or operating the dangerous business of motorcycle taxi (*okada*) in the context of uncertainty in Lagos, Nigeria (Chapter 9).

The perspective of the political economy of everyday life involves analysing the manifold attempts at imposing collective destitution on the people in the name of market logic or market imperative. It points us towards understanding the fact that neoliberal metrics cannot fully capture or express the many dimensions and the depth of Africans' lived experience and the macro as well as micro conditions that determine their lives. This approach also involves the investigation or analysis of the specific ways in which economic, political and social processes, institutions, practices and systems of *accounting* place value on, and thus govern, human life in different contexts. The placing of value and the government of human life happen in interaction with, or in response to, the *(il)logic* of discernible configurations of local and global economics, politics, social process, cultural rationality and history. How this (il)logic structures or determines the ways of living, livelihood and sustainable life in Africa is therefore critical. Here we are concerned with the logic as well as the illogic of discernible configurations of local and global processes in both temporal and spatial dimensions because we are mindful of how much of what concerns Africa is often assumed to be *irrational* in a global discourse dominated by the Western order of *ration*ality, one which limits or ignores Africa's *ration*ality. Indeed, analysis of 'the difference between rationality, rational choice and reason' (Guyer 2007b: 418) as well as the investigation of the limitations of Western (abstract) construction of rationality – particularly within neoliberal orthodoxy – in coming 'to grips with the messy realities of actual reasoning' (Guyer 2000: 1012) in Africa constitute some of the most innovative and refreshing ways of accounting for life in modern Africa. As a 'theory of behaviour' in Africa, Western accounts of rationality as evident in the concept of *Homo Economicus* (Pearson 2000) fail to capture the full range of the texture of economic and social life in the continent. Thus, we need to investigate and understand 'alternative forms of rationality and valuation that are developing in a context of constant crisis' (Geschiere et al. 2007: 38) as Bill Maurer (2007: 125–38) points out in the case of South Africa where 'calculative rationality continues to play a limited role and does not necessarily subsume other forms of valuation' (Geschiere et al. 2007: 40).

Contributors to this volume examine ways in which the processes of valuation, the placing of value on, and the governing of, human life fit or do not fit into the ascendant neoliberal order – even where the overbearing powers of this order often disrupt the lives of many Africans and expose them to various forms of precarity. The contributors' approach the political economy of everyday life through certain forms of convergence including how life acquires value (or is devalued) in the context of (i) money, currency and fiscal life struggles, (ii) labour, social lives and precarity; (iii) marginality, disaffection and bio-economic distress, and (iv) history, temporality, agency and democratic life (I will return to this later).

We take this approach in analysing the social process in modern Africa by engaging with – and, in some instances, also departing from – the intellectual oeuvre of one of the most influential (Africanist) economic anthropologists, Jane I. Guyer. Her intellectual project over more than four decades has been to study the ways in which Africans struggle to live a good life while constantly seeking for a better life in a context in which necessity and invention converge – as she elaborates in her work (Guyer 2002b) where her respondents insisted on *'kos'ona miran'* ('no other way') to live or attempt to live well. The concern with what constitutes the political economy of everyday life in Africa can be described as the central issue that has shaped and animated her scholarship.

An Introduction

Whether she is researching, reflecting on, articulating or analysing production (including in micro and macro contexts involving farming, family, gender, rural economy, etc.), or money (in relation to its instability, cultures and values, and the transactions and struggles associated with these), and the rationalities of market response and market engagement that reshape 'collective life in permanent ... and pervasive ways' (Guyer 1997a: 7), or the spatial dimensions of civil society in Africa (Guyer 1994), Guyer has placed the theories, practices and undercurrents of production, transactions, relations and exchange at the very heart of the politics of governance and the question of *rule* in modern Africa. This is done against the backdrop of her fundamental commitment to examining 'the context in which most people live most of their lives' (Guyer 1995b: 4) in Africa. Her work re-articulates in refreshing ways – to use the words of B. Radcliff (2001: 941) in the epigram above – the fact that market and politics are two important social mechanisms for the generation and distribution of wellbeing.

Though, like our key interlocutor, we take an Afro-optimistic tone in this volume, we recognize that many of the subjects of the chapters in this book use their agency within the political economy not only to *engage with* or *muddle through* their marginality, but also to reject or resist such marginality – as the chapters by Makhulu, Watts and Animasawun show. Also, it must be noted that not everyone in the universe that we cover in this book accepts the reality of their own marginality, as they define their own frameworks of engagement with modern life whether through religious movements (such as Boko Haram, as analysed by Watts), various types of cultural movements, art, music and other informal economic networks (legal, para-legal and even criminal) where they 'frame modernity with their own realities at the centre'.[6]

However, this volume is concerned with three elements central to Guyer's overall analysis of the political economy of life in Africa: agency, resilience/persistence and imagination. These elements, I suggest, make the seemingly 'irrational' (in the Eurocentric economic view) necessarily rational for most Africans. Also, these three themes, singly or jointly, run through the different contributions in this book.[7] Guyer alerts us to anthropology's deep engagement with the 'impressive power of what people do, persistently, and resiliently and imaginatively over a long period of time' (Guyer 1997a: 8). She argues that if we accept 'pure choice' as a form of institutional reflexivity' that is native to capitalism and liberal democracy, then it is evident that 'economics leaves open a very large terrain for empirical inquiry into the broad reasonableness of human behaviour and the foundations of differences among societies in their cultivation and implementation of "rationality"' (2000: 1014). Engaging with this 'large terrain' enables us to study how 'people the world over search – with all the mental and physical resources available to them – for ways of making a living in a globalized economy' while recognizing that people do what they do through all sorts of capacities including 'calcu-

---

[6] I thank one of the reviewers for pointing this out.
[7] One of the reviewers even suggested that each of the three themes could be used to divide the contributions into three parts.

lative reasoning' (ibid.). Therefore, as 'people manage the actualities of a desperately disturbed everyday life', which press them towards a 'combination of fantasy futurism and enforced presentism', a combination that seems 'specific to the lived implications of the economic policies' in Africa (Guyer 2007a: 409–10), their rationality would seem to challenge Western economic orthodoxies. Africans' persistent, resilient and imaginative engagement with their marginality in the global market and space point us to what is 'buried behind the repetition of actors and their shifting patterns', that is, Africans' capacity for 'rational adaptation to environment; passive resistance to a predatory state; [and their] faithfulness to cultural principles or ancestral dictates' (Guyer 1997a: 8).

In working with Guyer's penetrating perspectives and reflecting on the critical issues raised by her work, this volume contributes to the literature on the socio-economic and political processes in Africa by taking an approach that encourages us to pay greater attention to the popular systems of value and the concomitant processes of valuation and transaction that constitute the possibilities, opportunities and constraints placed on living, livelihood and life in specific social formations in Africa over the long term. This implies a multidimensional approach to the problem of living, livelihood and sustainable life as processes determined by economic as well as socio-cultural and political dynamics, where any of these dynamics can be salient, even though none over-determines the others. For instance, economic dynamics are constructed or constituted by, and interact with, socio-cultural and political dynamics, and are therefore sustained, elaborated or constrained by them. Guyer's oeuvre constitutes illuminating illustration of this reality.

The compositional nature of life – which in neoliberal terms might seem 'illogical' – is at the centre of the approach we embrace, particularly in terms of the unending symbiosis of the fiscal and the social in Africa. 'Market' – more specifically, *transactional* – forces are not independent of the social formations in which they emerge and which they serve. As many of the contributors to this volume show, whether affected, (re-)structured, or (over-)determined by external/global forces, the political economy of everyday life in Africa is a permanent transactional process that is in constant conversation with the logic and practices of specific social formations as well as global forces. In Guyerian understanding, for most Africans, there is 'no other way' to live than to engage in constant composition and re-composition – *necessitated invention*; they are forced to do so by local exigencies and/or transnational/global forces. The logic, precept and practices of the market are, therefore, in constant negotiation with other interactive forces including human agency – in both personal and associational senses. However, it is important to emphasize that what is at stake in this approach is *life itself* and the processes, transactions, institutions, politics, markets and policies that have the potential to sustain or obstruct the living of good life by the population in any specific context over the *longue durée*.

The political economy of everyday life in Africa has been shaped fundamentally by what Guyer describes as 'flexibility, negotiability, resilience, innovation, and entrepreneurship ... alongside the dangers of extraction

An Introduction

and marginality in the global economy' (2004a: 6). Boel Berner (2000: 281) contends that one of the two theoretical lessons that we can learn from the African experience is 'the importance of incorporating notions of flexibility and multiplicity into our understanding of [human] action'. In the light of this, Achille Mbembe (2000: 271) points to the specific form of 'sociology of circulation' that takes place in the 'time and space of flexibility and negotiability', adding that we need to develop 'a kind of governance approach that incorporates [such] basic things – these little things of everyday life, the moments where material conditions and meaning are intertwined, where people negotiate.' The emphasis on flexibility, negotiability, resilience, innovation and entrepreneurship is useful in organizing this volume because the contributors explore how such emphasis in the context of the interactions of the various dimensions of the political economy – fiscal, social, cultural, spatial, territorial, political, even *translational* – could provide a robust account of the social composition of life in modern Africa. We therefore want to 'trace some of [the] effects [of the larger economic processes] on people's mode of conduct and ways of understanding their lives' (Ferguson 1999: 12). Yet another critical advantage of the political economy of life approach is the articulation of the historical forces and undercurrents – local, but in interactions with the regional, national and/or the global – of the economic processes in any society and how the interactions of the economic, the social and the political in and through time and space help to constitute the conditions and possibilities, and also limitations, of life in specific contexts.

This approach also underscores the constant and unremitting interaction of structure and agency in the (re)production of material life – and the role that immaterial things/processes play in this interaction. In addition, the political economy of life perspective involves an examination of the different strands of bio-politics including 'the social, cultural, environmental, economic and geographic conditions under which humans live, procreate, become ill, maintain health or become healthy [and also their] living and working conditions … levels of economic growth and … standard of living' (Dean 1999: 99). Even though the idea of *political economy* has been approached as presenting limits to 'the bio-political aim of the optimization of the life of the population' (ibid.: 100; Inda 2005a: 5), a political economy of everyday life approach transcends this limitation by yoking the strictures and opportunities of the political economy to the life-optimizing potentials of bio-politics. This explains why in this volume we make socio-economic valuation speak to bio-sociality as evident, for instance, in Elisha P. Renne's chapter.

In the extant literature on Africa, the political economy approach to the study of society is yet to speak strongly to the emergent literature on the politics of life, as proposed in this volume. Since the waning of Marxist orthodoxy in African studies, the political economy approach has been adopted by leftist and progressive scholars as a way to account for the reality of actually existing societies in the continent. This approach is expressive in (i) Peter C.W. Gutkind and Immanuel Wallerstein's (1976) highly regarded book, *A Political Economy of Africa*, in which they emphasize Africa's dependence and underdevelopment, integration into and collaboration with the capitalist world system, modes of production, peasantization and proletarianization, class relations, alternative development strategies, etc. (Shaw 1978: 115); it is also expressed in (ii) Claude Ake's (1976, 1981) important intervention where he concludes that 'the main obstacles to development in Africa[8] ... can be removed only by abolishing the present relations of production', since economic development is impossible 'by humane incremental change' (Ake 1976: 23). However, the political economy approach has focused largely on (macro-)structural processes without paying sufficient attention to the effects of local (micro) and global (macro) structures on (individual) *life itself*.

Relatedly, the literature on the politics of life (Rose 2007; Inda 2005b; Biehl 2005), which engages with the politics of 'emergent form of life', that is, 'the vital lives of those who are governed', including a concern with the growing capacities of human beings and institutions to 'control, manage, engineer, reshape, and modulate the very vital capacities of human being as living creatures' (Rose 2007: 3), has raised questions about the centrality of the whole apparatus of *making live* and sometimes *letting die* in relation to the political economy – in areas as diverse as health and diseases, reproduction, nutrition and wellbeing, environment, labour, economic viability, credit worthiness, debt and indebtedness, etc. Yet, social science scholarship in/on Africa, with few exceptions (see, for instance, Fassin 2009), is yet to fully embrace the paradigm of the politics of life in analysing the social process – particularly, the political-economic processes. Despite this, following Foucault (2004), it is important to analyse the relationship between the political economy and the politics of life given that 'biopolitics is an extension of the economic rationale' (Fassin 2009: 45). Against this backdrop, this volume integrates the perspective of political economy and the politics of life in understanding the social process in contemporary Africa. Contributors interrogate and/or extend the focus on how economic questions structure – and are structured by – the social and the political in Africa.

Through her analysis of monetary, financial, fiscal, commercial and gendered relations in Africa, Guyer (1984a; 1984b; 1986; 1991; 1992; 2004b; 2007b; Stianse and Guyer 1999) has pointed to the political and social dimensions, as well as the salience of economic transactions and exchanges, and the ways in which the three areas of life in Africa reflect and refract one another. 'A distinguishing feature of Guyer's work', as Anthony T. Carter (2004: xi) correctly notes, 'has been her persistent concern with the individual lives behind the numbers produced in quantitative studies'. From the 'niche economy' (Guyer 1997a) – 'a new conceptual vocabulary', which she coined to 'depict the combination of multiplicity, finely graded hierarchy, relentless competition and ordered process' evident in rural economy in Yorubaland – to her influential analysis of wealth in people (Guyer 1995c), which raises awareness about the existence of 'multiple points of acknowledged overlap'

---

[8] Including the specific nature of the material base of African economies, ethnic conflict, one party system, the drift to military rule, the nature of class antagonism and economic stagnation.

An Introduction

(Duane 2010: 193) between things and people as constituting wealth, this volume draws on Guyer's work on Africa's economic experiences to interrogate economic, political and social life in Africa while engaging with the general scholarship on the non-Western world. We are sensitive to Guyer's constant attempts to dissolve homogeneousness or what is assumed to be homogenous, including her frontal battle against 'a too-hasty effort to homogenize actors and situations into globally relevant categories' (Guyer 2004b: 173), which have helped in illuminating our understanding of modern life in Africa.

The liberating thesis that foregrounds Guyer's oeuvre is relevant to the ways in which the contributors to this volume approach the political economy of everyday life in Africa. Robin Hahnel perhaps speaks directly to the intellectual concern that animates this volume when he describes it as one based on 'liberating theory'. Such concern is geared towards 'attempts to understand the relationship between economic, political, kinship and cultural activities, and the forces behind social stability and change, in a way that neither over- nor underestimates the importance of economic dynamics, and neither over- nor underestimates the importance of human agency compared to social forces' (Hahnel 2000: 1). Contributors to this volume examine (in)egalitarian economic and social formations and uncover the problems inherent in them, as well as the potentials for private and public good in these formations, processes and the agencies and structures that determine or can determine the solutions: market, law (economic and constitutional), institutions (local, national, or/and international), labour (formal and informal), health and diseases, history, conflict, spatial/territorial reconfiguration, the subaltern and elites, etc. This necessarily involves the examination of *what is to be done* as well as *what is to be undone*.

Whether exploring why 'money matters' (Guyer 1995a; 1995b) developing the idea of 'interface moneys' (Guyer 1995b), explaining 'money struggles' (Guyer et al. 2002), illuminating 'monetary transactions,' pointing attention to production, as opposed to 'demand,' or explicating how to 'feed African cities' (Guyer 1987) in the context of social history, urbanization, family, gender, land use and farming (Guyer 1980; 1984b; 1986; 1991), Guyer has raised critical questions about the challenges that people face in actually existing African societies and states, which are taken up by the contributors to this volume. To cite a few examples: why is life assumed to be equivalent to 'subsistence' while the economy is approached as 'export' – to the detriment of the domestic market (Guyer 1997a)? How do new forms of rural–urban relationships create new commercial and social orders that transcend the state? (ibid.) How do we explain 'the capacity of market engagement to reshape collective life in permanent and pervasive ways?' (ibid.: 7). What results from the convergence of two radically different economies as is the case for centuries in Atlantic Africa (Guyer 2004a)?

Because Guyer's *liberating scholarship* has been based also on a *complimentary holistic* approach that constantly links the different spheres of life (Hahnel 2000: 13), even while focusing largely on the economic sphere, this volume does not follow Marxist orthodoxy in presuming the dominance of the economic 'base' thereby ignoring the analysis of the social and political which interact with, and sometimes foreground, economic transactions or behaviour. Also, this volume departs from Afro-pessimism, while inviting scholars and others in the West to embrace Africa beyond the hackneyed prisms of 'backwardness, underdevelopment, irrationality, or primitiveness' (Barrett-Gaines 2004; see also Guyer 1995a; 1995b; 1995c).

Beyond Marginality:
Agency, Resilience/Persistence & Imagination

Jane Guyer's *Marginal Gains: Monetary Transactions in Atlantic Africa* examines 'marginal gains' in a region of the world (Atlantic Africa), which, despite the fact that it has been 'remotely global' (Piot 1999), remains on the margins of the world. Here, we recognize this marginality but seek to go beyond it to examine the fundamental opportunities offered, and the fundamental limitations imposed, by the marginality that compel most Africans using their agency, resilience, persistence and/or imagination to aim at *marginal* rather than *material* gains. As Sara Berry argues in Chapter 11, 'Africans are unusually attuned to [the] possibilities for "marginal gains"', not because they are 'more traditional, or less interested in material gains than people in other parts of the world, but because centuries of extractive trade and investment, imperial domination, and political transformation and turmoil have left their economies poorer, their share of global markets smaller, than other world regions'. Therefore, in dealing with and moving beyond Africa's recognized marginality, the contributors to this volume examine both direct and indirect, concrete (material) or symbolic (immaterial) interface between Africa and the world; how the global has historically determined the local context, and how the local context reacts creatively to global dynamic forces and change.

Given that '(i)nternal change has been persistently distinct' in Africa, though this change has not been merely 'directly derivative of the interface with Europe', change cannot be understood, in temporal terms, without engaging with the experiences generated by the interface (Guyer 2004a: 5). Despite the 'enormous obstacles' throughout history, as captured by Berry in her chapter, domains of life in Africa continue to expand as people creatively encounter momentous changes in the global context. The chapters in this book articulate different aspects of these domains of life and how human life is sustained within the constraints and opportunities of these domains.

Money Matters: Currency and Fiscal Life Struggles
It would seem needless to restate that money matters in our lives. Indeed, as Ralph Waldo Emerson quipped, for most people, '(m)oney often costs too much'. On a daily basis, the (in)ability to have or access (sufficient) money determines the quality of life. Yet, in Africa, people struggle to ensure that limited access to money or its insufficiency does not totally occlude value in

An Introduction

human life even as they deal with what Bill Maurer (2007: 126) describes as 'money's pragmatics'. What Guyer and others describe as 'money *struggles*' (Guyer et al. 2002, emphasis added) define the lives of most people who have to live on less than $2 dollars a day in Africa (see Chapters 6, 8 and 9 by Bolt, Makhulu and Animasawun respectively for instances of such 'money struggles'). The dilemmas of those caught up in such everyday fiscal life struggles perhaps led Mark Twain to modify the Biblical conclusion in stating that 'the lack of money is the root of all evil'.

One of the key concerns of Guyer's scholarship is to understand the historical evolution of currency, how it represents a crossing point in Africa's relationship with the West and the implications of this for modern life in the continent. From the precolonial to the contemporary currencies in Africa, indeed, 'throughout their entire history' (Guyer 1995b: 3), 'Africans have incorporated currency change of varying provenance: radical shifts in the prices of goods, the range of good to which money could be applied, the capacities of that money as a financial resource, the financial institutions to which they had access, and the physical nature of the acceptable currency.' She has also examined the dynamism of ordinary Africans in living with and living through currency changes, particularly currency instability – with their fundamental implications for fiscal lives. Money can be approached as 'an indicator [of capacity and confidence and how surplus extraction occurs] rather than as a fundamental phenomenon in itself' (ibid.: 5) as well as, literally, 'an object invested by its users with a whole penumbra of meanings' (ibid.). What is important, Guyer argues, is that both perspectives 'encourage us to move forward again into a more political economic as well as *cultural inquiry*, and try to marry the two' (emphasis added). The first in its formal and institutional senses as something that state and supra-state institutions compel us to use and depend on, and the other – based on the first – as a result of the fact that money is 'probably the single most important "thing/good" in ordinary people's ordinary lives' (ibid.).

In examining the economic subtleties of the everydaynesss of the lives of the 'ordinary' people in the margins – of the world, economy, political power, social organization, etc. – and the ways in which value and valuation (and the 'various modalities of valuelessness' – Butler and Athena 2013: 19) are determined and experienced, we cannot ignore, indeed, we must interrogate, 'the macro political and economic contexts in which ... the parameters of valuation are set' (Guyer 1995b: 4). Therefore, to be able to make sense of the political economy of ordinary people's lives over the *longue durée*, we need to address the macro contexts from the vantage point of the local/micro (ibid.). How have changes in the currencies, and the instabilities in fiscal lives that these bring about, been embraced or challenged over time in African communities? How has the 'long and complex experience' of Africans with currency change 'honed their skills at rapid adjustment to maintain the crucial equivalences of social life' (ibid.: 5)? And how can we read 'the money of people's experiences' which involves cultural inquiry (as evident in Chapters 1, 2 and 8) into the 'money of the state and ... the market' (ibid.: 6) – as evident in Chapter 4?

The Comaroffs in their exhaustive and magnificent analysis of cattle, currency and the politics of commensuration in South Africa show how commodification is central to the government of life and the regulation of living. They argue that 'at the heart of all "modern" colonialisms, a condition of their possibility perhaps, were mundane mechanisms that made inimical kinds of value, with different cultural roots, at once objectifiable, comparable, and negotiable'. In the South African frontier, the Comaroffs link money (and commerce, in general) to Christianity through a 'currency of conversion' which was also a 'currency of salvation' in the larger project of 'political contestation and incorporation at the edges of empire'. Their perspective helps us to understand the logic that reaches its ultimate travesty in contemporary African Pentecostalism where the love of money is emptied of its Biblical warning as the 'root of all evil'. Against the backdrop of the economic and social devastation wreaked by the Structural Adjustment Programme from the 1980s Africa, Pentecostalism sturdily embraced the Biblical take on money in Ecclesiastes 7:12 (KJV) as a 'defence'.

In Chapter 1, Jean and John Comaroff identify money, 'the ultimate currency of conversion, commerce, civility and salvation', as the factor at the centre of the negotiations and tensions in the varied conception of value by Africans and Europeans. Money was the *thing* or phenomenon with which the Protestant missions in Africa 'took the waxing spirits of capitalism, its specie and its signifying conventions, on a world-historical journey'. How different conceptions of value eventually clashed and coalesced around a 'modern' conception in Africa therefore raises the question of its implications for the total (re)organization of everyday life in colonial and postcolonial Africa including how the emergent conception of material value affected or (re-)determined the conception of the value of human life. However, there is a parallel in what the Comaroffs found among the Tswana in South Africa and what Guyer (1993, 1995c; Guyer and Eno Belinga 1995) found in Equatorial Africa in terms of wealth in people, even though in the latter case, cattle was 'the prime means of storing and conveying wealth in people and things'.

What the Comaroffs describe as the 'meliorative qualities of cash' raises interesting questions on how we can marry Guyer's concepts of wealth in people with that of wealth in things – with money as the '*ur*-commodity, condensing in itself the essential quality of all good/s' – in Africa. Is wealth in people ultimately geared towards producing wealth in things – particularly the *ur*-thing, Money?

In his excellent Chapter 2 on currency and conflict in colonial Nigeria, David Pratten takes up aspects of the questions of changes in currencies and the resultant instabilities in fiscal lives and how the 'long and complex experience' of Africans with currency change 'honed their skills at rapid adjustment to maintain the crucial equivalences of social life'. Developing Guyer's analysis of monetary transactions in Atlantic Africa, particularly in terms of 'the implications of money valuation in relation to social order and disorder', Pratten focuses on manilla currency exchange, which he argues, has often been ignored as an important factor in the various social upheavals for about a century before it was 'redeemed' in 1948. Examining how the political economy of colonialism provoked actions and reactions by the colonized in terms of what they saw as colonial obstacles to living a good life, he uses the famous Women's War of 1927 in Eastern Nigeria in a gendered explication of the relationship between the possibility of human flourishing and (colonial) taxation. Taxation as a form of governing lives by raising revenue provoked the protests led by women. Here, a crisis provoked by economic rearrangement (which was assumed to imply that women would be taxed) was approached as precipitating a new social order with implications for the political. Also, the leopard murder cases examined by Pratten shows how claims over women (and their bodies) led to fatalities in colonial Nigeria, principally because women's bodies were tied directly to men's economic fortunes. Women not only constituted means of livelihood for men and potentials for incurring debt in colonial Annang society, they constituted *life itself*.

In the light of this, Pratten argues that the specific spatial and gendered nature of the protests could only be understood when 'mapped onto the manilla region and a moment in the manilla exchange rate fluctuations' in the context of the implications for the rumoured taxation to be imposed on women. Thus, we can see how, as the Comaroffs argue in this volume, 'currencies of conversion, opened up new lines of distinction, new languages of value, new forms of inequity, new objects of desire, new possibilities of appropriation and exploitation'. Pratten emphasizes poverty and not profit as the basis of the protest. His chapter fully illustrates the fact that, in the cultural rationality of the people, the fundamental reason of the *economy* is about *making a living* and not so much about *making a profit*. This is demonstrated in the testimony which states that if women 'could not make a living, they might as well make a stand'. In this way, the political economy of everyday life in Atlantic Africa again reminds us that, against the backdrop of the opportunities provided and the constraints imposed by the economy, throughout human history, those who can't make a living in private have often been forced to take a public stand. This chapter further illustrates how changes in the political economy and its associated (fiscal) transactions can affect, or in fact, overturn the socio-political order, thus destabilizing or invalidating the process by which such order has reproduced itself for a long period. Such effect or destabilization has huge consequences for everyday life, particularly in relation to access to any currency which determines the social distribution of economic, social and political (dis)advantages.

Returning to what they describe as 'one of the most inspiring ideas in Guyer's rich oeuvre', that is, her 'consistent attention to "marginal gains" to be made by crossing disjuncture between different registers of value and knowledge', Peter Geschiere and Tristan Oestermann use Guyer's perspective on the role of 'composition' (in contrast to 'accumulation') to make sense 'of the chaotic developments during the boom in wild rubber' in the brief period of German rule in Kamerun (now Cameroon). The key question their Chapter 3 reflects on is how to relate the omnipresence of money in the forest zones of Equatorial Africa, even in 'the most intimate spheres of life', to Guyer's notion of 'composition' and 'multiple self-realization'. Geschiere and Oestermann show the implications of the combination of 'free' trade and coercion for human life in German Kamerun as the combination of, and confrontation between, these two forms 'led to considerable uncertainty, haste and violence'. The role of currency in socio-economic valuation is also important given that in the late nineteenth century when the German company, Gesellschaft Süd-Kamerun (GSK), entered the scene in Kamerun, ivory was the only commodity for trade. Ivory had exchanged for a long time with iron bars and European import goods used as currencies in the Congo Basin area. Therefore, it played 'a crucial role in local social relationships, especially as a means to pay bridewealth'. Also access to ivory, and by that fact, currencies, represented one of the 'pillars of the gerontocratic society'. Against this background, as the authors show, the new trade in rubber which gave power to young men who could harvest it individually – unlike the ivory trade controlled by the local big men – and sell to GSK produced a new 'form of valuation of rubber' posing 'a threat to the established gerontocratic social order.' Thus, new forms of economic and social lives were composed in this era for the purposes of multiple forms of self-realization. The need for rubber in the Metropole and the rubber trade not only encouraged the locals to eagerly participate in the devastation of their own lives but also led to atrocities by the Europeans against the local population. Thousands of human lives were lost. One clear implication of this chapter is that the extractive structures and processes of the political economy of everyday life (and its reproduction) frequently consume human lives. Extraction and expendability (of human lives) often converge.

Economic anthropology developed partly in the context of a particular concern with the way in which anthropological literature on the 'constitution and management of wealth' ignored economic theory or the work of economists (Guyer 2000: 1011, 1997a). Thus, Friedrich von Hayek's Nobel Prize lecture entitled 'The Pretence of Knowledge' is the departure point for Célestin Monga's Chapter 4 which reverses the gaze, as an economist takes up the ideas developed within the disciplinary framework of anthropology. As an economist, here Monga confronts macroeconomic issues as they relate to microeconomic life on the ground in contemporary Africa – with a measure of theoretical–philosophical reflection – thus pointing to how macroeconomics can feed into analysis in Africa and globally and then feed back into everyday lives.[9] Unlike in the other chapters in this section, Monga focuses on macro issues which are (and ought to be) informed by what he describes succinctly as 'stunning insights from the very practical analyses of how people perform economic relations on multiple and overlapping scales' as evident particularly in Guyer's work on households. Monga, a former World Bank economist, argues that macroeconomic view of growth should be complemented by microeconomic heterogeneity, thus emphasizing not only the 'importance of heterogeneity' but also the 'productivity behaviour

---

[9] I thank Jaqueline Mitchell for pointing out the need to emphasize this.

An Introduction

of agents'. Pointing to the limitations of *Homo Economicus*, Monga demonstrates the need to integrate the findings from social and economic anthropology in Africa into new (economic) methodological approaches. Again, he points strongly to the seemingly paradoxical, but actually 'rational', ways in which macroeconomic assumptions have been confronted by the reality of economic life in Africa. His overriding aim in his chapter is to put economic theory – and thus economic planning – in the service of the creation of greater possibilities for people in Africa to live better (fiscal) lives (cf. Monga 2016).

Labour, Social Lives & Precarity

'African originality' is a key factor in Guyer's (1997a: 8) analysis of the economic and social processes and institutions over the longue durée. Originality is important in relation to the constant challenges of life and living: uncertainty,[10] precarity and risk. For instance, in examining a rural community that supplies food to the Ibadan metropolis in south-western Nigeria, she identifies 'one set of actors ... who are encouraged by the proximity of the urban market and forced by the weakness of the state institutions of local governance, to create and manage their own social and economic diversity' (ibid.: 8–9). Facing precarity, these marginal people deploy their labour in the attempt to transcend their marginality by contributing to 'the creation of a competitive and responsive regional market that promises to be one of the most important social forms in West Africa's future' (ibid.).

In this section that considers labour and precarity – 'politically induced condition in which certain populations suffer from failing social economic networks of support more than others and become differentially exposed to injury, violence, and death' (Butler 2015: 33) – in relation to social lives, Frederick Cooper and Maxim Bolt take on different aspects of how to approach the political economy of everyday life in modern Africa. Cooper's Chapter 5, focusing on the labour question in African history, also examines the plight of young people in 'uncertain and conflictual political contexts' (on which Watts also focuses in Chapter 7). In a very rigorous analysis of how the past informs the present, Cooper argues – with a slightly different inflection from Watts – that the precarity that Africans are facing today is not a function of a particular phase of economic history but one that 'is an inherent characteristic of capitalist labour'. Africa's marginality is drawn into the centre of world history through the question of labour. Argues Cooper, '(w)hat links 1800 and 2000 is the unevenness of global economic relations'. Thus, the 'slave trade of the eighteenth and nineteenth centuries and the labour migration of the twenty-first have been possible because of the forging of connections among disparate parts of the world, and indeed because of increasing disparity'.

---

[10] Elizabeth Cooper and David Pratten in *Ethnographies of Uncertainty in Africa* (2015) argue that it is 'not only that contemporary life is objectively risky and unpredictable [in Africa] ... but that uncertainty has become a dominant trope ... in the subjective experience of life in contemporary African societies'. Therefore, people 'weave their existence' around 'incoherence, uncertainty, and instability', in a context in which uncertainty 'is not always and exclusively a problem to be faced and solved' but, more positively, 'a social resource' that can be used 'to negotiate insecurity, conduct, and create relationships, and act as a source for imagining the future'.

Noting how Guyer uses concepts to 'launch an inquiry' rather than to 'close off analysis', Cooper approaches labour in Africa in the context of the limitations of the earlier assumptions about the universality of the category. Analysing the African socio-economic reality in the long term in relation to the local and global conditions that led to the collapse of most African economies by the 1980s – resulting in the intervention of 'international financial organizations [that write off] rather than sustain African economies' – Cooper contends that the Structural Adjustment Programmes (SAP) imposed on African countries by the Bretton Woods institutions had deleterious effects on human lives. As James Ferguson (1999: 11) illustrates in the case of Zambia, the dramatic economic downturn worsened by structural adjustment 'has been paralleled quite closely by an equally dramatic downturn in life itself, a downturn so shattering as to shave a full five years off an average life within the span of a single decade'. SAP, Cooper argues, 'undermined the very sectors of African economies where labour had become the most stabilized, where workers might expect decent wages and a pension, and it sharply reduced state services that have equipped younger generations with the skills they needed for a changing world economy'. He therefore invites scholars to develop a conceptual apparatus to understand the political economy of everyday life, specifically in terms of comprehending the interface of precarity and 'freedom' in relation to African labour. How do we understand the 'continued movement of African labour outside the continent' and, thus, the shift from forced movement (in the era of slave trade and slavery) to an era of 'willing migrants' (in the age of globalization)? Given the precarity that is inherent in social organization of capitalist labour in Africa, is the idea of 'freedom' not an 'ideological construct' rather than a descriptive term? If the obverse of precarity is 'stabilization,' how do we approach the contemporary African state that constantly imperils the 'stable lives' of the population through massive divestments from the economic structures that make the living of good – and also *political* (bios), as opposed to *bare* (zoe) life in Agamben's (1998) perspective – life difficult, if not impossible? Is it possible to rethink and rework the possibilities of wellbeing or better life in Africa without addressing the question of labour – linking livelihood and dignity with work? Perhaps the most important take away from Cooper's insightful analysis is the critical point he makes about how and why *politics* and *struggle* are essential and unavoidable in the creation of the conditions for human wellbeing in Africa, conditions that will transform the present order that 'acclimatizes ['labourers'] over time to insecurity and hopelessness' (Butler 2015: 15).

The question of labour is also examined by Maxim Bolt in Chapter 6, who takes on some of the specificities of the holistic issues addressed by Cooper. Using ethnographic data informed by theoretical rigour, Bolt examines the navigation of (in)formality among migrant workers in the margins of South Africa. Here too, precarity – which Cooper insists is integral to capitalism – is produced by migrant labour. However, the precarity of economic life in South Africa is largely defined by the nature of political rule, institutions and processes – different phases of state surveillance – that determine legit-

An Introduction 19

imate residency and right to work. Therefore, in the lives of these migrant workers, precarity and documentality (Ferraris 2012) or 'government of papers' converge. As Matthew S. Hull (2012) shows in his book, *Government of Papers*, 'material forms of postcolonial bureaucratic documentation produce a distinctive political economy of papers' that governs life. Bolt deftly analyses how black workers on white farms 'navigate the terrains of formality' where 'a range of more or less official documents are key to workers' lives, strategies, and self-understanding'. Even though the Zimbabwean farm workers arrive with their Zimbabwean identity cards, once they are employed 'different identity documents attaching [them] to the farm enable new conditions of life'. This chapter illustrates in the particular context of labour how the political economy of everyday life simultaneously expands and narrows opportunities for living and living well. Risk and vulnerability are the attendant challenges faced by these farm workers in their attempt to access a better life. These workers are not notionally susceptible to risk, they actually risk their lives. Labour, in this context, is a way of risking life; therefore, the lives of these labourers are risked lives. Risking their lives through exposure[11] to health risks or harsh weather, among others, is the only condition by which they can go on living and hope to live a better life. Indeed, the political economy of everyday life involves various measures and channels of exposure that help to sustain life, but also place life in the line of injury or destruction (Butler 2015: 109). The Zimbabwean migrant workers are in what Butler (ibid.: 210) describes as a 'difficult bind' in that they face 'forms of power that exploit or manipulate [their] desire to live'. In their unofficial and official encounters with the state and its agencies, Bolt captures the abjection and excess (see Ferguson 1999: 234–8; Obadare and Adebanwi 2010: 1–28) that characterize the labour – life – of the underpaid, the overworked and the uninsured who survive at the margins of the political economy. The struggle for survival includes not only producing documents, it also involves *performance*. The workers need to perform to be able to convince their employers; thus, performing employability and, thereafter, hard work is as important as the reality of both. This important point compliments Sara Berry's argument (in Chapter 11) that managing market value is not based only on production; performance is also critical.

Marginality, Disaffection & Bio-Economic Distress

In Chapter 7 on 'Precarious Life' which involves 'living in the same now with no near future', an intellectual *tour de force* on Nigeria's political economic history and the forms of everyday life possible within it, Watts sets for himself an admittedly arduous task of converging three of Guyer's seemingly divergent observations on temporality, wellbeing and modernity's contradictions. Watts examines the relationship between poverty and violence, the temporalities of precarity and religious/secular doctrines in the context of

[11] Butler (2015: 139, 140) has argued that the word 'exposure' can help us to 'think vulnerability outside of the trap of ontology and foundationalism', partly because we can 'think vulnerability and agency together'.

modern secular national development in a typical African state – Nigeria. He presents the most refreshing scholarly attempt to link two of Nigeria's gravest national security challenges, the Niger Delta (oil-related) insurgency (about which he and many others have written a lot) and the latest, the Boko Haram (religious) insurgency in north-eastern Nigeria. The two insurgencies have totally transformed the everyday lives of everyone in two of Nigeria's six geopolitical zones, and beyond. Watts concludes that the two insurgencies are 'bequeathed by earlier crises and by a post-colonial history evident in the deepening crises of legitimate authority, the radical precarity of forms of rural and urban livelihood, particularly among generations of excluded youth, and the abject failures of secular national development'. The violence that dominates the everyday lives of the young insurgents in the troubled regions of Nigeria – and their victims – is not a mere reflection of the dominant order, argues Watts, it also expresses generative politics and presents moments of creativity that challenge and contest traditional notions of state territoriality. Watts' important observation about the creation of 'a vast space of alienation and exclusion' in which the contemporary African youth is neither citizen nor subject has led to the creation of a rural and urban middle class enduring what Giogior Agamben (1998) has described as 'bare life'.[12]

In a fascinating analysis of the personal 'debt trap' – or what she elegantly describes as a 'debt imperium' – in which many South Africans are ensnared in the era of liberalization as (non-)liberation, Anne-Maria Makhulu is inspired by Guyer's 'theory of deliberate incrementalism'. In Chapter 8, she uses this inspiration to reflect on the post-apartheid nation 'in which a new interface – namely between local and global markets – rather than affording ordinary South Africans opportunities for work and wellbeing has instead set the volatile and often unpredictable conditions of reproducing daily life'. As Maurer (2007: 126–7) has noted, in Africa, a 'vast number of things financial ... involve no exchange and no commensuration at all' but are about 'payments, efforts to avoid payments, the consequences of those efforts, and the creation and manipulation of debt'. South Africa's embrace of neoliberal reforms in the post-apartheid era, Makhulu demonstrates, has created a 'credit apartheid' and other contradictions (including the 'insurance racket') evident in the debtor–creditor relations which 'reconfigured the ways in which freedom was to be experienced in the day to day'. Miranda Joseph (2014: ix) recently reminded us of how 'debt is now *the determining economic* and thus social relation, superseding relations of production or consumption as the socially formative economic dynamic' (original emphasis). Indeed, the post-apartheid political economy is one in which the overarching relations of owing devalue the lives of most people and destroy their capacity to own – which Makhulu describes as a state of 'subjection and dispossession'. The state of affairs provokes those who have been marginalized in the ascendant

---

[12] Here, Watts chapter speaks directly to Gbemisola Animasawun's Chapter 9 on *okada* riders in Lagos and Maxim Bolt's unskilled farm hands who seek employments 'under conditions of extreme vulnerability' (Chapter 6).

An Introduction

neoliberal order to invoke the humanizing and liberationist mantra of the past: 'All Power!!! To the People!!!'

Work and the production of value, as Karl Marx concluded, are tied to temporality. Temporalities, Sarah Sharma warns in her book, *In the Meantime: Temporality and Cultural Politics* (2014: 8), 'are not times'. Rather, 'experiences of time depends on where [one is] positioned within a larger economy of temporal worth'. However, positioning within the larger economy happens in spatial terms too. Thus, like temporality, 'space is a co-producer of social relations' (ibid.: 10). Against this backdrop, it is important to reflect on how the political economy of everyday life often predisposes people to use time and space – and the relations they trigger or convoke – as strategies of survival (cf. ibid.: 145). In Chapter 9, in examining the social lives of 'marginal men', that is *okada* (commercial motorcycle) riders who are enmeshed in a particular time and space, in what he calls a 'struggle economy', Gbemisola Animasawun takes on Guyer's important perspective in *Money Struggles and City Life* on the pervasive 'chronic uncertainties' that define the 'domain of human struggles and achievement' in African cities. Animasawun shows how 'the phenomenon of greater informalization of the economy and the expansion of the "popular economy"' has provoked strategies by the urban poor to *struggle-manage*'. The struggle economy developed by the urban poor, and with which they cope, is described by Animasawun as 'aspects of the popular economy in urban Africa dominated by the most marginalized, whose incomes are unstable and chronically insufficient for survival in the expensive cities in which they work and live, and who, nonetheless, face extreme precarity and danger in the work with which they strive to make a living'.

The conflict that is inherent in, and integral to, the everyday relationship between these *okada* riders, organized as the Amalgamated Commercial Motorcycle Owners and Riders Association of Nigeria (ACCOMORAN), and the state, which is eager to regulate (including restricting or proscribing) them, is the focus of Animasawun's chapter. A paradox is revealed: State's men (as opposed to statesmen[13]), at some point, restricted or banned *okada* riders – for the sake of 'urban renewal' and 'security' – and at other times lifted the restriction or ban while mobilizing these riders to herald them during their electoral campaigns and as demonstrations of support among marginal people. In the end, *struggle economy* is defined not only as a struggle *against* the state but a struggle *for* livelihood, and in some cases, for life itself. Given the nature and dynamics of the political economy of everyday life in contemporary urban Africa, Animasawun correctly notes that 'African cities provide spectacular vistas of urban chaos, resilience, limited capacity for organization, potentials for improvement and the stark reality of striving for majority of its populace.'

A crucial aspect of the political economy of everyday life is the health of the population. Extraction of surplus in colonial Africa depended on human labour. Therefore, bio-sociality was crucial to the process of socio-economic valuation

---

[13] See Obadare and Adebanwi, 'Introduction' (2010: 3).

in every context of colonial exploitation. In Chapter 10, Elisha P. Renne considers specific forms of 'life politics' or bio-politics central to socio-economic valuation and the (re)composition of life in colonial Nigeria by analysing health and illness in a particular social context (see also Vaughan 1991: 1–28). She examines 'the intersections and disjunctions in the socio-cultural beliefs about Sopona [small pox] held by the residents of Ekiti Yoruba area of south-western Nigeria and the political economic context of British colonial officials' attitude to contain smallpox outbreaks.' Renne's chapter captures one major goal of bio-politics: the optimization of the life of the population (Inda 2005a: 5). Colonial government's regulation of lives and the health of the population transformed the treatment of smallpox, even though, at this point, it failed to transform the local people's conception of, and attitude towards, the diagnosis of the disease. The forced transformation of treatment had to be backed by governmental practices and disciplinary regimes including ordinances 'forbidding the worship of small pox juju (god, or orisa)' and one compelling parents and their children to attend vaccination events. The challenge of smallpox epidemic in this context and the different interpretations of its cause and remedy, Renne shows, point to 'different forms of political rule' in colonial Africa. However, with the embrace of Western education by the young people in this area, their conception of life and the biomedical means of sustaining life were substantially transformed. In the end, the triumph of Western biomedical logic and practices and the embrace of Christianity (which undermined belief in the gods and deities) constituted the instruments against ignorance, the spread of diseases and mass misery, thus giving more and more people the opportunity to live and contribute to the colonial economy based on cash crops.

Historicity, Temporality, Agency & Democratic Life
Drawing examples from ethnographic and historical studies of economic conditions and practices in Africa, Sara Berry reflects in Chapter 11 on how history adds value to things transacted in the market and 'how production of history and the constitution of market value inform and reflect each other'. History adds value not only to scarce and specialized things, it also adds value to 'a wide variety of marketed things that take account of the past in many different ways'. But everyday fiscal life struggles are not defined only by valuation and exchange relating to the past, they also have to do with newness and even things that do not yet exist. Berry provides some interesting examples of how the use of history or historicity in making claims to things of value – and the valuation of things in themselves – can illuminate fiscal life struggles. Claims to land constitute one such example in Africa. The colonial (and, in some cases, postcolonial) laws, which endorsed 'traditional' land tenure systems, have produced struggles between the 'first comers' and rival claimants through migration, conquest, alliance, and exchange – by the 'late comers'. These struggles oftentimes intersect with the concept and practices of citizenship. In many parts of Africa, such struggles are matters of life and death.

Berry provides two important perspectives regarding the reactions of people who live in the margins and/or are marginalized in the dominant

An Introduction   23

fiscal organization of their specific society and the world. One, marginalized people adjust notions and practices of custom/tradition/history to fit contemporary logic of the neoliberal market in its attitude to the 'past' and artefacts. They do this so as to partake of the benefits – through earning money – of the neoliberal market. The 'past', in this way, is turned into commerce and transaction. Two, marginalized people transform their knowledge of the local terrain into a skill or commodity which can be sold, or at least, offered for sale, in the market. By so doing however, they are also exposed to the instability – and uncertainties – of the market. Berry's core arguments in this chapter, I suggest, include the fact that people use history and historicity to add value to things and to confer value – economic and social, and ultimately, political, through endowing themselves with *political lives* – on themselves. The problem is that this same process can lead to devaluation. Berry pushes the argument offered by Guyer and Eno Belinga (1995) further by showing that people do not merely *embody* expertise (knowledge), they *manage* it through interaction; thus their *power* extends beyond embodiment to management. In the end, the market value that people manage daily is not based solely on production, but also on performance.

Using, as a departure point, a scene from a book by the anthropologist, historian, novelist, interpreter and translator of West African oral cultures and literatures into French, Amadou Hampâté Bâ (1901–91), Souleymane Bachir Diagne examines in Chapter 12 the question of historicity and historical agency through translation, which emphasizes 'meaning making of impressive magnitude and relentless resilience' (Guyer 2002a: ix) as well as Africans' capacity for 'rational adaptation to environment; passive resistance to a predatory state; [and their] faithfulness to cultural principles or ancestral dictates' (Guyer 1997a: 8). Diagne studies the figure of the interpreter as a colonial intermediary and what can be characterized as a move from interpretation to translation in the struggle for autonomy even within the context of colonial subjugation. The chapter provides a philosophical–linguistic outlook on the question of the centrality of translation within the political economy of colonial – and postcolonial – relations. An exploration of the life and work of a Malian interpreter, transcriber and translator, who belonged to the Sufi Order of Tijaniyya, leads Diagne to the analysis of Merleau-Ponty's (1964) affirmation that our postcolonial world marks the end of an 'overarching universal' and the era of what he called a 'lateral universal'. Within this lateral universality, translation (beyond interpretation) not only helps to insert the agency of the translator into the asymmetrical relationship of the colonial order, it intervenes in the political economy of religious freedom or freedom of conscience – which, in the case examined in this chapter, the hegemony of the French was constructed to obstruct or deny. Thus, translation in the Malian case showcases not only the 'flexibility, negotiability, resilience, innovation' (Guyer 2004a: 6) that undergird everyday life in Africa since the colonial encounter, but also shows that historical authenticity, in the contest of translation, 'duplicates the two sides of historicity' by engaging the translator as 'actor and narrator' (Trouillot 1995: 150).

Translation produced a dynamic process in which the loss of 'temporal power' was resisted through the maintenance of 'spiritual aura' as the cultural translator was also a mediator, not only within colonial relations, but in human history. Through the creation of 'reciprocity and respect', translators turn colonial relations of exploitation into resources for resistance and cultural restitution. Given that historicity of the human condition 'requires that practices of power and domination are renewed in the present,' as Michel-Rolph Trouillot (1995: 151) argues, only in the present of the colonial condition could the translator be 'true or false to the past [he chooses] to acknowledge'. Against the backdrop of the work of historians of colonialism who have examined the important actors in the 'third space', a space of hybridity in which these agents participated 'in the world of the imperium and that of the colonized', Diagne invites us to question 'the one-sided dimension of interpretation' so as to recognize the interpreter as one who can be 'a representative *par excellence* of the third space', one who 'exceeds the role of mere *truchement*' by becoming a translator.

Examining democratic rule from the prism of 'the dynamics of autonomy, resilience, co-optation and capitulation of micro (marginal, local) processes, structures and actors in their daily interactions and negotiations with the macro (dominant, national)' which Guyer promotes, Adigun Agbaje argues in Chapter 13 for a perspective in understanding 'the history of the travails of democracy' in Nigeria, embracing the Guyerian thesis through which 'popular responses ... to a harsh economic and political period of current devaluation' is socially expressed as 'no other way'. In the light of persistent practices of patronage and prebendalism in Nigeria's public life over time and across contexts, Agbaje presents a logic of 'no-other-wayness' that does not close off options, but constantly, consistently and innovatively opens up *other* ways. While the logic of *no other way* is (re)produced by the fundamental and inescapable need to overcome, if not escape, the constricting and restricting rules of extant institutions, rituals, methods, customs, ethos and routines (comprising *set* ways), its practices are characterized by unlimited innovation and inventiveness pressed in the service of collective (human) survival. In this context, there is *no option* other than constant and unending innovativeness and invention. In Agbaje's analysis, existing institutions, rituals, methods, etc. are not abandoned, but they are reinvented, transformed or remodelled to fit the emergent challenges in the course of life and living. Against this backdrop, the political scientist argues that even though the 'Nigerian experience has suggested for long that there may be no escape route from the pathological manner in which patron-client networks, relations and exchanges as well as prebendalism have structured the processes and dominant values undergirding everyday engagement in political and public life of elite and non-elite alike in manners that make democratic possibilities largely unattainable'; episodic and even systematic opportunities often arise for addressing if not challenging the 'toxic' networks, relations and exchanges that propel pseudo-democratic institutions and practices towards the violation of the quality of life, specifically, and human lives, generally. Therefore, in

An Introduction

understanding the specificity of the limitations that the configuration of the political economy of everyday life presents (in Nigeria, for instance), Agbaje contends that we need to focus on the 'escape routes as well as the tactics and strategies for broadening ... pro-democratic ways and means', even as anti-democratic forces consolidate and expand their vice hold on African polities.

Conclusion

On the whole, as one of the reviewers of this volume commented, we hope that the different strands of analyses about everyday life in Africa here could constitute the 'catalyst of a truly interdisciplinary conversation, that could simultaneously attract the interest of Africanists and other scholars who might be eager to apply the concepts and approaches developed here to other regions of the world'.

The political economy of everyday life approach invites us to pay attention to and study closely 'the context in which most people live most of their lives' (Guyer 1995b: 4) at specific contexts and conjectures, as well as over the long term. As it would be expected of a scholar who possesses such rigour and range, two of Guyer's important books (Guyer 1995a, 1997a) have attracted debates and discussions that culminated in special issues of journals.[14] Not surprisingly, some have described *Marginal Gains* (2004a) as 'bold,' while others have suggested that it is 'original' (see Guyer 2007: 184). The contributors to this book engage either in a general or specific way with different aspects of the question of the political economy of everyday life using their own expertise in different countries/regions of Africa while mobilizing ethnographies and intellectual reflections to interrogate the challenges and opportunities presented by the nature of life in modern Africa.

The nature of our approach in this volume is fitting, we believe, because we use the study of various forms of economic behaviour, for the most part, as entry points to understand the political and social life in Africa – or vice versa. The key themes with which the contributors grapple include: how people cope with, contest, confront, collaborate with and/or liberate themselves from the limitations of their economic environment by using not only fiscal resources, but also social and political facilities and opportunities. In confronting the fundamental issues that shape the political economy of everyday life in Africa, the contributors attempt to account for and discover or uncover what people (should) demand from their economy,[15] politics and socio-cultural processes. Also, they examine the interaction (or *non*-interaction) of the economic and the political and their implications for social life and living in modern Africa. By modern Africa, we do not mean only contemporary times. Our periodization covers Africa's modern encounter with the West, particularly from

---

[14] *African Economic History* 32, 2004; *African Studies Review* 50(2), 2007.
[15] Robin Hahnel (2002) proposes this question directly and succinctly in his book, *The ABCs of Political Economy*.

the fifteenth century onwards. As an interdisciplinary volume that includes contributions from four generations of African(ist) scholars from the disciplines of anthropology, political science, history, economics, philosophy, literature, sociology, geography and conflict studies, it is not surprising that there are diverse perspectives on how to understand the political economy of life.

Finally, it is easy to be gloomy about much of African economic and socio-political reality. The predatory economic order – complicated by political and social disorder – imposed on the continent which sees many, if not most, people as dispensable or even disposable, is reversible. The essays in this book, written from different intellectual traditions in examining the basic questions of everyday life, speak in different ways to the possibility of this reversal. Indeed, there is much about Africa that presses us towards hope. Still, we recognize, as Michael Jackson (2011: ix) reminds us, that human wellbeing is 'not a settled state but ... a field of struggle'. The contributions in this volume compel us to move away from a gloomy view of life and instead embrace one, which, by understanding and analysing actually existing structures and processes of life, ends up encouraging and promoting human wellbeing, liveable life or the good life, one which foregrounds human dignity.

References

Agamben, G. (1998). *Homo Sacer: Sovereign Power and Bare Life*. D. Heller-Roazen (trans.). Stanford, CA: Stanford University Press.
Ake, C. (1976). 'Explanatory Notes on the Political Economy of Africa'. *Journal of Modern African Studies*, 14(1): 1–23.
—. (1981). *A Political Economy of Africa*. London, New York: Longman.
Barrett-Gaines, K. (2004). 'Introduction: A Keener Look at the Evidence', *African Economic History*, Special Issue in Honor of Jane Guyer and 'An African Niche Economy (1997)', 32: 1–13.
Bates, R.H. (1983). *Essays on the Political Economy of Rural Africa*. Berkeley: University of California Press.
Berlant, L. (2007). 'Slow Death (Sovereignty, Obesity, Lateral Agency)'. *Critical Inquiry*, 33: 754–80.
Berner, B. (2000). 'Manoeuvring in Uncertainty: On Agency, Strategies and Negotiation'. In Boel Berner and Per Trulsson (eds), *Manoeuvring in an Environment of Uncertainty: Structural Change and Social Action in Sub-Saharan Africa*. Aldershot, UK: Ashgate.
Berry, S. (2007). *'Marginal Gains*, Market Values, and History'. *African Studies Review*, 50(2): 57–70.
Biehl, J. (2005). 'Technologies of Invisibility: Politics of Life and Social Inequality'. In Jonathan Xavier Inda (ed.), *Anthropologies of Modernity: Foucault, Governmentality, and Life Politics*. Malden MA: Blackwell.
Bierschenk, T. and J.-P. Olivier de Sardan (2014). *States at Work: Dynamics of African Bureaucracies*. Leiden: Brill.

Booth, D. and D. Cammack (2013). *Governance for Development in Africa: Solving Collective Action Problems*. London: Zed Books.

Butler, J. (2015). *Notes Towards a Performative Theory of Assembly*. Cambridge, MA: Harvard University Press.

Butler, J. and A. Athanasiou (2013). *Dispossession: The Performative in the Political*. Cambridge, UK: Polity Press.

Carter, A.T. (2004). 'Foreword'. In J.I. Guyer, *Marginal Gains: Monetary Transactions in Atlantic Africa*. Chicago, IL and London: University of Chicago Press.

Castells, M. (1996). *The Rise of the Network Society: The Information Age – Economy, Society, and Culture*. New York: Blackwell Publishing.

Chabal, P. (2009). *Africa: The Politics of Suffering and Smiling*. London: Zed Books.

Cohen, R. (1961/62). 'Everyday Life in Africa', *International Journal*, 17(1): 34–9.

Cohen, D.L and John D. (1996 [1981]). *Political Economy of Africa: Selected Readings*. Ann Arbor: University of Michigan Press.

Cooper, E. and D. Pratten (eds) (2015). 'Ethnographies of Uncertainty in Africa: An Introduction'. In E. Cooper and D. Pratten (eds), *Ethnographies of Uncertainty in Africa*. Basingstoke, UK: Palgrave Macmillan.

de Certeau, M. (1984). *The Practice of Everyday Life*. Berkeley and London: University of California Press.

De Herdt, T. and J.-P. Olivier de Sardan (2015). *Real Governance and Practical Norms in Sub-Saharan Africa: The Game of the Rules*. New York: Routledge.

Dean, M. (1999). *Governmentality: Power and Rule in Modern Society*. London: Sage.

Duane, A.M. (2010). 'Keeping His Word: Money, Love, and Privacy in the Narrative of Venture Smith'. In James Brewer Stewart (ed.), *Venture Smith and the Business of Slavery and Freedom*. Amherst: University of Massachusetts Press.

Fassin, D. (2009). 'Another Politics of Life is Possible'. *Theory, Culture & Society*, 26(5): 44–60.

Ferguson, J. (1999). *Expectations of Modernity: Myths and Meanings of Urban Life on the Zambian Copperbelt*. Berkeley and London: University of California Press.

—. (2006). *Global Shadows: Africa in the Neoliberal World Order*. Durham, NC and London: Duke University Press.

—. (2008). 'Global Disconnect: Abjection and the Aftermath of Modernism'. In Peter Geschiere, Birgit Meyer and Peter Pels (eds), *Readings in Modernity in Africa*. Bloomington and Indianapolis: Indiana University Press.

Ferraris, M. (2012). *Documentality: Why It is Necessary to Leave Traces*. Richard Davies (trans.). New York: Fordham University Press.

Foucault, M. (2004). *Security, Territory, Population: Lectures at the Collège de France. 1977–1978*. Michel Sellenart (ed.), Graham Burchell (trans.), Basingstoke, UK: Palgrave Macmillan.

—. (2008). *The Birth of Biopolitics: Lectures at the Collège de France, 1978–*

1979. Michel Sellemart, Arnold I. Davidson, Alessandro Fontana and François Ewald (eds), Graham Burchell (trans.), Basingstoke, UK: Palgrave Macmillan.

Geschiere, P., M. Goheen and C. Piot (2007). 'Introduction: Marginal Gains Revisited'. *African Studies Review*, 50(2): 37–41.

Gutkind, Peter C.W. and Immanuel Wallerstein (1976). *The Political Economy of Contemporary Africa*. Beverly Hills, CA: Sage.

Guyer, J. I. (1980). 'Food, Cocoa, and the Division of Labour by Sex in Two West African Societies'. *Comparative Studies in Society and History*, 22(3): 355–73.

—. (1984a). 'Naturalism in Models of African Production'. *Man*, 19(3): 371–88.

—. (1984b). *Family and Farm in Southern Cameroon*. Boston, MA: Boston University Press.

—. (1986). 'Beti Widow Inheritance and Marriage Law'. In Betty Potash (ed.), *Widows in African Societies: Choices and Constraints*. Stanford, CA: Stanford University Press.

—. (ed.) 1987. *Feeding African Cities: Studies in Regional Social History*. Manchester, UK and London: Manchester University Press for International African Institute.

—. (1991). 'Female Farming in Anthropology and African History'. In Micaela Di Leonardo (ed.), *Gender at the Crossroads of Knowledge: Feminist Anthropology in the Postmodern Era*. Berkeley and Los Angeles: University of California Press.

—. (1992). 'Representation without Taxation: An Essay on Democracy in Rural Nigeria, 1952–1990'. *African Studies Review*, 35(1): 41–79.

—. (1993). 'Wealth in People and Self-Realization in Equatorial Africa.' *Man*, 28(2): 243–65.

—. (1994). 'The Spatial Dimensions of Civil Society in Africa: An Anthropologist Looks at Nigeria'. In John W. Harbeson, Donald Rothchild and Naomi Chazan (eds), *Civil Society and the State in Africa*. Boulder, CO and London: Lynne Rienner.

—. (ed.) (1995a). *Money Matters: Instability, Values, and Social Payments in the Modern History of West African Communities*. Portsmouth, NH: Heinemann and London: James Currey.

—. (1995b). 'Introduction: The Currency Interface and its Dynamics'. In Jane I. Guyer (ed.), *Money Matters*.

—. (1995c). 'Wealth in People, Wealth in Things – Introduction'. *Journal of African History*, 36(1): 83–90.

—. (1996). 'Traditions of Invention in Equatorial Africa'. *African Studies Review*, 39(3): 1–28.

—. (1997a). *An African Niche Economy: Farming to Feed Ibadan*. Edinburgh, UK: Edinburgh University Press.

—. (1997b). 'The Food Economy and French Colonial Rule in Central Cameroun'. *Journal of African History*, 19(4): 577–97.

—. (2000). 'Rationality or Reasoning? Comment on Heath Pearson's "*Homo Economicus* Goes Native, 1859–1945"'. *History of Political Economy*, 32(4): 1011–15.

—. (2002a). 'Preface'. In J.I. Guyer, L. Denzer and A. Agbaje (eds), *Money Struggles and City Life*.
—. (2002b). '"Kos'ona Miran" ("No Other Way"): Necessity and Invention in Mechanized Farming'. In J.I. Guyer, L. Denzer and A. Agbaje (eds,) *Money Struggles and City Life*.
—. (2004a). *Marginal Gains: Monetary Transactions in Atlantic Africa*. Chicago, IL: University of Chicago Press.
—. (2004b). 'Concluding Remarks: Niches, Margins and Profits: Persisting With Heterogeneity', *African Economic History*, 32: 173–91.
—. (2007a). 'Africa Has Never Been "Traditional": So Can We Make a General Case? A Response to the Articles'. *African Studies Review*, 50(2): 183–202.
—. (2007b). 'Prophecy and the Near Future: Thoughts on Macroeconomic, Evangelical, and Punctuated Time'. *American Ethnologist*, 34(3): 409–21.
—. (2012). 'The Burden of Wealth and the Lightness of Life: The Body in Body-Decoration in Southern Cameroon'. In C. Panella (ed.), *Lives in Motion, Indeed: Interdisciplinary Perspectives on Social Change in Honor of Danielle de Lame*. Tervuren, Belgium: Royal Museum of Central Africa.
—. (2014). 'Pauper, Percentile, Precarity'. Keynote address to conference: 'The History of Poverty in Africa: A Central Question?' Columbia University, New York, 6 March.
—. (2016). '"The Craving for Intelligibility": Speech and Silence on the Economy Under Structural Adjustment and Military Rule in Nigeria'. In Jane I. Guyer, *Legacies, Logics, Logistics: Essays in the Anthropology of the Platform Economy*. Chicago, IL and London: Chicago University Press.
Guyer, J. I. and S.M. Eno Belinga (1995). 'Wealth in People as Wealth in Knowledge: Accumulation and Composition in Equatorial Africa'. *Journal of African History*, 36(1): 91–120.
Guyer, J. I., L. Denzer and A. Agbaje (eds) (2002). *Money Struggles and City Life*. Portsmouth, NH: Heinemann.
Hage, G. (2004). 'Towards a Political Economy of Life'. *What Would You Die For?* Manchester, UK, British Council.
Hahnel, R. (2000). *The ABCs of Political Economy*. London: Pluto Press.
Hope, K.R. (1997). *African Political Economy: Contemporary Issues in Development*. New York and London: M.E. Sharpe.
Hull, M.S. (2012). *Government of Paper: The Materiality of Bureaucracy in Urban Pakistan*. Berkeley and London: University of California Press.
Inda, J.X. (2005a). 'Analytics of the Modern: An Introduction'. In J.X. Inda (ed.), *Anthropologies of Modernity*.
—. (ed.) (2005b). *Anthropologies of Modernity: Foucault, Governmentality, and Life Politics*. Malden, MA: Blackwell.
Jackson, M. (2011). *Life Within Limits: Well-being in a World of Want*. Durham, NC and London: Duke University Press.
Joseph, M. (2014). *Debt to Society: Accounting for Life Under Capitalism*. Minneapolis and London: University of Minnesota Press.
Maurer, B. (2007). 'Incalculable Payments: Money, Scale, and the South African Offshore Grey Money Amnesty'. *African Studies Review*, 50(2): 125–38.

Mbembe, A. (2000). 'Everything Can Be Negotiated: Ambiguities and Challenges in a Time of Uncertainty'. In B. Berner and P. Trulsson (eds), *Manoeuvring in an Environment of Uncertainty: Structural Change and Social Action in Sub-Saharan Africa*. Aldershot, UK: Ashgate.

Merleau-Ponty, M. (1964). 'From Mauss to Levi-Strauss'. In M. Merleau-Ponty, *Signs*. Evanston: Northwestern University Press.

Mkandawire, T. (2015a). 'Neopatrimonialism and the Political Economy of Economic Performance in Africa: Critical Reflections'. *World Politics*, 67(3): 563–612.

—. (2015b). *Africa: Beyond Recovery*. Accra, Ghana: Sub-Saharan Publishers.

Monga, C. (2016). *Nihilism and Negritude: Ways of Living in Africa*. Cambridge, MA: Harvard University Press.

Ndulu B.J., S. O'Connell, R. Bates, P. Collier and C. Soludo (eds), (2008a). *The Political Economy of Economic Growth in Africa: 1960–2000. Vol. 1*. Cambridge: Cambridge University Press.

—. (2008b). *The Political Economy of Economic Growth in Africa: 1960–2000. Vol. 2*. Cambridge, UK: Cambridge University Press.

Obadare, E. and W. Adebanwi (2010). 'Introduction: Excess and Abjection in the Study the African State'. In W. Adebanwi and E. Obadare (eds), *Encountering the Nigerian State*. New York: Palgrave Macmillan.

Onimode, B. (1988). *The Political Economy of the African Crisis*. London and New Jersey: Zed Books.

Padayachee, V. (ed.) (2010). *The Political Economy of Africa*. New York: Routledge.

Pearson, H. 2000. '*Homo Economicus* Goes Native, 1859–1945: The Rise and Fall of Primitive Economics'. *History of Political Economy*, 32(4): 933–89.

Piot, C. (1999). *Remotely Global: Village Modernity in West Africa*. Chicago, IL: University of Chicago Press.

Radcliff, B. (2001). 'Politics, Markets, and Life Satisfaction: The Political Economy of Human Happiness'. *American Political Science Review*, 95(4): 939–52.

Roitman, J. (2007). 'The Efficacy of the Economy'. *African Studies Review*, 50(2): 155–61.

Rose, N. (2007). *The Politics of Life Itself: Biomedicine, Power, and Subjectivity in the Twenty-First Century*. Princeton, NJ: Princeton University Press.

Sharma, S. (2014). *In the Meantime: Temporality and Cultural Politics*. Durham, NC and London: Duke University Press.

Shaw, T.M. (1978). Review of *The Political Economy of Contemporary Africa* by Peter C.W. Gutkind; Immanuel Wallerstein. *ASA Review of Books*, 4: 115–18.

—. (1985). *Towards a Political Economy for Africa: The Dialectics of Dependence*. London: Macmillan.

Stianse, E. and J.I. Guyer (1999). *Credit, Currencies and Culture: African Financial Institutions in Historical Perspective*. Uppsala, Sweden: Nordic African Institute.

Terranova, T. (2009). 'Another Life: The Nature of Political Economy in Foucault's Genealogy of Biopolitics'. *Theory, Culture and Society*, 26(6): 234–62.

Trouillot, M.-R. (1995). *Silencing the Past: Power and the Production of History.* Boston, MA: Beacon Press.

Vaughan, M. (1991). *Curing Their Ills: Colonial Power and African Illness.* Cambridge, UK: Polity Press.

Part I

MONEY MATTERS:
CURRENCY & FISCAL LIFE STRUGGLES

1 Cattle, Currencies & the Politics of Commensuration on a Colonial Frontier[1]

Jean & John L. Comaroff

Prefatory Note

Encounters between different regimes of value – regimes divided by cultural space and time – presume mediation, translation, communication and, therefore, currencies, at once verbal and material, that objectify them. This, in turn, depends on one thing above all else: on mechanisms of commensuration, mechanisms that render negotiable otherwise inimical, apparently intransitive, orders of signs and practices. Without such mechanisms, which have often been the object of conflict and contestation, large-scale historical projects, like colonialism, would have made no sense, neither as a world-undertaking on the part of colonizers nor as a lived reality to those upon whose worlds it was wrought. Jane Guyer (2004: 13), in an acute reading of the West African archive, warns against the assumption that commensuration, especially that attributed to the alchemy of money, necessarily dissolves all distinctions between disparate scales and measures of worth. In Africa, she insists, non-equivalent exchange has been pervasive. If anything, it has been facilitated by the spread of quantifiable currencies: as people became adept at deploying monetary scales, they frequently used them for negotiating intervals, 'exchanging goods and services that were explicitly not the match of each other' (47). In similar spirit, the following essay interrogates the role of commensuration in the colonial encounter: how might the management of value conversion – efforts, that is, both to facilitate and to impede it – play into larger processes of political contestation and incorporation at the edges of empire?

Introduction

> Money is sacred, as everyone knows...
> (Barry Unsworth 1992: 325)

This essay explores a very specific obsession with very general historical implications: the effort of British Nonconformist evangelists – evangelists,

[1] An earlier version of this essay was published in *Archaeological Dialogues* 12(2), 2005: 107–32, and content is used by permission.

that is, from Protestant denominations other than the established Church of England – to introduce coinage, to replace beads and cattle with banknotes, among Tswana peoples in South Africa. At its broadest, it posits a post-Marxist argument, rooted in the concerns of both Marxist and liberal theory, about the salience of commensuration in the modernist construction of society and history; above all, in the forging of empires. For, we shall claim, at the heart of all 'modern' colonialisms, a condition of their possibility perhaps, were mundane mechanisms that made inimical kinds of value, with different cultural roots, at once objectifiable, comparable and negotiable – mechanisms, that is, which permitted the up- and downloading of unlike forms of wealth, both human and inanimate. Commensuration and objectification, standardization and abstraction, equilibration and convertibility, of course, all feature prominently in classic theories of commodification; also in theories of the workings of money. But their significance in the construction of modernity as an ideology of global scale, and in the encounter between Europe and its others, has not been adequately plumbed. Nor, we believe, have their various media, their poetics and magicality, been adequately theorized.

In order to make our general point, and to explore its further theoretical consequences, we interrogate processes of commensuration in one African colonial theatre, focusing on the material transactions they enabled across semantic frontiers; on their diverse, and differently endowed media, alike indigenous and imported; on their implications of the long run for cultural constructions of wealth; on their existential effects upon all involved. We ask why it was that the campaign to convert Tswana to Christianity, and to the ways of the West, concentrated so centrally on recasting their currencies: on teaching them to use cash, to make good by buying and selling goods, to commodify their labours by transforming the wages of sin into virtuous incomes. We trace how these ventures were challenged by African conceptions of value; how they called into being hybrid tokens of exchange and how they set in train struggles to domesticate new alchemies of enrichment amidst efforts to protect local means of storing wealth. We shall show that, for nineteenth-century colonial evangelists in South Africa, saving savages meant teaching savages to save. If Jesus was to redeem them, his sable followers had to learn to invest. Also to produce providentially, using God's gifts to bring forth the greatest possible abundance – or at least marketable surpluses. Only then would Africa become part of the Christian commonwealth and its sacred economy. Drawing 'native' communities into that body of corporate nations meant, first and foremost, persuading them to accept money, the ultimate currency of conversion, commerce, civility, salvation. In their endeavour to do this, the Protestant missions took the waxing spirits of capitalism, its specie and its signifying conventions, on a world-historical journey.

In recuperating that journey, we seek to make visible the hidden hand, sometimes the sleight of hand, behind the political economy of nineteenth-century European colonialism. Which returns us to the broad outlines of our argument: (i) inasmuch as the building of empires depended on processes of commensuration, on rendering epistemically equivalent

Cattle, Currencies & the Politics of Commensuration

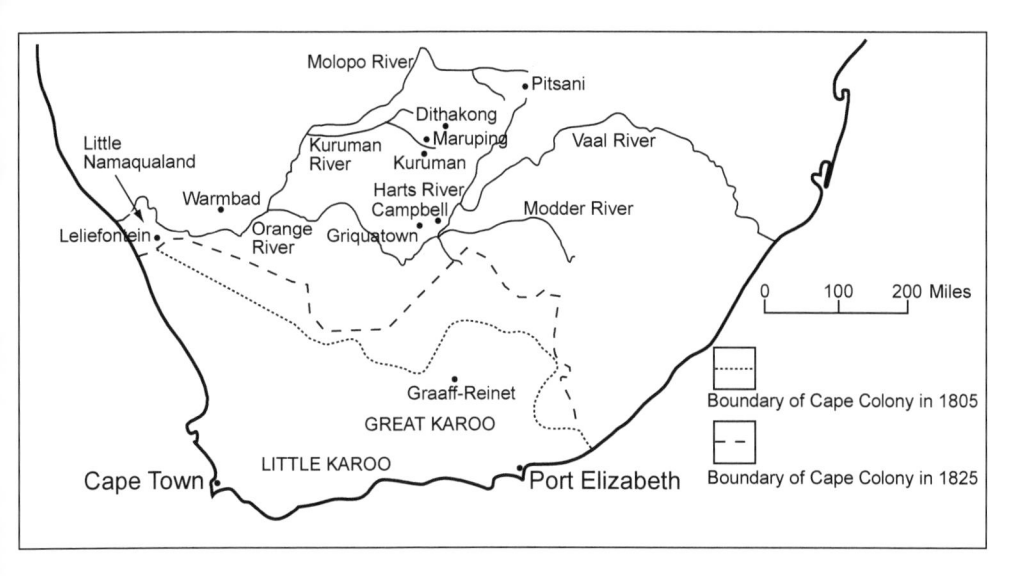

Map 1.1 Map of South Africa in the early nineteenth century

and transitive once incomparable objects and ideas, signs and meanings, it demanded media – beads, coin, contracts and the like – with the capacity, simultaneously, to construct, negate and transfigure difference; (ii) inasmuch as those media, those currencies of conversion, opened up new lines of distinction, new languages of value, new forms of inequity, new objects of desire, new possibilities of appropriation and exploitation, they took on magical properties; this because (iii) they appeared, in and of themselves, to objectify history-in-the-making, even to make history of their own accord. Which, we shall demonstrate, is why banknotes, beads and bovines became the objects of a protracted struggle in the South African interior; why, more generally, they became metonymic of the antinomies of value on which the colonial encounter, *tout court* was played out.

As this suggests, we seek here to make two species of theoretical claim. Both are instantiated by our South African story, both extend far beyond it. One is about 'modern' European colonialism, whose historical logic, we propose, is incomprehensible without an understanding of the processes of commensuration and conversion that allowed various worlds to be brought into the same orbit of being, both imaginatively and concretely – and made phenomenological sense of the politics, economics and semantics of the encounters to which it gave rise. The other is about commensuration itself and about the media upon which it depends: media are fetishized not merely because they congeal labour power and/or obscure relations embodied in processes of production, nor because they displace unspeakable passions from people to objects or vice versa, but because, being uniquely endowed things, they take on a social life of their own. Their genius, we shall show, does not lie in their being empty, or emptied, signifiers, just as their meaning does not derive simply from their relations to other, equally empty signs. It is owed in part to their intrinsic properties, in part to the moral, material and magical work they are made to do in the exigent course of history.

Species of Values, Value & Specie

Christian Political Economy: Secular Theology, Sacred Commerce
If early modern European political economy was a secular theology (Hart 1986: 647), contemporary Nonconformist theology sanctified commerce. During the 'second reformation' of the late 1700s, British Protestantism had refashioned itself with cultural fabric milled by the industrial revolution. Indeed, the interplay of church and business, realms never fully separate, produced a rich discourse, at once religious and temporal, about value and its production (Hempton 1984: 11; Waterman 1991: 3f). Eighteenth-century evangelicals, Rack (1989: 385f) claims, had been more influenced by the language of practical reason than their espousal of scripture and spirituality might suggest; similarly Warner (1930: 138), who long ago linked the 'empirical temper' of Methodist lore to the central place it accorded economics.

But the discourse of political economy, which fused a belief in the beneficence of existing economic institutions with a Whigish desire for reform, was especially audible among abolitionists and 'improvers' in the first years of the nineteenth century (Waterman 1991: 6). As a call to practice, moreover, it was particularly congenial to the spirit of the great evangelical societies. While liberal theory per se was seldom a subject of open discussion among missionaries to South Africa, most of them were guided, more or less, by its material and moral principles. Some actually did cite it as a charter for their labours: the London Missionary Society (LMS) Superintendent, John Philip (1828 1: 369), for example, quoted Adam Smith on the need to stimulate the indigent to industry, and David Livingstone (1961: 194) made mention of Malthus on the subject of reproduction. As this implies, Nonconformist theologians and their followers were advocates of moral deregulation. According to the 'New System' Calvinism of the Congregationalist clergy, all, not just the elect, were candidates for salvation. They also sought to remove the spiritual 'ceiling' that the Anglican hierarchy put in the way of aspiring dissenters (Helmstadter 1992: 15, 23). These men set all available means, including economic ones, to work for their cause. Likewise the Methodists: in line with early champions of free trade, John Wesley saw nothing intrinsically unworthy or antisocial in riches (Semmel 1974: 71f) – quite the reverse. The 'lusty zest' with which he advocated the quest for gain went further than most previous Puritans, who tended not to celebrate wealth but to condone it as a necessary compromise with evil (Warner 1930: 138f). For him, 'business' did not 'interrupt communion with God'. It was merely one of its channels.

'Business', in fact, seems to have served as a synecdoche for human action in the world,[2] just as 'usefulness' conveyed a sense of virtuous efficacy (Helm-

---

[2] As it did in Adam Smith's (1976: 14) phrase, 'the general business of society'.

stadter 1992: 9). Not that commerce did not pose its own dangers: Wesley's economic teachings were, in many ways, a lifelong effort to counter those implications of The Wealth of Nations that he saw to be corrupting (Outler 1985: 264). But therein lay the challenge: 'Make yourselves friends of the mammon of unrighteousness', he preached (1985: 266), citing Luke's injunction (16: 1–2) to redeem the potential of wealth. In his sermon on 'The Use of Money', he (1985: 267–8) chides fellow Christians for acquiescing in an 'empty rant' against the 'grand corrupter of the world'. The duty of the faithful was to deploy, to the greatest possible advantage, all that providence had provided. Money was a precious 'talent'. The word evoked both Biblical coinage and a sense of special, God-given capacity:

> [It] is of unspeakable service to all civilized nations in all the common affairs of life. It is a most compendious instrument of transacting all manner of business, and (if we use it according to Christian wisdom) of doing all manner of good.

Money, he went on (268), was 'food for the hungry' and 'raiment for the naked'. Even 'father to the fatherless' – surely one of the most genial images of cash in contemporary European moral discourse. As a compendious instrument, it was an *ur*-commodity, condensing in itself the essential quality of all good/s. Reciprocally, it could stand for all things, even the closest of human connections.

Wesley seems to have seen coin as the servant of existing laws of value and a neutral vehicle of trade; he subscribed to the 'commodity theory' of currency shared alike by classic liberal theorists and by Marx (Hart 1986: 643). Marx, of course, also stressed that money, as capital, was uniquely equipped to extract value from human producers. Wesley would himself inveigh against dishonest industry and fettered exchange, but not against the powers of cash itself. In his simpler moral economy, its poison was drawn if it was used in ways pleasing to God. And it made all virtuous effort measurable and commensurable, permitting the conversion of worldly enterprise into spiritual credit. In this sense, the most 'precious talent' of money was its capacity to enable mortals to 'trade up'. Salvation itself became obtainable on free-market terms. These fiscal orientations also suffused Wesleyan practice. 'As a voluntary organization', says Obelkevich (1976: 206), 'Methodism ... fostered in its members a new outlook, individual and collective, towards money'. Finances were a constant matter of concern, and collections were taken up for many causes, not least foreign missions. In Britain, as among African converts, a ceaseless stream of demands and appeals highlighted the meliorative qualities of cash.

The great evangelical societies, in fact, were run like businesses, with men of commerce actively investing their resources and managing their affairs (Helmstadter 1992: 10). In the field, the Nonconformists put their trust in the power of money to bring progress, and to place all things, even God's grace, within human reach. This faith in the creative powers of cash recalls Simmel's *Philosophy of Money*, perhaps the most refined statement of the nineteenth-century

European belief in the transformative power of coin. For Simmel (1978: 291), man was by nature an 'exchanging animal' and, by this token, an 'objective animal' too: exchange, in its 'wonderful simplicity', made both the receiver and the giver, replacing selfish desire with mutual acknowledgement and objective appraisal. Transaction, he went on, begets rationalization, and the more that values are rationalized, 'the more room there is in them, as in the house of God, for every soul'. Because of its unlimited convertibility (292), money was uniquely capable of setting free the intrinsic worth of the world to be traded in neutral, standardized terms, and so it enabled the construction of an integrated society of morally dependent, but psychically self-sufficient persons (297f).

While they might never have put it in just these terms, the Nonconformists missionaries in South Africa devoted much of their effort to making Africans into 'exchanging animals', an enterprise in which cash played a pivotal role. They, too, nurtured the dream of an expansive civil society built not upon savage barter but upon transactions among self-possessed, moneyed persons. According to this dream, the liberation of 'natives' from a primitive dependence on their kin and their chiefs lay in the creation of a higher order, a world of moral and material interdependence mediated by stable, impersonal media: letters, numbers, notes and coin.

There was, as everyone knows, another side to money: its longstanding Christian taint as an instrument of corruption and betrayal. In part, this flowed from the power of cash, indeed all instruments of commensuration, to equate disparate forms of value. It could dissolve what was unique, precious and personal, reducing everything to the indiscriminate object of private avarice: the Saviour, note, had been sold for 30 pieces of silver. What was more, the ability of coin to transpose different forms of worth enabled profitable conversions to be made among them; in particular, it allowed the rich to prosper by using their assets to control the productivity of others. Parry and Bloch (1989: 2f; cf. Le Goff 1980) remind us that this sort of profit was anathema to the medieval European church, which saw productive work as the only legitimate source of wealth and condemned, as unnatural, the effortless earnings of merchants and money lenders. Capitalism was to exploit the metabolic qualities of money in unprecedented ways, of course – especially its capacity to make things commensurable by turning distinct aspects of human existence, like land and labour, into alienable commodities. Protestantism would endorse this process by sanctifying desire as virtuous ambition; also by treating the market as a realm of provident opportunity. Yet its medieval qualms remained. As Weber (1958: 53) stressed, those Christians who most aptly embodied the spirit of capitalism were ascetics. They took little pleasure in wealth per se. For them, *making* money was an end in itself, a transcendental value. It gave evidence of ceaseless 'busy-ness' and divine approval.

In so far as money remained demonically corrosive, there was only one way to avoid its corrupting qualities: to let it go. If it was to generate virtue, it had visibly to circulate. Hoarded wealth was 'the snare of the devil' (Wesley 1986: 233). It made men forsake the inner life for superficial pride, luxury and leisure. The Divine Proprietor required that his stewards put its talent to work either by cycling it back into honest business or by giving it away in charity; the proper movement of wealth was both creative and positive. By those lights, exchange *was* production (Parry and Bloch 1989: 86). Nonconformists still held to a labour theory of value, but now the notion of industry was cast in terms of manufacture and the market, of wage labour, the circulation of wealth, and the productive character of capital.

For Nonconformists like Wesley, in short, assiduous effort and ethical dealing – the market, literally, as a 'moral' economy – were enough to curb the malignancy of money. Charity, itself a high yield investment in virtue, was the main means of redistributing wealth, a way to 'lay up ... treasures in the bank of heaven' (Wesley 1984: 629). Humble toil also paid spiritual dividends, but at a lower rate. In the here and now, Methodism tended to endorse existing labour relations; during the late 1700s, even child workers were said to profit from industrious discipline (Warner 1930: 151). And the just wage *was* just, for exertion in one's allotted calling was its own reward. Hence it behoved the faithful to strive ceaselessly to produce all they could, an injunction that gelled well with the expansive ethos of humane imperialism.

Read in this light, it is clear that the economic emphasis of missionary practice in South Africa expressed more than a mere effort to survive or even to profit. It expressed the spirit of liberal modernity, being part of the attempt to foster a self-regulating commonwealth, for which the market was both the model and the means; also, to induce what Unsworth (1992) has aptly termed a 'sacred hunger', an insatiable desire for material enrichment and moral progress. As we shall see, the task proved onerous, for the 'mammon of unrighteousness' was never easily befriended. By the mid-1820s, some of the more radical evangelicals in England were denouncing the reduction of human qualities to price. In the mission field, the Nonconformists were caught, time and again, in the double-sided implications of money. Meanwhile, the kind of value carried by coin would come face to face with African notions of worth, setting off new contrasts, contests and combinations.

Other Kinds of Value

The Southern Tswana world of the early nineteenth century bore some similarity to the one from which the missionaries set out. Stress was laid here, too, on human production as the source of value. Here, too, communities were understood as social creations, built up through the ceaseless actions and transactions of people eager to enhance their fund of worth. Here, too, exchange was facilitated by versatile media that measured and stored wealth, and permitted its negotiation from afar.

These parallels, we have argued (1992: 127f), are sufficient to cast doubt on the exclusive association of commodities and competitive individualism with industrial capitalism – or with modernity. But, by the same token, similar practices do not necessarily have the same genesis, constitution or meaning. Although Southern Tswana subscribed to a fundamentally humanist sense of the production of wealth, their understanding of value – and the way it vested in persons, relationships and objects – was different from that of their interlocutors from abroad. Thus, while early missionaries thought they detected in the Africans a stress on self-contrivance, a dark replica of Western economic man, they found, on longer acquaintance, that this person was a far cry from the discrete, enclosed subject they hoped to usher into the church. Indigenous 'utilitarianism', Tswana literati like Molema (1920: 116) insisted, was unlike European 'egoism'; the evangelists referred to the 'native' variant as 'selfishness'. Indeed, closer engagement of previously distinct economies on the frontier would reveal deep distinctions behind superficial resemblances, and would give birth to a dynamic field of hybrid subjects and signs.

The Setswana verb *go dira* meant 'to make', 'to work,' or 'to do'. *Tiro*, its noun form, covered a wide range of activities – from cultivation to political negotiation, cooking to ritual performance – which yielded value in persons, relations and things. It also produced 'wealth' (*khumô*), an extractable surplus (of beer, artefacts, tobacco, stock and so on) which could be further deployed to multiply worth. Sorcery (*boloi*) was its inverse, implying the negation of value through attempts to harm others and/or unravel their endeavours. *Tiro* itself could never be alienated from its human context and transacted as mere labour power; that experience still awaited most Southern Tswana. Rather, it was an intrinsic dimension of the everyday act of making selves and social ties.

This vision of the production of value, based on close human interdependence, bore little resemblance to that of liberal economics, which saw the commonweal as the fruit of impersonal transactions among autonomous beings. For Tswana, wealth inhered in relations. Which is why its pursuit involved (i) the construction of enduring connections among kin and affines, patrons and clients, sovereigns and supporters, men and their ancestors; and (ii) the extension of influence by means of exchanges, usually via the medium of cattle, which secured rights in, and claims over, others. But, while these rights and claims were constantly contested, the productive and reproductive properties of a relationship, be it wedlock or serfdom, could not be separated from the bonds that bore them (Molema 1920: 125; Schapera (1940: 77). The object of social exchange was precisely *not* to accumulate riches with no strings attached: the traffic in beasts served to knit human beings together in an intricate weave, in which the density of linkages and the magnitude of value were one and the same thing.

Because they were the means, *par excellence*, of building social biographies and accumulating capital, cattle were the supreme form of property here; they could congeal, store and increase value, holding it stable in a world of flux (Comaroff and Comaroff 1992: 139). Not surprisingly, their widespread use as currency in human societies was noted by early theorists of political economy (Smith 1976: 38; Marx 1967 1: 183). While Adam Smith (1976) judged them 'rude' and 'inconvenient' instruments of commerce, he appreciated that they embodied many of the elementary features of coin, being useful, alienable, relatively durable objects. Although standardized as species, moreover, stock come in different sizes and colours, genders and ages, and so might be utilized as tokens of varying quality and denomination. (Many African peoples, of course, have long elaborated on the exquisite distinctions among kine; among domestic bovines, that is, of either sex and any age). True, cattle are not as divisible as inanimate substances like metal and tend, therefore, to be more gross, slow-moving units of trade. But, as we shall see, Southern Tswana took this to be one of their advantages over cash, whose velocity they regarded as dangerous. Herds *were* moveable, of course, especially for purposes of exchange, a fact stressed by Marx (1967 1: 115); for him, the apparent self-propulsion of currency was crucial to its role in animating commodity transactions. Affluent Tswana men exploited this ambulatory quality, dispersing bridewealth to affines and loaning stock to clients as they strove to turn their resources into control over people. They also rotated animals among dependants, and between cattle posts, both as a hedge against disaster and as a way of hiding assets from the jealous gaze of rivals (Schapera 1938: 24).

It is as exchange value on the hoof, then, that cattle occupied a pivotal place in Southern Tswana political economy. Their capacity to objectify, transfer and enhance wealth endowed them with almost magical talents; much like money in the West. The beast, goes the vernacular song, is 'god with a wet nose' (*modimo o nkô e metsi*; Comaroff and Comaroff 1992: 127). This is a patent instance of fetishism in bovine shape – of the attribution to objects, that is, of value produced by humans – which suggests that the commodity is not specific to capitalism. At the same time, the case of Tswana stock also shows that commodification need not be an all-or-none process; and that it is always culturally situated in a meaningful world of work and worth. Here, for example, while animals enabled rich men to lay claim to the labours of others, they did not depersonalize relations among people. Quite the contrary: they drew attention to the social embeddedness of those very relations – while making them seem part of the natural order of things.

The complex qualities of cattle currency would intervene in mission efforts to transform the Southern Tswana sense of value. For beasts were enough like money to be identified with it, yet enough unlike it to make and mark salient differences. On one hand, they could abstract value. On the other, they did the opposite: they signified and enriched personal identities and social ties. The capacity of animals in Africa to serve both as instruments and as signs of human relationship has long been noted; the so-called 'bovine idiom' is an instance of the more general tendency of humans to use alienable objects to extend their own existence by uniting themselves with others (Mauss 1954; Munn 1977). Both in their individual beauty and their collective association with wealth, kine were ideal – and idealized – personifications of men. A highly nuanced vocabulary existed in Setswana to describe variations in colour, marking, disposition, horns and reproductive status (Lichtenstein 1973: 81; Sandilands 1953: 342). Named and praised, they were creatures of distinction. Not only did they bear their owners' stamp as they traversed social space (Somerville 1979: 230), they also served as living records of the passage of value along the pathways of inheritance, affinity, alliance and authority.

The intricate patterns of stock deployment among Tswana made it difficult for early European visitors to assess their holdings. Longer-term records suggest a history of fluctuations in animal populations, with cycles of depletion being followed by periods of recovery, at least until the end of the nineteenth century (Grove 1989: 164). But there is clear evidence of the existence, at the beginning of that century, of large and unequally distributed herds. Observers were struck by blatant discrepancies in cattle ownership, and by the unambiguous association – Burchell (1824 volume 2: 272) used the word 'metonymy' – of wealth in kine with power (cf. Lichtenstein 1973: 76f; Molema 1920: 115). Thus the chief was the supreme herdsman (*modisa*) of his people, a metaphor that captured well vernacular visions of value and political economy. Situated atop the *morafe* ('nation'), he presided over a domain marked, not by fixed boundaries, but by an outer ring of water holes and pasture – in other words, a range (Comaroff and Comaroff 1992: 141). Royal stock also built relations beyond the polity, being used to placate and to trade with other sovereigns.

It was not only chiefs who mobilized cattle as a currency of power: other men of position also accumulated stock and set up networks of alliance and patronage. Ordinary male citizens, however, relied on inheritance, bridewealth and natural increase to build their modest herds. Some – serfs, and others laid low – had no animals at all. They made up what Burchell (1824 2: 348) termed an 'ill-fated class', eternally dependent on their betters. In the bovine economy of the Southern Tswana, in sum, an indigenous 'stock exchange' underwrote inequalities of class, gender, generation and rank. As the pliable media used to forge all productive relations, human and superhuman alike, cattle were the quintessential form of social and symbolic capital. They moved men to intrigue, sorcery and warfare, to deep contemplation about the nature of life and worth, and, as Somerville (1979: 134) witnessed in 1801, to passionate public poetry.

Cattle were also a prime medium in the exchanges that, by the late eighteenth century, linked Southern Tswana to other peoples on the subcontinent, yielding beads from the Kora and Griqua to the south, and iron implements, copper jewellery and tobacco from communities to the north and north-east (Lichtenstein 1930 2: 409; Stow 1905: 449, 489). Bovine capital also gave access to the ivory and pelts desired by white travellers, who arrived in growing numbers from *c*.1800 (Shillington 1985: 11). Pack oxen enabled the long-distance haulage of *sebilô*, a sought-after hair cosmetic, from its source in Tlhaping territory (Campbell 1813: 170). But the earliest European explorers already noted that Tswana were reluctant to trade away their beasts. Somerville's (1979: 140) expedition to the interior failed in its mercantile objectives because of the '["natives"] unwillingness to part with their cattle'. The Englishman found this 'difficult to account for, since they convert them to no useful purpose whatever'.

Nonetheless, regional exchange networks were active enough to persuade the Europeans that they had stumbled upon the 'essential principles of *international traffic*', or 'mercantile agency in its infancy' in the African veld (Burchell 1824 2: 555; original emphasis). Andrew Smith (1939 1: 251), in fact, observed that chiefs managed production explicitly to foster alliances;

Cattle, Currencies & the Politics of Commensuration 45

they tried, as well, to monopolize dealings with foreigners and to control commerce across their realms (Campbell 1822 2: 194). Indeed, whites found these men aware of discrepancies in going rates for such items as ivory, and keen to profit from them. Notwithstanding the reluctance to sell beasts, occasions to traffic with Europeans – in the early years for beads, later for guns and money – were eagerly seized. When Lichtenstein (1930 2: 388) visited the Tlhaping in 1805, before a permanent mission was established, he noted that a 'general spirit of trade' was easily roused. The Africans kept up an energetic exchange until his party had naught left to sell. A few years on, Burchell (1824 2: 555) was struck by the existence of enduring trade partnerships (*maats*; Dutch) between individual Tlhaping and Klaarwater Khoi.

We shall come back, shortly, to the entry of the civilizing mission into Southern Tswana commerce. Already, however, two things are clear. The first is that the Africans had long channelled their surpluses into trade, bringing them a range of goods from knives and tobacco to widely circulating forms of currency. Of the latter, second, beads had become the most notable. By the turn of the nineteenth century,[3] they were serving as media of transaction that articulated local and global economies, linking the worlds of cattle and money (cf. Graeber 1996). Along with buttons, which were put to a similar purpose, they were portable tokens that, for a time, epitomized foreign exchange value beyond the colonial frontier. Beads were 'the only circulating medium or money in the interior', Campbell noted (1822 1: 246), adding that every 'nation' through which they passed made a profit on them. Different kinds composed distinct regional currencies; Philip (1828 2: 131) tells us that no importance was attached to particular examples, however beautiful, if they were 'not received among the tribes around them'. At the same time, African communities showed strong preferences, in the early 1800s, for specific colours, sizes, and degrees of transparency (Beck 1989: 220f).[4]

Even as they became a semi-standardized currency for purposes of external trade, beads served internally as personal adornments; in this they were like many similar sorts of wealth objects. Their attraction seems to have stemmed from the fact that particular valuables could be withdrawn from

---

[3] According to Beck (1989: 220), beads were introduced into Southern Africa by the Portuguese, and continued to find their way into the interior in small quantities after the establishment of the Cape Colony (Saunders 1966: 65). Only in the early nineteenth century, however, did sizeable mass-produced stocks arrive from abroad (Somerville 1979: 140). Metal rings and beads, especially of brass and copper, seem to have predated glass imports in long-distance trade (Stow 1905: 489).

[4] It is not clear (i) how much these observations actually applied to Southern Tswana; or (ii) the extent to which the alleged capriciousness of African demand was a matter of European ignorance. We find little record of rapidly shifting tastes among the Tlhaping people. A very early document (Saunders 1966: 65) suggests that they traded in blue beads. In 1801, Somerville (1979: 140) noted that they would only accept black and white ones; but blue reappears time and again in their preferences. In 1812, Burchell (1824 2: 569) confirmed that light blue, as well as black and white, were their favourites. In the 1820s, Campbell (LMS 1824) found that blue was still greatly desired, although by then darker shades tended to be chosen. Twenty-five years on, Livingstone (1959 vol.1: 151) observed that the Kwena preference – which, he implies, was a matter of changing 'fashion' – was for solid, bright shades of red, blue or white. By then, however, the bottom had fallen out of the bead market to the south (see below).

circulation for display, itself a form of conspicuous consumption.[5] But men of means also accumulated *hidden* stocks: 'their chief wealth, like that of more civilized nations, [was] hoarded up in their coffers' (Campbell 1822 1: 246; cf. Graeber 1996). Here it stayed, in precisely the manner abhorred by the Protestants, until favourable opportunities for trade presented themselves. Market exchange was, at this point, a sporadic activity directed at specific exotic objects. It was set apart from everyday processes of production and consumption.

Some observers stressed the monetary properties of beads: 'They answer the same purpose as cowrie shells in India and North Africa', wrote Campbell (1822 1: 246), 'or as guineas and shillings in Britain'. But others were struck by the differences. For a start, aesthetic qualities seemed integral to their worth. 'Among these people', offered Philip (1828 2: 131), 'utility is, perhaps, more connected with beauty that it is with us'. Simmel (1978: 73) would have said that the separation of the beautiful from the useful comes only with the objectification of value: the aesthetic artefact takes on a unique existence, *sui generis*; it cannot be replaced by another that might perform the same function. Such an artefact, therefore, is the absolute inverse of the coin, whose defining feature is its substitutability.

Among Southern Tswana, the increasing velocity of trade did render some media of exchange – first beads, then money – ever more interchangeable. But the process was never complete, and it did not eliminate other forms of wealth in which beauty and use explicitly enhanced each other. Indeed, the longevity of cattle currencies in African societies bears testimony to the fact that processes of rationalization, standardization and universalization are *always* refracted by social and cultural circumstance. In the cow, aesthetics and utility, uniqueness and substitutability complemented each other, colouring Tswana notions of value in general – and of money in particular. Black wage labourers in early twentieth-century South Africa, Breckenridge (1995: 274) notes, set special store by the physical qualities of metallic coins; in explaining their attitude, public intellectuals John Dube and Solomon Tshekisho Plaatje contrasted 'flimsy' paper money with 'the good red gold we know and love'. Comeliness and usefulness play off each other in the West as well, of course; modernists, after all, insist that form should follow function. The Tswana appreciation of prized beads and beasts, similarly, expressed a sense of 'attractiveness' that fused the perfect with the practical. Persons or objects possessed of it were thought to draw towards themselves desirable qualities dispersed in the world at large. Ornamental baubles or celebrated stock were the very epitome of attractiveness: held apart from the everyday cycle of exchange, they congealed precious potential.

Objects that come to be invested with value as media of exchange vary greatly over time and space, a point well demonstrated by the emergence of

---

[5] What seems significant in the use of the coin, jewel, bead or shell as personal adornment is that it be regarded as *intrinsically* valuable; not, like notes or credit cards, as tokens of value that resides elsewhere. Yet the distinction between 'real' worth and its representation is often hard to sustain.

new currencies as formerly distinct economic orders begin to intersect. Marx (1967 1: 83) once said that, when the latter happens, the 'universal equivalent form' often lodges arbitrarily and transiently in a particular commodity. So it was with beads, which had been mass produced for different ends in the West, but turned out to serve well, for a while, as a vehicle of commerce beyond the colonial border. Marx also added that, as traffic persists, such tokens of equivalence tend to 'crystallize ... out into the money form'. So, once again, it was with beads. While Tswana would accept various articles as gifts, these were of little use in trade. 'They want money in such a case', Campbell (1822 1: 246) found, 'that is, beads'. As transactions increased in volume, standards of value in the worlds linked by this new currency began to affect each other: merchants noted that rates charged by Africans in the interior rose and became more uniform.[6] By the 1820s, the demand for beads at the Cape had driven up prices dramatically, to the extent that missionaries tried to secure supplies from England at one-third of the cost (Beck 1989: 218f).

The bottom soon fell out of the frontier bead market, however (although not so further north; see Chapman 1971 1: 127). That market seems to have been sustained by the dearth of fractions of the rixdollar, the currency at the Cape in the early 1800s (Arndt 1928: 44–46). After 1825, Britain introduced its own silver and copper coinage to its imperial possessions, and paper dollars were replaced by sterling. Once the new supply had stabilized, and had filtered into the interior, its effect on bead money was devastating. In 1835, Andrew Smith (1939 1: 250) wrote that a white merchant

> inform[ed] me that when first he began to trade in this country about 1828, nothing was desired by the natives but beads, etc., but now they are scarcely asked for; indeed nothing is to be purchased by them [beads] but milk or firewood ... They understand reckoning money quite well, and if told the price of an article ... they reckon out the money with the greatest precision.

Ironically, while Tswana came to reckon in money, many traders preferred to deal in kind. But, even more important than changes in the cash supply, a shift was occurring in the structure of wants and in local notions of value. It was encouraged, above all, by the presence of the evangelists and by the entry onto the scene, at their urging, of a cadre of itinerant merchants and shopkeepers.

* * *

Here, then, were two distinct regimes of value, one European and the other African, whose engagement would have a profound impact on the colonial encounter. To the Nonconformists, economic reform was no mere adjunct to spirituality: virtue and salvation had to be made by man, using the scarce

---

[6] Earlier discrepancies – and the fact that they could mass-produce trinket cash – had, of course, been advantageous to the Europeans. In 1802, LMS clergy in the Eastern Cape actually contemplated setting up a button factory to assist their purchase of things like stock (Beck 1989: 214).

material resources bequeathed by providence for improving the world. Commercial enterprise allowed the industrious to turn labour into wealth and wealth into grace. Money was the crucial medium of convertibility in this. It typified the potential for good and evil given as a birth-right to every self-willed individual. Southern Tswana, upon whom the evangelists hoped to impress these divine possibilities, also inhabited a universe of active human agency, in which riches were made through worldly transactions. Exchange, in their case, was effected primarily through cattle. In contrast to cash, stock socialized assets, measuring their ultimate worth not in treasures in heaven, but in people on earth. We move, now, to examine how these regimes of value, already in contact in the early 1800s, were brought into ever closer articulation.

Extending the Invisible Hand

Civilizing Commerce, Sanctified Shopping: The Early Years

> You white men are a strange folk. You have the word of God ... but [your traders] are giving beads to the girls [and] corrupting the women of my people. [T]hey are teaching my people abominations of which even they were once ignorant, heathen as they are. Here are traders enough (Chief Sechele 1865).[7]

British observers in the early 1800s might have acknowledged that Southern Tswana showed a lively interest in exchange. But they also stressed the difference between 'native commerce' and orderly European business. Thus Burchell (1824 2: 536–9) noted that 'mercantile jealousy' had produced competing efforts to monopolize traffic with the colony to the south. He proposed a 'regulated trade for ivory ... with the Bichuana nations', to be vested in an authorized body of white merchants who would institute 'fair dealing' to the advantage of all. Like liberal economies before and since, his 'free' market required careful management.

The founding evangelists shared this trust in the beneficent effect of trade. Some said that the very 'sight of a shop' on mission ground roused savages to industry (Philip 1828,1: 204–5). The equation of civilization with commerce might have become one of the great clichés of the epoch. But, for the Nonconformists, it was far from a platitude. The point was not to create an exploitable dependency; although that did happen. Nor was it simply to play on base desire to make people give ear to the Gospel; although that happened too. It ran much deeper. Trade had a capacity to breach 'the sullen isolations of heathenism', to stay the 'fountain of African misery' (Livingstone 1940: 255). All of which made material reform an urgent moral duty. The optimism of the missionaries in this respect was to falter in the face of the stark realities of the colonial frontier. The Christians had eventually to

---

[7] These words were part of a message sent by the Kwena chief to Robert Moffat (Smith 1957: 171).

rethink their dream of a commonwealth of free-trading black communities, actively enhancing their virtue and wealth. But they continued to hold that the market would rout superstition, slavery, sloth; this even when, later in the century, market forces undercut their own idyll of independent African economies, compelling 'their' peoples to become wage vassals in their own land.

There was, in other words, more to championing commerce among heathens than merely making virtue of necessity, as some have suggested; although it *is* true that many pioneer evangelists had to exchange to survive (Beck 1989: 211). In fact, the most ardent advocates of free enterprise were often those most opposed to clergy themselves doing business. Livingstone (1857: 39) held that, while missionary and trader were mutually dependent, 'experience shows that the two employments cannot very well be combined in the same person'. Ironically, he was to be accused of gun running by the Boers. But then, on the frontier, the lines between prestation, purchase and profit were very fine indeed – and frequently in dispute. While traffic with peoples living beyond colonial borders was forbidden by law, missionaries were, de facto, exempt, except for the ban on selling liquor, weapons and ammunition. Dealings with Africans often went well beyond the procuring of necessities, involving considerable capital outlay. In the upshot, competition and accusations of dishonourable practice among the brethren soon became common (Beck 1989: 214). As early as 1817, the LMS at the Cape had had to confront the issue as a matter of policy. Its members agreed that, while trade was forced on them by the inadequacy of the Society's support, they should make their stations self-sustaining through agriculture and handicrafts. The quest for profit, however, was specifically discouraged.

From the first, Tswana associated evangelists, like all whites, with barter. Robert Moffat (Moffat and Moffat 1951: 18) reports that, when he and the Rev. Kay of the Wesleyan Methodist Missionary Society (WMMS) travelled among the Tlhaping in 1821, 'the Bootchuanas flocked around us with articles for exchange'.[8] The clergymen tended to be less than open in their formal correspondence about their dealings; this notwithstanding the fact that, in the 1820s, the mission societies considered entering the lucrative ivory business to raise funds for projects in the Colony (Beck 1989: 217; Moffat and Moffat 1951: 62). Cooperation between the Nonconformists and merchants was close: traders journeying beyond the Orange River tended to lodge at mission stations and often accompanied evangelists on their travels (Livingstone 1960: 141).

The Nonconformists also gave out goods for purposes other than trade. Early on they dispensed tobacco, beads and buttons to encourage goodwill, only to find that prestations came to be expected in return for attending church and school.[9] Few Tswana seem initially to have shared the European distinction between gifts and commodities, donations and payments. Yet one

---

[8] See also S. Broadbent, Matlwasse, 8 June 1823 (WMMS, South Africa Correspondence, 300).
[9] Mrs Hamilton, New Lattakoo, 16 February 1818 (CWM, LMS Incoming Letters (South Africa), 7–3–A).

thing *was* widely recognized: that whites controlled desirable objects. As a result, they soon became the uncomfortable victims of determined efforts to acquire those objects. Their correspondence declared that all Africans, even dignified chiefs, were inveterate 'beggars': that they persistently demanded items like snuff, which the missions were assumed to have in large supply, and that their behaviour violated Protestant notions of honest gain (Moffat and Moffat 1951: 63). It took a while for the Christians to realize that 'begging' was also a form of homage to the powerful (Price 1956: 166; Mackenzie 1871: 44f). Burchell (1824 2: 407), a naturalist and not a cleric, discerned that these requests were limited largely to a specific category of goods:

> [T]hey never asked for *sikháka* (beads); these being considered more especially as *money*, to be employed only as the medium of trade with distant tribes, and for the purchase of the more expensive articles; while *muchúko* and *lishuéna* (tobacco and snuff) being consumable merchandise, are ... regarded as a less important species of property. (Original emphasis)

A similar contrast between treasures and trifles seems to have obtained in the brazen 'theft', in the first years, of the evangelists' belongings, especially their produce and tools (Moffat and Moffat 1951: 57). Previous visitors, interestingly, had remarked on the virtual absence of pilfering.[10] Lichtenstein (1973: 75) was struck by the fact that only items *not* considered as property were ever taken. But Broadbent's account of the severe response of a Rolong chief to one such incident[11] makes it clear that the sudden presence of quantities of desirable goods had raised unprecedented problems of defining and maintaining ownership. The missionaries tended to see this as a lack of respect for private effects: Hodgson (1977: 336) mused, in 1826, on the 'precarious tenure upon which the natives [held] their possessions'. Obviously, conventions of acquisition, proprietorship and remuneration were being tested on both sides of the encounter.

As Beck (1989: 224) confirms, the evangelists introduced more European goods than did any other whites at the time. Their dealings eroded the local desire for beads and buttons in favour of a complex array of wants, primarily for domestic commodities like clothes, blankets and utensils. But this transformation, as we have suggested, entailed far more than the mere provision of objects. Changing patterns of consumption grew out of a shift in ideas about the nature, worth and significance of particular things in themselves, which, in turn, was set in play by the encounter of very different regimes of value. Thus, even where their uses seemed obvious, such goods as clothes and furniture were given meanings irreducible to utility alone, meanings which often made the Europeans uneasy (Comaroff and Comaroff 1997: chapter 5).

Yet more basic than this was the fact that, as the century wore on, it was less the missionaries than the merchants they brought in their wake who were responsible for the supply of goods. Discomforted by the image of men

---

[10] S. Broadbent, Matlwasse, 8 June 1823 (WMMS, South Africa Correspondence, 300).
[11] ibid.

of God haggling over the price of trinkets (Beck 1989: 213), most evangelists encouraged independent traders to settle on their stations. By 1830, John Philip (1828 1: 204f) had already publicized the success of his 'experiment' to have one open a store at Bethelsdorp:

> The sight of the goods in their windows ... produced the effect anticipated: the desire of possessing the articles for use and comfort by which they were constantly tempted, acquired additional strength on every fresh renewal of stimulus.

Money, he added, had gone up in the people's estimation. They had begun, enthusiastically, to bring produce to the trader to exchange for goods. Bechuanaland soon followed Bethelsdorp. The introduction of stores in this manner – all the better to instruct non-Western peoples in 'the economic facts of life' – was a high priority among British Protestants in many parts of the world; Miller (1973: 101) describes similar ventures in the Argentine in the 1930s.

Time would mute the idyll of cooperation between missions and merchants. Already in 1841, Mary Moffat (1967: 18), while reiterating the need to foster a desire for commodities, bemoaned the high prices charged by local dealers for 'worthless materials'. A decade later, Livingstone (1959 2: 152) wrote in acerbic terms about traders of all stripes. While they reaped huge profits, he complained, these men resented the evangelists, accusing them of driving up the price of African goods. While the whites squabbled over their dealings with Africans, Tswana sovereigns – witness the words of Chief Sechele – had their own reasons for being wary of merchants. The latter paid scant respect to longstanding mores or monopolies, being ready to buy from anyone who had anything desirable to sell; the purchase of ivory and feathers from Rolong 'vassals' in the Kalahari, for instance, cost the life of one businessman and his son (Mackenzie 1871: 130). Such friction was frequent beyond the mission stations (Livingstone 1959 2: 86). But even when storekeepers operated under the eyes of the evangelists, their behaviour often gave offence. Brawling, theft and sexual assault were common; Sechele banished two of them for an 'indecent' attack on a Kwena woman in broad daylight near Livingstone's home (Livingstone 1974: 120). No wonder that local rulers developed a 'well-known' reluctance to allow itinerant traders to traverse their territories (Mackenzie 1871: 130). Or that, later in the century, strong chiefs would try to subject European commerce to strict control (Parsons 1977: 122).

The evangelists would have to wrestle constantly with the contradictions of commerce. In embracing its virtues, they had to deal with the fact that the two-faced coin threatened to profane their sacred mission. Yet the merchants were essential in the effort to reform local economies by hitching them to the colonial market – and the body of corporate nations beyond.

Object Lessons
So the merchants remained on the mission stations – where they prospered. Storekeepers stocked all the quotidian objects deemed essential to a civil 'household economy' (Moffat 1842: 507, 502f): clothes, fabrics, furniture,

blankets, sewing implements, soap and candle moulds; the stuff, that is, of feminized domestic life, with its scrubbed, illuminated interiors. They also carried the implements of intensive agriculture, and the guns and ammunition required to garner the 'products of the chase', increasingly the most valuable of trade goods. Colonial whites abhorred the idea of weapons in African hands. But, by the 1830s, 'old soldier's muskets' were being sold for '6, 7 and 8 oxen', and three or four pounds of gunpowder for a single animal (Smith 1939 1: 232)[12] – although, after the mid-century, the expanding arms business was mostly in the hands of well-capitalized Cape entrepreneurs, a fact that would have far-reaching consequences for game stocks and for the economic independence of Southern Bechuanaland (Shillington 1985: 13f, 21f).

Mission accounts from the late 1800s show that European commodities had begun to tell their own story in the Tswana world. Wookey (1884: 303) wrote:

> Through the settlement of missionaries, and the visits of traders and travellers, the country became known and opened up. Cattle first, and then ivory, feathers, and karosses, were the principal things brought by the natives for barter. They were exchanged for guns and ammunition, cows, wagons, horses, clothes, and ... other things. To-day a trader's stock is not complete unless he has school material, stationery, and even books.

Ornaments, cooking utensils and consumables were widely purchased, as were coffee, tea and sugar. The foreign goods that seemed everywhere in use spoke of far-reaching domestic reconstruction.

At least in some quarters: the acquisition of these commodities required surplus production and disposable income, which was restricted to the emerging upper and middle peasantry. At the same time, despite their taste for European things, many wealthy men remained reluctant, save *in extremis*, to sell stock (Schapera 1933: 648). On the other hand, the market was particularly attractive to those excluded from indigenous processes of accumulation. Client peoples, for example, were easily tempted to turn tribute into trade – which is why some chiefs lost their monopolies over exchange (but cf. Parsons 1977: 120). Especially along the frontier, ever more Tswana, citizens and 'vassals' alike, entered into commercial transactions; as a result, they acquired manufactured goods well before the South African mineral revolution of the 1870s and the onset of large-scale labour migration. Small objects may speak of big changes, of course. Rising sales of coffee, tea and sugar marked important shifts in patterns of nutrition and sociality. They also tied local populations to the production and consumption of commodities in other parts of the empire (cf. Mintz 1985). As George Orwell (1962: 82) once said, in this respect, 'changes in diet are more important than changes of dynasty or even of religion'.

But Wookey's account also suggests that things had veered out of mission control (1884: 304):

---

[12] Smith (1939 1: 232) gives some insight into profit margins at the time, noting that an iron pot, costing 2½ rixdollars at the Cape, was sold in Tswana areas for 10 – four times the price.

> Changes, however, have taken place in the trade of the country. A few years ago many thousands of pounds' worth of produce annually changed hands and passed through to the colony. Now ivory has become scarce ... [and] the [ostrich feather] trade has dwindled down ... But another door was opening for the people ... I mean the Diamond Fields.

Proletarianization was an almost inevitable consequence of the economic revolution encouraged by the Nonconformist mission. Wookey (1884: 304) admitted that the material developments promoted by the evangelists had not been an 'unmixed good'; in this, he anticipated the concerns of African critics, voiced later, about the impact of sugar, alcohol and imported provisions on the health of black populations. Not only had new diseases appeared, but drink had become 'one of the greatest curses of the country'. The most profitable and addictive of commodities, its effects were a sordid caricature of the desire to make 'natives' dependent on the market. Despite Christian efforts to limit its distribution (Mackenzie 1871: 92), brandy was being supplied in ever growing quantities to Bechuanaland by the second half of the nineteenth century.

The issue was not trivial. Several Tswana rulers had already tried to banish brandy from their realms, and Khama III expelled traders who failed to comply (Holub 1881 1: 278). Plaatje (1996), using the black press, was to champion the Liquor Proclamation of 1904, a law prohibiting the purchase of 'white man's fire water' by 'natives' in South Africa. But the flow of alcohol had been eroding the cultural and physical defences of many frontier communities for decades. Holub's (1881 1: 236) graphic account of his tour of Tlhaping territory belies Wookey's paean to the positive, 'opening' effect of European commodities. It sketches a dark picture of the corrupting force of the colonial market:

> [M]en, in tattered European clothes, except now and then one in a mangy skin, followed by as many women ... and by a swarm of children as naked as when they were born, came shouting eagerly towards us. They were nearly all provided with bottles, or pots, or cans, and cried out for brandy ... They had brought all manner of things for barter for spirits. One man held up a jackal's hide, another a goat-skin; ... It was a disgusting scene ... One of the men made what he evidently imagined would be an irresistible appeal, by offering me a couple of greasy shillings.

In the nineteenth-century colonial imagination, as we have shown (Comaroff and Comaroff 1997: chapter 5), 'grease' evoked the clinging filth of savagery, the grime of uncontained bodies and unsavoury associations. Money was meant to promote the kind of industry and lifestyle that would dissolve its dirt. But in this instance it had failed, merely adding to the muck of heathenism, its own supposedly non-stick surfaces becoming coated with residues of depravity.

Accounts of this sort soon became more frequent. As new industrial centres sprang to life around the diamond fields, the satanic underside of commerce came all but to the Nonconformists' door. As it did, it exposed their naïvety in hoping to befriend the 'mammon of unrighteousness' by introducing Tswana to the market in a controlled, benevolent manner. By then, in any case, the traders they had brought into their midst had already helped to set a minor revolution in motion through the 'magic' of their commodities. That magic had ambiguous effects. It led, at one extreme, to the contrivance of a polite bourgeois life-world; also, among ordinary people, to forms of consumption in which objects were deployed in new designs for living, newly contrived identities, all of them stylistic fusions of the familiar and the fresh. At the other extreme, it conjured up the 'disgusting scenes' of poverty described by Holub and others. To be sure, the merchants had also given Southern Tswana practical lessons in the exploitative side of enlightened capitalism. From the very first, these entrepreneurs engaged in the infamous practice of buying local produce for a pittance and then, when food was short, selling it back at exorbitant profit.

The missionaries themselves had also played a crucial role in determining the ways in which Western objects and market practices had entered into Tswana life, however; as we have stressed, there is more to commodification than the mere provision of goods. The Christians set out to instil a 'sacred hunger', a sense of desire that linked refined consumption to a particular mode of producing goods and selves – and that encouraged continuing investment in civilizing enterprise. Above all else, this required a respect for the many talents of money.

The Objectification of Value & the Meaning of Money

> [M]oney's educational. It's far more educational than the things it buys.
> (E.M. Forster 1992: 133)

In so far as colonialism entailed a confrontation of different regimes of value, the encounter between Tswana and the missionaries was most clearly played out – and experienced – through the media most crucial to the measure of wealth on either side: cattle, money and the trade beads that, for a while, strung them together. Encounters of this sort, especially when they involved European capitalism in its expansive form, often ended in the erasure of one currency by another. But they sometimes gave rise to processes a good deal more complex than allowed by most theories of commodification. For value is born by human beings who seek actively to shape it to their own ends. Along the frontier, cash and cows became fiercely contested signs, alibis of distinct, mutually threatening modes of existence. The Nonconformists found themselves deeply mired in this struggle, not least in the early years.

To Tswana, it will be recalled, beasts were the prime means of storing and conveying wealth in people and things; also of embodying value in social relations. In fact, control over these relations was one of the objects of owning animals. Thus, while cattle *were* sometimes dealt on the foreign market, the bulk of both internal and long-distance trade seems to have been directed towards acquiring more stock.[13] In ordinary circumstances, barter never drew on capital; this is why Somerville's (1979: 140) party failed, in 1801, to persuade Tlhaping to part with bovines or to procure a single milk cow. Beads, here, stood for worth in alien and alienated form, circulating against goods on the external market, or those which had been freed from local entanglements. By being transacted with neighbouring people for animals, they could also be used to convert value from more to less reified forms.

But this currency had its own logic. With the increasing standardization of the bead market across the interior in the early nineteenth century, the value of certain resources in Tswana life was rendered measurable – and more easily negotiable. Articles formerly withheld from sale, or given only for cattle (such as karosses – garments of animal skin – made as personal property; Lichtenstein 1930 2: 389), became purchasable (Moffat and Moffat 1951: 262, 267). The Nonconformists encouraged this process of commodification, although their real objective was the introduction of money. Hence they used the token currency themselves to put a price on inalienable things, such as land and labour. Not only did they pay wages in it, but, in 1823, used it to acquire (what they thought was) the freehold on which their mission station was built (Moffat and Moffat 1951: 189, 113). Beads were also bartered for agricultural surpluses by both missionaries and merchants. There is even evidence – *vide* Sechele's outrage – that some traders offered Tswana women these baubles for sexual favours.

The effort of the missionaries to commodify African land, labour and produce, and to foster a desire for domestic goods, eventually helped to reorient the bulk of trade from the hinterland towards the Cape. This had the effect of limiting the viability of bead currency itself. The latter had served well as long as token transactions remained relatively confined in space and time; as long as they involved a narrow range of luxuries from a few external sources of supply; as long as exchange was sporadic and did not extend to the procurement of ordinary utilities. But once the ways and means of everyday life began to be commodified, and increasingly to emanate from the colonial economy, a more standardized, readily available, and widely circulating currency was needed to buy and sell them. So, as Tswana engaged with a broadening range of manufactures and middlemen in the 1830s, money quickly became the measure of worth. This, in turn, posed a threat to vernacular regimes of value that before had been kept distinct from foreign traffic. Even where coin did not actually change hands, it came to stand for the moral economy, the material values and the modes of contractual relationship propagated by the civilizing mission – and its world.

In spite of this, or perhaps because of it, the first attempts of the missions to teach the value of cash were not a success. Tswana evinced distrust in European tender, most notably in paper money. Not only was it suspected of being an easy medium of fraud, but its lack of durability was also a worry – for good

---

[13] There is evidence from elsewhere in South Africa that some African traders sold stock in order to use the cash they received to buy more at lower prices (Beck 1989: 214; Peires 1981: 100).

reason. Between 1806 and 1824, rixdollar notes were infamously fragile, and were thought unreliable by many whites as well (Arndt 1928: 44, 62). Later in the century, traders would pass illiterate Africans false bills – issued, in one case, by the 'Bank of Leather', entitling the bearer to 'the best Value' in 'London or Paris Boots & Shoes' in exchange for diamonds (Matthews 1887: 196).

Given the uncertainties of colonial currency, the evangelists did not always entrust the actual introduction of money, or the dissemination of its qualities, to the workings of the market. Occasionally they took matters into their own hands. Thus the Rev. Campbell had, on a tour beyond the colonial frontier in 1812–13, decided that the Griqua community merited consolidation both as a 'nation' and as a base for expanding LMS mission operations into the interior (Parsons 1927: 198). Crucial to the venture was a proper coinage (Campbell 1813: 256):

> It was likewise resolved, that as they had no circulating medium amongst them, by which they could purchase any small articles ... supposing a shop to be established amongst them ... they should apply to the Mission Society to get silver pieces of different value coined for them in England, which the missionaries would take for their allowance from the Society, having Griqua town marked on them. It is probable that, if this were adopted, in a short time they would circulate among all the nations round about, and be a great convenience.

God's bankers indeed! This mission money would be dubbed 'one of the most interesting emissions in the numismatic history of the British Empire' (Parsons 1927: 202; Arndt 1928: 128). Campbell set about ordering supplies of special coinage from a well-known English diesinker. We have record of four denominations, two each in silver and copper. 'Griquatown' and the amount were inscribed on one face, the symbol of the LMS on the other. The latter, a dove with an olive twig in its beak, aptly embodied the ideal of pacifying diffusion. Aesthetic considerations were significant on both sides: the Griqua expressly asked Campbell to obtain only silver pieces for them. Consistent with their views of beauty, Africans at the time preferred bright, shiny currency over duller coppers, a fact that seems to have had a tangible effect on the dissemination of this money (Parsons 1927: 199). Shipped to South Africa in two consignments in 1815 and 1816, it established itself in limited circulation (*pace* Arndt 1928: 127), a few examples turning up in places like Kimberley in later years.

The evangelists also deployed other means to foster respect for money. At issue, as we have said, was a moral economy in which its talents measured enterprise and enabled the conversion of wealth into virtue. If there was no cash in the African interior it had to be invented – or its existence feigned. The evidence shows that, even when little coinage was in circulation, missionaries used it as an invisible standard, a virtual currency, against which to tally the worth of goods, donations and services. In 1828, a few months after establishing an offshoot from the main Wesleyan station at Platberg, Hodgson wrote of his new school (WMMS 1829–31: 120):

1.1 Examples of Griqua Town coins

> We pay for it four shillings and sixpence per month rent; which sum, however, is raised by the children themselves, most of whom subscribe one halfpenny per week each, which they obtain by bringing us milk, eggs, firewood, &c., for sale ... The first week produced three shillings and ninepence; (the children having been requested to bring one penny each;) the second, two shillings and twopence.

Amidst a barter economy, the missions reckoned accounts with numerical exactitude. In the 1820s, the Methodists on the Eastern Cape frontier encouraged offerings of beads and buttons that would be rendered in shillings and pence according to current 'nominal' values (Beck 1989: 223). Also at issue in this small grinding of God's mills was the effort to encourage calculation. Counting – adding up, that is, the margins of profit and loss – enabled accounting, the form of stock-taking that epitomized puritan endeavour. The evangelists associated numeracy with self-control, exactitude, reason; school arithmetic, for example, was taught mostly in fiscal idiom, computation being inseparable from the process of commodification itself.

Numbers provided a tool with which to equate hitherto incomparable sorts of value, to price them and to allow unconditional convertibility from one to another. Quantification was iconic of the processes of standardization and incorporation, the erasure of differences in kind, at the core of cultural colonization. Hence the frequent association, in 'modernizing' contexts, of religious conversion with various forms of enumeration; an association well captured by Spyer's (1996) term 'conversion to seriality'. But it was also salient to the exacting logic of evangelical Nonconformism, with its need to measure conquests and count treasures. This emphasis on numbers cannot be taken to imply a trading of quality for quantity, however, as Simmel (1978: 444) might have implied in arguing that the reduction of the former to the latter was an intrinsic feature of monetization. The Protestants were also preoccupied with the *morality* of money, with the exchange of riches for virtue above price. They sought ceaselessly to reconcile these two dimensions of value. For, just as time always entails space, quantity always entails quality.

Still, by promoting the commodification of the Tswana world – where, in fact, cattle had long been counted[14] – colonial evangelism spawned a shift from the qualitative to the quantitative as the *dominant* idiom of evaluation. This shift had important consequences for control over the flow of wealth, as men of substance were quick to grasp. In effecting it, the Nonconformists were helped, and soon outstripped, by the European traders. Ironically, while these men preferred to do business by barter (see Wookey 1884: xx, above), they used monetary values to compute all transactions (Philip 1828,1: 205f) – including the wholesale purchase of local produce, for which they gave goods set at well-hiked retail rates, and the extension of loans, from which they extracted high interest (Shillington 1985: 221; Livingstone 1940: 92). In attempts, later on, to exert influence over prices and profits, some Tlhaping farmers would persuade merchants to pay them in cash for their crops (Shillington 1985: 222). But coin remained scarce for a long time and struggles to elicit it from white entrepreneurs would go on well into the twentieth century in some rural areas (Schapera 1933: 649). Not only did storekeepers benefit from conducting business by barter, mediated through virtual money; by using goods as token pounds and pence, they also limited the impact of rising prices in the Colony on those they paid in the interior. This form of cash in kind was a species of signal currency that had its (inverted) equivalent in Tswana 'cattle without legs', or cash as kine. Such were the hybrid media of exchange born of the articulation of previously distinct, incommensurable regimes of value. They expressed the efforts of the different *dramatis personae* to regulate the conversion of wealth in both directions. We return to them below.

While familiarity with the value of money did not always translate into the circulation of cash, it did bear testimony to the growing volume of Tswana production for the market. Most lucrative were the fruits of the hunt. As they gained access to guns, African suppliers became ever more crucial to the capital intensive colonial trade in feathers and ivory – until natural resources gave out (Shillington 1985: 24). But agriculture was also important, especially among the middle and upper peasantry. Surpluses were sold in increasing quantities, permitting the purchase of cattle, farming implements, wagons and other commodities. With the discovery of diamonds, but before the territory was annexed by Britain in 1871, Tlhaping, Kora and Griqua took part in the new commerce, finding stones and selling them to speculators for cash, wagons and beasts (Shillington 1985: 38; Holub 1881 1: 242). Matthews (1887: 94f) writes that, once this trade had been

---

[14] Early travellers reported that Tswana used 'decimal arithmetic' (Somerville 1979: 128), their numbers ending at 10. Later, Sandilands (1953: 110), a missionary linguist, described their numeration as 'logical ... but clumsy'. It is clear, though, that exact tallies were kept of stock, however many (Burchell 1824 2: 560). The decimal system was deployed in combination with the qualitative features of individual animals to effect an overall count.

Cattle, Currencies & the Politics of Commensuration

outlawed, traffic was conducted in an argot in which gems were referred to as 'calves'.

Although Southern Tswana soon lost all claim to the diamondiferous lands, many remained implicated in the local economy around Kimberley – wherever possible, converting their profits into livestock. Indeed, a report in the *Diamond News* in 1873 voiced the worry that, by turning their cash into animals, blacks were avoiding wage work (Shillington 1985: 68). Sir Gordon Sprigg, Prime Minister at the Cape, echoed this concern to white audiences on a tour of the Colony in 1878. '[L]arge troops of cattle and other stock [mean] idleness', he declared, to cries of 'Hear, Hear!'[15] Such anxieties were not baseless. But they focused only on Africans of means, underestimating the growing impoverishment of the interior. While most resources, even water, now had a price in Southern Bechuanaland (Holub 1881 1: 231, 246), the majority of Tswana were in no position to benefit from new market opportunities. Those with stock and irrigated lands might have been able to provision the diamond fields; however, as John Mackenzie observed, the 'poorer classes [were] often sadly disappointed'.[16] Many had already begun to sell their labour either to rural employers or in the Colony.[17]

Of the ironic history of Southern Tswana proletarianization we have written elsewhere (Comaroff and Comaroff 1987; 1997: chapter 4). Here it will suffice to make two points. First, the workings of the colonial economy, of the very mechanisms supposed to 'civilize' and enrich Africans, did more than just eat away at their material lives. It also perverted the effort of the Protestant mission to instil in them a commitment to the idea of self-possessed labour and enlightened commerce; to seed among them the persuasive hegemony of the market as sacralized place, practice and process; and to replace their 'primitive communism' with a lifestyle centred on refined domesticity, the nuclear family and money. Second, most Southern Tswana remained reluctant proletarians, with strong views about the terms on which they were willing to sell their labour. Even when hunger was rife, and jobs at the diamond fields were scarce, they were loath to toil on the Transvaal goldmines, where there was a great demand for employees, but where workers were known to be ill-treated (van Onselen 1972: 486; Cape of Good Hope 1907 G36: 20). In fact, observers noted repeatedly that labour migration was not driven by brute necessity. Among other things, it was tied, as an Inspector of Native Locations wrote in 1908 (Cape of Good Hope 1909 G19: 32), to the state of cattle holding; also, as we have said, to the desire of Tswana to invest, through various forms of stock exchange, in local social relations and political enterprises. It was just this, of course, that decades of colonial evangelism had been designed to transform.

---

[15] *Diamond Fields Advertiser*, 1 November 1878: 3.
[16] J. Mackenzie, Kuruman, 17 February 1882, Report for 1881 (CWM, LMS South Africa Reports, 2–1).
[17] Ibid.; R. Price, Kuruman, 29 April 1885 (CWM, LMS Incoming Letters (South Africa), 43–1-B); Mackenzie (1871: 521; 1975: 42f); Wookey (1884: 304f).

Stock Responses

Cattle, Currency & Contests of Value

> Cattle are our 'Barclays Bank' (Mhengwa Lecholo 1970)[18]

By the close of the nineteenth century, Southern Tswana communities had become part of a hybrid world in which markets and migration were more-or-less prominent; in which money had become a ubiquitous standard of worth; in which coin undercut all other currencies, including cattle. For many, this last development was neither inevitable nor desirable. Turning cattle into cash was not a neutral act. It entailed the loss of a distinctive form wealth and endangered their autonomy. Especially older men, whose power and position derived from their herds, sought to reverse the melting of everything to money. Even more, as we have noted, they tried constantly to convert all gains from the sale of labour or produce into beasts. Their orientation contrasted with that of the rising Christian literati, for whom universalizing media – cash, education, consumer goods – promised entry to a modernist, middle class commonwealth. Not that these families ceased to invest in beasts; correspondence among Southern Tswana elites at the time makes frequent mention of transactions in kine. But, as Chief Bathoen of the Ngwaketse wrote in 1909 to Silas Molema in Mafikeng, he would be happy to take payment for an old debt 'in cattle or money',[19]

The missionaries knew that livestock enabled Southern Tswana to sustain their independent existence – and to resist the invasive reach of Christian political economy. As Willoughby once put it:[20]

> [T]he whole cattle-post system has been alien to our work ... [T]he frequent absence of the people at their posts has been a break in all their learning, as well as an influence of an alien order.

Efforts to persuade men to harness their beasts to arable production might have been reasonably successful. But, for the most part, the evangelists had failed to decentre the 'alien order' inscribed in animals. They had not convinced Tswana to dispense with their herds or the social relations secured by them. Quite the contrary: in 1881, in Kuruman, '[t]he people [were still] almost all engaged in pastoral pursuits – either being themselves the owners of cattle, or as servicing those who are'.[21] What is more, their stock gave the Africans a potent resource – their own cultural expertise – in their dealings with whites. Here, to their obvious satisfaction, they were on home ground; here their own local knowledge gave them a clear edge; here, within the colo-

---

[18] Barclays Bank, a subsidiary of the British company, was one of the oldest financial houses in South Africa. Mhengwa Lecholo was a senior advisor to Chief Kebalepile of the Tshidi-Rolong.
[19] Bathoen, Kgosi ea Bangwaketse, Kanye, 18 March 1909 (Molema -Plaatje Papers, Aa 2.28).
[20] W.C. Willoughby, Palapye, 21 April 1896 (CWM, LMS Incoming Letters (South Africa), 53–1–D).
[21] J. Mackenzie, Kuruman, Report for 1881 (CWM, LMS South Africa Reports, 2–1).

nial economy, was one domain, one site of contest, from which they profited (Mackenzie 1887 1: 80). The corollary? By investing in wealth that served as a hedge against the market, they made themselves less dependent, conceptually and bodily, on the cycle of earning-and-spending on which the missions had banked to change their everyday lifeways. Through such ordinary deeds were grand colonizing designs eluded. For a time.

Other whites, in particular those eager to employ black labour, shared the uneasiness of the missionaries over the enduring African preoccupation with cattle. They, too, were aware that stockwealth allowed 'natives' some control over the terms on which they entered the market economy; hence Sprigg's fighting talk of animals, idleness and wage work. From the very start, the colonization of Southern Tswana society involved the gradual, deliberate depletion of their herds and the dispossession of their range. It was a process that gained momentum through the century. Early on, Boer frontiersmen tried to press Rolong communities into service by plundering their beasts, seizing their fountains and invading their pastures. Later, in the annexed territories of Griqualand West and Bechuanaland, settlers impounded 'stray' African stock in such numbers that government officials were moved to express concern (Shillington 1985: 99f). Exorbitant fees were charged for retrieving these beasts, cash that had to be borrowed from traders at the cost of yet further indebtedness. The Tswana sense that 'money eats cattle' (Comaroff and Comaroff 1992: 151) owed much to such experiences.

Apocalypse, then: Rinderpest
Several of the evangelists working on the unsettled frontier protested the blatant expropriation of African stock.[22] At the same time, they did not mask their relief when the rinderpest pandemic of 1896 seemed, along with overstocking and deteriorating pasture, to deal a fatal blow to Tswana herds. The Rev. Williams's response was fairly typical:[23]

> If the loss of their stock teaches the people the value of labour it will prove a veritable blessing in disguise. The wealth of the people has always been a hindrance to progress. So long as a man had a cattle post he cared little about anything else. The cattle have gone and larger numbers of the people are away at the Diamond and Gold Fields.

Similarly sanguine clergy elsewhere in Southern Africa reported that stricken populations were seeking refuge at missions (van Onselen 1972: 480f). Many of them cheered the apparent demise of pastoralism. A few, though, pondered its implications for the lingering ideal of viable Christian communities in the countryside. While the scourge would probably help their cause, mused Willoughby at Palapye, it had reduced 'the capital of the country' by some 50 to 60 per cent; and it had deprived Tswana of their protection from drought,

---
[22] Mackenzie (1887 1: 234f); cf. W. Ashton, Barkly West, 26 January 1887 (CWM, LMS Incoming Letters (South Africa), 44–5–A).
[23] H. Williams, Molepolole, Report for 1897 (CWM, LMS South Africa Reports, 3–1).

their income from transport riding and their main means of locomotion.[24] From his vantage in the more heavily agricultural district around Taung, John Brown saw a revisitation of the days of Moses, when 'all the cattle of Egypt died'. Wagons and ploughs lay idle, and 'women and girls, and in some cases men, [were] busy picking [at the ground] in the old way'.[25]

The Tswana experience of rinderpest was unquestionably apocalyptic in the short run. Stockowners large and small lost almost all of their beasts (Molema 1966: 196). The southernmost peoples, who were already land poor and widely dependent on wage labour, never fully recovered. Some communities in semi-arid regions turned to agriculture for the first time, only to be struck by locusts and drought. 'Not since the days of Moses', repeated the Rev. Williams, had there been such a cataclysm. '*Re hedile*', intoned a chorus of local voices, 'we are finished!'[26] Over the longer run, in fact, herds *did* recover in most places. But the impact of the devastation was inseparable from that of wider political and economic processes unfolding at the time; most immediately, from the protracted, at times violent, struggle of the Africans to withstand those who would deprive them of their autonomy.[27] Beasts were often implicated in acts of rebellion along the frontier; they became highly charged objects of contestation on both sides. For example, a farmer killed in an uprising in 1898 (Comaroff and Comaroff 1991: 290) was the keeper of an official cattle pound beside the Orange River. When government agents sought to halt the implacable advance of the pandemic by shooting entire herds of Tswana stock,[28] they were met with acute disaffection. Rumours spread that the authorities had introduced the rinderpest to reduce blacks to servitude (van Onselen 1972: 487). In the end, however, some rulers complied with the administration and received compensation. Cattle to cash once more.

Africans in the Cape called the rinderpest *masilangane*, 'let us all be equal' (van Onselen 1972: 483), a sardonic reference to its levelling effects and to the power of beasts to make or break people. While the pandemic had ruinous effects, it did not diminish the value of stock among Tswana. If anything, it enhanced the 'bovine mystique' (Ferguson 1985). Exploiting the transport crisis caused by the shortage of oxen, the upper peasantry were first to rebuild their herds – and, with them, the distinctions that comprised their world. Their understanding of the economic forces at work was epitomized in the relation of cattle to coin. Not only could coin eat cattle, but the replacement of the second was made possible by the first. Yet animals remained the preferred form in which to store money; a form which, barring catastrophe, allowed it to grow into, and accumulate, social worth. The association of beasts with

[24] W.C. Willoughby, Palapye, 21 April 1896 (CWM, LMS Incoming Letters (South Africa), 53–1–D).
[25] J. Brown, Taung, Report for 1896 (CWM, LMS South Africa Reports, 2–4).
[26] H. Williams, Molepolole, Report for 1896 (CWM, LMS South Africa Reports, 2–4); cf. Cape of Good Hope (1897 G19: 69).
[27] Annual reports published by the Department of Native Affairs in the Cape Colony at this time stress the high incidence of cattle theft around Kuruman and Vryburg (e.g. Cape of Good Hope 1899 G31: 60, 62).
[28] J. Brown, Taung, Report for 1896 (CWM, LMS South Africa Reports, 2–4); cf. Cape of Good Hope (1897 G19: 71f).

banks became a commonplace, making livestock synonymous with wealth at its most generative (cf. Alverson 1978: 124). In the event, cash came to be seen as the most fitting recompense for kine (Schapera 1933: 649), kine the optimum medium for the storage of cash. As we said earlier, they were alike special commodities. Both had an 'innate' capacity to equate and translate different sorts of value. And to produce riches. It is this capacity to commensurate that gives such media their magic. Because of it, they seem to bring about transformations, and so to make history, in their own right.

But cash and cattle were also different in one respect that no European political economist could have anticipated: their distinctive colours, their racination. Money was associated with transactions controlled by whites. It was the elusive medium of the trader, the hard-won wage paid to worker, the coercive currency of taxes levied by the state. It was also a highly ambiguous instrument. On one hand, it opened a host of new possibilities, typifying the culture of the mission and its object-world; and it made thinkable new materialities, new practices, new passions, new identities. Yet, in its refusal to respect personal identities, it also undermined 'traditional' monopolies, eroded patriarchal powers, displaced received forms of relationship – which is why, in part, many Southern Tswana rulers found their authority weakened, the centralization of their chiefdoms giving way, the hegemony of longstanding political and economic arrangements in question. 'Money', the vernacular saying goes, 'has no owner'; *madi ga a na mong*. In democratizing access to value, it put a great deal of the past at risk, sometimes in the cause of transitory desire. Formerly inalienable, intransitive values might now be drawn into its melting pot. In the name of debt, tax collectors could attach Tswana cattle and force men to sell their labour to raise cash.

Government Stock, Live Stocks
Meanwhile, many observers – besides the evangelists – were announcing the death of African pastoralism. Prematurely, it turns out. The Report of the South African Native Affairs Commission of 1903–4 (South Africa 1905: 54), concluded that 'money [has become] the great medium of business where formerly cattle were used'. In a post-pastoral age, it went on, Africans should be encouraged to use government savings banks. But the matter was not so straightforward. In 1909, a resigned Rev. Williams wrote to his superiors that, to Tswana, cattle were already like government bonds:[29]

> [T]the Native is very slow to part with his cattle ...Too often he will see himself, wife and family growing thin, whilst his cattle are increasing and getting fat, but to buy food with any portion of them is like draining his life's blood ... His cattle are like Government Stock which no holder will sell for the purpose of living on the Capital unless forced to do so.

The reference to 'life's blood' is telling. Williams understood that beasts, here, enabled a particular kind of existence. It was this, for Tswana, that made

[29] H. Williams, Kanye, Report for 1908 (CWM, LMS South Africa Reports, 4–2).

1.2 Cattle being herded in Mochudi. (Isaac Schapera early 1930s; reproduced courtesy Botswana National Museum and the estate of Isaac Schapera)

them capital in the first place. Indeed, any asset that did the same thing might be treated as if it were stock – even coin. But all too often coin did the opposite, consuming cows and threatening relations made through them. Ironically, it was referred to in Setswana as *madi*, an anglicism and a homonym for 'blood'. But this was blood, or perhaps blood-money, in a less sanguine sense. It connoted the alienable essence of the labourer, that part of her or him from which others profited (Comaroff 1985: 174). As Williams implies, selling cattle under coercive conditions was tantamount to selling lifeblood.

The Rev. Williams went on to say that Christian teaching *had* made inroads into the Tswana reluctance to sell beasts, that many were now willing to part with cattle when corn was scarce. But prices had fluctuated wildly on local markets: during the rinderpest (1896), a 'salted' (disease resistant) ox had fetched £30; by 1908, the finest animal brought £6 at most. No wonder, Williams concluded, contradicting what he had just said, that Tswana were slow to retail their stock. Returns on agricultural produce were also erratic. As a result, money was often scarce. Under these conditions, the capacity of kine to serve as the 'safe custody' of wealth was underlined. They were a bulwark against the ebb and flow of other, less stable stores of value – hence their enhanced mystique. Hence, too, the fact that they were exchanged only for coin or other forms of capital; in particular, wagons, ploughs and guns, which had become the primary means of producing wealth in a receding rural economy.

But, as importantly, cattle were also shares – live stocks as it were – in a social community and a moral economy whose reproduction they enabled. While overrule further eroded courtly politics in Southern Tswana chiefdoms, patronage continued to be secured through the loan of cows; young, educated royals seem, in the early 1900s, to have used their cultural capital to shore up family herds, and vice versa.[30] Court fines were levied in kine, and marriage involved the transfer of animals, late into the twentieth century. Significantly, where bridewealth came to be given in cash payments, the

---

[30] See e.g. a letter from Sebopiwa J. Molema in Kanye (where he was serving as Interpreter to the Magistrate) to Silas, his uncle, suggesting that he buy cattle there for him; S.J. Molema, Kanye, 2 September 1916 (Molema-Plaatje Papers, Ac 1).

latter was often spoken of as token beasts, 'cattle without legs' (Comaroff and Comaroff 1992: 148).

Endings, Continuities

Livestock, in sum, were still the medium for making the social connections that, by contrast to more ephemeral contracts, formed and reformed a recognizable social world. These 'signal transactions' (Sansom 1976: 145) – in nominal animal currency at a rate well below prevailing prices – distinguished privileged exchanges from ordinary commercial dealings. Legless cattle were a salient anachronism, an enclave within the generalizing terms of the market. Counted in cows but paid in coin, this notional cash-in-kine was the inverse of the cash-as-kind deployed by merchants to compel Africans to barter at non-competitive rates. Both virtual currencies served as modes of surge control that tried to harness the flow of value, if in opposite directions, by putting a brake on the rapid conversion from one form to another.

It was precisely because they experienced colonization as a loss of control over the production and flow of value that so many Tswana – as Tshidi-Rolong elders at the court of the late Chief Setumo Montshiwa reminded us recently – pinned their hopes on cattle in the early twentieth century. In them, it seemed, lay the means for recouping a stock of wealth and, with it, a sense of self-determination. This did not imply an avoidance of money or wage work. The Africans had been made dependent, to a greater or lesser degree, on the colonial marketplace; their access to beasts and other goods – not to mention cash – lay increasingly in the sale of their produce and/or their labour. Neither did it imply opposition to Christianity. By the turn of the century, most chiefs had joined the church, and many of their people followed suit, even if they were not, in the main, pious converts. The significant contrast in this world did not lie between Christian and non-Christian. It was between those for whom the values and relations inscribed in cattle remained paramount and those more invested, ideologically and materially, in the capitalist economy of turn-of-the-century South Africa. Cows, and the ways in which they were used, were the markers of this contrast. Rather than the bearers of a congealed, unchanging tradition, they were the links between two orders of worth. Thus, even where they served as icons of Setswana, they were hybrid signs of identity in the here and now; identity that was itself a matter of shifting relations and distinctions.

Remember too, in this respect, that stockwealth was not repudiated by those of more modernist bent; they tended to treat it like other forms of capital in a world of mercantilism, commerce and commodities. It was they – the educated children of old elites, the upper peasantry, and the petite bourgeoisie cultivated by the mission – who were heirs to the liberal vision of the early evangelists. Others, less able to ride the contradictions of colonial political economy and Protestant modernism, remained marginal to the conventions and the cultural practices of the marketplace. They sought to garner what they could of its wealth,[31] and to invest it in the social and material assets they knew and appreciated. This was to be an enduring strategy, visible even as the forces of global capital reshaped the post-apartheid Southern African periphery in the late twentieth century. In August 1995, the *Gaming Gazette* of the Sun International Corporation carried the story of a man, apparently of modest means, from Ramotswa in Botswana. He had hit the jackpot on a slot machine at the Gaborone Sun Hotel. Ralinki, his given name, would use his winnings to buy beasts. For Tswana, he explained, 'cattle are ... wealth, and it is traditional to have as many as possible to pass on to your sons'.[32]

* * *

Which brings us back to the matters with which we began.

World historical movements of social incorporation – nation building, colonialism, globalization, and the like – are all founded on a logic of commensuration and conversion: on the demand that inimical sorts of value – in respect of language and culture, wealth, beauty, even the idea of god – are made equitable and translatable; also, that irreconcilable forms of difference among people and things are rendered reducible, imaginatively and concretely, to common denominators. As our case shows, such processes of commensuration and conversion, and above all their enabling currencies, have often been the focus of concern, indeed of struggle, among people caught up on all sides of colonial encounters. These people tend to be minutely sensitive to the capacity of diverse media – money, beads, stock or whatever – to make or to resist convertibility and, therefore, the modes of exchange, abstraction, exploitation and incorporation that they allow; modes of exchange that sustain or threaten the autonomy, distinctiveness and control we often associate with the 'local'; modes of exchange, to return to Jane Guyer's (2004) founding observation, whose tendency towards non-equivalence opens up any number of possibilities for managing relations among persons and things. That is why currencies of conversion often come to be fetishized; why they seem to have a power all of their own; why they loom so large at times of great historical changes of scale in economy, society and culture. Hence the obsession on the part of European missionaries with inducting Africans into the use of money – and the equally impassioned investment, among Tswana, in retaining their wealth in kine. Conversion, after all, was not merely a matter of religious reform. It was the key mechanism of imperialism at large.

References

Alverson, H. (1978). *Mind in the Heart of Darkness: Value and Self-Identity among the Tswana of Southern Africa*, New Haven/London: Yale University Press.

[31] In fact the very poor had little or no stock, or any other assets. They depended on wage work, and whatever else came to hand, to eke out an existence for themselves and their families.
[32] 'Ralinki's Speedy P98 000 Win', *Gaming Gazette*, August 1995, 5(8): 2.

Arndt, E.H.D. (1928). *Banking and Currency Development in South Africa, 1652–1927*, Cape Town: Juta.

Beck, R.B. (1989). 'Bibles and Beads: Missionaries as Traders in Southern Africa in the Early Nineteenth Century', *Journal of African History* 30: 211–25.

Breckenridge, K. (1995). '"Money with Dignity": Migrants, Minelords and the Cultural Politics of the South African Gold Standard Crisis, 1920–1933', *Journal of African History* 36: 271–304.

Burchell, W.J. (1822–24). *Travels in the Interior of Southern Africa*, 2 volumes, London: Longman, Hurst, Rees, Orme, Brown & Green. Reprinted, 1967, Cape Town: Struik.

Campbell, J. (1813). *Travels in South Africa*, London: Black, Parry. Reprinted, 1974, Cape Town: Struik.

—. (1822). *Travels in South Africa ... Being a Narrative of a Second Journey*, 2 volumes, London: Westley. Reprinted, 1967, New York/London: Johnson Reprint Corporation.

Cape of Good Hope (1897). *Blue Book of Native Affairs, 1897 (G19–'97)*, Cape Town: Cape Times Ltd., Government Printer.

—. (1899). *Blue Book on Native Affairs (G31–'99)*, Cape Town: Cape Times Ltd., Government Printer.

—. (1907). *Blue Book on Native Affairs, 1906 (G36–1907)*, Cape Town: Cape Times Ltd., Government Printer.

—. (1909). *Blue Book on Native Affairs, 1908 (G19–1909)*, Cape Town: Cape Times Ltd., Government Printer.

Chapman, J. (1971). *Travels in the Interior of South Africa, 1849–1863: Hunting and Trading Journeys from Natal to Walvis Bay & Visits to Lake Ngami & Victoria Falls*, Part 1, Cape Town: Balkema. First edition, 1868.

Cobbing, J. (1988). 'The Mfecane as Alibi: Thoughts on Dithakong and Mbolompo', *Journal of African History* 29: 487–519.

Comaroff, J. (1985). *Body of Power, Spirit of Resistance: The Culture and History of a South African People*, Chicago, IL: University of Chicago Press.

Comaroff, J. and J.L. Comaroff (1991). *Of Revelation and Revolution*, Volume 1, *Christianity, Colonialism, and Consciousness in South Africa*, Chicago, IL: University of Chicago Press.

Comaroff, J.L. and J. Comaroff (1987). 'The Madman and the Migrant: Work and Labor in the Historical Consciousness of a South African People', *American Ethnologist* 14: 191–209.

—. (1992). *Ethnography and the Historical Imagination*, Boulder, CO: Westview Press.

—. (1997). *Of Revelation and Revolution*, Volume 2, *The Dialectics of Modernity on a South African Frontier*, Chicago, IL: University of Chicago Press.

Davies, H. (1962). *Worship and Theology in England from Newman to Martineau, 1850–1900*, Princeton, NJ: Princeton University Press.

Ferguson, J. (1985). 'The Bovine Mystique: Power, Property and Livestock in Rural Lesotho', *Man* (NS) 20: 647–74.

Forster, E.M. (1992[1910]). *Howards End*, O. Stallybrass (ed.), London: Penguin

Books. Reset and reprinted from the Abinger Edition, 1975.

Graeber, D. (1996). 'Beads and Money: The Visibility and Invisibility of Value', *American Ethnologist* 23(1): 4–24.

Grove, R. (1989). 'Scottish Missionaries, Evangelical Discourses and the Origin of Conservation Thinking in Southern Africa 1820–1900', *Journal of Southern African Studies* 15: 163–87.

Guyer, J. (2004). *Marginal Gains: Monetary Transaction in Atlantic Africa*. Chicago, IL: University of Chicago Press.

Hart, K. (1986). 'Heads or Tails? Two Sides of the Coin" *Man* (NS) 21: 637–56.

Helmstadter, R.J. (1992). 'The Reverend Andrew Reed (1787–1862): Evangelical Pastor as Entrepreneur', in R.W. Davis and R.J. Helmstadter (eds), *Religion and Irreligion in Victorian Society: Essays in Honor of R.K. Webb*, London/New York: Routledge.

Hempton, D. (1984). *Methodism and Politics in British Society, 1750–1850*, London: Hutchinson.

Hodgson, T.L. (1977). *The Journals of the Rev. T.L. Hodgson: Missionary to the Seleka-Rolong and the Griquas, 1821–1831*, R.L. Cope (ed.), Johannesburg: Witwatersrand University Press for the African Studies Institute.

Holub, E. (1881). *Seven Years in South Africa: Travels, Researches, and Hunting Adventures, between the Diamond-Fields and the Zambesi (1872–79)*, 2 volumes, translated by E.E. Frewer, Boston, MA: Houghton Mifflin.

Le Goff, J. (1980). *Time, Work and Culture in the Middle Ages*, translated by A. Goldhammer, Chicago, IL: University of Chicago Press.

Lichtenstein, M.H.C. (1930). *Travels in Southern Africa in the Years 1803, 1804, 1805 and 1806*, Volume 2, translated from the 1812–15 edition by A. Plumptre, Cape Town: The Van Riebeeck Society.

—. (1973). *Foundation of the Cape* (1811) [and] *About the Bechuanas* (1807), translated and edited by O.H. Spohr, Cape Town: A.A. Balkema.

Livingstone, D. (1857). *Missionary Travels and Researches in South Africa*, London: J. Murray.

—. (1861). 'On Fever in the Zambesi: A Note from Dr. Livingstone to Dr. M'William. Transmitted by Captain Washington, R.N., F.R.S., Hydrographer to the Admiralty', *Lancet* 2 (24 August): 184–7.

—. (1940). *Some Letters from Livingstone 1840–1872*, D. Chamberlin (ed.), London: Oxford University Press.

—. (1959). *David Livingstone: Family Letters 1841–1856*, 2 volumes, I. Schapera (ed.), London: Chatto & Windus.

—. (1960). *Livingstone's Private Journals 1851–1853*, I. Schapera (ed.), Berkeley: University of California Press.

—. (1961). *Livingstone's Missionary Correspondence 1841–56*, I. Schapera (ed.), London: Chatto & Windus.

—. (1974). *David Livingstone: South African Papers, 1849–1853*, I. Schapera (ed.), Cape Town: The Van Riebeeck Society.

LMS – London Missionary Society (1824). 'Kurreechane', *Missionary Sketches* (April) XXV, South African Library, Cape Town: South African Bound Pamphlets, no. 54.

Mackenzie, J. (1871). *Ten Years North of the Orange River: A Story of Everyday Life and Work among the South African Tribes*, Edinburgh: Edmonston & Douglas.
—. (1887). *Austral Africa: Losing It or Ruling It*, 2 volumes, London: Sampson Low, Marston, Searle & Rivington.
—. (1975). *Papers of John Mackenzie*, A.J. Dachs (ed.), Johannesburg: Witwatersrand University Press.
Marx, K. (1967). *Capital: A Critique of Political Economy*, 3 volumes, New York: International Publishers.
Matthews, J.W. (1887). *Incwadi Yami, or Twenty Years' Personal Experience in South Africa*, New York: Rogers & Sherwood. Reprinted, 1976, Johannesburg: Africana Book Society.
Mauss, M. (1954). *The Gift: Forms and Functions of Exchange in Archaic Societies*, translated by I. Cunnison, London: Cohen & West.
Miller, E.S. (1973). 'The Christian Missionary: Agent of Secularization', *Missiology: An International Review* 1:99–107.
Mintz, S.W. (1985). *Sweetness and Power: The Place of Sugar in Modern History*, New York: Viking.
Moffat, M. (1967). 'Letter to a Well-Wisher', *Quarterly Bulletin of the South African Library* 22: 16–19.
Moffat, R. (1842). *Missionary Labours and Scenes in Southern Africa*, London: John Snow. Reprinted, 1969, New York: Johnson Reprint Corporation.
Moffat, R. and M. Moffat (1951) *Apprenticeship at Kuruman: Being the Journals and Letters of Robert and Mary Moffat, 1820–1828*, I. Schapera (ed.), London: Chatto & Windus.
Molema, S.M. (1920). *The Bantu, Past and Present*, Edinburgh: W. Green & Son.
—. (1966) *Montshiwa, 1815–1896: Barolong Chief and Patriot*, Cape Town: Struik.
Munn, N.D. (1977). 'The Spaciotemporal Transformation of Gawa Canoes', *Journal de la Société des Océnistes* 33: 39–53.
Obelkevich, J. (1976). *Religion and Rural Society: South Lindsey, 1825–1875*, Oxford: Clarendon Press.
Orwell, G. (1962). *The Road to Wigan Pier*, Harmondsworth: Penguin Books. First edition, 1937.
Outler, A.C. (1985). 'An Introductory Comment on Sermons 34–36', *The Works of John Wesley*, Volume 2 (Sermons 34–70), A.C. Outler (ed.), Nashville: Abingdon Press.
Parry, J. and M. Bloch (eds) (1989). *Money and the Morality of Exchange*, Cambridge, UK: Cambridge University Press.
Parsons, H.A. (1927). 'The Coinage of Griqualand', *Spink & Son's Numismatic Circular* 4 (April): 197–201.
Parsons, N.Q. (1977). 'The Economic History of Khama's Country in Botswana, 1844–1930', in R. Palmer and N.Q. Parsons (eds), *The Roots of Rural Poverty in Central and Southern Africa*, London: Heinemann.
Peires, J.B. (1981). *The House of Phalo: A History of the Xhosa People in the Days of Their Independence*, Johannesburg: Ravan Press.
Philip, J. (1828). *Researches in South Africa; Illustrating the Civil, Moral, and*

Religious Condition of the Native Tribes. 2 volumes, London: James Duncan. Reprinted, 1969, New York: Negro Universities Press.

Plaatje, S.T. (1996). *Selected Writings*, B. Willan (ed.), Johannesburg: Witwatersrand University Press.

Price, E.L. (1956). *The Journals of Elizabeth Lees Price written in Bechuanaland, Southern Africa 1854–1883 with an Epilogue: 1889 and 1900*, U. Long (ed.), London: Edward Arnold.

Rack, H.D. (1989). *Reasonable Enthusiast: John Wesley and the Rise of Methodism*, Philadelphia, PA: Trinity Press International.

Sandilands, A. (1953). *Introduction to Tswana*, Tiger Kloof: London Missionary Society.

Sansom, B. (1976). 'A Signal Transaction and Its Currency', in B. Kapferer (ed.), *Transaction and Meaning: Directions in the Anthropology of Exchange and Symbolic Behaviour*, Philadelphia, PA: Institute for the Study of Human Issues.

Saunders, C.C. (1966). 'Early Knowledge of the Sotho: Seventeenth and Eighteenth Century Accounts of the Tswana', *Quarterly Bulletin of the South African Library* 20: 60–70.

Schapera, I. (1933). 'Economic Conditions in a Bechuanaland Native Reserve', *South African Journal of Science* 30: 633–55.

—. (1938). *A Handbook of Tswana Law and Custom*, London: Oxford University Press, for the International African Institute.

—. (1940). 'The Political Organization of the Ngwato in Bechuanaland Protectorate', in M. Fortes and E.E. Evans-Pritchard (eds), *African Political Systems*, London: Oxford University Press for the International African Institute.

Semmel, B. (1974). *The Methodist Revolution*, London: Heinemann.

Shillington, K. (1985). *The Colonisation of the Southern Tswana, 1870–1900*, Johannesburg: Ravan Press.

Simmel, G. (1978). *The Philosophy of Money*, D. Frisby (ed.), translated from the second enlarged edition [1907] by T. Bottomore and D. Frisby, London: Routledge & Kegan Paul.

Smith, Adam (1976). *An Inquiry into the Nature and Causes of the Wealth of Nations*, Volume 1, R.H. Campbell and A.S. Skinner (eds), Oxford: Clarendon Press. First edition, 1776.

Smith, Andrew (1939). *The Diary of Dr. Andrew Smith, 1834–1836*, Volume 1, P.R. Kirby (ed.), Cape Town: The Van Riebeeck Society.

Smith, E.W. (1957). *Great Lion of Bechuanaland: The Life and Times of Roger Price, Missionary*, London: Independent Press Ltd. for the London Missionary Society.

Somerville, W. (1979). *William Somerville's Narrative of His Journeys to the Eastern Cape Frontier and to Lattakoe 1799–1802*, E. and F. Bradlow (eds), Cape Town: The Van Riebeeck Society.

South Africa, British Crown Colony of (1905). *Report of the South African Native Affairs Commission, 1903–5*, Cape Town: Cape Times Ltd., Government Printer.

Spyer, P. (1996). 'Serial Conversion/Conversion to Seriality: Religion, State, and Number in Aru, Eastern Indonesia', in P. van der Veer (ed.), *Conversion to Modernity: The Globalization of Christianity*, London: Routledge.

Stow, G.W. (1905). *The Native Races of South Africa*, London: Swan Sonnenschein.

Unsworth, B. (1992). *Sacred Hunger*, New York/London: W.W. Norton.

van Onselen, C. (1972). 'Reactions to Rinderpest in Southern Africa, 1896–97', *Journal of African History* 13: 473–88.

Warner, W.J. (1930). *The Wesleyan Movement in the Industrial Revolution*, London/ New York: Longmans, Green.

Waterman, A.M.C. (1991). *Revolution, Economics and Religion: Christian Political Economy, 1798–1833*, Cambridge, UK: Cambridge University Press.

Weber, M. (1958). *The Protestant Ethic and the Spirit of Capitalism*, translated by T. Parsons, New York: C. Scribner's.

Wesley, J. (1984). *The Works of John Wesley*, Volume 1, A.C. Outler (ed.), Nashville, TN: Abingdon Press.

—. (1985). *The Works of John Wesley*, Volume 2, A.C. Outler (ed.), Nashville, TN: Abingdon Press.

—. (1986). *The Works of John Wesley*, Volume 3, A.C. Outler (ed.), Nashville, TN: Abingdon Press.

WMMS – Wesleyan Methodist Missionary Society (1829–31). 'Boschuana Country: Extract of a Letter from Mr. Hodgson, dated Bootchnaap, November 24th, 1828', *Missionary Notices Relating Principally to the Foreign Missions* 6 no. 164, August 1829: 120.

Wookey, A.J. (1884). 'South Bechuanaland, Some Changes Which Have Taken Place', *The Chronicle of the London Missionary Society* (September): 303–7.

2 Currency & Conflict in Colonial Nigeria

David Pratten

Money is mundane, but it is a mundane mystery to most who use it.
(Jane Guyer 1994: 26)

This chapter examines a central theme in Jane Guyer's analysis of monetary transactions in Atlantic Africa – the implications of money valuation in relation to social order and disorder in Nigeria. It revisits the case of manilla currency exchange that she has discussed extensively in relation to calculation, ranking and political legitimacy (Guyer 2004, 2009). The manilla exchange rate is often ignored as a contributory factor in the various social upheavals of the region in the period before the manilla was 'redeemed' in 1948.[1] Following Guyer's lead, and drawing on the pioneering scholarship of Naanen (1993), this chapter argues that manilla currency exchange critically exposed fault lines in gender relations and crucially amplified the social and economic tensions that contributed to two of the most significant conflicts in Nigeria during the colonial period – the Women's War (1929) and the 'man-leopard murders' (1943–8).

The 'oil rivers' region of south-eastern Nigeria had been a hub of Atlantic trade from the sixteenth century onwards. Located between two of the 'oil rivers' flowing south to the coast, the Annang territory discussed here lay adjacent to Ogoni and Igbo communities across the Imo River to the south and west, and to the Ibibio across the Qua Iboe River to the north-east. The economic basis of these neighbouring hinterland communities shifted during the nineteenth century from slaves to palm-oil exports.[2] The effects of the fluctuations of the global palm-oil market were intensified in this region because of a peculiar economic feature, dual currencies of shilling and manilla.[3] The

---

[1] Archival abbreviations refer to the National Archives of Nigeria, Enugu (NAE), Rhodes House Library, Oxford (RH), the Public Records Office of Northern Ireland (PRONI), and The National Archives, Kew (TNA). For an overview of currency instability in south-eastern Nigeria over the past century see Ekejiuba 1994.
[2] The ethnic landscape of the nineteenth century 'oil rivers' saw the Kalabari, Bonny and Efik control overseas trade, while the Aro Igbo acquired a similar monopoly in overland trade.
[3] Originally introduced to the West African coast by the Portuguese as a bracelet at the end of the fifteenth century, the manilla was manufactured in Birmingham by the mid-nineteenth century. Annang manillas were calculated in bundles and could be counted in two ways, as multiples of ten, or of twenty (*okuk kiet* – ten manillas; *edip òkpòhò* – twenty manillas). Over 100 manillas could also be counted in multiples of twenty or as an equivalent number of goats since a goat was worth 100 manillas (*ebut* – 100 manillas). Very large amounts also had particular names *nduo okpo* – 400 manillas and *ukpuho* – 8,000 manillas).

manilla currency was originally introduced to the West African coast by the Portuguese as a bracelet. With the expansion of European trade from the late seventeenth century onwards, currencies became specialized between local uses and trading at the coast (Jones 1958; Latham 1971; Northrup 1978: 157–64). The brass rod, the currency used in Calabar, had been supplanted by British currency by the turn of the twentieth century. Elsewhere on the coast (between Oron and Ikot Ubo) copper wire currency was displaced by the shilling and the penny by 1920. Yet, elsewhere in Calabar Province, particularly in the Annang-speaking Ikot Ekpene, Abak and Opobo Divisions, the local manilla currency proved to be a durable medium of exchange until the late 1940s. The palm-oil trade was a significant source of wealth, and much of it had been retained in manillas which was relatively stable in exchange terms.

Wealth in the palm-oil economy of south-eastern Nigeria under colonial rule at the turn of the twentieth century was critically determined by the manilla–shilling exchange rate. By 1948 the manilla was redeemed and demonetized at a rate of one per 3d (three old British pennies) or four manillas per shilling – precisely the rate of exchange obtaining almost a century before in 1856. While this might suggest that the manilla had been a very stable currency it would overlook a volatile history of exchange-rate fluctuations. Across West Africa, the acceleration of commercialization and accompanying instabilities in prices and money supplies during the early twentieth century were accompanied by a destabilization of the social and institutional processes through which claims on goods and services were defined and legitimated (Berry 1994: 300). As Guyer (2004: 12, 81) has argued, currency fluctuations would 'implicate different constituencies'. In the two case studies compared here, it is evident that the fluctuations of the exchange rate produced clear winners and losers in the local economy – a complex matrix of farmers vs the salaried class, women producers vs male traders that would in turn map onto corresponding patterns of protest and violence, perpetrators and victims.

The Women's War

The Women's War of 1929 is rightly recorded as a significant moment in the history of south-eastern Nigeria and beyond. Within the legacy of indirect rule it has been seen as one of the great revolts by 'stateless' communities against the imposition of state hierarchy (Mamdani 1996: 41). The events in Calabar and Owerri Provinces are generally considered the culmination of misguided colonial policies on chiefs, tax, palm oil and courts. To replace the demands of forced labour and bolster the position of the government-sanctioned 'warrant chiefs', the first tax was due to be levied across southern Nigeria in April 1928. The tax assessment was calculated as an income tax on the population of adult men. In the palm-oil-rich divisions of Calabar Province each man paid 7 shillings tax which was collected by the chiefs of the village. In total £85,000 was collected in the first tax collection in 1928.

While the success of the 1928 tax inspired optimism in senior official circles and led to a more rigorous assessment in 1929, the tax was perceived quite differently by its payers: 'the people here imagine that the tax was a levy, or a kind of collective fine on a large scale. The real difficulties may begin when the people realize that tax collection is an annual event'.[4] As the censuses to establish the nominal tax rolls began for the following year, these 'difficulties' did, indeed, materialize. The reassessment was postponed in Abak during September 1929 following opposition from the chiefs. In November, when the tax census in Bende Division in neighbouring Owerri Province included counting wives, children, goats and sheep, rumours spread that women were also to pay tax (Noah 1985: 28).

The rumour spread quickly, and had reached Opobo Division in Calabar Province via palm-oil middlemen and palm-wine dealers within the next few days. The residents of Ukam in the Ikpa clan of Opobo Division were therefore well aware of the significance of the arrival, unannounced, of a young cadet, R.F. Floyer, his interpreter and two messengers on 2 December 1929. Floyer was conducting the tax reassessment, for which he employed a system of enumerating male adults by means of a 'factor', a calculation that estimated the ratio of houses, property and beds to taxable men.[5] To ensure that they told the truth Floyer took the 'town chiefs' to an 'Idem' shrine and made them swear an oath that they had not concealed men or houses.[6] As the counting took place women started shouting in protest, young men threatened the Assistant District Officer, and scuffles broke out. As Floyer's two messengers ran for the police, he and his clerk were beaten up. At a subsequent meeting in Ukam the villagers explained the fears that led to this attack: that they were going to be made to pay more tax, that they had heard women were going to be taxed, that the Government was going to sell their palm trees, and that villagers feared the chiefs were going secretly to sell land to the Government.[7]

Three similar riots were reported in Owerri Province before a European doctor drove his car through a protesting crowd in Aba killing two women on 11 December. This was the catalyst that turned a simmering set of protests to mass violence. Merchants' factories were attacked at Umuahia, Aba, Imo River, Nbawsi, Omoba and Opobo, and Native Courts were attacked across the region.[8] Despite the association of the 1929 riots

---

[4] Notes on the History of Taxation affecting Eastern Province and more especially Calabar Province, February 1933, RH: Mss.Afr.S. 1000(1).
[5] Floyer had tested his 'factor' in Essene where he calculated the factor to be 0.42, or 42 men per 100 'doors'. Report of the Commission of Inquiry appointed to inquire into the disturbances in the Calabar and Owerri Provinces, December 1929, 1930, RH: 723.13.s.4/1930.
[6] In Ukam the Chiefs would claim that the system resembled the process by which chiefs would order a dead man's goods to be counted and seized (by which they most likely meant if the man had been killed by m̀bìàm). Notes of Evidence taken in the Calabar and Owerri Provinces on the Disturbance, 1930, RH: 723.17.s.1.1929.
[7] Notes of Evidence taken in the Calabar and Owerri Provinces on the Disturbance, RH: Mss 723.17.s.1.1929.
[8] For a more detailed account of the Women's War see Afigbo 1966, 1972; Gailey 1970; Ifeka-Moller 1975; Akpan and Ekpo 1988; Dike 1995; Falola and Paddock 2011; Matera et al. 2012.

with the Igbo trading town of Aba, the theatre of the subsequent violence also included Utu Etim Ekpo, Ika, Ikot Ekpene, Abak, Itu, Ikono, Okopedi and Opobo. It was here, in the Ibibio and Annang region in the south-west of Calabar Province, that 55 women died and 50 more were wounded in extensive clashes that the women involved called *ékóŋ íbáàn*, the Women's War (Van Allen 1976).

Set against the depression, and a dramatic slump in produce prices for palm oil, the women directed their anger not only at the question of tax, or the economy, but at the imposition of unfamiliar 'warrant chiefs' by the colonial regime and at the judgements they provided in the new courts, and as such they struck at the very heart of the colonial project. The subsequent commissions of enquiry established to investigate the causes of the Women's War highlighted a combination of factors as causing the riots: the taxation scheme, corrupt and illegitimate chiefs, and economic hardship because of the depression. Later commentators have argued that women were not targeting any one constituency but re-aligning the balance of all men's relations to women (Ifeka-Moller 1975; Matera et al. 2012: 236).

Yet, despite the array of factors, both immediate and more remote, that contributed to the outbreak of women's protests in 1929, a key puzzle remains. Why these women? Why were these women so upset about the rumoured tax, and why did Ngwa Igbo, Annang and Ibibio women rebel in Owerri and Calabar Provinces and not those elsewhere in the eastern Provinces who were similarly affected by prices, chiefs and tax? The report of the Commission of Enquiry stated that no evidence was presented to show why some areas rose in the riots and others did not: 'We have not before us evidence to show why other parts had not disturbances. To enquire into that would have extended unduly the labours of this commission'.[9] The answers to this puzzle, I argue, lie with the way in which the protests mapped onto the manilla region, and a moment in the manilla exchange-rate fluctuations in which the introduction of taxation, especially on women, was critical.[10]

The shifting balance of power wrought by the palm-oil economy in western Calabar Province had a profoundly gendered impact. This transformation was accompanied by significant changes to underlying gender relations in which women's control of palm-oil processing and kernel marketing exposed tensions within the household over the control of money and labour. By the late 1920s some women had gained de facto control over palm-oil production, as well as distribution, by pledging palm plots (Ardener 1953: 900). Introduced a decade earlier, cassava (manioc) was also rapidly becoming an important crop, especially for women for whom cassava cultivation added to their labour burden, but also to their potential economic return. But despite

[9] Report of the Commission of Inquiry appointed to inquire into the disturbances in the Calabar and Owerri Provinces, December 1929, RH: Mss 723.13.s.4/1930.
[10] The focus on currency exchange is of course one of a range of further factors limiting the unrest to Owerri and Calabar Provinces, including the shared cultural institutions and ideology of the women involved, the persuasions of local leaders and the force of the colonial military response; see Pratten 2007.

these longer-term trends, it was poverty, not profits, that led to the events of 1929.[11]

The region was hard hit by the collapse of agricultural produce prices during the 1920s and the consequent rising cost of living. A four-gallon tin of palm oil was sold for 15s 6d in Aba during the post-First World War boom which peaked in 1925–26, but had fallen to 5s 10d in 1929 (Jones 1989: 96).[12] The prices of imported goods also increased and were compounded by a rise in import duties – a head of tobacco rose from 6d to 9d; VH gin from 11s to 15s. Songs from the period lamented the poverty that the changing terms of trade effected:

> Stand and hear all so that you can laugh at my poverty
> Still stand and hear all, hear all and laugh at my honesty
> Still stand and hear all
> People buy fowls for two manillas – cut cow and enter into *inám*;
> Still stand and hear all
> Stand and hear all and laugh at my poverty
> Still stand and hear all
> I buy a fowl for ten manillas – my own became ashes
> Still stand and hear
> Still stand and hear and laugh at my poverty[13]

The economic strains were manifest in domestic tensions where households engaged in the palm and kernel oil industry functioned on the basis of cash and gift exchanges between husbands and wives. Once it is harvested from the tree, wives buy the palm fruit from their husbands. This transaction, which takes place before the oil is processed, is known as palm money (*òkpòhò áyôp*). It was women, therefore, who were responsible for the subsequent processing, boiling and squeezing the palm fruit oil (*álân áyôp*), for drying, cracking and squeezing the remaining kernels (*álân ísíp* – kernel oil), and for trading both oil and kernels at the market. As Basden testified in his evidence to the commission of enquiry into the Women's War:

> Most of the trade in this country is in the hands of the women, and the complaint which they came and expressed to us was that there was no margin of profit at all, and as they could not make a living, they might as well make a stand ... They do not understand the fluctuations of prices.[14]

When in March 1929 UK prices for palm oil and kernels dropped abruptly, followed immediately by corresponding price falls in the markets of Calabar

---

[11] As I have outlined elsewhere (Pratten 2007), this emphasis on the impact of taxation and related economic factors should be seen to complement analyses that have emphasized political grievances that came to the fore in the Women's War. See also Falola and Paddock 2011.
[12] At Umuahia the palm oil price (per 4 gallon tin) fell from 13s before the depression to 7s 4d in 1928, and 5s 11d in 1929. See Akpan and Ekpo 1988:.13. See also Onwuteaka 1965: 277.
[13] Feast song (íkúɔ úsɔ̀rɔ̀) in Ibibio Notes nd, WUL: Jeffreys Papers File: 256; *inám* is an elderhood complex with expensive initiation fees.
[14] Notes of Evidence taken in the Calabar and Owerri Provinces on the Disturbance, RH: Mss 723.17.s.1.1929.

Currency & Conflict in Colonial Nigeria

and Owerri Provinces, farmers faced a significant cut in their standard of living. The concentration of women's labour in palm-oil production and marketing, as well as their roles as food farmers and petty traders, therefore, provides a significant explanation as to why it was women of the palm belt, and not men – who were similarly affected by the general economic downturn – who joined the revolt (Martin 1988: 112, 117). However, the effects of this economic shock on local gender relations was amplified by the economic dynamic brought about by underlying currency exchange rates.

The areas within Calabar and Owerri Provinces in which the disturbances took place mapped precisely onto the 'manilla currency zone', and the effects of the falls in palm-oil prices and tax demands on local producers were critically aggravated by the falling manilla exchange rate in 1929. The manilla was a resilient currency because of its role in the palm-oil trade and because it was a means of storing wealth. In fact it was proving a sound investment as the manilla had begun to appreciate from the turn of the twentieth century. From 1902 to 1912 the local exchange appreciated by almost 1 manilla each year. In August 1914, young men from Atam and Efiat complained to the local mission that 1 shilling was being exchanged for 9 manillas.[15] This trend was attributed to the increase in trade at Opobo and the settled conditions there relative to the 1880s. As Table 2.1 illustrates, the exchange rate was very sensitive to price fluctuations, and rises in produce prices for palm oil and kernels caused the manilla to appreciate. When produce prices were high the supply of British currency increased and the manilla appreciated as more sterling chased the relatively fixed quantity of manillas. Conversely, when there was a depression of palm-oil prices, resulting in the contraction of the supply of sterling, the manilla depreciated against sterling. Though there are anomalies, the broad and consistent way in which palm-oil price changes are mirrored in manilla–shilling exchange rates can be seen in Table 2.1.

The introduction of British currency to the manilla zone at the turn of the century had been based on the assumption that the West African token money would displace the manilla, though it was afforded legal status and could be tendered as payment for court fees and fines. An embargo was imposed on the importation of manillas in 1904 which served to fix the overall supply of manillas (though this was actually declining because of attrition, hoarding and its diversion to ritual purposes). By 1907 nickel cash was beginning to percolate into the manilla area. Early attempts to stabilize the exchange rate between manillas and sterling in Uyo and Opobo (at 12 manillas to the shilling) failed to take off and although the manilla's status as legal tender was withdrawn in 1911, the colonial state was unwilling to pay the price of manilla redemption. Proposals to demonetize and redeem the manilla in 1913 were dismissed by Governor Sir Frederick Lugard who stated at the time:

> I am not prepared to consent to saddle the general taxpayers of Northern and Southern Nigeria with the cost of solving the difficulties with which the Opobo clique of merchants are confronted, or to defer important and urgently needed

---

[15] Diary, J.W. Westgarth, 29 August 1914, PRONI: D/3301/CB/1.

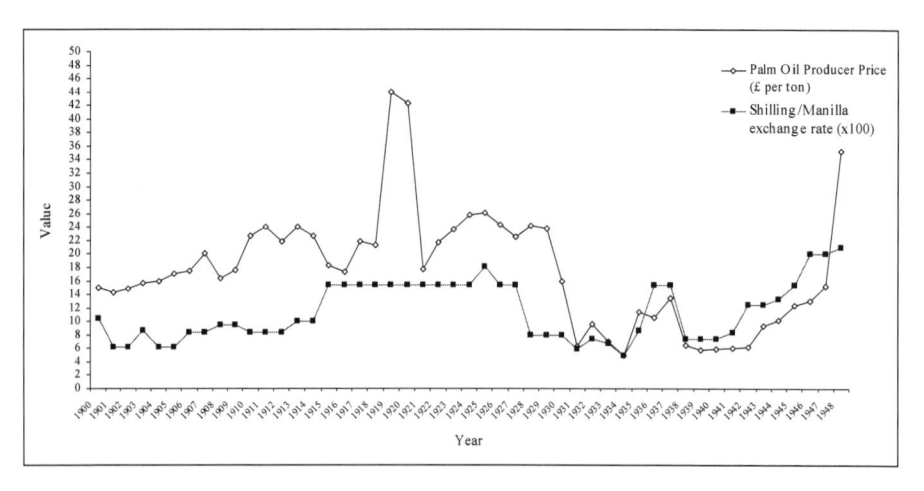

Table 2.1 Manilla exchange rate and palm oil price, 1900–1948. (Adapted from Naanen, 1993: 431. Naanen cites the following sources in the compilation of the manilla exchange rate figures: Helleiner, 1966, 'Manillas, 1948–49', NAE: IKOTDIST 13/1/482)

> public works by applying a large sum of public revenue to an attempt to solve in a hurry by heroic means, a problem which in due course will, in my opinion, solve itself by natural laws.[16]

The link between manillas and palm oil, however, could not be broken by the natural laws to which Lugard referred. Paper money distributed during the First World War was extremely unpopular and throughout the period the trading firms adopted the manilla in preference because of its stability. An Opobo-based firm at one time carried a stock of over one million manillas. This practice was checked after the war with the introduction of the Manilla Ordinance in 1919, which prohibited Europeans from using the manilla as currency.[17] Thereafter manillas were confined to trade in local markets and the stocks of manillas previously held by Opobo merchants passed to oil middlemen – which further displaced the British currency in the local economy.

The exchange rate itself was determined by two factors, the demand and supply of the two currencies and the price of palm oil, the region's main export crop. The way in which the currency market operated is best explained by the main palm-oil buyers at Opobo, the United African Company:

> An African middleman, let us suppose, sold a quantity of palm oil to the Company's manager on the wharf, for which he was paid in money of the West African Currency Board. The middleman then went to the Company's store and used some of this money for the purchase of trade goods, which he intended to carry back to

---

[16] Cited (much later) in Draft Report on Manilla Currency, 1946, NAE: OPODIST 1/1/2.
[17] Manilla Ordinance Cap 125 Vol. II L/N: 1151 Lagos, 1923. This explains the static exchange rate recorded in Table 2.3 when the palm oil price rocketed during the early 1920s.

his district for sale. With the remainder of his money he then approached one of the manilla dealers and bought manillas from him at the current rate. He then had manillas, and also goods which he could sell in the oil-producing districts. He returned to his village and sold the merchandise for manillas, he then purchased more palm oil, which he brought to the Company's wharf or 'beach' at Opobo; and the series of transactions was then repeated. The main feature of this trade was the use of manillas to purchase produce. The producer, operating direct or through intermediaries, used manillas to purchase imported merchandise or local goods and services in his village market or in Opobo – and it was these returning manillas which fed the manilla market in Opobo. (United Africa Company 1949: 46)

The manilla–shilling exchange rate affected everyone. Commodity producers and traders, who dealt mainly in manillas, needed to exchange them for sterling with which to conduct official transactions such as paying tax and dealing with the European firms. Those who were paid in sterling, the salaried wage earners, had to buy food or locally produced goods and services, which required them to exchange their shillings for manillas. Exchange-rate fluctuations, however, affected these two groups alternately. When produce prices were low, the manilla depreciated and commodity producers' purchasing power declined. At the same time the shilling appreciated and the wage earner's purchasing power increased. When the palm-oil price was high, however, the manilla appreciated and commodity producers' purchasing power increased, but as the shilling depreciated so the wage earner's purchasing power decreased. The net effect of the exchange-rate fluctuations therefore was to magnify the impact of palm-oil export prices, and to create two sets of economic players, manilla-holding women (producers and traders in the oil economy) and shilling-dealing men (of the chiefly and salaried classes linked to the local administration).

The intimate link with palm-oil prices led to a fluctuating pattern of currency instability. Agitation for the demonetization and abolition of the manilla came from the salaried classes, who were always at an economic disadvantage in the manilla-using areas. To the manilla-owning peasantry it was not the manilla that fluctuated in ratio to cash, but cash that fluctuated in relation to the manilla, whose value in terms of goods was relatively constant. In turn, women traders also expressed their frustrations with the exchange rate against the colonial currency. During the market riots in Calabar in 1925, for instance, women sought to prohibit the use of European coins, along with protesting the imposition of tolls, men planting cassava, rising food prices, and excessive 'dowries' (Akpan and Ekpo 1988: 18–20). As a result of these tensions, schemes for the progressive redemption of the manilla were devised throughout the 1920s, but were dismissed one by one. Many of the proposed manilla redemption schemes involved allowing litigants to pay fines in manillas, rather than in sterling, so that they could then be destroyed. A 1922 proposal calculated that 350,000 manillas might be disposed of annually in this manner at a cost of £3,000 per annum in foregone court income.[18]

---

[18] Annual Report, Abak Division, 1922, NAE: CALPROF 5/13/110.

It was assumed that the introduction of tax in sterling would displace the manilla currency. Ironically, it was precisely because this could not happen that the tax riots took place. The tax demand introduced in 1928 was only payable in West African currency. At this time there was only £10 million in Nigeria, a per capita figure of around 10s if it was all in circulation. The per capita figure of West African currency was much lower in the 'manilla zone' than elsewhere, and since the tax rate was 7s it met with an extreme currency scarcity and 'complete economic upset'.[19] Tax collection during the depression years created severe problems and consequent heavy recourse to money lenders who exploited the situation and the exchange rate of the manilla:

> [M]oney changers held out for as much as 19 [manillas] to 2/-. The normal rate at that time is about 13 to 2/-. By keeping these manillas until January when they are 6 to the shilling the money changers will make 50% profit in 5 months. The serious part of this is that in order to pay 7/- tax a man has to change the equivalent of 10/- in manillas. This is a great argument for the abolition of manillas. Low produce prices have made tax payment more difficult.[20]

The drain on cash due to tax was such that the shilling almost disappeared from the area after the 1928 tax, and the manilla, already dropping because of low produce prices, slumped in value. Using a broad regional average of shilling–manilla exchange the manilla depreciated rapidly from 6.5 manillas per shilling in 1927 to 12.5 manillas per shilling in 1928 and 1929 (Naanen 1993: 431). The impact of the second year of tax was therefore not only felt most acutely within the manilla zone but the currency slump it generated disproportionately affected women: 'her fluid wealth is in manillas and on her falls the brunt of the manilla fluctuations and the consequent losses'.[21]

As we have seen, women were the marketers of palm oil and therefore felt the impact of manilla depreciation more quickly and more acutely than men. The falling manilla critically undermined women's buying power relative to the imported goods they increasingly demanded of their husbands, and to the shilling, which they would have had to buy from money lenders had the tax rumours been true. If women were the losers during this economic watershed, then it is also significant that the targets of their protests, the men of European firms, court clerks and messengers, who exchanged shillings for manillas, were the winners as their purchasing power increased.[22]

Seven years after the Women's War, while reviewing ongoing tensions caused by the manilla exchange rate, the District Officer M.D.W. Jeffreys realized that this aspect of the local political economy had never been considered in the context of the events of December 1929. Jeffreys argued that the subsequent enquiries into the Women's War had completely missed its true origin; the manilla was not once mentioned in the commission of enquiry's

---

[19] Land Tenure in Nigeria by M.D.W. Jeffreys, 1 October 1936, NAE: CSE 1/85/6334.
[20] Annual Report, Abak Division, 1930, NAE: CALPROF 2/11/10.
[21] DO Special Duties to Assistant Treasurer, Calabar, 15 May 1933, NAE: IKOTDIST 13/1/482.
[22] Initially, court summons fees were paid in manillas and then shillings. Court sitting fees were 5 shillings per member and 10 shillings to the President (Groves 1936: 55).

Currency & Conflict in Colonial Nigeria

report. He concluded that local currencies such as the manilla should have been redeemed, and calculated that £75,000 spent on the redemption of the manilla would have prevented the Women's War.[23]

* * *

After the Women's War and throughout the inter-war years one economic issue in Calabar Province above all preoccupied the school-educated, salaried class of the 'reading public': 'the Manilla menace'. The boom-bust cycle of the 1930s had dramatically exposed the currency instability within the manilla area. In the slump years the manilla depreciated with one shilling exchanged for 20 manillas in 1934. Just two years later, in the boom year of 1936, however, the manilla had appreciated and one shilling was exchanged for 5 manillas. A sharp depreciation marked the late 1930s when the exchange rate stood at 13 manillas to the shilling between 1938 and 1940, but the manilla appreciated rapidly in line with the rising price of palm oil as commodity prices were increased as part of the war effort. During 1942 the shilling lost a third of its value against the manilla in less than six months, by 1943 the average exchange rate was 8 manillas per shilling, and by the end of the war one shilling was exchanged for just 5 manillas (see Table 2.2).

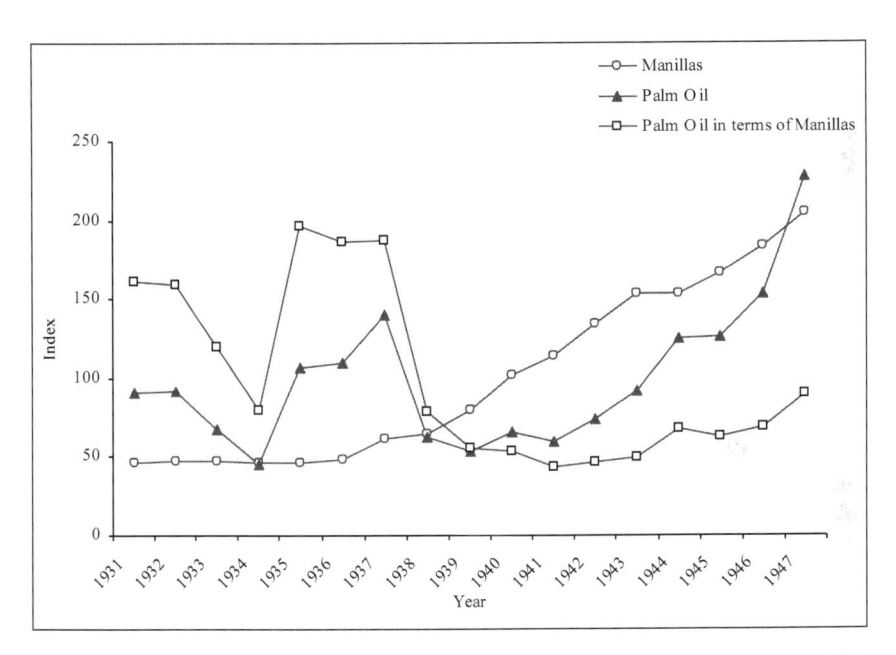

Table 2.2 An index of manilla exchange rates and palm oil prices, 1931–1947. (United Africa Company, 1949)

---

[23] Land Tenure in Nigeria by M.D.W. Jeffreys, 1 October 1936, NAE CSE 1/85/6334. The extent to which Jeffreys' view was shared by his contemporaries is not clear; in the margin of the report next to the calculation, however, someone had written 'what nonsense'.

In practical terms domestic budgeting was relatively straightforward when the manilla–shilling exchange rate was 1s to 12 manillas since there was effective parity between a manilla and a penny. Yet the introduction of British currency denominations in the manilla zone was insufficient and ineffective. Daily purchasing of small quantities in the food 'chop' markets required small denominations of currency which was not matched by the limited supply of half-pennies and tenths. At the same time the conversion rates of such small denominations against the manilla were difficult to calculate; only the shilling was large enough to ascertain its manilla equivalent. The lack of small denominations led to price inflation for those paying in shillings. Food costing 3 manillas was worth 4½ pence when the exchange rate was 8 manillas to the shilling, but the seller would ask for 6 pence as it was the nearest equivalent available coin.

The impact of the wartime economy on the key indices of the palm-oil price and the shilling–manilla exchange rate for residents in the manilla districts fell disproportionately on those who received their incomes in West African currency. While wartime economic conditions were hard for commodity producers and wage earners alike, the fluctuations of the manilla exchange rate during the war years exacerbated the situation for the salaried class. Sharp increases in the price of imports during the war (a rise of 226 per cent between 1939 and 1945) were not matched by increases in commodity export prices (which rose by only 180 per cent). The cost of living therefore soared and while the national picture was one of high inflation and declining real wages, in the manilla zone the position was further aggravated for those paid in 'coin' by the sharp appreciation of the manilla in 1942. A reduction in the exchange rate from 12–13 manillas for a shilling to 6–8 for a shilling marked almost a 50 per cent reduction in the purchasing power of salaried employees like the labourers and clerks employed by the Government and the trading firms who were buyers of local goods and foodstuffs which had to be paid for in manillas. The impact of price rises and the exchange rate was acutely felt in Abak Division where salary earners in mission and local administration employment complained of a shortage of food and that 'at present yams and rice can only be obtained by wealthy people' (*Nigerian Eastern Mail* 11 August 1945).

Faced with mounting pressure, the Government responded in 1943 with the Manilla Currency (Amendment) Ordinance which empowered local councils to fix the exchange rate. A scheme at Opobo to standardize the manilla at the rate of 8 for 1 shilling was introduced under the Ordinance but failed because traders refused to abide by it when the manilla was steadily appreciating in line with rising palm-oil prices. In March 1944 a committee representing the Civil Service Union along with the 'Yoruba, Igbo, Efik, Hausa and Cameroons Community' in Ikot Ekpene petitioned the government on the manilla problem. Their concern was that the Ordinance that allowed Native Authorities to standardize the manilla rate was not applied to Ikot Ekpene where the rate had fallen to 6 manillas to the shilling, and that without intervention the trend would continue:

> It is now known that every 1/- rise in the price of palm produce denotes the going down in the number of manilla exchange and eventually devaluation of the King's money. But since the need for oil for war works may necessitate further rise in prices, there is likelihood of value of manilla currency rising as high as one for one shilling if no steps are taken.[24]

Committees like this, along with meetings of the literary clubs, quickly adopted the editorial lead of the leading local newspaper, the *Nigerian Eastern Mail*. A salary of £5 per month was reduced to £2.10s in the manilla markets, the paper reported, and the unfortunate average earner was confronted with the universal rise in prices of all commodities with only 50 per cent of their purchasing power. The *Mail* and its 'progressive' readers petitioned continuously during the war for the government to end the 'manilla menace' and for it either to standardize the exchange rate or remove the currency from circulation:

> This ancient anachronism has been a thorn in the flesh of workers in the Manilla area who receive their pay in his Majesty's coin. The illiterate persons and market women from whom the worker has to buy his daily food have almost a superstitious regard for the Manilla and will receive payment in no other form of currency. It is obvious that the erratic fluctuation of the exchange rate of the Manilla for coin of the realm can hit the worker cruelly hard and at times practically reduce the purchasing power of his salary in the market by as much as fifty per cent. (*Nigerian Eastern Mail* 18 March 1944)

In this light it has been suggested that during and immediately after the war these economic pressures had reached such a state that the potential was high for 'a major economic crisis with unpredictable political repercussions in the manilla belt' (Naanen 1993: 439).

The Man-Leopard Murders

The man-leopard murders took place against this fast-changing wartime political and economic landscape. Between 1943 and 1948 almost 200 mysterious deaths were recorded in the districts of Abak and Opobo under Calabar Province. The victims appeared to have been killed by stabbing, usually in a manner that mimicked a wild leopard attacking its prey, from behind and biting at the neck and throat. By the end of the investigation, 96 men were convicted of murder, 77 of whom were executed. The subterfuge of a leopard-style attack, with copy-cat mutilations, created doubts over the identity of the killer, whether man or beast, from the outset. The shape-shifting powers that the killers were said to invoke – in Annang they were known as Ekpe-Owo, 'the leopard men' – only heightened an air of mystery that was compounded by contradictory and fragile evidence. In the British press these cases were reported as 'the strangest,

---

[24] Community Committee, Ikot Ekpene to Resident, Calabar, 20 March 20 1944, NAE: IKOT-DIST 13/1/482.

biggest murder hunt in the world'.[25] During the three years of investigations, hundreds of police officers were drafted into the districts to conduct patrols and raids; special sessions of the Supreme Court were held to hear 'man-leopard' cases. By the end of 1946 the two districts were under curfew, and subject to a Peace Preservation Ordinance which gave the authorities the power arbitrarily to search and arrest suspects. This was the largest breakdown of law and order in the region since the Women's War.[26]

Those closest to the investigation feared that the origin of the so-called 'man-leopard' murders would probably never be discovered with any degree of certainty, and that the events would remain shrouded in mystery. Speculation over the motives for the murders fell broadly within two camps – ritual versus revenge. The official verdict as presented on 10 February 1948, by the under-secretary for the colonies to the British Parliament was that the 'real motive behind all the murders was ritual'. The precise composition of the ritual aspect was not always fixed but centred on the possible role of a central shrine (like the Long Juju of Arochukwu associated with slave dealing), the organization of the killers in an initiatory cult (the 'leopard society'), and the orchestration of the murders by diviners (*ídíoŋ*). An alternative police theory linking the murders to 'revenge' motives came to light as the murder investigations unfolded during 1946 and revealed a pattern that in each and every case the accused had a personal grudge against the victim.[27] As a result, official opinion shifted away from the belief that an organized society was directing the murders for ritual purposes, and towards the idea that those accused of committing murder were part of, or had hired, a band of professional assassins, a 'native form of "Murder Incorporated"',[28] compelled by the 'Corsican vendetta'.[29]

In August 1946, a review of the 65 murders that had been investigated showed that among the victims more females than males had been killed; 27 victims were men, 29 were women, 6 were boys and 15 were girls. Why were so many of the victims female? The gender distribution of the victims suggested that these crimes were set against tense domestic dynamics. Indeed, the suspected motives for the 97 confirmed 'leopard murders' to 17 November 1947 revealed revenge and jealousy, especially linked to unresolved court cases concerning brideprice, land and debts, as the prime motives for the leopard murders (see Table 2.3).[30]

---

[25] Daily Mail 30 June 1947.
[26] The Ordinance meant it was possible to give the Resident more evidence than he might normally see in a criminal case and it enabled him to order an arrest on suspicion alone. The cost of stationing troops or police in districts proclaimed under the Ordinance was also to be levied punitively upon the inhabitants (Ibhawoh 2002: 66).
[27] General Report on the activities of the Police on Special Duty in the Abak and Opobo divisions – December 1945 to May 1946, 27 May 1946, NAE: CALPROF 13/1/8. The fact that no strangers were killed during *ekpe-owo* seemed to confirm that the killings were 'personal matters'.
[28] A Report on the Leopard Society Murders, 1951, RH: Mss.Afr.s.1784 (18).
[29] Comments on Notes of Mr D.C. Neillands on the Leopard men by F.R. Kay, 21 May 1946, NAE: CALPROF 17/1/1595.
[30] In the case of 60 additional deaths which were investigated, making a total of 157, the motives were uncertain.

Currency & Conflict in Colonial Nigeria

Motive	No. of murders
Revenge	19
Jealousy	17
Dispute over dowry	16
Dispute over land	9
Non-payment of debt	6
Dispute over succession to children and property	6
Refusal to allow sexual intercourse	4
Dispute over ownership of property	4
Dispute over 'Esusu' society contributions	2
Dispute over inheritance of widow	1
Concealment of another murder	1
Non-apparent	12
Total	97

Table 2.3 Motives of the 'man-leopard murders', 1947. (Source: Officer Administering the Government, Nigeria to the Secretary of State for the Colonies, 30 December 1947, TNA: CO 583/294/3)

That this range of court cases, divorce, debt and land would come to the fore was no coincidence. These were precisely the long-term, often protracted, investments that had been disrupted by the introduction of colonial currency. The process of monetization had profound effects on marriage, land-holding and debts across colonial Nigeria, of course (Bohannan 1959), but the uncertainties of a fluctuating exchange rate where long-term debts became convertible to other currencies amplified the process.

The pattern of court case disputes was closely linked to the investment priorities of senior men during the inter-war period. During this period wealthy elders chose to consolidate their positions through the defence and appropriation of assets (wives, credit and land) in litigation. Hence, village elders across this region between the wars had 'showed little inclination to switch their land, capital and labour resources into fresh uses. Instead, they concentrated on issues of ownership and power and began to re-establish their claims to land and palms within the new colonial judicial system' (Martin 1988: 78). Senior men, therefore, were using the courts to secure access to rights in productive resource and the courts were employed by elders to underpin new property rights based on cash. It is the nature of these contested rights that the murder investigations illuminate more fully, and here the clue to the relevance of courts and cases to the man-leopard killings is in understanding precisely what was at stake not only for the winners, but especially for the losers of this litigation.

The prevalence and contentious nature of the cases that came to court during the mid-1940s rested on the peculiar vulnerability of rights in land, debt and wives. In each instance arrangements for securing these rights were based on a process of deferred exchange based on trust: land pledges might span generations before redemption, loans might pass through several successors before being repaid, and brideprice would constitute many years of labour service along with intermittent payments of gifts and money before a marriage was finally agreed. The impact of monetization was most especially felt on precisely this set of longer-term ranges of exchanges. Despite vociferous complaints about immediate, everyday transactions (like tax and food), the effects of the persistence and fluctuations of a parallel shilling-based currency within the manilla zone were acutely felt in those transactions that concerned the reproduction of the long-term social order. As these exchanges tended to be correlated to central moral precepts, so monetization, commoditization and the peculiarities of the dual currency system would expose the social fault lines of Annang society (Parry and Bloch 1989).

Each type of case was a form of debt but it was precisely because the conditions for completing contracts were in confusion that debt cases proved so contentious in the mid-1940s. The redemption of debts was dependent on a number of factors including economic stability, trust between the parties involved, and recourse to effective sanctions. Yet each of these necessary conditions was in turmoil during this period. The terms of trade were in decline, recourse to legal sanctions in the Native Courts was slow, expensive and unpredictable, and trust forged on a belief in the efficacy of oath-swearing was also undermined by both the expanding Christian congregations, and by a ban on its use as a judicial instrument in the Native Courts.[31]

The combined influence of arbitrary interference by colonial officers, of chiefs capitalizing on their positions as court assessors, and of the collapse in the relations of exchange contributed to bring apparently mundane small legal claims to the top of the list of the murder motives. One instance of legal innovation above all figured at the heart of the murder enquiries and focused on the relationship between these microeconomics and the man-leopard murders. This concerned a controversial innovation in the matrimonial sphere, the so-called 'one manilla divorce':

> Many stories as to what incites these wicked men to wage merciless and relentless war on their innocent country men, mainly womenfolk, have been told ... it is heard on all sides that the alleged vexing decision by the District Officer that a woman might be permitted to divorce her husband with 'one manilla' has had some part to play.[32]

As brideprice during the war years had risen to several thousand manillas the ruling apparently made by District Officer Kay that reduced the amount refunded in a divorce settlement from the wife's family to the husband to just one manilla was destined to provoke controversy. There was no substantive

---

[31] Nigeria 1953, Report of the Native Courts (Eastern Region) Commission of Inquiry, Lagos: Government Printer: 51.
[32] *Nigerian Eastern Mail*, 26 January 1946.

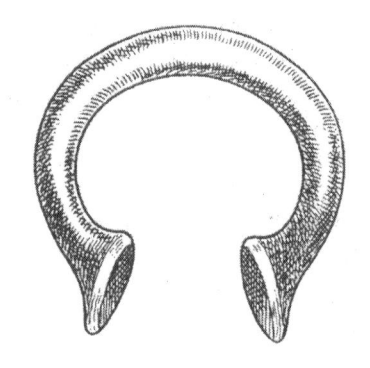

2.1 Line drawing of manilla currency. (Julie Boast, reproduced with kind permission from G.I. Jones, from *Slaves to Palm Oil: Slave Trade and Palm Oil Trade in the Bight of Biafra*, Cambridge African Monographs 13, Cambridge: African Studies Centre, 1989).

evidence that a 'one manilla divorce' was ever actually granted but, as it was reported at precisely the moment the leopard murders went public, it was unsurprising that connections were drawn, as here in the *Mail*'s letter page:

> Now, dear Editor, have you ever asked yourself why it is that mainly women are attacked? Is it because they are weak and helpless? No! The answer is far from it. One of the alleged causes of the revival of the activities of the [leopard] society is that a high official ruled in Abak Division that all divorced women pay their husbands only one manilla to compensate the dowry that they paid on their behalf. The enraged husbands therefore take up this nasty revenge and terminate the lives of such women.[33]

Marriage was the primary reason why men went into debt in Annang society and for this reason, as well as the importance of agricultural labour during and immediately after the war, it was imperative that wives remained in the marriage. Where there was a divorce, however, husbands wanted their bridewealth refunded immediately so that they could retire their debts and re-marry (Byfield 1997: 87). Divorce litigation emerged as the stated motive in a significant proportion of cases. 'Dowry' disputes accounted for 16 of the 97 murders for which motives were established. Six further murders centred on disputes over children, and four involved the refusal by women to have sex with their husbands.

Underlying these dynamics of dispute and revenge was the manilla. Exchange-rate fluctuations served to amplify the impact of the economic dynamics during and immediately after the Second World War on particular groups. Accounting for the winners and losers of these fluctuations provides an informative economic context to the man-leopard killings. During the war years the manilla appreciated significantly from a low of 13 manillas to the shilling to a high of 4 to the shilling in 1947. In April 1946 at the height of the 'man-leopard' episode the exchange rate across Ibibio country was 5 manillas for 1 shilling (*Nigerian Eastern Mail* 27 April 1946). Those who exchanged manillas for shillings – taxpayers, court litigants and women traders – saw their purchasing power increase steadily as a result of the manilla's appreci-

---

[33] *Nigerian Eastern Mail*, 2 March 1946.

ation. At the same time those exchanging shillings for manillas, the salaried class of colonial auxiliaries and their dependants felt the post-war economic situation more severely.

This is not to identify the murderers but to highlight that they were committed by men who were apparently frustrated at their inability to realize debts held in manillas that in terms of their shilling equivalent were worth more than ever. Debts calculated in manillas, such as brideprice refunds, contribution club debts and land pledges began to appreciate rapidly in shilling terms, and the amounts involved became more significant over time for those already dependent on salaries paid in shillings. Brideprice, as we have seen, was calculated in manillas. Yet calculations were made only in relation to the shilling equivalent. Since there was no fixed exchange rate people preferred to make all payments of brideprice in manillas because 'they hope of its fluctuation to make more than the face amount'.[34] The exchange rate evidently had a critical effect, and otherwise innocuous debts had become matters of life and death.

Perhaps the crucial factor in determining the significance of the exchange-rate fluctuations during the man-leopard murders was the question of uncertainty itself. Agitation for and discussion of the redemption of the manilla was widespread throughout the war years and the imminent buying up of the entire stock of manillas was common knowledge. During his annual tour of the province in 1946 the *Mail*'s editor, J.V. Clinton, addressed popular concerns about the 'manilla problem'. The question was, should it be standardized or abolished? Whatever happened, Clinton argued, it should be done with full consultation especially as 'women had a strong interest in the manilla and might not approve of its abolition' (*Nigerian Eastern Mail* 11 May 1946).

> The manilla areas are amongst the least settled of any part of Nigeria, were the focal point of the Aba riots in 1929, have been the scene subsequently of minor outbreaks of disorder and at present include the area of the human leopard murderers. Any misunderstanding of Government's intentions, or any misrepresentation of them, or indeed any rumours of an attempt of Government not to act in good faith – however unjustified – might very well set a spark to the tinder and result in disastrous consequences.[35]

While the direct effects of exchange-rate fluctuations on gender relations and the upheavals of the Women's War and the man-leopard murders are not recorded in the historical register, it seems that they were on the tip of the tongue of contemporary observers.

---

[34] Manilla as used in the Eastern Provinces, 1949, RH: Mss.Afr.s.1556/7(b). Offiong has suggested that brideprice repayments were being paid in sterling during the 1940s, a depreciating currency (Offiong 1989: 68). This does not seem to have been entirely the case. Rather, brideprice and its refund was calculated in terms of both currencies simultaneously: 'It was common ... in the Native Court for refund of dowry to be 5 pounds in manillas at six manillas to the shilling, and no litigant would be satisfied if any reviewing officer attempted to render this either as 'six hundred manillas' or as 'five pounds' (Grey 1951: 63). Clearly the manilla–shilling exchange rate was the critical determining factor.
[35] Draft Report on Manilla Currency, 1946, NAE: OPODIST 1/1/2.

In April 1946 the decision was finally taken at the regional level to abolish the manilla within a period of two years and was put to the public in October 1946.[36] The precise timing and rate of the redemption, however, were not known and were therefore subject to considerable speculation. Uncertainty over the future of the manilla incited a wave of claims and counter-claims over debts. Questions over the currency's future introduced an economic imperative to those creditors holding debts in manillas. Claims to these debts needed to be established quickly and formally, and the debts themselves had to be liquidated while exchange rates were high and before they were set arbitrarily by the colonial authorities.

Conclusion

Various local efforts at exchange-rate stabilization between 1946 and 1948 failed. By early 1948 the increase in the production of palm produce and the award of 'cost-of-living' allowances to civil servants meant that the exchange rate in Opobo had shifted sharply with the manilla appreciating from 12 to 4 to the shilling (*Nigerian Eastern Mail* 31 January, 24 May 1947). Speculation that the manilla was to be redeemed only served to sustain its appreciation against the shilling. Manilla redemption proposals were more coolly received by women than by men, and the authorities recognized that '[f]rom a political point of view, the unknown factor, and a dangerous one, is represented by the women'.[37] When the redemption started on 1 October 1948, the (most common) òkpòhò manilla was exchanged at four to the shilling (*Nigerian Eastern Mail* 11 September 1948). In addition to the exchange available at banks and commercial firms, manillas were also accepted in payment of official taxes and dues for the first time. By 1949 the manilla redemption exercise had removed 23,175,890 manillas valued at £289,562. 13s.[38]

Comparing the fates of indigenous currencies in colonial Nigeria, Jane Guyer argued that 'Manillas were more deeply implicated in the male economy of palm oil and prestige' (Guyer 2004: 12). I hope to have shown in this chapter that while the manilla was indeed a symbol of masculine power, of ritual and tradition, and of initiation and ceremony, it was also deeply embedded in mediating ambiguous, competitive and conflictual gender relations. As Guyer has demonstrated so powerfully 'all money valuation must implicate the social order' (ibid.: 82), and in the cases demonstrated here currency conversions were also implicated in social dis-order.

---

[36] Annual Report, Calabar Province, 1949, RH: MSS Afr.S.1505.4.
[37] Ibid.
[38] Ibid.

References

Afigbo, A. (1966). 'Revolution and Reaction in Eastern Nigeria, 1900–1929: The Background to the Women's Riot of 1929', *Journal of the Historical Society of Nigeria* 3(3): 539–57.

—. (1972). *The Warrant Chiefs: Indirect Rule in Southeastern Nigeria, 1891–1929*. London: Longman.

Akpan, E. and V. Ekpo (1988). *The Women's War of 1929*, Calabar: Government Printer.

Ardener, E. (1953). 'A Rural Oil-Palm Industry', *West Africa 1909* (26 September): 921–3.

Berry, S. (1994). 'Stable Prices, Unstable Values: Some Thoughts on Monetization and the Meaning of Transactions in West African Economies', in *Money Matters: Instability, Values and Social Payments in the Modern History of West African Communities*, J.I. Guyer (ed.), Portsmouth, NH and London: Heinemann and James Currey: 299–313.

Bohannan, P. (1959). 'The Impact of Money on an African Subsistence Economy', *The Journal of Economic History* 19(4): 491–503.

Byfield, J. (1997). 'Innovation and Conflict: Cloth Dyers and the Interwar Depression in Abeokuta, Nigeria', *Journal of African History* 38: 77–99.

Gailey, H. (1970). *The Road to Aba: A Study of British Administrative Policy in Eastern Nigeria*. New York: New York University Press.

Guyer, J.I. (1994). 'Introduction: The Currency Interface and its Dynamics', in *Money Matters: Instability, Values and Social Payments in the Modern History of West African Communities*, J.I. Guyer (ed.), Portsmouth, NH and London: Heinemann and James Currey: 1–33.

—. (2004), *Marginal Gains: Monetary transactions in Atlantic Africa*, Chicago, IL: Chicago University Press.

—. (2009). 'Manillas, Money and the Cost of Legitimacy in the mid-20th Century: A Royal Account in Eastern Nigeria', in C. Eagleton, H. Fuller and J. Perkins (eds), *Money in Africa*, London: The British Museum: 28–44.

Ekejiuba, F. (1994). 'Currency Instability and Social Payments Among the Igbo of Eastern Nigeria, 1890–1990', in J.I. Guyer (ed.), *Money Matters: Instability, Values and Social Payments in the Modern History of West African Communities*. Portsmouth, NH and London: Heineman and James Currey.

Eyo, E. (1979). *Nigeria and the Evolution of Money*, Lagos: Central Bank of Nigeria in association with the Federal Dept. of Antiquities.

Falola, T. and A. Paddock (2011). *The Women's War of 1929: A History of Anti-Colonial Resistance in Eastern Nigeria*, Durham, NC: Carolina Academic Press.

Grey, R. (1951). 'Manillas', *Nigerian Field* 16(2): 52–66.

Ibhawoh, B. (2002). 'Stronger than the Maxim Gun: Law, Human Rights and British Colonial Hegemony in Nigeria', *Africa* 72 (1): 55–83.

Ifeka-Moller, C. (1975). 'Female Militancy and Colonial Revolt: The Women's War of 1929, Eastern Nigeria', in Ardener, S. (ed.), *Perceiving Women*, London: Malaby Press: 127–57.

Jones, G. (1958). 'Native and Trade Currencies in Southern Nigeria during the Eighteenth and Nineteenth Centuries', *Africa* 28: 43–54.
—. (1989). *From Slaves to Palm Oil: Slave Trade and Palm Oil Trade in the Bight of Biafra*, Cambridge, UK: African Studies Centre.
Latham, A. (1971). 'Currency, Credit and Capitalism on the Cross River in the Pre-Colonial Era', *Journal of African History* XII(4): 599–605.
Mamdani, M. (1996). *Citizen and Subject: Contemporary Africa and the Legacy of Late Colonialism*. Princeton, NJ: Princeton University Press.
Martin, S. (1988). *Palm Oil and Protest: An economic history of the Ngwa Region, South-Eastern Nigeria, 1800–1980*, Cambridge, UK: Cambridge University Press.
Matera, M., M. Bastian and S. Kent (2012). *The Women's War of 1929: Gender and Violence in Colonial Nigeria*, New York: Palgrave Macmillan.
Naanen, B. (1993). 'Economy Within an Economy: The Manilla Currency, Exchange Rate Instability and Social Conditions in South-Eastern Nigeria, 1900–48', *Journal of African History* 34(3): 425–46.
Noah, M. (1985). 'The Role, Status and Influence of Women in Traditional Times: The Example of the Ibibio of Southeastern Nigeria', *Nigeria Magazine* 53: 24–31.
Northrup, D. (1978), *Trade Without Rulers: Pre-Colonial Economic Development in South-Eastern Nigeria*, Oxford: Clarendon Press.
Offiong, D. (1989). *Continuity and Change among the Traditional Associations of Nigeria*. Zaria: Ahmadu Bellow University Press.
Onwuteaka, V. (1965). 'The Aba Riot of 1929 and its Relation to the System of "Indirect Rule"', *Nigerian Journal of Economic and Social Studies* 7(3): 273–82.
Pratten, D. (2007). *The Man-Leopard Murders: History and Society in Colonial Nigeria*. Edinburgh and Bloomington, IN: Edinburgh University Press and Indiana University Press for the International African Institute.
United Africa Company (1949). 'The Manilla Problem', *Statistical and Economic Review* 3: 44–56.
Van Allen, J. (1976). 'Aba Riots or Igbo Women's War? Ideology, Stratification and Invisibility of Women', in N. Halfkin and E. Bay (eds), *Women in Africa*, Stanford, CA: Stanford University Press: 59–85.

3 Coercion or Trade? Multiple Self-realization during the Rubber Boom in German Kamerun (1899–1913)

Tristan Oestermann & Peter Geschiere

One of the most inspiring ideas in Jane Guyer's rich oeuvre is her consistent attention to 'marginal gains' to be made by crossing disjuncture between different registers of value and knowledge. Especially her work from the 1990s on the role of 'composition' (in contrast to 'accumulation') as characteristic to economic agency in Equatorial Africa was most inspiring for both of us in our research in that area – notably for our efforts to make sense of the quite chaotic developments during the boom in wild rubber that marked so deeply the brief period of German rule in Cameroon (see Guyer 1993, 1986; Guyer and Eno Belinga 1995).[1] No wonder, because there is a clear regional overlap: Guyer's examples in these articles come from the forest zones of Equatorial Africa, where the rubber boom took especially dramatic forms – in Cameroon under German rule as much as in the two Congos under the Belgians and the French. But even more than the regional fit, the original implications of these ideas were most stimulating to us. To simplify a very fine-grained line of argumentation: for Guyer it can be misleading to speak of 'accumulation' if one wants to understand the strong rivalry among 'big men' that marked relations in this area (as it still does). She proposes to use the term 'accumulation' in contexts where the aim is to accumulate the same on the same (as in capitalist accumulation: money on money). The rivalry between big men in her examples from Equatorial Africa is rather marked by 'composition' – the possibility of composing bundles of different forms of value and knowledge in order to claim pre-eminence; Guyer speaks also of 'multiple self-realization'. Or to simplify even further: excellence in any field could be invoked in order to prevail in the confrontations with other big men that marked everyday life in these societies with their strong emphasis on personal achievement.

To one of us (Oestermann 2013), these ideas were inspiring for his efforts to make sense of the apparent readiness among many locals to become involved in the production and trading of wild rubber, a new product, the uncertain valuation of which developed under chaotic and often quite violent circumstances.[2]

[1] See also Guyer 2004 where she develops these ideas in a more general analysis of the key role of 'marginal gains' as typical for African economies by the 'linking of disjunctive value registers' according to multiple scales of enumeration.
[2] Oestermann 2013; cf. also his present PhD project at the Humboldt University on 'Kautschuk, Arbeit und Gewalt in Kamerun während der deutschen Kolonialzeit, 1884–1914' (Rubber, Work and Violence in Cameroon under German Rule, 1884–1914), supervised by Andreas Eckert with Peter Geschiere as second supervisor.

This eagerness was in striking contrast with the prevailing stereotypes among the German colonizers about the indigenes' inborn *Faulheit* (laziness) that would make violent coercion the only way to spur them on to productive labour. Clearly, there was another layer to this confrontation. For Geschiere, this trend in Guyer's explorations was also most stimulating in a more general sense – to understand the rapid monetization of each and every aspect of daily life in the villages of the Maka in the northern part of the forest zone, with whom he did his main research. Commoditization seemed to have no limits in this society. 'These women turn everything into a market', as his assistant sighed when he was confronted with a new 'custom' with women blocking the road during a funeral and asking all passers-by for some money (Geschiere 1982, 2000, 2005). To what extent can the present-day omnipresence of money in these societies, even in the most intimate spheres of life, be related to Guyer' notions of 'composition' and 'multiple self-realization'?

In this chapter, we propose to discuss first some special aspects of the boom in wild rubber in German Kamerun. The violence that marked this episode was certainly not exceptional. Around the same time similar 'booms' developed in forest areas all over the world and with similar shocking displays of violence (as in Congo or in Amazonia, to mention two of the most notorious examples). What was particular to German Kamerun was that the government allowed and to a certain extent encouraged the development of two different forms of trade next to each other: through a concessionary regime and through 'free' trade – both forms being increasingly in direct competition. This was a special factor encouraging violence, but it also allows for comparing the implications of different forms of valuation.

In the later parts of this chapter, we will sketch a few examples, based on written historical sources, oral history and on ethnographic observations, that can in particular highlight the relevance of Guyer's explorations on the linking of 'different registers of value' and 'composition'. In the conclusions we hope to expand on the wider relevance of these interpretations to understand subsequent developments in the area.

The Rubber Boom in German Kamerun: Struggles over Valuation

The Cameroon rubber trade was part of a global phenomenon. Technical revolutions like the invention of vulcanization in 1851 and especially of the pneumatic tyre in 1888, together with the recovery of capitalist economies in the 1890s, created a rapidly rising demand for rubber. It was used for all kinds of purposes: from rubber dolls or shoes to electronic isolators, tyres for bicycles and later cars. The boom began in the early 1890s and ended abruptly in 1913 when the plantations in Southeast Asia, created with British capital during the boom years, flooded the global market with cheap rubber of a better quality, pushing expensive wild rubber into the margins. Before this, one region after the other – especially in dense tropical forest zones – became the scene of chaotic wild rubber booms. At first, most of wild rubber came from *Hevea* trees in Brazil. But as demand exceeded supply year after year, leading to rapidly increasing prices, other tropical regions became sources of rubber as well. Thus Africa became the second largest source of rubber, gained by tapping certain *Landolphia* vines and *Funtumia elastica* trees to supply the expanding rubber industries of Europe and the USA (see Tully 2011).

In Africa, two models of rubber production developed: one based on straightforward coercion and another one based on 'free' trade (at least formally free but in practice always marked by a wide array of hidden or not-so-hidden forms of violence).[3] The latter model was found in the coastal regions of West Africa where rubber was harvested by African producers in the hinterland, transported to the coast by African entrepreneurs and then sold to European merchants. This trade in rubber already began in Gabon in the 1850s, in Angola in the 1870s, followed by Sierra Leone and the Gold Coast in the 1880s, and by Southern Nigeria, Cameroon and others in the 1890s (see Harms 1975; Christy 1911: 1–21; Patterson 1975: 60). In Equatorial Africa, the coercive model of rubber production was introduced in the Congo Free State in 1892, when the State gave huge territories as concessions to European corporations (see Harms 1983; Gann and Duignan 1979; Hochschild 1998). These firms enjoyed trade monopolies for rubber and ivory that excluded competitors. Additionally, they had the right to collect taxes and to police the population of their territories. As taxes were collected in rubber, this product was not acquired through trade; rather every man was forced to bring a fixed quota of rubber to the concessionary firms' factories every two weeks. Any resistance met fierce repression by the companies' militias or the State's army (see Harms 1975, 1983; Gann and Duignan 1979; Hochschild 1998). For some time, this system provided such immense profits for the Congo Free State that also France and Germany introduced the concession regime – at least some traits of it – in their own Central African colonies (the French Congo and Cameroon) in 1898.[4]

But what made Cameroon a special case in the history of the rubber trade in Africa was the fact that here the two models – the 'free' trade and the coercive model – coexisted while they were kicked out in the two Congo colonies (Coquery-Vidrovitch 1972: 238–42; Obdeijn 1983). From 1899 on, a concessionary company, Gesellschaft Süd-Kamerun (GSK), worked from Moloundou in the extreme south-east of the newly acquired territory. But, especially after 1903, it would be in fierce competition with German firms who had established factories on the Batanga Coast in the south-west of the colony (the so-called Batanga-Firmen) over the rubber tapped by the local population in

---

[3] This distinction is made by several authors (see, for instance, Harms 1975: 74; Amin 1972: 504).
[4] For the French Congo, where 40 concessions were granted, see Coquery-Vidrovitch 1972. In Cameroon the Colonial Office only licensed three concessions: Gesellschaft Süd-Kamerun (GSK), Gesellschaft Nordwest-Kamerun (GNK), Gesellschaft Nordkamerun (the latter never set foot on Cameroon). See for GSK and GNK Ballhaus 1968 and for the GNK Michels 2004. However, it should be noted that concessions without any rights of sovereignty also existed in West African colonies like Ivory Coast and Lagos as well. Cf. Omosini 1979: 30ff; Munro 1981: 268ff.

the interior. It was this confrontation of two forms of exploitation that led to special patterns of uncertainty, haste and violence.[5]

In 1898, the German Colonial Office granted a large concession in the southeast to the GSK to open up the area to German commerce. At this time, the German free trade firms from the Batanga Coast like Randad & Stein, C. Woermann, and others still limited their activities to the coastal regions and the Yaoundé station.[6] Hostile reactions of the populations near the coast and the difficult accessibility of the terrain blocked the further advance of the trading firms into the interior. The colonial officer Ernst von Carnap-Quernheimb was the first German (and the only one until 1903) who in 1897/8 managed to pass from Yaoundé over land to the south-east of the Cameroon colony, but he did so by circumventing the inaccessible forest areas, rather following from Yaoundé the border between forest and savannah until he reached the Kadei/Sangha river in the east of the colony by which he could navigate down to its south-eastern tip and then further down over the Congo river network (see von Carnap-Quernheimb 1898).

Indeed, of crucial significance for the development of the rubber trade was that the whole south-eastern area of Cameroon is part of the Congo Basin. In contrast to the Sanaga, Nyong and Ntem rivers that flow westwards, more-or-less straight to the Cameroonian coast, the south-eastern rivers flow eastward into the Congo river system. Therefore, this part of the colony was most easily accessed by travelling the Congo and Sangha rivers upstream. Thus, to his dismay, von Carnap-Quernheimb discovered that the Belgian and Dutch companies Société Anonyme Belge pour le Commerce du Haut-Congo (SAB) and the Nieuwe Afrikaansche Handels-Vennootschap (NAHV), both mainly active in the Congo Free State, had already entered the area allotted to the Germans over this river system, and were already trading in ivory there (von Carnap-Quernheimb 1898; Kaeselitz 1968: 34; Ballhaus 1968: 105). This created great indignation among the Germans, both in the colony and in the metropolis, all the more so since around this time the unexpected value of wild rubber, reputed to be available in large quantities especially in this far-distant part of the colony, became clear. Under mounting pressure to save the profits of the German colony for German companies, the authorities decided to grant a concession for the whole south-eastern area to two German colonial financiers, the lawyer Julius Scharlach and the tycoon Hugo Sholto Douglas. Both were in close contact with the Belgian company (SAB) that had become dominant in the area. Out of this collaboration the Gesellschaft Süd-Kamerun was born as the concession holder (Ballhaus 1968: 105f).

In fact, Belgian interests played a key role in the granting of the concession. As the director of the Kolonial-Abteilung – the German Colonial Office – von Buchka, when his concession policy came under pressure, declared in

---

[5] On the competition between GSK and the Batanga-Firmen see also Kaeselitz 1968, Ballhaus 1968, Wirz 1972.

[6] The Germans had founded this 'Jaunde' station already in 1889, close to the border with the savannah; it was, therefore, seen as a potential link to access the circuits of the Hausa trade in the northern parts of the colony, of which the Germans originally had high expectations.

the Reichstag on behalf of the colonial administration that the licensing of a concession to a financially strong German–Belgian joint venture seemed the only way to develop the remotest part of Southern Cameroon, that was unfortunately also the richest in rubber. However, he wisely concealed the fact that the mighty holding company of the SAB, the Compagnie du Congo pour le Commerce et l'Industrie (CCCI), had threatened the colonial administration to block the only access to the area via the Congo for any German enterprise if the CCCI's business interests were not protected by the granting of a concession to a new company in which it would take a considerable part.[7] Indeed, given the geographical, administrative and commercial conditions, the colonial administration had little alternative. In order to at least partly engage German commerce in the mercantile exploitation of south-eastern Cameroon, it agreed to experiment with the concessionary model in the colony.[8]

However, the concession that was given to the GSK differed significantly from the model practised in the Congo Free State and the French Congo. It did not grant the corporation any rights of sovereignty. All efforts by the GSK to get the right to police the population of its concession or to collect taxes from it were blocked by colonial authorities in Berlin.[9] Invoking the principles of the Congo Free Trade Zone, of which south-eastern Cameroon was part, not even a formal trade monopoly was granted to the GSK (Ballhaus 1968: 106). The company only enjoyed a de facto monopoly in its first years, because potential competitors – mainly the Batanga-Firmen from the coast – still did not manage to penetrate that far into the forest interior, while the Belgian SAB factories were incorporated and the Dutch NAHV was bought out (Ballhaus 1968: 128f). But formally, the concession only allowed for the acquisition of land: the GSK was given the right to take into possession the 'crown land' of its zone – that is all the land not in actual use of the population and regarded as 'ownerless'. Moreover, it enjoyed a pre-emptive right to buy up land in possession of the locals (Ballhaus 1968: 106).[10] Thus, the German authorities opted for a quite limited concession model. Especially after 1903, these limitations allowed the Batanga-Firmen to penetrate the concession area with a different conception of trade. As noted, the coexistence of the two forms of trade would have dramatic consequences.

Two Forms of Trade

From 1899 to 1903, the GSK enjoyed benevolent protection and support from the colonial administration (Rudin 1938: 293f; Ballhaus 1968: 128f). Its representatives accompanied the civil and later military authorities during

---

[7] BArch (Bundesarchiv Berlin) R 1001/3442: Reichard to Puttkamer, Berlin 6 July 1898: 6–9; Marchal 1952: 688f; Geschiere 2005: 255.
[8] BArch R 1001/3442: Note by von Puttkamer, not dated, p. 11f.
[9] BArch R 1001/3443: Protocol of the 6th board-meeting of the GSK, Brussels, 25/04/1900, p. 155; BArch R 1001/3445: Protocol, 23/12/1903: 87ff. Ballhaus 1968: 102 mentions that those rights were not given to the GSK but still suggests that the company worked like the Congo Free State corporations.
[10] The text of the concession can be found in René 1905: 220ff.

Coercion or Trade? The Rubber Boom in German Kamerun

their expeditions to explore the concession, most of which was still blank space on the maps. GSK agents also made their own exploratory trips into the rainforest to establish trade relations along the rivers Dja, Boumba and Bek, and even up to Bertoua which lay outside of the concession (see Ballhaus 1968: 128f; Kaeselitz 1968: 35ff; Jäckel 1909: 264f). The German military not only protected the GSK's agents, they also attacked communities that refused to cooperate with the concessionary company. Moreover, there is evidence that the GSK, like its sister companies in the Congo Free State, could order military attacks whenever this seemed necessary to its agents. The latter could even ask for soldiers who, under the command of GSK agents, forced the population to cooperate with the firm.[11] Interestingly, conflicts between the GSK and the population did not so much arise from coercive measures to make people tap rubber – apparently many people were eager to bring rubber to the GSK's factories[12] – but rather from the necessity to recruit porters for the company's caravans. As hardly any river in the concession was navigable for more than a short distance, and beasts of burden could not survive for long time in the area infested by tsetse flies, every commodity had to be carried by humans along the narrow paths of the forests (Wirz 1972: 92). Most often, local people refused to carry the goods and the rubber of the GSK. Thus, when a village was successfully subdued, talks took place 'in presence of a representative of the company' and 'after consulting the company's representative', peace terms implied almost everywhere the forced recruitment of carriers (von Stein 1904: 86).[13]

However, the year 1903 marked a turning point in the rubber trade since, from then on, the colonial authorities quite openly encouraged the coexistence of 'free' trade next to the concession arrangement. As said, the GSK enjoyed until then the protection of the colonial administration and hence a de facto trade monopoly, but it was going to lose both in the course of the succeeding years. Already in 1898 and 1898, in the very first years after the Colonial Office had granted the GSK concession, it came under sharp criticism in the Colonial Council, the press, and the Reichstag, the main reasons being the dominance of foreign capital and the exclusion of other German trading interests (see Ballhaus 1968: 112–16).[14] Moreover, the authorities both in Cameroon and in Germany became increasingly disappointed with the GSK's deficient investments in the zone. In consequence, the initial policy of support and protection was increasingly abandoned. When in early 1903 the GSK tried to have its land purchases confirmed, the local and metro-

---

[11] BArch R 175 F FA 1/131: Langheld to administration, Moloundou, 31/12/1900: 48; BArch R 1001/8114: Scheunemann to governor, Besam, 20/12/1904: 140.
[12] See below for an attempt to explain this in relation to Guyer's notions.
[13] See also BArch R 1001/3448: Scheunemann to Gouvernement, bivouac Ateke, 27/07/1905: 146f. See also Hausen 1970: 164, Rüger 1960: 195.
[14] The GSK was indeed dominated by the Belgians in its first years. Most of its shareholders were Belgians and it was steered from Brussels by the well-known Belgian colonial explorers and capitalists Alexandre Delcommune and Albert Thys. Only in 1903 did it move its headquarters to Hamburg. But still, the Belgians continued to play a significant role in the administration of the GSK. Cf. Ballhaus 1968: 110, BArch R 1001/3444: 11th board meeting of the GSK, Brussels, 23/08/1901, without pagination.

politan bureaucracy tended to delay the approval of these acquisitions further and further (clearly against the spirit of the concession allocated to the GSK in 1898).[15] Since 1901, the local colonial authorities, impatient with the slow development of the concession, began to look for possible ways to open the area for rival traders. The local head of administration at the time, Hauptmann Ludwig von Stein zu Lausnitz, insisted that the underlying reason for all the problems was lack of competition. Therefore, he took energetic measures to create a safe and reliable route between the remote south-east and the coast, so that the companies based on the Batanga Coast could access the zone. In 1903, he succeeded in making the journey through the forest area to the coast, thus opening the way for the Batanga-Firmen (see Ballhaus 1968: 129).[16]

1903 was also the year of a powerful surge in the price of rubber in Hamburg. Connected with a renewed uptrend of the German industry, this was another stimulus for the Batanga-Firmen, their African subcontractors and trading partners (especially the Bulu from the coastal hinterlands) to venture themselves into the GSK concession (see Wirz 1972: 32; Burhop 2011: 79; Ausbüttel 1922: 55–8).[17] However, these new forms of direct competition, from which von Stein expected so much, soon led to a chaotic situation in the south-east. An important reason was the continuing uncertainty about the status of the GSK claims on land, the approval of which was delayed time and again. This encouraged the Batanga-Firmen and their representatives on the spot to quickly try to get out as much rubber as possible of the territory by whatever means (Wirz 1972: 138).[18] After all, the GSK's claims could be confirmed any time. Indeed, GSK agents intervened on several occasions against traders from the Batanga Coast, confiscating their rubber stocks, which they considered to be stolen from GSK land (Ballhaus 1968: 146). A feverish rush for rubber set in, with GSK and Batanga-Firmen in fierce competition over the rubber produced, causing the concessionary company to write furious complaints to the Colonial Office in Berlin, while the Batanga-Firmen through their headquarters in Hamburg were putting pressure on the same Office and on the deputies in the Reichstag in whatever way they could (see Ballhaus 1968: 166f). Soon the free traders had the edge over the concessionaires. There were several incidents in 1903 and subsequent years of locals violently ousting or even killing GSK agents in favour of their Batanga-competitors (see Hoffmann 2007: 152; Kaeselitz 1968: 40; von Stein 1904; Scheunemann 1904: 766).[19]

In order to understand the population's apparent preference for the traders

[15] Cf. for example BArch R 1001/3445: GSK. Bericht für das vierte Geschäftsjahr, 12/12/1903: 69f, BArch R 1001/3446: Stuebel to GSK, Berlin, 08/08/1904: 41f, minute of a conference about the land question in the GSK concessionary area, 11/06/1904: 44f.
[16] Denschrift über die Regelung der Landfrage im Konzessionsgebiet der Gesellschaft Süd-Kamerun 1905: 2, BArch R 1001/3450: von Stein to Gouvernement, Atok, 04/12/1905: 188, von Stein 1901c.
[17] Statistisches Reichsamt 1935: 722.
[18] BArch R 1001/8114: Scheunemann to Gouvernement, Besam, 20/12/1904: 138.
[19] Preuß 1904, BArch R 1001/4291: Lämmermann to Gouvernement, 25/05/1906: 22f.

Coercion or Trade? The Rubber Boom in German Kamerun

from the coast, it is enlightening to have a closer look at the differences between the ways in which the Batanga-Firmen and the GSK were mobilizing and valuating rubber. Guyer's notions of 'composition' and 'multiple self-realization' can be of great help here. Of utmost importance was the fact that rubber was a new commodity for the people in the concessionary zone (see Wirz 1972: 108).[20] When the GSK entered the scene in 1899, the only trade item was ivory. At that time, people did not produce rubber – whether they refused to do it or just did not know how remains unclear. After all, rubber was not a commodity in south-eastern Cameroon until the very end of the nineteenth century. Ivory, however, had already been traded for decades against metal bars and European import goods that were used as currencies in the Congo Basin in precolonial times (see Harms 1981; Guyer 1986, 2004: 31–40). Alongside the items against which it was exchanged, ivory played a crucial role in local social relationships, especially as a means to pay the bridewealth.[21] Access to ivory and thereby local currencies was one of the pillars of the gerontocratic structure of society. Since hunting for ivory required the coordination of a larger group of men, or special ties to groups of Baka hunters who exchanged ivory against metal and agricultural products, it was controlled by elders/big men (see Wirz 1972: 104; Harms 1981: 41; Hardin 2011: 114; Kilian-Hatz 1992: 68; Koch 1913: 261; Petersen 1938: 65f). This institutionalization of the ivory trade made it easy for outsiders, like the Belgian SAB, the Dutch NAHV and later the German–Belgian GSK, to enter into trade relations for acquiring this commodity.

By contrast, wild rubber had never been a product of interest, indeed it was hardly ever harvested, and certainly not exchanged. No institutionalized ways existed for procuring or distributing it. This delayed the development of the rubber trade. Indeed, both the GSK and the colonial administration saw it as their task to actively teach the population how to gather rubber. As von Stein reports, on all expeditions to explore the concession, soldiers and employees of the GSK were giving 'a detailed practical demonstration of the production of rubber in every bivouac to the still absolutely ignorant inhabitants of the country'.[22] While the ivory trade was still dominated by local big men, rubber could be harvested by young men individually. Of special importance is that the GSK set up a network of factories and posts – some of which it took over from the SAB, its Belgian predecessor – where people were encouraged to come and bring their products to exchange them for the highly desired European goods. This arrangement opened up new opportunities for the advancement of younger men. Indeed, everybody could go into the forest, tap rubber, bring it to the GSK's factories and posts, and get paid with the same currencies as were paid for ivory (see Wirz 1972: 107; Geschiere 2007: 51ff).[23] This way, the GSK unwittingly enabled social mobility inside the soci-

---

[20] Oral accounts state that rubber actually was used locally – cf. Zouya Mimbang 2013: 139. Whether this is true or not, in no way was it a commodity before the Germans arrived.
[21] For ivory and bridewealth in Cameroon (mainly at the coast) cf. Wirz 1972: 103; Quinn 2006: 33, Guyer 1986, 1993.
[22] BArch R 1001/8114: von Stein to Colonial Office, Berlin, 15/02/1904: 76.
[23] A sketch of the network of GSK factories and posts can be found in the protocol of its sixteenth

eties of the forest. In fact because of its form of valuation, rubber posed a threat to the established gerontocratic social order.

In contrast, the Batanga-Firmen explicitly based their trade on their relationships with big men and elders. An important reason for this was the increasing distance between their factories on the Batanga Coast and the areas ever further into the interior where rubber was still available. While the GSK form of trade encouraged the producer to come to fixed posts, the trade of the Batanga-Firmen was based on mobility, their caravans contacting villages over increasing distances. This meant also that their agents mainly worked through local leaders, in the tracks of the ivory trading networks to and from the coast, thus fitting into pre-existing gerontocratic networks (see Geschiere 2007: 53; Wirz 1972: 117).

German and British ivory traders had been active on the Batanga Coast since the early second half of the nineteenth century, and commercial relations therefore were established for quite a while when the rubber boom set in. As at most places along the coast, traders used the 'trust' system: European merchants advanced imported goods as credit to African entrepreneurs who used them to acquire ivory, and later rubber. With the European goods as currency, they visited big men in the hinterland who became their more-or-less fixed trading partners. These partnerships were usually established by kinship, marriage or alliance and were part of a long supply chain of similar trade relations that stretched very far inland.[24] By means of this system, ivory and later rubber passed through many hands until it reached the coast where the African entrepreneur paid off the trust. This system seems not to have been altered by the emergence of the rubber trade: African merchants still advanced European goods to local big men who made their dependants tap rubber. Thus, the elders still controlled the bulk of prestige goods – currencies and commodities – necessary for marriage payments.

But it would definitely be wrong to understand this trading system as static. Under the conditions of colonialism and the rubber boom, it was constantly changing. As noted, well into the 1890s, most of the hinterland was blocked for European traders by African groups who protected their share in the above-mentioned system. But, little by little, the colonial authorities managed to subdue the peoples of the hinterland and to open up these regions for European trade.[25] Simultaneously, the rubber frontier moved ever further inland

---

(contd) board meeting, 05/02/1903 – see Archiv der Freiherrn von Stetten: 415. It mentions factories at Moloundou, Yukadouma, Beri, Dume, Ngato, Bidjum, Moohul, Matulli, Kul, Dongo. At the end of the year, the GSK had 11 factories, 12 posts and worked with a staff of 32 Europeans and 618 Africans in south-eastern Cameroon (BArch R 1001/3445: Gesellschaft Süd-Kamerun. Bericht für das vierte Geschäftsjahr, 12/12/1903: 69f). Cf. also what Richard von Stetten, the nephew of one of the GSK directors, wrote in 1906 to his parents before taking over the GSK post at Nginda: 'I do not have the intention to follow the principles of my lazy predecessors and other factory leaders – that is, to stay at the factory and to make the blacks come to me. I will rather close the factory from time to time and visit the villagers in the wider environment with 15 to 20 carriers with trade goods in order to buy up ivory.' (Archiv der Freiherrn von Stetten: 415).

[24] For a perspicacious sketch of this system of chains of exchange links that worked mostly without the establishment of regular markets, see Wirz 1972: 100.

[25] The military destruction of the existing trade networks that blocked the advancement of German merchants is described by Kaeselitz 1968, Hoffmann 2007, Rudin 1938.

Coercion or Trade? The Rubber Boom in German Kamerun 101

because the resources near the coast were quickly depleted due to overexploitation. According to the judge Lämmermann, who had to look into the deeper reasons for the *Unruhen* (disturbances) in the forest area that necessitated a large-scale military expedition in 1906–7, a new transformation of the old trust system had been developed in 1902 – allegedly by the firm A. & L. Lubcke.[26] It was to be called, using a Pidgin term, the 'trade-back' system, and became the object of fierce debates. In the factories on the coast, African and later also European intermediary traders received European import goods as 'trust' with which they went to their trading partners as before. But now the new political situation allowed them to go ever further inland with ever-larger caravans of carriers, leaving import goods with the elders of every village on the route. When they made their way back, they collected the equivalent of the goods in rubber and brought it to the coast. The big question was, of course, what was 'equivalent' in this exchange – all the more so since, for rubber as a new commodity, hardly any established standards of value had emerged (Geschiere 2005). However, it will become clear that, despite dramatic changes in their trading system, the Batanga-Firmen, particularly when they reached as far out as the GSK concession, had the advantage to relate to locally established forms of exchange that supported the social hierarchy of these gerontocratic societies.

When the Batanga-Firmen started trading inside the concessionary zone, this had drastic effects. Where local big men had a chance to trade with merchants from the coast, they preferred them to the GSK agents. Indeed, there is a striking coincidence between the appearance of the Batanga traders in the south-east and the first acts of violence, already mentioned, against the GSK agents – for instance it was in December 1903 that the GSK agent Charles Monnier was killed in Bidjum after his colleague Kundenreich tried to put pressure on the local big man (Harms 1981).

All over the world, the trade in rubber had a hasty and chaotic character. An obvious reason was that the available resources were often quickly exhausted so that traders were constantly looking for new and as yet untapped areas. However, in German Kamerun this rushed character was particularly encouraged by the nervous competition between the GSK as the concession holder and the trading houses from the coast. Especially the ongoing uncertainty as to whether the coastal traders had or had not access to the concession made the competition all the more fierce.[27] A well-known quote from Schutztruppenoffizier Hans Dominik, the great empire builder of German Kamerun sums up the turbulent developments most cogently:

> However, I know from experience what is the state of an area where the struggle for this gold of the jungle has been waged. The lust for quick money, the fear of competitors vanquishes all scruples and the locals are intoxicated as well: they slaughter their animals, do not sow or harvest anymore, but only make rubber,

[26] BArch R 1001/4291: Bl. 15–26: Bericht Oberrichter Lämmermanns, 25/05/1906. See also Wirz 1972: 116.
[27] Cf. BArch R 1001/8114: Scheunemann to governor, Besam, 20/12/1904:140.

rubber. Happily for the country, the wave rolls on when the rubber is exhausted. But then follow the caravans marching through, then food shortages arise and then it comes to violence. (Quoted in Wirz 1972: 137 and note 191)[28]

Indeed, from 1903 on, the rubber boom in the Cameroonian forest zone became a real race for the available resources, with traders and agents losing any consideration they might have had for the fate of the region's population. Batanga traders and GSK agents alike tried to prevent people trading with their competitors, and even used violence to this end. The rubber trade was therefore more and more accompanied by atrocities against the population, committed by free traders, GSK agents and the caravans of both (see Rüger 1960: 229; Ballhaus 1968: 176; Hausen 1970: 188). Escalating violence increasingly blocked people's willingness to participate in the rubber trade, leading directly to the violent turmoil that ultimately plunged the land into chaos after 1905. The military repression by the large-scale *Süd-Expedition* led by Hauptmann Peter Scheunemann cost thousands of lives and only ended in 1907 (see Kaeselitz 1968; Hoffmann 2007).

Rubber & Self-realization

Striking in the sombre quote from Dominik above is his emphasis on the active involvement of the locals in the *Taumel* (intoxication) of the rubber boom. Indeed, the differences between the trade forms of the GSK and the Batanga-Firmen may have been significant, but noteworthy in both contexts was the active role of the local producers. An important difference with the concessionary regimes in the Belgian and the French Congo was the fact, already mentioned, that in German Kamerun the concession holder did not have the right to tax the population, while in the Congo the concession holders could simply oblige the locals to bring specified quantities of rubber to the factories as a form of obligatory tax – and it was this entitlement to tax that made the concessionary regime in the Congos so coercive and violent – the GSK did have to offer some sort of payment to the people who came to bring their rubber to the factory.[29] In the locals' exchanges with the repres-

---

[28] See also Archives nationales Yaoundé, nr. 544, Bl. 63ff, Dominik 06/03/1906.
[29] Of course, the GSK also applied much coercion and violent pressure on the population, but it is significant that this mainly concerned the recruiting of carriers (who had to transport the goods between the factories and the central post in Moloundou from where it could be transported over the river) and not so much the harvesting of rubber itself. The GSK reports are full of complaints about the stubborn unwillingness of the locals to accept to work as carriers. Indeed, for these kinds of services it often had to take recourse to *Strafarbeiter* (punitive labourers) who throughout the colony played a crucial role in solving the Germans' eternal *Arbeiterfrage* (labour problem). Often GSK agents worked closely together with the administration and the *Schutztruppe* to punish rebellious villages, and then the GSK would profit from the *Strafarbeiter* that the village had to deliver as sign of its subjection (cf. Rüger 1960). But, as shown above, such forms of coercion did not seem necessary to make the population produce rubber. At most, coercion was used to force people to deliver to the GSK and not to its rivals – which reinforces the impression that no force was required to make people harvest rubber. Apparently the attraction of the European trade goods was enough of a motivation.

Coercion or Trade? The Rubber Boom in German Kamerun 103

entatives of the Batanga-Firmen, violence and coercion did certainly occur, but the causes were mostly disagreements about what could be considered as the proper equivalent in rubber for the European trade goods that the caravan had deposited in the village on its way out. Also in these forms of *trade-back Verfahren* (method) no direct coercion seemed to be necessary to make the people harvest rubber.

Let us have a closer look at the reports on such encounters and confrontations to clarify what was at stake. We owe to *Hauptmann* Scheunemann, who played a central role in the administration and the 'pacification' of the Sanga-Ngoko district (that included most of the GSK concession) after 1903, several quite caustic sketches of life at a GSK factory, deep in the forest. Scheunemann introduces the following description of how 'trade' took place at an unnamed GSK factory as a 'textbook example':

> At nine in the morning, the native arrives at the factory with a few kilos of rubber (his money) in order to buy some little things: cleavers, flintlocks, iron wire. But the lord of the factory is still asleep. His 'Rose'[30] announces the buyer. The trader is unhappy with the disturbance. He has a headache and gives first the order 'Wait'.[31] The native modestly sits down in a corner and waits. When at noon the *Bigman* is finally ready with toilet and breakfast, he deigns to accept the rubber from the black man. Since the scales just broke down, he makes an estimation, and he is kind enough to give the negro a piece of red cloth. However, the latter timidly expresses the wish to look around in the store since this time he would rather like to buy a different piece of cloth, instead of the red one he bought already several times, and he wants a few other things. This request is roughly refused with the remark that blacks are not allowed to enter this sacred space (no problem that this clearly implies that the buyer might be a thief). But today the lord of the shop wants to be nice – after all he has a hangover! So he kindly gets a rusted cleaver and a box of damaged matches, and says magnanimously to his clerk: 'Tell the monkey, I dash him this on top!' But now something terrible happens. The native has the audacity to ask for a smaller cleaver rather than this big one ... This stretches the big man's patience too far. He just finds one word that he thunders at the miserable fellow: 'move!' The black buyer is thrown out! With the proud conscience that he has confirmed the authority of the white race over and against these *niggers*, the lord of the shop sits down and takes another cognac. The highest principles of modern retail trade, 'big turnover, small profit,' turns into its opposite in south-east *Kamerun*, especially in these factories in the interior that can only be accessed over the Congo river. The preceding example of the red cloth comes from a GSK factory. These sad remainders of the textile industry, real fun-fair junk, are still piled up in great quantities in the GSK factories, and have to be sold to the natives for prices that are bureaucratically fixed at the Gröninger street in Hamburg [the address of the GSK's main office – TO/PG]. It is the same with many other trade goods.[32]

---

[30] Presumably his African concubine.
[31] Interestingly, Scheunemann uses several expressions in Pidgin English in his text (in italics – as in the present translation). Apparently, Pidgin, very common on the Cameroonian coast, had already penetrated this far into the interior only a few years after the Germans entered this part of their colony.
[32] BArch R 175 FFA 1/67, p. 94–122; *Hauptmann* Scheunemann, *Jahresbericht* 1904/1906: 117 ff.

A contrasting example of the trade in ivory comes from the same area – from a novel by Erich Robert Petersen (1938), based on his experiences when he worked as a GSK agent. Petersen worked for the company 1910 to 1914 and in his texts, as a practitioner, gives quite valuable information about how trade was conducted. His account corresponds with Scheunemann's official report and those of other traders.[33] The story tells how a fictive German trader creates a factory in a village of the Missanga Häuptling Apacka:

> The factory is hardly under the roof, when Apacka makes his appearance as the first customer of 'his' white man. He brings a big elephant tusk with him. With a magnanimous gesture he turns around and indicates to his servants that they have to place the heavy tusk at the feet of the white man. He does not want any payment – beware! Here in the bush, under Europeans the tusk has a value of two hundred Marks, and under the natives the same number of *midjoko* (copper spirals – the local money). But the big headman Apacka offers it as a present to the white men with his best wishes. Of course Kusumba [the African name of the German – TO/PG] knows this kind of dirty sorcery but he shows himself to be deeply moved and offers the generous king a counter gift from his stock that equals the tusk's value ... The completion of this exchange of gifts and the appropriate show of friendship takes more than two hours, with half of the villagers getting involved in one way or another. When the Häuptling's servants have finally managed to collect all the copper spirals, pieces of cloth, knifes and containers in order to carry them to Apacka's hut, other villagers are already lining up with their bundles of *Gummiwürsten* (rubber 'sausages') for the white man. (Petersen 1938: 63ff)

The examples suggest indeed that there were important differences between the older trade in ivory – through the big men and with some ceremony – and the trade in rubber, more by individuals coming to the GSK factories. A similar contrast is, for instance, suggested by Georg August Zenker, the famous botanist who acted for seven years (1889–95) as leader of the 'scientific station' at Jaunde/Yaoundé. In those years Jaunde was an isolated outpost, far from the coast (between 1890 and 1894 Zenker was only twice visited by German expeditions). In an article published in 1895, he notes the growing importance of rubber in the area:

> Until a short time ago, only ivory could grant access to European trade goods. But, in the last two years, rubber began to play this role as well. Indeed, it is rubber that made young Jaunde men, who now laboriously check any Landolphia vine they can find, go down to the coast – while earlier on they would never have dared to go further than the first Ngumba village (Zenker 1895: 64; Wirz 1972: 107).[34]

---

[33] For another trader's account see Richard von Stetten, footnote 23.

[34] It is to be noted that Zenker describes the very first phase of the rubber trade in the interior when apparently producers tried to go down themselves to the coast to the European factories there (the Ngumba/Ngoumba live just inland from the Batanga coast and served initially as intermediaries in the trade; they tried for several years to block the penetration of European traders and their caravans into the interior in order to protect their advantageous role as middlemen). After 1900 all this changed when the factories on the coast sent caravans ever deeper into the forest (via the *trade-back Verfahren* already mentioned); then the traders

Striking, again, is the eagerness and the rapidity with which producers took advantage of the new opportunities. This is all the more noteworthy if one takes into account that (in contrast to ivory) rubber was a completely new product. For the Europeans, its increasing value may have come about quite abruptly. But for the locals it must have constituted a complete surprise. Moreover, the rubber resources were often not that easy to find. Reports refer to harvesters who got lost in the dense forest looking for *Gummi* often in quite inaccessible places (see Petersen 1939: 71f). The colonials, both the traders and the authorities, were also very worried about the complete lack of local knowledge for harvesting the rubber from the available trees and lianas. For instance, as described above, the GSK together with the administration organized detailed courses how to tap at tree. Apparently, these courses were attended by the villagers, eager to tap as much as possible. In order to profit from the expanding rubber trade, local people soon developed new techniques of gathering the rubber to sell to the traders. Hauptmann von Stein mentions that Konabembe men invented a special knife for harvesting rubber,[35] Petersen describes an apparatus for climbing trees, invented by Mkako (Petersen 1939: 71f). Both the young men and their elders were ready to use these new forms of expertise for the 'composition' of 'bundles of knowledge' which, in Guyer's terms, were so important for 'multiple self-realization' in the forest area.

Of course, this reaction 'from below' emerged in a context marked by extreme violence: constant forced labour was levied by the government in order to meet its insatiable demand for labour for its own projects (roads, cleaning the river, porterage) in this thinly populated area of difficult access. Both the traders and the GSK were also desperate to recruit porters in sufficient numbers, and were happy to use all sorts of coercion when the supply of rubber by the locals was unsatisfactory. The short boom in wild rubber in German Kamerun was as violent as in other parts of the world during the same period. But in contrast to the Congos, where concession holders had complete sovereignty over their zone, violence and physical coercion were not the main means for making people produce rubber. Rather, struggles over the value of the product, the fierce competition among the various firms involved in the trade, and struggle to its access led to violent confrontations. As the trader Bernhard Lehning told one of his employees, when he entered the village of Assobam with his caravan, he menaced the chief with a revolver pointing to his head, to *allow* his people to trade with him.[36] The strong emphasis on violence in the literature concerned should not hide the fact that villagers' eagerness to get access to the European goods made them often quite keen to profit from these new opportunities.

Consider the following incident that became the occasion for the large-scale Süd-Expedition that was supposed to definitely 'pacify' the area

---

(contd) and their caravans came to the villages where the rubber was produced, and apparently contacted the big men rather than the young (who still did the harvesting while their elders controlled the exchange for European trade goods).

[35] BArch R 1001/8114: von Stein to Colonial Office, Berlin, 15/02/1904: 81.

[36] Staatsbibliothek zu Berlin Ms. germ. oct. 1355 Sauer, Fritz (1919): Meine Fahrt zum Aequator. Süd-Kameruner Erinnerungen:116f.

between the Dja and the Nyong. In 1905 the German trader Hinrichsen of the Bremer Westafrika-Gesellschaft was murdered in the village of Häuptling Ebolobingon (probably near present-day Ayos). According to Hauptmann Scheuneman, the leader of the subsequent Süd-Expedition, Hinrichsen had been highly imprudent, underestimating *die Habgier der Eingeborenen nach den Schätzen der Kaufleute* (the natives' cravings for the merchants' treasures). Apparently Hinrichsen had left a pile of European goods in Ebolobingon's village. On his return he expected to pick up a commensurate quantity of rubber (but commensurate according to which standards?) Hinrichsen was not satisfied with what the villagers had gathered and started negotiating. But since they remained stubborn, he got so furious that he fired a shot over the chief's head. Whereupon Ebolobingon's brother, thinking that he was attacking the chief, killed Hinrichsen with one shot (see Geschiere 2007: 52, 2005: 255f; Scheunemann 1907: 347–52).[37] The event illustrates how easily things could go wrong in the uncertain negotiations (if one can use that word for just firing in the air) about the value of the new product. But it illustrates at the same time that despite all uncertainty and mutual distrust some sort of trade arrangement was worked out. Hinrichsen did not exert violent pressure to make Ebolobingon's people harvest rubber. Apparently this was not necessary. Indeed, differences of opinion about what was a commensurate quantity of rubber for the goods that the German had left in the village led to his killing.

In later phases violent confrontations came about when caravans became bigger and their provisions became ever more of a problem in the often already depleted zones they were trekking through. As indicated above, there was no violent pressure needed to make the natives go into the forest to tap rubber. Apparently, they quickly realized that this newly discovered 'gold of the forest' could provide them access to the much coveted Western products.

This view on what was going on during the chaotic rubber boom in German Kamerun, stressing the locals' eagerness to profit from a new opportunity – indeed, what one would expect following Guyer's highlighting of a tendency towards 'multiple self-realization' and the 'composition' of 'different bundles of knowledge' in Equatorial Africa – contrasts in striking ways with the current colonial stereotypes of those days. Like other colonizers, the Germans never tired of complaining about the 'laziness of the natives' and their 'reluctance towards any form of labour' (Eckert 1999: 507)[38] – characteristics that are hard to reconcile with, for, instance, Zenker's report quoted above that as soon as rubber acquired some value in the exchanges with the Europeans, Yaoundé young men were most eager to undertake the perilous trip down to the coast in order to profit from this new opportunity.

It rather seems that the reluctance of the German authorities to impose the concessionary system in a similar coercive form as the French and the Belgians

---

[37] In the early 1920s the American Presbyterian missionaries created a station in a place they called Ebolobingon (sometimes they refer also to the Ebolobingon as a group). Apparently, for them the name was an equivalent for 'Yebekollo' and the place was near Ayos (see Foreign Missions Manuscript – Presbyterian Historical Society, Philadelphia files RG 142–8–42m and 46).

[38] For quotes lamenting African 'laziness' from a GSK agent cf. Koch 1913.

Coercion or Trade? The Rubber Boom in German Kamerun

did in the Congos – a reluctance apparently reinforced by the manifest role the Belgians had to play in the new concessionary company and maybe also by the clamorous protests of the Batanga-Firmen advocating their form of 'free' trade which would be more in the interest of German business – allowed some space for local initiative in harvesting rubber. And the locals were clearly most eager to make use of this space – apparently the brutal forms of physical coercion for which Leopold II's Congo became so notorious were not necessary for this. In Cameroon it was rather the violence and rapacity that followed from the uncertainties of the competition between different colonial groups – the GSK defending its concession and the Batanga-Firmen trying to break it open – that blocked such local initiatives and led to a general resistance. But the special circumstances of the rubber boom in this area highlighted local initiative rather than *Faulheit* (laziness) or *Arbeitsscheu* (reluctance to work).

Money: An Uncontained Force?

The eagerness in the local response to the new opportunities offered by the chaotic rubber boom in German Kamerun fits with a broader picture of developments in this area: with the rapid penetration of money into all spheres of life that seems to be characteristic of the forest societies. Indeed, one can speak of an abrupt and almost total process of commoditization which is all the more striking since in these areas – certainly further into the interior – the impact of the European trade must have been a true upheaval.[39] Until the invasions by the Germans (the military, the GSK agents, the caravans of the Batanga-Firmen), trade in these areas was underdeveloped – at least if one compares with the societies of the west (Bamiléké) or the north (Hausa-Fulani) of present-day Cameroon. In the forest area, commerce between the small family villages remained mostly limited to exchanges fitting within the network of kinship and affinity between these villages.[40] Yet, it is precisely in this area that money and European goods very rapidly penetrated throughout

---

[39] The general tendency in more recent literature (cf. Parry and Bloch 1989, and see Geschiere 2000) to distinguish monetization and commoditization is of little use for understanding developments in this area. Parry and Bloch attack Marx's view of money as a general leveller (putting everything on sale) since in their view many societies succeed(ed) in containing the circulation of money to certain spheres; Western capitalism would be an exception in this respect. Developments in the forest area of Cameroon rather seem to fit with the Marxian interpretation: there is hardly any effort to contain money to certain spheres of exchange; indeed, the tendency of money to break through all social barriers (certainly through the barriers around so-called 'prestige goods') seems to be even more marked here than in the West. In this sense monetization and commoditization seem to coincide here: money turns everything – also personal acts, like sex or work inside the family, and even people themselves – into a commodity. See further Geschiere 1994 and 2000.

[40] Cf. Wirz' sketch of how in precolonial days traders would create networks between the villages based on personal relations; cf. the complaints by the first penetrators of these zones – the GSK agents but also the American Presbyterian missionaries who arrived in some areas along the upper Nyong prior to the Germans – about an absolute lack of provisions: there were simply no possibilities to exchange food for money or other goods. See, Foreign Missions Manuscripts, Presbyterian Historical Society, Philadelphia, files RG55–1–26 and RG 142–8–50; and, for GSK agents, Oestermann 2013: 26.

society, also in the more intimate spheres of exchange: into bridewealth and funeral payments and other kinship exchanges.[41]

A recurrent element in Geschiere's ethnography of everyday life in Maka villages in the forest area of Cameroon is indeed the omnipresence of money in all walks of life (Geschiere 1994, 2000, 2007). Fierce haggling over money dominates highly personal moments. The wild mourning rituals at a funeral are constantly interrupted by vocal struggles over the amounts to be paid between the various family groups involved. Marriage celebrations often become very tense occasions because of the harsh negotiations over bridewealth and concomitant payments. On all these occasions, people haggle over money, mentioning very specific amounts and using arguments that in other societies – for instance in the West – are seen as more appropriate to a market situation. This omnipresence of money came all the more of a surprise to the anthropologist in view of the endless complaints in reports by colonial and subsequent developers that 'these' people are insensitive to the value of money and incapable of accumulation. Moreover, the ever-further monetization of relations – also, for instance, for work in the family: it is becoming quite normal that a child expects to be paid for some work for his mother – turned out to be a most dynamic process. Remember, for instance, the example quoted in the introduction to this article: women launching a new 'traditional' payment during a funeral by obliging all male passers-by to pay some money; and remember especially the somewhat shocked comment by Geschiere's assistant: 'these women turn the funeral into a market'.

A concrete example of how rapid and complete the impact of money must have been in this society is the abrupt loss of value of the *mimbesh*, bundles of iron bars that functioned as a prestige good in the exchanges between the families. They still figure in the stories of the elders about the bridewealth, but it seems that already in the 1930s they lost all value. In those years (after the abrupt collapse of the rubber boom in 1913) some money became finally available to the villagers through the cultivation of cocoa. Then it became almost immediately the core of the bridewealth payments, completely replacing the old *mimbesh*. How quickly the devaluation of the latter occurred is illustrated by the fact that still now, when people clear a new field for their wives, often a package of *mimbesh* suddenly drops from a tree that is felled. This is always the occasion for laughter and all sorts of jokes about the stupidity of the elders

---

[41] Geschiere's data on the payment of the bridewealth in the Maka area only go back to the 1930s (in the 1970s some elderly women gave detailed information on the composition of the bridewealth that had been paid for them around that time; they still could quote the exact amount of money that had been paid for them – then already the main item in the bridewealth). For the preceding decades, the French officials, who administrated this area since 1915, never stopped complaining about the total absence of money in the villages and the apparent incapacity of the locals to produce anything for the market. Since wild rubber had lost its value (from 1913 on), the French were looking for alternative cash-crops (palm oil, peanuts) but did not succeed with these. The consequence was that it was hardly possible to collect tax from the villages (a fact which was quite detrimental to the record of any official serving in this area). This changed very gradually in the 1930s through the incipient production of cacao – see below; Geschiere 1994 and 2000.

Coercion or Trade? The Rubber Boom in German Kamerun 109

from former days. People will say that this must have been a treasure hidden by one of these elders in the forest. In the old days, the men did not have a house of themselves. In daytime, they sat in a *mpanze*, an open hut, at the fire of the elder of the settlement; at night they slept in the kitchen of one of their wives. Consequently, the elders hid their treasures – for instance, the prestige goods received at the marriage of one of their daughters – in the forest, telling only a confidant the exact place. Now people will say that these *mimbesh* had so completely lost their value that the elders did not even take the trouble to go and look for them in the forest.

Indeed, the all-pervasive role of money in the forest societies has become a subject of lively debate in present-day Cameroon: it is the grist of powerful and quite vicious ethnic stereotypes about the Beti, the main forest group, who since 'their' President Paul Biya came to power (1982) are seen as being in control of the state. With the return of ethnic classification in public debate in the 1990s (openly referring to ethnic identities was not done during the preceding decades when nation building and hence the celebration of national citizenship was the prevailing discourse, powerfully supported by the state's disciplinary sanctions[42]) the supposed opposition between these Beti and the Bamiléké from the western highlands has become a fixed adage. The latter, seen as dominant in the national economy, are supposed to be experts in accumulation even at the cost of their own kin. In contrast, the Beti are supposed to be unable to keep their money: this is why they have to 'eat' the state in order to be able to satisfy the unrelenting demands of their own family. Such stereotypes will be invariably accompanied by the general comment: *Ah oui, la chèvre broute où elle est attachée* (Well, the goat eats where it is tethered) (see Bayart 1989 and 1996).[43] In this highly stereotypical image of the Beti, there is the idea that money has become an uncontained agent, precisely because it penetrates all relations and this makes strategic accumulation almost impossible. This is also the popular explanation of why, despite heavy support from the regime since 1982, there is no Beti bourgeoisie emerging that could compete with the Bamiléké bourgeoisie that seems to be in control economically.

Such views have a long history, as may be clear from an example that takes us back, again, to German times. In 1913, Paul Rohrbach, a German journalist from the *Frankfurter Zeitung*, travelled along the road from Kribi on the coast to Yaoundé in the interior. This road had been cleared with great difficulties at the end of the 1890s to facilitate the rapidly growing rubber trade. According to some estimates (Wirz 1972: 1317), already in 1903 a daily average of about 1,000 carriers would have used it. In 1913 Rohrbach was also surprised to see so many people travelling along it. But he was even more intrigued to see in many villages groups of women standing along the road, singing a cheerful song. On his request, his 'boy', who spoke *Neger-Englisch*, translated their song:

---
[42] For an elaboration of this, see Basile Ndjio 2016.
[43] See also Warnier 1993 about special traits of the kinship arrangements among the Bamiléké to block the 'strategies of disaccumulation' that emanate from family pressures (there is a clear, if implicit, contrast with relations among the Beti elites here).

> We are happy to sleep with the strangers who pass
> But they have to pay us well
> Else we run away when they want to have us

Whereupon his young servant added: 'Oh, these Yaoundé people, they like money too much.'[44]

The servant's comment in particular is striking. There is a remarkable contrast here with the later complaints of the French administrators that these people were insensitive to *la loi d'offre et de demande* (the law of supply and demand). Instead, it seems that the villagers were so keen on earning money that they did it by means which were fairly shocking to both the European and his servant from the coast. It rather seems, therefore, that these societies knew remarkably few barriers to the spread of money: even sex was commoditized on an unprecedented scale.[45]

The quick response of the forest people during the violent rubber boom in Cameroon to new possibilities to value a product that until then had had no value at all clearly fits in with a larger configuration. The abrupt confrontation of the forest societies with forms of market economy that were quite different from that with which they were accustomed did not lead to withdrawal – as predicted by the colonial stereotypes. On the contrary, it triggered such a materialistic embrace – inspired by a true obsession with the new European goods as new forms to attain prestige – that money turned society inside out, especially the local kinship arrangements. Guyer's insights into people's preoccupation with the 'composition' of different forms of knowledge and value as expressing a deep urge towards 'self-realization' clearly have great potential for understanding the specific trajectories of monetization/commoditization of these societies.

---

[44] *Frankfurter Zeitung*, 25/05/1913; see also BArch R 1001/4226:57.

[45] Rohrbach's rapid sketch is convincing since it corresponds to certain elements in the anthropological literature on the area. A general trend in these forest societies is that people see it as normal that a woman's sexual favours entitle her to some sort of counter-service (her lover has to clear a field in the forest for her, file her cleaver, bring her bush-meat and, most of all, give her regular presents). Moreover, according to Laburthe-Tolra – the great ethnographer of the Beti group – it used to be common practice among them that girls were often betrothed when they were still children. Moreover, it was quite normal that this first, pre-arranged marriage ended in divorce. Then the girl was allowed a kind of interlude during which she could have several affairs. Girls in this phase were even supposed to show off with a cord with knots for each lover they had had – before embarking on a more permanent marriage (cf. Laburthe-Tolra 1981: 236; Vincent 1976). However, it must have been quite new that after German 'pacification', girls could offer their favours to complete strangers. Apparently the sudden influx of carriers along the new road, who had at least some money to offer, led to a novel commercialization of sex on a much larger scale.

References

Amin, S. (1972). 'Underdevelopment and Dependence in Black Africa: Origins and Contemporary Forms'. *Journal of Modern African Studies* 10(4): 503–24.

Ausbüttel, J. (1922). 'Die deutsche Kautschukwarenindustrie'. Dissertation, Würzburg.
Ballhaus, J. (1968). 'Die Landkonzessionsgesellschaften'. In H. Stoecker (ed.), *Kamerun unter deutscher Kolonialherrschaft. Studien*, 2 vol. Berlin: Rütten & Loening: 99–180.
Bayart, J.-F. (1989). *L'État en Afrique – La politique du ventre*. Paris: Fayard.
—. (1996). *L'Illusion identitaire*. Paris: Fayard.
Burhop, C. (2011). *Wirtschaftsgeschichte des Kaiserreichs 1871–1918*. Göttingen: Vandenhoeck & Ruprecht.
Christy, C. (1911). *The African Rubber Industry and Funtumia elastica ('Kickxia')*. London: J. Bale, Sons & Danielson.
Coquery-Vidrovitch, C. (1972). *Le Congo au temps des grandes compagnies concessionnaires, 1898–1930*. Mouton, Paris: Le Haye.
'Denkschrift über die Regelung der Landfrage im Konzessionsgebiete der Gesellschaft Süd-Kamerun' (1905), *supplement of the Deutsches Kolonialblatt* 24.
Dumett, R. (1971). 'The Rubber Trade of the Gold Coast and Asante in the Nineteenth Century: African Innovation and Market Responsiveness'. *Journal of African History* 12(1): 79–101.
Eckert, A. (1999). 'Arbeitergeschichte und Geschichte der Arbeit in Afrika'. *Archiv für Sozialgeschichte* 39, 502–30.
Fenske, J. (2010). '"Rubber will not keep in this Country." Failed Development in Benin, 1897–1921'. *MPRA Paper* 23415.
Gann, L.H. and P. Duignan (1979). *The Rulers of Belgian Africa 1884–1914*. Princeton, NJ: Princeton University Press.
Geschiere, P. (1982). *Village Communities and the State: Changing Relations Among the Maka of South-Eastern Cameroon Since the Colonial Conquest*. London/Boston/Melbourne: Kegan Paul.
—. (1994). 'Parenté et argent dans une société lignagère'. In J.-F. Bayart (ed.), *La réinvention du capitalisme*, Paris: Karthala, 87–117.
—. (2000). 'Money versus Kinship: Subversion or Consolidation?' *Asia Pacific Journal of Anthropology* 1(1): 54–78.
—. (2005). '"Tournaments of Value" in the Forest Area of Southern Cameroon: "Multiple Self-Realization" Versus Colonial Coercion during the Rubber Boom (1900–1913).' In W.M.J. van Binsbergen and P. Geschiere (eds), *Commodification: Things, Agency, and Identities* (*The Social Life of Things* Revisited), Münster: LIT: 243–66.
—. (2007). 'Regional Shifts: Marginal Gains and Ethnic Stereotypes'. *African Studies Review* 50(2): 43–56.
Guyer, J.I. (1986). 'Indigenous Currencies and the History of Marriage Payments', *Cahiers d'Études africaines* 104(26): 577–610.
—. (1993). 'Wealth in People and Self-Realization in Equatorial Africa', *Man* 28(2): 243–65.
—. (1996). 'Traditions of Invention in Equatorial Africa', *African Studies Review*, 39(3): 1–28.
—. (2004). *Marginal Gains: Monetary Transactions in Atlantic Africa*. Chicago,

IL: University of Chicago Press.

Guyer, J.I. and S.M. Eno Belinga (1995). 'Wealth in People as Wealth in Knowledge: Accumulation and Composition in Equatorial Africa', *Journal of African History* 36: 91–120.

Hardin, R. (2011). 'Concessionary Politics: Property, Patronage, and Political Rivalry in Central African Forest Management'. *Current Anthropology* 52(3): 113–25.

Harms, R.W. (1975). 'The End of Red Rubber: A Reassessment'. *Journal of African History* 16(1): 73–88.

—. (1981). *River of Wealth, River of Sorrow: The Central Zaire Basin in the Era of the Slave and Ivory Trade, 1500–1891.* New Haven and London: Yale University Press.

—. (1983). 'The World ABIR Made: The Maringa-Lopori Basin 1885–1903'. *African Economic History* 12: 125–39.

Hausen, K. (1970). *Deutsche Kolonialherrschaft in Afrika. Wirtschaftsinteressen und Kolonialverwaltung in Kamerun vor 1914.* Zurich and Freiburg i.Br: Atlantis.

Hochschild, A. (1998). *King Leopold's Ghost: A Story of Greed, Terror, and Heroism in Colonial Africa.* New York: Houghton Mifflin.

Hoffmann, F. (2007). *Okkupation und Militärverwaltung in Kamerun. Etablierung und Institutionalisierung des kolonialen Gewaltmonopols 1891–1914*, 2 vol. Göttingen: Cuvilier.

Jäckel, H. (1909). *Die Landgesellschaften in den Deutschen Schutzgebieten. Denkschrift zur kolonialen Landfrage*, Jena: Fischer.

Kaeselitz, R. (1968). 'Kolonialeroberung und Widerstandskampf in Südkamerun (1884–1907)'. In H. Stoecker (ed.), *Kamerun unter deutscher Kolonialherrschaft. Studien*, 2 vol., Berlin: Rütten & Loening: 11–54.

Kilian-Hatz, C. (1992). '"Denn Komba hat den Wald für dich gemacht": Der Wald in Wirtschaft und Weltanschauung der Baka im südlichen Kamerun'. In M. Bollig and D. Bünnagel (eds), *Der zentralafrikanische Regenwald. Ökologie, Geschichte, Wirtschaft*, Münster/Hamburg: LIT: 65–72.

Koch, C.W.H. (1913). 'Die Stämme des Bezirks Molundu in sprachlicher, geschichtlicher und völkerkundlicher Beziehung'. *Baessler-Archiv* 3(6): 257–312.

Laburthe-Tolra, P. (1981). *Les seigneurs de la forêt*, Paris: Karthala.

Marchal, A. (1952). 'Philippson (Franz-Moïse)'. *Biographie coloniale belge*, vol. 3: 688f.

Michels, S. (2004). *Imagined Power Contested: Germans and Africans in the Upper Cross River Area of Cameroon 1887–1915*, Münster: LIT.

Munro, J.F. (1981). 'Monopolists and Speculators: British Investment in West African Rubber, 1905–1914'. *Journal of African History* 22(2): 263–78.

Ndjio, B. (2016). 'Leadership, Nation and Subjectivity in Cameroon: Ahidjo's "Citizenization" and Biya's "Autochthonization" in Comparative Perspectives'. In E. Obadare and W. Adebanwi (eds), *Governance and the Crisis of Rule in Contemporary Africa: Leadership in Transformation.* New York: Palgrave Macmillan.

Obdeijn, H. (1983). 'The New African Trading Company and the Struggle for Import Duties in the Congo Free State, 1886–1894'. *African Economic History* 12: 195–212.
Oestermann, T. (2013). *Das schwarze Gold des Regenwaldes. Kautschukhandel und Gewalt im Konzessionsgebiet des Gesellschaft Süd-Kamerun, 1898–1906*. Unpublished Master's Thesis, Humboldt Universität, Berlin (history department).
Omosini, O. (1979). 'The Rubber Export Trade in Ibadan 1993–1904: Colonial Innovation or Rubber Economy'. *Journal of the Historical Society of Nigeria* 10(1): 21–46.
Osborne, E.L. 2004. '"Rubber Fever": Commerce and French Colonial Rule in Upper Guinée, 1890–1913'. *Journal of African History* 45(3): 445–65.
Parry, J. and Bloch, M. (1989). 'Introduction'. In J. Parry and M. Bloch (eds), *Money and the Morality of Exchange*, Cambridge, UK: Cambridge University Press: 1–33.
Patterson, K.D. (1975). *The Northern Gabon Coast to 1875*, Oxford: Clarendon Press.
Petersen, E.R. (1938). 'Kusumba, der weiße Händler'. In P. Ritter (ed.), *Afrika spricht zu Dir. Selbsterlebnisse deutscher Kolonialpioniere*, Mühlhausen-Thüringen: Bergwald 2nd edn: 57–97.
—. (1939). *Gummi aus Kamerun*, Berlin: Safari.
Preuß, P. (1904). 'Bericht des stellvertretenden Chefs der Verwaltung des Ssanga-Ngokogebiets, Preuß, über eine Expedition nach Kul und Alaman'. *Deutsches Kolonialblatt* 25: 762–5.
Quinn, F. (2006). *In Search of Salt: Changes in Beti (Cameroon) Society, 1880–1960*, New York and Oxford: Berghahn.
René, C. (1905). *Kamerun und die Deutsche Tsâdsee-Eisenbahn*, Berlin: Mittler & Sohn.
Rudin, H: R. (1938). *Germans in the Cameroons, 1884–1914: A Case Study in Modern Imperialism*, New Haven, CT: Yale University Press.
Rüger, A. (1960). 'Die Entstehung und Lage der Arbeiterklasse unter dem deutschen Kolonialregime in Kamerun (1895–1905)'. In H. Stoecker (ed.), *Kamerun unter deutscher Kolonialherrschaft. Studien*, 2 vol. Berlin: Rütten & Loening: 149–242.
Scheunemann, P. (1904). 'Bericht des Oberleutnants Scheunemann über die Expedition zur Unterdrückung der Unruhen im Djem- und Ndsimu-Gebiet'. *Deutsches Kolonialblatt* 25: 765–70.
Statistisches Reichsamt (1935). 'Die Entwicklung der Kautschukpreise seit 1820'. *Wirtschaft und Statistik* 15(19): 722f.
Tully, J. (2011). *The Devil's Milk: A Social History of Rubber*, New York: Monthly Review Press.
von Carnap-Quernheimb, E. (1898). 'Kamerun: Expedition v. Carnap'. *Deutsches Kolonialblatt* 10: 272–4.
von Stein, L. (1901). 'Expedition des Freiherrn von Stein'. *Deutsches Kolonialblatt* 20: 742–6.
—. (1904). 'Bericht des Oberleutnants Freiherrn v. Stein über die Expedition

gegen Kunabembe'. *Deutsches Kolonialblatt* 3: 82–9.
Vincent, J.-F. (1976). *Traditions et transition: Entretiens avec des femmes Beti du Sud-Cameroun*. Paris: Berger-Levrault.
Vos, J. (2009). 'Of Stocks and Barter: John Holt and the Kongo Rubber Trade, 1906–1910'. *Commodities of Empire*, Working Paper No. 12.
Warnier, J.-P. (1993). *L'esprit de l'entreprise au Cameroun*, Paris: Karthala.
Wirz, A. (1972). *Vom Sklavenhandel zum kolonialen Handel. Wirtschaftsräume und Wirtschaftsformen in Kamerun vor 1914*, Freiburg i.Br.: Atlantis.
Zenker, G.A. (1895). 'Yaúnde', *Mittheilungen von Forschungsreisenden und Gelehrten aus den deutschen Schutzgebieten* 8(1): 36–70.
Zouya Mimbang, L. (2013). *L'Est-Cameroun de 1905 à 1960. De la 'mise en valeur' à la marginalisation*, Paris: Harmattan.

4 The Macroeconomics of Marginal Gains
Africa's Lessons to Social Theorists

Célestin Monga

Introduction

In his 1974 Nobel Prize lecture titled 'The Pretence of Knowledge', Friedrich von Hayek chastised his fellow economists about their love affair with analytical approaches that mimicked physics or biology, especially after their discipline had 'been conceded some of the dignity and prestige of the physical sciences'. He argued forcefully and convincingly that some of the gravest errors of economic policy are a direct consequence of this 'scientific error' (von Hayek 1974). Decades later, his criticism of economic methodology in general is still valid and has been endorsed by a wide range of economists, including some of the most influential in the field (Solow 2008, 2009; Krugman 2008; Stiglitz 2010; Caballero 2010). The 'scientific' validity of economic methods has become even more controversial in the aftermath of the 2008–09 Great Recession, and for a good reason: the crisis confirmed once more that the assumptions of markets as optimal institutions where rational and generally well-informed agents make individual decisions that eventually serve the interests of society as a whole were misleading. Yet, these assumptions remain the foundations on which modern economic theory is built.

Jane I. Guyer's work of social and economic anthropology, which focuses on the grey zones between formal and informal economies where various patterns of confrontations and collaboration constantly take place, sheds light on how economic agents facing hard budget constraints but eager to conform to sets of social norms make decisions, how the productive economy in such settings actually works, how the division of labour among heterogeneous groups takes form, and how the money is managed to serve as a unit of account, a medium of exchange and a store of culture, meaning and value. It is to their own detriment that macroeconomic theorists have not paid more attention to the stunning insights from the very practical analyses of how people perform economic relations 'on multiple and overlapping scales of value'.

This chapter, which draws on Monga (2011, 2015), builds on some of the insights from Guyer's landmark book, *Marginal Gains: Monetary Transactions in Atlantic Africa* (2004) and discusses the state of macroeconomic theory today to suggest a few lessons that social theorists could draw from the study of Africa. The critique of economic orthodoxy in this chapter focuses on what the discipline has been missing by neglecting the work of anthropologists such as Jane I. Guyer, not on the need for some heterodox economics in the African context – this has been well-articulated by authors such as Thandika Mkandawire, Christopher Cramer and Ha-joon Chang.[1] The second section begins with some of the puzzling basic questions on the mystery of economic growth, which reflect the ineffectiveness of current macroeconomic knowledge. The third section sketches an example of a macroeconomic approach that takes into account the type of findings that anthropologists bring to the corpus of social science knowledge. The following section outlines the rationale for post-macroeconomics, and the philosophical theoretical path ahead for macroeconomic modelling. The chapter closes with some concluding thoughts.

A Few Lingering Questions on the Growth Mystery

Let's start with the idea that economic growth is generally good for poverty reduction, global prosperity, peace and stability. For a long time, economists believed that the growth potential of any given country depended primarily on its volume of natural resources, the quantity and the quality of its human capital or investments, and its use of the technology available. It was the sparkling intuition of Solow's growth model. The levels of technology and productivity available were considered to be exogenous to the model, and were more or less regarded as public goods. Advances in growth theory especially through the endogenization of productivity (technology being considered as a private good) have generated a new wave of research that integrates into the models some factors previously identified only intuitively. However, the progress of knowledge has not led to a clear understanding of the specific factors that allow countries to grow at a given point in time – let alone the specific policies to be implemented in order to generate sustained growth. In fact, despite the progress, many respected macroeconomists still come up with doubtful assertions about the reasons for economic failures or successes.

Nowhere is this more evident than in the study of Africa's poor macroeconomic performance, which has been alternately attributed to: the absence or abundance of natural resources; the rather high number of landlocked countries; the brutality of its tropical climate; the narrowness of its market or the weakness of its social and political institutions (Sachs and Warner 1997).

Lacking natural resources or having too much of it? Japan has had neither. Yet, its economic history, which was marked by two atomic bombs, suggests that it never needed them. Compare its endowment in natural resources to the extraordinary geological wealth of the Democratic Republic of Congo, which may have largely contributed to impoverishment and political bank-

---

[1] See for instance Mkandawire (2014) and Cramer and Chang (2015). They convincingly highlight the need to integrate history, politics and social theory into economic thinking about Africa.

The Macroeconomics of Marginal Gains

ruptcy. Yet, the idea that countries with very many natural resources suffer a 'resource curse' (the paradox of plenty) does not hold and cannot be generalized: Qatar, Dubai, and even Botswana have been able to use their natural resources to kick start their respective economic development processes.

Being a landlocked country? Switzerland has been one for as long as one can remember. Yet, it exploited that condition to rigorously assess its strategic options and to choose an optimal growth strategy: its geographical location has perhaps forced it to establish good, mutually profitable relations with its neighbours, as its policy makers understood that their country's economic success is dependent on that of the neighbouring states.

Hot and humid climate? Dubai is not in a place known for the gentleness of its temperatures, but this has not prevented capital holders of the world from going there to invest their savings and even build their second homes which often remain unoccupied. Just as Dubai, Gabon, Congo, Angola or Sudan have huge oil reserves, no retired American or Japanese billionaire will consider going there to settle and enjoy his or her fortune.

Narrow markets? The size of Singapore or the modest population of Costa Rica did not prevent them from positioning themselves as major exporters and from making huge gains from their policy choices. With reduced transportation costs, major technological progress and a greater coordination of trade policies facilitating exchanges, the potential market of any small African country is no longer limited to its borders. The Chadian market or the Burundian market is actually the world market, provided that they are able to improve their business environment.

Weak and ineffective political institutions? While there is a lot of empirical research pointing to large macro effects of 'governance' on growth, it is still unclear what that concept means precisely. In fact, it is extremely difficult to identify specific quantitative measures of institutional quality that are really significant in statistical models of growth. The typical measures of institutional quality such as 'government effectiveness' that are often used in empirical growth investigations rely on surveys of perceptions by the private sector of the government's behaviour, not on the well-established and sustainable institutional features for which they are proxies (property rights, enforcement of contracts, etc.). It is puzzling that some countries that have been praised for economic successes and poverty reduction often perform poorly on governance indicators (i.e. China or South Korea prior to 1980). Many drivers of growth such as trade, education or even governance, are endogenous and the empirical literature has not convincingly disentangled their effects. Moreover, most institutional factors associated with growth such as property rights are not easy to establish (in some countries, they have resulted from decades or even centuries of socio-political changes). This has led some researchers to conclude that 'there is no relationship between growth and constitutional measures of institutions' (Glaeser et al. 2004).

These paradoxes and many others are enough to justify a reassessment of the intellectual foundations of traditional macroeconomics, and to explore new theoretical and epistemological approaches from the kind of micro analyses carried out by anthropologists. It is clear from Guyer's work for instance (2004, 1995), that there is a need for post-macroeconomic thinking (Monga 2011), an approach to the discipline that constantly integrates new knowledge from other disciplines of the social sciences and the humanities to traditional macroeconomics.

The Analytics of Humility

Some economists have taken too seriously 'the dignity and prestige of the physical sciences' conferred to their discipline as a licence to simplify everything – including feelings, values and behaviour – and to allocate monetary value to all social practices. Guyer and some of the best exegetes of her anthropological work have rightly criticized that aggressive push for economic formalization, which they see as analogous to colonial conversion, 'a strategy intended to tear apart and reconfigure existing systems of social practice and meaning. It is unlikely ever to be achieved because existing multiple scales of valuation do important work in formatting and reformatting social relations. Formalization in this part of Africa will remain partial, just another scale of transactional possibility' (Green n.d.).

One can object to excessive, mechanistic and meaningless simplification of complex social practices without throwing away the baby with the bath water. Economics will retain its unique status among the social sciences only if it can use formal models and numbers to codify its knowledge and make it easily teachable and reproducible. But it will endure and gain even more credibility if it also goes beyond the rigid constraints of simplified modelling to enrich its toolbox with findings and lessons from other disciplines. Economic knowledge benefits enormously from the technical rigour of mathematical models but it needs not be restricted to such models.

A key feature in the approach suggested here as post-macroeconomics is the idea that economics should maintain its drive towards analytical rigour and even formalization. A consequential mistake made by the first generation of development economists in the 1950s was to assume that they could build a credible and consistent sub-discipline from some sort of 'pragmatist thinking', and by ignoring the pressures to produce mathematically consistent analyses. That intellectual attitude was largely justified by the difficulty of telling their story of poverty traps and the impossibility at the time to confront market structure in a formal way. They believed that the aggregate behaviour of a whole economy dominated by oligopolistic rather than perfectly competitive industries was the way to go. They were right in their suspicion of having to assume perfectly competitive markets but did not have the analytical tools to prove it. In fact, economists were only able to formalize their intuition in the 1980s and 1990s.[2]

---

[2] The first successful attempt to translate the key points made by early development economists into a simple, formal model is found in Murphy et al. 1989.

Unfortunately, their intellectual strategy of neglecting formal models only generated hostility and contempt from mainstream economics, as it left out the clarity of reasoning and assumptions that underline any given theory. The strict adherence to a discursive style eventually meant that development thinkers had to use parables and metaphors to make complicated points such as economies of scale (which implies imperfect competition), so crucial to their theories. This could only lead to some fuzziness, despite the pertinence of their ideas. The choice of a methodological path should be clear. Modelling is always part of economic thinking, either explicitly, or implicitly. As Krugman (2008) points out, 'the problem is that there is no alternative to models. We all think in simplified models, all the time. The sophisticated thing to do is not to pretend to stop but to be self-conscious – to be aware that your models are maps rather than reality.'

Since this may sound rather general, let us go back to the important issue of economic growth, outline what could be the methodological path ahead, and sketch a formal exposition of why macroeconomics would be enriched by a clear rehabilitation of the kind of microeconomic knowledge that can be derived from the work of Guyer and others in social anthropology. At the outset, it must be said that most mainstream macroeconomists acknowledge the rather disappointing results of the current frameworks for growth analysis, which have so far yielded little actionable results. The existing models of growth in cross-country analyses are almost invariably based on the assumption of representative firms and representative consumers. In real life – and that is the reason why countries with similar conditions and policies may perform quite differently – there is a lot of heterogeneity in behaviour for firms and consumers, both within and across countries. From a methodological viewpoint, the study of growth must give more prominence to models where attention is given to the agent (household or firm).

For sure, economists have learned a few things about the general conditions that are conducive to growth. Cross-country empirics have highlighted broad differences between high-income countries by identifying three types of variables that are correlated to growth: (i) structural variables such as productivity, physical capital, labour force or educational attainment; (ii) institutional variables such as the 'quality of institutions' (too often arbitrarily defined) or governance; and (iii) policy variables such as macroeconomic stability, investment climate, financial development or trade openness (though the current crisis has shattered the consensus on what these variables should be).

But these lessons are not very helpful as countries vary enormously with regard to conditions under which they can generate and sustain high growth. Over the past decades, China and Chile have adopted very different policies but were able to grow comfortably. Korea and Taiwan have chosen different degrees of government intervention in their economies but have done quite well over a long period of time. Qatar has recorded high growth rates despite its mediocre governance indicators, while other major oil producers such as Gabon or Nigeria have performed poorly.

These puzzling facts have forced economists to explore new directions in growth research. They are not yet centring their mathematical tools and attention to all the findings from social anthropology but they are much more willing to entertain the possibilities of assumptions that are radically different from those underlying the still-dominant neoclassical model. Paying more attention to individual firms and households would require a different approach to macroeconomic modelling, one that explicitly recognizes heterogeneity as a first step to the study of what Guyer (2004: 20) has called the 'multiple and overlapping scales of value'.

In the quest for economic growth, such an approach could be expressed formally as follows: suppose in a given country that the output of each agent i, indexed by $i = 1,2,...N$, is q_i.

For simplicity, let's assume that all agents have identical production functions and that each agent's output is

(1) $$q_i = a_i f^i(k_i, l_i)$$

with q representing the agent's endowment in physical capital, l his/her human capital, and a productivity.

(2) $$Q = \sum_i q_i \; ; K = \sum_i k_i; \text{ and } ; L = \sum_i l_i$$

From these macro aggregates, one can write

(3) $\bar{q} = Q/N$ as the average output and the average output is $\bar{a} = (1/N) \sum_i a_i$

The marginal productivity of capital endowment of type j (physical or human) for agent i is MP^i_j, with

(4) $$\overline{MP_j} = (1/N) \sum MP^i_j$$

We can then write the growth of aggregate output, $\hat{Q}$, to the sum of the following two components:[3]

(5) $$\hat{Q} = \hat{\bar{a}} + \frac{K}{Q} \overline{MP_k} \; \hat{K} + \frac{L}{Q} \overline{MP_l} \; \hat{L}$$
$+$

(6) $$\sum \frac{(q_i - \hat{q})}{Q}(\hat{a}_i - \hat{\bar{a}}) + \sum \frac{k_i}{Q}(MP^i_k - \overline{MP_k})\hat{k}_i + \sum \frac{l_i}{Q}(MP^i_l - \overline{MP_l})\hat{h}_i$$

Equation (5) expresses the fact that growth is the result of aggregates and averages, while equation (6) stresses the importance of differences in the levels and growth rates of productivity among agents. The former is about micro-

---

[3] I thank Luis Serven for drawing my attention to this way of formulating the problem.

The Macroeconomics of Marginal Gains

economic heterogeneity, while the latter is about the macro view of growth. This approach recognizes the problem of endogeneity of economic agents and raises issues of aggregation. But it remains perhaps too abstract and a bit too general for operationalization. It therefore needs to be complemented by one that highlights both the difficulty of model specification, and the importance of heterogeneity and productivity behaviour of agents.

The treatment I offer here is a streamlined version of the exposition in Bourguignon (2006) and Monga (2007). Starting again from the standard accounting identity of a stylized economy where all agents have the same production function, the growth of output, $\hat{Q}$, can be attributed to the growth of the capital stock, $\hat{K}$, the growth of labour supply or possibly human capital, $\hat{L}$, and total factor productivity growth, $\hat{A}$. Considering that a is the capital share of income and $(1 - a)$ is the share of other factors in national income, that identity can be written:

$$(7) \qquad \hat{Q} \equiv a\hat{K} + (1 - a)\hat{L} + \hat{A}$$

That identity can then be enriched by introducing behavioural relationships linking growth in each production factor to a set of variables Z (determinants of growth) that describe the initial conditions, policy variables, and institutional environment of the economy. In a reduced form model, aggregate growth, $\hat{Q}$, would be a function of Z and a set of parameters β. That is the realm of most of growth empirics. But it is generally carried out in a linear and unrealistic way. The more complex and detailed one could be in the specification of the function $f(\beta, Z)$, the closer we would be to understanding the heterogeneity of economic agents in any given country. However, given the data limitation, it is currently difficult if not impossible to estimate such complicated models in a meaningful way. As we take into consideration the fact that economic agents in any given country are heterogeneous and that we need to differentiate them by levels of productivity for instance – not to mention their objective functions, endowment in physical or human capital, access to credit or constraints – then we realize that equation (7) can be made more explicit. Focusing on firms and assuming that they all have the same shares of capital and labour coefficients (a and $1 - a$) with different productivity levels, A_i, Bourguignon (2006) has suggested that we consider the production function for firm i is as:

$$(8) \qquad q_i = A_i . k_i^a . l_i^{1-a}$$

That gives us the standard growth accounting identity as

$$(9) \qquad \hat{Q} = a \sum_i w_i \hat{k}_i + (1 - a) \hat{L} + \sum_i w_i . \hat{A}_i$$

where $\hat{k}_i$ is growth in capital stock of firm i, $\hat{A}_i$ is total factor productivity growth for firm i, and w_i is firm i's share of effective capital (where 'effective capital' is capital stock weighted by the productivity term). In this formulation and despite the stringent assumption of firms having identical shares of capital and labour, it is easier to see that the three sources of aggregate growth (the three terms on the right hand side of the equation) display a new dynamics: first term represents overall increase in capital behind which lies the investment behaviour of individual firms, with an important role being played by the reallocation of capital across firms; because of the assumption of perfect labour market competition, the second term remains unchanged; and the third term reflects aggregate productivity growth, which is derived from differentiated productivity gains of individual firms weighted by their shares in effective capital. The next logical step is to introduce behavioural relationships that would link Z policy and institutional variables to firm level investment behaviour and productivity growth. While this would clearly yield more insights on the heterogeneity of firms and the sources of growth, it would also highlight the complexity of the micro–macro linkages. That is only one way among many in which economic theorists could think of integrating the findings of social anthropology into new methodological approaches.

Some marginal gains are underway and many macroeconomic theorists acknowledge the need to update their old methodological framework, which relies primarily on the 'neo-Keynesian model' and postulates three relations: (i) an aggregate demand relation, where production is determined by demand, which itself depends on anticipations made by agents regarding future production and future interest rates; (ii) a relation based on the Philips curve, where inflation depends on production as well as on anticipation of future inflation levels; and (iii), a relation of monetary policy, which reflects in the model the idea that monetary policy can be used to influence prevailing real interest rates.

The availability of new powerful software and computers now makes it possible to carry out complex and simultaneous calculations. Macroeconomics is no longer concerned solely or primarily with the resolution of differential equations systems. New methods such as dynamic stochastic programming, which simultaneously integrate some of the lessons of microeconomics (consumer and employee utility maximization, value maximization by companies, rational anticipations, detailed specification of imperfections, etc.) represent a breakthrough in economics.

Macroeconomists working on African economies have shown that, the basic neo-Keynesian model, which has been expanded to take into account many imperfections, especially those found in credit or employment markets could be strengthened even further (Collier and Mayer 1989). But some fundamental issues remain: first, the amount of detailed and disaggregated information necessary for the use of these new *dynamic stochastic general equilibrium models* (DSGE) seldom exists in many poor countries. Also, the meaning of the structural parameters often generated by DSGE models has become so doubtful (Canova and Sala 2006) that 'this may be a case in which technology has run ahead of our ability to use it, or at least to use it best' (Blanchard 2008: 24).

In addition, the micro–macro linkages are still ignored in DSGE models, as well as the heterogeneity of households and firms, which are too quickly

The Macroeconomics of Marginal Gains

rapidly amalgamated in randomly created generic categories. Again, the study of African economies sheds light on the need to explicitly address issues of aggregation. In the African context, the very idea of household (an economic concept that applies to all persons living under the same roof, regardless of whether they are linked by family ties) poses conceptual challenges to statisticians and demographers (van de Walle 2006). The same is true for firms, a term so general and so broad that it could be quite misleading in economic modelling exercises.

The solution to such difficulties is not for macroeconomists to content themselves with structural parameters generated from industrialized economies but rather, to complement macroeconomic analyses with microeconomic, country studies, and lessons from thematic monographs from other disciplines. Far from weakening the identity of macroeconomics and diluting it, it would enrich it and strengthen the credibility of the entire discipline of economics. It must be acknowledged that the suggestion to move from traditional macroeconomic modelling to post-macroeconomics would open up a wave of technical and complex methodological issues, and perhaps even raise some controversies. Yes, research in the social sciences should not be concerned about complexities and controversies if they all lead to better understanding of the tasks ahead, and humility. The next section offers some semantic clarification and outlines the general expository strategy for the research agenda ahead.

The Philosophical & Theoretical Path Ahead

Since it defined itself as a social science that uses the methodology of the physical sciences, economics has faced some serious intellectual challenges, which have become even more salient in the aftermath of the global financial crisis and recession. The shortcomings of economic methodology certainly do not invalidate everything learned from it. However, they point to major gaps in knowledge and point to the need for improvements in traditional approaches. Fortunately, advances in research in other social sciences – especially in anthropology, sociology, psychology and political science – provide valuable new insights that can strengthen the status of economics as a dominant academic discipline, one with a much richer foundation for theory.

Post-macroeconomics should not be understood as another *metanarrative* of the end of *metanarratives*.[4] True, to theorize certain key features of the new macroeconomics as *post*, is, of course, to assume *ipso facto* another narrative. However, my use of the prefix *post* here suggests and emphasizes much more than temporal posteriority. Post-macroeconomics should follow *from* macroeconomics more than it follows *after* macroeconomics. In fact, I do not envisage new macroeconomic theories that will emerge from the current crisis as a complete rejection of all of the previous knowledge of the discipline.

---

[4] That is the way J.-F. Lyotard (1984) framed postmodernity.

My theorizing of post-macroeconomics is therefore neither systematically oppositional, nor hegemonic. I do not advocate a 'dialectic opposition' between macroeconomics and post-macroeconomics. Rather, I suggest that the latter builds on the former and goes beyond it. Post-macroeconomics should not necessarily be against macroeconomics. While there needs to be some repudiation of the founding assumptions that led to the desire for a unique grand theory constrained by its own technical limitations, the goal should be to avoid the kind of dichotomist approaches that have led to the validation of a dominant, if not unique, way of thinking about economics. An important lesson from the recent global economic crisis is the realization that macroeconomics should no longer position itself as an antecedent analytical framework that claims to a certain exclusivity of understanding – a positioning that led to theoretical macroeconomists to derive from unrealistic assumptions many ineffective or harmful policies in areas as diverse as banking supervision, financial regulation, monetary policy, etc. Post-macroeconomics suggests a rejection of that claim of exclusivity, and stresses the importance of enriching economic theory with new methodological assumptions and new knowledge. *Post-* should thus image in macroeconomics the meaning of *meta* in classical metaphysics.

To be specific about what post-macroeconomics entails:

- It is the rejection of the analytical consensus that has characterized mainstream macroeconomics for decades, and which assumes that there is a single methodological route to knowledge, comparable to what Appiah (1992: 143) called 'exclusivism in epistemology, metaphysical realism (there is one truth, which is exclusivism in ontology), each underwritten by a unitary notion of reason'.
- It is the rejection of monism in the design of analytical frameworks in macroeconomics, and its overthrow by a conception of economics as irreducibly plural, drawing insights from various perspectives from other disciplines of the social sciences and beyond.
- It reacts against the self-righteousness and the elegant but mathematically simplistic and often misleading models that have been used for public policy around the world since the methodological convergence between new-Keynesians and new-classical economists.

The need for such epistemological nuances is actually nothing new, and certainly not to researchers who worked on Africa – and developing economies in general. For decades, many researchers had argued that economics had nothing to fear from enriching itself with lessons and advances from other disciplines (see for instance Ela 1990; Galbraith and Monga 1994; or Mkandawire and Olukoshi 2002). Unfortunately, these suggestions were either neglected or dismissed upfront within what was then arbitrarily considered mainstream economics. The global crisis has led even Nobel Prize winners to acknowledge that the problem facing economists and policy makers today is mostly intellectual – it is the need to confront the systematic failure of thinking, especially on the part of macroeconomists. Akerlof

The Macroeconomics of Marginal Gains

and Shiller (2009) for instance, identify five elements in what they call 'animal spirits', the omission of which blocks conventional economics from either understanding today's crisis or providing pertinent solutions to policy makers for dealing with it. They are: confidence or the lack of it in the market place; concern for fairness by economic agents who are often puzzled by the behaviour of some people in crisis situations; corruption and other antisocial behaviour; 'money illusion', which makes agents susceptible to being misled by purely nominal price movements and not changes in real values; and the reliance on 'stories', which justifies herding behaviour.

Guyer and other social anthropologists may be pleased to know that there is now widespread acknowledgement that conventional economic models fail to fit the facts in almost all aspects of observable economic behaviour. To put it bluntly, 'the theories economists typically put forth about how the economy works are too simplistic' (Akerlof and Shiller 2009; see also Acemoglu 2009; Friedman 2009; Colander et al. 2004). What is at stake now is how to incorporate 'animal spirits' into economic theory, and to make macroeconomic frameworks more relevant to the analysis of everyday problems. Unfortunately, the analytical strategy suggested by leading theorists still falls short of the needs. After succeeding in highlighting both the rigidity and narrowness of mainstream macroeconomic thinking, and its disastrous implications for policy, Akerlof and Shiller's attempt to 'clean up macroeconomics and make it more scientific' also fails to offer a convincing alternative. The main reason is that they propose an unrealistic approach to the search for a better theoretical strategy. Discussing what is usually included in conventional economic theory and what is not, they basically suggest to start with a square divided into four boxes, denoting motives that are economic or non-economic, and responses that are rational or irrational. They then observe that current economic models fill only the upper left-hand box, as they only answer the question: how does the economy behave if people only have economic motives and respond to them rationally. To understand exactly what they suggest, I offer below my own visual illustration of their argument, which shows that macroeconomists have so far focused on Box 1 in Illustration 4.1, and neglected Boxes 2, 3 and 4.

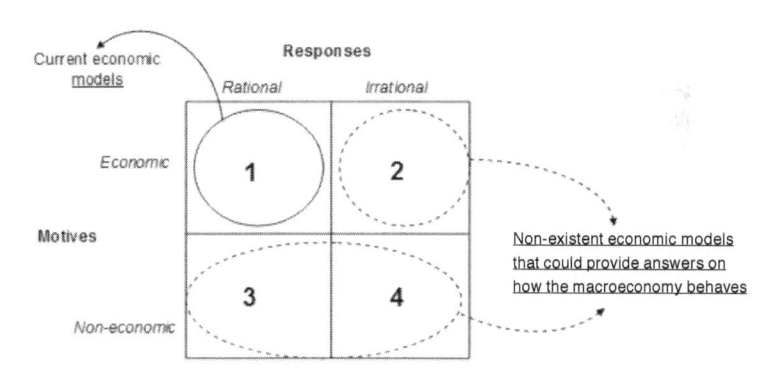

Table 4.1 The search for a theoretical strategy (Célestin Monga)

Of course, the main problem with such a schematic analysis is that it relies on arbitrary definitions of what constitute 'economic' or 'non-economic' motives, and what are to be considered 'rational' or 'irrational' responses. If someone who chooses to buy organic coffee instead of the regular food store brand because it tastes better, that is presumably an 'economic' motive. But what if the choice is motivated also by the supposed low impact of organic coffee on the environment and the higher income revenue from coffee farmers? Likewise, poor household heads who take their children out of school after an economic crisis because they have lost a fraction of their already low income and need extra help to compensate for it may be acting 'irrationally': they deprive their children and their society of the opportunity to build a much needed human capital. Still, given their situation, pulling children from school is a 'rational' way of getting extra labour at their disposal to cope with negative shocks. These examples show that the distinctions between 'economic' and 'non-economic' motives and between 'rational' and 'irrational' responses are not very useful pillars for designing a rigorous theoretical macroeconomic framework. As Friedman pointed out, 'an "economic" motive is whatever economists include in their theories of how people behave. And since different economists are always proposing different theories, what constitutes an "economic" motive can differ from one theory, and one economist, to another' (2009: 43).

The reconstruction of the analytical framework for studying key macroeconomic questions must also take into account the specific nature of each social environment, and adjust to changing times. Much can be learned from the study of African economies, recent advances in growth research, and lessons from other sub-disciplines of economics and various fields of the social sciences. All this new knowledge can help address the theoretical deficit in economics, and outlines the frontiers of post-macroeconomics.

Economists have long been either dismissive of or nervous about such thinking, which they perceive as unjustified legitimation of socially constructed differences in humans (agents) – and for good reason: accepting the prevalence of intrinsically different modes of thinking and patterns of behaviour among people or social groups raises serious methodological questions and challenges the very boundaries of economics (Malinvaud 1991). At a more abstract level, it can also open the door to ethical questions and crude prejudices of the type that led many to believe that the 'economic man' did not exist in Africa (Jones 1960).[5]

---

[5] Already in 1960, Jones pointed out with mordant irony the rapid and erroneous conclusions of the many researchers in various disciplines who found in the 'strange' behaviours of the economic agents in Africa the 'proof' that those people had peculiar motivations. Commenting on the analyses of African behaviours reported by Western experts, he wrote: 'They have come home with stories of all sorts of peculiar, seemingly irrational responses to economic stimuli and innovation. Stories of farmers who refuse to harvest the cotton crop the government has required them to plant, or who refuse even to plant the food crops needed for their very subsistence, of cattle that are valued for the shape of their horns rather than for their flesh, of laborers who cannot be induced to work overtime even by attractive bonuses, of consumers who refuse to buy unfamiliar but nutritious foods available at low prices although their supply of the traditional staple is exhausted, of producers who react to higher prices or lower production costs by

The Macroeconomics of Marginal Gains   127

Fortunately, the terms of the debate have been clarified in recent years, polemics has subsided, and there has been much intellectual progress on such questions. Mainstream economists have done a much better job explaining the methodological reasons why 'economic imperialism' should not be a source of shame but rather of pride in the social sciences (Lazear 2000). In doing so, they convincingly expanded the scope of their discipline. Even leaving aside the advent of the behavioural revolution in economics, it is now clear that economics has opened up (Colander et al. 2004) and enriched its traditional methodological tools by studying non-monetary interactions (Glaeser and Scheinkman 2003), social interactions and social norms (Manski 2000; Loury 1977), and making the case for a more rigorous exploration of the variety of human motivations and behaviour (Akerlof and Kranton 2010; Basu 2010; Akerlof 1984; Sen 1977).

In their quest for a richer set of tools, economic theorists could draw many lessons the work carried out by anthropologists in the African context. One central question on which research by Guyer (1981, 1986, 1997; Guyer and Peters 1987) and others have already generated much critical information is the fundamental motivation of households and firms as agents. It is at the heart of economic theory and has been answered for hundreds of years (since Adam Smith) to be only about profit maximization. Research on Africa sheds light on the inaccuracy of that fundamental postulate of economic theory. Like most economic agents elsewhere in the world, households, workers and companies moving in the African context make decisions they see as optimal, based on the quality and cost of the information available to them and according to the circumstances and changes in supply and demand. But contrary to the suppositions of microeconomic theory, they are capable of simultaneously having a multiplicity of objectives that do not fit into the simplifying modelling techniques imposed by the maximization postulate. Their utility functions are much richer and more complex than that which appears in textbook diagrams.

Individual interest is not always their sole motivation. Altruistic, social, spiritual or even philosophical objectives are equally at work in business relations. For instance, people give much of their time and money to social activities with the goal of helping improve the quality of life in their communities – this even when it is not necessarily in their own direct interest to do it. Throughout the continent, entire villages are equipped with rural paths, wells, schools, libraries and dispensaries financed anonymously by citizens whose only profit is the feeling of having done what seemed logical to them in a context of chronic government failure. Even in the West, where the frenzied cult of profit seems to dominate social interactions and justify the theoretical postulate of the maximization of a utility reduced to its financial aspects, notions like the public good or the general interest are greatly valued

---

(contd) reducing their output, of prices determined by custom that are stubbornly resistant to changes in supply or demand, and of consumers who spend their money on spectacle frames without glasses, shoes to be worn slung over the shoulders, and nostrums that have no effect other than to turn the urine purple' (1960: 107).

in relations between economic agents, justifying the dictum often attributed to Winston Churchill: 'We make a living by what we get. We make a life by what we give.'

Conclusion

Economic theorists have long promoted the idea of universally representative agents who are self-interested and exclusively motivated by the pursuit of maximum profit in anything they do, whether in the realm of commercial transactions or in non-monetary domains of life. While these important assumptions have allowed for simple and elegant modelling techniques that describe and predict human thinking and decision making – and granted the discipline of economics a methodological status comparable to that of hard sciences – it never helped predict or avert major financial and economic crises, resulting in heavy human costs and consequences.

The time has come for an intellectual aggiornamento in the social sciences. The methodological consensus that has underlined economics must be reconsidered. Contrary to Malinvaud, who defined a rather narrow field of investigation for the discipline and advised macroeconomists 'not to divert his/her focus towards the explanation of institutional, social or technical evolutions' (1991: 30), I have argued in this chapter that macroeconomics should renew itself and update its stock of knowledge. Without throwing away the baby with the bath water, it is possible for macroeconomists to question some of the fundamental features of their dominant model, – a model founded on the rationality of economic agents and the efficiency of the markets, even in situations involving asymmetric information – to break loose from the diktat of the single existing methodological approach, and to draw lessons and tools from microeconomics and other disciplines of the social sciences.

It is both refreshing and ironic that it is research on Africa (a region of the world where there has been a debate in the economic literature on the existence of the rational 'economic man') that is providing some of the best clues on the existence of multiple rationalities and overlapping value scales, destined to enrich economic methodology and knowledge. It is now a well-documented fact that economic problems and the challenges of development are often of a different nature in Africa than those observed in industrialized countries. Yet for decades, African policy makers and central bank governors have simply, but regrettably, replicated in their respective contexts the dominant macroeconomic models used in western economies. The ineffectiveness of this approach has sustained the analytical shallowness of economic thinking on Africa.

Thanks to pioneering work by social and economic anthropologists like Guyer, questions can be raised about the relevance of some of the most widely used macroeconomic frameworks, and the effectiveness of some of the pillars of development thinking. Challenges to the pertinence of the main assumptions in dominant macroeconomic models not only force researchers to reflect

The Macroeconomics of Marginal Gains

on the validity of the neo-Keynesian or neoclassical frameworks. They also lead to the reassessment of fundamental policy issues such as the determinants of consumption, investment and savings; the proper role of the government in the economy in general and in financial systems in particular; the appropriate goals and instruments for monetary policy; the effectiveness of fiscal policies in an increasingly globalized world; and many other important topics.

This methodological evolution obviously poses a serious identity problem for macroeconomics: should the discipline, like other social sciences, venture into distant territories to seek answers to economic problems – even at the risk of drowning in the broad corpus of the social sciences? Or should it continue to limit its aspirations to activities it can handle, quantifying and calculating with precision – even at the risk of being viewed as a sensitive, sectarian and overly formalized discipline, incapable of rendering a genuine account of reality of life? In truth, the debate is actually about much more than academic turf battles. It is in fact about intellectual integrity, and the heavy financial, and intellectual costs of bad ideas and methods for human lives.

References

Akerlof, G.A. (1984). *An Economic Theorist's Book of Tales*, Cambridge, UK: Cambridge University Press.
Akerlof, G.A. and R.E. Kranton (2010). *Identity Economics: How Our Identities Shape Our Work, Wages, and Well-Being.* Princeton, NJ: Princeton University Press.
Akerlof, G.A. and R.J. Shiller (2009). *Animal Spirits: How Human Psychology Drives the Economy, and Why It Matters for Global Capitalism.* Princeton, NJ: Princeton University Press.
Acemoglu, D. (2009). *Introduction to Modern Economic Growth.* Princeton, NJ: Princeton University Press.
Appiah, K.A. (1992). *In my Father's House: Africa in the Philosophy of Culture.* New York: Oxford University Press.
Basu, K. (2010). 'The Moral Basis of Prosperity and Oppression: Altruism, Other-Regarding Behaviour and Identity', *Economics and Philosophy*, 26(2): 189–216.
Blanchard, O. (2008). 'The State of Macro', working paper no. 08–17 (August), Cambridge, MA: MIT Department of Economics.
Bourguignon, F. (2006). *Economic Growth: Heterogeneity and Firm-Level Disaggregation.* PREM Lecture (May). Washington, DC: World Bank.
Caballero, R.J. (2010). 'Macroeconomics After the Crisis: Time to Deal with the Pretense-of-Knowledge Syndrome', *Journal of Economic Perspectives*, 24(4): 85–102.
Canova F. and L. Sala. (2006). *Back to Square One: Identification Issues in DSGE Models.* Working Paper no. 583, Frankfurt am Main: European Central Bank.

Colander, D., R. Holt and B. Rosser Jr. (2004). 'The Changing Face of Mainstream Economics', *Review of Political Economy*, 16(4): 485–99.

Collier, P. and C. Mayer (1989). 'The Assessment: Financial Liberalization, Financial Systems, and Economic Growth', *Oxford Review of Economic Policy*, 5(4): 1–12.

Cramer C. and H.-J. Chang, 2015. 'Tigers or Tiger Prawns? The African Growth "Tragedy" and "Renaissance" in Perspective', In C. Monga and J.Y. Lin (eds), *The Oxford Handbook of Africa and Economics*, Vol. 1, *Context and Concepts*, New York: Oxford University Press: 483–503.

Ela, J.-M. (1980). *Le cri de l'homme africain*. Paris: L'Harmattan.

—. (1990). *Quand l'Etat pénètre en brousse: les ripostes paysannes à la crise*. Paris: Karthala.

Friedman, B.M. (2009). 'The Failure of the Economy and the Economists', *The New York Time Review of Books*, 28: 42–5.

Galbraith, J.K. and C. Monga (1994). 'Où en est l'économie du développement aujourd'hui?' *Afrique 2000 – Revue africaine de politique internationale*, 18: 69–75.

Glaeser, E. and J.A. Scheinkman (2003). 'Non-Market Interactions'. In Mathias Dewatripont, Lars Peter Hansen and Stephen J. Turnovsky (eds), *Advances in Economics and Econometrics: Theory and Applications, Eighth World Congress*, Vol. I. Cambridge, UK: Cambridge University Press: 339–70.

Glaeser, E., R. La Porta, F. Lopez-de-Silanes and A. Shleifer (2004). 'Do Institutions Cause Growth?' *Journal of Economic Growth*, 9(3): 271–303.

Green, M. (n.d.). 'Jane Guyer's Marginal Gains', *Society and Space*, http://societyandspace.com/material/discussion-forum/books-of-the-decade/green?iframe=true&preview=true/feed (accessed 19 February 2017).

Guyer, J.I. (1981). 'Household and Community in African Studies', *African Studies Review*, 24(2/3): 87–137.

—. (1986). 'Intra-Household Processes and Farming Systems Research: Anthropological Perspectives'. In Joyce L. Moock (ed.), *Understanding African Households and Farming Systems: A Key to Agricultural Growth*. Boulder, CO: Westview.

—. (ed.) (1995). *Money Matters: Instability, Values and Social Payments in the Modern History of West African Communities*. Portsmouth, NH: Heinemann.

—. (1997). 'Endowments and Assets: The Anthropology of Wealth and the Economics of Intrahousehold Allocation'. In Lawrence Haddad, John Hoddinott and Harold Alderman (eds), *Intrahousehold Resource Allocation in Developing Countries: Models, Methods, and Policy*. Baltimore, MD: Johns Hopkins University Press.

—. (2004). *Marginal Gains: Monetary Transactions in Atlantic Africa*. Chicago, IL and London: The University of Chicago Press.

Guyer, J.I. and P. Peters (1987). 'Introduction'. Special Issue, 'Conceptualizing the Household: Issues of Theory and Policy in Africa'. *Development and Change*, 18(2): 197–214.

Jones, W.O. (1960). 'Economic Man in Africa', *Food Research Institute Studies*, I(2): 107–34.

Krugman, P. (2008). 'What to Do', *New York Review of Books*, 55(20).
Lazear, E.P. (2000). 'Economic Imperialism', *Quarterly Journal of Economics*, 115: 99–146.
Loury, G. (1997). 'A Dynamic Theory of Racial Income Differences'. In P. Wallace and A. LaMond (eds), *Women, Minorities, and Employment Discrimination*, Lexington, MA: Lexington Books.
Lyotard, J.-F. (1984). *The Postmodern Condition: A Report on Knowledge*. Minneapolis, MN: University of Minnesota Press.
Malinvaud, E. (1991). *Voies de la recherche macroéconomique*, Paris: Editions Odile Jacob.
Manski, C.F. (2000). 'Economic Analysis of Social Interactions', *The Journal of Economic Perspectives*, 14(3): 115–36.
Mkandawire, T. (2014). 'The Spread of Economic Doctrines and Policymaking in Postcolonial Africa', *African Studies Review*, 57(1):171–98.
Mkandawire, T. and A. Olukoshi (eds) (2002). *Between Liberalisation and Oppression: The Politics of Structural Adjustment in Africa*, Dakar: CODESRIA.
Monga, C. (2007). 'L'aide est-elle un obstacle à la croissance?' Paper presented at the conference on 'Aide publique au développement, 50 ans après', Dakar, 7 December.
—. (2011). 'Post-Macroeconomics: Lessons from the Crisis and Strategic Directions Ahead', *Journal of International Commerce, Economics and Policy*, 2(2): 1–28.
—. (2015). 'Principles of Economics: African Counter-narratives'. In C. Monga and J.Y. Lin (eds), *The Oxford Handbook of Africa and Economics*, Vol. 1, *Context and Concepts*, New York: Oxford University Press.
Murphy, K.M., A. Shleifer, R.W. Vishny (1989). 'Industrialization and the Big Push'. *The Journal of Political Economy*, 97(5): 1003–26.
Sachs, J.D. and A. Warner (1997). 'Sources of Slow Growth in African Economies', *Journal of African Economics*, 8: 335–76.
Sen, A.K. (1977). 'Rational Fools: A Critique of the Behavioral Foundations of Economic Theory', *Philosophy & Public Affairs*, 6(4): 317–44.
Solow, R.M. (2008). 'The State of Macroeconomics', *Journal of Economic Perspectives*, 22(1): 243–9.
—. (2009). 'How to Understand the Disaster', *The New York Review of Books*, LVI(8): 4–8.
Stiglitz, J.E. (2010). *Freefall: America, Free Markets, and the Sinking of the World Economy*. New York: W.W. Norton.
Van de Walle, E. (ed.) (2006). *African Households: Censuses and Surveys*. Armonk, NY: M.E. Sharpe.
von Hayek, F.A. (1974). 'The Pretence of Knowledge', Nobel Lecture, www.nobelprize.org/nobel_prizes/economic-sciences/laureates/1974/hayek-lecture.html (accessed 21 February 2017).

Part II

LABOUR, SOCIAL LIVES & PRECARITY

5
From Enslavement to Precarity? The Labour Question in African History

Frederick Cooper

It is a particular pleasure to contribute to this engagement with Jane Guyer's work. Jane and I have known each other since the beginning of both our careers. We were junior faculty members at Harvard, Jane in Anthropology, me in History, during the late 1970s and we were both part of a lively community of Africanists in the Boston area. Since Harvard had a tradition of faculty not talking to each other – and African studies there was particularly moribund at the time – we usually got together at Boston University's African Studies Center, for a time located in a rambling old house on the Brookline–Boston border. In the 1980s, there was a diaspora of Africanists from Boston-area universities – including the migration of Jane and Sara Berry to Johns Hopkins and me to Michigan – a process that makes this period of exchange and mutual influence particularly poignant in, at least, my memory.

There is more than nostalgia to the interest that this period holds. It was formative in terms of the theoretical incisiveness that characterized the study of Africa, and Jane was very much part of the movement both to raise questions and to innovate in the conceptual apparatus, within and beyond her discipline. Anthropology had a long track record in the study of Africa, and that meant it had a closet-full of concepts that had to be sorted through, perhaps to be discarded, perhaps to be reinvigorated. History was starting from a more naïve, or perhaps less overburdened, position, for the mere claim that Africans had a history was enough of a founding principle for the field in the 1960s. What historians were to make of that fact was not so clear. A formative moment in the rethinking process came when the African Studies Committee of the Social Science Research Council (SSRC – a committee that was abolished some years later in a fit of anti-area-studies hubris) commissioned for the African Studies Association meeting of 1980 a series of presentations on important conceptual issues. It had the temerity to ask younger (i.e. untenured) scholars to present some of these studies, beginning a process that the SSRC pursued for some years. Jane presented a paper on 'Household and Community' (Guyer 1981) and I did one on 'Africa and the World Economy' (Cooper 1981).[1] Jane's paper scrutinized a transition from classic

---

[1] The other two were 'States and Social Processes in Africa', by John Lonsdale, who was somewhat more senior than Jane and me, but not yet the widely admired expert on the history of Kenya, and Wyatt MacGaffey, 'African Ideology and Belief'. These and subsequent essays in the SSRC-commissioned series were published in *African Studies Review*, beginning with 24 (2/3) 1981.

approaches in anthropology, in which 'kinship' was the keyword, to the more 'sociological' concepts of household and community. She made clear that these new concepts, like the old, could not be seen as the givens of social units, but needed to be examined in the context in which they were developed and transformed. The 'ism' of constructivism had not yet secured its place in scholarly fashions, but in any case the innovative dimension of her essay was not just in its overall perspective, but in the specific analysis in dynamic terms of how relationships among people did or did not produce social forms that could be characterized as 'community' or 'household'. The emphasis was on relations and change, not on static characteristics of collectivities.

Jane's conceptual work was not simply deconstructive. She brought into common usage what have become useful conceptual categories too. Prominent among these is the use she made of the notion of 'wealth in people', turning away from economistic notions of wealth to focus on relationships, in particular asymmetrical relationships, that is on the accumulation of power by individuals or groups by making themselves the centre of networks of connection, through mixtures of coercion and attraction. Her work on money is both empirically rich and conceptually sophisticated. In all her work, the greatest interest of a concept is in the varied ways in which it can be deployed. Her effort is to use a concept to launch an inquiry, not to close off analysis by slotting something definitively into a category. This attention to concepts – and their deployment and refinement in connection with detailed empirical work in a wide range of domains – has characterized Jane's work ever since the heyday of Boston-area Africanism.

The Labour Question in African History

That brings me to the principal subject of this essay, how to think about another set of concepts and particularly the changing way in which they have been used since the 1970s. I am thinking about the labour question. This was a subject of considerable interest to Africanists in the 1970s, more so than at any time since. It is not hard to recognize that work can take an enormous variety of forms, anything in any context that produces something – a use value in Marx's terms (Atkins 1993). The concept of labour is relational, the production of commodities for the benefit of others, the production of exchange value (again in Marx's terms), and the systematization on a regional, national or global scale of structures that allow for some people to get others to produce values for them. Equally important in Marxist theoretical terms is the conceptual dimension of capitalism, the subsuming of relationship among people to relationships among things, the notion that 'labour power' is a commodity like any other despite its origins in human effort and the human will, the claim that the terms under which people work or do not work are determined by impersonal market forces rather than the action of individuals or collectivities, and the treatment of property – or lack thereof – as a legal fact independent of the history that produced the distribution of property (van der Linden 2008; Lucassen 2006).

In the 1970s and into the 1980s, the most indicative word in scholarship on labour in Africa was 'making'. The reference was to E. P. Thompson's famous book, first published in 1963, *The Making of the English Working Class*. Africanists wanted to say that Africans could be workers too, and the titles – and for the most part the contents – of these interventions presumed a certain expectation of linearity. Africans had been entering the wage labour force in increasing numbers and were continuing to do so; they were acquiring an ever stronger sense of themselves as workers; they were engaging in union organizing and strikes as proper workers should do (Sandbrook and Cohen 1975; Crisp 1984; Lubeck 1986; Higginson 1989).[2] In many places wage workers in the most vulnerable sectors – mines, railways, ports – achieved some notable successes in bringing the gains workers in Europe had achieved to Africa: union recognition, 'breadwinner's' wages, pensions.

But if one approach to the category of labour was to presume a universal model – but really based on a simplified reading of European history – and insist on Africa's place within it, historians and anthropologists also kept coming up with complications and distinctions. Some of the earliest – and best – work in urban anthropology was suggesting that urban labour and urban lifestyles reflected both the patterns of social relationships that African workers brought with them and the fragmented, conflictual and uncertain nature of social life in the late colonial and early independence periods.[3]

For some, the distinctiveness of forms of labour outside of Europe was the object of theorization at as high a level of generalization as the proletarianization model. World systems theory posited a neat differentiation between one form of labour in the 'core', another in the 'periphery', and hybrid forms in the 'semi-periphery'. Marxist theorists proposed that capitalist labour relations could develop in parts of Africa because non-capitalist relations in other parts paid the costs of reproduction – caring for children, elders and other non-wage-workers – thereby lowering the costs of wage labour below that of a fully proletarianized economy. Neither theoretical approach left much room for workers to make their own history, but it was precisely this danger that worried colonial regimes: that workers would not come forth when needed or would strike when needed too much, making use of whatever resources they could find in urban or rural, capitalist or non-capitalist social relations (Wallerstein 1974; Meillassoux 1975; Cooper 1981).

What was missing was awareness of the volatility and variety of forms of political and social relations: as workers used their earnings to develop small-scale enterprises or their kinsmen's farms, or as women found niches in urban production and marketing as well as rural production, as young

---

[2] In view of my criticisms of the 'making' model that follows, it should be added that these are all works of high quality and did much to open up the subject of African labour history.
[3] One of the most innovative and insightful of such works was Georges Balandier, *La sociologie des Brazzavilles noires* (1955), but the theme is a major one in the urban anthropology of the 1950s and 1960s.

men found that personal clientage to 'big men' could be more fruitful than wage labour. Especially in uncertain and conflictual political contexts, the possibilities of collective action were more varied than the classic European story of worker mobilization. The importance of state action was underestimated too, particularly the way in which African political elites who had used organized labour as a constituency against colonial regimes, later sought to co-opt or repress any social movement that they could not directly control. Economically, the post-independence economy was capable of supporting growth spurts – particularly around certain export commodities – but conditions for long-term accumulation of capital, by either national bourgeoisies or foreign corporations, were constrained by the volatility of relations of production and the difficulties of making a breakthrough in a world economy rigged against them (Jerven 2010).[4] Because 'gatekeeping' – political rulers' efforts to keep a tight lid on the economic realm they could best control, the interface between national and overseas economies – made politics into a zero-sum game, violent conflict over control of the gate became frequent in much of Africa and made conditions of accumulation all the more uncertain (on gatekeeping, see Cooper 2002).

Neither the proletarianization thesis nor arguments that explained structures by reference to their functionality for world capitalism could come to grips with the volatility and blockages of African economies in the 1960s and 1970s, nor with the crisis that followed the world recession, the contraction of markets for African exports, and the willingness of international financial organizations to write off rather than sustain African economies. 'Structural adjustment' undermined the very sectors of African economies where labour had become the most stabilized, where workers might expect decent wages and a pension, and it sharply reduced state services that might have equipped younger generations with the skills they needed for a changing world economy. The confluence of the brittleness of gatekeeper states and the capacity of the world economy to write off much of a continent revealed the limits of explanatory schemes that presumed that one knew what one meant by the category of 'labour'.

In Search of Categories

Casting about for new categories, some scholars came up with the notion of an 'urban informal sector'. The concept is still in use in the 2010s. For some users of this concept, 'informalization' is a worldwide phenomenon. Some Africanists insist, however, that 'African economies are the most informalized in the world'. Non-waged economic activities, unregulated by law and unprotected by social regulations or services, became increasingly visible – not that they were new. Often, women took on increasingly important roles in supporting families as the 'male breadwinner' notion was pushed aside and economies provided fewer full-time, wage-paying jobs (Meagher 2016: 485; see also Tripp

---

[4] Leys (1978), at different times, argued both sides of the question of whether the form of capitalist development in Kenya was highly dependent on foreign control or could give rise to a relatively autonomous pattern.

1997; Hart 1973). 'Urban informal sector' was an evocative but sloppy concept: the urban informal sector was not specifically urban; it was not informal, since relations among producers was quite complex and often highly organized; and it was not a sector, for economic activities of different sorts overlapped each other. To the extent that there was something specific about its operations, it was defined negatively and not by economic role or structure but by state regulation, or rather the absence thereof (see Cooper 1983).

That something other than contractually bound, state-regulated forms of work were becoming increasingly salient – although they are found in many time periods and many places – was an important subject for inquiry. The conceptual tools to analyse such forms in all their specificity were harder to pinpoint. What were the relationships of the 'big men' to the varied categories of market sellers, street vendors, artisanal apprentices, beggars and small-scale economic enterprises over whom they exercised different degrees of control? Did these vulnerable workers constitute a sort of 'reserve army of the underemployed', available to serve the wealthy, government officials acting beyond their state roles, or even people with only slightly better resources than those they possessed? What were the interfaces between such entrepreneurs and state actors, or perhaps to state actors who privatized economic activity to themselves? There was in fact a great deal of empirical work in the 1980s and 1990s addressing such questions, but whether finding an overall label for such complex processes helped or hindered the endeavour is not so clear.[5]

Some scholars found in the activities of this vaguely specified domain not just something to lament – the loss of jobs that paid decent wages and provided a decent career path – but something to celebrate – the energy and skill of the small-scale entrepreneur. Who will gain and what will change from that deployment of energy and skill is less evident. A young man, who in the 1970s would have sold tiny packets of peanuts in the streets of Dakar or in the 2000s low-denomination phone top-up cards, finds a niche because his labour is worth so little that an entrepreneur can employ him to sell things to people too poor to spend a significant some of money at a time. The activity works 'by dividing a given activity in ever-finer morsels' (Ferguson 2015: 106). Whatever label is attached to such a situation, can it be seen as a step to a more vibrant economic future or as a symptom of relations that turn ever more inward?[6]

Scholars of labour have long been motivated by a sense of possibility – that a working class might come together to make its own future. In much of Africa,

---

[5] As Breman (2013: 136) points out, 'informality is a multi-class phenomenon, structured by multiple levels of exploitation'.

[6] The 'bottom-of-the-pyramid' argument, coming out of business schools, claims that Africa, in fact, has much to offer to global capitalism. It has lots of cheap labour to capture and multinational sellers of products divisible in small units can find markets among relatively poor people if they can get low-paid middlemen to distribute them. This business strategy envisions large-scale incorporation of Africans as entrepreneurs (but actually as disguised workers) and as consumers; whether it will do much to induce structural change or reduce poverty is very much in question. (See Meagher 2016; Dolan and Roll 2013; Dolan and Rajak 2016).

disillusionment set in with the travails of the post-independence decades and especially the economic crisis that began in the 1970s. In Southern Africa, the enthusiasm for labour history was more persistent: the very endurance of white domination – and labour's role in the struggle against it – gave intellectuals a sense that a more open future could at least be imagined and had to be fought for. But for many historians, the reaction to the disheartening present in the realm of work was to turn to other subjects. Anthropologist Jean Copans (2014) complains of the eclipse – partial to be sure – of labour studies in the social sciences more generally.[7] The phenomenon was not unique to African studies, and the desertion of social and economic history is sometimes referred to as 'the cultural turn', another unfortunate choice of words reflecting the tendency of scholars to follow the pack in whatever direction it seems to be going. There are signs of revival, most notably through the efforts of the research group 'Work and Human Life Cycle in Global History' at the Humboldt University in Berlin since 2008, and the new research brought together more recently in *International Labour and Working Class History*.[8]

Connections & the Ambiguity of 'Free' Labour

Meanwhile, scholars were slowly becoming aware of something that also seemed new. Africa was exporting people, especially as European and North American economies revived while African productive activities did not. Remittances were becoming a necessity to the survival of significant portions of the population in some African countries (see Gupta, Pattillo and Wagh 2009).

Here we need to look back at a longer connection of Africa with Europe and the Americas, a topic that has not been entirely well served by divisions of labour among scholars, for whom 'slavery' was one domain on inquiry with its coterie of specialists, 'labour' another. In the long run, there has been a vast change in how Africans came to participate in the dynamics of capital accumulation outside the continent. In 1700 or 1800, Africans were sent by force across the Atlantic to work on slave plantations. Many died along the way. In 2000, Africans were taking their own initiative to cross the Mediterranean to Spain or Italy or the Atlantic to the Canary Islands, seeking wage labour. Many died along the way. Yesterday's migrants were coerced; today's migrants are at one level the freest of the free: they not only agree to leave Africa for Europe, but they go to great effort and great risk to do so.

In the nineteenth century, many slaves of African descent rebelled or escaped from the plantations. Now, undocumented workers from Africa living in Europe try to avoid expulsion back home. Africans working in Europe,

---

[7] Anruta Chhachhi (2014: 906) similarly notes the 'eclipse of "labour" in development policies/studies' since the 1980s, but sees the beginning of a revival, both in terms of labour mobilization in different parts of the world, and in scholarship. Scholars of South Africa retained – not surprisingly – a stronger interest in labour history and labour studies generally than did their colleagues whose research interests lay elsewhere.

[8] *International Labour and Working Class History* 86 (Fall 2014). In introducing the excellent studies in this volume, its editors, F. Barchiesi and S. Bellucci, point to the fall and revival of interest in labour history.

and indeed many working in Africa, live in precarious situations, but it is a precarity characteristic of capitalist economies – the 'choice' between the job and starvation – underscored by the precarity characteristic of displacement, vulnerability to state controls over immigration, the need to construct new webs of connection, the capacity of employers to exploit the vulnerabilities of people who move across borders without the documentation that states now consider proper.

'Precarity' has become the fashionable new concept in labour studies. It seems to mark the transition from a period when capital was striving to insure that it could extract surplus value from a large and growing – and potentially dangerous – work force to a situation in which more and more workers have become unnecessary, disposable. But the term has also been criticized precisely because precarity is an inherent characteristic of capitalist labour rather than of a particular phase of economic history.[9] It is relative job security and relatively good social benefits that are unusual in capitalist economies, and they are the contingent product of a particular conjuncture in twentieth-century world history. These social arrangements, the argument goes, are now under fire as that conjuncture has passed. If critics of the current state of things invoke the dangers of 'precarity', the defenders of the current economic order refer to capitalist economies' need for 'flexibility'.

What links 1800 and 2000 is the unevenness of global economic relations. The slave trade of the eighteenth and nineteenth centuries and the labour migration of the twenty-first have been possible because of the forging of connections among disparate parts of the world, and indeed because of increasing disparities.

Do we have the conceptual apparatus to understand both the continued movement of African labour outside the continent and the shift from coerced movement to a situation where Africans take the initiative, becoming in François Manchuelle's (1997) expression 'willing migrants'? Here is not the place to deliver a full explanation, only to point to the conceptual issues at stake in thinking about it. We are not dealing with a succession of labour forms but with complex and shifting patterns of intersection. One recent trend in labour history is to soften the distinction between 'free' and 'coerced' labour. The more problematic of the pair is 'free', for it is more an ideological construct than a descriptive one. European states in the nineteenth century did not simply leave it to the market to insure a labour supply and labour discipline. Masters and servants legislation, penal sanctions for leaving a job and anti-vagrancy legislation added a strong measure of state coercion to incentives to work. In the colonial empires, rulers and employers found new ways of subordinating labour – including long-distance connections that moved Indians, Chinese and others across long distances to plantation zones, deploying the fetishism of the labour contract to assimilate their status to 'freedom' (Stanziani 2009, 2014). The ideological act of making plausible

---

[9] Marcel van der Linden (2014) notes both the long history of precarity and the recent expansion of people falling into that category, in wealthy as well as poor countries. See also Standing 2011. For a critique of Standing's version of this concept (see Breman 2013: 130–8).

a distinction between slave and free labour – turning slave labour into a bounded and excisable category – was itself a basic part of the development of capitalism.

Even during the height of the slave trade in the early nineteenth century, non-slave labour performed vital tasks in Africa, recruited and supervised through channels of clientage and extended kinship. 'Kru' from the region that became Liberia were noted sailors, including on slave trade vessels.[10] Part of the dynamism of African societies was the possibility of a leader attracting men who had become, or chose to become, detached from their communities. Their 'labour' might be war or it might be porterage or commerce, and the relationships involved were not necessarily those of the anonymous individual and the anonymous employer, so we are not necessarily dealing with the commodification of labour in the Marxist sense of term. We are dealing with a wide grey area between labour power as a marketable commodity and labour power appropriated through enslavement. Labour takes other forms as well: in households, for example, where men and women, boys and girls might work under the direction of others and might or might not share equally in the fruits of labour. Over the life course, an individual might progress from a subordinate relationship to a commanding one, or an individual could be held in a long-term subordination. Debt bondage and pawning are also ways of allocating labour, and the ability of people to shape their conditions of work – let alone their remuneration – varies greatly. Historians have shown in some instances how relatively benign systems of labour allocation become exploitative, particularly when hitched to expanding markets (see Cooper 1977; Stanziani 2014). In any case, the relationship between production for local consumption, regional markets, and long-distance commerce is neither simple nor stable. What we mean by labour in Africa needs to be examined in all its specificity and all its variety, just as it should be in other parts of the world.

We also have to be careful about thinking of Africa as a single unit. At one level of generalization, it is possible to argue that the relatively low population density of much of the continent and the capacity of people in such a context to form relatively strong notions of kinship made it difficult for elites in much of Africa to exploit 'their' people. But it is the highly differential nature of those qualities that help to explain the asymmetries of power within the African continent that in turn interacted with the asymmetries of power at a global scale. The would-be ruler might take advantage of geographic conditions that allowed for higher population density or access to long-distance trade routes, or temporary imbalances in the size or coherence of lineages to attract more and more followers and thereby be able to marry more women or capture more slaves and thereby accentuate differentiation. But such a process might also encourage local communities or kinship groups to move

---

[10] Jeffrey Gunn is working on a thesis for York University stressing the role of 'headmen' in the organization of Kru labour. Earlier work by Brooks (1972) and (Frost) 2002 on the Kru has documented the importance of this form of non-slave labour in (among other places) the slave trade. See also Coquery-Vidrovitch and Lovejoy (1985) and Rockel 2006.

away. The consequence, in some places, was the externalization of relations of power: better to extract labour from outside the boundaries of the political unit a king was establishing (Cooper 1981; Bayart 1999). The external slave trade – going back many centuries across the Sahara desert, developing across the Atlantic Ocean in the fifteenth century – offered an outlet, lowering risks of supervision of slave labourers while forgoing the possibilities of directly exploiting their labour. As some West African kingdoms developed military, administrative and judicial institutions capable of reproducing such a system, they often tried to shift among such possibilities.

But the conjuncture of West and West Central African societies with tendencies towards externalization of power relations and labour supplies with the growing demand for plantation labour in the Caribbean in the context of worldwide rivalries among imperial powers produced an insidious – and transformative – dynamic, making it hard for societies that did not build themselves up through such external connections to protect their people from enslavement.[11] In some regions, especially in coastal West Africa, powerful, militaristic, slave-exporting empires persisted over time; in others, states rose, fought each other and collapsed. Either dynamic produced thousands of slaves.

When Britain led other European states into acting against the slave trade, some African rulers feared that the loss of the external outlet would lead to a crisis of control.[12] But some such polities adjusted, exporting slave-grown commodities instead of the human beings who produced them. The slave trade within Africa became an object of attack from anti-slavery movements in Europe around the mid-nineteenth century, eventually becoming a justification for colonization. But colonizing powers were more concerned with the fetish of slave labour than its complex and diverse practices, rather quickly coming to realize that their political stability and economic viability depended on relations with the very elites whose violent practices they had been condemning. They did not always recognize that slaves would sometimes take matters into their own hands, and make use of the many fissures in the apparatus of control by colonial regimes and their African intermediaries to migrate or to seek a new balance between autonomy and dependence.[13]

---

[11] A new wave of scholarship on the slave trade focuses on the mechanisms that made it work, including networks that linked the sources of slaves to the ports where the intersection was made with networks coming out of Portugal and then other European states, shaping a system of movement of people, goods, and capital across the Atlantic Ocean (Green 2012; Nwokeji 2010; Heywood and Thornton 2007). It is unlikely that such a system could have developed if it were not for imperial power, for the sugar islands that harboured most slaves needed protection from rival powers, pirates and slave revolts. But the source of slaves lay, with the partial exception of the Angola-Kongo region and a number of enclaves, outside of territory annexed by the European empires. Both European and African states tried to exercise control over the trade, but traders often tried to ply their trade across imperial boundaries.

[12] For a recent entry into the literature on abolition, see Everill, 2012.

[13] A growing literature points to the persistence of relations of dependence between descendants of slave-owners and descendants of slaves in parts of Sahelian West Africa, even as many ex-slaves (especially males) left the region to seek alternatives elsewhere. A fine recent study is Rossi 2015.

In much of Africa not deeply affected by slavery or the slave trade, the question of relative autonomy of cultivators – faced with a colonial state whose presence was highly uneven and African elites whose capacity to manipulate the system in their own favour was quite varied – led to a patchwork of economic conditions across the continent. There were islands of European-controlled plantations or mines surrounded by large labour catchment areas; zones where African farmers developed sophisticated systems of labour mobilization in the production of cocoa, coffee, palm oil or other commodities, and accumulated considerable wealth and influence; regions where outlets for produce were limited by the miserable state of colonial infrastructure, and the ability to pay taxes or buy imported goods depended on wage labour; and large zones where the Africans could hold off efforts to exploit them but could generate little in the way of an economic surplus.

In the colonial period, neither 'free' nor 'coerced' labour was an unambiguous category, although in some cases – King Leopold's Congo or the building of the Congo–Ocean railway in French Equatorial Africa – one comes very close to unalloyed coercion and brutality. But the category question was itself part of the history. Just as colonial governments had to be careful about what they labelled slavery because they often depended for revenue and order on the very slaveholding elites they had criticized, they dissembled about their own recruitment practices. Labour was not necessarily a commodity available for purchase, especially for the prices private or public enterprises wanted to pay, let alone in conditions that could entice anybody with any say in the matter. Recruitment most often depended on imperial intermediaries – usually referred to as chiefs – and they were trying to manipulate the colonial system as it manipulated them. Colonial regimes tried to represent much of what they did as labour 'traditionally' owed to a chief, as the equivalent of military service, or as a lesson in the value of work that would eventually benefit Africans (Fall 1993).

The actual operations of recruitment took place in a murky world. As a British official in Kenya put it, obtaining labour from a chief for the benefit of white settlers 'depended on how far he could be induced to exceed his instructions' (Cooper 1980). This meant that critical questions concerning labour could not be posed forthrightly.

But the category game was still being played. Missionaries and humanitarian groups campaigned to define and excise forced labour from the repertoire of colonial power, even if they usually defined forced labour narrowly – as the use of official coercion for private profit or the abuses of government recruitment – and did not penetrate the patterns of land seizure and power that actually shaped the conditions of labour. The League of Nations in 1926 not only insisted that abolishing slavery was an imperative for all colonial governments, but asked the International Labour Organization (ILO) to find 'the best means of preventing forced or compulsory labour from developing into conditions analogous to slavery'. Invocation of the century-old tradition of anti-slavery in this context abstracted the dichotomy of free and coerced labour from the complex web of power and social relations in which labourers actually existed. In practice, British humanitarian organizations, as well as the government, were likely to single out other countries – Portugal, Liberia – for their coercive practices, an argument that did not lack validity even if it was a self-serving effort to define a proper sort of colonialism (see Allina 2012; Higgs 2012; Keese 2013; Jerónimo 2015).[14]

The process of abstraction in the League and ILO's characterization of slavery and forced labour would carry considerable ideological weight: whatever was not declared coerced was exonerated in terms of the principal moral criteria these institutions were applying to colonial labour. The ILO convention of 1930 insisted that colonial powers ban its use for private purposes and severely regulate its use for public projects. As critics of the ILO pointed out, banning forced labour assumed there was such a thing as free labour, that there existed individuals detached from community, land and culture who stood alone in the labour market. That contention also assumed – although they would not have said it this way – that capitalism had already remade African society.

The tendency to treat free labour as a fetish in colonial circles – or among free-market purists today – should not lead us to invert these conceptions and treat the labour question in Africa as if a single category of racialized subordination explains the actual lives of people throughout the continent. The efforts of Africans, as individuals and as communities, to defend themselves against subordination need to be taken seriously, as does, in some places, the ability of some Africans – the cocoa planters of the southern Gold Coast are the classic example – to create a modest prosperity for themselves, using forms of labour mobilization that don't easily fit into categories of 'capitalist' or 'peasant' agriculture (Berry 1993). Whereas, as Marie Rodet suggests, colonial regimes focused recruitment on young men, hoping to extract labour without disrupting what they regarded as African norms of family life, Africans were often trying to put together family life in their own ways. Women might provide much of the labour that kept a wage labour force alive, play a bigger role in agricultural labour than regimes intended, and participate in migratory initiatives to get away from forced labour and to try to establish a more family-oriented pattern of work and social life (Rodet 2014).

Forced labour had something of a revival during World War II – now in the name of fighting Hitler (Vickery 1989). Although it was formally repudiated after the war by France and Britain, it came back in the form of compulsory labour to construct new villages when thousands of people in Kenya, Algeria, and elsewhere were displaced to keep them away from guerrilla movements. Compulsion was used in soil conservation programmes, justified as saving Africans from their supposedly backward agricultural practices – actions that led to much anger and in some cases violence.

---

[14] An ambitious programme for the study of forced labour in Africa has been conducted under the direction of Alexander Keese, funded by the European Research Council.

Imagining a Working Class

Meanwhile, the category game was being played, notably by France and Britain, in a different way. Pre-war colonial regimes betrayed their sense that Africans might work, but they weren't really workers. This attitude was reflected not only in the resort to forced labour, but also in the absence of any serious effort to consider wage labour as a social problem, requiring the kind of state interventions in the realm of 'industrial relations' or 'welfare' that were the hallmark of the mid-twentieth-century western European state. Typical of the inter-war years was the refusal of several British colonies to organize a 'Labour Department'; instead, officials insisted, labour problems could be handled by a 'Department of Native Affairs'. This attitude changed rather quickly during and immediately after the war, as strike waves in ports, railways and mine towns confronted officials with the existence of workers. If the initial reaction of, for example, British officials to the first mine strikes in the late 1930s was to try to stuff workers back into the tribal bottle – through forced repatriations to home villages and designation of chiefs in mine towns – it soon became clear that they would not fit.

French and British governments both sought a new strategy, to demarcate a wage working class and to develop institutions to promote its welfare and keep it under surveillance. Officials described what they were doing not as creating a proletariat – but as 'stabilization'. That meant treating those men who worked for wages as true workers, likely to spend their lives in the mines or on a railroad. They needed to live with their families and had to be paid enough to support a family, removed from the backwardness of village life and under the watchful eyes of doctors, nurses, teachers and bureaucrats. In effect, administrators were saying was that it was impossible, except perhaps in the very long run, to remake all of African society around the concepts of work as practised – or at least imagined – in capitalist Europe, but one could do so with a small but essential fraction of the African population. That this would further fragment African society was considered a step, albeit not a leap, towards 'modernizing' Africa.[15]

Such programmes did not necessarily produce the kind of bounded working class officials wished to see. The 'male breadwinner' might use his wages to support his wife's engagement in petty trade or perhaps his own move out of wage labour; he himself might be more intent on becoming a 'big man' in the sense practised by his ancestors and relatives rather than the acultural worker and urbanite of the colonial imagination. The relationship of the categories of gender and labour were much more complicated in practice than in the visions of colonial 'reformers'; the line between those included in this colonial vision and those excluded was never very clear (Lindsay 2003; Rodet 2014). In any case, stabilization was not proletarianization. It reflected the fact that capitalist relations of production had not spread throughout the African countryside – along the model of Marx's *Capital* – but were

---

[15] These paragraphs are based on Cooper, 1996.

concentrated in a small number places. Late colonial governments wanted to exercise more thorough control over the workers in those regions and sought to wean them from their connections to the backward countryside, hoping that a working class so bounded would be orderly and productive. Not surprisingly, workers in such stabilized sectors – railways, mines, docks – were frequently capable of using their strategic position to escalate demands for better pay and working conditions. Moreover, the highly differentiated nature of the late colonial economy produced tensions among Africans as well as between Africans and government officials.

One of the underutilized categories of Marxist theory is primitive (sometimes translated as original) accumulation, the conditions that made possible the process that drove capitalist development. Marx's chapter on this subject in *Capital* (1977) gets away from the abstract reasoning of most of the text to present an historical analysis of the roots of capitalism in Great Britain, focusing on the forceful removal of most cultivators from land and the legal and administrative structure that enforced this social, political and coercive process. Keeping primitive accumulation in mind, one can focus on specific processes in Africa by which people acquired productive resources and excluded others from them – land, productive trees, nodal points on trade routes. In South Africa, the alienation of land went further than any place else, complicated by the racialized nature of the process and the fiction that Africans maintained the integrity of pre-capitalist societies. Elsewhere, there were specific regions where such alienation took place, and more where differential access to land and other resources took forms more complicated than a dichotomy of 'land alienation' and 'communal land tenure'.[16] In still others, Africans were able to straddle – with varying degrees of autonomy and security and over the individual life cycle or the family unit – between wage labour and agriculture in the context of family and community. In recent decades, governing elites and foreign investors have been buying up land, not necessarily using it in very productive ways, but leaving large numbers of people without either the security that access to land through kinship and community had once provided or any realistic possibility of supporting themselves through wage labour (Goldstein and Udry 2008).

If 'proletarianization' in the classic sense produced a dynamic capitalist economy that eventually made it possible for workers in parts of Europe to make a claim, however tenuous, to a greater share of the surplus they produced, 'stabilization' in the African context was itself unstable. The countryside in post-independence Africa was constrained by lack of infrastructure or investment and with, population rising faster than productivity (especially as mortality rates declined), the old labour catchment labourers began to produce more migrants than the stabilized sectors could employ. Migrants were willing, but they had to go ever further afield, not least to Europe, where in the 1950s the demand for their labour was growing. During the *trente glorieuses* in France – the three decades of economic

---

[16] The literature on land in Africa is slowly growing. For a recent entry see Lentz 2013.

growth following World War II – French leaders showed little anxiety about the fact that people from the French colonies, who at this time had the rights of citizens, were using those rights to seek work in metropolitan France. It was only later, as part of a global economic downturn and increasingly exclusionary notions of citizenship, that barriers against such movement were raised (Manchuelle 2014).

Precarity & Flexibility
Here is where one has to be careful about the concept of precarity. As Jan Breman and Marcel van der Linden note, the protections afforded workers in Europe and (to a significantly less extent the United States) are a product of special circumstances of the twentieth century, not least the power and potential threat of labour movements, fear of a socialist alternative, the rise of mass consumption, and attempts by elites, especially in democratic societies, to build cross-class coalitions and foster something like what the French are fond of calling 'solidarity'. They make clear that this model is under threat, that more and more labour contracts are short term and that benefits are called into question in the name of 'austerity' or 'flexible labour markets'. But they are careful to point out that the gains of social democracy are strongly defended, and it is not clear that the cause is lost (Breman and van der Linden 2014). Even extreme right-wing movements often defend the welfare state; their goal is to confine its benefits to a narrowly defined citizenry. Arguments that the South is the future of the North substitute teleology for political analysis (for example Comaroff and Comaroff 2012). Nor do they take into account one of the biggest actors on the world labour scene, sometimes held responsible for the degradation of working conditions in manufacturing elsewhere – but especially in Europe and North America – China. In such contexts, much is made of the low wages of Chinese workers, but not of the fact that the rise in the standard of living and the reduction of poverty in China are almost unprecedented in world history. Wages have gone up in China, enough so that Chinese industries are sometimes moving to other countries, including in Africa, in search of cheaper labour.[17]

So we need to keep in mind the partly successful struggles of labour movements, supported by the political movements of the day, for minimum wages, family allowances, pensions, the rights to unionize and to strike – in Europe in the early twentieth century, perhaps in China in the early twenty-first, and in French and British Africa in the 1940s and 1950s, at a time when colonial powers were insecure of their future.

If 'precarity' today has any meaning, it is as the reverse of 'stabilization'. As James Ferguson has described with particular poignancy, mineworkers in the early postcolonial years in Zambia had good reason to believe that they had achieved a degree of security through stable jobs, that they would have

---

[17] Friedman (2014) argues that while state repression has blocked the development of a labour movement in China, worker resistance at the level of the firm has been effective, bringing about concrete gains and pushing the state to adopt policies more favourable to labour. On the differing experiences of labour for Chinese enterprises in Africa, see Lee (2009).

resources for their children's education and pensions for themselves. But the unions that had provided a measure of collective protection were undermined by the state, wages were eroded by inflation, and under structural adjustment the jobs security, pensions and social services workers had come to expect were cut away. With the failure of the industry and massive layoffs, the future that stabilization had promised to this set of workers was taken away from them, leaving a legacy of bitterness. What kept mineworkers from a worse fate was the fact that they never quite fit into the category that stabilization had prepared for them, and they had some access to resources outside of the 'formal' economy of Zambia (Ferguson 1999).

South Africa went much further along the proletarianization axis than any other state in sub-Saharan Africa, but it was a racialized version of capitalism that was imposed, one that stuck to the fiction of Africans as 'tribesmen'. The fiction became increasingly unsustainable long before the end of apartheid, but distinctions within the African population developed further and have become more acute since 1994. South Africa has to come to grips with the importance of the non-working class, which has been excluded from much of the gains of post-apartheid South Africa. Indeed, the low-paid worker and the migrant worker are likely to be regarded as less than true citizens, for citizenship – and indeed human worth – is, in the minds of South Africa's governing elites, linked to productive work that is available to only a fraction of the population. Some argue that the South African state should get away from the equation of both livelihood and dignity with work and think of mechanisms like basic income grants that allow people to get by, independent of whether they work (Barchiesi 2011; Ferguson 2015).[18] But even such an argument presumes that the only work that needs to be done is that for which capital is willing to pay.

The prejudices that many elites – European and African – have these days in regard to precarious workers bear a resemblance to those held about Africans in general 80 years ago: they are accused of not having a culture that is amenable to work or to life in the so-called modern world. In such a conception, the problem is not the nature of work in today's capitalist economy, but the inadaptability of certain people to work. Such arguments have powerful backing within international financial organizations and in some African governments, but they are still that –arguments. They are not an essence of contemporary capitalism. Struggles continue: the mobilization of workers still takes place; young men still take to the streets. The labour question, as Laurent Bazin (2014) has recently argued in *Politique Africaine*, remains a profoundly political question.

The ILO felt compelled to name a new programme at the end of the 1990s: the 'Decent Work Agenda', in effect an admission that much work was not decent. The notion implies 'opportunities for work that is productive and

---

[18] The premise that capital in Africa no longer needs so many workers is questioned by among others Meagher (2016: 487), who argues that multinational capital is finding new uses of workers, as long as they are cheap, particularly to reach customers of modest means. See also the critique of Ferguson's argument about work and dependence in Rossi 2016.

delivers a fair income, security in the workplace and social protection for families, better prospects for personal development and social integration, freedom for people to express their concerns, organize and participate in the decisions that affect their lives and equality of opportunity and treatment for all women and men' (ILO 2014). Implicit in the programme's definition is that forms of labour widely practised today, in Africa and elsewhere, deprive people of dignity and security. Whether the ILO has any plausible remedies for this situation is in question.

Yet the story of today's precarious workers is not one of generalized misery, although there is plenty of that. It is unevenness, differentiation, within African societies as well as between them and the 'North' with which scholars have to come to grips. Driving through the growing suburbs of Dakar, one sees a proliferation of two-storey houses, some obviously under construction for many years, not just a dichotomy between the luxurious villas of a small elite and the misery of the slums. Much of this construction has been paid for by Senegalese working in France, Italy, the United States and elsewhere, who continue to send money home. The *Mouride confrérie* (an Islamic brotherhood) helped migrants to establish themselves abroad – particularly in trade – and has accumulated considerable wealth in the hands of leading marabouts and in the community surrounding the great mosque of Touba.[19] Some of those workers in France established legal residence or took French nationality before the crackdown on immigration in the 1970s; others cannot leave France for fear of not being able to get back in. Africans in France, if they are documented, have the benefits of the French welfare state, whose failings appear tolerable compared to the lack of social security in Senegal, Mali, Burkina Faso and other countries in Africa. They are on the better side of the crevice that now exists between the labour markets, even if in human terms the two remain intimately connected. For the '*sans papiers*', the situation is difficult, for they are subject to deportation, or exploitation by employers who know their vulnerability.

Conclusion

Unevenness is not simply a matter of layered categories: upper, middle, lower classes, stable workers vs precarious workers. It is a matter of relationships. People without resources seek patrons, and patrons seek clients. Such asymmetrical relationships are found at every level of society, from beggars who are organized by exploitative patrons, to taxi and bus drivers who depend on access and protection, to businessmen who seek a contract or a concession. The importance of vertical linkages remains one of the most important dimensions of politics, often left out of scholarship that

---

[19] Buggenhagen (2012) writes of 'global circuits' of Senegalese, stressing that they were not movements of anonymous labour power but organized patterns closely connected to the networks established by the Mouride brotherhood, in which migrants engage in trade as well as labour and retain close ties to Senegal, especially to the Brotherhood's spiritual capital of Touba.

From Enslavement to Precarity? 151

assumes people act in accordance to categories assigned to them (Fourchard 2011).

Are scholars – let alone policymakers – capable of making sense of how asymmetrical connections change? Can they come to grips with two factors that elude both evolutionary and structuralist theories, namely the importance of specific conjunctures and the importance of politics and struggle? Perhaps social scientists' liking for distinguishing one 'epoch' from another, for example between 'Fordist' and 'post-Fordist' forms of capitalist production, puts too much emphasis on coherent patterns of transition and not enough on overlapping, contested, variable labour forms. Social protections are strongly defended in Europe – although there is less to defend in the US or UK. There are further reasons to be cautious about the future, including the reception migrants will be getting in Europe (or for that matter the United States). The aging population of Europe may in a decade or two make Europe dependent on immigration from Africa and elsewhere to supply its labour needs. The interconnections that characterize our time may also spread awareness of the social costs of current arrangements, and we might see more mobilizations against those who profit from the exploitation of low-paid workers in Asia and Africa. The incapacity of African states to protect their populations from the vagaries of world markets and international financial institutions, to sustain the social services built up in the 1950s and 1960s, and to allow citizens to participate in decisions affecting their wellbeing all require historical explanation more complex than the naming of epochs. Prognostications for the future require more work to be convincing than just extrapolating from a recent trend.

The temptation remains – as it has in relation to so many domains of African studies – to treat forms of labour as signs of the particularity of life in Africa. There are neo-abolitionist literatures today that publicize the problems of 'slavery now' or 'child labour'. These are real issues, but the difficulty is to treat them as such without falling into the trap of thinking of them as another peculiar feature of African culture (for a more compelling view see Spittler and Bourdillon 2012). Of at least equal concern are the conditions facing 'real' wage workers in much of Africa, the dismantling of social services in the era of structural adjustment and the painful economic conditions that drive people to risk their lives in a small boat trying to get to Sicily or the Canary Islands, in short the terms on which Africa is connected to the rest of the world.

If some theorists respond to the seemingly 'global' nature at which questions of work and efforts to control workers (and non-workers) play out with fantasies of a 'multitude' that will get together to remake the world (Hardt and Negri 2000), others have not given up hope on reinvigorated labour movements, on protests that have arisen in places from Tunisia to Greece over miserable conditions of work and life, on growing publicity being given to extreme and growing inequality within nations, on international networks that bring attention to consumers of the conditions under which their commodities are produced, and on the possibility of more rigorous 'formalization' of labour by regional or international organizations (Breman 2013; van der Linden 2014; see also, Bazin 2014: 13–14).[20]

There is a great deal of interplay between demands on the state – in the name of citizenship – and demands on capital, as workers, and there is overlap, over the life cycle, in regard to families and communities, between 'formal' and 'informal' workers, between the 'precariat' and the 'salariat'. Political action will flow from relationships – of people to the means of production and to each other – and political relationships will cross categories. Analysing networks, mobilizations and institution building across categories will help us understand the successful movements for progress in the past and possibilities for the future.

'Precarity' and 'flexibility', 'coercion' and 'freedom' are blunt instruments for understanding how people participate in wage labour, their vulnerabilities as workers, the place of labour in their life course, and the way in which elites regard them. Marx's conception of the two sides of freedom – freedom from coercion and freedom from access to the means of production – was ironic, intended to reveal what free labour ideology concealed, that the idea of a person making a 'free' choice in a labour market is really a fetish, a symbolic structure that conceals complex notions of power that open up some possibilities and constrain others. The study of labour in colonial Africa suggests that colonial rulers eventually learned, notably in the 1940s, that they could not rely on fetishes. But they themselves were ill equipped to analyse the different worlds of work out of which Africans emerged and which they constructed within the colonial system. They were taught lessons by African workers, and they slowly learned that they had to think about – and try to manipulate – the social context in which workers were recruited and in which they worked, formed families, and lived their lives. Hoping that they could engineer a new world for African wage workers – by taking them out of their African context – was yet another illusion, but it was an illusion that, for a time, labour movements could use to make claims for decent wages and benefits. The colonial version of a working class excluded the majority of people who worked.

The postcolonial version did so as well. The number of people who fit into the category of the wage worker in postcolonial Africa did not grow as expected, while it was the category of the excluded – variously known as customary labour, informal labour and precarious labour – that grew. Those categories both reveal and conceal the circumstances and struggles of the men and women who are Africa's workers. As Jane Guyer has demonstrated in her own research, it is more fruitful to work *with* categories than to work *within* them.

---

[20] Chhachhi (2014) refers to the efforts of the South Asian Garment Workers Network to campaign for a South Asian Living Wage in the garment sector and cites other border-crossing mobilizations, particularly among the most 'marginal' workers.

References

Allina, E. (2012). *Slavery by Any Other Name: African Life under Company Rule in Colonial Mozambique.* Charlottesville, VA: University Press of Virginia.
Atkins, K. (1993). *The Moon is Dead! Give Us Our Money! Cultural Origins of an African Work Ethic, Natal, South Africa, 1843–1900.* Portsmouth, NH: Heinemann.
Balandier, G. (1955). *La sociologie des Brazzavilles noires.* Paris: Colin.
Barchiesi, F. (2011). *Precarious Liberation: Workers, the State, and Contested Social Citizenship in Postapartheid South Africa.* Albany, NY: SUNY Press.
Barchiesi, F. and S. Bellucci (eds) (2014). 'African Labour Histories: Introduction', *International Labour and Working Class History*, 86: 4–14.
Bayart, J.-F. (1999). 'Africa in the World: A History of Extroversion', *African Affairs* 99: 217–26.
Bazin, L. (2014). 'Le Travail: Un phénomène politique complexe et ses mutations conjoncturelles', *Politique Africaine* 133: 7–23.
Berry, S. (1993). *No Condition is Permanent: The Social Dynamics of Agrarian Change in Sub-Saharan Africa.* Madison, WI: University of Wisconsin Press.
Breman, J. (2013). 'A Bogus concept?' *New Left Review* 84: 130–8.
Breman, J. and M. van der Linden. (2014). 'Informalizing the Economy: The Return of the Social Question at a Global Level', *Development and Change* 45: 920–40.
Brooks, G.E. (1972). *The Kru Mariner in the Nineteenth Century: An Historical Compendium.* Liberian Studies Monograph Series No. 1. Newark, DE: Liberal Studies Association of America.
Buggenhagen, B. (2012). *Muslim Families in Global Senegal: Money Takes Care of Shame.* Bloomington, IN: Indiana University Press.
Chhachhi, A. (2014). 'Introduction: The Labour Question in Contemporary Capitalism', *Development and Change* 45: 895–919.
Comaroff, J. and J.L. Comaroff (2012). *Theory from the South, or How Euro-America is Evolving toward Africa.* Boulder, CO: Paradigm.
Cooper, F. (1977). *Plantation Slavery on the East Coast of Africa.* New Haven, CT: Yale University Press.
—. (1980). *From Slaves to Squatters: Plantation Labour and Agriculture in Zanzibar and Coastal Kenya, 1890–1925.* New Haven, CT: Yale University Press.
—. (1981). 'Africa and the World Economy', *African Studies Review*, 24 (2–3): 1–86.
—. (1983). 'Introduction: Urban Space, Industrial Time, and Wage Labour in Africa'. In *Struggle for the City: Migrant Labour, Capital, and the State in Urban Africa.* Beverly Hills, California: Sage: 7–50.
—. (1996). *Decolonization and African Society: The Labour Question in French and British Africa.* Cambridge, UK: Cambridge University Press.
—. (2002). *Africa since 1940: The Past of the Present.* Cambridge, UK: Cambridge University Press.
—. (2014). *Citizenship between Empire and Nation: Remaking France and French*

Africa, 1945–1960. Princeton, NJ: Princeton University Press.

Copans, J. (2014). 'Pourquoi travail et travailleurs africains ne sont plus à la mode en 2014 dans les sciences sociales: Retour sur l'actualité d'une problématique du XXe siècle', *Politique Africaine* 133: 25–44.

Coquery-Vidrovitch, C. and P. Lovejoy (eds) (1985). *Workers of African Trade* (Beverly Hills, CA: Sage.

Crisp, J. (1984) *The Making of an African Working Class: Ghanaian Miners' Struggles 1870–1980*. London: Zed.

Dolan, C. and K. Roll (2013). 'Capital's New Frontier: From "Unusable" Economies to Bottom-of-the-Pyramid Markets in Africa', *African Studies Review*, 56(3): 123–46.

Dolan, C. and D. Rajak (2016). 'Remaking Africa's Informal Economies: Youth, Entrepreneurship and the Promise of Inclusion at the Bottom of the Pyramid', *Journal of Development Studies* 52(4): 514–29.

Everill, B. (2012). *Abolition and Empire in Sierra Leone and Liberia*. Houndmills, UK: Palgrave Macmillan.

Ferguson, J. (1999). *Expectations of Modernity: Myths and Meanings of Urban Life on the Zambian Copperbelt*. Berkeley, CA: University of California Press.

—. (2015). *Give a Man a Fish: Reflections on the New Politics of Distribution*. Durham, NC: Duke University Press.

Fourchard, L. (2011). 'Lagos, Koolhaas and Partisan Politics in Nigeria', *International Journal of Urban and Regional Research* 35: 40–56.

Friedman, E. (2014). 'Alienated Politics: Labour Insurgency and the Paternalistic State in China', *Development and Change* 45: 1001–18.

Frost, D. (2002). 'Diasporan West African communities: The Kru in Freetown and Liverpool', *Review of African Political Economy*, 29(92): 285–300.

Goldstein, M. and C. Udry (2008). 'The Profits of Power: Land Rights and Agricultural Investment in Ghana', *Journal of Political Economy* 116: 981–1022.

Green, T. (2012). *The Rise of the Trans-Atlantic Slave Trade in Western Africa, 1800–1589*. Cambridge, UK: Cambridge University Press.

Gupta, S., C.A. Pattillo and S. Wagh (2009). 'Effect of Remittances on Poverty and Financial Development in Sub-Saharan Africa', *World Development* 37(1): 104–15.

Guyer, J.I. (1981). 'Household and Community in African Studies', *African Studies Review*, 24 (2–3): 87–137.

Hardt, M. and A. Negri (2000). *Empire*. Cambridge, MA: Harvard University Press.

Hart, K. (1973). 'Informal Income Opportunities and Urban Employment in Ghana', *Journal of Modern African Studies*, 11: 61–89.

Heywood, L. and J. Thornton (2007). *Central Africans, Atlantic Creoles, and the Foundation of the Americas, 1585–1660*. Cambridge, UK: Cambridge University Press.

Higginson, J. (1989). *A Working Class in the Making: Belgian Colonial Labour Policy, Private Enterprise, and the African Mineworkers, 1907–1951*. Madison, WI: University of Wisconsin Press.

Higgs, C. (2012). *Chocolate Islands: Cocoa, Slavery and Colonial Africa*. Athens,

OH: Ohio University Press.
ILO (2014). 'Decent Work'. Geneva: International Labour Organization. www.ilo.org/global/topics/decent-work/lang--it/index.htm (accessed 27 November 2014).
Jerónimo, M.B. (2015). *The 'Civilizing Mission' of Portuguese Colonialism, 1870–1930*. Houndmills, UK: Palgrave Macmillan.
Jerven, M. (2010). 'African Economic Growth Recurring: An Economic History Perspective on African Growth Episodes, 1690–2010', *Economic History of Developing Regions* 25: 127–54.
Keese, A. (2013). 'Searching for the Reluctant Hands: Obsession, Ambivalence, and the Practice of Organizing Involuntary Labour in Colonial Cuanza-Sul and Malange Districts, Angola, 1926–1945', *Journal of Imperial and Commonwealth History*, 41: 238–58.
Lee, C.K. (2009). 'Raw Encounters: Chinese Managers, African Workers and the Politics of Casualization in Africa's Chinese Enclaves', *The China Quarterly*, 199: 657–66.
Lentz, C. (2013). *Land, Mobility, and Belonging in West Africa*. Bloomington, IN: Indiana University Press.
Leys, C. (1974). *Underdevelopment in Kenya: The Political Economy of Neo-Colonialism*. Berkeley, CA: University of California Press.
—. (1978). 'Capital Accumulation, Class Formation and Dependency: The Significance of the Kenyan Case', *The Socialist Register*, 15: 241–66.
Lindsay, L. (2003). *Working with Gender: Men, Women, and Wage Labour in Southwest Nigeria*. Portsmouth, NH: Heinemann.
Lonsdale, J. (1981). 'States and Social Processes in Africa: A Historiographical Survey', *African Studies Review*, 24 (2–3): 132–226.
Lubeck, P. (1986). *Islam and Urban Labour in Northern Nigeria: The Making of a Muslim Working Class*. Cambridge, UK: Cambridge University Press.
Lucassen, J. (ed.) (2006). *Global Labour History: A State of the Art*. Bern: Peter Lang.
MacGaffey, W. (1981). 'African Ideology and Belief: A Survey', *African Studies Review*, 24 (2–3): 227–74.
Manchuelle, F. (1997). *Willing Migrants: Soninke Labour Diasporas, 1848–1960*. Athens, OH: Ohio University Press.
Marx, K. (1977). *Capital*. Vol. 1. Ben Fowkes (trans.). New York: Vintage.
Meagher, K. (2016). 'The Scramble for Africans: Demography, Globalisation and Africa's Informal Labour Markets', *Journal of Development Studies* 52: 483–97.
Meillassoux, C. (1975). *Femmes, greniers et capitaux*. Paris: Maspero.
Nwokeji, G.U. (2010). *The Slave Trade and Culture in the Bight of Biafra: An African Society in the Atlantic World*. Cambridge, UK: Cambridge University Press.
Rockel, S.J. (2006). *Carriers of Culture: Labour on the Road in Nineteenth-century East Africa*. Portsmouth, NH: Heinemann.
Rodet, M. (2014). 'Forced Labour, Resistance, and Masculinities in Kayes, French Sudan, 1919–1946', *International Labour and Working Class History* 86: 107–23.

Rossi, B. (2015). *From Slavery to Aid: Politics, Labour, and Ecology in the Nigerien Sahel, 1800–2000*. Cambridge, UK: Cambridge University Press.
—. (2016). 'Dependence, Unfreedom and Dependence in Africa: Towards an Integrated Analysis'. *Africa* 86: 571–90.
Sandbrook, R. and R. Cohen (eds) (1975). *The Development of an African Working Class*. London: Longman.
Spittler, G. and M. Bourdillon (eds) (2012). *African Children at Work: Working and Learning in Growing Up for Life*. Münster, Germany: Lit Verlag.
Standing, G. (2011). *The Precariat: The New Dangerous Class*. London: Bloomsbury.
Stanziani, A. (2009). 'Labour Institutions in a Global Perspective, from the Seventeenth to the Twentieth Century', *International Review of Social History* 54: 351–8.
—. (2014). *Bondage: Labour and Rights in Eurasia from the Sixteenth to the Early Twentieth Centuries*. New York: Berghahn Books.
Tripp, A.M. (1997). *Changing the Rules: The Politics of Liberalization and the Urban Informal Economy in Tanzania*. Berkeley, CA: University of California Press.
van der Linden, M. (2008). *Workers of the World: Essays toward a Global Labour History*. Leiden: Brill.
—. (2014). 'San Precario: A New Inspiration for Labour Historians', *Labour* 11: 9–21.
Vickery, K. (1989). 'The Second World War Revival of Forced Labour in the Rhodesias', *International Journal of African Historical Studies* 22: 423–37.
Wallerstein, I. (1974). *The Modern World System*, 4 vols. New York: Academic Press.

6 Navigating Formality in a Migrant Labour Force

Maxim Bolt

Introduction

Stack after stack of pallets, each piled high with crates of oranges, await the trucks that will take them from the farm of Grootplaas, located on South Africa's border with Zimbabwe, to the port of Durban on South Africa's Indian Ocean coast. From there, ships will take them to countries across Europe, the Middle East and East Asia. Different crate designs signal different agents, buyers and brands. The logos of British supermarkets and American citrus providers (even though South African oranges reportedly cannot be sold in the United States) jostle with those of Capespan fruit agents and the local Limpopo Valley trade name. Michael, Grootplaas's personnel manager and packshed administrator, moves between the pallets, dressed in a white coat and armed with a clipboard. Key to his role is producing the labels that detail each pallet's journey. As they sit next to the loading bay, the pallets of oranges evoke industrial-scale production, global connections, and the clinical formality of factories in the fields. Certainly, this is a long way from the old stereotypes of South African farms as quasi-feudal, anachronistic backwaters.

At the very centre of the packshed's network of conveyor belts, and the gantries overlooking them, is Michael's harvest-time office. Visible to all, it is a statement about the importance of paperwork in the work of the farm. Alongside the export labels and documents lie Grootplaas's personnel records, for which Michael is also responsible as personnel manager. These follow Michael in a bank of filing cabinets, as his work moves seasonally between the packshed and the farm's workshop. The contents tell one version of work and life on the border farms. Applications for employment, contracts, South African documents for 'normalization' (regularization), and records of dismissal all speak in a corporate register – 'thank you for your interest in our company', the application for employment declares. But, among these documents, Zimbabwean departure permits signed by thumbprint speak of another reality – of migrant workers fleeing the estate, even without their official identification.

Working on the border farms involves constantly relating to official and semi-official documents and institutionalized arrangements. This is doubtless what we expect of formal employment. But what exactly is the nature of formality here? While substantial intellectual energy has been invested in understanding what informality is (e.g. Hart 1973; MacGaffey 1991; Roitman 2004; Meagher 2010), the 'formal sector' is more often taken for granted. Elsewhere (Bolt 2012), I have argued that formal work on South Africa's border farms is underpinned by informal livelihood strategies, yet also orders them spatially. Workers not only supplement their incomes through business in the labour force's residential compound and through cross-border trade, but even acquire formal employment on the farms as a means to anchor existing business activities. Meanwhile, formal employment incorporates migrants into social arrangements that organize space and time: work routines and attachment to the farms mitigate the extreme transience of the border itself; labour hierarchies bring round-the-clock authority that extends into the labour compound (see Bolt 2015). Building on an understanding of such interdependence, this chapter aims to go further. Jane Guyer (2004) has usefully explored 'formalities' in the plural, suggesting a more fragmented picture than an overarching notion of 'the formal'. Here my aim is to begin to unpick what is actually formal in formal employment itself. How does formality – given that it is not actually a thing – emerge as an effect of social relations in and beyond a workforce?

Beyond the packshed, with its labelled, bar-coded crates and its conveyor belts for grading and boxing fruit, formality is not so much a uniform mode of employment and life, as a diverse mosaic of connections to officialdom. State institutions 'see' (Scott 1999) Grootplaas through spotlights such as inspections, permits and employment contracts. Navigating these spotlights takes skill on the part of Grootplaas's white farmers. They learn how to present the farm while continuing to operate according to their own rules. When it matters, local labour practices built on vulnerability and dependence are framed in officially acceptable ways. In the process, state and farm institutions interlock. Together, they shape workers' lives, through inclusion in and exclusion from narrowly circumscribed modes of formal regulation.

Meanwhile Grootplaas's black workers also navigate the terrain of formality. Worker committees foreground idioms of due process, yet they are co-opted into existing, personalized hierarchies. Crucially, a range of more-or-less official documents are key to workers' lives, strategies, and self-understandings. Many migrants arrive with little other than their Zimbabwean identity cards and sheaves of qualification certificates, whose power comes from the presumed durability of their meaning and value through time. Once employed, different identity documents attaching workers to the farm enable new conditions for life. For workers as much as for their employers, using documents takes adeptness: deciding when to reveal them; taking them beyond the purposes for which they were originally intended; converting between different forms of official and semi-official identity. Between the two extremes archived in Grootplaas's filing cabinets – corporate personnel records and abandoned identity cards and papers – is a world in which workers negotiate their everyday lives and their possibilities for the future.

Recent scholarship has explored the place of documents in governing people and space, and in the ways people 'acquiesce to, contest, or use this

Navigating Formality in a Migrant Labour Force

6.1 The Grootplaas packshed, with Michael's office at its centre (© Maxim Bolt)

governance' (Hull M.S. 2012b: 1). In what Matthew Hull describes as the 'political economy of paper', documents are 'graphic artefacts [whose] 'circulation ... creates associations among people that often differ from formal organisational structures' (ibid.: 18). His particular focus is on bureaucracies. But, whether in offices or on remote border estates, such associations have far-reaching consequences. For Maurizio Ferraris, documents are formalized 'traces' – 'inscriptions' that attest in officially recognized ways to people's past acts and current status (2013: 253–4). Publicly acknowledged 'traces' take on particular significance, in a place where migrants attempt to achieve a degree of stability amidst transience. Papers are crucial to farm workers' attempts to shape their circumstances, even as the very conditions in which they are required to do so ensure a precarious workforce. What I present here, then, is a story about brokering formality through social relations, in which official and semi-official paperwork becomes the focal point for negotiation because of its apparent fixity of meaning.[1]

Taken together, these perspectives invite a view of formal production and employment that foregrounds *specific* connections between workers, between workers and employers, and between the workplace and state officials. It

[1] This account is based on 17 months of ethnographic fieldwork (November 2006 to April 2008), during which I lived in Grootplaas's labour compound. During the citrus harvest, I also worked (not for pay) in a picking team in the orchards and, more briefly, grading fruit in the packshed. While much of farm life on the border has remained unchanged since 2008, and I therefore write in the present tense to avoid an undue sense of distance, I draw attention to relevant changes in the text and footnotes.

examines people's attempts to control and stabilize the meanings of such connections, through particular objects and processes. On the margins of an African economy in which 'the formal' appears structurally more dominant (Guyer 2014) and looms larger in people's imaginations (Barchiesi 2011) than in most places on the continent, workers and employers nevertheless encounter formalities (in the plural) as a constellation of points through which to navigate.

Fragmented Formality on South Africa's Margins

Grootplaas is one of a string of family-run crop estates, located on the southern bank of the Limpopo River, which marks South Africa's border with Zimbabwe. Many of these farms are large and high-profile. Grootplaas itself employs 140 permanent workers, plus 460 seasonal workers during the picking season. The farm reached one million crates of citrus in 2007, during my fieldwork, and its oranges and grapefruits were being sold in British and other EU supermarkets, as well as in the Middle East and East Asia. It had even been selected by one supermarket for an experimental agreement, in which small numbers of oranges would be transported by high-cost express flight – because the oranges did not have to be preserved by waxing the skins, they could be used in marmalade production in the UK. Grootplaas's neighbour claims to be the largest cotton producer in the country, his profitability shored up by his own gin, which enables him to cut out the middleman. Another border farmer claims to be the largest supplier of tomatoes for a household brand of ketchup.

Tied into global supply chains, Grootplaas is regulated through both state and non-state inspections. The Department of Labour, for example, visits the border farms for periodic evaluations of working conditions. GLOBALG.A.P (formerly EUREPGAP), a standards agency that certifies produce for European markets, surveys hygiene conditions as well as 'worker welfare'. Some supermarkets have their own, even stricter investigation processes. It is during all of these, of course, that the filing cabinets of worker records become important, as they stand for proper procedure on the farm.

This appears to be indicative of a South Africa of far-reaching formality, in which the economy is dominated by regulated international linkages, oversight is the basis of a pervasive infrastructure, and life in the workforce has different rules from life outside. Scholarship on wage labour in southern Africa has long explored the implications of inclusion in export-oriented enclaves (e.g. Gluckman 1961; Moodie with Ndatshe 1994). As elsewhere, such as in India (see Holmström 1976, 1984; Breman 1999), formal employment comes to appear as a kind of fortress, with sharply defined – albeit permeable – outer walls. In a seminal analysis, Seekings and Nattrass (2005) argue that this sphere needs to be expanded to allow more people in, while Callebert (2014) has recently responded by foregrounding the existing dependencies between the formal and the informal. Either way, what emerges is a world in which formality is a 'sector', and in which workers' livelihoods might plausibly be addressed in the universalist, material/structural idiom of a 'standard of living' (Guyer 2014: 149).

But in workplaces like Grootplaas, it is not clear that speaking of the formal 'sector' in universalist idioms is helpful. The official linkages with Grootplaas are spotlights, and limited ones at best. Especially at its margins, South Africa has historically been characterized by limited state capacity, and a high degree of institutional blindness and incoherence (Bolt 2015; MacDonald 2012). Today, 'the people' remain largely illegible to bureaucrats responsible for governing the right to settle in the country (Hoag 2010). On South Africa's farms, assumptions persist that white landowners have a kind of sovereign, paternalist authority over their territory and 'their people', further complicating what it means for estates like Grootplaas to come under state purview (see e.g. Rutherford 2008). Even in a post-apartheid era of minimum wages, required work conditions, and stipulated access to housing, determining what exactly is formal in farm employment is no simple matter.

Grootplaas is, in fact, locally thought to be subject to more frequent Department of Labour inspections than other farms because it is especially easy to access from the local tourist resort. Officials, I was told by Grootplaas's founder, can report having seen the border farms without going too far out of their way. This broadly suits the farmers on the Limpopo, too, since Grootplaas's worker accommodation is some of the best in the area. Thus, in comparison to some of the other border farms, formality appears to be most clearly in evidence at Grootplaas itself. Non-state investigations are more thorough, and may involve the inspector staying on site in the farm's own guest accommodation. Nevertheless, workers do not speak up in cases where conditions are considered dangerous, perhaps out of fear of repercussions from their employers. Private dissatisfaction expressed to me, for example about the risks of burning the packaging from chemical fertilizer without protective masks, did not translate into public complaint. Meanwhile, attention to life in the labour compound outside work time is cursory at best. An inspection is announced, the moment arrives, few workers even encounter the assessment, and then it is all over. Otherwise, as a Human Rights Watch report (2006) found, shortly before my fieldwork, legal frameworks relating to living conditions are enforced in partial and selective ways on the border's estates.

Needless to say, such arrangements serve to protect employers. But not all of this patchiness favours them. The farmers feel their own incorporation into state infrastructures to be selective and incomplete. They pay tax. But their electricity comes directly from the national provider, Eskom, via their own substation. Their water comes from boreholes and the river. They gather and burn their own waste. They grade their own dirt roads, even those that are marked on the map as public thoroughfares. Some farmers build small schools for workers' children, staffed by publicly employed teachers. But I would often spend the morning waiting with pupils for the teacher to arrive, only to find that he had 'run errands' in town, or even that he was catching up with friends in one of the labour compounds. During my fieldwork, a Department of Health mobile clinic began coming to the farms, but its visits were rare and infrequent. A clinic was later established in the compound through the efforts of Doctors Without Borders. The farms draw few resources from the municipality, and a whole range of state employees is conspicuously absent. With undigitized personnel records and extremely slow internet connections, the farms often feel a long way away from state infrastructures. Different state institutions stand for particular kinds of regulation, with different interplays of attention and absence. But they generally manifest themselves through a kind of scaling, encompassing effect – their power to arrive virtually unannounced, or even not to arrive at all (see Ferguson and Gupta 2002).

In this fragmented picture, the army and the police are stark exceptions to a general rule of state neglect. For workers and farmers, much everyday interaction with state employees means negotiating the presence of border garrisons and police patrols. Understanding this means appreciating the border's wider context. Since 2000, Zimbabwe has seen a crisis involving the collapse of its currency, supply shortages and political violence. Many people have responded by crossing into South Africa – by 2009, Doctors Without Borders (2009) estimated, it was 3,000,000, although such approximations are rudimentary because of the large number who climbed through the border fence undetected. Many, including some with considerable education, were unemployed before they came. For others, the value of their pay evaporated in the wake of acute hyperinflation – around 150,000 per cent by 2008 (*Guardian* 2008), according to conservative estimates.[2] Meanwhile, supporters of the opposition have fled persecution. A large number of Zimbabweans, with varied regional, ethnic and class backgrounds, have sought work on farms across the border, now sharing conditions of extreme vulnerability (Rutherford and Addison 2007; Rutherford 2008).

The large-scale migration of Zimbabweans into South Africa led to a flurry of hostile media reporting, as well as popular xenophobia throughout South Africa (see Morreira 2010). On the border during the period of fieldwork, this translated into a regime of frequent, aggressive police deportation raids.[3] Police *bakkies* (pick-up trucks) would sweep into the compounds and run down seasonal labourers who were left exposed by the bare grids of worker accommodation. Deep tyre marks in tight circles around trees confirmed stories of *bakkies* chasing Zimbabweans through the bush. Fearing discovery, seasonal workers would often avoid their rooms altogether, instead enduring bitter winter nights hidden in dry riverbeds. Beyond the farms, they lacked freedom

---

[2] Hyperinflation ended in 2009 – the Zimbabwean Dollar was abandoned, and Zimbabwe officially adopted foreign currencies including the US Dollar and South African Rand as legal tender. But the draw of access to South African Rand, and the lack of livelihood opportunities in Zimbabwe, has meant that employment in South Africa continues to be of crucial significance for many.

[3] In 2009, the deportation of Zimbabweans was suspended. But, coinciding with the end of a programme to register undocumented Zimbabweans en masse (the Zimbabwe Documentation Project), which only reached a minority of Zimbabweans in South Africa, deportations recommenced in late 2011.

Navigating Formality in a Migrant Labour Force

of movement; and farmers could easily dismiss them, even denouncing them to the police just before month-end to avoid payment (see Human Rights Watch 2006). On the other hand, farmers saw the deportation of workers as tiresome. Replacing them meant paperwork, and deported employees would often climb back through the fence and reclaim their jobs days later. As for the police, their aggressive presence was only matched by their absence when it came to keeping the peace.

It is worth noting that, however exceptional the specific circumstances of the border today, such labour arrangements have a longer history – one characterized by cross-border migrants who faced crisis at home (Werbner 1991; Bolt 2015) and coercive, highly exploitative conditions in their search for employment (van Onselen 1976; Bradford 1993; Murray 1995). In contemporary South Africa, a floating reserve of migrant labour has enabled farmers to respond to market liberalization (Johnston 2007). The experiences of farm workers described in this chapter thus represent an extreme case of a wider historical and contemporary trend.

In any case, even this coercive dimension of state attention is localized in important ways. Farmers regularly meet police and army chiefs to negotiate how their workers might be left alone by border patrols. Indeed, during my fieldwork, the border's white military commander paid them regular social visits. As I discuss later in the chapter, one result is that the farms produce their own ID cards, part of a longer story of ill-defined accommodations between 'formal' regulation and farmers' government of their own workforces. Meanwhile, farm workers have themselves localized the army presence. During the harvest, soldiers escort police raids onto the farms. But even in that part of the year, the same soldiers also spend weekends at the farm compounds' *shebeens* (illegal bars), looking for beer and company. Housed in garrisons numbering ten or so, located every few kilometres, they are often bored and lonely. Hailing from other parts of the country, many find it difficult to converse with the majority of TshiVenda- and ChiShona-speaking workers (the former is the language of the border, while the latter is the majority language of Zimbabwe). The farm compounds nevertheless represent concentrations of people. Soldiers seek out women for sex. Meanwhile, they rely on senior male workers for insight into the border setting. Those workers in turn draw on soldiers, with their apparently incontestable official positions and uniforms, to mediate disputes in the labour force and underwrite everyday vigilante justice. At one point, soldiers even assembled a football team, so that they could compete in the tournament held between the teams of the different farm workforces. While soldiers' connections to the workforces are multifaceted, their connection to their commander is more attenuated. Reportedly, concrete indicators of soldiers' on-the-ground performance are limited: holes cut in the border fence by would-be migrants; bullets fired on border duty; people detained. Between these are the complex realities of actually serving in a border garrison. What the soldiers' situations foreground is the tenuous connections to officialdom beyond the area, and the ways these intersect with, and are mobilized within, on-farm arrangements.

This is true even when particular concerns focus official attention. Shortly before my fieldwork, meningitis swept through the border farms' compounds. News coverage and the sustained surveillance of the municipality's health services brought increased scrutiny from other departments. According to one senior worker, this soon meant inspections relating to water and housing. The farmer, Willem, maintained that there was nothing wrong with worker accommodation. But, at the time, seasonal workers who could not fit in the compound's brick buildings slept in a large tent. A point of contention became the fact that access to limited accommodation was up to that point allocated at the whim of the foreman. Favoured workers lived in brick structures, others in the tent.

Such moments are rare, but their lasting effect is in inflecting arrangements on the farm itself. A new, brick 'hostel' was an improvement on the tent, but it remained the least desirable housing. Its residents spent as much time as possible outside, and reported massive overcrowding and concerns about tuberculosis. The allocation of rooms therefore remained contentious. Indeed, long after state and media attention had subsided, the impact of the meningitis episode was the creation of a worker-run Housing Committee. Composed of two permanent workers, who rotate in and out of the roles, it is hardly a model of impersonal decision making. For Marula, the foreman, the main everyday role of the Housing Committee's two members is to summon people to audiences with him, at the court he has built outside his house. In the allocation of housing itself, perhaps unsurprisingly, nepotism continues to dominate. A moment of intensified state attention produced a veneer of formality inside the workforce, an idiom of due process. This was quickly adapted to serve existing notions of personalized workforce hierarchy once official concern receded. Here, then, a formalized committee is best seen as the debris of earlier, momentary connections to officialdom. The same could be said of other structures, such as the procedure for implementing a UK supermarket's corporate social responsibility scheme. In that case, project management was delegated to Michael, the personnel manager, which rendered him a broker between supermarket foundation and farm. What this meant on the ground, in the compound, was that Michael attempted to convert his position into the basis of expanded paternalist authority outside work time (see Bolt 2016).

What all of this amounts to is a fragmented mosaic. The spotlights of official attention here are disconnected and multiple. Each is a point of partial regulation that sustains highly personalized hierarchies characterized by acute dependencies. What requires more sustained attention, therefore, are the particular points of connection, and the brokering of particular relationships within and beyond the workforce, that generate a sense of formality. These often revolve around particular official and semi-official documents, with their apparent authority. The next section focuses on their uses by workers, in negotiating everyday recognition, security and legitimacy in the workforce, in a wider context of precariousness. I begin with the contract itself.

Formality from the Contract Outwards

The farm's contracts represent a juxtaposition of formal categorization and fixity, on the one hand, and half-hearted and flexible execution, on the other. They demand a description under 'position of employee', and some specification of where on the estate the recruit will work. Hours of work and daily pay are specified. Three lines for completion by hand at the foot of the page – 'on behalf of employer', 'date', 'employee' – suggests a parallel symmetry in the employment situation. But, within this rubric, matters are left as vague as possible. Most employees are simply 'farm hands'. The workplace of those not based in the packshed is usually 'lands', the estate's vast hectares of orchards, and even this is subject to transfer as required. The contract may not actually be signed by the employee at all.

As for hours and pay, the form of the contract gives the impression that clock time predominates across the farm (see Thompson 1967). While the packshed, run around its conveyor belts, somewhat conforms to this model (if one turns a blind eye to periods of unpaid 'preparation time'), picking in the orchards is actually remunerated through team-based piece rates. Workers are paid for the number of trailers their team have filled per month, divided by the number of pickers in their group (usually 30). Days of picking work have broadly similar lengths (ten hours rather than the eight hours that appear on the contract), but even this varies according to whether there is a backlog at the packshed or whether, conversely, there is a rush to finish a particular batch. Far from the abstract regularity implied by the contract, then, workers' actual experiences of work revolve around the rhythms of gang labour. Pace is maintained by calls from supervisors and other colleagues (see Bolt 2010). Workers are aware of how fast they are working largely in relation to neighbouring teams, as supervisors chalk tallies onto the backs of trailers and compete aggressively with one another. Indeed, the value of labour comes to be experienced through praise and admonishment, collective effort and rivalry.

By the end of each month, workers are unable to tell whether their pay reflects their labour at all. Rather, payday is experienced by seasonal workers as a ritual affirming the formality of the contract. One at a time, they 'sign' for pay with a thumbprint, at a table outside the office, in return for a paper packet adorned with dot-matrix typescript. This announces employee and remuneration details, but workers can only check the contents against the number on the outside. Individualized, abstracted and calculated out of sight in the farm offices, it appears to have little to do with the last month's exertions. All of this, of course, is useful for employers. The fact that workers cannot pick fast enough to make up their theoretical daily rate (the national minimum wage) does not bring any risk of added state scrutiny. Reportedly, the South African state's loss of test farms since apartheid means that it cannot investigate how quickly farm work can reasonably be accomplished. Farmers must simply ensure that they set their piece rates at the same levels as one another, in conversation with lawyers.

Much of the contract has only a tenuous relationship with recruits' lives on the farm. But it does have a place in a chain of documentation. Understanding this chain is crucial to understanding how workers live through and around paperwork – their claims to formal identities of various kinds. Anthropologists have recently highlighted the ways bureaucratic documents are grist to the mill of everyday negotiation and manipulation, and how they actively shape the networks that result (see e.g. Riles 2006; Hull M.S. 2012a, 2012b). Useful here is Elizabeth Hull's insight that 'material certificates, documents and ... aesthetics ... are essential' to an institution's appeal to formality (Hull E. 2012: 172). Yet, as Reeves (2013) has shown in relation to labour migrants in Moscow, the use of official and semi-official documents depends on mobilizing them in convincing performances. It is important to extend these insights into analyses of workforces, if we are to examine critically what is formal inside formal employment. In a workforce like Grootplaas, documents work as fragmentary badges of formality – as putative connections to officialdom. Yet this is far from simple. Formality appears to emerge from documents, because of people's investment in ensuring or defending their authority and efficacy. But these documents are in fact focal points in the relationships through which the legitimacy of formality comes to be experienced. To all this, we need to add another dimension – how workers convert between documents, and in the process create a degree of unity from this fragmentary picture.

To appreciate a worker's experience of formal employment, and of conversion through a chain of documents, it is worth imagining arriving on the border. This means braving the Limpopo River alone or in groups, climbing through the double razor-wire fence, and finding oneself on one of the farms. The crossing comes with its own dangers, from drowning or crocodile attacks when the river is in flood, to abuse, assault or rape by border gangs (*magumaguma*) or South African soldiers (see SPT 2004). Migrants' transience is inflected by the 'loss of coherence and unity' characteristic of crisis (Vigh 2008: 10), undermining any attempts to plan for the future. In Zimbabwe (see Hammar 2014; Jones 2014), as elsewhere, fast-shifting, unpredictable circumstances require constant navigation, as personal projects collapse, and norms formerly taken for granted cease to produce intended effects (Vigh 2008; see also Mbembe and Roitman 1995). Transience, of course, has spatial as well as temporal dimensions. On the Zimbabwean–South African border, the search for shelter and work while dodging patrols and deportation raids makes for a fugitive existence. Conversely, being incorporated into one of the farm workforces offers provisional residence and new possibilities for planning.

But the experience of transience goes beyond a lack of rootedness in place. For many who have travelled a long way, the border is a place where they are total strangers – isolated and unknown. The white game farmer who trains soldiers to track 'border jumpers' routinely finds the bodies of exhausted, dehydrated migrants under trees in the bush, empty water bottles still in hand. The quality of their footwear indicates whether this fatal journey was preceded by other, more successful trips; cheaper, Chinese-manufactured shoes reportedly show that their wearer is a first-timer, whereas nicer shoes suggest earlier migratory achievements. But the migrants in question become mere cases. They are specific only in terms of the clues they provide to a tracker. Photographs of their corpses remain logged on his computer as testament to his own experience.

Even in less extreme cases, some long-distance migrants initially float through the border area like ghosts. Strangers pass through the farms' labour compounds, taking water and occasionally some unfinished *vhuswa* (TshiVenda: maize-meal porridge) from a doorway en route. At least many adult residents of the border try to be hospitable. Migrants who stop over comment on the fact that workers offer shelter and food when they can. But the isolation of being unknown is starker when the residents are children. On one occasion, I waited to speak to a black game farm manager at his remote house. Meanwhile, I chatted to his children and those of Grootplaas's foreman – the latter had accompanied me to visit their friends. Before the manager returned, a man in ragged clothes walked up the dirt path asking for water. Without hesitation, the children threw rocks at him and drove him away. They were adamant that he represented a threat and that giving him the benefit of the doubt was too much of a risk.

Guyer (2004) points out that formality often appears to people in Africa through the apparent fixity of more-or-less official documents. This has particular implications amidst the transience of the Zimbabwean–South African border. In this world of enduring dislocation, migrants' documents – as socially recognized 'inscriptions' of people's histories (Ferraris 2013) – represent a particular kind of stability. Zimbabwean national identity cards – durable metal plates – bear their owners' personal information, including area of origin. Sheaves of certificates bearing histories of qualifications – school and even university grades, courses taken alongside employment in administration or IT, proof of training from public health NGOs – are carefully protected, ready to be revealed and mobilized at the right moment. Countermanding the footloose experience of migration, then, are groups of objects whose meaning once appeared unimpeachable. In their capacity to connect past lives to future possibilities, such formal (official and semi-official) documents belong to a wider category of prize possessions among migrants. Lists of contact numbers in South Africa (see Hall 2013) cast previous relationships as chances for shelter and employment. Photo albums recall happier days and comfortable families, acting both as memories and as assertions of former status.

While the aura of official documents comes from the apparent stability of their meaning, acquiring work and gaining traction on the border means mobilizing these documents in specific interactions. The meaning of identity cards appears obvious, but it is precisely the way they stand for their owners that enables them to become points of apparent fixity around which workers and job seekers negotiate their positions. Officially, the recruitment of seasonal workers happens in the open – by the gates of the farm workshop

6.2 New arrivals at Grootplaas struggle to get their identity cards and papers into the hands of a senior worker, during recruitment (© Maxim Bolt)

yard, a stone's throw from the administrative offices. Hardship, a senior worker and keeper of the employment register, stands on a low wall and collects the cards from throngs of outstretched hands. Hopefuls towards the back of the crowd hand their cards forward. Others, who realize that any struggle is futile, stand back from the melee, their cards hanging from their hands beside them. But the real significance of identity cards' centrality in recruitment emerges off-stage, as migrants attempt to give them to senior workers. The understanding is that, if a senior figure takes one's card, one will be given work. The importance of patronage is a lesson quickly learned by new arrivals, and the risks of giving up one's card should not be underestimated. One group of workers managed to hand their IDs to the foreman, after which he promptly lost them. They found themselves in a strange limbo: on the farm's books but, for several days until the cards reappeared, at risk of losing any officially recognized identity. As we will see below, once migrants acquire alternative badges of officialdom, a few are willing to abandon their Zimbabwean cards altogether.

Those who do secure a job enter the world of farm paperwork. The first stage is a formal 'application for employment', whose discursive register is conspicuously removed from the racialized world of South African agriculture, and stark subordination by both white farmers and black foremen and supervisors. On the one hand, the closing statement on the form reads: 'Thank you for your interest shown in our company'. On the other, recruits' fingerprints are then taken and they line up for photographs, during which they are exposed to objectification and humiliation by management – on one occasion, the white secretary loudly complained about the smell of their bodies. Information is sought. After asking for the 'applicant's' title, home address, nationality, place and date of birth, marital status, and children's particulars, the application form demands an assessment of linguistic ability in Afrikaans, English and other languages, and requests references. But little is corroborated. Linguistic ability is largely determined by self-assessment. When I was shown through the personnel records, I found only two references from previous employers, both simply describing the worker's departure as a matter of 'seeking greener pastures'.

This, then, is the moment when the contract appears. We have already seen how little of it bears resemblance to the world beyond the filing cabinet where it is stored. But the contract does have three clear external referents: the recruit's ID document number; whether he or she has submitted copies of 'school, academic, apprenticeship (completed) or any other educational qualifications'; and the employee number allocated by the farm, which then takes on its own life. We have already seen how central a recruit's ID card is to his or her experience of getting a job. The same may be said of certificates. While, like the ID card, their meaning appears simply obvious, some skill is involved in mobilizing them. Michael, the personnel manager, underlined the point, in a discussion one day about his own arrival. He characterizes his own past in terms of his education, marked by the accumulation of formal qualifications: O-levels, and diploma courses in Personnel Management, Office Management and Administration, Computers, and Modern Management. But when he came to Grootplaas, he said, he had to keep his raft of skills and credentials a secret from other workers to avoid any enmity from them. Only when it became clear that there was no permanent employment available for him as a manual labourer did he discretely disclose his qualifications and obtain a 'management' job.

Indeed, the risks of revealing certificates were borne out during my fieldwork. One seasonal worker, Jameson, was clearly set apart from other workers by his collared shirt tucked into once-pressed trousers, and by the fact that he always wore gold-rimmed glasses. Keen to be taken out of picking work, he approached Michael with his qualifications. He had, after all, passed not only his A-levels, but also a Bachelor's degree and a postgraduate diploma. In addition, he had travelled to Nairobi and attained a certificate in entrepreneurial development. His previous employment was equally striking for a farm worker: as a teacher, in a post office, and for the Zimbabwe Election Support Network and the National Constitutional Assembly. Hyperinflation had eroded his earnings to the point where he left home to seek employment in South African Rand. Revealing his background was a double-edged sword. Within a couple of weeks, Jameson secured a clerical job in the packshed. However, it was not long before he was demoted and sent back to the orchards. Bad relations had developed between him and Michael, and it was widely rumoured (including by Jameson himself) that he had really been demoted because his qualifications and experience constituted a threat to

Michael's own educated status and position. Jameson was right – certificates should be revealed quietly, and only to those who will not see them as a threat. In Michael's case, he had taken them straight to the farmer, not to a fellow worker.

The third external referent on the contract, the farm ID number, points forward into employment; it takes on a life of its own after recruitment. That is because it is the basis of a worker's farm ID card. Responding to huge delays in processing seasonal workers, farms make laminated employment cards and issue them to workers. Ad-hoc agreements between farmers, police and army mean that patrols generally accept the cards from workers so long as they remain on the estates. These, then, are recognized documents attesting to sponsorship by white farmers, which protect black workers and offer them a degree of security, in a world where farmers are understood to have some sovereignty over their land. Moving around on the border road, or elsewhere off the estates, is more dangerous. Nevertheless, employment cards offer increased stability for livelihood strategies on the farms – waged and otherwise. Their value is attested to by the market in forgeries that has developed in the Zimbabwean border town of Beitbridge.

The understanding on which farm ID cards are built has its own history. In the 1990s, the farms on the Limpopo were considered part of a 'special employment zone' in the vicinity of the border, in which the usual bureaucratic processes could be bypassed (see Rutherford 2010). Special permits allowed Zimbabweans to enter South Africa if they were linked to a specific farmer, and the South African border authorities even established an 'informal' border post at a garrison by the farms so that farmers could pick up recruits literally on the edge of their estates (see Lincoln and Maririke 2000). Even so, it was understood that many workers would cross illegally and expect regularization on the farms themselves. While the special employment zone has long been discontinued, and farmers' corporate permits for workers are the same as elsewhere in the country, this understanding continues. Seasonal recruits are always regularized after they start work. Their existence is also always negotiable, sometimes tacitly legitimated and sometimes requiring more explicit mediation. Throughout, it is they who bear the risk.

The historical resonance of farm IDs – the fact that migrants' engagement with space depends on privately issued proof of attachment to white landowners – is not lost on workers. For newcomers, the cards stand for racialized agricultural arrangements that seem peculiarly anachronistic. For veteran workers, these arrangements are simply a continuation of what came before. In any case, the cards' material form underlines the power relations for which they stand. As a 'graphic genre' (Hull M.S. 2012b: 15), these documents are distinguished by the fact that they stand for the private authority of farmers and their families, yet they are in effect semi-official. Each is homemade, cut from a piece of paper prepared on a home computer. On each, a cartoon-style, Clipart image of a fruit tree dominates. A star-shaped hole is punched into the edge of the rough lamination

Navigating Formality in a Migrant Labour Force 171

for each month of employment, confirming for any patrol that the bearer has been working continuously on the estate since the card's stated date of issue. Such an extension of private power over workforces has long characterized white agriculture in the region, in what Rutherford (2001) has called 'domestic government'.[4]

In any case, at this point workers begin to be treated as officially legitimate. Yet this is uneven – it has to be negotiated and renegotiated. Moreover, whereas permanent workers' demeanours mean that they are rarely even checked for documents, seasonal workers' palpable nervousness means that they are constant objects of suspicion. Given the market in forgies, farm ID cards may not be enough to prevent arrest if workers flee when the police arrive. It does not help that, unlike the pieces of paper that workers carry once they have been fully regularized, farm IDs bear no photographs. The cards are ambiguous: *semi*-official (at least in the way they are treated by representatives of the state), *usually* accepted, *probably* issued by a farmer, but forged with relative ease.

Gradually, workers receive work permits from Home Affairs. This process is itself mediated – in this case by Michael, the personnel manager. Faced with large numbers of workers who need permits, Michael can exercise a degree of choice in whose he processes, and when. Especially during the harvest, when there are hundreds of recruits and many never receive legal documents, handling paperwork confers a great deal of power. Who is processed depends on connections. Michael can afford to neglect some arrivals, or even use his influence to demand favours or build dependencies. In other cases, attempting to do so brings the wrath of other senior workers. In fact, Michael was assaulted in his office, precisely for attempting to deny paperwork to a female seasonal worker with powerful kin. As for those who are selected, Michael takes groups of 10 or 15 to the border post in a pick-up truck, commandeering the farm's senior driver. There, each has to be furnished with Zimbabwean travel documents. During the period of fieldwork, this was an Emergency Travel Document ('ETD', a photocopied sheet of paper, in place of a passport[5]), to which their photograph would be stapled. The South African authorities would then affix a small, blue short-term visa to the back. Over time, as it disintegrated and became softer and darker, this sheet of paper was often adorned with stamps and further adhesive visas, depending on work and movement. But, for those migrants who had one, an ETD became a basic record of formal employment. Alongside the work permit itself, the ETD's photograph, blue visa sticker, and stamps were together crucial for negotiating encounters with border patrols.

Here too, then, processes of brokering and attempts to shape social relations are key as workers build personal histories through documentation.

---

[4] It also, doubtless, offers a relatively easy way to forge workable documents in Beitbridge. It is worth noting that, while forgery offers perspectives on ordinary people's engagements with the state (see e.g. Ismail 2010), this case is unusual precisely because of the mediating role of employers and their own documents.
[5] ETDs were developed to streamline the documentation of Zimbabwean farm workers, because of a shortage of passports. Access to Zimbabwean passports has since improved.

Meanwhile, work permits transcend their apparently obvious purpose. Whereas they attach a worker to a particular employer, for a fixed period, many workers see these documents as passports to more open-ended mobility. These are unambiguously state documents, and police on the roads are assumed not to be able to check immediately whether the permits of absconded workers have been cancelled. So many seasonal workers head for Johannesburg, armed now not only with their certificates and contact numbers, but with pieces of paper – a permit and a visa-adorned travel document – that appear to legitimate them in terms that are less personalized and less localized than the farm ID cards. Of course, the provisional and temporary usefulness of this documentation underlines not only migrants' strategies, but also the acutely vulnerable conditions in which they make decisions.

The possibilities for conversion are most starkly visible among workers who become permanent. A number of permanent workers appear as South African citizens in the records. Many of these were in fact Zimbabwean-born, but they acquired South African identity documents while working on the border farms. How this is done is of course difficult to determine, since the subject is sensitive. But rumours are suggestive. One way, I was told, is to find a South African who will stand as a foster parent for a fee. A letter from an employer confirming long-term service offers the simplest (and a legal) way to acquire a South African ID (although not citizenship). But apparently many workers are hesitant about approaching the South African Department of Home Affairs in this manner – perhaps the result of farm workers' marginalization beyond the farms, however influential they are inside workforces. Instead, employers in the area have been known to turn a blind eye and confirm their workers' South African credentials. Given that it is in their interests to have stable core workforces, it is perhaps not surprising that they are seen as willing to do so and even as actively supportive of such efforts.

In whatever way workers gain their South African identity documents, their successful use requires finesse. Some workers take different names, to avoid any suspicion at roadblocks of their being Zimbabwean. But in that case, they need to be able speak the language their name suggests. Others, who do not change their names, need to be ready to pay off officials. Meanwhile, there are difficult decisions about how far to go in seeking South African documentation. Acquiring a South African ID on the basis of long-term residence certainly feels more stable than living on renewable six-month work permits.[6] But once that decision has been taken, it is difficult to upgrade to citizenship – one exists in the database as a Zimbabwean. One senior worker was instead holding out for a passport, and therefore used a fraudulent ID document, in which he was a South African, even though he was entitled to

---

[6] During the Zimbabwe Documentation Project (see Note 3), some permanent workers were able to acquire four-year South African visas. But this depended on being physically present at the farm when Home Affairs officials visited – and many workers were not – highlighting the contingent nature of access to documents.

one as a long-term Zimbabwean worker. He decided to use a South African Venda name, but he was caught out by police on the road, because of his limited knowledge of South African Venda places and language. The farmer was called, he was let out of prison, but he was back to square one with his documentation. Months later, I was told that he now faced problems using a new set of South African documents that used his real name. Its spelling marked him out as a non-South African (Zimbabwean Ndebele names, like his, are similar to South African Zulu names, but are sometimes spelled differently), and he was left paying regular bribes. Documents' apparent fixity of meaning gives them a powerful allure. But, even as the ultimate goal of regularization as a South African citizen comes within reach, these documents remain subject to processes of everyday negotiation in which possibilities are starkly constrained. They are foci in the framing of relations with officialdom, but not ones that determine outcomes in any simple way.

Conclusion

What we have seen here is a long way from the usual reification of 'formality' as a form of employment or a sector. Rather, here we have a multiplicity of regulatory lenses, with different purposes and different effects. And there are different engagements with state officials – Home Affairs in issuing permits, soldiers and police in controlling movement and settlement – that shape workers' day-to-day existence. Even the issuers of Zimbabwean ID cards and school certificates play their parts here, remotely.

The fragmentary mosaic of multiple formalities that I have depicted reflects the equally fragmentary nature of 'the state', as a series of overlapping agencies and institutions (see Abrams 1988). The view from South Africa's margins renders these fragmentary formalities especially visible. Far from constituting a thick system of regularities, official spotlights on South Africa's northern border are limited. The networks created by documents are relatively sparse and reflect this fractured reality. For workers, using them often means negotiating with farmers, work supervisors, and others, adding to the multiplicity. In turn, this patchwork of formal rubrics sustains the power of farmers and their foremen in steeply hierarchical labour arrangements, enabling inequitable labour conditions to persist.

Nevertheless, for workers, documents also make up a register of formality that opens up possibilities under adverse conditions. Indeed, formality emerges from attempts to connect up the diversity of documents and official encounters. Workers learn to convert between different documents, using them like stepping-stones. The goal is to realize an identity that carries weight with an increasing range of state officials. From below, the unity of formality is the result of a chain of encounters, with documents as their focus, which together hold out tantalizing but often elusive promise.

References

Abrams, P. (1988). 'Notes on the difficulty of studying the state', *Journal of Historical Sociology* 1(1): 58–89.

Barchiesi, F. (2011). *Precarious Liberation: Workers, the State, and Contested Social Citizenship in Postapartheid South Africa*. Albany, NY: State University of New York Press.

Bolt, M. (2010). 'Camaraderie and its Discontents: Class Consciousness, Ethnicity and Divergent Masculinities among Zimbabwean Migrant Farmworkers in South Africa', *Journal of Southern African Studies* 36(2): 377–93.

—. (2012). 'Waged Entrepreneurs, Policed Informality: Work, The Regulation of Space and the Economy of the Zimbabwean-South African Border', *Africa* 82(1): 111–30.

—. (2015). *Zimbabwe's Migrants and South Africa's Border Farms: The Roots of Impermanence*. Cambridge, UK: Cambridge University Press.

—. (2016). 'Accidental Neoliberalism and the Performance of Management: Hierarchies in Export Agriculture on the Zimbabwean-South African Border', *Journal of Development Studies* 52(4): 561–75.

Bradford, H. (1993). 'Getting away with Murder: "Mealie Kings", the State and Foreigners in the Eastern Transvaal, c.1918–1950', in P. Bonner, P. Delius and D. Posel (eds), *Apartheid's Genesis, 1935–1962*. Braamfontein: Ravan Press.

Breman, J. (1999). 'The Study of Industrial Labour in Post-Colonial India – The Formal Sector: An Introductory Review', *Contributions to Indian Sociology* 33(1): 1–41.

Callebert, R. (2014). 'Transcending Dual Economies: Reflections on "Popular Economies in South Africa"', *Africa* 84(1): 119–34.

Doctors Without Borders (2009). 'Beyond Cholera: Zimbabwe's Worsening Crisis', 17 February. http://www.msf.org/sites/msf.org/files/old-cms/source/countries/africa/zimbabwe/2009/Zimbabwe_Beyond_Cholera_Feb09.pdf

Ferguson, J. and A. Gupta. (2002). 'Spatializing States: Toward an Ethnography of Neoliberal Governmentality', *American Ethnologist* 29(4): 981–1002.

Ferraris, M. (2013). *Documentality: Why it is Necessary to Leave Traces*. Richard Davies (trans.) New York: Fordham University Press.

Gluckman, M. (1961). 'Anthropological Problems Arising from the African Industrial Revolution', in A. Southall (ed.), *Social Change in Modern Africa: Studies Presented and Discussed at the First International African Seminar*. Oxford: Oxford University Press.

Guardian, The (2008). 'Zimbabwe Inflation Passes 100,000%, Officials say', 22 February. www.theguardian.com/world/2008/feb/22/zimbabwe (accessed 28 August 2013).

Guyer, J.I. (2004). *Marginal Gains: Monetary Transactions in Atlantic Africa*. London: University of Chicago Press.

—. (2014). 'Gains and Losses in the Margins of Time: From West and Equatorial History to Present-Day South Africa, and Back', *Africa* 84(1): 146–50.

Hall, R. 2013. 'Hierarchies, Violence, Gender: Narratives from Zimbabwean Migrants on South African Farms', in B. Derman and R. Kaarhus (eds), *In the Shadow of a Conflict: Crisis in Zimbabwe and its Effects in Mozambique, South Africa and Zambia*. Harare: Weaver Press.

Hammar, A. (2014). 'The Paradoxes of Class: Crisis, Displacement and Repositioning in Post-2000 Zimbabwe', in A. Hammar (ed.), *Displacement Economies in Africa: Paradoxes of Crisis and Creativity*. London: Zed Books.

Hart, K. 1973. 'Informal Income Opportunities and Urban Employment in Ghana', *Journal of Modern African Studies* 11(1): 61–89.

Hoag, C. (2010). 'The Magic of the Populace: An Ethnography of Illegibility in the South African Immigration Bureaucracy', *PoLAR: Political and Legal Anthropology Review* 33(1): 6–25.

Holmström, M. (1976). *South Asian Factory Workers: Their Life and World*. Cambridge, UK: Cambridge University Press.

—. (1984). *Industry and Inequality: The Social Anthropology of Indian Labour*. Cambridge, UK: Cambridge University Press.

Hull, E. (2012). 'Banking in the Bush: Waiting for Credit in South Africa's Rural Economy', *Africa* 82(1): 168–86.

Hull, M.S. (2012a). 'Documents and Bureaucracy', *Annual Review of Anthropology* 41: 251–67.

—. (2012b). *Government of Paper: The Materiality of Bureaucracy in Urban Pakistan*. Berkeley, CA: University of California Press.

Human Rights Watch (2006). *Unprotected Migrants: Zimbabweans in South Africa's Limpopo Province*. Volume 18, No. 6 (A). New York: Human Rights Watch.

Ismail, O. (2010). 'Deconstructing Oluwole: Political Economy at the Margins of the State', in W. Adebanwi and E. Obadare (eds), *Encountering the Nigerian State*. New York: Palgrave Macmillan.

Johnston, D. (2007). 'Who Needs Immigrant Farm Workers? A South African Case Study', *Journal of Agrarian Change* 7(4): 494–525.

Jones, J.L. (2014). '"No move to make": The Zimbabwe Crisis, Displacement-in-place and the Erosion of "Proper Places"', in A. Hammar (ed.), *Displacement Economies in Africa: Paradoxes of Crisis and Creativity*. London: Zed Books.

Lincoln, D. and C. Maririke (2000). 'Southward Migrants in the Far North: Zimbabwean Farmworkers in Northern Province', in J. Crush (ed.), *Borderline Farming: Foreign Migrants in South African Commercial Agriculture*. Southern African Migration Project Migration Policy Series No. 16. Cape Town, SA: Idasa.

MacDonald, A. (2012). 'Colonial Trespassers in the Making of South Africa's International Borders 1900 to c.1950'. PhD thesis, University of Cambridge.

MacGaffey, J. (1991). *The Real Economy of Zaire: the contribution of smuggling and Other Unofficial Activities to National Wealth*. London: James Currey.

Mbembe, A. and J. Roitman (1995). 'Figures of the Subject in Times of Crisis', *Public Culture* 7(2): 323–52.

Meagher, K. (2010). *Identity Economics: Social Networks and the Informal Economy in Nigeria*. Woodbridge: James Currey.

Moodie, T.D. with V. Ndatshe (1994). *Going For Gold: Mines, Men and Migration*. Berkeley, CA: University of California Press.

Morreira, S. (2010). 'Seeking Solidarity: Zimbabwean Undocumented Migrants in Cape Town, 2007', *Journal of Southern African Studies* 36(2): 433–48.

Murray, M. (1995). 'Blackbirding at "Crooks' Corner": Illicit Labour Recruitment in the Northeastern Transvaal 1910–1940', *Journal of Southern African Studies* 21(3): 373–97.

Reeves, M. (2013). 'Clean Fake: Authenticating Documents and Persons in Migrant Moscow', *American Ethnologist* 40(3): 508–24.

Riles, A. (2006). 'Introduction: In Response', in A. Riles (ed.), *Documents: Artifacts of Modern Knowledge*. Ann Arbor, MI: The University of Michigan Press.

Roitman, J. (2004). 'Productivity in the Margins: The Reconstitution of State Power in the Chad Basin', in V. Das and D. Poole (eds), *Anthropology in the Margins of the State*. Oxford: James Currey.

Rutherford, B. (2001). *Working on the Margins: Black Workers, White Farmers in Postcolonial Zimbabwe*. London: Zed Books.

—. (2008). 'An Unsettled Belonging: Zimbabwean Farm Workers in Limpopo Province, South Africa', *Journal of Contemporary African Studies* 26(4): 401–15.

—. (2010). 'Zimbabwean Farmworkers in Limpopo Province, South Africa', in J. McGregor and R. Primorac (eds), *Zimbabwe's New Diaspora: Displacement and the Cultural Politics of Survival*. Oxford: Berghahn.

Rutherford, B. and L. Addison (2007). 'Zimbabwean Farm Workers in Northern South Africa', *Review of African Political Economy* 34(114): 619–35.

Scott, J.C. (1999). *Seeing Like a State: How Certain Schemes to Improve the Human Condition have Failed*. New Haven, CT: Yale University Press.

Seekings, J. and N. Nattrass (2005). *Class, Race, and Inequality in South Africa*. Scottsville: University of KwaZulu-Natal Press.

SPT – Solidarity Peace Trust (2004). *No War in Zimbabwe: An Account of the Exodus of a Nation's People*. Port Shepstone: Solidarity Peace Trust.

Thompson E.P. (1967). 'Time, Work-Discipline and Industrial Capitalism', *Past and Present* 38: 56–97.

van Onselen, C. (1976). *Chibaro: African Mine Labour in Southern Rhodesia 1900–1933*. London: Pluto Press.

Vigh, H. (2008). 'Crisis and Chronicity: Anthropological Perspectives on Continuous Conflict and Decline', *Ethnos* 73(1): 5–24.

Werbner, R. (1991). *Tears of the Dead: The Social Biography of an African Family*. Edinburgh, UK: Edinburgh University Press.

Part III

MARGINALITY, DISAFFECTION
& BIO-ECONOMIC DISTRESS

7 Precarious Life
Violence & Poverty under Boko Haram & MEND

Michael J. Watts

The relationship between existential precarity, moment to moment, and the long processes of a 'structure-in-crisis', is a question for empirical study of exactly how the effects of an improbable structural condition are generated, perpetuated and inserted into ongoing life. The diagnosis of longevity then opens up a wide and long force-field that demands empirical study.
(Jane Guyer 2016a)

This chapter engages with three broad themes addressed in Jane Guyer's (2007, 2016a, 2016b) recent work: temporalities and near futures (and especially the temporalities of immediate precarity and deep or structural time), modernity's aporias (the doctrines of the religious and the secular in relation to the contradictions and failures of modern secular national development) and the figure of the pauper or more properly the relations of violence and poverty. Much of Jane's work has of course built upon her hugely influential exploration of the cultural and political economy of Nigeria, a part of the world that has struggled throughout its postcolonial history with the failures of secular development, with the challenges of building a democratic future in a pluri-ethnic federal system, and with stark realities of political violence that surfaced almost immediately after independence with the descent into the Biafran civil war. Nigeria will be my crucible too in this chapter but I want to view the trio of concerns through the lens of the two insurgencies that have arisen since the return to civilian rule in 1999.

Boko Haram and the Movement for the Emancipation of the Niger Delta (MEND) arose in different parts of the country and appear to share few family resemblances. They are of course very different. One is draped in the language of true Islam, the full implementation of shari'a law, a rhetoric of restoration and purity, and a hostility to any sense of multi-religious tolerance linked to Boko Haram's deepening affiliations with global jihadist networks. The other is resolutely secular and modern; it appears to resemble a militant civic nationalism calling for 'resource control' and constitutional reform (including of fiscal federalism). One is situated in the dry (and increasingly desiccated) northern savannahs, a Hausa-Fulani and Kanuri dominated region operating within the relics of the nineteenth-century Sokoto Caliphate and the Bornu Empire; the other in the complex multi-ethnic swamps and creeks of the Niger Delta operating on the ruins as it were of the slave trade in the Bight of Biafra, and the nineteenth-century palm-oil city states. One stands at the epicentre of the Nigerian oilfields, the lifeline of the Nigerian economy since 1960; the other at a geographical remove from oil production operating in the former and the now declining heartland of the former Nigerian colonial export economy: groundnuts, cereals and cotton, and of a textile industry now devastated by Chinese competition.

While both of these regions have historically been mired in rural and urban poverty, they also share common *paradoxical* qualities. Militancy emerges, in each case, following the return to civilian rule in the context of the slow and uneven maturation of electoral democracy. Both insurgencies arose at a time when in some respects the region's prospects had markedly improved. Boko Haram emerged in the wake of the adoption of shari'a law across the 12 northern states (i.e. in the context of a deepening control by Islamist forces in northern Nigeria, historically the seat of political power in the country). MEND arose from the creeks of the Niger Delta in 2005 in the wake of changes in 1999 of the federal revenue allocation (a sharp increase in percentage allocated to the oil-producing states through the so-called derivation principle) which meant that a region historically marginalized in economic terms was awash in oil monies. In other words these insurgencies are complexly – one might say inversely – related to political and economic exclusion. I want to account for these quite different insurgencies, and their paradoxes, by invoking what Jane Guyer calls the relations between 'existential precarity, moment to moment, and the long processes of a structure-in-crisis'. My argument is that both Boko Haram and MEND arose in frontier spaces standing at the edge of the state, each shaped by what I shall call the twin logics of the petro-state: the dialectical centralization and decentralization mechanism of state-captured oil rents, and the forms by which the class settlement of the petro-state (a 'provisioning pact') simultaneously fragments space and forms of authority. The consequences of the operations of these twin logics, always locally and regionally specific, was to create a youth crisis, a generation living radically precarious lives excluded not simply from the market but from all forms of state, customary and religious authority. These frontier existences at the edge of the state constituted a fertile social space within which differing armed non-state actors, shaped by their cultural and historical traditions, launched what Mike McGovern (2012) calls a violent politics of *ressentiment*.

Each insurgency was bequeathed by earlier crises and by a postcolonial history evident in the deepening crises of legitimate authority, the radical precarity of forms of rural and urban livelihood, particularly among generations of excluded youth, and the abject failures of secular national development. All of these conspired to produce spaces and social conditions in which these violent expressions of political society were not simply forms of predatory clientelism as Bayart argues of African politics in general (Bayart 2009) but also instances of generative politics that surface at the interstices of everyday life (Lefebvre 2008). My task is to show how everyday life – in my case everyday life occupying the same 'now' but not the same place nor the same lived history (what Gramsci – see Buttigieg 1992 – called non-contemporaneity) – carries traces of both the dominant order of power, yet elicit episodic expressions of generative politics (Jeffrey and Dyson 2014) and moments of creativity that in Lefebvre's account are a product of the multiple, nested and overlapping spaces associated with forms of state territoriality. Insurgencies then throw into sharp relief the fragility and contradictory operations of political pacts secured, especially in Nigeria's postcolonial state that has exhibited the contradictions of an oil-fuelled passive revolution. Youth mobilization and expressions of what Mannheim (1972) called 'generational consciousness' must bear the stamp of patrimonial struggles over inequitably distributed resources. Yet it is equally true that the precarity of everyday life can generate vital moments and critical durations (Johnson-Hanks 2002) – conjunctural in Gramscian terms – in which recognition politics and rights talk may coexist with often violent forms of predation and insurgency. In this sense, I shall argue, MEND and Boko Haram express what Ludwig Wittgenstein called 'family resemblances', a kinship that grows from the order of power – the same now – which helped midwife each insurgency.[1]

Insurgencies are typically construed as armed movements by non-state actors seeking to contest state power in the course of which they typically establish their own territories, identities and forms of rule. Insurgent combat techniques as forms of contentious politics possess their own formal properties: small, mobile irregular forces, campaigns of targeted assassination, sabotage, kidnapping and strategic mobility, cross-class social composition of youth combatants, operations within, and among, the territory and agents of the ruling state power, and not least their reliance, whatever their ideological orientation, in differing degrees upon local populations, more of less coercively, for material support (Weinstein 2007: 29). Naturally, insurgencies can and do differ radically in their political and ideological orientation. Clapham's typology (1998), for example, historically and ideologically classifies African insurgent movements: liberationist (anti-colonial), separatist (secessionist or autonomist in orientation), reformist (radical reform of the state), and warlord (directed towards leadership change within the status quo). Both Boko Haram and MEND have attributes of separatist, reformist and warlord insurgencies yet, as I hope to show, none of these categories singly or collectively quite capture their contours, dynamics, impulses and character.

---

[1] This is not to suggest of course that Boko Haram's utterly appalling acts (beheading, rape, murderous attacks) and its anti-Enlightenment philosophy can be unproblematically placed on the same ground as MEND's invocation of constitutional reform and resource control. *Differing* forms of precarity politics can nevertheless be situated on a common canvas of the dialectics of, to invoke Gramsci again, the 'absolute historicism', 'absolute humanism' and 'absolute earthliness' required to grasp the forms in which forms of rule operates through the integral state (see Thomas 2009).

The Irresistible Rise of Insurgent Power

On 26 August 2011, an armed neo-Salafist[2] Islamist group popularly referred to as Boko Haram, whose origins can be traced to the Kanuri heartland in Bornu State in the north-east of Nigeria, detonated a large explosive device in central Abuja, the capital of the country. Though its origins seem to date back to Islamic study groups in the mid-1990s, Boko Haram had become a visible presence in and around Maiduguri by 2003 and its charismatic leader Mohammed Yusuf, a controversial preacher born in Yobe State in 1970, had garnered a large following with connections in both elite religious and political circles in and outside of the north-east. At its inception, Boko Haram was not violent and its horizon was local, but by 2011 it had left a trail of wreckage across the ten northern states, engaging in direct military confrontations with security forces but also targeting traditional rulers, clerics, politicians and civilian populations deemed to be hostile to their goal of implanting a full and pure shari'a (HRW 2012). Particularly after the killing of Yusuf while in police custody in 2009, tactics and operations escalated to include attacks on religious and political leaders, churches, schools and universities, beer halls and banks, culminating in an astounding jail break releasing 800 of its incarcerated followers in Bauchi in 2010.

The massive car bomb that was detonated in the United Nations compound in Abuja, located in the diplomatic zone in the centre of the city close to the US embassy, killed 23 persons with more than 100 seriously injured. Housing 26 humanitarian and development agencies, the building is the UN's main office in Nigeria. Within ten days, two videos were released to the media that included 25 minutes of speeches by the alleged UN bomber who is seen holding an AK-47 automatic rifle. A man claiming to be a spokesman for the sect told local news services that the alleged bomber was Mohammed Abul Barra, a 27–year-old married man from the north-eastern city of Maiduguri. In the videos a young man speaks in measured tones wearing a striped shirt, a turban and what appears to be a suicide vest. At other moments in the videos, the UN is referred to as a 'forum of all the global evil' and praises are offered to Osama bin Laden, the al-Qaeda leader killed by US Special Forces in Pakistan two months prior.

Boko Haram's origins can be traced back to Salafist-inspired prayer groups in the north-east of Nigeria in the 1990s but also to the rise of a charismatic and influential cleric Mohamed Yusuf who by 1994 had become the 'emir' of a radical group – the Movement for the Revival of Islam (JTI) – whose members included radicalized affiliates of the Islamic Movement for Nigeria (IMN) associated with a prominent Shia cleric Ibrahim Al-Zazaky (de Montclos 2014; Pantucci and Jesperson 2015). The larger context was the splin-

---

[2] Salafism has a deep history within Islam. In its modern iteration, Salafi refers to a follower of a modern Sunni movement known as Salafiyyah – which is related to, and sometimes includes, Wahabbism, and sometimes the two terms are seen as synonymous. Salafism has become associated with literalism, restorative Islam and with the controversial idea that violent jihad against civilians is a legitimate expression of Islam.

7.1 Mothers of some of the 276 girls adopted by Boko Haram participating in the #BringBackOurGirls campaign that became a global movement involving celebrities all over the world. (Oluwafemi Ipaye; reproduced courtesy *TheNEWS*, Lagos, Nigeria)

tering of sacred authority within the landscape of Nigerian Islam as new groups challenged the hegemony of the Sufi brotherhoods (Comolli 2015; Walker 2016; Smith 2015). By 2002 Yusuf's influence had grown within Bornu where he emerged as a major critic of the government implementation of shari'a. Under his influence, and amidst considerable debate and acrimony among splintering Islamist groups, Boko Haram was born in 2002 (Thurston 2016). Although its beginnings were peaceful, by December 2003 Boko Haram was engaged in direct military conflict with security forces; these attacks became more audacious and confrontational over the period 2003-9 culminating in the extrajudicial killing of Yusuf by the Nigerian military in 2009. In the wake of Yusuf's death the movement went underground and reappeared under the leadership of Abubakar Shekau which proved to be a turning point in terms of the escalation and scale of attacks. Since 2010 the movement has laid waste to vast tracts of the north-east. By 2016 1.5 million people had been displaced (many thousands to Niger, Chad and Cameroon), and over 20,000 killed, the majority Muslim. 2014 witnessed a massive escalation in the scale and character of violence. Fatalities increased by 150 per cent over 2013; 400 conflict events accounted for over 7500 deaths the majority of which were perpetrated in remote border communities (ACLED 2015). Another 11,000 deaths were attributed to Boko Haram in 2015, marked by large-scale abductions (the 276 Chibok girls were famously kidnapped in April 2014) and increasingly vile terrorist actions (beheading, the deployment of young female suicide bombers, sexual violence and slavery) and enhanced terrorization of civilians. In March 2014 Boko Haram established a caliphate in Bornu and added substantial territorial gains in Yobe and Adamawa States. By March 2015 the group had pledged allegiance to the Islamic State and claimed its reincarnation as ISIS's 'West Africa province' (Wilayat Gharb Ifriqiya) (Thurston 2016).

About ten months before the Boko Haram attack in Abuja, two massive car-bomb attacks had been launched against the diplomatic heart of Nigeria's high-modernist capital. On 1 October 2010, amidst the Golden Jubilee celebrations marking the 50th Independence Day anniversary, three car bombs were detonated, two outside the justice ministry and a third near Eagle Square where President Goodluck Jonathan sat with hundreds of Nigerian and foreign dignitaries. Twelve people were killed and many more seriously injured. The State Security Service (SSS) claimed it had, just days before the attacks, foiled other plans to detonate at least six car bombs on 29 September in the Three Arms Zone in central Abuja that houses the presidential palace, parliament, the Supreme Court and also the SSS headquarters. Shortly afterwards, MEND, the armed group fighting for what it calls 'resource control', issued an electronic statement apparently penned by their shadowy public relations person, Jomo Gbomo:

> The Movement for the Emancipation of the Niger Delta (MEND) deeply regrets the avoidable loss of lives during our bomb attack in Abuja on Friday October 1, 2010. Our hearts go to the families of those killed who we know were sympathetic to our cause. The irresponsible attitude of the government security forces is to blame for the loss of lives. They were given 5 days prior notice [and] the security forces were also warned one full hour to the first bomb blast ahead of the general alert sent to the media and told to steer the public from all parked cars which was not done.

In an earlier email to the Nigerian security agencies and to the foreign diplomatic community, MEND warned of the prospect of attacks and disruption because, as they put it, 'for 50 years, the people of the Niger delta have had their land and resources stolen from them'. In spite of this admission, President Goodluck Jonathan, himself an indigene of the Niger Delta, immediately absolved MEND of responsibility for the attacks. Yet within two days Henry Okah,[3] a purported operative and arms supplier for MEND, was arrested in South Africa, as were his brother and four others accused of master-minding the attacks.

A raft of non-state armed groups had emerged across the Niger Delta oilfields in the wake of the return to civilian rule in 1999, and with the dramatic appearance of MEND in late 2005 – by far the most militarily capable and well organized of the militant movements to have arisen – the region had descended into what one commentator called a 'zone of insurrection' (Adunbi 2015; Oriola 2013; Obi and Rustad 2011; Watts 2016). MEND exploded out of the creeks of the western Niger Delta promising to close down the oil industry unless a number of political demands (including the release of

---

[3] See http://odili.net/news/source/2012/may/6/508.html (accessed 2 May 2016).

7.2 Movement for the Emancipation of the Niger Delta (MEND) militants on a canoe (© Ed Kashi; reproduced by kind permission)

a number of key Ijaw figures and compensation for oil spills). Within a matter of days, close to one-third of national output was shut in. The situation rapidly deteriorated as MEND launched ever more audacious and well organized attacks on oil infrastructure and on government security forces, reaching a nadir in June 2008 with an extraordinary assault on Shell's massive Bonga platform 75 miles offshore, shutting in 10 per cent of national oil output in one dramatic event. According to *The Report of the Technical Committee of the Niger Delta* (RTCND), in the first nine months of 2008 the Nigerian government lost a staggering $23.7 billion in oil revenues due to militant attacks and sabotage. By some estimates the losses to the Nigerian Treasury between 2003 and 2009 amounted to over $100 billion. By May 2009 oil production had fallen by over a million barrels per day, a decline of roughly 40 per cent from the national average output five years earlier. On 13 May 2009, federal troops – a dedicated regional force called the Joint Military Task Force (JFT) established in 2003 – launched a full-scale counter-insurgency against what the government saw as violent organized criminals. The militants in return launched ferocious reprisal attacks, gutting Chevon's Okan manifold which controlled 80 per cent of the company's shipments of oil. Over a two-month period from mid-May to mid-July, 12 attacks were launched against Nigeria's $120 billion oil infrastructure. Of Nigeria's 300 operating oil fields, 124 were shut by mid-July 2009. Since 2006 conflict deaths, by some estimates, were running at 1500 per year. Perhaps as many as 100,000 people had been

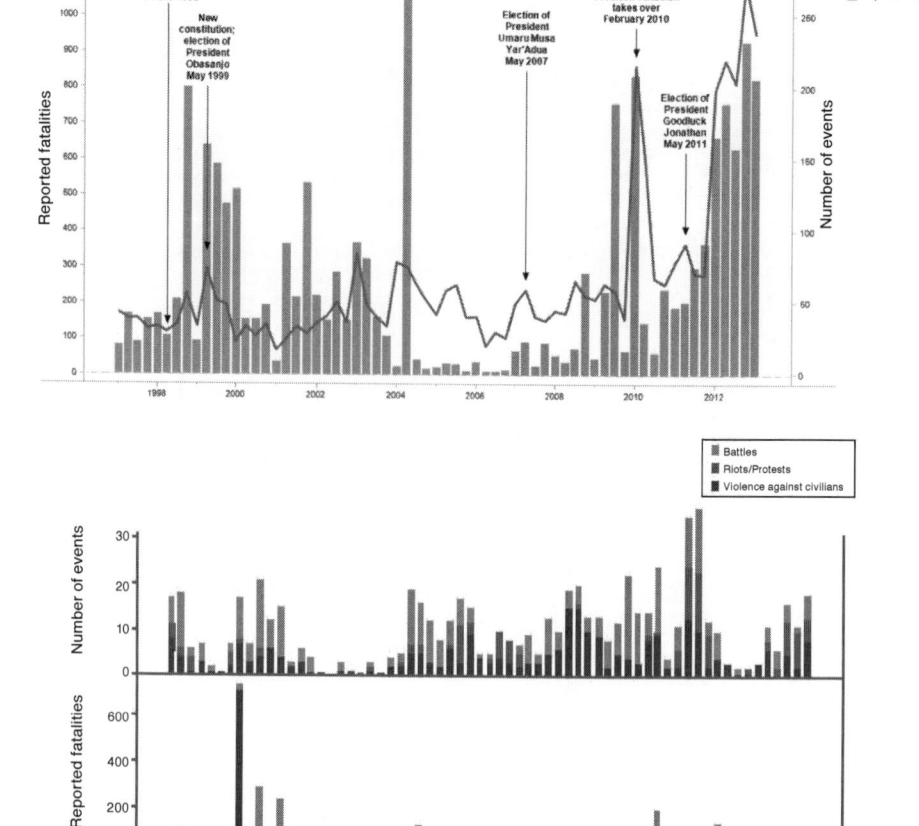

186   **Marginality, Disaffection & Bio-Economic Distress**

7.3 Conflict Events and Reported Fatalities, Nigeria, 1997 to March 2013. (Source: Armed Conflict Location & Event Data Project (ACLED), Country Report: Nigeria April 2013 (www.acleddata.com/wp-content/uploads/2013/04/ACLED-Country-Report_Nigeria_April-2013.pdf; accessed 23 February 2017)

internally displaced by June 2009. Faced with the prospect of a long drawn out military struggle – and profound questions of whether the security forces could prosecute a successful campaign against MEND in the creeks – the government announced an amnesty on 24 June 2009.

These twin assaults confirmed what most Nigerians already knew: that the country confronted two home-grown insurgencies.[4] Inevitably, the 2010–11 Abuja attacks – indeed the larger patterns of violent conflict since the early 2000s (see Illustration 7.3) – appear as a return of the repressed, or at the least

---

[4] The language of insurgency remains a question for some. Nwajiaku (2012) inexplicably uses scare quotes when she describes the Niger Delta 'insurgency' and like Paul Collier (2007) seems to believe that it is either organized crime, or at least does not warrant the term. For Boko Haram, the term insurgency is widely deployed by the press, the military and policy intellectuals.

a terrifying echo of earlier eruptions: the Maitatsine movement crushed by the armed forces in Kano in 1980, and the brutal repression of the Ogoni mobilization by Abacha's military junta ending with the hanging of Ken Saro-Wiwa and his comrades in 1995. But the scale of the violence – and the military capabilities of Boko Haram and MEND – suggested something altogether of a different order and of a much darker cast. The insurgencies confirmed by many the sense that Nigeria was – to use the parlance of the policy world – a 'fragile and conflicted state' that was 'too big to fail'. The near future looked bleak. By 2016 Boko Haram accounted for over 20,000 mortalities and the displacement of 2.5 million people. The federal amnesty offered in 2009 – and taken up by some 30,000 militants – had brought a measure of peace to the Niger Delta, yet the defeat of Goodluck Jonathan in the 2015 elections and the prospect of the radical constriction of the post-amnesty programme by President Buhari triggered the emergence in early 2016 of a new militant group, the Niger Delta Avengers, whose attacks on oil infrastructure, in several months, shut in almost one million barrels of oil.

The Ordering of Power

> [Authoritarian leviathans] that survive strictly through patronage and spending – what I call 'provision pacts' instead of 'protection pacts' – will gradually squander their remunerative power and find themselves increasingly vulnerable to debilitating fiscal crises. The point is not that such regimes are incapable of enduring [but] that they suffer from the political equivalent of a 'birth defect'. (Dan Slater 2011: 19)

Nigeria is customarily seen as an exemplary instance of petro-affliction in extremis. If the country is a catastrophic showcase for the failures of oil-led secular national development,[5] Nigeria is of course one of Africa's economic powerhouses and is now the largest economy in Africa, averaging around 8 per cent annual gross domestic product (GDP) growth over the past decade (World Bank 2013). Yet a decade of impressive economic growth, coupled with its US$1 trillion in oil and gas earnings over the past half century, have not translated into either significant increases in employment or widespread improvements in the wellbeing and life chances of the majority of its citizens. Wage employment is low and falling; only 12 per cent of the labour force is in paid employment (Oyefusi 2012), unemployment rates increased over the decade to 2009 and, according to the World Bank more than 40 per cent of the country's young people are unemployed (this is almost certainly a serious underestimate). The total poverty headcount rose from 27.2 per cent in 1980 to 65.6 per cent in 1996 and recent figures from the Central Bank of Nigeria show that, in a 20–year period (1980–2000) those in poverty increased by 400 per cent. In half of Nigeria's 36 states, the estimated poverty headcount

---

[5] There is a large literature of this sort on the 'resource curse'; see for example Collier (2007); Ross (2012); Humphreys et al. (2007).

increased between 2004 and 2010.[6] Overall, Nigeria's human development index (HDI) for 2013 shows a gradual improvement from 2005 to 2011 but the country's global HDI ranking fell from 142nd in 2010 to 153rd in 2013. In the phrasing of one IMF report, Nigeria's oil revenues have 'not significantly added to the standard of living of the average Nigerian' (Sala-i-Martin and Subramanian 2003: 4). Inevitably these failures and seemingly intractable structural impediments cast a long shadow over the optimistic assessments of Nigeria's short-term future.

Since the end of the civil war in 1970, oil and gas revenues have dominated the country's political economy and it is this dependency that is often seen to have over-determined Nigeria's litany of developmental failures and its political dynamics (and by implication the portfolio of appropriate policy options). The 'Dutch Disease',[7] the costs of volatility and poor governance produce a well catalogued litany of state deficits. Squandered opportunities, endemic corruption, and the failure of the state to provide basic public goods have contributed to a deep sense of pessimism and massive state-sponsored outlays on global rebranding have done little to arrest bleak predictions regarding the country's future. Nigeria's inventory of governance indicators make for especially grim reading and offer a sad accounting of postcolonial political leadership. Patterns of state dysfunction and institutional deficit are endemic; many forms of public authority are seen to be illegitimate and unjust, and they display a range of deficits – in transparency, monitoring and participation – that erode effective forms of fiscal accountability, bureaucratic competence, regulation, and government service delivery (Amundsen 2010; Humphreys et al. 2007: 265; Watts 2011).

Oil has seeped indelibly into the country's political, economic and social lifeblood and has become an essential part of the conflicted national political space (Soares de Oliveira 2007). In 2013, over 80 per cent of government revenues, 90 per cent of foreign exchange earnings, 96 per cent of export revenues and 15 per cent of GDP was accounted for by oil and gas revenues (World Bank 2014). Spliced into existing ethno-religious and class cleavages, oil has bequeathed a profound legacy for both political culture and competition. Most obviously, the capture of substantial oil rents by the state severed public taxation from state revenue and contributed to the rapid growth of centralized power, even as the political settlement – what Slater (2011) in another setting calls a 'provisioning pact' – and the ferocious struggle over oil rents drove societal fragmentation, splintering and dispersion. A cardinal political conundrum for the rentier state is how to share power and oil resources in a fractious multi-ethnic federal system. Practically speaking, Nigeria's experience has been enduring, and serial conflicts, with all of their attendant costs,

---

[6] Nigeria's Multidimensional Poverty Index (MPI) for 2008 estimates that 54.1 per cent of the population suffers multiple deprivations, while an additional 17.8 per cent is vulnerable to multiple deprivations. The breadth of deprivation (intensity) in Nigeria, as calculated by the average percentage of deprivation experienced by people in multidimensional poverty, is 57.3 per cent.

[7] The negative impacts of sudden inflow of foreign currency as a result of the discovery of large oil reserves, and the resulting currency appreciation that discourages the export market.

driven by vicious, and often violent, struggles over access to oil revenues – a process usually construed as predation and looting. In the wake of the return to civilian rule in 1999, there has been a dramatic escalation in ethnic, religious and political violence, illustrated in part by Boko Haram and MEND.[8]

The main beneficiaries of a political economy constructed around oil rents are a diverse and fractious class of politicians, civil servants, high-ranking military officers, and business interests, who constitute a form of elite cartel. Accounts of Nigeria's political architecture are almost always grounded in a rentier state and the vast neo-patrimonial edifice through which political networks are deeply imbricated with public office to provide vast opportunities for illicit gain. Other social classes, more peripheral to the centres of power, are the indirect beneficiaries of state largesse as public sector employees.[9] The construction of Nigeria's elite cartel – perhaps the most durable feature of the country's state building in the petroleum era – is the product of an exclusionary political settlement that limits most gains to a narrow selection of notables from specific regions and segments of the population. There is a pervasive culture of impunity surrounding these political classes. The logic of the political order entails buying off powerful groups and individuals so that they do not become a threat (co-optation); permitting some benefits to trickle down to purchase consent and legitimacy; and building powerful coercive apparatuses to ensure compliance (coercion) (Humphreys et al. 2007: 264). This political settlement, in short, has been profoundly shaped by the ways in which oil was inserted into a multi-ethnic federal system and has direct implications for long-term legitimacy, political stability and forms of public authority.

The ordering of power wrought in some way by oil is strikingly different from the situation that Slater (2011) describes in Southeast Asia. He argues that the growth and development trajectories there after the Second World War were shaped by the rise of what he calls durable 'authoritarian leviathans'. These regimes arose because contentious class politics were seen by powerful classes as endemic and unmanageable – that is to say their security and class positions are threatened by urban insurrection, radical redistributive demands and communal tensions. The revolutionary situations across much of Southeast Asia during the Cold War meant that elites supported state centralization as a bulwark against popular mobilization from below. These threats, in short, sustained state-centred coalitions and pacts, which facilitated state building. In the first instance this was through the state's coercive apparatuses, but more generally through building durable state institutions. Different sorts of 'protection pacts' emerged through coalitions among state officials, economic elites, middle classes and communal elites unified by 'shared support for heightened state power and tightened authoritarian

---

[8] President Jonathan declared a state of emergency in three northern states in May 2013, but efforts to restore order have been trailed by civilian casualties, refugees and serious allegations of atrocities perpetrated by security forces.
[9] Nearly three-quarters (72 per cent) of the government budget consists of recurrent costs (*Business Day*, 25 September 2012: 1).

controls' (Slater 2011: 15), reflecting particular orderings of power. State capacity, military cohesion and party strength were held together – that is to say politically ordered – by forms of extraction (flows of resources particularly around direct taxation), institutions and historical experiences that convince powerful social forces that 'they have more to fear from each other than the state' (ibid.: 20).[10] These pacts were infrequently democratic but they did build durable institutions, forms of public authority and in most cases significant growth and development achievements.

Nigeria offers a quite different story. Anti-colonial nationalism there had its origins in the 1930s among Western-educated southerners who led the pan-ethnic Nigeria Youth Movement (NYM), and drove the constitutional reforms implemented by the British. But the class configuration in Nigeria looked very different from the Cold-War, left-inspired armed struggle politics of post-war Southeast Asia – the unique and 'alarming profile', as Ben Anderson (1998: 7) dubbed it. The Second World War *did* propel radical nationalist sentiments in Nigeria because economic conditions deteriorated and also because the war, for the first time, spurred the first taste of government services. In Nigeria there were three radical anti-colonial nationalist mobilizations – the so-called Zikist Movement with its labourist and socialist leanings rooted in the east, the radical populism of Aminu Kano and Northern Elements Progressive Union (NEPU) in the north, and a growing Nigerian Labour movement that memorably organized a national strike over wages and cost-of-living allowances in 1945 – but they were all relatively weak. None could claim any explicit and enduring connection to socialist or communist politics, and during the 1950s they were in any case largely integrated into the emerging political parties that were overwhelmingly ethnic in orientation. The colonial state also came down hard on any radical organizations or movements through imprisonment, co-optation, transfer to another state as they did with Aminu Kano, or simply by banning such organizations, as in the case of the Zikist Movement in 1950.

The contentious politics that finally mattered – endemic and unmanageable – and capable in Slater's terms of providing the material basis for a protection pact, came shortly after dependence, a product of what Falola and Heaton (2008) call the 'fears of domination'. The First Republic, in fact, unravelled terrifyingly quickly. The British had bequeathed to the north a fragile hegemony over two unruly regions and a political culture of intimidation. Northerners feared domination by the south (Awolowo's AG) and Azikwe's NCNC, and the prospect that better-educated southerners would be a dominant presence in the federal bureaucracies (and in some quarters of business). The south feared that the north would Islamize the country and divert resources to the impoverished north. The army, while small, was staffed predominantly

---

[10] In this sense Slater's argument turns on two claims: that the most profound forms of post-war contentious politics were generative of revolutionary impulses, and that differing (geographically and nationally specific) counter-revolutionary reactions explain divergent Southeast Asian pathways of the authoritarian leviathans. The specific forms of contention, and the antecedent conditions prevailing in differing precolonial states, matter to the *forms* of coalitional pact.

by northerners but led by southerners, especially Igbo. The production of an elite coalition across deep ethnic and religious suspicions and cultural–religious difference proved to be especially fraught. The commodity Marketing Boards were regional and political too, raising substantial surpluses by indirectly taxing millions of peasant producers of groundnuts, cotton, cocoa and palm oil; captured by the regional political parties each funded increasingly venal and violent party political machines. The federal coalition quickly fell apart and in short order the national censuses in 1962 and 1963, on which revenue sharing and allocation of federal seats were based, triggered intense struggles, rigging and political violence. The national and regional elections also proved to be especially violent and massively fraudulent on every level as the parties jockeyed for power. The 1965 elections in the west produced a state of emergency, as two political factions fought over what appeared to be their marginality from the federal centre. As the First Republic was about to implode, a group of Igbo officers in January 1966 led a military coup; two major northern political leaders and the Governor of the Western Region were killed. But six months later a northern-led counter coup displaced Major General Ironsi (an Igbo) in response to what was perceived to be an Igbo putsch that culminated in a 1967 Decree to abolish the federation as such. By this time relations between the Military Governor in the east – Colonel Ojukwu – and the new military junta at the federal level had broken down, particularly as ethnic violence spun out of control in the north where more than 80,000 Igbo were slaughtered, many by the military (Anthony 2002). All this led Ojukwu to question whether the Igbo should or could live within a federal Nigeria. Despite frantic last minute negotiations, he declared on 30 May the independence of the Eastern Region, and the establishment of the Republic of Biafra. The revolutionary moment, clearly, was regional and ethnic, and decidedly not driven by class. The implications were profound.[11]

What sort of political order emerged from these contentious politics, that is to say a regional separatist movement that turned into a civil war consuming two million lives over a brutal and bloody two and half years before federal forces finally defeated the Biafran army in January 1970? In one sense the contours are clear: the Nigerian bourgeoisie – both industrial and agrarian – was relatively weak, politics remained deeply ethnic in tenor but the federal centre (and the military) had gained enormous power and authority as a result of the war. The Nigerian army had barely 10,000 recruits in 1967; at the end of the war it had over 250,000. The danger with militarization as authoritarian politics is that it neither assists in the process of institution building outside of the military itself, nor does it necessarily provide a ground for pacts between civilian and military elites, particularly if the depth of communal sentiment and ethnic division shapes the recruitment and organization of the military itself (which had been a running sore within the Nigerian military). Class conflict was muted, and communalism, which can potentially constitute a transcendent threat capable of providing resources

[11] The literature on the Biafran War is substantial as indeed is that on the First Republic (see Forsyth 1969; Diamond 1988; Osaghae 1998).

for a permanent protector, seemed to have contradictory effects. The horror of Biafra and its historical memory is etched into the political psyche of Nigeria and is often mobilized – 'the danger of sliding back into civil war' – during moments of crisis as a rationale for state powers. But whether communal strife (and civil war conducted in its name) is capable in itself of galvanizing state officials and economic elites to reduce their factional interests for the sake of a wider protection pact is always an open question, and in most cases (Nigeria included) seems an unlikely prospect. A civil war, if regional in character, does not necessarily constitute a radical threat to other elite groups and classes (outside of the contested region itself) even if it does, of course, provide a sense of national insecurity for which the military's power, funding and centralized organization – and possibly cohesion – can be enhanced. A strong military without robust societal and elite class linkages, which was certainly the outcome of the Biafran war, is unlikely to produce administrative and state capacity – what Michael Mann (1988) calls infrastructural power.

What makes the Nigerian case more than militarization – after all military rule, as a dominant trajectory, was interrupted by a civilian interregnum between 1979 and 1983, and since 1999 the military has withdrawn from direct political rule as such – was the presence of two other structural forces. The first is the enduring power and dominant presence – the antecedents of which were laid long before the authoritarian leviathan emerged in the 1970s – of ethno-religious communalism. Powerful centripetal forces were at work – separatism, communalism, regionalism – all of which rested upon a tortured, fractured and weak imagined community called the Nigerian nation (Nigerian as a 'mere geographical expression' as one postcolonial leader put it). As a consequence, the overdetermination of ethnic exclusivity and ethno-regional (community) mobilization, as the basis for claims making and doing politics, propelled the forces of fragmentation. In Southeast Asia, Slater sees the fragmented cases as the products of episodic and largely manageable crises around the birth of authoritarianism, and a splintering of shallow coalitions that followed; the elites concern for self-interested economic largesse provided a weak foundation for authoritarian durability and institutional coherence, and 'highly personalized regimes' predominated (2011: 24). This logic was, as we have seen, operative in the period between 1945 and the outbreak of civil war in Nigeria. Of course, after 1970 military rule was the defining character of the authoritarian leviathan but it proved incapable of either raising extractive (direct tax) revenues, or building robust institutions. If military rule was fully instantiated in Nigerian political life by the 1970s, the logic of ethnic and religious fracturing among a small capitalist class and among the political classes at the expense of anything like class consolidation, continued apace. Political parties, to the extent they existed, were marginally organized on the basis of ideological positions related to class or strategy. Doing politics was a self-reinforcing set of relations forged between the electorate and politicians driven by intense competition between communities, regions and ethno-religious groups over access to state resources. But, as it turns out, it was geology and geography that were to prove decisive in how this deadly configuration of fragmentation and militarization was to play out and gave Nigeria's its particular specificity.

The game changer was the discovery and exploitation of massive oil and gas resources, and the quite rapid development of an oil complex (Watts 2011). The foundational contentious politics of the 1960s coincided with the moment at which the sources of state revenue shifted dramatically from indirect taxing of peasants to rents derived from petroleum and other hydrocarbons, resources that were constitutive, in part, of what the civil war was fought over (the oil resources were located in the territory claimed by Biafra). In short, significant quantities of oil – capable during the oil-boom years of the 1970s of accounting for upward of 85 per cent of government revenues and 98 per cent of export revenues – provided a resource flow that did not require the sort of protection pact upon which direct revenues through taxation could be levied. The Nigerian state's statutory monopoly over oil, establishing joint ventures with transnational oil companies and its own national oil company, permitted the direct capture of oil rents. The rentier political order put in place after the defeat of Biafra came to be constructed around twin principles: the capture of oil revenues (which rested on a sort of state dispossession and a politics of resentment); and the political mechanisms (revenue mobilization and allocation as it is called in Nigeria) by which oil revenues were sown within a fragile and contested federation (which also as we shall see produced a politics of dispossession and resentment). The politics of fiscal federalism ruled the day.

Oil in this sense played a contradictory role. Its capture by the state had a strong centralizing effect but the political mechanisms by which the revenues were to be distributed (by fair means or foul) in a federal system wracked by ethnically based claims had the effect of decentring and fragmenting the polity. One the one hand, oil funded a strong military and a raft of new federal institutions, on the other it drove a vast multiplication of states and local governments (from four states in 1967 to 36 currently, and from roughly 50 local government councils to almost 800 now) and the creation of a vast state-salaried class all of which emboldened sub-national forms of identification. Oil was a national resource controlled by the state, deployed in the service of building an oil nation and a state territory; but at the same time oil as geography, as landed property and as oil rent generated a raft of other more-local territorial identities (oil-bearing chiefdoms, oil minorities and so on) as communities of various stripes struggled for their cut of the action. Oil, in short, provided a unique colouration to the provisioning pact – holding Nigeria together and yet pulling it apart. It is from these contradictory dynamics that the two insurgencies emerged.

The weakness of a powerful and organized Left, deeply institutionalized ethno-regionalisms and a state radically dependent on oil collectively shaped the sort of elite pact and the authoritarian institutions – the provisioning dynamics in a militarized and fragmented political order – that are the hallmarks of the Nigerian case. But provisioning pacts, for fiscal and market as much as political reasons, are unstable. With the onset of the Fourth Republic there has been a gradual and jagged shift towards a civilian 'protection pact', constructed still around the provisioning logic of oil, but given form by a growing middle class, a cross-regional dominant party (the People's Democratic Party – PDP), a nascent bourgeoisie, and a raft of federal institutions geared to moving money. In Slater's typology, Nigeria appears as one part militarism, one part political fragmentation, yet is radically unified by the central presence of oil. Oil fed the military machine but it also lubricated a vast patronage and rent-seeking system by which the regional and ethno-religious tensions were sometimes dampened, and sometimes exacerbated, as each community attempted to feed at the federal trough. In such redistributive and patrimonial systems, the dialectics of centrifugal and centripetal forces are always put to the test of the stability of revenue flows (the global oil market in this case). Oil is a commodity that has been distinguished historically by its market volatility but since the return to party politics, however, the arc of prices has been, for the most part, upward. Peak oil, Asian demand and speculative finance capital worked, in principle, to permit the oil wealth to continue to purchase a modicum of political consent, a shallow hegemony perhaps, within a factitious federalism at the expense of robust institution building. If institutions primarily serve the purpose of shifting money, or of converting public office into a personal prebend, then the possibility of not just institutional accountability but of any sort of Weberian bureaucratic instrumental rationality will be remote – it produced what Adebanwi and Obadare (2010) call excess and abjection. If the provisioning pact possessed its own internal logic of social reproduction and its own durability, structurally it tottered on the edge of implosion.

The design of the institutional mechanism by which oil wealth was to be distributed in a multi-ethnic federal system – fiscal federalism – which distributes revenues both vertically (from the federal centre, the level at which oil revenues are grasped, to state and local governments) and horizontally (the metrics by which the value of the allocations are determined), thus became the principle and enduring site of elite contest. In Nigeria, as elsewhere, exclusionary political settlements are associated with high levels of violence and political conflict.[12] Yet, enduring institutional failure must not blind us to the fact that the combination of oil and nation building has produced a *durable* and expanded federal system (including the national rebuilding after the Biafran war), a multi-party *partial democratization* (albeit retaining an authoritarian cast) and important forms of *institution building* (increasing separation of powers, more autonomy of the judiciary, a gradual improvement in electoral processes and a proliferation of civil society organizations). The reality is that the state has been informalized for particular purposes, vested with certain state capabilities and made 'functional' (networks, pacts, coalitions)

---

[12] There is a grave danger in seeing Nigeria exclusively through the monochromatic and often deterministic lens of the resource curse. After all so-called institutional traps reflect *political choices* and a resource-curse analysis has little to say about what particular political choices are made and why, or about the institutional effects of such decisions and the ways in which patrimonial regimes can deliver very different political and economic outcomes (Booth 2012).

in particular ways. Clearly the state has not been vested with the capabilities required for fully representational politics, to promote economically productive or socially equitable investments, or deliver public goods – justice, security, services, livelihoods – effectively and democratically. At the same time, the state has grown the capacities of security and control, through both public and private institutions, to co-opt elites while re-directing and patronizing popular discontent, to secure oil installations and infrastructure, and to provide the political infrastructure for the system to reproduce itself and withstand shocks. It has become an effective instrument to garner the loyalty of powerful groups and individuals, and direct benefits to particular constituencies. It has enabled extraordinary illicit wealth to be accumulated and secured, with impunity, over time.

Nigeria's provisioning system therefore could secure elite privileges for long periods through military rule and a robust security state, but did not require investment in non-coercive and effective public institutions to diversify the economy or impose a tax on business elites to finance security or services to reproduce labour. Rather, the provisioning pact created at the sub-national level a vast fragmentation of different forms of public authority – secular, religious, chieftainly, and so on – each in the near term competing, unstable and unable to contain the politics of dissent or conflict (the 'crises of authority'), but nevertheless *in toto* durable because of the twin capabilities of coercion and patrimonialism. The durability of the provisioning system tends to produce conditions of 'ungovernability' at the same time as selective forms of effective investment by the state ('asymmetric capabilities'). Yet these twin processes can, and do, contribute to insecurity, injustice and violence. Put differently, these pacting arrangements – in the Nigerian conjuncture of the post 1960s lubricated by and constructed through centralized oil revenues – were the form in which a passive revolution was achieved from above.

The Politics of Precarity

If the 1970s oil boom converted Nigeria overnight into a petro-state, oil revenues underwrote the provisioning system of authoritarian rule. Two logics underwrote the provisioning pact, each of which substantiated a politics of dispossession and *ressentiment* (McGovern 2012). The first was the capture of oil rents by the state though a series of laws and statutory monopolies (the 1969 Petroleum Law being the foundation stone). In effect the conversion of oil into a national resource conferred two things: first it became the basis of claims making. That is, citizens could, in virtue of its national character, plausibly claim their share of this national cake as a citizenship right. Second, it flew in the phase of robust traditions of customary rule and land rights. The logic of indigeneity and the authorization of communities' forms of rule in effect institutionalized a parallel system of governance associated with chieftaincy in the south or Caliphal rule in the north. Its life was further prolonged as indigeneity as a category enshrined in the Nigerian constitution; in a multi-ethnic polity indigenes looked to customary institutions as a source of legitimacy and authority and nowhere more so than around question of access to and control over land. Oil nationalization trampled on local property systems and land rights and complicated the already tense relations between first settlers (indigenes) and newcomers.

For the Nigeria Delta and its 60 ethnic groups, the raft of oil laws inevitably was construed locally as expropriation and dispossession – the loss of 'our oil'. These claims were inevitably expressed in ethnic terms (our land, our oil) and marked the emergence of so-called oil minorities (a postcolonial invention) not only as a political category but as an entity with strong territorial claims. The fact that oil companies, as co-signatories to joint ventures with state, were in turn compelled to pay rent – always vague and indeterminate – to oil-bearing communities (which typically meant undisclosed cash payments to chiefs, councils of elders and ruling big houses), converted an already contested arena of land rights into a charnel house of violent struggles over 'who owns the oil' and on what basis (lineage, clan, ethnicity, first settlers). The resentments over corrupt chiefs and elders, over oil spills and lack of corporate accountability, the massive ecological footprint of the industry, of ineffective local government, and community squabbles over territorial boundaries, often adjudicated by remote and corrupt commissions, all ran deep. In the north, where oil was not located, less ethnically heterogeneous Muslim populations stood in a more attenuated relation to oil expropriation. Here it turned in part on the basis for northern communities – states, local governments, Muslim *umma* – getting their share of the national cake. Resentments turned on the extent to which the Delta was perceived to be capturing disproportionate shares of oil wealth, but also in terms of the consequences of oil monies on the operations of the state itself and of a Muslim community that had lost its moral compass; which points to the second logic of the provisioning pact.

The history of the political and institutional mechanisms by which revenues were be allocated with a federal system – both vertically (from federal centre to state and local government) and horizontally (the metrics by which the value of the allocations were to be determined) – contains much of what post-Independence Nigeria has been about: how the provisioning pact works and what are its driving forces. Suffice to say that the sources of public revenue in Nigeria are proceeds from the sale of crude oil, taxes, levies, fines, tolls, penalties and they accrue in general to the Federation Account. The Federation Account excludes the derivation account by which a percentage (currently 13 per cent) of revenues from resources flow directly to their states of origin; enhanced derivation necessarily benefits the oil-producing states. It also excludes the various federal government dedicated accounts and so-called 'first charges' (including Petroleum Trust Funds, National Priority Project Funds, External Service Funds, NNPC Joint Venture Payment Account). The balance of the total federally collected revenues is paid into the Federation Account, which is currently roughly 60 per cent of the total, down from over 90 per cent in 1970. Oil revenues are the main source of public

Violence & Poverty under Boko Haram & MEND

revenue, accounting for about 80–85 per cent of the total. In the period 2001–10, oil revenues averaged 27 per cent of GDP while tax revenues averaged 6.4 per cent. In 1992 the vertical allocation system – the proportion of revenues allocated to differing tiers of government – was changed to 48.5 per cent, 24 per cent and 20 per cent for federal, state and local government respectively. The current vertical allocation – adopted by then Minister of Finance, Dr Ngozi Okonjo-Iweala in March 2004 – is 48.5 per cent, 26.72 per cent and 20.60 per cent for federal, state and local government respectively (with 4.18 per cent for special funds, and 13 per cent derivation). Local governments and states rely overwhelmingly (over 70 per cent for local governments, over 50 per cent for the states) for their revenues on the Federation Account – that is to say, the dependence on centralized oil revenues have been at the expense of other forms of internal revenue generation. These figures confirm, of course, the centralizing effect of capturing oil rents but the details, hammered out in a raft of revenue commissions over half a century, are the subject of intense contestation and controversy.

The broad contours of the revenue allocation process are clear. The federal centre captures a disproportionately large share of the revenues; the states and local governments depend heavily on statutory allocations. Since the 1960s the principles of allocation in effect demolished the principle of derivation, reducing it from 50 per cent to roughly 1 per cent between the mid-1960s and mid-1980s. Fiscal centralization reflected a calculus by which monies for developmental purposes were re-directed away from the centres of oil production to non-oil ethnic majority states. The federal centre became a hunting ground for contracts and rents of various kinds. Derivation politics, and the loss of revenues within the allocation process, inevitably became axes of contention between the Delta and the federal centre, and laid the basis for what became in the 1990s the Delta's clamour for 'resource control'. Since Obasanjo's return to power in 1999, the federal centre has tried to balance the growing agitation, and growing militancy, over derivation from within the Delta against the array of political forces rooted in the hegemony of powerful northern and southern political interests. Abuja drew a line in the sand in its refusal to meet the Delta's demands of 25 per cent derivation or more during the 2005 National Conference and in the struggle over offshore oil resources (a Supreme Court decision affirmed Federal control over oil resources in 2002). But the debates over a just derivation and the revenue sharing process continue unabated.

What is incontrovertible is that as a consequence the oil boom since the late 1990s, the vast windfall oil profits as prices rose to $70 per barrel, and the upward pressures on derivation has collectively injected a vast influx of monies into the Delta through the state and local government structures and through dedicated interventions such as the Niger Delta Development Commission (NDDC) and the new Ministry of the Niger Delta. Currently Rivers and Delta States, for example, receive in excess of $1 billion in federal revenues each year. From 2004 to 2010, the four largest oil-producing states received at least $2 billion each year such that, to take one example, in the first six months of 2006 the 23 local governments in Rivers State received more than $115 million in federal allocations. Nobody believes the full complement of statutory allocations are received in their entirety by the oil-producing states and the extent to which, at state and local levels, monies are corrupted is simply staggering (the Human Rights Watch report *Chop Fine* (HRW 2007) detailed the massive fiscal haemorrhages at the local government level[13]). The prevailing senses of dispossession and resentment that fuelled the insurgency have not diminished as successive waves of petro-revenues coursed through the region but have deepened and intensified. In the zero-sum logic of provisioning, a Niger Delta rich in oil money implies fewer revenues to the north.

What were the developmental consequences of a revenue allocation system rooted in the militarized and fragmented politics of the post-Biafra period? Provisioning politics produced neither state capacity nor disciplined accumulation but a catastrophic combination, of waste, draft, institutional erosion and economic misery. The provisioning in a system is not just patronage unhinged but of a system that resembles a huge potlatch, constituted by what Peters (2011: 60) calls 'a set of loosely interlocking patrimonial cones' manifested as factions, cliques and groups within ministries, state institutions, the judiciary and the security forces. At its dysfunctional best, to quote the former head of the Economic and Financial Crimes Commission, Nuhu Ribadu, the state is 'not even corruption. It is organized crime' (*The Economist* 28 April 2007: 56). By most conservative estimates almost $130 billion was lost in capital flight between 1970 and 1996. Over the period 1965 to 2004, per capita income fell from $250 to $212 while income distribution deteriorated markedly. GDP per capita and life expectancy have, according to World Bank estimates, both fallen. Nigeria appears close to the top of virtually everyone's global ranking of corruption, business risk, lack of transparency, fraud and illicit activity. To argue, as the International Monetary Fund has, that $700 billion dollars may have contributed to a decline in the standard of living – that many more Nigerians are poorer today than they were in the late colonial period is mind boggling and at the same time a condemnation of the Nigerian provisioning pact.

What oil-development meant for everyday life is a textbook example of what Guyer (2016b) calls modernity's aporias. It is sometimes hard to gasp the contours of the failures of secular nationalist development. From the vantage point of the Niger Delta – but no less in the barracks of the vast slum worlds of Kano, Port Harcourt or Lagos – oil-development is a pathetic and cruel joke. Over the last five years, the rate of theft of oil has fluctuated between 50,000 and 300,000 barrels of oil per day, the variability driven by the electoral cycle, oil prices, and the ups and downs of local militancy. Organized by a syndicate of bunkerers linking low-level youth operatives and thugs in the creeks to the highest levels of the Nigerian military and political classes and

---

[13] As Murray Last (2007: 609) notes, the creation of these Local Government Authorities (LGAs), 'to whom huge sums are disbursed each month from the federal oil-revenue account in Abuja, has made access to LGAs' funds of the utmost significance: any individual who can share in the control of his LGA has potentially untold riches coming to him personally'.

to the oil companies themselves (HRW 2007, 2005), it is a multi-billion-dollar business.

The gradual return to electoral politics in the Fourth Republic – which in effect produced a sort of turbo-charged release of ethnic, sectional and communal interests within the political sphere – has been dramatic. One part of this is the consolidation of a hegemonic trans-regional political party (the PDP). In practice the political order is now marked by serial electoral fraud and thuggery and the proliferation of ethno-religious violence across the country. The lethal combination of failed development and violent democracy has unleashed three new decentralizations: first, the decentralization of corruption (associated with, in the case of the Delta, the vast increase in revenue flows associated with the increase of derivation to 13 per cent) particularly to the lower tiers of government; second, the democratization of the means of violence (or the extent to which the state monopoly of the violent means of destruction has been undercut by the widespread deployment of arms locally by militia and other militant groups); and third, the rise (in part associated with changing revenue allocation) of enormous power and wealth at the level of the state governors and politicians ('godfathers' in local parlance) who have become not only counterweights to the federal centre but godfathers in their own right.

The regional experiences of this authoritarian leviathan, while exhibiting family resemblances, also reveal sharp differences in kinship. In the Niger Delta, geographical proximity to the oil resource, an all too intimate connection with transnational oil companies, and not least the devastating ecological footprint of the oil complex, conjured up a politics of resentment over fiscal allocation principles, but also a demand for community rights, the need for accountability among local governments, and how redress might be sought from the violations perpetrated by the security forces. The failure of local government, of transnational capital, of security forces, and the failures of customary rule (the chiefs pocketing so-called community rents) populate one large universe of abjection, all draped in the overarching language of dispossession.

In the north, where the forces of neoliberal dispossession were concurrent with the adoption of shari'a law in the 12 northern states, resentments grew from dwindling state resources, a precipitous decline in human security, and the crumbling of both the old emirate system and of local government. Insurgent Islam not surprisingly was directed against the failures of secularism, Western development and the fortunes of the *yan boko* (the Western educated). Dispossession entailed the loss, as it were, of material and ideological legitimacy: the moral and political failings of the state, the loss and decay of customary values and forms of authority, a sort of ideological expropriation by organized Islam, and not least the decay of the state apparatuses and the perceived diminution of Muslim power within the federation (northern power was seemingly usurped both in the wake of the death of President Yar Adua, and by the success of Niger Delta militancy in capturing a larger slice of the oil cake). All human security indexes were astoundingly low. As Lubeck

(2010) has shown, malnutrition is almost twice the national average in the shari'a states; the human poverty index is 45.88 compared to 27.8 in the non-shari'a states; female literacy in the north is 17 per cent compared to 69 per cent in the south; the percentage of married women using contraception is 3.4 per cent in the shari'a states compared to 14 per cent nationally; and not least total fertility rates in the north are over seven per woman making for a massive youth bulge (the comparable figure in the Niger Delta is 4.7). Overall the picture is one of economic descent and declining per capita income coupled with radically declining health and education standards, but also of a crisis of legitimacy for the institutions of secular national development, and for northern ruling classes facing growing hostility from millions of *talakawa* (commoners). As Last (2007) puts it, northern youth have occupied a world of material, political and spiritual insecurity.

Nigeria's Fourth Republic and its violent democracy points to the unravelling of a hegemonic bloc that had presided over the country's emergence as a major oil power. But the Nigerian leviathan retained a certain durability through a process of what one might call involution. Oil revenues were, all things considered, buoyant, electoral politics increasingly violent but contained, and the manic drive to capture rents in the name of community and party did not radically compromise what Gbrie (2005) calls the 'raw networks' of the police and army. What has emerged vividly is a deep crisis of authority and legitimacy across a slate of governing institutions – a vast political space of illegitimacy. Argenti (2007), in discussing the Cameroon, talks of the 'double marginalization' of youth as traditional and national authorities failed.

Nigeria offers up something much worse: multiple crises of authority rooted in the evisceration of a raft of customary and formal state institutions, all casualties of the ordering of power in the petro-provisioning system.

First the federal state has failed to deliver development and is synonymous with graft ('carry go' as the local vernacular has it); but this is no less the case with the institutions with which most Nigerians have some modicum of direct contact (namely local governments, elections and the judiciary, all of which are utterly bankrupt).

Second, the institutions of customary rule – whether the relics of the old emirate system in the north or the chieftaincy systems in the south – are no longer legitimate systems of authority either, and most youth feel excluded from their gerontocratic orders. Niger Delta chiefs are not unusually violently ejected from office by rebellious youth angry at their pocketing of monies paid to them by oil companies for purportedly community development. The gerontocratic order is in effect upended. The emirs and their retinues continue to function but are increasingly marginal to the lives of many Muslims in the north.

Third, religion itself as a system of authority is in question. Some northern clerics are tainted by their connection to state actors and agents; equally, the ferocious debate within the Muslim community – and the harsh debates between the Sufi brotherhoods and Muslim organizations like Yan Izala (see below), IMN and Kala Kato – reveal that what constitutes legitimate Muslim practice and authority, in spite of the adoption of shari'a law, is in question. The massive growth of Pentecostal and evangelical Christianity across the Delta certainly commands enormous power and allegiances among communities for whom the ideology of self-improvement and material gain has much appeal. But it too is tainted by big politics and in any case plays no role whatsoever in the politics of resource control.

Finally there are the security forces – especially the police and army – whose purpose is ostensibly to provide protection and impose law and order. In practice the police have become objects of utter contempt, not only for their corruption (the endless roadblocks and taxes levied on vulnerable travellers for example) but because of the extent to which so much of the urban and rural violence in both regions has been triggered by excessive police actions. The postcolonial history of violence in the north and south is littered with the wreckage of state repression, extrajudicial killings and undisciplined security forces. The fact that the police in the north are referred to popularly as dogs, and the fact that the mobile police (the infamous 'MOPOLS') are held in such scorn across the oilfields says much about popular imaginings of the state.

The involution of the wider political order – coupled with crises of social reproduction in the rural and urban slum worlds of the northern savannahs and the Delta creeks – produced a fertile soil in which the two insurgencies could grow, gaining momentum on the back of the *longue durée* of dissent. But these conditions, one might argue, are endemic across the continent – the recognition of a continental youth crisis is a case in point – and insurgencies remain an exception rather than the rule. Organized militancy and the rise of non-state armed groups did not appear fully-formed from within the rich loam of despotism, exclusion and truncated aspirations; insurgency is a social achievement as McGovern (2012: 205) calls it, and this is where the organization of the war machine (Hoffman 2011) – the making of forms of solidarity, modes of organization, ideological formation and the like – comes into play.

Crises of Authority: Boko Haram & MEND Compared

Violence is the occasion to invent. (Hoffman 2011: 250)

The origins of the two insurgencies represent a sort of historical reversal: a previously marginal and politically disenfranchised Niger Delta is inserted into the centre of Nigerian politics at the same time that economic and social conditions in the north – historically the seat of postcolonial political power – have declined precipitously. Both MEND and Boko Haram blossomed when the military withdrew from political life as a purportedly democratic Nigeria took shape. I want to argue that my tale of two insurgencies arises from the intersection of a profound crisis of authority and rule on the one hand, and the politics of precarity on the other. These two force fields are rooted in the ordering of power in the Nigerian authoritarian leviathans, and the creation of political pacts arising from deep crises of contentious politics. Boko Haram and MEND share family resemblances – they are products of the same authoritarian leviathan – despite the obvious fact that one is draped in the language of religion and restoration (but, as we shall see, modernity) and the insistence that Nigeria should become transformed into a true Islamic state, while the other is secular and civic (and also modern) wishing to expand the boundaries of citizenship through a new sort of federalism. There are striking commonalities in the social composition of the armed groups and their internal dynamics; each is deposited at the nexus of the failure of local government, customary institutions, and the security forces (the police and the military task forces in particular). Each, nevertheless, is site specific: a cultural articulation of dispossession politics (Lieven 2012) rooted in regional traditions of warfare, in particular systems of religiosity, in very different sorts of social structure and identity, and in very different ecologies (the semi-arid savannahs of the north, and the creeks and forests of the Niger Delta). In both cases extra-economic state coercion and ethico-moral decrepitude of the state figures centrally, as does the politics of resentment (McGovern 2012) that it generates. Conflicts, as McGovern (ibid.: 36) notes in the regional conflicts in Côte d'Ivoire, reveal much about the tensions between the normative and actual order of society, and the deep structural contradictions within a cultural field that drive inter-generational, class and other social dynamics. This is no less the case with Boko Haram and MEND.

Boko Haram & the Politics of Takfir[14]

Boko Haram was born in the aftermath of 9/11 and inevitably has been shaped by discursive shifts with the global Muslim world, and the concept of global jihad (Mustapha 2014; de Montclos 2014). The group's origins seem to be traceable to an Islamist study group in the mid-1990s. When its founder, Abubakar Lawan, left to pursue further studies at the University of Medina, a committee of shaykhs appointed Mohammad Yusuf as the new leader. In 2003, Yusuf ousted the shaykhs – charging them with corruption and failure to preach 'pure Islam' (Vanguard (Lagos), 4 August 2009) – and founded a movement known as the Yobe Taliban, rooted in a largely rural, impoverished Kanuri region of Yobe State, approximately 70 kilometres from the state capital, Danmaturu. Modelled on al-Qaeda and the Taliban, and self-consciously imitating their dress and affect, followers believed that the adoption of shari'a in the 12 northern states since 2000 was partial and incomplete. After conflicts between members of the movement and local villagers escalated, the Yobe State Council compelled the sect to move, and they decamped to a remote location near the border with Niger; the new base was named 'Afghanistan' and the group adopted the moniker 'Taliban' of Yobe. Between 2002 and 2009, Boko Haram as the group was popularly referred to, clashed with local villagers and police and dispersed to various

[14] This section is drawn from the path-breaking work of Lubeck (2010) on the changing face of Islam in northern Nigeria; and by Forest (2012); Militant Leadership Monitor (2012); Tanchum (2012); Committee on Homeland Security (2011); Isa (2010); Cook (2011) on Boko Haram.

locations across the north-east making Maiduguri a new hub. The 32-year-old Yusuf established a religious complex with a mosque and an Islamic boarding school in Maiduguri, along with a prayer group which he called 'people committed to the propagation of the Prophet's teachings and jihad'.

On 11 June 2009 an encounter with the police turned violent – conflict being triggered by the seemingly trivial issue of a local helmet law that Boko Haram flouted during a funeral procession to bury some of their members who died in a car accident. Perceived by the police as an open defiance of authority, in the subsequent conflagration 17 persons were hospitalized. Anger at what were perceived to be heavy-handed police tactics subsequently triggered an armed uprising in the northern state of Bauchi, and spread quickly into the states of Borno, Yobe and Kano. The violence began on 26 July when Boko Haram members attacked and destroyed the Dutsen Tanshi Police Station in Bauchi. Over the next four days, in Maiduguri, Lamisulu and Gamboru, members attacked the State Police headquarters, a primary school, a maximum security prison, the national Directorate of Employment, the Makera Police Station, the Police Mobile College barracks and several churches: 50 civilians, 22 suspected militants, two police officers and one prison officer died. On the same day, the group attacked several targets in nearby Yobe, including the Calvary Baptist Church, the National Population Commission and the Federal Road Safety Commission office. In Kano, members attacked the Wudil Police Station. All of this suggested a far larger network of recruits and leaders. On 30 July 2009, in a violent confrontation in Maiduguri, security forces captured and killed Boko Haram's leader in what human rights groups have deemed an extrajudicial killing. Yusuf's execution was videotaped by soldiers and later broadcast on television. In total, nearly 800 people were killed in the uprising.

The death of Yusuf marked a turning point for the Boko Haram. Driven underground – many of its leaders reportedly fled to other parts of Nigeria, as well as neighbouring countries – the group adopted a new and more radical leadership in Imam Abubakar Shekau, considered a spiritual leader and operational commander, in Kabiru Sokoto, the alleged mastermind of the Christmas 2011 attacks, and in Shaikh Abu Muhammed. For many members of the sect, the unjust circumstances surrounding the death of Yusuf served to amplify pre-existing animosities towards a secular state seen to have abandoned Islam and the protection of Muslims. By 2010, Boko Haram re-emerged determined to seek vengeance against the Nigerian state and Boko Haram militants carried out violent operations against government targets in the north including an astounding assault on a Maiduguri prison and a bombing in the city of Jos that killed more than 80 people. In June 2011, Boko Haram militants bombed the Police headquarters in Abuja, and finally carried out the suicide attack against the Abuja UN headquarters two months later.

To grasp Boko Haram's dynamics – particularly its goal to restore true Islam and to wage war against unbelievers – requires an understanding not simply of the spiritual and economic insecurity of its recruits but of the fragmentation of and contestation within segments of organized Sunni Islam in the north and associated various revitalization movements seeking reform (*tajdid*). Lubeck (2010) has laid this out brilliantly in his account of how the authoritarian leviathan and its developmental failures were read through the cultural lens of *tajdid* in order to fully implement shari'a as a means for Muslim self-realization. The dominant Sufi brotherhoods associated with the ruling emirate classes came into conflict with a conservative modernizing movement emerging in the 1960s led by Abubakar Gumi (himself supported by radical Muslim populists critical of the ascriptive and reactionary system of the Sufi Brotherhood and old emirate social structure). Gumi's formation was linked to his exposure to Saudi patronage and to Salafist groups like the Muslim Brotherhood, adopting the doctrines of Sayyid Qutb and the willingness to condemn Muslims as *takfir* (unbelievers) for adopting un-Islamic practices (*bidah*). In founding a mass based organization in 1978 – Yan Izala – to provide a modern interpretation of shari'a he represented not just a reformist movement within northern Islam but an all-out assault on Sufism. The movement drew sustenance during the economic recession of the1980s because the call for shari'a law invoked a sense of economic and political justice for the poor, and a type of open egalitarianism, as Lubeck says, that appealed to youth. But at this point the reformist movement fractured and fragmented among with more-or-less militant and radical assessments of what sort of Islamic restoration was required. Splits within Yan Izala, and the rise of a new Shi'ite group, *Yan Brothers*, drawing inspiration from the Iranian Revolution, coupled with the wars in Afghanistan and Iraq and the encompassing war on terror, provided the ground on which a charismatic leader could emerge recruiting impoverished youth and Qu'ranic students locally and within a transnational space – the Chad Basin – wracked by poverty, conflict and violent accumulation, but also capable of gaining adherents in high political places within state bureaucracies.

Boko Haram's critique of the state and its apparatuses – during the 2011 elections they assassinated clerics, politicians, and destroyed schools and police stations – was inseparable from the violence of the army and police, confirming for the insurgents the utter decay of the state. There is evidence to suggest that well-placed politicians supported the group, that the recruits went underground across the border into neighbouring states to avoid state repression, and that Boko Harm has acquired ideological and material support from Islamic terrorist organizations in Algeria, Somalia and elsewhere.[15] At the same time, the organization appears to have fractured, reflecting sectarian differences over killing civilians and military strategy,[16] but also the diffi-

---

[15] On 30 November 2011 the US House of Representatives Committee on Homeland Security released a headline-grabbing report, 'Boko Haram: Emerging Threat to the US Homeland', which claimed increasing collaboration between the group and al-Qaeda in the Lands of the Islamic Maghreb (AQIM) and al-Shabaab. The US declared Boko Haram a foreign terrorist organization in November 2013.

[16] The suggestion is that Boko Haram has split into three factions: one that remains moderate and welcomes an end to the violence; another that wants a peace agreement; and a third that refuses to negotiate and wants to implement strict shari'a law across Nigeria. On 19 July 2011, a group calling itself the Yusufiyya Islamic Movement (YIM) distributed leaflets widely in Maiduguri denouncing other Boko Haram factions as 'evil'. The authors of the leaflet, asserting the

culty of maintaining organization and coherence among a heterogeneous pan-ethnic, and transnational body of recruits. Whether Boko Haram represents a full manifestation of a global jihadi movement at this point is hard to say; many of its grievances concern local issues such as police brutality and the reconstruction of mosques and the release of prisoners. But there is no question that the ideology of religious renewal has provided a powerful social adhesive from which charismatic leaders like Yusuf could build a utopian community. At the same time the connections with al-Shabaab and al-Qaeda in the Maghreb – to say nothing of the escalation of horrific murders of civilians since the 2014 kidnapping of the female students at Chibok – and the complex fissions and factions emerging from the movement all suggest a form of revolutionary Islam that is still evolving.

MEND & the Political Geography of Insurgency[17]

MEND emerged in the western Delta in the creeks south of Warri, a major petro-city of the region. The political agenda of MEND was not clear in the weeks of late December 2005 except that it self-identified as a 'guerrilla movement' whose 'decisions, like its fighters, are fluid'. In fact, in a press release by email, PR man Jomo claimed that MEND was apolitical and its fighters 'were not communists ... or revolutionaries. [They] are just very bitter men' (Bergen Risk Solutions 2007). But in spite of a welter of email denials – calling an Oporoza-based Ijaw militant group the Federated Niger Delta Ijaw Communities (FNDIC) a tribal assembly, claiming to have co-opted other militant groups in the eastern Delta, rejecting any connection with oil bunkering (theft), and claiming that it was not an Ijaw militia group – there was in fact a clear political platform. In a signed statement by field commander Tamuno Godswill in early February, MEND's demands were clearly outlined: the release of three key Ijaw prisoners, the immediate and unconditional demilitarization of the Niger Delta, and the immediate payment of $1.5 billion compensation from Shell approved by the Nigerian National Assembly covering four decades of environmental degradation. In an interview with Karl Maier on 21 February 2006, Jomo made it clear that MEND had 'no intention of breaking up Nigeria', but also had no intention of dealing directly with government which 'knows nothing about rights or justice'. Resource control meant that the states would 'directly manage' oil. Other communiqués reiterated that these demands were not pecuniary and 'we shall receive no money from any quarters' (*Vanguard*, 4 February 2006).

The emergence of MEND in 2005 represents a moment in a longer arc of political mobilization that reached a watershed moment with the 1998 Kaiama declaration that founded the Ijaw Youth Congress (IYC) – an Ijaw youth group that grew out of their frustrations with more-conservative Ijaw

---

(contd) legacy of founder Mohammed Yusuf, distanced themselves from attacks on civilians and on houses of worship. The split in Boko Haram appears to be so serious that one representative of its moderate faction was killed after negotiating with former Nigeria President Olusegun Obasanjo.
[17] This section draws from Watts (2005, 2011); Nwajiaku (2012); Ikelegbe (2006a, 2006b); Ukiwo (2007); Courson (2009); Obi and Rustaad (2011).

elders and their organizations (most especially the Ijaw National Congress), and the growing state militarization of the region since 1990. Their declaration carried more than a faint echo of Boro's 12 Day Revolution launched in 1965 in which he reminded his followers, to 'remember too your petroleum which is being pumped out daily from your veins and then fight for your freedom' (Boro 1982, 117). Kaiama marked a massive cross-delta (and cross-ethnic) mobilization through mobile parliaments and youth organizing, and an explicit strategy to diversify tactics associated with the struggle. The question of militancy was always an object of debate within IYC – and indeed it preceded IYC since the so-called first Egbesu war in which Bayelsa State youth took on security forces occurred in the late Abacha years. A second Egbesu war emerged in 1999 from the deliberate attempts of the state to suppress the political project expressed at Kaiama. Militants in turn, as they had in the first war, occupied flow stations and provided protection for oil companies, the proceeds of which were invested in arms. But IYC also helped spawn its own offspring – the Niger Delta People's Volunteer Force (NDPVF) of Asari Dokubo was one, and arguably the most important – and drew into its ranks all manner of disaffected youth groups in such places at Okrika, Eleme and Nembe in a shifting set of alliances in which the borders between criminality, Mafia-like vigilante groups and politically organized insurgents was difficult to discern. These militants were not in any obvious sense – as some have argued for Sierra Leone – a predominantly urban lumpen-class raised on a diet of drugs, rap and alienation, without intellectuals and without ideology. As survey data shows (Watts 2011), many were of rural and small-town backgrounds who were the casualties of exclusions from the chieftainship and lineage systems of the Ijaw, as much as local government and the labour market, many of whom were hounded and bombed by the military task forces for their trouble.

MEND's genesis reflected a complex regional geography. The emergence of the group shifted the struggle dramatically to the western Delta – the so-called Warri axis. Here a similar set of grievances and struggles were playing out wrapped up with the complex ethnic politics of Warri, city the failures of the companies to provide meaningful benefits to host communities, and the militancy of women – most famously against Chevron in Ugborodo in 2003 (Ukeje 2004).

As Ukiwo (2007) has shown, Ijaw marginalization stemmed from a long history of struggle over trade during the nineteenth century in which Itsekeri peoples emerged as a comprador class to the European trading houses (and thereby cutting off the Ijaw). The western Ijaw built up a reputation as 'truculent' and 'pirates' and actively resisted colonial rule until the 1920s when they were located into a new Western Ijaw Division cut out of the Warri Division. By the 1940s the Gbaramantu clan – which is central to MEND's political dynamics and one of 60 clans in the Ijaw diaspora across the Delta – was involved directly in claims over land (with the Itsekeri) and by the 1970s, in the wake of the establishment of oil operations by Chevron and Shell in the mid-1960s, violent conflicts had occurred over the oil-bearing lands near Ugborodo. It was from this axis that MEND dramatically emerged in late 2005, having grown from an earlier history of militant youth groups – the Egbesu Boys of Africa, the Meinbutu Boys, Feibagha Ogbo, Dolphin Obo, Torudigha Ogbo – in the Warri region dating back to the early 1990s and before (Courson 2009). These Ijaw fighters were war-hardened during the inter-ethnic violence of the Warri crisis in the late 1990s, but in contrast to the east, Ijaw militants were not co-opted by a state government. Conversely, in the Eastern Region around Port Harcourt, militant groups were co-opted by powerful regional politicians and often deployed for electoral violence. Here the militants were funded, armed and shaped by political godfathers anxious to both dampen the youthful energy of the IYC and to re-direct it to political ends during the election cycle. When these groups began to fall out with the political class and fought among themselves often over payment – this was the heart of the violent battles between Dokubo and Ateke Tom's Niger Delta Vigilante in 2003–4 – insurgent sentiments were channelled into criminal enterprises like oil theft. As a consequence the horizons of militant groups talking resource control were in practice often local and pecuniary. Groups became fragmented and splintered – new commanders and militias sprouted – without any identifiable trans-Delta leadership or political direction, and with none of the coherence and military might of MEND in the west.

The challenge for MEND and the western Ijaw was whether it could provide a Delta-wide centralized leadership among militant groups, fractured by clan, lineage and ethnicity, around an ideology of resource control. Solidarity and leadership was provided by charismatic leaders like Chief Government Ekpemupolo, alias Tomopolo, but equally important was the role of indigenous religious practices, not the dominant Pentecostalism but the local spirit world and the Egbesu cult. Egbesu (in a manner strikingly similar to the complex meanings of the word jihad for northern Muslims) invoked an indigenous sense of warriorhood but also of truth and moral purity in a disordered world (Golden 2012). Over the decades, the Egbesu (the powerful Ijaw god of war and justice) and its cosmological order were revived in the political mobilization of the Ijaw. In the period up to the counter-insurgency launched in May 2009, meetings among commanders across the Delta under Tomopolo's direction suggested something like a unified, if volatile, command. But as with Boko Haram, the sectarian tendencies – in this case the splintering off of so-called commanders like Farah and John Togo, and Boyloaf, many of whom had no discernable political project – represented an enormous challenge for Tomopolo or anyone to exercise authority over the welter of splintering groups many of whom claimed to act under the sign of MEND or use it as a sort of political franchise.

In part, this fragmentation reflected different local responses to the serial failures of the state – military transgressions by the military task forces, failures to negotiate meaningfully – but also to the complex internal divisions within an Ijaw community cross-cut by lineages, clans and chieftaincies, and ethnic and territorial disputes. The lure of oil played a decisive role here as a constellation of groups struggled for access to oil rents, often compounded by the role of the oil companies that dispensed vast cash payments to chiefs, youth groups and vigilantes in an attempt to secure the flow of oil, often backfiring as militants and youth fought among themselves and with the gerontocratic order (WAC Global 2003; Watts 2011, 2005). The logic of struggles over oil in its various forms – as landed property, revenues, cash payments, compensation, rents – had the effect of not just splintering territory and identities but of dispersing political energies. When the United Nations Development Programme identified 150 hotspots in host oil communities, many were local, isolated and disconnected from the larger structural crisis of social reproduction that affected all youth. For this reason the production of a coherent political platform in the name of resource control, to say nothing of the sorts of rebel governance and alternative development seen in Sierra Leone, have proved to be impossible. The acknowledgements that the federal government paid a whopping $40 million in the 12 months to August 2012 to four Niger Delta warlords – Dokubo Asari, General Ateke Tom, General Ebikabowei Boyloaf Victor Ben, and General Government Tompolo Ekpumopolo – to guard the country's oil pipeline[18] in the wake of a largely failed post-amnesty rehabilitation and reconstruction programme, is not just another instance of the state attempting to purchase compliance in a fashion that undercuts the likelihood of a coherent political project among aggrieved youth (and is sure to engender further intra-group dissent), while failing to guarantee a longer-term peace.

Generation, Authority & Precarity

> In nineteenth-century Ireland and Italy, periods of profound transformation and historical trauma united particular age cohorts and shaped generational consciousness. The deep upheaval caused by the revolutionary wars in Italy and the Great Famine in Ireland heightened generational solidarity within the nationalist movements that emerged in their aftermaths. In Ireland it appears generational consciousness was sustained among the same age cohort at different times. Both the Fenians and Risorgimento nationalists consciously appealed to youth and projected a rupture with previous generations. The rank-and-file volunteers in both movements were comprised of younger men, for whom fighting in a rebellion not only expressed their political commitments, but was also a means of crossing the threshold to 'manhood'. (Wheelan 2014: 965)

Boko Haram and MEND are not in any single sense the product of single causes, any more than are their goals and missions singular and uniform. Each resides, to return to Jane Guyer's suggestion, at the intersection of the moment-to-moment existential precarity, and the long processes of a 'structure-in-crisis'. If each is in some way expressive of a structural crisis of youth that is deeply embedded in what I earlier called the multiple crises of legitimacy and authority, then one might claim plausibly that there is a

---

[18] See http://allafrica.com/stories/201208250274.html.

powerful thread linking youth militancy to a political order that, as Hoffman (2011: 67) says 'denies them recognized forms of authority'.

The significance is threefold. First, the two insurgencies must be located on a wider social field of conflict. In the Delta, MEND is one of a raft of conflicts on the oilfields in both rural and urban settings engendered by disputes of oil-property, struggles over corrupt chieftainship, violence among and between youth groups and security forces over access to oil company contracts and rents, inter-ethnic battles over electoral wards, local government boundaries and territorial authority (including oil-bearing lands), violent exchanges over bunkering territories by competing militias, vigilante groups offering protection services, and the deployment of young men by politicians for electoral thuggery. In the same way, Boko Haram must be located on a larger canvas of Muslim vigilante groups (*Hisbah*), conflicts between Christian and Muslim communities, the incessant violent episodes with state security forces, conflicts between Muslim organizations over legitimate religious practice and so on. There is often traffic in youth across and between these sites of conflict which speaks to a second question. MEND is not simply an expression of Ijaw militancy any more than Boko Haram is of Muslim fundamentalism. This is not a claim that both insurgencies are pan-ethnic – there is a sense in which this may be true – but rather that in the same way that youth may move between differing sorts of conflicts (their polymorphousness) so too are the boundaries between the core concerns of youth – citizenship, masculinity, religious identity, authority – quite porous. As Hoffman (2011: 13) points out, the overlap between nationalist sentiment, economic exclusion, religious ideology and gender in Sierra Leone are such that existentially 'these forces are interchangeable ... the dividing line between them effectively erased'.[19] If these spheres are not readily separable in practice this is because the life of youth is deeply multi-valent, embedded in multiple and contradictory forces shaping contemporary global capitalism and the postcolonial condition.

Second, each insurgency too has a unique historical trajectory while being shaped by the same now. One links youth and Islam dating back to the nineteenth jihad of Usthman Dan Fodio, the turn-of-the-century establishment of colonial native administrations, which opened up opportunities for *yan boko* (Western-educated youth), and to the formation of the first political parties in the 1950s (Last 2005). More recently, the rise of a transnational Islamism and the armed groups such as al-Qaeda in the Maghreb (AQIM) and al-Shabaab in Africa has provided a new and different historical frame, and a source of inspiration for groups like Boko Haram. In the Delta, the earlier struggles of the Ogoni people, the heroics of Ijaw rebel Isaac Boro in the 1960s, the earlier proto-nationalism of the ethnic minorities in the 1920s and 1930s and, earlier still, the anti-colonial struggles of King Jaja and Governor Nana in the 1890s, are all fully part of the ideological frame of MEND's militants.

---

[19] In the work on the civil defence force militias in Sierra Leone, Peters (2011), Hoffman (2011) and Richards (1996) all make the point that the ethnic character (the 'Mendeness') of the movement was only one expression of a broader constellation of discourses on the state, lineages, spirituality, self-defence, civic rights and so on.

Finally, I want to return to Jane Guyer's long interest in social structure. Notwithstanding the radical difference in the details of two very different forms of generative politics, one cannot help but be struck by the wider historical resonances with youth and generational struggles, as exemplified in Wheelan's (2014) exemplary account of the relations between nationalism, agrarian conflict and generational consciousness in nineteenth-century Ireland and Italy. The Irish Republican Brotherhood (IRB) – the Fenian movement – was a militant secret society that emerged in the wake of the Great Irish Famine, 1845–52. The Fenians staged an abortive rebellion in 1867 and also played a role in the mass movement for agrarian reform during the Irish Land War (1879–82) and the Plan of Campaign (1886–91). In Italy, revolutionary activity in the early 1830s – followed by the uprisings and wars of 1848–49 and 1859–70 – not only created the new Kingdom of Italy but produced widespread rural unrest in the south of the peninsula that became known as brigantaggio (brigandage) and between 1861 and 1865 was furiously repressed by the state. In the nineteenth century, as Wheelan shows, young people were excluded from the electoral process, held little or no security over their labour, and remained tied to social structures in which inheritance and upward mobility were in play. The alternative – migration to urban centres for employment – conferred its own stresses and strains. While there is no simple relation between these conflicts and youth as such, it is striking that forms of identity (national, gender) and distinctive generational contestation with the old orders (the ancient regime) – what I have seen in terms of forms of authority – play a foundational role.

Fenian and Risorgimento nationalists in turn raise a final point and this speaks to the politics of precarity. The precarious classes or precariat (Standing 2010) has its origins in the analysis of emergent forms of labour insecurity under 'industrial citizenship' in advanced capitalist states confronted by neoliberal reforms of welfare. Standing emphasizes the lack of a work-based identity, the long shadow over their future, a distinctive structure of social income and of an emergent status as a denizen with few entitlements and rights. There is, of course, a version of the precariat in the global South: the lexicon is different, namely a wageless life, an informal proletariat and active unemployment. The precariat of the global South is not confined to the urban slum world captured by Mike Davis (2005) but gestures to rural areas where often differentiation and recession, coupled with demographic growth and collapsing social structures, produce something like a 'rural slum' as Paul Richards (1996) calls it. The rural communities in the Niger Delta creeks and on the savannahs of Bornu, marked by unemployment, land scarcity, ecological degradation and the exclusion from forms of state and customary authority, make Richard's invocation quite apt. Precarious classes at both ends of the world system are internally unstable, heterogeneous, differentiated and differentiating; denigrated of a clear class identity, lacking esteem and social worth, and, as Davis says, largely dispossessed of fungible labour power and with little access to the culture of collective labour. The youth crisis as I have described it – young men in particular of differing education statuses and prospects who are violently shed from customary institutions like clan, lineage, village, chieftaincy, by religious authorities and by the state – points to the floating, fluid, insecure precarious classes of Bornu and Bayelsa.

Precarity, as Paret notes (2013), is associated politically with the demand that they be recognized as members of a political community. It is a matter of status, and belonging; they want inclusion, dignity, equality, justice. These sorts of moral and ethical claims – the politics of recognition is how Nancy Fraser (2009) puts it – became, as Paret says, points of leverage for what Holston (2008) calls 'insurgent citizenship', providing the leverage for redistribution or allocative struggles, and for representation struggles for membership (these are again Fraser's terms). What seems to matter in regard to differing sorts of precarious politics is the political-economic composition of the precarious classes and how they experience their structural exclusion and their cultural-historical contexts, and their relations to capital and the state. Precarious classes then reflect differing political orientations associated with differing goals and targets that emerge from the overlapping social spaces they inhabit.

In this sense the generative politics I invoked at the onset have differing qualities among the two insurgencies I have described. MEND could be construed as a continuation of postcolonial nation building, in which the orientation of the struggle is inclusivist, focused on allocative equality and following insurgent citizenship. Boko Haram may, in its restorative rhetoric, invoke senses of Islamic popular justice and of 'true Islam' but, at heart, it is exclusivist, and its relation to the nation-state (indeed to state power) remain ambiguous and unclear. Here one might profitably return to Bloch's theory of non-synchronism which opens the way to seeing a given historical moment as a co-presence of the contemporary and past social orders. If MEND and Boko Haram inhabit a nation enmeshed in the contemporary world of Nigerian petro-capitalism, they live in a 'now' defined by the determinations and utopian desires of earlier historical moments. How these nonsynchronous contradictions with capitalist modernity express themselves may produce radically different forms of generative politics.

References

ACLED (2013) *Country Report: Nigeria*. Armed Conflict Location & Event Data Project, prepared by Caitriona Dowd. www.acleddata.com (accessed 2 May 2016).
—. (2015). *Conflict Trends # 33*. www.accleddata.com (accessed 2 May 2016).
Adebanwi, W. and E. Obadare (eds) (2010). *Encountering the Nigerian State*. London: Palgrave.
Adunbi, A. (2015). *Oil Wealth and Insurgency in Nigeria*. Bloomington, IN: Indian University Press.
Amundsen, I. (2010). *Good Governance in Nigeria: A Study in Political Economy and Donor Support*. Norad Report Discussion No. 17/2010. Oslo: Norad.

Anderson, B. (1998). *The Spectre of Comparisons: Nationalism, Southeast Asia, and the World.* London and New York: Verso.
Anthony, D. (2002). *Poison and Medicine: Ethnicity, Power and Violence in a Nigeria City 1966–1986.* London: James Currey.
Araias, E. and D. Goldstein (eds) (2010). *Violent Democracies in Latin America.* Durham, NC: Duke University Press.
Argenti, N. (2007). *The Intestines of the State.* Chicago, IL: University of Chicago Press.
Bayart, J.-F. (2009). *The State in Africa: The Politics of the Belly.* London: Longman.
Bergen Risk Solutions (2007). *Security in the Niger Delta.* Bergen, Norway: Bergen Risk Solutions.
Booth, D. (2012). *Development as a Collective Action Problem: Addressing the Real Challenges of African Governance.* African Power & Politics Programme, Policy Brief No. 9 (October). London: Overseas Development Institute.
Boro, I. (1982). (ed. T. Tebekaemi), *Twelve Day Revolution.* Port Harcourt: Umeh Publishers.
Buttigieg, J. (ed.) (1992). *Antonio Gramsci: Prison Notebooks* vol. I. New York: Columbia University Press.
Clapham, C. (ed.) (1998). *African Guerillas.* London: James Currey.
Cole, J. and D. Durham (eds) (2006). *Generations and Globalization: Youth, Age and Family in the New World Economy.* Bloomington: Indiana University Press.
Collier, P. (2007). *The Bottom Billion.* London: Oxford University Press.
Cook, J. (2011). *Boko Haram: A Prognosis.* Working Paper. James Baker Institute for Public Policy, Houston,TX: Rice University.
Comolli, V. (2015) *Boko Haram: Nigeria's Islamist Insurgency.* London: Hurst.
Courson, E. (2009). Movement for the Emancipation of the Niger Delta. *Discussion Paper 57*, Uppsala: Nordic Africa Institute.
Davis, M. (2005). *Planet of the Slums.* London: Verso.
de Montclos, M.-A. (2014). *Boko Haram: Islamism, Politics, Security and the State in Nigeria.* Leiden: African Studies Centre.
Diamond, L. (1988). *Class, Ethnicity and Democracy in Nigeria.* Syracuse, NY: Syracuse University Press.
Falola, T. and M. Heaton (2008). *A History of Nigeria.* Cambridge, UK: Cambridge University Press.
Forsythe, F. (1969). *The Story of Biafra.* London: Penguin.
Forest, J. (2012). 'Confronting Terrorism of Boko Haram in Nigeria'. *Florida: JSOU Report 12–5.*
Fraser, N. (2009). *Scales of Justice.* New York: Columbia University Press.
Gberie, L. (2005). *A Dirty War in West Africa.* Bloomington, IN: Indiana University Press.
Golden, R. (2012). *Armed Resistance: Masculinities, Egbesu Spirits and Violence in the Niger Delta.* Department of Anthropology. New Orleans, LA: Tulane University.
Guyer, J.I. (2007). 'Prophecy and the Near Future: Thoughts on Macroeco-

nomic, Evangelical, and Punctuated Time', *American Ethnologist*, 34(3): 409–21.
—. (2015). 'Response: One Confusion After Another: 'Slander' in Amos Tutuola's Pauper, Brawler and Slanderer (1987)', *Social Dynamics*, 41(1): 69–72.
—. (2016a). 'Money in the Future of Africans'. In B. Goldstone and J. Obarrio (eds), *African Futures: Essays on Crisis, Emergence and Possibility*. Chicago, IL: University of Chicago Press.
—. (2016b). *Legacies, Logics, Logistics: Essays in the Anthropology of the Platform Economy*. Chicago, IL: University of Chicago Press.
Hoffman, D. (2011). *The War Machines*. Durham: Duke University Press.
Holston, J. (2008). *Insurgent Citizenship: Disjunctions of Democracy and Modernity in Brazil*. Princeton, NJ: Princeton University Press.
HRW (2007). *Chop Fine*. New York: Human Rights Watch.
—. (2012). *Spiraling Violence*. New York: Human Rights Watch.
Humphreys, M., J. Sachs and J. Stiglitz (eds) (2007). *Escaping the Resource Curse*. New York: Columbia University Press.
Ikelegbe, A. (2006a). 'Beyond the Threshold of Civil Struggle'. African Study Monographs. Centre for African Studies, Kyoto University, Kyoto, 27(3): 87–122.
—. (2006b). The Economics of Conflict in the Oil Rich Niger Delta Region of Nigeria, *African and Asian Studies* 5(1): 23–55.
Isa, H. (2010). 'Militant Islamic Groups in Northern Nigeria.' In W. Okumu and A. Ikelegbe (eds), *Militias, Rebels and Islamic Militants*. Pretoria: Institute of Security Studies.
Jeffrey C. and J. Dyson. (2014). 'I Serve Therefore I Am: Youth and Generative Politics in India', *Comparative Studies in Society and History*, 56(4): 967–94.
Johnson-Hanks, D. (2002). 'On the Limits of Life Stages in Ethnography: Towards a Theory of Vital Conjunctures', *American Anthropologist*, 104(3): 865–80.
Last, M. (2005). 'Toward a Political History of Youth in Muslim Northern Nigeria 1750–2000'. In J. Abbink and I. van Kessel (eds), *Vanguard or Vandals*. Boston, MA: Brill.
—. (2007). 'Muslims and Christians in Nigeria: An Economy of Panic', *The Round Table: The Commonwealth Journal of International Affairs*, 8.
Lefebvre, H. (2008). *Critique of Everyday Life*. Vol. I. London: Verso.
Lieven, M. (2012). 'The Politics of Dispossession'. PhD dissertation, University of California, Berkeley, Department of Sociology.
Lipschitz, R., P. Lubeck and M. Watts (2007). *Convergent Interests*. Washington, DC: Center for International Policy.
Lubeck, P. (1985). 'Islamic Protest under Semi-Industrial Capitalism: "Yan Tatsine Explained"'. In J.D.Y. Peel and C.C. Stewart (eds), *Popular Islam South of the Sahara*. Manchester, UK: Manchester University Press, 369–90.
—. (2010). Nigeria: Mapping the Shar'ia Movement. CGIRS Working Paper: University of California, Santa Cruz.
Mann, M. (1988). *States, War and Capitalism: Studies in Political Sociology*. Oxford: Basil Blackwell.

Mannheim, K. (1972) [1936]. 'The Problem of Generations'. In P. Altbach and R. Laufer (eds), *The New Pilgrims: Youth Protest in Transition*. New York: David McKay, 101–138.

McGovern, Mike (2012). *Making War in Côte d'Ivoire*. Chicago, IL: University of Chicago Press.

Meehan P. and J. Speier (2011). *Boko Haram: Emerging Threat to the U.S. Homeland*, U.S. House of Representatives Committee on Homeland Security, Subcommittee on Counterterrorism and Intelligence, Washington DC.

Militant Leadership Monitor (2012). *Special Report on Boko Haram*. Washington DC: The Jamestown Foundation.

Mustapha, A.R. (2014). *Sects and Social Disorder: Muslim Identities and Conflict in Northern Nigeria*. Woodbridge, UK: James Currey.

Nwajiaku, K. (2012). 'The Political Economy of Oil and Rebellion in Nigeria's Niger Delta', *Review of African Political Economy* 132: 295–314.

Obi, C. and S. Rustad (eds) (2011). *Oil and Insurgency in the Niger Delta*. London: Zed Books.

Okonta, I. (2005). *When Citizens Revolt*. Trenton, NJ: World Africa Press.

Oriola, T. (2013). *Criminal Resistance?* Farnham, UK: Ashgate.

Oyefusi, A. (2007). 'Oil and the Propensity for Armed Struggle in the Niger Delta Region of Nigeria'. *Post Conflict Transitions Papers No. 8 (WPS4194)*. Washington, DC: World Bank.

—. (2012). *Wealth Sharing Arrangements for Economic Growth and Conflict Prevention/Resolution: Nigeria Case study on Linkages between Natural Resources Extraction and Conflict*. Abuja: The World Bank.

Paret, M. (2013). 'Precarious Politics: Citizenship based Class Struggles in the US and South Africa'. PhD dissertation, Sociology. Berkeley, CA: UC Berkeley.

Pantucci, R. and S. Jesperson (2015). *From Boko Haram to Ansaru*. Occasional Paper. London: Royal United Services Institute.

Peters, K. (2011). *War and the Crisis of Youth in Sierra Leone*. Cambridge, UK: Cambridge University Press.

Richards, P. (1996). *Fighting for the Rainforest*. London: James Currey.

—. (2011). 'A Systematic Approach to Causal Explanations of War', *World Development*, 39.

Ross, M. (2012). *The Oil Curse: How Petroleum Wealth Shapes the Development of Nations*. Princeton, NJ: Princeton University Press

Sala-i-Martin, X. and A. Subramanian (2003). *Addressing the Resource Curse: An Illustration from Nigeria*. IMF Working Paper. Washington, DC: International Monetary Fund.

Slater, D. (2011). *Ordering Power*. Cambridge, UK: Cambridge University Press.

Smith, M. (2015). *Boko Haram: Inside Nigeria's Holy War*. London: Tauris.

Soares de Oliveira, R. (2007). *Oil and Politics in the Gulf of Guinea*. London: Hurst.

Standing, G. (2010). *The Precariat*. London: Palgrave.

Tanchum, M. (2012). 'Al-Qa'ida's West African Advance', *Israel Journal of International Affairs*, VI(2).

Thomas, P. (2009). *The Gramscian Moment: Philosophy, Hegemony and Marxism*. Amsterdam: Brill.

Thurston, A. (2016). *The Disease is Unbelief: Boko Haram's Religious and Political Worldview*. Analysis Paper 22. Washington, DC: Brookings Institution.

Ukeje, C. (2004). 'From Aba to Ugborodo: Gender Identity and Alternative Discourse of Social Protest among Women in the Oil Delta of Nigeria', *Oxford Development Studies* 32(4): 605–17.

Ukiwo, U. (2007). 'From 'Pirates' to 'Militants': A Historical Perspective on Anti-State and Anti-Oil Company Mobilisation among the Ijaw of Warri, Western Niger Delta', *African Affairs* 106(425): 587–610.

UNDP (2005). *Niger Delta Human Development Report*. Abuja: United Nations Development Programme.

WAC Global Services (2003). *Peace and Security in the Niger Delta*. Port Harcourt: WAC Global Services.

Walker, A. (2016). *Eat the Heart of the Infidel*. London: Hurst.

Watts, M. (1997). 'Black Gold, White Heat: State Violence, Local Resistance and the National Question in Nigeria'. In S. Pile (ed.), *Place and the Politics of Resistance* (pp. 33–67). London: Routledge.

—. (2005). 'Righteous Oil? Human rights, the oil complex and Corporate Social Responsibility', *Annual Review of Environment and Resources* 30: 373–407.

—. (2006). 'Empire of Oil: Capitalist Dispossession and the Scramble for Africa', *Monthly Review* 58(4): 1–16.

—. (2007). 'Petro-Insurgency or Criminal Syndicate?' *Review of African Political Economy* 144: 637–60.

—. (2010). 'Oil City: Petro-Landscapes and Sustainable Future'. In G. Doherty and M. Mostafavi (eds), *Ecological Urbanism*. Baden, Switzerland: Lars Muller.

—. (2011). 'Blood Oil'. In Stephen Reyna and Andrea Behrends, Stephen Reyna and Gunther Schlee (eds), *Crude Domination: An Anthropology of Oil* (pp. 49–80). Oxford: Berghahn.

—. (2016). Provisioning Pacts, Political Settlements and Peace-Building: A Case Study of Insurgency in the Niger Delta, Nigeria and the Amnesty-DDR Program (2009–2015). Unpublished manuscript, University of California, Berkeley.

Weinstein, J. (2007). *Inside Rebellion*. Cambridge, UK: Cambridge University Press.

Wheelan, N. (2014). 'Youth, Generations and Collective Action in Nineteenth-Century Ireland and Italy', *Comparative Studies in Society and History* 56(4): 934–66.

World Bank. (2014). *Nigeria Economic Report*: Abuja: The World, Bank.

8 The Debt Imperium
Relations of Owing after Apartheid

Anne-Maria Makhulu

Money is dangerous, beyond calculation, a destroyer as well as a builder of social ties, aleatory in its origins and effects. (Jane Guyer, *Marginal Gains* 2004: 11)

Introduction

In sub-Saharan Africa in the last decade or so 'bottom-of-the-pyramid' (BoP) or 'bottom billion capitalism' has taken off. So has the associated scholarship (see for example Cross and Street 2009; Dolan and Roll 2013; Blowfield and Dolan 2014). The literature spans two distinct sets of disciplines: economics, business and development studies, on one hand, keen to think about the global margins as sites of new opportunity, and those disciplines in the interpretive social sciences and humanities, on the other, that see a new market logic at work on the global limits and about which there is some significant scepticism. In the main, the extension of micro-finance and the creation of new consumer markets aim at the *inclusion* of populations previously presumed extrinsic to capital. If in the past the poorest and most vulnerable were the subjects of 'Third World' development, they are now understood as capable of unleashing entrepreneurial potential that will bring about economic development as a consequence of sound business practice at the bottom (see for example Hart 2005; London 2009; cf. Roy 2010). Rather than 'uplifting' the poor, the new economics of 'bottom billion capitalism' casts the poor as 'stakeholders' and 'change agents' eager to use commercial acumen as a means to *self*-empowerment. Yet, predictably, the spread of BoP schemes also involves the spread of new technologies of 'capture' (Deleuze and Guattari 1987) that not only formalize previously informal modes of livelihood, but also routinely produce new relations of subjectivation (Elyachar 2005; also see Lazzarato 2011). Such technologies not only presume knowledge of the poor, they also derive from such knowledge the means to new modes of governance over marginal and vulnerable populations.

My focus in this chapter is on South Africa and the forms of financial inclusion ostensibly afforded by the rise of 'bottom-of-the-pyramid' efforts there. As such, financial inclusion bears specific consideration in the face of South Africa's transition to democracy and embrace of neoliberalism.

The Debt Imperium: Relations of Owing after Apartheid

8.1 Women participating in South Africa's SaveAct initiative. This involves, according to SaveAct, the creation of voluntary savings groups in rural communities for people to 'save and grow their money'. (© Anton Krone; reproduced courtesy SaveAct, South Africa)

8.2 Participants in SaveAct's programme, which 'facilitates the formation of savings and credit groups in rural communities as a simple but effective tool to fight poverty'. (© Nicolas Pascarel; reproduced courtesy SaveAct, South Africa)

Whereas in many parts of the world such forms of economic inclusion may be relatively new, in South Africa the country's poor have long been both excluded from formal institutions such as banks, insurers, and the like, and yet, have laboured *within* rather than beyond the formal economy. Denied access to bank accounts, black South Africans were already integrated into formal wage labour relations beginning in the late nineteenth century. This particular set of circumstances gave rise, early on, to the creation of alternative and parallel institutions of saving and lending even as blacks shopped and consumed within the formal sector. This apparent paradox of economic life remains a central feature of what it means to be poor in South Africa. Consigned on one hand to survivalism owing to high levels of post-apartheid unemployment, nevertheless, most poor South Africans buy food staples, clothes and utilities in formal supermarkets, shops, and through parastatals. This fact places an additional burden on poorer households in which levels of informally acquired income are quite disproportionate to those much higher levels of purchasing power normally required for participation in the formal consumer marketplace.

Several observations follow: for one, poor South Africans persist in their reliance on financial self-help schemes such as savings and lending clubs – including SaveAct's initiative of establishing 'in rural communities ... voluntary savings groups that allow people to save and grow their money' and 'fight poverty' (see Illustrations 8.1 and 8.2; for other examples, see Bähre 2007; Makhulu 2010) – even as banks and insurers have moved to build 'bottom-of-the-pyramid' client bases; they also increasingly depend on state issued social grants (Ferguson 2015); finally, many resort to forms of deliberate incrementalism – a concept I borrow from Jane Guyer's work and upon which I will elaborate below. These last enable poorer households to survive through careful budgeting and given strategies for making 'marginal gains' (Guyer 2004).

Credit Apartheid & Other Inherited Contradictions

In *Money from Nothing*, Deborah James rightly observes that the emergence of subprime markets in South Africa parallels processes elsewhere, even as the post-apartheid debt crisis *preceded* the global financial meltdown of 2008 (James 2014). In the 1990s, the banking and financial services sector was already engaged in efforts at 'banking the unbanked', responding to justifiable criticism that a vast majority of black South Africans had historically been excluded from the savings and loan and credit industries. Beyond redressing a form of 'credit apartheid', South Africa's financial institutions were doubtless motivated by the promise of profit leading in part to the extension of loans to lower-middle- and middle-class consumers. Between about 1995 and 2000 not only did the financial sector broaden and deepen its reach; informal institutions did the same while in turn becoming thoroughly financialized (see in particular Makhulu 2010).

The Debt Imperium: Relations of Owing after Apartheid 219

Crucial to the story of South Africa's political transition then are those debtor–creditor relations that, in a sense, reconfigured the ways in which freedom was to be experienced and in the ways that households were afforded material goods, food, shelter and a minimal sense of wellbeing, if not, on occasion, enabling the satisfaction of specific desires that might otherwise have remained unfulfilled. But this is surely a duplicitous freedom in the sense that the extension of credit and the relations of indebtedness that are a direct consequence, while appealing to principles of free choice (and in a sense indebtedness has become the very expression of free choice), nevertheless rob individual and collective subjects of both economic and political sovereignty (see in particular Makhulu 2010; also see Joseph 2014; Martin 2002). Recent events have betrayed the deceit of South African democracy as debt has come to substitute for the means to adequate material redress. From Julius Malema's outspoken denunciation of President Zuma's raiding of the public coffers, to the massacre of Lonmin striking miners at Marikana who sought nothing more than a pay increase, to the 'poo wars' (see for example Robbins 2014: 1–3) – a scatological assault on local government for its failure to provide basic infrastructure, including toilets, in many of the informal settlements – South Africans have been protesting, in increasing numbers, the material deprivations of post-apartheid life, which have been shored up through formal and informal credit.

The realities of financial liberalization have in turn defined two theoretical camps in the now burgeoning literature of post-apartheid political economy. If some have noted the significant role played by the state in what Seekings and Nattrass have called a 'distributional regime' (2005) in post-apartheid South Africa and in so doing argued that distributional operations should be understood as the antithesis of neoliberalism (also see Ferguson 2007; Krige 2012), radical critics have argued the contrary. For those on the Left the state is both central to understanding the transition – its efforts at reconstruction and development, land reform, and the extension of welfare payments to all sections of the population – and to neoliberal policies (Bond 2005; Hart 2013; Marais 1999, 2011). In other words, even sites of state distribution can and must be conceived as sites of the proliferation of neoliberalism itself. 'Today, neoliberalism encompasses a wide range of efforts to organize society according to principles of market rationality ... Rather than shrinking the state, neoliberals have worked to restructure it and harness its capacities' (Soss et al. 2011: 2–3).

The much-decried 'jobless growth' of the late 1990s and early 2000s saw the productive sector transformed as job shedding shrank the agricultural, manufacturing and mining industries. Notably, as in many other societies, transitioning away from a strictly Fordist regime – though, as I have written elsewhere that shift in South Africa has to be defined very expressly in relation to the legacy of *racial* Fordism (Makhulu 2012) – the service sector, and specifically financial services, grew significantly. Yet, FIRE industries, that is, finance, insurance and real estate (see for example Sassen 1991), arguably produce little of material value; their tendency to speculation depending less on any real productive capacity and more on the fact of capital in circulation and credit in particular (Harvey 2007; Foster and Magdoff 2009; cf. LiPuma and Lee 2004). As Foster and Magdoff argue (2009: 45),

> today's banks have themselves become massive borrowers. Financial institutions of all types now accumulate huge quantities of debt as they attempt to make money with borrowed money. This debt undertaken by financial institutions for the purpose of speculation has little to no stimulatory effect on production. Relatively few people are employed in the process of speculation (say, per billion dollars borrowed and speculated with) compared to other more productive uses for that capital.

This shift from productive to service sectors – a transition to post-Fordism after a fashion (Makhulu 2012) – defined the 'problem-space' (Scott 2004) in which banks extended unsecured credit to the nominally employed. Commentators have tended to be concerned primarily with a salaried middle class burdened by enormous debt, yet, even those belonging to the un- and under-employed have been trapped by the net cast both by formal and informal money lending institutions (*pace* James 2014; cf. Makhulu 2015; Bond 2013). Barchiesi strikes the most satisfactory balance between the two positions when he notes in *Precarious Liberation* that the material realities of the post-apartheid era have to be reckoned in the conjuncture of wage work and the multiple dependencies that emerge from job shedding (Barchiesi 2011). Specifically, for those employed in the mining sector, the fact of earning a wage has to be accounted for in relation to households of extended kin all of whom depend on the meagre earnings of a given head of household. These are not, in other words, the salaried class to which James refers, thus throwing up a much more significant problem of definition. Who, precisely, in South Africa makes up the middle class or middle classes? Are these miners whose wages support upward of 40 dependants and other extended kin; are these teachers, nurses, and police – members of the petty bourgeoisie – earning minimal salaries?

The undoing of 'credit apartheid' and the emergence of policies for 'banking the unbanked' though aimed at righting the injustices of the past also speak volumes of the intensification of debtor–creditor relations in South Africa. For even if, according to Lazzarato, such relationships function as a central organizing logic of twenty-first century life almost everywhere, South Africa's history plays into this relationship in very particular ways (cf. Lazzarato 2011). Already a grossly unequal society in 1994, given the many systematic indignities of apartheid and the settler colonialism that preceded it – among these, land expropriation, mass deskilling, forced removals and dispossession – those inequalities deepened *after* 1994 suggesting that the inherited contradictions of apartheid political economy had played into the processes by which South Africa's markets were then globalized (see for example Alexander et al. 2012). Earlier, I proposed that South Africa's post-apartheid debt crisis *preceded* debt crises elsewhere. In prefiguring the 2008 credit crunch,

The Debt Imperium: Relations of Owing after Apartheid 221

this postcolony – as postcolonies are very often wont to do (see for example Makhulu et al. 2010) – anticipated a structural predicament in the metropolitan centres. Such financial storms and eddies breaking first on African shores (Comaroff and Comaroff 2006: xi) or, if not first, then in their most palpable, most hyperextended form, in so doing produced newer relations of absolute or financial power.

Interestingly, public and media attention to the South African crisis of indebtedness came to a head in 2010, the very year of the FIFA (Fédération Internationale de Football Association) World Cup, a year in which South Africa was supposed to reap the benefits of several prior years of infrastructural investment: the construction of stadia, light rail and bus services, tourist venues, hotels and the like. Yet, abruptly, in the months preceding the World Cup, South Africa lost several hundreds of thousands of additional jobs. Indeed, in an article published in the *Mail & Guardian* in December 2010, Mazibuko Jara, co-convener of the Conference of the Democratic Left, noted:

> The magical year of 2010, a year of millennial promises and expectations, is drawing to an end, with South Africa still facing multifaceted social, economic, political and ecological crises. In 2010 we saw continued profit maximisation by an economic elite, poor service delivery, growing unemployment, increasing inequalities, sustained inequities in land ownership, the brutalisation of women at home and in their communities, still very high levels of HIV infection and many other social and economic problems.[1]

Jara spoke of the climate in the post-apartheid polity in several ways, but perhaps most notable were his remarks concerning the 'continued profit maximisation of an economic elite'. How might we understand 'profit maximisation' in the context of overall deepening poverty? What logic might be at work and how, precisely, do such surpluses come into being? The larger question, and about which much ink has been spilled, not least most recently by Thomas Piketty, concerns the ever-widening gulf between those who own and those who earn (Piketty 2014). In a National Union of Metalworkers of South Africa (NUMSA) media release in 2010, the union drew important connections between prevailing conditions of contingency, un- and under-employment, and the central banking system, concluding that the lowering of interest rates and a tightening of exchange controls might ameliorate the problem of an economy opened up to global risk.[2]

NUMSA's spokesmen went on to highlight the dramatic rise in unemployment and intensifying urban poverty since 1994 observing that 'with

---

[1] See Mazibuko Jara, 'It's Time For a New Left Politics: Can the Poor and the Middle Classes Open a Path to Change the Country?' *Mail & Guardian* 17–22 December 2010: 34, available at http://mg.co.za/article/2010-12-21-its-time-for-new-left-politics (accessed 26 July 2016).
[2] See 'The Treasury and SARB are Failing to Manage Our Economy to Promote Growth and Development – *We Need Much Lower Interest Rates and Tighter Exchange Controls!*' NUMSA Submission to the Joint Meeting of the Standing Committee on Finance and Select Committee on Finance (National Assembly and National Council of Provinces), Hearings on the 2010 Medium-Term Budget Policy Statement (MTBPS), Committee Room E249, Second Floor, National Assembly Wing, 10 November 2010.

the exception of 2004, every year since liberation in 1994 until 2009' profit rate increases had far exceeded increases in wages.[3] A point that anyone from Thomas Piketty to David Harvey has argued characterizes the historical unfolding of capitalism, generally, and more narrowly the course of those post-industrial economies in which finance reigns supreme. Harvey has compellingly argued that insofar as the 'rate of return on capital (r) always exceeds the rate of growth of income (g)' necessarily the share of the social surplus enjoyed by labour is wont to decrease. 'This ... is and always has been "the central contradiction" of capital.'[4] For Piketty, this fact can explain the historically continuous process by which the system of capitalism fosters greater and greater inequality (cf. Harvey 2010).

In *Capital in the Twenty-First Century* Piketty's treatment of income versus wealth is thoughtful enough, but inasmuch as declining income is shored up by the massive expansion of credit, there is surely more to be debated than the mere fact of growing inequality in places as different as contemporary France and South Africa. Larger profits for a smaller number – 'r' or the rate of return, something Piketty claims is calculable[5] – relies, as Foster and Magdoff have already noted, on financialization and its basis in accumulation by dispossession or wealth accumulation for the few at the cost of the many. Is this not 'bottom-of-the-pyramid' capitalism at its most egregious? Further, the increasing speed with which the rate of return on capital is achieved must be understood in relation to interest bearing capital (cf. Marx 1991 and Harvey 2007) as the primary mechanism by which capital 'as a mysterious and self-creating source of interest' brings about 'its own increase', as Marx was wont to opine (1991: 516). Bearing no trace of its origins in social relations, finance capital is a form of 'self-valorising value' (ibid.).

So how to more fully understand the relationship between South Africa's financial sector, apparently limitless rates of return, and the increasing tendency towards the redundancy of vast numbers? Noting just such a relationship in late 2010, Nic Dawes, writing in the *Mail & Guardian*, argued that South African regulators, analysts, and even Trevor Manuel (former Finance Minister) himself, had been seemingly ignorant of the relationship between financialization and redundancy as the 2008 crisis spread to South Africa wiping out 'more than a million jobs [and] about five years of employment creation'.[6] Yet, in a sense, the story begins much earlier.

South Africa's economic problems date back to the 1970s and have persisted in the face of market integration efforts since 1994 (cf. Arrighi 1994; Harvey 2003). If the apartheid economy was organized around 'uneven and combined

---

[3] Ibid.: 2.
[4] Available at http://davidharvey.org/2014/05/afterthoughts-pikettys-capital (accessed 26 July 2016).
[5] For David Harvey there is some question as to whether Piketty has been successful in this regard.
[6] See Nic Dawes, 'The Map is Not the Territory: The Financial Crisis is an Opportunity to Rethink South Africa's Place in the World', *Mail & Guardian* 13 December 2010 – 6 January 2011: 17, available at http://mg.co.za/article/2010-12-23-the-map-is-not-territory (accessed 26 July 2016).

The Debt Imperium: Relations of Owing after Apartheid 223

8.3 Men seeking loans wait for a money lender advertising 'cash finance' and 'cash loans' in Marikana. (© Nadine Hutton)

development' – a system of labour reserves feeding industrial concerns in the country's cities (see for example Wolpe 1972, 1975; also see Ashman et al. 2011a) – financialization inevitably exacerbated the uneven capitalist geography left behind by the old regime. South Africa went on to sustain fully six currency crashes in the period 1996 to 2011 and a sizeable real estate bubble. The latter led to an expansion of the consumer credit market, mortgages for the most part (see for example Desai and Pithouse 2004), and to unsustainable lending driven by consumerism. For ordinary borrowers, high interest rates set by the Reserve Bank – a strategy for belatedly integrating South Africa into the global financial system – generated unserviceable levels of debt (cf. Lazzarato 2011).

The August 2014 collapse of the micro-lender, African Bank, and the antics of its former Chief Risk Officer (CRO) resonate not only because the bank was over-leveraged, but because its profit margins derived precisely from forms of lending at the bottom.

'F*** them, f*** them'; this from the former CRO, Tami Sokutu, of the African Bank, South Africa referring to thousands of former borrowers ruined as a consequence of the bank's risky lending and Moody's downgrading of the bank's debt to junk. African Bank Limited (ABL) had already been reassessed at level Caa2 on 12 August 2014: 'Caa2 obligations are obligations judged to be of poor standing and subject to very high credit risk', according to the NASDAQ.[7] Asked whether people would be right to blame him (Sokutu) for

---

[7] Available at www.nasdaq.com/investing/glossary/c/caa2 (accessed 26 July 2016). African Bank was relaunched after 20 months of curatorship, 4 April 2016.

not having done a better job of controlling lending at the bank, Sokutu's answer was simple: 'They will be right to say, "I'm f****d"'[8]

As elsewhere, the South African financial sector, including both large and micro-lenders, has grown significantly in the last decade, while assessments of its size vary quite radically. Ashman, Fine and Newman contend, for example, that the financial sector can be understood as '*appropriating* one fifth of GDP' (2011a: 186, emphasis added). By contrast, the 2011 National Treasury report, 'A Safer Financial Sector to Serve South Africa Better',[9] estimates the financial sector, comprising banks and insurers, as well as public and private pension funds, to constitute a significantly smaller 10.5 per cent of annual gross domestic product while employing only 3.9 per cent of the employed (Ashman et al. 2011b: 3).

Whatever the discrepancies in estimates of the size and significance of the financial sector, there is agreement that some responsibility rests with the South African Reserve Bank – given its ability to set interest rates, exchange controls and other aspects of monetarist policy – to establish the preconditions for a freer and fairer market in which the financiers might not gain such great advantage. Such recommendations aside, South Africa's difficulties exceed any remedy the Reserve Bank might offer. These difficulties include: massive structural unemployment (of the order of 26.7 per cent by official estimate);[10] the risk exposure to South African markets brought on by neoliberal reforms (cf. Bourgouin 2012); and the new 'imperatives of financialization' (Ashman et al. 2011b: 7) – what Lazzarato has called a 'politics of subjection' (2011: 10).

The Insurance Racket

In early 2013, I started receiving a series of emails from my long-time friend and research assistant, Gugulethu (Gugs for short), who is based in Cape Town. When we first worked together in the late 1990s and early 2000s I was researching a project that would eventually become *Making Freedom: Apartheid, Squatter Politics, and the Struggle for Home* (2015). Focused on the decades leading up to the political transition and the period immediately following South Africa's first democratic elections, *Making Freedom* was concerned with understanding a long history of migration between the former Transkei and Ciskei territories and metropolitan Cape Town. I was particularly committed to understanding the ways in which African migrants and their families had settled, first illegally, on the city limits setting up makeshift homes and

---

[8] Available at http://afkinsider.com/68953/south-africas-failed-bank-top-executive-says-f-poor-borrowing (accessed 26 July 2016).
[9] Available at www.treasury.gov.za/documents/national%20budget/2011/A%20safer%20financial%20sector%20to%20serve%20South%20Africa%20better.pdf (accessed 26 July 2016).
[10] See 'Quarterly Labour Force Survey: Quarter 1, 2016', available at: www.statssa.gov.za/publications/P0211/P02111stQuarter2016.pdf (accessed 26 July 2016). Significant drops in the unemployment rate since 2003, when it was almost 40 per cent, have been reversed in the last year or so with South Africa recording significantly increased levels of unemployment in the first quarter of 2016.

The Debt Imperium: Relations of Owing after Apartheid

informal settlements – shantytowns as they were referred to then – and how over time their place in the city came to be authorized if only tacitly.

Gugulethu had lived through a very significant period in the history of informal settlement residing first in Crossroads and then later moving to a site-and-service scheme[11] planned by the Cape Provincial Administration (CPA) and located only a half mile away. Despite the political tumult of the late 1980s and early 1990s – a period during which many school age South Africans dedicated themselves to 'liberation *before* education' – Gugs had not only finished secondary school at the aptly renamed 'Mandela High', but, by the late 1990s, had gone on to read social science at the University of the Western Cape. Aside from being well educated, he was a popular local figure and in due course was elected to political office. Grassroots politics, especially in the Western Cape, involve longstanding chauvinisms that pit former migrants against city folk. Colonial- and apartheid-era categories classified African people in terms of their levels of education, their adherence to 'custom', and willingness to convert to Christianity, in so doing determining the degree to which Africans had responded positively to the 'civilizing' efforts of Europeans. Echoing such concerns, South African ethnographers long noted the use of terms like 'school' versus 'red'[12] to characterize those who attended mission schools versus those who remained wed to 'traditional' ways of life (Wilson and Mafeje 1963; Mayer 1963). Inevitably, such asserted differences disrupted black solidarities that threatened the supremacy of the racial state. But, even after 1994, these distinctions persisted organizing political and social life in the townships and informal settlements on Cape Town's limits. Gugs, despite his degree, despite his struggle credentials – a Comrade who organized students in the 1980s – was rejected by ANC (African National Congress) brass on grounds he was an *igoduka* or country type; a migrant without the appropriate cultural capital.

But in the end, it was Gugs' heartfelt advocacy of his constituents – black Capetonians living on the social and economic margins – that was his undoing. Gugs lived in the informal settlements alongside those he represented; he lived through the long delays in the delivery of housing and services; the winter flooding, the poorly constructed homes, the joblessness; and in so doing his values came to be defined through those daily, concrete encounters with others in turn defining a concrete politics (Gibson 2012; also see Fanon 1963). His expectations were his constituents' expectations, his demands their demands, but, in a political climate that was increasingly defined by vote buying and empty promises, such integrity was not only problematic, it

---

[11] Site-and-service schemes have a long and tortuous history in South Africa. They are generally leased or purchased plots of land on which local or provincial government lays on basic infrastructure. These became pervasive in the 1980s when the South African state was seeking 'viable' alternatives to formal housing provision and used the promise of such schemes to win hearts and minds.

[12] The reference to 'red' refers to the use of red clay by Xhosa women in the rural areas as facial adornment; something, that in principle, educated, urban Africans did not use. Ironically, however, the application of calamine lotion in quite similar fashion among urban Xhosas goes some way to undermining such a binary opposition.

exposed the hypocrisies of the new state. Eventually, Gugs was ousted from the ANC; he was also falsely accused of improper financial conduct by the Democratic Alliance (DA) (the opposition) for which he was briefly sanctioned before his case was thrown out in the Cape Town Magistrate's Court.

A long period of unemployment followed. Gugs applied for a number of Council jobs, mostly positions requiring skills in community outreach, development facilitation work and public relations between Council and local communities on the Cape Flats – that part of the city most in need of redevelopment. In turn, without formal solicitation, I wrote a series of heartfelt letters of reference suggesting that Gugs was ideally suited to such work, which of course he was. I had known Gugulethu for 15 years or so, first encountering him in the context of efforts to redevelop the informal settlement where he resided. I argued that his prior experience as a local activist, during the darkest period immediately preceding 1994, coupled with his education, had more than prepared him for the fraught inter-institutional work required of a Community Liaison Officer or CLO.

I noted that over the years I had witnessed countless examples of Gugs' tireless efforts in advocating on behalf of people living in the most precarious of conditions: spending hours on the phone in his office, going door to door, communicating about the process of development, housing delivery, beneficiary lists, and so on. I also relayed how in late 2008, in the lead up to the general elections, Gugs rallied other community leaders in the Philippi East area to come to the rescue and support of Zimbabweans, Somalis and others who were placed at tremendous risk in the townships as anti-foreigner sentiment intensified. In fact, Gugs eventually spearheaded an effort to place foreign nationals in a series of school buildings and community halls, organizing local people to guard those buildings until the violence subsided. Philippi East, all thanks to Gugs, had become a safe zone in the midst of deadly xenophobic attacks against foreign-born Africans,[13] mostly small business owners, who were perceived to be centrally responsible for the high levels of unemployment that persisted almost 20 years into South Africa's new democracy. Finally, I went on to add:

> I can think of no one better equipped to serve as a departmental communicator. Mr. Sokothi knows the informal settlements through and through: he understands the needs of people in those communities, their long histories of waiting for delivery, the day to day routine difficulties and challenges of living on the Flats. Besides, he is fluent in both Xhosa and English and thus able to communicate across both sides of the negotiating table. He understands current guidelines from his previous work and has the competencies required for the post from being employed in a formal office situation.

---

[13] 'South Africans Take Out Rage on Immigrants', Barry Bearak and Celia W. Dugger, *New York Times* 20 May 2008, available at www.nytimes.com/2008/05/20/world/africa/20safrica.html?_r=0 (accessed 26 July 2016). Also see 'Analysis: The Ugly Truth Behind SA's Xenophobic Violence', Khadija Patel, *Daily Maverick* 28 May 2013, available at www.dailymaverick.co.za/article/2013-05-28-analysis-the-ugly-truth-behind-sas-xenophobic-violence/#.VTwc4GZDS84 (accessed 26 July 2016).

The Debt Imperium: Relations of Owing after Apartheid   227

While I wrote heartfelt references, Gugs, belatedly, found employment. Radically different from his experiences as both an activist and then a public official, in early 2013 he was, at long last, contracted to a large insurance firm, which, for the sake of discretion, we will call Old Progressive.

The email correspondence to which I earlier referred now came fast and furious. Though he had finally secured employment Gugs was essentially broke. In the two or so years in which he had been without work Gugs had racked up a significant amount of unsecured debt, mostly on a Woolworths' store credit card as well as a Discovery card. Notably, Woolworths, one of South Africa's leading retailers, modelled on Britain's Marks and Spencer chain, beginning in 1994, transformed its store credit model. Previously, in-store credit was extended at zero per cent interest with the obligation to total pay off within six months – an arrangement that essentially transformed Woolworths into a primary lender. We would do well to recall that South African market reintegration in the mid-1990s was achieved through a number of distinct strategies including interest rate hikes and the development of financial services. Those in the business of extending credit, in many instances, appeared to pay little to no attention to those to whom it extended unsecured loans. After an initial boon in corporate profits, vast numbers of those with store credit cards inevitably defaulted. 'Analysts noted that WW (Woolworths), in some cases, had extended credit to "a sector of the population who had neither the knowledge nor the income to service [credit cards] just yet," leading to a mountain of bad debt' (Yoffie and St. George 1997: 8–9). Such claims, after the fact, deny of course the motivation to make profit from the bottom – a seemingly essential strategy in a country that, at the time, had more than 40 per cent unemployment. Where else to bleed profit than from the poor and unemployed and from the extension of loans?

Setting aside the now predictable claims of lenders with regard to borrower financial illiteracy – a claim that conceals the role of lenders in the undoing of borrowers – Woolworths and other retailers who turned aggressively to the use of store credit cards were intent on building new forms of brand loyalty at a moment when the new post-apartheid African consumer held such promise. They were also keen to defray the higher costs of the old in-store credit model when 'implicit finance charges and bad debt costs were built into selling prices' (Yoffie and St. George 1997: 8). 'To Be the Best: More for Less', Woolworths' early 1990s business mantra, credit had to be seen to shore up the gap between bad debt and corporate profitability. Other food and clothing chains quickly turned to the promotion of credit cards too. These included Edgars, Foschini, and Pick 'n Pay – staple retailers and supermarkets – frequented by ordinary South Africans, many of whom by the late 1990s were facing extended or permanent unemployment.

At Old Progressive (OP), 'a proudly Level 2 empowerment contributor company' – which is to say that OP complies with the Broad-Based Black Economic Empowerment scorecard (see for example Mangcu et al. 2007) – another kind of predation was at work. Gugs wrote to me a few months into his new job to report that, as yet, he had not been paid. He was employed in the sales department where performance targets were linked to earnings, specifically commission. Gugs had been hired, along with an army of other black entry-level employees, with the aim of opening up new sales 'territory' in African areas of the city of Cape Town, which, till that point had remained inaccessible to OP. Former African Group Areas, which were previously uncaptured by large banking and insurance operations under apartheid, now became increasingly attractive as sources of *incremental* surplus, following Guyer (1995, 2004). Though most sales were conducted over the phone in the OP offices, that Gugs had a driver's license and owned a car from his days as a local government official, was regarded as a selling point. Furthermore, he lived in the very area of the city in which OP hoped to effect new 'market penetration', speaking directly to Guyer's notion of 'wealth-in-people', those deep social and economic networks upon which Africans had always relied, and that were now sought by corporate insurers as a source of profit (see Guyer 1993). Skilled as a political negotiator and community facilitator, never mind his Bachelor's degree in social science, Gugs was regarded as an 'asset' mostly by dint of his access to a new and untapped consumer demographic (see for example Guyer 2014).

Between March and July 2013 Gugs' monthly sales targets rose from R11,500 to R37,000.[14] Nevertheless, he came very close to meeting increasingly impossible targets. That first month he brought in R11,098 in sales and by July R34,323. Still, he was regarded as an underperformer. Then in August, having made the numbers, the insurance policies Gugs sold went unprocessed ahead of the month-end deadline and he promptly 'lost' R19,000 in commission. By early December, he was anticipating a shortfall of R30,000 on his latest sales target, leaving him uncompensated and yet expected to pay for transport, phone calls, and other miscellaneous expenses associated with working at OP. Gugs' final target for 2013 was set at R85,000 – a more than 600 per cent increase from the beginning of his time working for OP. It was evidently a pyramid scheme or, as Gugs put it, a 'game' in the face of absurd targets, shifting expectations, and lost paperwork, while he and his fellow salesmen were required to sign up for seminars in which attendees were divided into teams who then had to compete with one another for additional incentives; in the end, Gugs' remuneration amounted to little more than approximately $300 a month.

Persistent corporate profit maximization in South Africa relies, albeit not exclusively, on the profit to be made at the bottom or what Deborah James identifies as 'money from nothing' in her book of the same title – a national project of financial inclusion, mostly through access to credit, which comes to be dubbed a mode of enfranchisement (James 2014). Julia Elyachar's work on 'markets of dispossession' in Egypt where the *right* to indebtedness emerges as a key concept in the development of credit markets in the global South is also critically relevant here. She notes that 'empowerment debt' in Egypt does 'more than earn profits for banks, new rents for the state, and new sources of

---

[14] Throughout 2013 the South African currency hovered at approximately R10 to the US Dollar.

The Debt Imperium: Relations of Owing after Apartheid 229

illicit income for state functionaries. It help[s] to reshape a field of power in which the poor ha[ve] to change, even if they [remain] poor' (Elyachar 2005: 211).

There are varied ways in which poor, working and middle-class South Africans are captured by the credit market, or for that matter insurance. Debt, insurance premiums, and other financial instruments and vehicles – both formally and informally issued – bridge the gap in opportunity that post-apartheid political economy has conjured. On the one hand, the new access to loans, to banking, to credit, and yes, to insurance, promises to realize material and consumer desires and, on the other, marks the inception of a descent into debt servitude and foreclosure (Desai and Pithouse 2003, 2004). It also marks new and impossible relations of owing even as debt, to an extent, can sustain, if only temporarily, the conditions for the reproduction of life.

Thus far, I have spoken of the many corollaries of financialization: structural unemployment, foreclosures and subprime housing markets, as well as the turn to informal work. Elsewhere I have written of the ways in which women, most particularly, have laboured to ease household deprivations through membership of informal savings clubs (Makhulu 2010), which enable fore-planning, saving and redistributional care (Polanyi 2001) in the deployment of meagre wages, social assistance payments and other sources of income. For Gugs, the terms of repayment and restitution were less clear, though he relied increasingly on his brothers' wages to sustain him and his late parents' home as a place of shelter and family support, suggesting the degree to which wealth-in-people was critical to his survival. Yet, ultimately, such relations of owing produce subjection and dispossession. This is of course the central paradox of the new financial speak, which assumes that 'banking the unbanked' or lending to those without credit history operates to liberate or enfranchise those previously excluded from formal economic institutions.

Liberalization versus Liberation

The tension between the imperatives of finance (credit, insurance and profit) and the lived realities of post-apartheid political economy – the surge in debt across class lines, the emergence of a subprime mortgage market, its associated foreclosures – is perhaps best articulated in the terms of liberalization versus liberation. The former represents the so-called 'freeing' of the market; the latter, ostensibly, the freeing of a people long oppressed by colonial and apartheid yokes. South African neoliberalism, like neoliberalism more generally, assumes a ready conflation of the freedom of the market with political freedom: that 'human well-being can best be advanced by liberating individual entrepreneurial freedoms and skills' (Harvey 2005: 2). Gugs saw all too well the paradox. Having only a few days before attempted something akin to the unionization of the sales force, Gugs captured the power of finance to oppress and disenfranchise in one of a final series of emails to management in December 2013. Listing in detail the various insurance policies he had sold for the month (including the policy numbers) and the ways in which each of these was submitted to central office via fax by a particular date only to be rejected by the system, that, or intentionally ignored by someone responsible for data processing. Gugs pointedly outlined the nature of the insurance racket. The response from head office was predictably managerial. The language was empty of content, dismissive of grievance, and focused on targets. In this case targets amounting to more than 100 per cent:

> Good day everybody. Just a comment from my side – it is extremely difficult to assist an individual who does not follow the right sales process [sic] Gugulethu must follow the right process [sic] We are also aiming to get to 133% where we won't have issues like this. Trust you understand – THE AREA MANAGER.[15]

In turn, Gugulethu relied on political language – a language of justice, a language borrowed from the anti-apartheid struggle, and from Mandela himself. Describing the earlier confrontation with his boss he invoked a whole history of struggles for dignity and self-empowerment, if only performed in the minutest of acts of defiance. He notes:

> I also raised my concern with our new area manager ... many of my colleagues were shocked to hear me speaking so harshly about the condition under which we are working. I reminded them of what Madiba [Mandela] said about his first day at Robben Island after sentencing when the official wanted to know why his hair was uncut ... Madiba quickly used that moment to show his power by responding harshly so as to make his mark ... you don't just bow to anyone ... you stand up.

Amandla!!! Ngawethu!!!/All Power!!! To the People!!![16]

With that battle cry drawn from the days of the anti-apartheid struggle and directed at the heart of corporate South Africa, Gugulethu had had enough and resigned on the spot.

* * *

There are many things one might say about OP, about the insurance racket, and a very conspicuous and growing dependency on the fortune at the bottom – a fortune that is captured deliberately and incrementally in order to create corporate profit. Desai and Pithouse (2004) have noted the particular force of interest rate hikes and their direct and devastating effect on urban housing markets, putting many homes underwater and leading to the eviction of homeowners too poor to pay arrears. Political liberation accompanied by economic liberalization prioritized contractual obligations over and above the rights of people. This was abundantly clear in early 2002 as the banks urged the authorities to initiate mass evictions on the margins of the city of Cape Town:

[15] Email correspondence dated 6 December 2013.
[16] Email correspondence dated 5 December 2013.

The Debt Imperium: Relations of Owing after Apartheid

> The Western Cape government's attack on the poor of Khayalitsha [sic] at the beginning of 2002 was swift and brutal. In January 2002 evictions took place daily. More than two thousand households faced eviction. Elsewhere in the country people were being evicted from council housing. But in Mandela Park the complainants were banks. Banks are important, even revered. When the bank's lawyers get nasty, the state must be seen to immediately respond to their court orders lest boardroom whispers begin about South Africa's commitment to the rule of law. (Desai and Pithouse 2004: 855)

Homeowners and council housing tenants regard the right to housing as a right of the new dispensation – it is, after all, part of the Bill of Rights and explicitly articulated in Section 26. For Gugs, as a former activist, such an understanding of the value of the market in relation to the value of persons makes a good deal of sense. Yet, his corporate employer, evidently, held to a distinct social vision even in the face of new and emerging post-apartheid conditions. Gugs' vision is of a world organized through a moral economy; OP's a vision of profitability by any means.

The continuities between the formal and informal or moral economies in South Africa are many (see for example Ashman et al. 2011a; Bond 2013). Those continuities across formal lending and township loan sharking, for example, have very particular consequences for the already vulnerable. The extension of unsecured credit by banks to the nominally employed dovetails with the practices of micro-finance on one hand and various *gooi-gooi* or pyramid schemes in the townships,[17] on the other, encouraging over-leveraging and eventually leading to aggressive debt collection. For Gugs, however, the place of continuity between the formal and moral resided in the very fact of selling life insurance. Even as he attempted, month by month, to meet the impossible targets set by OP, he also continued to attend regular meetings for his local burial society – the place where the real work of insuring against death is done, less so than the claims of companies like All Life to shoring up the risk of death and debt by insuring the uninsurable including those HIV seropositive policy holders. Operating in a long tradition of alternative or parallel institutions – given South Africa's history of financial exclusion from formal banking and insurance – burial societies, much like informal rotating credit schemes, have served to ensure against death and to guarantee, not only money for burial costs, but most critically, the presence of others in death. Burial societies, unlike formal insurers, rely on group membership to safeguard against the worst possible fate, that is, being without moral and social support. Again, wealth-in-people is centrally at issue. In the tradition of 'penny capitalism' (see for example Comaroff and Comaroff 1997) with its own deliberate incrementalisms, burial societies and other similar institutions build moral worlds – presumably the kind of moral worlds that one former Comrade would be only too pleased to inhabit. Its moral and political mantra, 'Amandla!!! Ngawethu!!! – All Power!!! To the People!!!' is a window into a vision of the world that challenges the predatory excesses of neoliberalism.

---

[17] *Gooi-gooi* refers to an in-and-out investment.

Conclusion

In her Introduction to *Money Matters: Instability, Values, and Social Payments in the Modern History of West African Communities*, Jane Guyer notes something at once ordinary and critically significant to the longue durée history of monetization in the region. In the colonial 'interface' between Africans and Europeans, 'worrying (that is producing a folk theory)' about money took 'more time and imagination than much else' (Guyer 1995: 5–6). Interface currencies tended to be variable, remarkably volatile, and difficult to convert. Guyer goes on to suggest that Atlantic Africans were generally disposed to structural instability, which, in its turn, shaped complex and long-distance transactions. Anticipating her later work, *Marginal Gains*, such exchanges presumed 'indefensibly small increments' that nevertheless remained 'highly motivating' (2004: 25–6). For Guyer, inasmuch as these were gains of small quantity, very often hard won on the limits of empire, these always involved rational and strategic action through which incremental costs were assessed in relation to incremental returns.

Guyer's theory of deliberate incrementalism, if I might call it that, has inspired me to think about the contemporary South African milieu in which a new interface – namely between local and global markets – rather than affording ordinary South Africans opportunities for work and wellbeing has instead set the volatile and often unpredictable conditions for reproducing daily life.

As against the Atlantic Africans at the centre of Guyer's work – involved in long-distance trade in the colonial context – in the mid-1990s, following the democratic transition, South Africans confronted a new kind of conjuncture that grew out of the state's embrace of neoliberal reforms. During the apartheid years, most black South Africans were consigned to unskilled and low-wage jobs. Yet those very same subjects of the labour relation came to be enormously well organized such that trade unions would play a central role in the anti-apartheid struggle – making demands not only for themselves, but also for a free South Africa, more generally (see for example Roux 1964; Feit 1967; Breckenridge 1995; Crankshaw 1997). At the end of apartheid, as South Africa's markets submitted to reform, South African labour came to be understood as 'indisciplined' and over-compensated. A process of job shedding that was well underway in the late 1980s now accelerated to dismantle a whole structure of industrial and agricultural wage labour as the rush for the bottom took jobs to China and other parts of Asia and investors and employers went in search of a 'cheaper' and more 'compliant' workforce (cf. Hart 2002). It was in this sense of an interface between local and global competition that those without work were left to ponder the relative advantages of the old regime. It also left a majority worrying with considerably more frequency about money (see for example Ashforth 2000).

Some who recall the era of migrant-dependent wage work (Hunter 2010) are nostalgic for its certainties notwithstanding its abuses: the extreme workplace exploitation, on one hand, and the ways in which households were cruelly separated by hundreds of miles, on the other, given South Afri-

The Debt Imperium: Relations of Owing after Apartheid

ca's reliance at that time on migrant labour – a system that critics referred to as 'racial Fordism' (see Gelb 1987). Such nostalgia remains age-specific, however, differing significantly from the modes of aspiration to upward mobility emerging among 'born frees' – the generation born after the end of apartheid. Particularly in urban contexts, young people engage in ritually destructive acts burning money and expensive commodities, including designer clothes, in ways that gesture at the dilemmas of declining wage work and the threat this poses to fulfilling desires or fantasies of the affluent life. *I'khothane*, derived from the Zulu word *ukukhothana*, meaning to 'lick like a snake', involves playful or performative competition paralleling institutions like potlatch (see for example Mauss 1990; Bataille 1991) in which participants aim to earn prestige and respect in their peer group through forms of destructive consumption (see Makhulu 2012). To be sure, without any basis in experiences of real work, the logic of *i'khothane* appears to turn on an almost occult faith in the possibilities for wealth accumulation (through wanton destruction) in the near total absence of income-generating activities (see for example Comaroff and Comaroff 2000). Yet how different is this from the corporate commitment to making money from the bottom and from imagining that genuine surplus value might be derived from lending to the poor?

Shoring up the gap between desire and wish fulfilment remains both a tactical and strategic challenge while the discourse of an emergent black middle class squares in no way with the extant conditions for upward mobility. Recent research conducted by Grace *Khunou* and Detlev Krige on what it means to be black *and* middle class in contemporary South Africa, stresses both a widespread reluctance among the country's black and upwardly mobile to being labelled middle class, and the heavy reliance of those who have recently enjoyed a degree of socio-economic mobility on debt as a mechanism for social climbing.[18] One or two black entrepreneurs – Cyril Ramaphosa (Deputy President from 2014) and mining magnate, Patrice Motsepe (South Africa's wealthiest man in 2012) among them – doubtless stand in for black financial success, while in reality the elusive 'middle' remains only tenuously distinguishable from a wage earning working class and, in some instances, a growing 'precariat' (Standing 2011).

Historically, the undue burdens borne by black households in South Africa situated them within the mobile nexus of the rural and the urban as women, particularly, shored up gaps between remittances and domestic needs. Since democratization women have persisted in long-range planning to accommodate small flows of income both from formal and informal work (Makhulu 2015). But, with a growing inequality gap in South Africa, *corporate* capital has likewise turned to methods of incremental 'capture' (Deleuze and Guattari 1987) by looking to the 'fortune at the bottom' (Prahalad 2010). Commercial banks that, in the past, served very few of South Africa's poor and black

---

[18] See 'Why Is It Difficult To Be Black and "Middle Class"?' Grace Khunou and Detlev Krige, *Mail & Guardian* 8 November 2013, available at http://mg.co.za/article/2013–11–07–why-is-it-difficult-to-be-black-and-middle-class (accessed 26 July 2016).

working class, now offer savings accounts geared to small depositors – both as a matter of compliance with post-apartheid banking legislation and in the effort to make money through transaction fees, while insurers like All Life have seen fit to take on an otherwise fraught niche in a country with record levels of HIV infection and high levels of premature mortality. Arguing that life insurance need not focus on historical behaviour, as is the actuarial convention in evaluating insurability, instead, All Life claims to promote responsible future health best practices for HIV-positive and diabetic clients, all the while charging very high premiums.

As Rosalind Morris has noted, the post-apartheid 'speculative economy has a new object' (2008: 209) in insurance inasmuch as the management of both health and risk play out by an actuarialization of the costs of life and death in the context of the country's HIV/AIDS epidemic. Insurance 'enacts the value-producing dimension of risk while seemingly offering techniques with which to contain it' (ibid.). Setting up a distinction between those who are HIV-positive and those who are not, companies like All Life attempt to capitalize on illness, fear and the inevitable. They also focus on capturing segments of South African society previously left unserved, given colonial and apartheid racisms. Efforts to insure the uninsurable and bank the unbankable also mark a growing dependency on the financialization of small or marginal sums, as South African corporate capital comes to increasingly rely on the bottom of the socio-economic pyramid (cf. Elyachar 2005).

References

Alexander, P., T. Lekgoa, B. Mmope, L. Sinwell and B. Xezwi (2012). *Marikana: A View from the Mountain and a Case to Answer*. Johannesburg: Jacana Media.
Arrighi, G. (1994). *The Long Twentieth Century: Money, Power, and the Origins of Our Times*. New York: Verso.
Ashforth, A. (2000). *Madumo: A Man Bewitched*. Chicago, IL: University of Chicago Press.
Ashman, S., B. Fine and S. Newman (2011a). 'The Crisis in South Africa: Neoliberalism, Financialization and Uneven and Combined Development'. *Socialist Register* 47: 174–95.
—. (2011b). 'Amnesty International? The Nature, Scale and Impact of Capital Flight from South Africa'. *Journal of Southern African Studies* 37(1): 7–25.
Bähre, E. (2007). *Money and Violence: Financial Self-Help Groups in a South African Township*. Boston, MA: Brill.
Barchiesi, F. (2011). *Precarious Liberation: Workers, the State, and Contested Social Citizenship in Postapartheid South Africa*. Albany, NY: SUNY Press.
Bataille, G. (1991). *The Accursed Share: An Essay on General Economy*, Volume 1, trans. Robert Hurley. New York: Zone Books.
Blowfield, M. and C. Dolan (2014). 'Business as a Development Agent: Evidence of Possibility and Improbability'. *Third World Quarterly* 35(1): 22–42.

Bond, P. (2005). *Elite Transition: From Apartheid to Neoliberalism in South Africa*. London: Pluto Press.
—. (2013). 'Debt, Uneven Development and Capitalist Crisis in South Africa: From Moody's Macroeconomic Monitoring to Marikana Microfinance Mashonisas'. *Third World Quarterly* 34(4): 569–92.
Bourgouin, F. (2012). 'On Being Cosmopolitan: Lifestyle and Identity of African Finance Professionals in Johannesburg'. *Ethnos* 77(1): 50–71.
Breckenridge, K. (1995). '"Money and Dignity": Migrants, Minelords and the Cultural Politics of the South African Gold Standard Crisis, 1920–1933'. *Journal of African History* 36: 271–304.
Comaroff, J. and J.L. Comaroff (2000). 'Millennial Capitalism: First Thoughts on a Second Coming'. *Public Culture* 12(2): 291–343.
—. (2006). *Law and Disorder in the Postcolony*. Chicago, IL: University of Chicago Press.
Comaroff, J.L. and J. Comaroff (1997). *Of Revelation and Revolution, Volume Two: The Dialectics of Modernity on a South African Frontier*. Chicago, IL: University of Chicago Press.
Crankshaw, O. (1997). *Race, Class and the Changing Division of Labour under Apartheid*. London: Routledge.
Cross, J. and A. Street (2009). 'Anthropology at the Bottom of the Pyramid'. *Anthropology Today* 25(4): 4–9.
Deleuze, G. and F. Guattari (1987). *A Thousand Plateaus: Capitalism and Schizophrenia*, trans. Brian Massumi. Minneapolis, MN: University of Minnesota Press.
Desai, A. and R. Pithouse (2003). '"But We Were Thousands": Dispossession, Resistance, Repossession and Repression in Mandela Park'. *Centre for Civil Society Research Report* 9: 1–30.
—. (2004). '"What Stank in the Past is the Present's Perfume": Dispossession, Resistance, and Repression in Mandela Park'. *South Atlantic Quarterly* 103(4): 841–75.
Dolan, C. and K. Roll (2013). 'Capital's New Frontier: From "Unusable" Economics to Bottom-of-the-Pyramid Markets in Africa'. *African Studies Review* 56(3): 123–46.
Elyachar, J. (2005). *Markets of Dispossession: NGOs, Economic Development, and the State in Cairo*. Durham, NC: Duke University Press.
Fanon, F. (1963). *The Wretched of the Earth*. New York: Grove Press.
Feit, E. (1967). *African Opposition in South Africa: The Failure of Passive Resistance*. Hoover Institution on War, Revolution and Peace. Stanford, CA: Stanford University.
Ferguson, J. (2007). 'Formalities of Poverty: Thinking About Social Assistance in Neoliberal South Africa'. *African Studies Review* 50(2): 71–86.
—. (2015). *Give a Man a Fish: Reflections on the New Politics of Distribution*. Durham, NC: Duke University Press.
Foster, J.B. and F. Magdoff (2009). *The Great Financial Crisis: Causes and Consequences*. New York: Monthly Review Press.
Gelb, S. 1987. 'Making Sense of the Crisis'. *Transformation* 5: 33–50.

Gibson, N. (2012). 'What Happened to the "Promised Land"? A Fanonian Perspective on Post-Apartheid South Africa'. *Antipode* 44(1): 51–73.

Guyer, J.I. (1993). 'Wealth in People and Self-Realization in Equatorial Africa'. *Man* 28(2): 243–65.

—. (1995). *Money Matters: Instability, Values, and Social Payments in the Modern History of West African Communities*. Portsmouth, NH: Heinemann.

—. (2004). *Marginal Gains: Monetary Transactions in Atlantic Africa*. Chicago, IL: University of Chicago Press.

—. (2014). 'Pauper, Percentile, Precarity'. Paper delivered at the History of Poverty in Africa Conference, Columbia University, 6 March.

Hart, G. (2002). *Disabling Globalization: Places of Power in Post-Apartheid South Africa*. Berkeley, CA: University of California Press.

—. (2013). *Rethinking the South African Crisis: Nationalism, Populism, Hegemony*. Durban: University of KwaZulu-Natal Press.

Hart, S. (2005). *Capitalism at the Crossroads: The Unlimited Business Opportunities in Solving the World's Most Difficult Problems*. Upper Saddle River, NJ: Prentice Hall.

Harvey, D. (2003). *The New Imperialism*. New York: Oxford University Press.

—. (2005). *A Brief History of Neoliberalism*. New York: Oxford University Press.

—. (2007[1982]). *The Limits to Capital*. Chicago, IL: University of Chicago Press.

—. (2010). *The Enigma of Capital: And the Crises of Capitalism*. Oxford: Oxford University Press.

Hunter, M. (2010). *Love in the Time of AIDS: Inequality, Gender, and Rights in South Africa*. Bloomington, IN: Indiana University Press.

James, D. (2014). *Money from Nothing: Indebtedness and Aspiration in South Africa*. Stanford, CA: Stanford University Press.

Joseph, M. (2014). *Debt to Society: Accounting for Life under Capitalism*. Minneapolis, MN: University of Minnesota.

Krige, D. (2012). 'Fields of Dreams, Fields of Schemes: Ponzi Finance and Multilevel Marketing in South Africa'. *Africa* 82(1): 68–90.

Lazzarato, M. (2011). *The Making of the Indebted Man*. Amsterdam: Semiotext(e).

LiPuma, E. and B. Lee (2004). *Financial Derivatives and the Globalization of Risk*. Durham, NC: Duke University Press.

London, T. (2009). 'Making Better Investments at the Base of the Pyramid'. *Harvard Business Review* 87(5):106–13.

Makhulu, A.-M. (2010). 'The Search for Economic Sovereignty'. In Makhulu et al., *Hard Work, Hard Times*.

—. (2012). 'The Conditions for after Work: Financialization and Informalization in Post-Transition South Africa'. *PMLA* 127(4): 782–99.

—. (2015). *Making Freedom: Apartheid, Squatter Politics, and the Struggle for Home*. Durham, NC: Duke University Press.

Makhulu, A.-M., B.A. Buggenhagen and S. Jackson (eds) (2010). *Hard Work, Hard Times: Global Volatility and African Subjectivities*. Berkeley, CA: University of California Press.

Mangcu, X., G. Marcus, K. Shubane and A. Hadland (eds) (2007). *Visions of

Black Economic Empowerment. Auckland Park, SA: Jacana Media.
Marais, H. (1999). *South Africa, Limits to Change: The Political Economy of Transition*. New York: Zed Books.
—. (2011). *South Africa Pushed to the Limit: The Political Economy of Change*. New York: Palgrave.
Martin, R. (2002). *Financialization of Daily Life*. Philadelphia, PA: Temple University Press.
Marx, K. (1991). *Capital: The Process of Capitalist Production as a Whole, Volume III*. London: Penguin Books.
Mauss, M. (1990[1950]). *The Gift: The Form and Reason for Exchange in Archaic Societies*. W.D. Halls (trans.). London: Routledge.
Mayer, P. (1963). *Townsmen or Tribesmen: Conservatism and the Process of Urbanization in a South African City*. Cape Town, SA: Oxford University Press.
Morris, R. (2008). 'Rush/Panic/Rush: Speculations on the Value of Life and Death in South Africa's Age of AIDS'. *Public Culture* 20(2): 199–231.
Piketty, T. (2014). *Capital in the Twenty-First Century*. Boston, MA: Harvard University Press.
Polanyi, K. (2001). *The Great Transformation: The Political and Economic Origins of our Times*. Boston, MA: Beacon Press.
Prahalad, C.K. (2010). *The Fortune at the Bottom of the Pyramid: Eradicating Poverty through Profits*, 5th edn. Upper Saddle River, NJ: Prentice Hall.
Reinhart, C.M. and K.S. Rogoff (2011). 'From Financial Crash to Debt *Crisis*'. *American Economic Review* 101(5): 1676–1706.
Robbins, S. (2014). 'Poo Wars as Matter Out of Place: "Toilets for Africa" in Cape Town'. *Anthropology Today* 30(1): 1–3.
Roux, E. (1964). *Time Longer Than Rope: A History of the Black Man's Struggle for Freedom in South Africa*. Madison, WI: University of Wisconsin Press.
Roy, A. (2010). *Poverty Capital: Microfinance and the Making of Development*. London: Taylor & Francis.
Sassen, S. (1991). *The Global City: New York, London, Tokyo*. Princeton, NJ: Princeton University Press.
Scott, D. (2004). *Conscripts of Modernity: The Tragedy of Colonial Enlightenment*. Durham, NC: Duke University Press.
Seekings, J. and N. Nattrass (2005). *Class, Race, and Inequality in South Africa*. New Haven, CT: Yale University Press.
Soss, J., R.C. Fording and S.F. Schram (2011). *Disciplining the Poor: Neoliberal Paternalism and the Persistent Power of Race*. Chicago, IL: University of Chicago Press.
Standing, G. (2011). *The Precariat: The New Dangerous Class*. London: Bloomsbury Academic.
Wilson, M. and A. Mafeje (1963). *Langa: A Study of Social Groups in an African Township*. Cape Town, SA: Oxford University Press.
Wolpe, H. (1972). 'Capitalism and Cheap Labour-Power in South Africa: From Segregation to Apartheid'. *Economy and Society* 1(4): 425–56.
—. (1975). 'The Theory of Internal Colonialism: The South African Case'. In I. Oxaal, T. Barnett and D. Booth (eds), *Beyond the Sociology of Development:*

Economy and Society in Latin America and Africa. London: Routledge.

Yoffie, D. and A. St. George (1997). 'Woolworths South Africa'. *Harvard Business School*, 9–798–026: 1–21.

9 Marginal Men & Urban Social Conflicts
Okada *Riders in Lagos*

Gbemisola Animasawun

Many of us (okada riders) are not happy with the ban because we see okada business as the only thing we could do. No need of any capital base and it's very lucrative. There are some of us who conspire with armed robbers and other criminals like hired killers for the sake of money from okada charter. (Moyo Fabiyi *P.M. News* 20 November 2012)

We have okada too in Rwanda. It is a lucrative business. A good number of people are doing okada business in Rwanda. But their activities are well-regulated. There are rules and regulations that define the limit of their operation. We also organise them into groups, such as association of owners and association of operators. The groups help in ensuring that the rules and regulations are duly observed. Because we have rules, institutions and structures in place, we do not have much problem with okada operators. (Rwandan President, Paul Kagame, quoted in Ilevbare 2013)

@desmondc03: FOOTBALL inside POLITICS: Governor Fashola who's a Manchester untd fan has rendered 80 per cent of Chelsea fans (okada rider) jobless in Lagos. (Nwachukwu Egbunike 2012)

'Struggle' Economy & City Life

In her preface to the important volume, *Money Struggles and City Life*, Jane Guyer (2002: ix-xvi) raises interesting questions about the ways in which those of us who live and work in urban Africa witness what de Certeau (1984) describes as the 'practice of everyday life', which 'encompasses systems of employment, provisioning, and meaning-making of impressive magnitude and relentless resilience' (Guyer 2002: ix). In reflecting on the 'domain of human struggles and achievement' – particularly in Ibadan and other urban centres in southern Nigeria – within which 'chronic uncertainty is pervasive' (ibid.: x), Guyer argues that '(c)ase studies have to be a source both of data for analysis and of witnessed documentation of the realities of life' (ibid.). In this chapter, I take up the task that she commended to African(ist) scholars in the 'context of the intellectual and empirical challenges' of 1990s Nigeria by focusing on an otherwise marginal phenomenon, albeit one that reflects the deep crisis of urban life in Africa in the post-structural adjustment era – an era which still bears not only the structural, economic, including fiscal,[1] and social disasters imposed by Structural Adjustment Programmes, but also dramatizes the consequences of authoritarian rule with its attendant lack of urban planning.

Focusing on 'the wretchedly negligent, repressive and rapacious military government of Sani Abacha (1993–1998)', Guyer (ibid.: xi) describes the challenges of popular urban life in Nigeria in this period to include:

> petro shortage, personal insecurity, long interruptions in electricity and water service, multiple road blocks ... and sheer worry about the futures ... the shocking waste of hope and energy as children failed to get medical care, very brilliant students failed to shape careers, farmers and traders failed to get goods to market before they rotted ... Life was fearful and profoundly discouraging.

While the situation in Nigeria in general – and urban areas specifically – has improved slightly since Guyer made this observation, particularly with the end of repressive military regime and the enthronement of democratic rule, life in urban Nigeria remains as Guyer concluded in late 1990s: fearful and profoundly discouraging.

Therefore, in this chapter, I show why the case study approach for which Guyer argued in this environment remains 'first and foremost ... a moral and political imperative, as well as a pragmatic solution to the penury of resources for research [in Nigeria]' (2002: xi). In examining social conflicts provoked by the phenomenon of greater informalization of the economy and the expansion of the 'popular economy' as evident in the *okada*[2] (commercial motorcycle) as a popular means of transportation in urban Lagos, I engage with what Guyer (ibid.) has succinctly described as one of the strategies 'within popular economy that has continued to provide for and employ people in spite of massive theft, idiosyncratic intervention, and policy incoherence at the top' in Nigeria.

Here, I take her emphasis on popular economy as reflected in what I will call *struggle economy* to capture how claims by and against those at the margins of the economy are 'articulated and put forward into the public realm' (Guyer and Denzer 2013: 57), on the one hand, through government's laws and actions, and on the other hand, through protests and demonstrations by the marginalized. Struggle economy points to those aspects of the popular economy in urban Africa dominated by the most marginalized, whose incomes are unstable and chronically insufficient for survival in the expensive cities in which they work and live, and who, nonetheless, face extreme precarity and danger in the work with which they strive to make a living. Even though people employ different forms

---

[1] Guyer emphasizes currency devaluation as a major consequence of this era (2002: xi).
[2] Okada is the name of a town in Edo State in southern Nigeria, the hometown of one of Nigeria's prominent millionaires Gabriel Igbinedion, founder of the first domestic airline established in the 1980s named 'Okada Air', after which the motorcycle taxi in most urban areas in Nigeria is named.

Marginal Men: *Okada* Riders in Lagos

9.1 A crowd of *okada* riders in Lagos (reproduced courtesy *TheNEWS*, Lagos, Nigeria)

of resistance in the struggle economy, the economy also makes sense to them as they 'appear to be somewhat accustomed to [the] turbulence and policy confusion' (Guyer 2004: 8) responsible for their unstable income and precarious existence.

The Motorcycle Taxi in Contemporary African Cities

African cities provide spectacular vistas of urban chaos, resilience, limited capacity for organization, potentials for improvement and the stark reality of striving for the majority of their populaces. More than five decades ago, Peter Gutkind (1963), while decrying the insensitivity of governments, described African cities as places with large numbers of men who clutter cities, choking corridors of government offices, milling around building sites, docks, bus parks, markets, shopping centres, pouncing on car owners to wash or watch. The reality has not changed much since then. In fact, the intensity of what he described has increased as the explosion of populations and rural–urban migration put greater pressure on infrastructures, the economies and therefore lives of the denizens of cities in Africa. As Africa continues to urbanize in what Patrick Chabal (2009: 154) describes as a 'dizzyingly rapid pace', life is 'unremittingly bleak' for most young people in cities.

In their 'relentless determination to mitigate the effects' (Guyer 2002: xi) of the harsh economic realities on the continent, many young people have devised diverse means of striving and surviving. The lack of accommodation in the formal sector for both the educated and uneducated has pushed many into diverse forms of legal, para-legal and illegal trades and entrepreneurship. This partly explains the proliferation of markets on major roads and street corners many of which emerge in contradiction to set rules by government at different tiers. This phenomenon brings about frequent confrontations that in many instances lead to violence between the traders and state authorities. These confrontations have not only turned the streets to sites of struggles and conflicts (Adebanwi 2012: 1), they also mirror, new 'temporal horizons' as 'new configurations of [social] power ... and plausible social action form and reform' (Guyer 2002: xi). The inevitability of socio-economic and political conflicts in the contemporary African city is understandable because most of these cities 'are growing demographically without necessarily developing economically or politically along any of the known pathways of the past' (ibid.: xii). In most cases, African cities are not industrializing, they not 'centralizing administrative functions and connecting them to regional policies ... They are not growing because of opportunity but rather because the countryside has often become a more difficult place to make a living, in some places because of disorder' (ibid.).

One of the defining features of African cities in the last three decades has been the exploding demographic growth accompanied by the lack of government capacity to provide infrastructure and services for the growing population. One of the areas where this is obviously felt is the transport sector which has given rise to disparate actors including motorcycle taxi operators, commonly known in Nigeria as *okada* riders. This important, and needed, informal urban transportation system complicates the challenges of urban governance. Richards (2009) describes the *okada* as a motorcycle taxi found in many congesting cities in the developing world. The motorcycle taxi has different popular names across sub-Saharan Africa and the global South. It is called *zemidjan* in Benin and Togo, *bendskin* in Cameroun, *okada* in southern Nigeria and Accra, Ghana, *achaba* in northern Nigeria, *kabu-kabu* in Niger, *peen peen* in Liberia, *pikipiki* in Kenya and *boda-boda* in Uganda and Kenya. In Indonesia, it is called *ojek; habal-habal or skylab* in the Philipinnes; *motoesai rap chang* in Thailand; and *xeom* in Vietnam (Mungai 2014). In African towns and cities, the activities of the riders have created a motorcycle economy based on the types of micro-businesses undertaken within the larger economy from Douala to Lagos, Accra to Dar es Salam and Kinshasa to Kigali (Olvera et al. 2012).

In most of these cities, there are three main actors in the motorcycle economy. These are the dealers who in most cases are rich business men who import the motorcycles, mostly from China and India. Next on the ladder are the owners comprising individuals and cooperative societies who sometimes pay for the motorcycles in instalments, with interest in most instances. Occupying the lowest rung of the ladder are the drivers who operate on terms given to them by either the cooperative societies or individual owners who will or cannot drive them. Out of the three, the worst affected by government bans are the drivers who in most cases face the danger of starving without a job while they also must service debts owed to the owners and sometimes the dealers.

In a comparative study of Nigeria, Cameroon and Uganda, Ajay Kumar (2011: 1) argues that 'governance failure and weak (transport) sector performance' and failure in tailoring economic and political policies to local contexts constitute the underlying cause of the conflict between the *okada* riders and governments across many African cities. The remote factors that have made the motorcycles taxi riders indispensable could be located in the failure of government control and provision of bus transport services that coincided with the effects of the Structural Adjustment Programmes of the 80s and 90s Africa. Realizing their inability to sustain the full and partial subsidies it had offered, governments left the sector without any plan for its management, thus leaving it open and accessible to all comers, including *okada* operators.

Increasingly, the *okada* drivers have continued to provide speed, relative comfort, home deliveries, flexibility and access to thinly populated neighbourhoods or remote parts of the cities that are not commercially viable for large buses and taxi cabs. Their presence continues to have impact on everyday city economies, settlement patterns, safety and security, and street trading. Contrary to the assumption by some that they serve only the poor, *okadas* occupy a strategic position as the main driver of e-commerce as attested to by the leading actors in Nigeria (for instance, Jumia and Konga) because they ensure prompt delivery of goods ordered online to the doorstep of customers (Mungai 2014) thereby meeting the needs of the middle class.

However, the relationship between the *okada* riders and many governments in Africa is dogged by frequent violent expression of disaffection owing to proscriptions, restrictions and disputes over exorbitant levies charged by government agents. Since it constitutes a refuge for many jobless young men and a means of augmenting income for many students and civil servants, proscribing the motorcycle taxis from the most lucrative routes pitches the government against a critical mass of the population comprising the poor and the middle class who largely depend on their services. In places like Kigali, Rwanda the government has been able to enforce strict licensing laws and helmet regimes as a way of curbing their excesses and reducing road accidents without necessarily making them lose their incomes.

However, Murdock (2013) reports that it has been difficult to achieve such a balance without threatening livelihoods of those on the margin in places like Lagos, because they are 'far more lawless and hectic than Kigali.' The resistance against bans in some African cities such as Lagos can be understood in the context of the view of a driver in Lagos who states that 'the danger of driving a motorcycle is much less than the danger of starving without a job' (ibid.). Similarly, a *boda-boda* driver from Kampala, Sam Kibuuka, asserts that 'I would rather ride a *boda-boda* than starve to death' (Ssenkaaba 2013). This reveals the everyday hunger and fear of starvation as critical in understanding not only the operation of the motorcycle taxis, but also the desperation of the riders. Urban governments seem to ignore this when they ban motorcycle taxis, even though they claim that the ban is also in the interest of the riders.

The frustrations and resistance of the *okada* riders in the Ghanaian capital, Accra, is not different from Lagos going by the accounts of Martin-Otteng Ababio and Ernest Agyemang (2015: 25). The riders, sustained by the mutually dependent relationship with the middle class, have remained 'an unofficial but thriving mobility option' despite government banning.

There has thus emerged a seeming alliance between the marginal men and the urban middle class to disobey or ignore the government. This is understandable given that, as Kumar and Barrett (2008) found in a study of 14 major African cities (including Lagos) that are 'stuck in traffic', there is an average of six seats to every 1,000 residents on the large buses while there are 30–40 seats to 1,000 residents in middle-income countries of Latin America, Eastern Europe, the Middle East and Asia (World Bank, quoted in Kumar and Barrett). Therefore, the acuteness of the shortage of options for mobility in Africa persists. Consequently, the motorcycle taxi riders, despite the associated risks to themselves and the threats to safety and security in cities, will remain 'king in African cities' (Mungai 2014).

Lagos State Government versus Okada Riders: When Enforcement Clashes with Striving

The frequent clashes and tense relationship between members of the Amalgamated Commercial Motorcycle Owners and Riders Association of Nigeria (ACCOMORAN) and other associations of commercial motorcycle riders and many state governments in Nigeria provide a veritable context for examining how resistance and conflict between the state and urban marginal men or the underclass have defined the political economy of everyday life for the latter across Nigerian cities. In Lagos, the erstwhile capital of Africa's most populous country, the demographic details of the *okada* riders graphically depicts marginal men as explained by Mehretu et al. (2000: 14) as those individuals and communities locked in a 'complex situation of disadvantage and experiencing vulnerabilities arising from hostile environmental, cultural, social, political and economic factors'. Miller (1987: 30) posits that such people have no 'economic alternative'. Given the fact that a majority of Nigerians live on less than $2 a day, it is clear that the vast majority of Nigerians live on the margins – economic, social and political. As result of this, many have devised legal, para-legal and illegal means of surviving; ranging from street hawking to selling of foreign currencies and petroleum products, and others like begging, prostituting, touting, etc. Evidently, the streets of commercial cities such as Lagos are a platform for meeting the needs of both the law-abiding citizens and the outlaws.

As one of the means of work and survival, the *okada* phenomenon has become a permanent feature of urban life in Lagos and all other Nigerian cities. It is seen by some as an informal and alternative means of 'mass transit'. Kayode Oyesiku (2002) traces the steady rise and ubiquity of *okadas* on roads across cities in Nigeria since the 1970s to the unaffordable cost of new vehi-

Marginal Men: *Okada* Riders in Lagos 245

9.2 'Mass transit': this *okada* rider with seven passengers is both a reflection of the crisis of urban mass transit in Lagos and of the danger to safety that the *okada* riders constitute. (Reproduced courtesy *TheNEWS*, Lagos, Nigeria)

cles, deterioration of intra-city transport systems and upsurge in the population of many cities. Therefore, as population increased, the number of vehicles available for transportation was decreasing. In 1983, there were 16,500 vehicles registered for public transportation and by 1988, the figure had reduced to 1,500 amidst a rapidly growing population, which made the emergence of an alternative means of intra-city transportation expedient (Ikeano and Akinrolabu 1991). Olubomehin (2012) argues that the economic depression of the 1980s was the impetus for the search of an alternative means of intra-city transportation such as the *okada*, which has since become a permanent feature in Nigerian cities.

Okada as a means of commercial transport began in southern Nigeria in Calabar in the early 1970s and in Yola in northern Nigeria and increased nationwide after the mass retrenchment of civil servants in 1975/76 (Adesanya 1998). The use of *okada* as a means of public transport in Lagos started in the 1980s in the Agege suburb as a part-time means of supplementing earnings after work hours by people in paid employment (Kumar 2011). By the early 1990s, it had become a principal or only means of employment and by the 2000s, when democracy was restored, it became the major item of poverty eradication/alleviation programmes of state governments across the country.

Until they were banned or restricted, *okada* riders plied all routes including highways in Lagos metropolis and environs such as Epe, Ikorodu, Badagry,

Mushin, Oshodi, Alimosho, Ikeja, Victoria Island, Obalende and Surulere. Commuters found them effective both in the urban centres and the rural suburbs. For instance, Kujenya (2014: 7) states: 'Live in Lagos and you would see them – *okada* riders on the move often with two or more males aboard or in some cases, with a female sandwiched within them. Many believe their intentions are solely commercial driven, while others believe there is more to them.' Tola Adeniyi (2014) describes a typical picture of riding on the *okada* as humiliating especially for women because of 'the indignity of having to roll up your skirts past your knees, sometime revealing your underwear? A respectable housewife, a corporate lady, a college principal, all having to sit behind a stinking dirty *okada* rider? Some-times body hugging' in order not to fall off. Thus, this common everyday means of transportation for most Lagosians is one that involves a measure of humiliation.

In addition to being a faster means of mobility, the *okada* was initially hailed and celebrated as a veritable alternative to white-collar jobs. At the inception of the Fourth Republic in 1999, the *okada* served divergent purposes. While it was used as a distributive good by patrons within the political class in wooing swing voters and retaining core voters, especially the subalterns, it eased mobility for many commuters in urban areas with their traffic gridlocks. Also, it helped mobility in the rural areas where there is no efficient public transportation system just as it offered a source of livelihood for the riders. The Governor of Edo State and former leader of the Nigerian Labour Congress (NLC), Adams Oshiomole, even identified with the *okada* riders as members of the working class as the debate on whether to ban them or not was raging. Upon his re-election in 2013, Oshiomole said 'It is a class issue and I belong to the working class, so I cannot ban *okada*. First, I believe that *okada* is a response to certain deficit in our intra-urban transportation system' (Inyang 2012). A former governor of Anambra state, Peter Obi, also expressed similar sentiment 'I agree that *Okada* contributes to crime, but we must also accept that many of them are also good people and we cannot punish the multitude because of the sins of a few' (*Information Nigeria* 2014).

However, owing to an increasing number of deaths and maiming of commuters, including cases of criminality involving the use of the *okada*, many state governments had to either ban or restrict *okada* riders to limited routes. This decision had its harshest impact in Lagos metropolis, being the commercial nerve of the country and the city with the most mobile economy in Nigeria. This decision precipitated instant reaction from the *okada* riders under aegises such as ACCOMORAN, which saw the ban as a form of direct state violence that threatened their livelihood. Clashes between the affected *okada* riders and law enforcement agents of the state and federal government have become common, leading in some cases to loss of life. For instance, Aondoana Tavershima, a 24 year old *okada* rider, was shot dead at close range by men of the Nigerian police attached to the Maroko Police Station in Lagos on Thursday 11 November 2014 for refusing to stop after he was flagged down. The policemen rushed to clandestinely bury him at the Lekki beach where a fellow cyclist saw them and went to inform the relatives of the deceased. Linda, the sister of Aondoana, revealed that the divisional police officer of the Maroko Police Station offered her ten million naira to conceal the matter but she refused. Also, sometime in 2013, three policemen of the Rapid Response Squad (RRS) killed one Lekan Ajayi in Ikorodu, a Lagos suburb, which precipitated a further clash with youths in the community that resulted in the death of another protester. The police claimed that they shot the *okada* rider in self-defence because, after he was flagged down, other *okada* riders came to the scene to join in beating up the policemen and it was in the ensuing brawl that he was shot.

While not excusing the killings by the police as they tried to enforce the 2012 traffic law of Lagos State, there is always a common display of 'team spirit' by *okada* riders as they stick up for one another whether they are right or wrong and even in the face of obvious danger. Michael Peel (2010: 91) quotes the secretary of the Somolu branch as boasting that '[w]hen we are riding *okada*, we are one ... we protect the interests of the *okada* rider – whether right or wrong'. Peel recalls that in 2005, around Ikeja, an *okada* rider crashed into a car belonging to a military officer who promptly stepped out of the car and shot him dead. Acting in 'team spirit' other *okada* riders started destroying everything in sight and at the end properties worth millions of naira were destroyed (ibid.). Orimogunje, secretary of the Somolu branch of the *okada* riders association, states that the spontaneity of the team spirit in such situation arises from the deep-seated anger they nurse against the rest of the society because many of them are in the business out of 'choicelessness, it's a system you enter by force ... that's what brings our solidarity – people united by frustration. It's like particles attracted by magnet' (ibid.).

Civil society activists in Nigeria have rejected the argument offered by the state governments for banning or restricting the *okada*s as 'anti-people'. For instance, Ilevbare stated:

> The restriction on *okada*s is not only a lazy approach to problem solving, but pedestrian, unjust, inhumane, callous and vicious. Taxis and buses are used for the famous 'one chance,'[3] why weren't they banned? Militants and pirates use[d] speed boats to bunker oil and attack ships on the high sea. Were they banned even at the height of the Niger-Delta militancy? For years, Nigerian airlines have become flying coffins leading to the death of hundreds, not even the lives of prominent Nigerians were spared. Aircrafts and air travel should have been banned! It becomes glaring why *okada* riders are singled out for ban, throwing their families and dependants deeper into the abyss of privation. For such an anti-people move to be taken somewhat hastily without due consultation with stakeholders, to a large extent, is an indication that these state Governors have lost touch with the common man. (Ilevbare 2013)

Politically, recent elections in Osun and Ekiti States in South-West Nigeria have confirmed the potency of the agency of the subalterns or informal workers especially the *okada* riders, so much that open association with them became a vote-seeking tactics for candidates seeking to unseat incumbents

---

[3] 'One chance' is an urban phrase, which in this context, means quick-get-away street theft.

in the two states. Conscious of the electoral backlash, the incumbents in such states had to make conscious efforts to assuage their fears by assuring them that the number of routes they ply would not be reduced and that their use of *okada* to earn their livelihood would not be curtailed even though it contravened a core aspect of their administration's policy on security, urbanization and public safety. The potency of the agency of this class of marginal men was further demonstrated with the defeat of the incumbent Governor of Ekiti State, Kayode Fayemi, on 21 June 2014, partly explained as depicting the political cost of not appealing to the *okada* riders who constitute a significant percentage of marginal men and voters (*The Economist* 2014).

Since 2012, when the new traffic law came into effect in Lagos, there had been no love lost in the relationship between the Lagos State Government and the *okada* riders. Attempts to enforce this law and resistance against it often precipitated skirmishes disrupting public peace and security while hindering the free flow of traffic which the law seeks to enhance. The ban and resultant clashes have received condemnation and commendation virtually in equal measures, with critics condemning it as an inhuman neoliberal urbanization excuse.

Against the background of this crisis, this chapter analyses the conflict between the Lagos State Government and the *okada* riders based on spectacles of clashes witnessed and reported within neighbourhoods in the Lagos metropolis. It conceptualizes *okada* riders in a revised sense of Robert Park's (1928) 'marginal man', while being sensitive to Guyer's (2004: 25) point about the 'multiferentiality' and 'ambiguity' of the term 'marginal'. For my purpose, I approach marginal men as those living and sharing in the social life of the city, even though they are not quite accepted as properly belonging to the urban space in which they try to find a place. Subsequently, they don't fully belong to the city, yet they are no longer entirely of the place from which they came. The economic, social and political marginality of the marginal men predispose them to an economic life involving 'indefensibly small increments' (ibid.) of gains within the African popular economy. I also find Johan Galtung's (1996) theory of structural violence useful in explaining how government policies are experienced as 'pain' from the prism of the *okada* riders. Besides revealing the perceived conflict insensitivity of the proscription, the chapter argues that the organized resistance against the ban challenges the assumption of lack of agency by those in the informal economy and teases out the hollowness of initiating poverty alleviation interventions or economic empowerment programmes oblivious of sustainable livelihood in Nigeria.

In Lagos, the constant confrontations between state authorities and members of ACCOMORAN typify a classical example of how citizens encounter the state (Obadare and Adebanwi 2010), just as it resonates the argument of Chabal (2009: 106–7) of the need to survey Africa's political economy through the prism of individuals and groups engaged in economic activities within the broader context of what he describes as 'politics of striving'. Chabal (2009: 106) argues that scholars ought to deepen analysis of political economy in

Africa by seeking answers to questions touching on how people face up every day to the need to work. What does work mean to marginal men? How do they strive to secure a decent life and, when possible, improve their conditions?

Agential & Structural Causations of Social Conflicts: Marginal Men & State Policies

Early studies on marginality were led by geographers in the 1930s that focused on the social and spatial dislocations in areas described as *problem areas* following the Great Depression, the Second World War and the struggles for liberation in the global South (Mehretu et al. 2000). Generally, marginality as evident in spaces housing a mix of political, cultural, social, economic and environmental problems is summed up by Mehretu and Sommers (1992) as a complex condition of disadvantage lived by people facing vulnerabilities arising from such problems. Adisa (1997) has observed that lesser attention has been devoted to the people living in the margins of the society. Recently, much intellectual effort has been made to explain the factors that push people to the margins.

One of these is contingent marginality, described by Castells (1989: 172–97; cf. Guyer 2004: 25–6) as what befalls individuals who find themselves in situations wherein they are least or not prepared to cope socially and economically. Factors implicated in the inability to cope could be cultural restrictions, insufficient or obsolete labour skills, lack of information and cultural restrictions. As explained by Mehretu et al. (2000: 92), susceptibility or vulnerability to contingent marginality arises from sudden loss of capacity to socially, locationally, culturally and/or ecologically deal with the market. The market in this context includes the implications of the regulatory roles of the government and its self-regulatory effects on people (Chabal 2012).

Systemic marginality results from the difficulties felt by people and communities in a system and space where distribution is inequitably constructed through hegemony (Mehretu et al. 2000). Systemic or hegemonic marginality differs from market-induced marginality because it defies market reforms as a corrective measure. This is because it stems from a conscious plan by an existing hegemony to perpetuate its political control, social exclusion and economic exploitation (Mingione 1996). The history of hegemonic marginality can be described as specific to each community depending on the historical configuration of power within it. Examples would include the inequity and oppression suffered under apartheid in South Africa and Rhodesia, ethnically targeted exclusionary practices in countries like Rwanda, Ethiopia and Sudan, and policies that (in)advertently marginalize ethnic and religious groups leading to horizontal inequalities (Stewart 2009) in countries like Nigeria and Côte d'Ivoire where autochthony confers and denies rights. In many African countries, it remains at the base of agitations for secession and ethnic militancy. However, the susceptibility of ethnic minorities to hegemonic marginality is not peculiar to Africa.

There is also *collateral* marginality experienced by people not because they have markers of vulnerability but because they are found in a geographic or social milieu dominated by victims of both hegemonic and structural marginality (Mehretu et al. 2000). Most of the people experiencing collateral or temporal marginality are aid workers, missionaries and journalists who are compelled to reside or operate in such spaces temporarily. Such spaces are avoided by tourists and direct foreign investment. *Leveraged* marginality emerges in the context of skewed economic relations in most instances. Mehretu and colleagues illustrate this as a derivate of contingent or systemic marginality.

The term marginality has also been linked to other concepts like exclusion, inequality, injustice and spatial segregation (Perlman 2004) based on realities in places like Brazil since the country's return to democracy. This was due to the growth in drug trafficking, illegal arms business and gangs, whose activities have been constructed by the local press as the violence of the margins and latched on by rap and funk musicians to construct a narrative of revolt against state injustice (ibid.). The spate of violence has led to a fear of the 'marginalized' in the Brazilian context. Also, since the 1990s, the concept of marginality has been reviewed in academic parlance especially in the context of its use to describe poverty in the first world cities (ibid.) and describing the very poor mostly found in the black ghettos of the United States and in the slums of Europe. In these places, marginality resonates with descriptions like the *underclass, new poverty, new marginality* or *advanced marginality*. This plethora of concepts constitutes attempts by scholars and policy makers to describe the situation of the poor.

In applying marginality as a concept to describe the living realities of the poor, Katzman et al. (1999) came up with a consensus that 'social exclusion' aptly captures 'marginality', while Moser (1998) advances the argument that specific kinds of 'assets' represent the 'survival strategies' of the poor. In the context of Nigerian cities, the *okada* may qualify as an 'asset' for the marginalized or politically excluded. *Okada* riders are described as 'marginal' and 'marginalized' and not 'socially excluded' in this chapter, cognizant of their electoral power and agency, especially during elections. This is in line with the argument of Ward (1976) that marginality implies being outside the formal institutions of formal labour, which may not necessarily mean that such a class does not have socio-political agency.

In Africa and most of the global South, the poor have responded through new forms of socio-economic organizing to the inability of the state to fulfil its welfare obligations, which has thrown up new patterns of self-provisioning and employment, thus producing micro- and macro-entrepreneurs (Portes and Hoffman 2003). Also, in many cities, from Buenos Aires to Rio de Janeiro, Aba to Kano and Lagos, new forms of associational life are emerging and conferring an unprecedented agency on socio-political actions that vote seekers have found too attractive to ignore. This has influenced the conception and implementation of most poverty alleviation programmes by state governors since 1999 in Nigeria. However, the same phenomenon has turned into a source of instability and threat to public peace since the decision by many state governments to opt out of the once friendly relationship with the *okada* riders.

Instability in Nigeria can be analysed broadly as arising from a tapestry of violent and non-violent conflicts. This can be broadly categorized as conflicts between disparate peoples on one hand and conflicts between the state and her citizens on the other. In the category of conflicts among its peoples are conflating issues including religion, ethnicity, access to land, and autochthony among others. Other sites of citizen-to-citizen violence and conflicts in Nigeria include socio-cultural and religious practices that legitimize exploitation and abuses against women and the girl child even in peace times. Such practices fall within the purview of the cultural sub-set of Johan Galtung's (1996) theory of structural violence.

Against the backdrop of this understanding of structural violence, for many Nigerians life has become a perpetual struggle and resistance of violence from the home to the public space. For those who cannot 'fight' by subscribing to ethnic or religious warlordism in the economic jungle that many African cities have become, options open to them are migration through both legal and illegal routes or living on the margin. Despite the launch of the Millennium Development Goals (MDGs) followed up by the Sustainable Development Goals (SDGs), virtually none of the Goals can be seen to have improved the lots of those on the margin in sub-Saharan Africa, with the exception of Ghana that met both the poverty and hunger components of the MDGs through a robust agricultural reform (Annan 2012: 173). Realities across much of the continent affirm the 'Third World' appellation of Africa as a continent dismissed by Elizabeth Harwick in 1979 as 'having no future' (Clarke 2008: 20) because of some social characteristics. Joseph (2013) cautions that recent economic figures of growth in Africa should not be celebrated because what is actually being bred is 'discordant development', with growth negated by a rising poverty rate owing to lack of jobs and increasing numbers of young graduates and other school leavers. However, Annan (2012) opposes any bludgeoning push towards accepting Africa's current parlous state as given or irredeemable, based on the sustained success stories coming from countries like Madagascar and Botswana as telling examples of what right choices and decisions can bring.

From the preceding it is evident that 'discordant development' has pushed more people to the under-world of the economy in Africa, while setting many against the state, against their communities and forcing them into acts that negate the ethos and beliefs of their communities. Chabal (2009: 157) explains that the economic and socially marginalized class of young men and women has been pushed to the margin where they struggle to survive through different types of jobs that come their ways'. Most studies on economic inequalities in urban centres have dwelled on the causes and degree of social and spatial inequalities using the differentials of the quality of living (Mehretu et al. 2000). Also, the causality of this in the emergence of criminal gangs and insecurity has also attracted sufficient attention

(Adisa 1997). However, not much has been done in engaging how those on the margins, such as the *okada* riders who have elected not to go into criminality, are coping and how their quest for survival brings them into conflict with the state.

Apart from the greed grievance and the inherent contingent theories of conflicts, the objectivist and subjectivist explanations find resonance in the context of structure and agency towards a fuller understanding of causations of conflicts and attendant instability. The objectivists posit that the structure is the precipitant of violent conflicts in societies (Gorman 2011). They locate the causes of social conflicts in institutions, systems and dynamics that are not obvious. Therefore, for the objectivist, slavery, sexism, caste systems and other discriminatory practices are causes of conflict and instability that should not be ignored. In contrast, the subjectivists argue that conflict ensues once the parties (agents or actors) express incompatible aspirations (ibid.). This implies that conflicts do not occur in a given setting or relationship until the parties express incompatible goals even when there are structural indices visible to the objectivist.

The conflict between the Lagos State Government and the *okada* riders can be interpreted as one that moved from objectivist to subjectivist social conflict. It was objectivist with the signing into law of the Road Traffic Administration and Vehicle Inspection Law of Lagos State Law Number 4 on 2 August 2012 and became subjectivist with the resultant resistance and clashes between the *okada* riders and the law enforcement agencies. The stage was thus set for marginal men to interrupt the mapping and planning of the city by the government (Manton 2013). Contemporary Lagos can be described as suffering from acute over-urbanization. This is a situation in which the population grows much faster than the urban economies (UN-Habitat 2010: 278), with symptoms that include high unemployment rates, slum proliferation, social polarization and crime.

Lagos & the Marginals

African cities present few success stories of ongoing efforts by governments to instil order and sanity. However, the shrinking formal economic spaces have led to increasing casualization and informalization of work, and different forms of self-employment such as the class of okada riders. In pointing us towards the compositional nature of life in contemporary urban Africa as an 'asset' in the 'mitigation of poverty', Guyer (2014a: 146–50) alerts us to how increasing casualization and informalization are no longer marginal, but central in understanding what AbdouMaliq Simone (2004: 3) described as 'cities where livelihood, mobility, and opportunity seem to be produced and enacted through the very agglomeration of different bodies marked and situated in diverse ways'.

In the account of Baker (1974), Lagos was a heterogeneous town comprising peoples of diverse origins even during the colonial period. This conferred an eclectic face on the town accompanied by gradual stratification and contrasting lifestyles (Fourchard 2006). Despite the different cultural backgrounds of these groups and the inequitable distribution of wealth between them, settlements continued to grow and this made the maintenance of order complicated (ibid.). This trend continued until the Fourth Republic when the administration of then-Governor Bola Tinubu commenced a project aimed at the revitalization of the historical core of Lagos Island in order to reverse the economic and environmental decline of the last two decades (Lagos State Government 2012). According to the Lagos State Governor, 'our vision is to make Lagos State the reference point of harmonious physical development in Nigeria through best practices and physical planning and development matters' (ibid.: 5).

Much of the efforts at expanding the infrastructure to meet the needs of Africa's fastest growing city have failed because the population increase in Lagos often quadruples the rate of the expansion of infrastructure. This is particularly evident in the multi-ethnic and even multi-national[4] nature of the *okada* riders in Lagos. As the economic crisis in Nigeria deepens, more and more people move to urban areas, particularly the urban areas of south-western Nigeria, especially Lagos. This region of Nigeria has experienced the lowest frequency of widespread violence compared with other geopolitical zones in the country since Nigeria returned to democratic rule in 1999.

However, despite the expressed determination of the government on urban renewal, it was conscious of the need to tread cautiously in the transport sector in order to strike a balance between technocratic ambitions and patronage demands (de Gramont 2015). This could be traced to the political agency of the National Union of Road Transport Workers (NURTW), another commercial drivers' association, dating back to the Second Republic. The need to relate cautiously and sensitively in the transport sector stems from a cognition that actions perceived to be against commercial bus drivers and their trade would have been a sacrilege against one of the 'five gods' determining outcomes of elections in Nigeria (Fayemi 2009, quoted in Adebanwi and Obadare 2011: 326). Due to their numbers and voting strength they were in the class of constituencies for the buying of bulk votes, as observed by Collier (2010). This created an air of licentiousness for the NURTW members leading to the worsening of the traffic situation which the Tinubu administration (1999–2007) could not frontally curb. However, the vision and drive to make Lagos State the epitome of harmonious physical development and urban order assumed a wider dimension from 2007 when Tinubu was succeeded by Governor Raji Fashola, described as the 'actualiser' – with Tinubu described as the 'dreamer'.

---

[4] Some are from neighbouring countries such as Togo, Niger and the Republic of Benin.

Okada Riders & the Crisis of Restriction

The initial applause that greeted the appearance of *okada* riders on Lagos roads can best be appreciated in the light of the extent of time and pain experienced as a result of indefinite stays in traffic. Richards (2009: 210) argues that the 'go-slows' (as Nigerians popularly call congested traffic) have become 'go-stops', that is, the flow of traffic has changed from being sluggish to being at a standstill. In such instances, public peace and order can get disrupted. Richards (ibid.) reports that:

> What little self control Lagos drivers have goes straight out of the window. Normally sane men become maniac, driving up kerbs or the left hand lane to turn right at the junction only to block the way completely and cause grid lock making other drivers to go out and remonstrate.

Remonstrations and sudden exchanges of blows and altercations as a result of bashing of cars, due to 'go-stops' that eventually become 'go-bumps' when vehicles bash one another, are not the only disruptions of order that are triggered by Lagos traffic. Richards (ibid.: 214–17) satirically dissects the types and causes of long traffic lines as a major permanent feature of the streets of Lagos.

The first type of hold up is the 'pothole hold up'. This is occasioned whenever there is a hole in the middle of the road that often gets deeper until it is big enough to contain a truck oftentimes due to neglect. The second type is the 'flood hold up' that emerges after heavy downpours fill the pot-holes or truck-holes. The third type of 'hold up' is the 'broken down vehicle jam', following the breakdown of one or more vehicles, usually in the middle of the road. Images of such vehicles with their owners pushing with one arm while steering with the other arm have been common on Lagos roads, especially prior to the enactment of the Lagos traffic law in 2012. Also, queues for fuel at petrol stations generate sudden hold ups, as do the police check points, actually extortion points where a series of human rights abuses are committed. Another type of hold up and accidents usually involves scenes of commercial bus drivers making U-turns in wrong places especially in busy narrow roads thereby rendering adjacent traffic stationary, and sometimes causing crashes leading to loss of life and limb. The most recent type of traffic hold up is caused by banks and other owners of business premises who fail to provide parking places for their customers. The phenomenon of hold ups makes 'the distance between home and workplace … like travelling from Egypt to Canaan, only in this case there is no promised land' (Richards 2009: 219).

In order to avoid being trapped in traffic, most commuters in Lagos find the *okada* a ready means of escape. For some reasons, they are seen as constituting nuisances because, anywhere there is commotion, they are present. Some of the reasons that informed their description as 'nuisances' by Richards (2009) stems from their destructive and reckless manner of driving, leading to frequent damages to wing mirrors of vehicles, and crashes.

In an interview with the Commissioner for Transport in Lagos State, Kayode Opeifa (2007–15), he revealed that Lagos has an estimated 1.4 million registered vehicles and about 600,000 that go in and out of the city per day at a ratio of 224 vehicles per kilometre as at 2015. Against the background of the inadequacy of roads and the terrible state of most of them, traffic in Lagos became a crime- and conflict-generating phenomenon that the government could not ignore. The determination of the government to ensure order, peace and safety on Lagos roads informed the 2012 Traffic Law and the establishment of other agencies like the Kick Against Indiscipline (KAI) and the Lagos State Transport Management Authority (LASTMA), performing sanitary and traffic law enforcement functions. According to Kayode Opeifa, these two organizations were used as platforms to rehabilitate and reintegrate former street urchins ('Area Boys') into more dignifying means of livelihood, and enhancing street and neighbourhood security.[5]

The *okada* men typify a classical example of men living on the margin within an over-urbanized city. Most of them are migrants from other parts of the country and neighbouring countries with qualifications ranging from University degrees to school certificates, to drop-outs and the uneducated with none. Many of them resided under bridges until the coming of KAI, when they sought accommodation in the slums across the city and in some cases, established their own communes. Others converted their bikes into make-shift beds under the bridges after the KAI men would have closed for the day. Some also found refuge around the mosques from where they would generally leave before the first Muslim call to prayers around 5 a.m.

As everyday people, the typical *okada* men's day starts as early as 3 or 4 a.m., especially on weekends in areas where the night life is very boisterous. However, on weekdays, they usually resume business around 5 a.m. when they transport residents of Lagos living on the mainland – in order to escape the traffic – to the Island. Some of them do home pick-ups for passengers, taking their children to school, and sometimes conveying the entire family, first taking the children to school before taking the parents to work. Also, some of them do this for their wives and children before they begin the business of the day while others just ply their routes for passengers. Oftentimes by 10 a.m. many of them break to eat and/or take some locally brewed alcoholic drinks to keep them going. The commonest of the drinks is called *paraga*, an alcoholic herbal drink, but there are others such as *ogogoro*, a strong home-brewed beverage made from the juice of raffia palm trees. Also, they are known consumers of Indian hemp and cigarettes. All of these are very important for the *okada* riders because they supply them the 'fuel' to perform within the economy of struggle. To determine the fares charged by the *okada* riders, a lot of factors are taken into consideration, not the least the costs of their own 'fuel'. The haggling process and eventual fares charged by *okada* riders provides an opportunity to appreciate the mix of people in the trade, their anxieties and aspirations.

---

[5] Interview, Kayode Opeifa 24 September 2014, Ibadan, Nigeria.

As a point of everyday interactions, the demography of *okada* riders consists of a mélange of unemployed artisans, professionals, (il)literate youths and natural-born chancers (Peel 2010). In determining the fares charged, haggling is done mindful of certain variables. Fasakin (2002) enumerates factors underpinning the fares charged by operators. These include garage fees, the newness of the *okada* and its passenger-conveying capacity, daily operational hours, terms of ownership, drinking habits of the operators, sex, having other source(s) of employment, family size, saving towards acquiring one's *okada* and motive for entering the business. Other payments influencing the fares charged include taxes paid to the local government, the police to forestall arrests after flouting the laws, and 'areas boys' (street urchins) many of whom control different parts of many cities in Nigeria. However, at the end of the business day, they eke in averagely amounts in the range of 1,000 to 3,000 naira daily (data from 2010; GB pound £2.50 to £7.50, US dollar $3 to $9.50 as at February 2017). While defiance of traffic laws brings them in collision with the government through the police, finding the right amount of change for the commuters has always been the cause of altercations and conflicts between them and commuters, sometimes degenerating into brawls. Despite these instances, the *okada* riders have become practically indispensable for many commuters for reasons ranging from the convenience of taking passengers to their doorsteps and ability to meander their ways through traffic, thus helping many in the corporate world to keep appointments. Peel (2010: 89) describes how their behaviour elicits cheers and condemnation: 'if you are in a car or bus, you curse their incessant horn-blowing and gadfly dodging across lanes; if you are late for a meeting you will cheer your *okada* driver as he rides roughshod over traffic laws to get you to your appointment in time'. Given the rare convenience they offer commuters, there is bound to be support for them from across class divides as expressed in the tweet quoted in the third epigraph where the rivalry between the fans of Manchester United and Chelsea football club fans was seen as the reason why Fashola, a Manchester United fan, endorsed a policy that adversely affected *okada* riders because most of them are fans of Chelsea football club.

The ban pitched civil society organizations against the Lagos State Government as several protests were held to protest it. Many of these were held under the aegis of leading civil society organizations like the Committee for the Defence of Human Rights (CDHR), Path of Peace Initiative (PPI) and the Federation of Informal Workers Organizations of Nigeria (FIWON) (Ugbodaga et al. 2012). Izuekwe et al. (2012) reports that placards with inscriptions like 'You gave us no job, we gave ourselves one and you are killing us for it', 'They say *okada* riders are robbers, who gave them the guns?' and 'Fashola give me my vote back' were displayed during the protests. In an address at one of the protest rallies, Comrade Abiodun Aremu the Vice-Chairman of the Nigeria Labour Congress conveyed the mood of the protesters thus:

Marginal Men: *Okada* Riders in Lagos

9.3 A civil society group, Joint Action Front (JAF) was in the forefront of the protests in support of the *okada* riders. (Reproduced courtesy *TheNEWS*, Lagos, Nigeria)

> [W]e are here to tell the Lagos State government that enough is enough of the humiliation of poor people. The law banning okada is a bad law. This is the beginning of the struggle to liberate the poor people in Nigeria and the struggle must continue until we win. (Izuekwe et al. 2012: 2)

Policemen also made money out of the ban, as their routine night patrol became an avenue to clamp down on them. At one time the Lagos Police Command was in custody of over 3,000 seized motorcycles and this triggered a violent protest from the *okada* riders who attacked more than 300 luxury buses belonging to the Lagos State Government (Ugbodaga 2012a) in apparent expression of Ted Gurr's (1970) frustration aggression theory.

Eventually, the majority of the *okada* riders were compelled to relocate to their various states while *okada* riders from neighbouring countries such as Ghana, Togo, Chad and Niger had to find other means of livelihood as a result of the ban and clampdown by policemen and officials of LASTMA, the Lagos State agency responsible for compliance. However, those who stayed had to negotiate new terms of doing business with the Nigeria Police and LASTMA. After a while, the *okada* riders became known as 'Any Time Money (ATM)' in a perversion of the abbreviation of Automated Teller Machine (ATM), based on the fact that they constituted instant sources of money through bribery and extortion for the LASTMA men and their counterparts in the police. This shows how state agents exploit the marginality of others whose situation has been made precarious by harsh laws of the state. Over time, the *okada* riders have become accustomed to negotiating their ways through bribes and they even knowingly break aspects of the traffic law.

As observed by the author during field work, the policemen operate(d) in an ambush-like manner by suddenly emerging from hidden places to pounce on the *okada* riders who usually have to stop suddenly, sometimes leading to accidents in which the passenger, the rider and the policemen would sustain injuries. If no injury is sustained, the passenger is allowed to go while the negotiation between the policemen or LASTMA officials as the case may be, commences. If the *okada* rider has sufficient money ranging from 2,000 to 3,000 naira, the *okada* rider is released immediately. If the *okada* and/or the rider is taken to the Police Station, the rider or owner in some cases will have to pay a bribe as high as 5,000 naira to ensure release of the motorcycle, or risk permanent confiscation and/or trial and three years' imprisonment upon conviction. However, the bribe given to policemen is considered a milder option by many of the *okada* riders interviewed. This is because, according to them, if an *okada* is seized by a LASTMA official, rather than a police officer and it is taken to their office the chances of 'negotiation' are close to zero because the official penalty which is 'non-negotiable' is 20,000 naira and/ or three years in jail. In instances of arrests where the *okada* riders feel they outnumber the policemen, they usually decide to resist the impounding of their motorcycles which often triggers clashes between them and the law enforcement agents, which can lead to fatalities and casualties.

In a focus-group discussion with some members of the top hierarchy of the *okada* riders' association, the consensus of opinion revealed a feeling of betrayal by the government given the roles they play(ed) during elections. One interviewee said: 'Before election in 2011, [Governor Raji Fashola] gave helmets and vests to *okada* riders. The *okada* riders were behind Fashola everywhere he went to campaign, then they were not armed robbers and they were not causing accidents. Weeks after he got the second term, he started chasing them everywhere.' Many of them cited their 'selfless' contributions during elections with some of them revealing that they helped politicians to snatch ballot boxes during elections so that the politicians can stuff the boxes with illegal pre-cast ballots to rig elections. They also feel treated as inferiors to commercial bus drivers whom they believe bear lesser risks than them during elections. A respondent stated: 'it is easier to snatch a ballot-box and take off on an *okada* than using a car'. The respondent also referred to many occasions when the *okada* riders constituted part of the motorcades to venues of campaigns for Governor Fashola. They described regretfully that they feel 'used and dumped' since Fashola is in his second and last term, and is therefore no longer in need of their votes.[6]

---

[6] State decided to lift the restriction on *okadas* given the promise made by the rival Peoples' Democratic Party (PDP) candidate that he would lift the ban if elected into office. This points to the electoral value not only of the *okada* riders but their dependants, customers and sympathizers.

Marginal Men: *Okada* Riders in Lagos

9.4 Several *okada* riders accompanying Governor Fashola (standing left through the open roof of the vehicle) during his re-election campaign in 2007. (Reproduced courtesy *TheNEWS*, Lagos, Nigeria)

Optics of the State: Justification of the *Okada* Restriction

A common narrative that can be teased out from the statements of the governors who banned and/or restricted the *okada* riders across the country can be summed up as attempts to prevent crime, ensure security and impose order on the streets. Also, implied in some of their narratives is their frustration with the nagging crisis of urbanization. The decision to ban and/or restrict *okada* riders in different areas across the Lagos State came into being through a bill signed into law on 2 August 2012 and published as Law No. 4, 'A Law to Provide for Road Traffic Administration and Make Provisions for Road Traffic and Vehicle Inspection in Lagos State and other Connected Purposes' (Lagos State Government 2012: 149). However, the ban would not have attracted the controversy it did but for the history of the relationship between the *okada* riders and the Lagos State Governor when seeking votes. Another cause of controversy was the police claim that 73 per cent of armed robbery cases in Lagos prior to the ban involved *okada* riders (Ugbodaga 2012b).

Three months after the ban, the Governor of the State, Raji Fashola, a Senior Advocate of Nigeria (SAN), revealed that records from 25 general hospitals indicated that auto-accidents involving *okada* riders dropped from 646 to 525 representing 18.73 per cent reduction during those three months, while deaths recorded from *okada* crashes dropped from 14 to 8 per cent, indicating a 42.86 per cent reduction. This was considered worthy of celebration by the Government because at one time in the city's main orthopaedic hospital, a ward was designated '*Okada* Ward': it was exclusively for patients of *okada* accidents. Also, within the same period the office of the Commissioner of Police, Lagos State revealed that reported cases of armed robbery dropped by 30 per cent in September and 60 per cent to the end of October (Ugbodaga 2012b). By the end of 2012, over 12,000 motorcycles had been impounded with over 50 *okada* riders convicted under the 2012 Lagos Traffic Law (ibid.). The Lagos State Government reiterated that the restriction is about preserving lives, insisting that by banning the activities of *okada* riders on 495 out of the 9,700 routes in Lagos, the intention is to ensure safety of lives and enhance security of the citizens. But, for the *okada* riders, the law restricted or, in some cases, terminated their only means of livelihood, thus representing a devaluation of their labour and a threat to their lives, and making resistance and violent clashes with law enforcement agents unpreventable.

Conclusion:
Reconciling Urban Renewal with the Needs of Marginal People

Urban renewal efforts by state governments in Nigeria have increasingly become sources of conflict between the state and people on the margins, especially streets traders who are mostly women and *okada* riders who are mostly men. Despite the need for urban renewal in African cities, the process cannot be oblivious of its implications for the economic wellbeing of those affected, including *okada* riders. Therefore, there is an urgent need for a reconciliation of the urban renewal programmes of the state and the challenges of livelihood to urban marginals such as *okada* riders. An urban renewal plan that is not mindful of integrating the potential victims such as those who might become economically displaced will in no time become a threat to peace and security, and will imperil the renewal programmes in the long run. This is because men on the margins get pushed to the wall when their sources of livelihood are disrupted, and the attendant reactions will surely have terrible effects on urban peace and security. In the event that such men are displaced by state decisions on urban renewal, it is important to create choices for them so that they do not end up being without any choice.

In the light of this, a peace and conflict impact assessment of all phases of urban renewal initiatives would help in anticipating and being proactive in responding to likely areas of tension or conflict. As witnessed during fieldwork, the brutality and repression demonstrated by the law enforcement agencies (LASTMA and the police), saddled with the responsibility of implementing the restrictions and/or control of *okada*, often trigger violent confrontations.

Of equal importance is a conscious measurement of the economic displacement brought about by urban renewal on people in the margins such as *okada* riders. This is why the state must reckon with the fact that the informal sector where the *okada* riders are located provides opportunities for making a living to people struggling for survival (Lourenço-Lindell 2004). It also houses the highest number of workers, with huge numbers of dependants.

The conflict arising from *okada* riders and state agencies typifies the implications of not placing programmes of poverty alleviation on a framework of sustainable livelihood. A paradox is observed in Nigeria in that, at a point in time, the same governors banning or restricting *okadas* were struggling to outdo one another in giving out *okadas* as 'assets'[7] of poverty alleviation to young men. Some politicians actually used *okadas* as distributive goods for both core and swing voters. In Oyo state, south-western Nigeria, Governor Adebayo Alao-Akala (2007–2011) made the distribution of *okada* motorcycles a cardinal point of his poverty alleviation programme, while erstwhile Governor of Borno in north-eastern Nigeria, Senator Ali-Modu Sherif, once distributed 5,000 *okadas* to beneficiaries (Itodo 2005). Politicians also used them to facilitate easy carting away of ballot boxes on election days as part of rigging ploys, as already mentioned. This explains the gradual softening of the enforcement of the law on *okada* riders close to elections, as the incumbent political party and the opposition in Lagos State begin to court the *okada* riders for bulk votes. Therefore, just as weapons given out during elections are hard to retrieve after elections because they become sources of livelihood albeit illegally for their possessors, *okadas* given out in exchange for votes eventually end differently as real means of poverty alleviation, or threats to security and safety of the people.

However, a sustainable livelihood framework (Levine 2014) will ensure employment-generating growth targeted at the mass of youths who constitute the highest percentage of the *okada* riders. This will foster an economic growth hinged on building the capacity of the poor to have a decent living (Nussbaum 2006). Also, it is important to recognize that the marginal, the poor, do not necessarily go away from society when they are economically or spatially displaced. Rather, they scatter or regroup to generate new means of survival which may also become another source of crises in the future. Hence, it is expedient to initiate and sustain policies that will not set the grounds for its recreation. Envisioning and implementing policies must not lose sight of the safety and security of people and the environment, while empowering the poor as active agents to make positive contributions to society as whole. This, I suggest, is at the core of Guyer's scholarship on everyday life at the margins of the economy.

---

[7] As discussed earlier, Guyer (2014b) has argued that '[f]or an anthropological examination, the composition of what are now considered to be "assets" in the mitigation of poverty should move to the center of concern.'

References

Ababio, M.O and E. Agyemang (2015). 'The Okada War in Urban Ghana: A Polemic Issue or Policy Mismatch?' *African Studies Quarterly* 15(4): 25–44.

Adebanwi, W. (2006). 'Abuja' (pp. 83–102). In S. Bekker and G. Therborn (eds), *Capital Cities in Africa: Power and Powerlessness*. Dakar and Cape Town: CODESRIA.

—. (2012). 'Glocal Naming and Shaming: Toponymic (Inter)national Relations on Lagos and New York Streets', *African Affairs* 111(445): 640–61

Adebanwi, W. and E. Obadare (2011). 'The Abrogation of the Electorate: An Emergent African Phenomenon', *Democratization* 18(2): 311–35.

Adekanye, J.B. (2007). *Linking Conflict Diagnosis, Conflict Prevention and Conflict Management in Contemporary Africa: Selected Essays*. Ibadan: Centre for Gender, Governance and Development.
Adeniyi, T. (2014). 'The Okada Generation', *The Sun*, 23 July.
Adesanya, A. (1998). *The Use of Motorcycle for Transport: The Situation in Ibadan*. Monograph Series (No. 6). Ibadan: Nigerian Institute of Social and Economic Research (NISER).
Adisa, J. (1997). 'Lagos: Street Culture and Families in the Street' (pp. 89–136). In G. Herault and P. Adesanmi (eds), *Youth, Street Culture and Urban Violence in Africa*. Ibadan: Institute for French Research in Africa.
Annan, K. (2012). *Interventions: A Life in War and Peace*. New York: Penguin Books.
Baker, P.H. (1974). *Urbanization and Political Change: The Politics of Lagos, 1917–1967*. Berkeley, CA: University of California Press.
Boas, M and K.C. Dunn (eds) (2007). *African Guerrillas: Raging Against the Machine*. Boulder, CO: Lynne Rienner.
Castells, M. (1989). *The Information City*. Oxford: Blackwell.
Chabal, P. (2009). *Africa: The Politics of Suffering and Smiling*. London and New York: Zed Books.
—. (2012). *The End of Conceit: Western Rationality after Post-Colonialism*. London and New York: Zed Books.
Clarke, D. (2008). *Crude Continent: The Struggle for Africa's Oil Prize*. New Delhi: Profile Books.
Collier, P. (2010). *Wars, Guns and Votes: Democracy in Dangerous Places*. London: Vintage Books.
de Certeau, M. (1984). *The Practice of Everyday Life*. Berkley, CA: University of California Press.
de Gramont, D. (2015). *Governing Lagos: Unlocking the Politics of Reform*. Washington, DC: Carnegie Endowment for International Peace.
Fasakin, J.O. (2002). 'The Willingness to Pay for the Services of Commercial Motorcycles in Akure, Nigeria', *Cities* 17(6): 447–52.
Fayemi, K. (2009). 'An Insider's View of Electoral Politics and the Struggle for Electoral Reform in Nigeria'. Paper presented at the Panel on Ten Years of Civilian Rule in Nigeria at the *African Studies Association Annual Conference*, New Orleans, LA, 19–22 November.
Fourchard, L. (2006). 'Lagos', (pp. 65–82). In S. Bekker and G. Therborn (eds), *Capital Cities in Africa: Power and Powerlessness*. Dakar and Cape Town: CODESRIA.
Friedmann, J. and C. Weaver (1980). *Territory and Function*. Berkeley, CA: University of California Press.
Galtung, J. (1996). *Peace by Peaceful Means: Peace and Conflict Development and Civilization*. OSLO: International Peace Research Institute (PRIO).
Gorman, E.O. (2011). *Conflict and Development: Development Matters*. London and New York: Zed Books.
Gurr, T. (1970). *Why Men Rebel*. Princeton, NJ: Princeton University Press.
Gutkind, P.W.C. (1963). 'Tradition, Migration, Urbanization, Modernity and

Unemployment: The Roots of Instability', *Canadian Journal of African Studies*, 3(2): 343–65

Guyer, J.I. (2002). 'Preface' (pp. ix-xvi) In J.I. Guyer, L. Denzer and A. Agbaje (eds), *Money Struggles and City Life: Devaluation in Ibadan and Other Urban Centers in Southern Nigeria, 1986–1990*. Portsmouth, NH: Heinemann.

—. (2004). *Marginal Gains: Monetary Transactions in Atlantic Africa*. Chicago, IL and London: The Chicago University Press.

—. (2014a). 'Gains and Losses in the Margins of Time: From West and Equatorial History to Present Day South Africa', *Africa* 84 (1): 146–50

—. (2014b). 'Pauper, Percentile, Precarity': Keynote Address presented at Conference on The History of Poverty in Africa: A Central Question? Columbia University, New York City 6 March.

Guyer, J.I. and L. Denzer (2013). 'Prebendalism and the People: The Price of Petrol at the Pump' (pp. 53–77). In W. Adebanwi and E. Obadare (eds), *Democracy and Prebendalism in Nigeria: Critical Interpretations*. New York: Palgrave Macmillan

Ikeano N. and F. Akinrolabu (1991). 'Transportation: Commuters tell Story of Woes', *Daily Times*, 8 February.

Ilevbare, T. (2013). 'The Okada Ban and the Insensitivity of State Governors', www.newsdiaryonline (accessed 17 June 2013).

Information Nigeria (2014). 'Why I Didn't Ban Okada As Governor Of Anamabra – Obi', 28 October. www.informationng.com/2014/10/why-i-didnt-ban-okada-as-governor-of-anamabra-obi.html (accessed 22 April 2016).

Inyang, I. (2012). '"I Belong to the Working Class, so I Cannot Ban Okada" – Governor Oshiomhole'. *Daily Post* 10 November. http://dailypost.ng/2012/11/10/i-belong-working-class-i-ban-okada-governor-oshiomhole (accessed 22 April 2016).

Itodo, J. (2005). 'Borno Earmarks N1billion for Motorcycle Procurement', *Financial Standard: Arewa Business*, 24 October.

Izuekwe, C; Dedeigbo A and F. Toheeb (2012). '4 Activists, Okada Riders Arrested', *P.M News*, 10 October: 1.

Joseph, R. (2013). 'Discordant Development and Insecurity in Africa' (pp. 14–16), *Top Priorities for the Continent in 2013 Foresight Africa*. Brookings: Africa Growth Initiative

Katzman, R., L. Beccaria, F. Filgueira, L. Golbert and G. Kessler (1999). *Vulnerabilidad, activos y exclusión social en Argentina y Uruguay*. Santiago, Chile: OIT.

Klot, J.F. and V.-K. Nguyen (2009). 'Introduction' (pp. 606–22). In J.F. Klot and V.K Nguyen (eds), *The Fourth Wave of Violence, Gender, Culture & HIV in the 21st Century*. Paris: UNESCO.

Kujenya, J. (2014). 'Okada: Nigeria's Cat and Mouse Game', *The Nation*, Lagos, 7 September: 10.

Kumar, A. (2011). *Understanding the Emerging Role of Motorcycles in African Cities: A Political Economy Perspective*. SSATP Discussion Paper No. 13: 1–32. Urban Transport Series. Washington, DC: The International Bank for Reconstruction and Development/The World Bank.

Kumar, A. and F. Barrett (2008). *Stuck in Traffic: Urban Transport in Africa.* http://siteresources.worldbank.org/EXTAFRSUBSAHTRA/Resources/Stuck-in-Traffic.pdf (accessed 15 June 2015).

Lagos State Government of Nigeria Official Gazette. No. 27 Vol. 45, 3 August 2012. 'A law to provide for road traffic administration and make provisions for road traffic and vehicle inspection in Lagos State and other connected purposes'.

Levine, S. (2014). *How to Study Livelihoods: Bringing a Sustainable Livelihoods Framework to Life.* Working Paper 22. London: Secure Livelihoods Research Consortium: 1–17.

Lourenço-Lindell, I. (2004). 'Trade and the Politics of Informalization in Bissau, Guinea-Bissau' (pp. 84–98). In K.T. Hansen and M. Vaa (eds), *Reconsidering Informality: Perspectives from Urban Africa.* Uppsala: Nordiska Afrikainstitutet.

Manton, J. (2013). '"Environmental Akalism" and The War on Filth: The Personification of Sanitation in Urban Nigeria', *Africa* 83: 606–22.

Mehretu, A. and L.M. Sommers (1992). 'Macro and Microspatial Marginality in Developed Pluralistic Societies' (136–46). In O. Gade (ed.), *Spatial Dynamics of High Land and High Altitude Environments.* Boone, N.C: Apalachian State University.

Mehretu, A., B.W. Pigozzi and L.M. Sommers (2000). 'Concepts in Social and Spatial Marginality', *Geografiska Annaler: Series B, Human Geography* 82(2): 89–101.

Miller, S.M. (1987). 'The Pursuit of Informal Economies', *Annals of the American Academy of Political and Social Science,* 493: 26–35.

Mingione, E. (1996). *Urban Poverty and the Under Class: A Reader.* Oxford: Blackwell.

Moser, C. (1998). 'The Asset Vulnerability Framework: Reassessing Urban Poverty Reduction Strategies', *World Development* 26(1): 1–19.

Mungai, C. (2014). 'Why the "Annoying" Motorbike Taxi is King in Africa's Cities, and Smart Firms like Jumia and Konga Love Them', http://mgafrica.com/article/2014-11-11-that-annoying-motorbike-taxi-to-the-rescue (accessed 15 July 2015).

Murdock, H. (2013). 'Nigerian Motorcycle Taxis Driven Away by Ban', www.voanews.com/a/nigerian-motorcycle-taxis-driven-away-by-ban/1789196.html (accessed 20 July 2015).

Nussbaum, M.C. (2006). 'Poverty and Human Functioning: Capabilities as Fundamental Entitlements' (pp. 47–75). In D. Gursky and R. Kanbur (eds), *Poverty and Inequality.* Stanford, CA: Stanford University Press.

Obadare, E and W. Adebanwi (2010). 'Introduction: Excess and Abjection in the Study of the African State' (pp. 1–28). In W. Adebanwi and E. Obadare (eds), *Encountering the Nigerian State.* New York: Palgrave Macmillan.

Olubomehin, O.O. (2012). 'The Development and Impact of Motorcycles as Means of Transportation in Nigeria', *Research on Humanities and Social Sciences* 2(6): 231–9.

Olvera, L.D., D. Plat, P. Pochet and S. Maïdadi (2012). 'Motorbike Taxis in the

"Transport Crisis" of West and Central African Cities', *EchoGeo*, 20: 2–15.

Oyesiku, O.O. (2002). *From Womb to Tomb*. 24th Inaugural Lecture, Olabisi Onabanjo University. Ago Iwoye: OOU Press.

Park, R.E. (1928). 'Human Migration and the Marginal Man', *American Journal of Sociology* 33(6): 881–93.

Peel, M. (2010). *A Swamp Full of Dollars Pipelines and Paramilitaries at Nigeria's Oil Frontiers*. Ibadan: Bookcraft.

Perlman, J.E. (2004). 'The Metamorphosis of Marginality in Rio de Janeiro', *Latin America Research Review* 39(1): 189–92.

Portes, A. and K. Hoffman (2003). 'Latin American Class Structures: Their Composition and Change during the Neoliberal Era', *Latin American Research Review* 38(1): 41–82.

Richards, K. (2009). *Insider Outsider*. Ibadan: Bookcraft.

Simone, A.M. (2004). *For the City yet to Come: Changing African Life in Four Cities*. Durham, NC and London: Duke University Press.

Smith, B.C. (2003). *Understanding Third World Politics: Theories of Political Change and Development*. New York. Palgrave Macmillan.

Ssenkaaba, S. (2013). 'Boda Bodas: A Deathtrap at Your Beckon', *New Vision* (Kampala), 6 June.

Stewart, F. (2009). *Horizontal Inequalities and Conflict: Understanding Group Violence in Multi-Ethnic Societies*. Oxford: Centre for Research on Inequality, Human Security and Ethnicity.

The Economist (2014). 'Why Reform is So Hard', 25 June. www.economist.com/blogs/baobab/2014/06/politics-nigeria (accessed 14 June 2016).

The Sun (2014). 'Why I didn't Ban Okada in Anambra', Lagos, 27 July.

Ugbodaga, K. (2012). 'Relative Calm on Lagos Roads', *P.M News*, 13 November: 1.

—. (2012). 'Okada: 57 Councils Join Forces to Enforce Ban', *P.M News*, 15 November: 1.

Ugbodaga, K., E. Eromosele and A. Dedeigbo (2012). 'Okada Riders Protest Ban on 475 Roads', *PM News*, 8 October: 1.

UN-HABITAT – United Nations Human Settlements Habitat (2010). *The State of African Cities 2010: Governance, Inequality and Urban Land Markets*. Nairobi: UN-HABITAT.

Ward, P.M. (1976). 'The Squatter Settlements as Slum or Housing Solution: Evidence from Mexico City', *Land Economics* 2(3): 330–446.

10   Sopona, Social Relations & the Political Economy of Colonial Smallpox Control in Ekiti, Nigeria

Elisha P. Renne

Aina (my sister) and I were the next victims of smallpox in our household. She was the first to go down with a fever. Then, one night, I refused my favourite pounded yam from Yeye, my grandmother. She broke down in tears, blaming Baba (smallpox) for afflicting me. I had no appetite but was in the throes of a very high fever. I was laid on the floor, like my sister, and in spite of the blazing firewood fire provided for us, I was shivering and shaking. Within a few days, I lost consciousness. I have no recollection of the events in my life during that period. When I came round, my little sister, who was less than a year (she was born in October 1944) was nowhere to be seen. She had succumbed to the infection. Naturally, I was moved to tears. My grandmother consoled me lovingly and admonished me to be brave, because it was taboo to cry and mourn over a victim of smallpox.

(Adelola Adeloye, *My Salad Years* 2009: 94)

Introduction

As the terrifying experience of Professor Adelola Adeloye in Ikole-Ekiti in 1945 indicates, Sopona or Baba – as the deity associated with the disease, smallpox, was known – was lethal for some of its victims while others survived. Yet, Adeloye had been vaccinated in school. The unpredictable consequences of contracting smallpox reinforced local beliefs about the deity, Sopona, whose arbitrary power was often immune to the blandishments of Western medicine. Not surprisingly, Sopona was widely feared throughout Ekiti, which affected people's actions when it appeared. People were forbidden to 'cry and mourn over a victim of smallpox' for fear of provoking the deity's anger over the possibility that humans might question its actions in the selection of those whom it had affected. It was believed that if Sopona were to see someone crying for a family member, that the remaining members of the household would be stricken as well. This conceptualization of Sopona – as a dangerous orisa (deity) that possessed a person but which could be placated and treated by devotee priests and priestesses (awuro Sopona), contrasted with British colonial officials' conceptualization of smallpox – as a virus with particular symptoms and aetiology that could be prevented through inoculation. These two views of the disease framed approaches to disease control, which also reflected particular forms of political economy. One was locally based on kingship, priests and broadly based control of agriculture, trade and craft production, the other on a more distant regime of prime ministers, parliament and health departments, with agriculture, trade and manufacture largely controlled by a smaller group of individual owners. Yet, despite these very different explanations of affliction and death associated with distinctive forms of governance, there were also areas of overlap in Ekiti and British ways of thinking about Sopona and smallpox. For example, while their explanations of the means of contagion differed, both priests and colonial officials (and their surrogates) saw the deity's work or the disease, respectively, as highly contagious and believed in the importance of isolating those exhibiting symptoms. Nonetheless, the policing of communities affected by smallpox reflected the repressive power of the colonial state, which, along with British officials' use of biomedical discourse as a way of differentiating Africans, contrasts with the operation of 'biopower' postulated by Foucault, whereby state power is supported by individuals' internalized biomedical ideas about themselves and their bodies (Vaughan 1991: 10–11). Indeed, during the period discussed in this paper, British colonial health services were very minimally funded; it was only after World War II that colonial health care was more widely provided (Pearce 1980: 93). Thus while Foucault's conception of bio-politics 'as a form of government taken by a new dynamic of forces that, in conjunction, express power relations that the classical world could not have known' (Lazzarato 2002: 101) may be useful in thinking about this post-war expansion of the colonial medical service in Ekiti, it does not explain the situation in remote rural areas in south-western Nigeria in the 1920s and 1930s.[1] Rather, through colonial differentiation of Africans on the basis of ethnicity or race, British authorities established political control through their policy of 'indirect rule', instituted through a Native Authority system of 'traditional' rulers (Beidelman 2012: 291).

In this chapter, I consider the intersections and the disjunctions between the socio-cultural beliefs about Sopona held by residents in the Ekiti Yoruba area of south-western Nigeria and colonial officials' attempts to contain smallpox outbreaks as a way of better understanding the political-economic context of British colonial rule. As reflected in the case examined here, colonial attitude towards diseases – and therefore, disease control – was shaped by the specific organization of the political economy of domination. Governing lives, particularly in ways that serve economic exploitation and expropriation, involves sustaining the lives of those who constitute the labour pool. One particular outbreak of smallpox in Iye-Ekiti in 1929, described in

---

[1] In the context of smallpox, it would be interesting to think about Foucault's arguments about biopower and bio-politics in relation to the Smallpox Eradication Programme (SEP) that was instituted by the World Health Organization in 1967. The following year, the SEP received assistance in Nigeria from Center for Disease Control epidemiologists (Renne 2010: 27). This intervention suggests a bio-politics at the intersection of both international governmental organization and national government power with local ideas about medicine and disease during the early Independence era in Nigeria.

archival documents, provides a focus for the discussion, although Ekiti individuals' experiences of Sopona and of colonial vaccination efforts provide the backdrop for their sometimes contrary views.

Sopona in Ekiti

Before the British gained political control through the incorporation of the area of south-western Nigeria associated with the Ekiti-Yoruba kingdoms within the boundaries of the Lagos Protectorate in 1893,[2] particular priests – *awuro orisa* Sopona – who specialized in the worship of Sopona used various techniques to prevent, cure and treat towns and villages when Sopona appeared (Hopkins 2002: 202; Ojo 1966). In Itapa-Ekiti, if villagers heard that Sopona was present in nearby villages, they did two things to prevent Sopona from entering their own. First, the *awuro orisa* made sacrifices for Sopona at a shrine in the forested area outside of the village known as Igbo Kiti Oja, as one older man described:

> There is a particular place where they used to make *ojubo* [sacrifice] for Sopona ... Those people, the *aworo orisa*, were the ones making the sacrifice and only they knew it ... The *aworo* used a particular cloth, when they were making a sacrifice, they would hang a big white cloth near the shrine and would pass through it. Also, when they wanted to enter the shrine, they had to change their clothes and wear white cloth. They were just doing it as if it were a church service. They would do it so that Sopona would not come, they made appeasement.[3]

Second, they attempted to prevent Sopona from entering and spreading in the town by fumigation, using a type of *agbo* (herbal infusion) which they sprinkled on people, houses, crossroads and paths entering the town.

> They used leaves to prevent Sopona from coming into the town. They would gather leaves together and put them in water, after that they would go and look for *opa elelesinrin* [a type of plant]. That is what they used to dip in the water to spray people. They would do that in every area, they would even go to all the entrances of the town, they would spray them with this mixture.[4]

In the event that these sacrifices, medicinal spraying and prayers were unsuccessful and Sopona entered the town, there were particular symptoms which indicated that a person was affected. As was the case with Adelola Adeloye, loss of appetite or disinterest in favourite foods and feverishness were two early symptoms. One older man in Itapa-Ekiti who experienced smallpox when he was in his twenties described his memories:

---

[2] Later, in 1899, the Northeastern District of Yorubaland (encompassing Ijesa and Ekiti regions) was formed. Twelve years later Ekiti Division was established, with a divisional administrative centre built in Ado-Ekiti in 1914 (Renne 2003: 77).
[3] Interview: anonymous informant, 11 July 2010, Itapa-Ekiti.
[4] Ibid.

> When it starts, you begin to sweat, that's the first symptom ... Then you will have headache and start to feel dizzy. Then you will see yourself as if you are going mad. For example, you can be wearing a cloth, you may just remove it anywhere, anyhow and try to hit any person you see ... And you may even try to jump out of a window. And people will try to hold you. If they ask an afflicted person questions, s/he can't reply because s/he can't understand [i.e., outside of the realm of human social relations, a mad person]. And the person will be trying to get up, get up. It started as if one is experiencing madness. The person might have even gotten up and started running or they may take a cutlass and would try to go into the bush. And people would start holding the person. Then that person would be weak, unable to do anything; after some time the spots will start to come out. That is the way that Sopona affected people. Once they had discovered that it was Sopona that was affecting the person, they would go to look for *emu* [palm wine] and other things to add to it, they would mix these things together to appease Sopona. They will kneel down and prostrate to appease the *orisa*.[5]

This possession of a person's body by Sopona, literally a form of spirit possession, transformed the afflicted person's body into a sort of shrine where people would prostrate, regardless of the age of the person possessed by Sopona. Thus a small child could be greeted by a prostrating elder:

> When you see those people [with spots], you prostrate and greet the person. It is the things that come out that make people prostrate like that, saying, 'Baba, please don't affect me!' Even the time that Sopona affected me, people were calling me, 'Baba, Baba!' People started rubbing their hands and pleading.[6]

People also took care to attend to the slightest wishes of those whom Sopona had touched:

> For example, assuming they are pounding yam, you may say that you don't want to eat it, then you may say that you want to eat *amala* or beans. And if the person is not ready [with the food], the affected person will be shouting, 'It's taking too long!' They will quickly add salt and then bring it to the person to eat.[7]

These events would have taken place in Itapa-Ekiti around 1940. Five years later in Ikole-Ekiti, Adeloye (2009: 96) experienced a similar sort of treatment after he had recovered:

> Another memorable occurrence was the deferential treatment I received from all and sundry as a fortunate survivor of smallpox. I was treated with obligatory respect. Everybody fawned on me. It was believed that the disease had imbued me with extrasensory, paranormal ability, the gift of prophecy and powers of divination [i.e., superhuman powers]. Anything I ordered was done promptly and without

---

[5] Interview: anonymous informant, 22 June 2011, Itapa-Ekiti.
[6] Ibid. The gesture of rubbing one's hands together may be seen in church when people are praying, pleading for God's assistance.
[7] Ibid. Salt was used to make the food tasty but not red palm oil since red was Sopona's colour and would possibly offend the deity.

question. Even my father had to obey my instructions. I became an instrument of the gods. (Adeloye 2009: 94).

Treating Those Possessed by Sopona

Once a person had been identified as having been possessed by Sopona, *awuro orisa* specialists were called to make sacrifices to the *orisa* and to accompany the affected person to the outskirts of town or village where a small hut would be built to house the person as they convalesced. One of the *olorisa* would stay with the person, making offering to Sopona to facilitate recovery. 'They will beg Sopona. "Is it rat that you want, is it fish that you want?"', as one man put it:

> The *olorisa* are the ones who take care of the affected person, appeasing and begging Sopona. There were no doctors then, the *olorisa* were treating the person. They would be prostrating daily to the affected person, asking what Sopona will take to leave the affected person ... It was very powerful. But as they were begging, it would go little by little.[8]

The reasoning behind this isolation helps to explain local understandings of how Sopona was spread. Sopona could not be seen,[9] except by the *awuro orisa* who had special vision, and in its manifestations seen on its victims' bodies, through its spots. 'The *orisa* they call Sopona, they can't see it, it only comes through the air', as one man explained. He continued:

> The reason why they are taken to the forest, this will prevent others from getting it because it can be spread by the breeze. The breeze can bring the odour (*ategun o maa mu oorun*) of Sopona. Because if someone can smell it, they may get infected.[10]

Once the person had been sequestered in the bush, another series of actions relating to colonial government regulations were begun:

> Those who discovered the case will go to inform the Owatapa (the king of Itapa). Then the Kabiyesi will send a message to the [district office] where the *wole* [literally, 'look house' – name for government sanitary inspectors] stay. The *wole* who were there working, the king will say this is what is happening in my town. So they will send a *wole* to come to the town. The *wole* will first come to the king and the king will explain that the person is from a particular family. The king will now send some people to the family house of the Sopona sufferer and the *wole* will go to the place in the forest where the affected person stays and will fumigate the place. That fumigation will prevent the air from blowing Sopona to the town.[11]

---

[8] Interview: anonymous informant, 11 July 2010, Itapa-Ekiti.
[9] Samuel Johnson (1976[1921]: 28) wrote that Sopona was represented by 'a broom made from the branches of the bamboo palm, stripped of its leaves', although none of the people I spoke with in Ekiti described Sopona in this way. It was possible that Sopona was represented differently in different parts of Yorubaland.
[10] Interview: anonymous informant, 11 July 2010, Itapa-Ekiti.
[11] Ibid.

The government sanitary inspectors' actions after a smallpox outbreak – fumigation and isolation – paralleled the work done by the *olorisa* on the appearance of Sopona. However, government officials also had medical means of preventing the spread of smallpox through inoculation.[12] Although the man who described the work of the *wole* only mentioned fumigation of family houses, it is also possible that they vaccinated all of the family members and villagers whom they could find at the same time.

Colonial Efforts to Control Smallpox in Ekiti

Medical officials in the Ministry of Health enacted a vaccination ordinance that established rules, procedures, and penalties for smallpox vaccination measures in the colony of Nigeria (Schneider 2009). This system of formulating ordinances and making them public through the circulation in the government *Gazette* reflected a form of government based on writing, even when these published ordinances might be widely ignored. Thus while published vaccination ordinances supported smallpox vaccination initiatives in southern Nigeria which began early in the twentieth century,[13] it was not until the early 1920s when lanolinated calf lymph was imported – to replace the earlier, less effective dry lymph – that vaccination increased, tripling the numbers of people vaccinated between 1919 and 1920 (Horn 1952). However, in Ekiti, early vaccination efforts appeared to focus on smallpox outbreaks, rather than overall vaccination campaigns. Thus in 1926 and 1927 in the Southern Provinces (of which Ekiti was part), vaccination was carried out during small local outbreaks (ibid.). Suspected cases of smallpox were to be reported by village heads (as described for Ekiti above) to district health officials. Subsequently, sanitary inspectors, under the supervision of colonial health officials, travelled to the affected town or village and sought to contain the outbreak. The report of one such outbreak in Iye-Ekiti in 1929 provides a glimpse of how such a response worked.

Outbreak in Iye-Ekiti, April 1929

On 13 April 1929, the Ajero of Ijero at Iye, a sub-village of the District notified the District Officer at Ado-Ekiti of an outbreak of smallpox in the small village of Iye-Ekiti, near Ishan-Ekiti (Map 10.1). The District Medical Officer,

---

[12] While none of the men interviewed knew of Hausa-Fulani healers performing inoculation in Ekiti, inoculation had been practised in Northern Nigeria, mainly by Fulani and Hausa specialists, who took pus from the pox of infected individuals, which was then rubbed on cuts made in the arms of those being inoculated (Herbert 1975: 544; Smith 1954: 46). However, this form of arm to arm inoculation could lead to death (because the strength of the transmitted virus was not controlled) and it was banned by the British (Vaccination Ordinance of 1917, Chapter 53, section 15). During outbreaks of smallpox in Kabba Province in 1926–7, the senior sanitary officer of the Northern Provinces, Kaduna, sent out a memo 'to ascertain if the Natives are practicing inoculation', which he sought to stop (Davies 1928).

[13] The 1917 Vaccination Ordinance was published in the *Nigerian Gazette* in 1918.

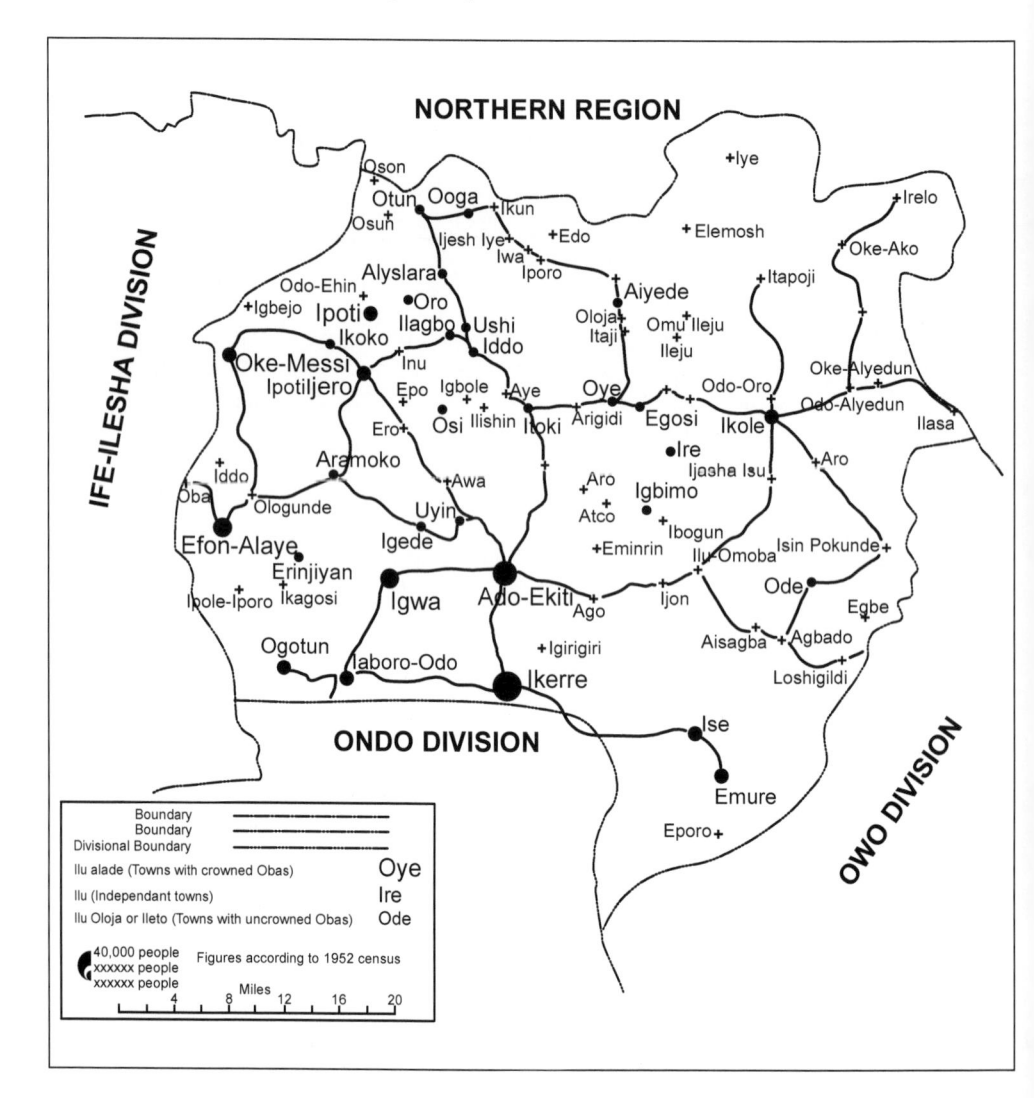

Map 10.1 Map of Ekiti, 1952, showing the location of Oye-Ekiti, Ishan-Ekiti, Iye-Ekiti, Itapa-Ekiti, Ikole-Ekiti, and Efon-Alaye. (from G.F.A. Ojo, *Yoruba Culture*. London: University of London Press, 1966)

D.F. Moore, the Assistant District Officer, the government vaccinator, the NA sanitary inspector, and eight policemen went to the town and gave the following instructions.

1. Any patients [are] to be isolated in a house selected for that purpose. One volunteer from each family who has been nursing the affected patient to stay with the patient in isolation.
2. Other contacts not to be isolated on account of the whole village being considered contact.

3. Spraying of infected houses.
4. Rooms in which known sick to have been [must be] closed.
5. Complete vaccination of this town and its neighbour [this would have been Ishan-Ekiti].
6. Closing of the Town to trade by Policing but people allowed to go to farm on being given slips.
7. Food to be brought to isolation compound not to patients.
8. If any difficulty of getting food arrangements to be made with the Bale of neighbouring town for a selected few to visit Market of this town to obtain food for village.
9. Police to be on guard on roads and isolation house and to assist vaccinator.
10. Complete clear up of the town, full clearing and all rubbish burnt.

This list, cited in the official report, was amended with two additional handwritten instructions, namely: the 'Government Sanitary Inspector [be] placed in charge of operations'; and: a 'complete roster of village to be taken and police search of all compounds of both towns for new infections' (Moore 1929a). By 1 June 1929, the Medical Officer reported: 'All staff have been returned and preventative special measures discontinued.' For the period from 13 April to 27 May 1929, 1,065 people had been vaccinated in Iye-Ekiti (as well as at the neighbouring villages of Iporo, Iyesha (Ijesha-Iye), and Eda; see Map 10.1), although the elderly and pregnant women were not vaccinated. The officer noted that there were 19 cases of smallpox since mid-April with one death (Moore 1929b).[14]

What is particularly interesting about this outbreak is that apparently the village head did not report it to District health officials. Rather, it was the district head, the Ajero of Ijero-Ekiti, who did so, much to the consternation of the acting District Officer, Ekiti Division:

> I have seen the Bale and his Chiefs and informed them that their conduct in hiding this outbreak is disgraceful in view of my recent instructions regarding infectious diseases to be reported immediately. (Sullen 1929)

The acting District Officer, Ekiti Division, also noted that the 'Ajero of Ijero proposes to deal with the Bale and his Chiefs in his Native Court'. Precisely what, if anything, consequently happened is not indicated in the official

---

[14] More recently in July-September 2014, a variation of this containment exercise was carried out, mainly in southern Nigeria, after the outbreak of the Ebola virus. Health officials used a combination of isolation wards in hospitals and contact follow-up to stop the spread of the virus. By early October 2014, 894 contacts had been identified and followed, 11 patients with confirmed Ebola were discharged, and seven had died. While initially there were some problems in the responses of the public and political leaders (who did not understand the seriousness of the disease) as well as some health workers (who refused to care for Ebola patients), information and training by the health personnel at the Emergency Operations Centre contributed to the effective implementation in this government-led response (Shuaib et al. 2014). An acceptance of the government's legitimacy in leading this public health programme also contributed to its success; on 20 October, the World Health Organization declared Nigeria to be Ebola free (WHO 2014).

reports, exemplifying the way that the distance – both social and physical – between Ekiti residents and colonials officials meant that the latter often 'did not know exactly what happened on the ground' (Beidelman 2012: 292)

Iye-Ekiti in 2010

The village known as Iye-Ekiti is located along a narrow paved road that begins at Oye-Ekiti and continues north through Ayedun-Ekiti and Ishan-Ekiti. We stopped at a 'storey' (two-storey) building to inquire about whether there were any elders in the village who might remember or heard stories of the 1929 outbreak of smallpox in Iye-Ekiti described in the colonial officials' account which I had found in the Nigerian National Archives at Ibadan. This event would have occurred 81 years prior to the sunny July day we'd set out to visit the village. We were directed to a house in Oriegun Quarter, which, like the other parts of the town, consisted of a mix of single- and two-storey mud- or concrete-block houses, plastered with concrete with louvre windows and tin roofs. We waited outside on benches on the cemented front stoop for the owner, Chief G.O. Kupolati. On his return, he opened the double doors of his well-stocked traditional medicine shop located in the front of his house and we entered (Illustration 10.1).

Chief Kupolati remembered episodes of smallpox in Iye-Ekiti, although it is possible that his memories reflect stories he had heard as a child, or his experiences of similar but later quarantines of the village. However, he made several points that coincided with the colonial report, supporting the accuracy of his account:[15]

> Yes, we had that Sopona here during the 1920s, but I can only speak for this town. I'm 85 so I can easily know what happened then. The majority of people affected were carried to the bush to treat them. They would never allow the infected people to stay in the town, they were treated in the bush. When the *oyinbo* [European] people brought all the things they were using, they gave people medicine [i.e., vaccinations] to prevent them from getting it. Those who were treated in the bush, they were brought back to the town and many people died. After the *oyinbo* came, the *olorisa* [traditional priests] withdrew, but some of them continued to treat people for Sopona. They used *ero* to rub people's bodies.[16] But when the *oyinbo* came, they were giving vaccine so when Sopona came it did not affect them so much. They would make a mark and put cream on it. But some people, after getting vaccinated they would be shivering – but it didn't affect me like that. It was only the ones who were yet to be infected [who were vaccinated]. The *oyinbo*, perhaps they heard about the outbreak in Lagos or Ibadan, so they sent their representatives – it was Nigerians who were sent to give the medicine. I was about nine years old

---

[15] Indeed, these overlapping descriptions of the events in Iye-Ekiti also support the accuracy of colonial officials' accounts, whose authors were subject to pressure to write reports which put them in the best light (Chanock 1985).

[16] The word, *ero*, means propitiation rather than medicine. Buckley (1985: 231) notes the reticence surrounding discussion of the specific ingredients of *ero*, similar to the fear that older Ekiti villagers feel when speaking of Sopona.

10.1 Chief G.O. Kupolati (in white), with companions, in his traditional medicine shop, Iye-Ekiti, July 2010. (© E.P. Renne)

then. The people then, the majority ran into the bush because they were afraid of the vaccine. But the *oyinbo* discovered it, so they had policeman who guarded the roads to the bush. They would only allow people holding a note confirming their vaccination who were allowed to pass. The *awuro orisa* had a particular place to worship Sopona and they used white cloth at this place ... The ones who carried the corpse, [buried] it and made sacrifices, they were very strong *olorisa*. During that time of the outbreak, there was not a single *awuwo orisa* who objected, they were very happy, they were not annoyed at all. They considered it as a sort of help to them. They didn't want people to die.[17]

Chief Kupolati's description of the smallpox outbreak coincided with Assistant District Officer's accounts in several ways. He noted that individuals with smallpox were treated in their homes, rather than sequestered in the bush; that colonial officials learned of the outbreak from someone outside the village; and that people leaving the quarantined village required a note to do so (point 6 from the ADO's list). His comment that it was 'Nigerians [i.e., Native Authority sanitary inspectors] who were sent to give the medicine' also coincided with Moore's handwritten addition that the 'Government Sanitary Inspector [be] placed in charge of operations', Yet he did not mention the Bale of Iye's failure to notify government of the outbreak and his attempt to have smallpox cases treated by *awuro* Sopona, as was done in the past. Furthermore, Chief Kupolati stated that Sopona priests fully supported the colonial intervention, while also noting that some priests continued to worship Sopona and that some people attempted to evade smallpox immunization for

[17] Interview: Chief G.O. Kupolati, 11 July 2010, Iye-Ekiti.

fear of the vaccine. This inconsistency in his description – that Sopona priests fully supported colonial health officials' efforts while some pursued their own means of placating Sopona – may be explained as an idealized interpretation of events, that the denizens of Iye-Ekiti had *olaju* [were 'enlightened'] and had fully supported the 'civilizing mission' of the British (Peel 1978).[18] Yet this resistance to colonial smallpox practices reflected a very different explanation of affliction, with Sopona viewed as a deity who 'came with creation', as opposed to seeing a progression of symptoms – fever, lack of appetite and the appearance of smallpox pustules – as an infectious disease, as it was defined by the British. These distinctive interpretations reflected both different forms of treatment as well as different forms of political rule.

Resistance to Smallpox Vaccination in Ekiti

In some ways, the great deference shown to the deity, Sopona, paralleled everyday social relations and practice, e.g., of juniors' mandatory show of respect towards elders and of the punishments meted out by elders for the social infractions of juniors. Furthermore, it was believed that just as the spirit of an ancestor could be reborn in a child (Adeyanju 2003), so the spirit of Sopona could come to inhabit the body of a victim. If the person survived, s/he would become a descendant of sorts, an *awuro* Sopona, who would be immune from the future ravages of Sopona. Thus Sopona priests and priestesses would make offering to the deity as one would to an ancestor and could care for others whom Sopona affected. Colonial officials' efforts to prevent smallpox through vaccination and quarantine, without making sacrifices to Sopona or respecting the deity's powerful seniority, were seen by some priests as risky behaviour that could incur Sopona's wrath. So despite the 1917 Vaccination Ordinance 'forbidding the worship of the smallpox juju (god, or *orisha*) and [the] heavy fines [which] were inflicted on many of its priests' (Schram 1971: 159),[19] *awuro* Sopona continued to perform sacrifices during the 1950s and 60s in Ekiti and elsewhere Yoruba south-western Nigeria. Enforcement of the Ordinance was untenable because of the secrecy surrounding *awuro* Sopona practices and the thinness on the ground of colonial officials and Native Authority sanitary inspectors. For example:

> Sanitary inspectors were responsible for large areas and since they generally travelled by bicycle, their coverage would be intermittent at best. The sanitary

[18] That this was not always the case was evident from a case of smallpox detected in 1970 in Amayo-Ilorin, Kwara State, where the chief denied knowledge of smallpox for fear of being deposed by government officials for hiding cases. In other rural parts of Kwara State, villagers also continued to resist vaccination up through the early 1970s (Fenner et al. 1988: 886).
[19] A similar attempt in Northern Nigeria to restrict the worship of *bori* spirits had a similar perspective: 'His Excellency the Governor directs that Residents are to urge on the Native Administrations the desirability of suppressing wherever possible all practices connected with bori' (Alexander 1910). One Hausa woman, Baba of Karo, describes the popularity of *bori* dances in the 1950s in Karo (a town in Kano State), which suggests that attempts to suppress *bori* worship in the north, like those outlawing Sopona, were equally ineffectual (Smith 1954: 233).

inspector appointed by the Health Superintendent, Ondo Province, in 1951, was 'responsible for Ijero, Iddo, Osi, Otun, Ishan, Aiyede, Itaji, Oye, and Ikole'. (Ekiti Div 1/1, File no. 995, p. 8, cited in Renne 2003: 246 n13)

Government officials were more inclined to follow up on outbreak reports or rumours that some *awuro* Sopona were intentionally infecting people with smallpox as a way of preserving their power (Bascom 1984: 91; Morgan 1979: 3).

Maintaining regular supplies of viable imported calf lymph vaccine was also a problem. In 1930, when a Native Authority vaccinator was sent to vaccinate villagers after a smallpox outbreak in two Bunu Yoruba villages in Kabba Division, he was unable to do so since he had no lymph vaccine (Rue 1930). However, during the 1940s, colonial officials increased their focus on widespread smallpox vaccination and, when necessary, enforcing vaccination acceptance through government programmes and visits to primary schools. As Schneider (2009: 214) notes: 'By the 1950s reports began to admit that the problem was not contagious travellers or effectiveness of vaccines but reaching enough people and following procedures strictly enough for those vaccinated.'

Smallpox Vaccination in Ekiti in the 1940s

In 1945, colonial officials amended the original 1917 Vaccination Ordinance to include a notice form and procedures for compelling both parents and their children to attend vaccination events. These events were to be announced by medical health officers and carried out according to rulings determined by local Native Authority officials (Jakeway 1945). Consequently many people in Ekiti presently in their mid-70s received smallpox vaccinations during campaigns held in the late 1940s and early 1950s (Illustration 10.2), as one man in Itapa-Ekiti explained:

> When the *oyinbo* [Europeans] came, they called some people *oninomba* (owner of the mark; vaccinator), they were *wole* people then. They would bring vaccine (*abere*), and using a machine, they would press the needle [gun] and the machine would cause the injection in the arm, then they would put cream on it. They said that we should not wash it and that the mark (*nomba*) would be there forever. That thing, it was for Sopona. So when Sopona came, it would not be killing people, the *abere* would just suppress its power. Before, Sopona did kill people but the *abere* suppressed the power of Sopona. At that time, I wasn't affected by Sopona, they just gave it to me to prevent Sopona from affecting me. I was sixteen years old then.

Adelola Adeloye received his vaccinations at a school in Ikole-Ekiti, although a razor blade rather than a needle-gun was used to produce cuts for the introduction of the smallpox vaccine:

> At school, we were vaccinated against the raging fever. Each pupil received two cuts with the blade on the outside of the upper arm into which a jelly-like substance

10.2 'SMALLPOX made me BLIND', poster by Ernest Hough. (From R. Bowret, 'Vaccination', *The Nigerian Teacher*, 1936, No. 3, p. 45)

was squirted. If the wound became infected, you were lucky, as it meant that you had developed some resistance to smallpox. The wound was subsequently dressed with lemon-juice. If, on the other hand, the skin lacerations dried up spontaneously, you were unprotected and vulnerable to infection. I received eight of those cuts, four on the left and another four on the right arm. None of them took. (Adeloye 2009: 93)

It is not clear why Adelola Adeloye's vaccinations did not take. It was possible that the lanolinated lymph vaccine which needed to be kept under refrigeration had lost its potency on the road from Lagos to Ekiti. While Adeloye was not discouraged by this vaccine failure and his subsequent bout of smallpox – he later went on to become professor and chair of the Department of Neurosurgery at University College Hospital, Ibadan, the uncertain quality of early vaccines contributed to the belief held by some that Sopona could not be prevented or cured by Western medicine, voiced by one chief in Itapa-Ekiti:

> They can't use medicine ... Sopona was not the type of thing they can do anything for, they can't give medicine for it. They cannot do any medicine for the person, just prostration because it has a spiritual cause. If they try to bring medicine to cure it, it can't work.

Indeed, this continuing belief in the deity, Sopona, was evident in an attitudinal survey conducted in 1967 in several sections of metropolitan Lagos, where 1,849 individuals were questioned about their views of smallpox, of its causes, and of possible measures for its prevention (Morgan 1979). The most common explanation was the dry, hot weather of the Harmattan season, which Morgan (ibid.:17) suggests was an indirect attribution to Sopona, whom people preferred not to refer to by name.[20] This explanation was followed in number by spiritual causes. 'Only 6.1 percent of respondents described smallpox as a germ-borne or communicable disease' (ibid.: 13–14). Indeed, one young man, a secretary with secondary school education, working at the University of Lagos Teaching Hospital at the time, told Morgan that 'vaccination did not prevent smallpox, and that we should watch our step' (ibid.:20). Yet many educated young people in twenty-first-century Ekiti no longer think this way, having learned about smallpox and its eradication through vaccination programmes; some may not know of the deity, Sopona. They also subscribe to a form of political rule by which federal, state, and local government bodies – ministries and departments of health – are responsible for disease control. Some older people, however, have other explanations for Sopona's absence.

The Disappearance of Sopona

Sopona no longer appears in Ekiti towns and villages. Rather, according to some older residents, its junior brother, the *aburo* Sopona, known as measles or by the Yoruba names of *kurukuru*[21] or *ile gbona* (literally, hot land) has taken Sopona's place although, with the presence of government primary health care vaccination programmes, it is seen less frequently.[22] As one older man in Itapa-Ekiti observed: 'It's not the real Sopona they are treating now, it's *kurukuru*, the *aburo* Sopona.' Indeed, smallpox and measles may also be referred to as *omoiya*, as two children from the same mother, according to an older chief, also in Itapa-Ekiti:

> Through the medicine given to people now, the person will be playing, it doesn't kill anymore. It was after that that Sopona turned into *kurukuru* [measles]. They are *omoiya* – they are children of the same mother. Since then, *kurukuru* will affect people but they will not die. So they are different. Sopona has the power to kill.

This connection made between smallpox and measles may be seen in descriptions of measles elsewhere in Ekiti. When asked about the cause of measles, some people in the town of Efon-Alaye (see Map 10.1) related 'its prevalence with the hot air in the dry season' (Adetunji 1991: 1382). The term for measles, *ile gbona*, 'hot land', refers to the hot, dry season associated with measles outbreaks. That this term was also an alternate name for smallpox

---

[20] In mentioning the weather, people also referred to 'frying palm kernels' and 'roasting corn', practices which were believed to anger Sopona (Morgan 1979: 17; see also Johnson 1976: 28).
[21] *Kurukuru* may refer to a kernel-less corncob husk (see Renne 1994) – perhaps making reference to the pitting left on the skin of some who experienced measles. Measles is translated as *eeyi* (or *arun eeyi*) in the 1913 Church Missionary Society dictionary (CMS 1979: 90).
[22] The level of measles vaccination in Ekiti State is very high, suggesting widespread availability and acceptance of this vaccine. According to the 2013 Nigerian Demographic and Health Survey, over 85 per cent of children ages 12–23 months had received measles vaccination (National Population Commission and ICF International 2014).

suggests the close connection between measles and smallpox made by some. Indeed 'two respondents called it [measles] 'messenger of god' and associated it with smallpox' (ibid.).

The conceptual connection made between Sopona and *kurukuru* (or *ile gbona*) are reflected in these parallel ways of thinking about the causes, symptoms and treatments of both smallpox and measles – and perhaps reflect an oblique criticism of the inadequacy of the Federal Government's provision of primary health care in Nigeria. In an interesting reversal of the earlier accusations of colonial officials that *awuro* [priests of] Sopona intentionally spread smallpox, one diviner-herbalist (*babalawo*) interviewed by Adetunji (1991: 1382) believed that, 'doctors hated measles and that they could give the child a "death" injection [an injection given to kill a child if the disease was dangerously contagious] if the disease did not heal quickly'. Also, ideas about the importance of a specific progression of smallpox symptoms for the recovery process are similar to beliefs about the symptoms of measles and the appearance of measles pox.

According to one respondent, measles 'beheads' the child internally if the child does not pass out the spots inside the stomach. If hospital drugs were to be used at all, it was believed that the spots must still be allowed to come out. Finally, measles, like smallpox, was identified by a 'measles odour': for those with good olfactory organs, smelling was enough to identify the disease, while those who were not good at recognizing its odour could depend on persistent high temperature and observation of stool colouration (Adetunji 1991: 1382–3).

Yet while measles may still be seen, Sopona has left towns and villages in Ekiti, as was the case with other, more localized, *orisa* who disappeared when their shrines were destroyed or abandoned as towns expanded and new roads were built. 'God has put an end to it over 30 years ago', one man observed. Its younger brother, measles (*kurukuru*) has taken its place, although its susceptibility to Western medicine, which includes measles vaccine, has reduced its presence in Ekiti as well.

Conclusion

People in Lagos in the early 1970s still spoke of Sopona and the deity's priests in hushed tones, and many believed that vaccination could not work even as they participated in the mass smallpox immunization efforts there (Morgan 1979). More recently, older people in Itapa-Ekiti also lowered their voices when speaking of Sopona, describing the deity as resistant to Western medicine. 'The *oyinbo* [European] can treat and cure Sopona elsewhere but not here', one man explained.

However many younger people, if they know of Sopona at all, attribute the disappearance of smallpox to vaccination campaigns which eventually eradicated it (Fenner et al. 1988). Rather than a direct consequence of colonial efforts to criminalize the worship of Sopona, this shift in the belief in the power of Sopona to the belief in the efficacy of Western medicine reflects other social processes set in motion through colonial rule, specifically mission schools and government health programmes, as well as a particular form of governmentality, which, while imperfect in its implementation of primary health care, has fostered expectations of such care. Thus it is particularly appropriate that recent vaccination events in Itapa-Ekiti are held at the Methodist Church Primary School grounds. For it was Western education that enabled younger people to learn of a different, biomedical, explanation for the affliction which their elders attributed to Sopona. It was Christianity that undermined beliefs in deities, such as Sopona, associated with Yoruba religion and traditional rule based on a system of kings and priests-councillors (Hocart 1970). Changes in the prevailing political economy based on new forms of social relations as well as beliefs about the world and explanations of death and illness, rather than the imposition of government prescriptions – ordinances decreeing vaccination, banning Sopona worship, and requiring quarantines of villages, led to the eventual demise of Sopona in the minds of younger, Western-educated, Christian women and men in Ekiti.

Yet one may be a Christian without entirely forsaking older beliefs, or while expressing scepticism about the prevailing forms of government and economic neoliberal reforms introduced in the 1980s in Nigeria. Perhaps the remark of the diviner-herbalist at Efon-Alaye about 'death injections' given to children suffering from severe cases of measles provides some insight into this perspective. When colonial officials banned Sopona priests from attending to smallpox victims, they did so because they believed – largely on the basis of hearsay since it was unlikely that they would have seen *awuro* Sopona practices – that the priests were contributing to the spread of smallpox. Their attribution of nefarious practices to *awuro* Sopona also dismissed the legitimacy of the priests' knowledge and authority, which itself was imbricated in a particular way of social life. Similarly, the *babalawo* who claimed that medical doctors killed their very ill patients questioned the morality of Western biomedicine, which while capable of miraculous cures, undermines more holistic approaches to illness, challenges the legitimacy of ancestral knowledge, and has introduced expensive forms of health care beyond the reach of many Nigerians. In her extensive work, Jane Guyer (2004: 23) has looked 'for whatever gives persistent shape to a pervasive experience of flux and change'.[23] For some older residents of Ekiti, the fact that, while Sopona has left the junior of Sopona – *kurukuru*/measles – remains, provides evidence for them of the continuing relevance of system of traditional rule – associated with chiefs and *babalawo* diviners-herbalists, a form of political economy associated with the Ekiti Yoruba past.

---

[23] While outside of the purview of this chapter, one might consider this experience 'of flux and change' through a comparison of the economics involved in Nigerian government's provision of health care and the economics of health care provided by traditional health and pharmacies for residents of rural Ekiti during the Independence era.

References

Adeloye, A. (2009). *My Salad Years: The Primary School Years*. Ibadan: BookBuilders.

Adetunji, J.A. (1991). Response of Parents to Five Killer Diseases among Children in a Yoruba Community, Nigeria. *Social Science & Medicine* 31(12): 1379–87.

Adeyanju, F. (2003). *The Life and Times of Pa Francis Adeyanju of Itapa-Ekiti*. In E. Renne (ed.), Ibadan: BookBuilders.

Alexander, D. (1910). 'Notes on Bori'. *Official Gazette (Northern Nigeria)* Supplement 11, no. 8: xxi, Nigerian National Archives, Kaduna.

Bascom, William (1984[1969]). *The Yoruba of Southwestern Nigeria*. Prospect Heights, IL: Waveland Press.

Beidelman, T.O. (2012). *The Culture of Colonialism*. Bloomington, IN: Indiana University Press.

Bowret, R. (1936). 'Vaccination', *The Nigeria Teacher* 3: 44–7.

Buckley, A. (1985). *Yoruba Medicine*. Oxford: Clarendon Press.

Chanock, M. (1985). *Law, Custom and Social Order*. Cambridge, UK: Cambridge University Press.

CMS – Church Missionary Society (1979[1913]). *A Dictionary of the Yoruba Language*. Ibadan: University Press.

Davies, L.W. (1928). 'Outbreak of Smallpox' (28 February). LokProf 130/1921, Nigerian National Archives, Kaduna.

Fenner, F., D.A. Henderson, I. Arita, Z. Jezek and I.D. Ladnyi (1988). *Smallpox and Its Eradication*. Geneva: WHO.

Guyer, Jane (2004). *Marginal Gains: Monetary Transactions in Atlantic Africa*. Chicago, IL: University of Chicago Press.

Herbert, E. (1975). 'Smallpox Inoculation in Africa', *Journal of African History* 16(4): 539–59.

Hocart, A.M. (1970[1936]). *Kings and Councillors*. Chicago, IL: University of Chicago Press.

Hopkins, D. (2002). *The Greatest Killer: Smallpox in History*. Chicago, IL: University of Chicago Press.

Horn, D.W. (1952). Notes on Smallpox in Nigeria. Vaccination Campaign Reports, 1949–1954. KAD-MOH 5/1, File No. 52, Vol. I. Kaduna: Nigerian National Archives.

Jakeway, F.D. (1945). 'An Ordinance to Amend the Vaccination Ordinance'. *Nigerian Gazette*, No. 16 of 1945: 273–5.

Johnson, S. (1976[1921]). *The History of the Yorubas*. Lagos: CSS Bookshops.

Legg, S. (2006). 'Governmentality, Congestion and Calculation in Colonial Delhi', *Social & Cultural Geography* 7(5): 709–29.

Lazzarato, M. (2002). 'From Biopower to Biopolitics', *Pli* 13: 99–113.

Moore, D.F. (1929a). 'Small Pox at Iye a Village near Ishan'. Ondo Prof 1/1, File 262B No. 9 1928. Ibadan: Nigerian National Archives.

—. (1929b). 'Small Pox Outbreak at Iye'. Ondo Prof 1/1, File 262B No. 9 1928.

Ibadan: Nigerian National Archives.

Morgan, R. (1979). 'The Sopono Cult and Smallpox Vaccinations in Lagos'. Working Paper No. 11, African Studies Center. Brookline, MA: Boston University.

National Population Commission (NPC) (Nigeria) and ICF International (2014). *Nigeria Demographic and Health Survey 2013*. Abuja, Nigeria and Rockville, MD: NPC and ICF International.

Ojo, G.J.A. (1966). *Yoruba Culture*. London: University of London Press.

Pearce, T.O. (1980). 'Political and Economic Changes in Nigeria and the Organization of Medical Care', *Social Science & Medicine* 14B: 91–8.

Peel, J.D.Y. (1978). '*Olaju*: A Yoruba Concept of Development', *Journal of Development Studies* 14(2): 139–65.

Renne, E. (1994). 'Things that Threaten: A Symbolic Analysis of Bunu Yoruba Masquerades', *RES* 26: 100–112.

—. (2003). *Population and Progress in a Yoruba Town*. Edinburgh: University of Edinburgh Press; Ann Arbor, MI: University of Michigan Press for the Intl African Institute.

—. (2010). *Politics of Polio in Northern Nigeria*. Bloomington, IN: Indiana University Press.

Rue, E.V.M. (1930). 'Outbreak of Smallpox.' LokProf 130/1921, ACC No. 68. Kaduna: Nigerian National Archives.

Schram, R. (1971). *A History of the Nigerian Health Services*. Ibadan: University of Ibadan Press.

Schneider, W.H. (2009). 'Smallpox in Africa during Colonial Rule', *Medical History* 53(2):193–227.

Shuaib, F., R. Gunnala, E. Musa, F. Mahoney, O. Oguntimehin, P. Nguku, S. Nyanti, N. Knight, N. Gwarzo, O. Idigbe, A. Nasidi and J. Vertefeuille (Centers for Disease Control and Prevention) (2014). Ebola Virus Disease Outbreak – Nigeria, July-September 2014. *Morbidity and Mortality Weekly Report* 63(39): 867–72.

Smith, M.F. (1954). *Baba of Karo*. New Haven, CT: Yale University Press.

Sullen, A.P. (1929). 'Small pox at Iye a Village near Ishan'. Ondo Prof 1/1, File 262B No. 9 1928. Ibadan: Nigerian National Archives.

Vaughan, M. (1991). *Curing Their Ills: Colonial Power and African Illness*. Stanford, CA: Stanford University Press.

WHO – World Health Organization (2014). 'Nigeria is now Free of Ebola Virus Transmission.' (20 October). Available at www.who.int/mediacentre/news/ebola/20–october-2014/en (accessed 17 November 2015).

Part IV

HISTORICITY, TEMPORALITY, AGENCY
& DEMOCRATIC LIFE

11 History as Value Added? Valuing the Past in Africa

Sara Berry

Introduction

Historical narratives figure prominently in contemporary African affairs. Since the late 1980s, international initiatives seeking to 'democratize' African governments and decentralize governing institutions have prompted widespread debate, sometimes conflict, over land claims, citizenship, eligibility for political office, and the relevance of historical precedents for social and political entitlements in the present. Describing the return of electoral politics to a northern Beninese town in the early 1990s, Bako-Arifari wrote that 'history [was] a subject of permanent discussion' (1997: 6). By linking authority and resource access to precise delineations of territory and ownership, neoliberal projects for protecting property rights and decentralization intensified debates over local and national belonging, prompting people to search for historical precedents to guide and legitimate social and political action in the present (Bierschenk et al. 2000; Chauveau 2000; Lentz, 2013; Tsikata and Yaro, 2011; Amanor 2012).

Understandings of the past have also been brought to bear in negotiating value in the marketplace. As competition over land and landed property increased in the years after independence, contestants engaged in a vigorous search for historical precedents to validate their claims and discredit those of their rivals. Historical imagination plays a role in a wide array of economic transactions, from the purchase and sale of 'antiquities', to loans, outlays on environmental protection, and the production and transmission of historical knowledge itself.[1] Drawing examples from a variety of ethnographic and historical studies of economic conditions and practices in Africa, this chapter reflects on history in the marketplace, asking how history adds value to things transacted in the marketplace, and how the production of history and the constitution of market value inform and reflect on each other.

---

[1] I am using the term 'transactions' to refer to transfers – loans, gifts, bequests as well as equivalent exchanges – as a reminder that most, if not all transfers evoke some kind of return, cf. Graeber 2011. By the same token, I use the terms 'buyer' and 'seller' to denote protagonists in all kinds of market transactions.

Markets for History:
Objects, Activities, Landscapes & Knowledge

History enters into the negotiation of market value in different ways.[2] Writing of things with 'historical value, derived from acts of production, use or appropriation that have involved the object in the past', David Graeber refers specifically to heirlooms – objects preserved and handed on from one generation to the next – and the rich body of anthropological writings that has accumulated on them (2011: 105). The present discussion suggests that history adds value not only to scarce and specialized heirlooms, but also to a wide variety of marketed things that take account of the past in many different ways. History figures in the valuation not only of things that are old or linked to bygone times and places, but equally in exchanges of things valued for their newness (perishable foods, novel designs, etc.) and things that do not yet exist. Newly made clothing, utensils, tourist facilities or theme parks that replicate or invoke bygone objects and practices are cases in point.

As transactors argue over the authenticity of competing historical narratives, interpretations of tradition, or attributions of public versus private ownership, markets flourish alongside (and in some cases because of) the debates. After describing some of the many kinds of things that rise in value when they are deemed to be historical, I take a closer look at processes of valuation, asking how narratives of past events, allusions to particular historical moments, or invocations of 'timeless' tradition are brought to bear in market transactions, how the production of history figures in the constitution of market value and vice versa, and what each might tell us about the other.[3]

Objects
Many authors have described particular kinds of marketable objects that are likely to fetch higher prices, in both local and international markets, if prospective buyers identify them as expressing, or deriving from, societies or cultural practices of the past. Such items may be grouped into two broad categories: 'traditional' goods, which replicate or resemble items that were produced and consumed in former times, and 'antiquities', or items that were

---

[2] I use the term 'negotiation' to emphasize the interactive character of market price formation, not to suggest that actors in any particular market are equally endowed with power or resources.

[3] This essay uses examples from historical and ethnographic literature on Africa, but similar points could be made about valuation and value added in other parts of the world. If, as Jane Guyer has suggested, Africans are unusually attuned to possibilities for 'marginal gains' (Guyer 2004), this is not because Africans are somehow more traditional, or less interested in material gain than people in other parts of the world, but because centuries of extractive trade and investment, imperial domination and political transformation and turmoil have left their economies poorer, their shares of global markets smaller, than those of other world regions. Recent evidence of rising rates of growth and increasing economic inequality in African countries not torn apart by or struggling to recover from brutally destructive warfare suggests that Africa is very much part of the global economy, but a part often disadvantaged by the particular conjuncture of extractive investment, contested top-down rule, and limited outlays on human and material infrastructure that characterized the continent's history for much of the twentieth century.

History as Value Added? Valuing the Past in Africa

made at some time in the past and have survived to the present. *Babban riga*, the embroidered garments that are worn today by notables in Zaria and other northern Nigerian cities, are an example of the former. Modelled on styles that date to the nineteenth century, the robes display their owners' ability to afford expensive garments and reassert the importance of 'traditional' political hierarchies in contemporary times (Renne 2004).

Comparable examples are legion: traditional designs and styles are incorporated in all kinds of consumer goods, from clothing, ornaments, furniture and utensils, to hairstyles, music and cuisine, that find ready markets (and imitators) not only in their localities or countries of origin, but around the world. Many are purchased by affluent consumers who have the means to satisfy even 'basic needs' such as food and clothing with a variety of novel and/or exotic goods; others find their way into private collections or museum displays.

Another category of objects that often bring high prices when marketed to those who can afford to pay for them includes goods that were produced and/or used a long time ago. Wood carvings and other art objects are a case in point. Whether presented as the unique creations of individual artists or admired for their aesthetic qualities, Yoruba, Akan, Mande, Zulu sculptures often replicate 'traditional' forms, seeking to appeal to consumers of the past as well as connoisseurs of art. The most highly valued of all are 'antiquities' – art objects made in the past and preserved by their owners for their ritual importance as well their aesthetic appeal. As Chris Steiner pointed out in his illuminating study of the global trade in Ivorian wood carvings, 'this is the category of goods which interests serious (i.e., investment-oriented) African art collectors and dealers' (Steiner 1994: 33–4). Professional Ivorian traders 'wander from village to village searching for art' objects that they know will bring high prices from collectors in Paris or New York if they are or appear to be old, and relaying information on collectors' preferences to contemporary carvers, who adjust their own work accordingly. The looting of archaeological sites is another unfortunate example of the market value of antiquities.

Activities
'Traditional' styles and historical allusions are also common in many contemporary forms of performative art – music, dance, film, etc. – as well as in domestic and commercial activities, such as cooking and food processing,[4] that influence demand for foodstuffs, equipment and related commodities. Purchases of foodstuffs for home consumption or the preparation of cooked food for sale (whether in restaurants or from vendors on the street) are two mundane examples that touch on the lives and living standards of entire populations. Encouraged by government efforts to attract foreign tourists as well as by expanding global markets for popular art styles, displays of chiefly regalia, revivals of festivals that had fallen into abeyance, or performances of 'traditional' music and dance – from

---

[4] The current popularity of 'ancient grains' in baked goods and breakfast cereals marketed in the USA is one example.

jali (or *griots*) on stage in Bathurst, Bamako or Boston to the ubiquitous 'Maasai dancers' whose red-check blankets and dangling earrings have become standard fare in tourist hotels on both sides of the continent – seek to re-enact the past for present consumption (See, inter alia, Austen 1999; Witz et al. 2001; Ebron 2002; Macgonagle 2006). The works of African filmmakers such as Ousmane Sembène and Adama Drabo, who explore historical and traditional themes in rich and complex detail, have also found audiences, and markets, around the world.

Landscapes
Traces of history, in particular landscapes, have long been a focus of popular, scholarly and political interest in many parts of the world. Historic sites – places that either bear visible traces of human activity in the past, such as buildings or the debris of earlier human habitation, or have been marked in some way to commemorate historical events and actors – are often valued as public assets – part of a 'heritage' that allows people in the present to know themselves and/or others through direct encounters with their pasts. Consumers' interest in historic sites, in turn, gives rise to a range of economic transactions, from investment in preserving or restoring historically significant sites and structures, to outlays on what might be called 'clio-tourism' – reconstructed scenes, episodes or lifeways of former times, that offer visitors simulated encounters with bygone people and places.

In the late twentieth century, most projects of historic preservation and/or re-enactment have to attract private as well as public capital in order to succeed. Museums, monuments and national archives built or taken over from colonial regimes by newly independent African governments as symbols of national pride, have suffered in recent years as states' financial resources have dwindled. In the meantime, private investors have begun to show interest in the potential of clio-tourism, sponsoring trips to historic locations, buildings, etc., or even following the example of some corporations in North America and Europe by creating historical theme parks. Examples may be found in Paulla Ebron's study of *jali* (oral historians and musicians) in Gambia, which includes an account of a 'homeland journey', in which African American winners of a contest sponsored by McDonald's visited author Alex Haley's ancestral home in Gambia (Ebron 2002: chapters 5 and 7), or Carolyn Hamilton's insightful essay on Shakaland, a theme park built in South Africa in the late 1980s to celebrate, and market, the famous nineteenth-century Zulu leader (Hamilton 1998: 187–205). In both cases, history was filtered through the contemporary media – Haley's book and film, Roots, and the South African TV mini-series 'Shaka'.

Paradoxically, landscapes may also be valued for the *absence* of human history. Tourists and conservationists seek out 'natural' habitats supposedly untouched by human intervention to study, admire and preserve. Like historic site preservation and clio-tourism, environmental protection and eco-tourism are big business these days, attracting billions of dollars from public agencies and private corporations, as well as large outlays from the

History as Value Added? Valuing the Past in Africa

burgeoning non-profit sector of the global economy.[5] Like sites of historic human activity, historic nature spans the contested boundary between public and private investment and access. Inspired by justifiable concern over the exhaustion of non-renewable natural resources, many environmental protection programmes are predicated on historical imaginations, informed by the widely held belief that restoring natural habitats to the state they are known or imagined to have attained at some (often undefined) point in the past is a public good that ought not to be left to the dictates of unregulated market exchange.[6] In response to these concerns, environmental projects in Africa have attracted large amounts from governments seeking to promote eco-tourism, and non-profit institutions, many organized and financed outside of Africa. As the international conservation movement has grown, African governments and private enterprises have also sought to tap the expanding international market for eco-tourism, with varying degrees of sensitivity and success. The frequency with which local people have been displaced to make way for nature preserves and/or wealthy foreign tourists underscores the exploitative potential of both public and private investment in 'natural history'. Are nature and/or the past forms of property? If so, to whom do they belong? (McGregor 2009; Bassett and Cormier-Salem 2007).

Knowledge

Questions about the past as property also arise with respect to the production and circulation of historical knowledge itself (see, e.g., Handler 1991). Knowledge of the past is frequently acquired and transmitted quite independently of market transactions, of course, but historical expertise may also command a price, in more ways than one. Professional historians who make their living by studying history and teaching it to others are to be found in most societies today, as are archivists, curators, genealogists, and so forth. History holds a central place in school curricula and scholarly research, generating a market for historical expertise from which many teachers and academics make their living, but other kinds of market transaction also give rise to demand for historical knowledge. Museum collectors, tourists, concert audiences, individual consumers all want to know what historical events and processes are represented or incorporated in the things they buy, and whether their historicity is authentic, before deciding whether to buy and how much to pay. In many cases, tracing the provenance of objects (relics, works of art) and activities lends weight to claims of historical significance, and adds value

---

[5] The literature is too large to cite. Useful collections may be found in Anderson and Grove 1987; Beinart and McGregor 2003; Bassett et al. 2007 (also Grove 1995).

[6] Like the international architects of market liberalization, international conservation organizations have frequently claimed the right – indeed, the authority – to set agendas of economic policy and investment in African countries in the name of a kind of global public interest in preserving natural habitats and resources for present and future generations of humans (and other species). See, e.g., Hulme and McMurphree 2001; Giles-Vernick 2002; Alexander et al. 2003. 'Restorations' of altered landscapes to some imagined 'original' form should be distinguished from efforts to preserve landscapes *as they are* from destructive forms of natural resource exploitation, or real estate projects that level terrain and raze vegetation in the name of low cost 'development'.

to the knowledge of experts – from academicians to *jali*, respected elders, or tour guides – who provide the information.[7] Historians' ability to convert knowledge into cash or its equivalent depends, in turn, on the credulity of consumers as well as on the depth and breadth of their own understanding and the manner and context in which their knowledge is transmitted.[8]

As provenance adds value to objects and art works, so people's ability to gain value through market transactions is influenced by what might be called their market biographies – chronicles of previous activity that attest to their knowledge, reliability and honesty.[9] I am referring not to inspirational pamphlets – inexpensive African counterparts to the 'best seller' accounts of the lives and woes of individual celebrities that have come to occupy a sizeable niche in the American book trade – but to more-or-less formalized equivalents of credit scores – ratings based on chronicles of debt and expenditure by individuals and enterprises – that are used by banks and other financial intermediaries in wealthy economies to assess the risks of lending to a particular borrower. In principle, market biographies or histories of market performance by particular agents allow people to study the past performance of potential customers or suppliers, in order to assess their reliability and the likely costs of doing business with them. Creditworthiness (sometimes conflated with the more emotionally charged concept of 'trust') consists in large part of others' access to knowledge about a potential buyer's or borrower's history of profit, loss, repayment and default.

In a recent work, Graeber points out that unpaid debts act to sustain social relationships. As long as a debt remains unpaid, borrower and lender share a piece of unfinished business, obliging them to interact in order to complete the transaction. (If, as in Bourdieu's (1977: 5–9) formulation, the main difference between a sale and a gift is the amount of time that may elapse before the receiver reciprocates, gifts may be said to work in the same way as a debt). Once a debt is repaid, however, 'both parties can walk away and have nothing further to do with each other ... [repayment] destroys the very reason for having a relationship' (Graeber 2011: 122). Logically, this is true, but it is not the end of the story. Repayment of a loan finishes the interaction between lender and borrower for that transaction but, by demonstrating to the lender that the borrower is able and willing to repay, it also lays the groundwork for more loans – and a continued relationship – in the future. Each completed

---

[7] Faced with shrinking opportunities for income and employment, Africans are often keenly attuned to the possibilities of turning historical and 'traditional' knowledge to economic advantage. See, e.g., Tom Bassett's article, discussed below, on the revival of Mande hunters' associations in Côte d'Ivoire as purveyors of traditional skills (knowledge of natural habitats and protective 'medicine') that found new uses in the Ivorian political economy of the 1990s (Bassett 2003).

[8] When historical precedents add value to present transactions, secondary markets may emerge for related historical records, often posing challenges for institutions and individuals who are responsible for protecting and preserving them. During my research in Asante, I heard stories circulated by both litigants and researchers about documents that disappeared from state or university archives after being requested by someone involved in a land or chieftaincy dispute.

[9] Analogous in some ways to the 'social lives' of things or forests, discussed in Appadurai 1988 and Hecht et al. 2014, respectively.

sale, repaid loan, or reciprocated gift adds a chapter to the buyer's market biography, enhancing her reputation for reliability and helping to prolong her relationships with her providers.

Where market actors have regular recourse to the requisite technologies, market 'biographies' may be compiled and circulated electronically, by banks, credit card companies and other financial intermediaries (sometimes without the knowledge or consent of their subjects). They also circulate in the form of stories, rumours and testimonies, through personal networks and 'informal' as well as 'formal' channels of regulation and exchange. Access to information about the likely behaviour of prospective transactors plays a major role in what economists call 'transactions costs'. Like the value of an object, the price of a loan or the promise of a future purchase or sale depends in part on what lenders and borrowers know, or think they know, about each other as well as about the provenance of objects, activities or ideas to which the loan or futures contract applies.[10]

History, or historicity,[11] figures in the making of claims to things of value as well as in the valuation of things themselves. Reinforced by colonial laws that endorsed 'traditional' land tenure, debate over claims on African land – how they're made, how they are or ought to be governed, and their significance for trajectories of social, economic and political change – has become a virtual sub-discipline of scholarship and debate on contemporary African affairs.[12] In many areas, descendants of 'first comers' – those who first settled on the land in question – vie with rivals who argue that the first comers' claims have been superseded by later events – migration, conquest, alliance, spiritual intervention, exchange – in which access to and control of land passed from its 'original' inhabitants to 'late comers' and their descendants.[13] Far from subsiding with the development of commercial land markets and the introduction of formal processes of land registration and titling, appeals to historical precedents and debates over their validity and relevance have multiplied in recent years, as land values rose and competition over land claims intensified.

Land registration programmes such as Kenya's Swynnerton Plan,[14] or land reforms launched in the 1990s under the aegis of structural adjustment, sought to replace verbal appeals to 'custom' with documents – title deeds, sales

---

[10] For African examples, see many of the essays in Guyer 1995 and Stiansen and Guyer 1999.
[11] M.-R. Trouillot's term for what happened in the past (historicity 1) and what people think (and say) about what happened (historicity 2) (Trouillot 1995).
[12] Since the publication of Elizabeth Colson's seminal essay, 'The impact of the colonial period on the definition of land rights' (1971), scholarship on African land arrangements has grown exponentially. For overviews of some of this literature see, among others, Bassett and Crummey 1993; Juul and Lund 2002; Berry 2002; Peters 2004; Kuba and Lentz 2006; Claassens and Cousins 2008.
[13] Illustrative examples from a now voluminous literature may be found in Bassett and Crummey 1993; Juul and Lund 2002; Benjaminsen and Lund 2003; Kuba and Lentz 2006; Lentz 2013.
[14] Initiated in 1954, the Swynnerton Plan aimed to promote agricultural production and prevent a recurrence of Mau by turning Kikuyu cultivators into landholding peasants with secure rights to clearly specified pieces of land and a vested interest in supporting the government that guaranteed them (Sorrenson 1967).

receipts, leases, loans and wills – meant to secure land tenure and consolidate multiple, overlapping claims into clear-cut rights of ownership and use. They did not, however, reject 'tradition' or historical precedents as legitimate grounds for claiming ownership. Rather than resolve or silence claims based on past events or 'timeless' traditions, land registration has often worked to reinvigorate them.[15] As land pressure grew and competition over land intensified, raising the stakes in the search for historical precedents, debates over the legitimacy of competing claims proliferated, adding to the value of historical knowledge and expertise. The proliferation of precedents and (often unresolvable) debates over their interpretation has neither prevented the commercialization of land transactions and displacements of poor and/or politically marginalized people, nor withered away as land markets expanded and prices climbed.[16]

In the last 50 years, claims on land – which are often based on membership or belonging in a lineage, community or ethnic group, or region – have intersected with claims to citizenship in postcolonial nations, reflected, for example, in frequent use of the term 'citizenship' to refer to local as well as national identity. Scholars have written extensively on the implications of contested or reconstituted belonging for political mobilization, governance and social conflict, as well as the many ways in which historical narratives are invoked and interpreted in debates over who is entitled to the privileges of citizenship, and who is not.[17] Claims to belonging may, in turn, affect the terms on which people gain access to land, pay taxes, or engage in market transactions.[18]

Process: How History Adds Value in the Market

Knowledge of the past is an ongoing process rather than a finished product. '[F]acts are not created equal: the production of traces is always also the creation of silences' (Trouillot 1995: 28), and access to them is uneven. Accounts of past events and practices are unavoidably selective, and many are ignored, suppressed, or intentionally or unintentionally forgotten. Trouillot wrote primarily about historical scholarship, but his observations apply equally to market transactions. Environmentalists elide histories of human exploitation

---

[15] Comparable in some respects to the archives of customary court records produced under colonial rule (Roberts 1990; Chanock 1985). During frequent visits to the Kumasi branch of the (then) National Archive of Ghana over a period of six months in 1993, I met only one other academic researcher: everyone else had come to the archives in search of evidence to use in a land case or chieftaincy dispute.

[16] Richard Levin's study of land claims and traditional rule in Swaziland provides an extended example of land concentration carried out in the name of tradition (Levin 1997). See also Claassens and Cousins 2008; MacGaffey 2013; and current efforts by Zulu king Zwelithini to claim a large portion of south-eastern South Africa under the newly reopened Land Restitution Amendment Act, on the grounds that the entire area was forcibly confiscated from his forebears by colonial authorities and subsequent white minority regimes.

[17] Like land claims, claims to citizenship and belonging are subjects of a rich literature. Examples include Geschiere 2009; Kuba and Lentz 2006; Mamdani 1996; and many others.

[18] In addition to sources cited above, see Juul and Lund 2002; Soares 2005; among others.

History as Value Added? Valuing the Past in Africa

in landscapes they seek to preserve and market to eco-tourists as 'pristine'. Construction crews raze buildings 'to make way for development'; monuments are destroyed in the name of religious or political 'reform'; records of past land transactions 'disappear' from the archives; 'traditional' artefacts, rituals and institutions are refurbished, or manufactured, to attract tourists and/or collectors.

The production of antique objects for cosmopolitan art markets is tellingly depicted in Christopher Steiner's *African Art in Transit*. Realizing that 'there was more money to be made in the trade in antiquities than ... in ... other "tourist" carvings', Ivorian traders sought out old objects in villagers' houses, and plied dealers and tourists with '"pedigrees" [of] an object's market history (how it was acquired, where it comes from, etc.)' and explanations of its 'cultural meaning and traditional use. Both types of information are constructed to satisfy perceived Western taste, and ... to increase the likelihood of sale' (Steiner 1994: 136). In some cases, carvers produce 'antiquities' directly to take advantage of consumers' taste for the old as well as the exotic. Dogon carvers in Mali 'smear ... new carvings with kitchen soot, bury them for a few weeks near a termite mound, soak them in millet gruel, and dry them in hot ashes, all to give them the highly valued patina of ritual use' (van Beek 1988: 64, quoted in Steiner 1994: 184, note 2).

Paulla Ebron's account of a 'heritage tour' to Senegambia, sponsored by McDonald's, illustrates the way people's emotional and epistemological stakes in the past may be imbricated in commercial transactions.

> Travel routes in such contemporary 'return' journeys to the continent are maps of collective memory; the visit becomes a 'revisit' with aims to attend to the trauma created by the capturing of African bodies taken to the New World as slaves.
>
> Yet it was difficult to ignore our sponsorship by the giant hamburger chain. The most intimate memories of reunion with 'Mother Africa' were moments anticipated by clever marketing strategies, moments that helped create what McDonald's has called, in another context, 'McMemories'. (Ebron, 2002: 190–1)

Taking shape in daily interactions among tourists, sponsors, tour guides and the villagers, traders, hotel staff and others whom the travellers met in Dakar and Juffure, the 'value' of the Americans' week-long encounter with history is not easily reduced to a single standard of measurement.[19] Ebron's account recalls others in which history may be said to add value to sites and experiences in the present through performative encounters between individuals or groups of people. Writing of *oríkì*, a genre of Yoruba verbal art replete with historical allusions, Karin Barber depicts another kind of performative encounter in which value is created, rather than simply transmitted, through the encounter between performer and listener. *Oríkì*, Barber explains, 'enhance' and 'empower' the person to whom they are addressed.

---

[19] For a stimulating discussion of multiple, often concurrent standards of measurement in West African monetary systems and market exchanges, see Guyer 2004.

As the performer chants, her 'subject is visibly affected ... he seems to expand, to take on afflatus, to be profoundly moved' (Barber 1991: 75). In other words, history figures in the production of power, or political value, as well as market value.

In similar vein, Hamilton suggests that each carefully staged encounter between tourists, tour guides and Zulu villagers at the South African history theme park, Shakaland, 'did more than simply market Zulu history and culture [or] provide new knowledge; its real product was "experience"' (Hamilton 1998: 203–4) During the social and political upheavals of the early 1990s, Hamilton argues, Shakaland provided a safe space in which white visitors could interact, however briefly, with Zulus, and begin to imagine a new future for South Africa. '[D]eveloped as a site for the production of both history and social ideas', Shakaland succeeded, in part, by presenting 'a fantasy experience [in which] the ideas that it advanced so successfully disguised their political potency and seeped unchallenged into popular consciousness' (ibid.: 205). Its owners also profited from the marketability of the past.

Hamilton's analysis illustrates a point made explicitly by Barber, who compares the interactive dynamic of *oríkì* performances to Bakhtin's concept of utterance as dialogic: 'it only has meaning because it occupies the space between a speaker and a hearer' (Barber 1991: 36). The value of *oríkì* is intertextual and dynamic: it inheres neither in the performer's words nor in the audience's reception of them, but emerges and grows in the 'space' of their interchange. A similar point may be made about the way history adds value to the different kinds of marketed goods described in this chapter – and, indeed, about market values in general. Supply and demand, conceptualized in neoclassical economic analysis as stylized representations of the capacities and intentions of prospective buyers and sellers, 'create' market value at the point of intersection between them. In effect, each market price is an interactive instant in an ongoing social drama in which transactions among myriad independent buyers and sellers converge to constitute 'a market', and both individual prices and the social demography of the market may change from one moment to another. That the social drama is conventionally suppressed in most formal economic analysis does not mean it is not there.

Attributes of pastness may also reduce market value, as happens when commodities deemed too old, worn out or outmoded lose political cachet. Such a case is vividly described in Thomas Bassett's account of traditional hunters in northern Côte d'Ivoire (Bassett 2003). Responding to a rising number of cattle thefts in the 1980s, Mande hunters (*donzow*) took it upon themselves to protect their neighbours' livestock. Drawing on their knowledge of the local terrain and sources of spiritual protection lodged within it, they were able to apprehend cattle thieves that had eluded the police for some time, restoring animals to their grateful owners and earning a reputation for invincibility that rested on their expert knowledge of 'traditional' arts of hunting and healing as well as local environments. Buoyed by their success against cattle thieves, hunters expanded their repertoire, offering themselves as knowledgeable agents of environmental protection as well as security, and earning a healthy level of respect from the police as well as their neighbours.[20] As their reputation spread, hunters enjoyed a brief interlude of public acclaim and prosperity.

In 1995, the *donzow* reached national prominence when President Henri Bédié recruited them as 'guards' for his re-election campaign, but the invitation was rescinded when alarmed aides warned Bédié that voters might link the *donzow* to the *kamajor*, Mende hunters whom many suspected (wrongly) of complicity in the brutal insurrections then ravaging Sierra Leone and Liberia. Repudiated by politicians and officials, and facing renewed enforcement of national laws against game hunting, Ivoirian hunters ended up poorer than they had been before stepping forward to help their neighbours ward off cattle thieves (Bassett 2003). Like notoriously volatile prices of agricultural commodities and raw materials, the value of the hunters' skills, specialized knowledge and associated spiritual powers first spiked and then plummeted in rapid succession, illustrating both the interactive character and the fragility of market values in general, as well as values added by history.

In the 'roots' tour to Gambia, Shakaland, and the political rise and fall of the *donzow ton*, history added value through some form of performance. Historical scenes, events and practices were not just invoked but re-enacted, allowing consumers to experience as well as witness the past. Much the same may be said of artefacts, musical performances or nature preserves, as art collectors, tourists or audiences pay money to engage with the past. In these, as in any other kind of market purchase, it is fair to ask 'what they have acquired in exchange for their payments?'

'Our History is Our Secret'

So far, this discussion has focused on connections between historical knowledge or imagination and market prices. They may also be compared. Market prices, like historical understandings, are dialogic: they inhere neither in demand or supply but come to be in the interactions between them – just as historical knowledge or experience is continually remade in the interactive space between purveyor and consumer. (These interactions may, of course, take place through a chain of brokers, processors, teachers, etc., rather than face to face.)

According to market theory, commodities gain value when they are scarce, whether in nature or by design. But history is more than a commodity: it is valuable but it is not scarce (Berry 1997: 1236). 'The production of historical narratives involves the uneven contributions of competing groups and individuals who have unequal access to the means of producing it' (Trouillot

---

[20] The hunters' effectiveness was enhanced by their reputation for spiritual power, itself linked to their knowledge of the bush. Even the police were afraid of them: 'Our bullets do not kill them; they have mystical powers. When we catch them we take off their clothes in order to remove their amulets [then] we take them to the police station.' A gendarme to a journalist, quoted in Bassett 2003: 23.

1995: xviii). Addressed explicitly to 'the various layers of silences' in historical accounts of the Haitian Revolution, Trouillot's book illuminates historiographical practice in general, reminding us that all historical narratives are selective, dwelling on parts of the past deemed valuable or significant by the narrators, while 'silencing' inconvenient historical truths (ibid.: 44).

Trouillot focuses on aspects of the past that are suppressed, invisible or unheard. In other cases, knowledge of the past is hidden in plain sight. It may be kept from view or relayed only to a few, but everyone knows that it's there. In an essay entitled 'Secret knowledge as property and power in Kpelle society: elders versus youth', William Murphy ascribed Kpelle elders' authority over youth to their 'ownership' of secret knowledge concerning 'medicine ... substances, utterances, actions and even organizations which are believed to possess unusual powers', adding that 'another important domain of owned knowledge is history', specifically the 'recent history of individual families who settled in a particular area' (Murphy 1980: 197). Family histories of migration and settlement figure significantly in determining ownership and belonging, just as knowledge of genealogy 'places' living persons in social frameworks and locates them in space. 'When elders meet to settle a disagreement, each presents his version of the past which bears on the matter until a consensus is reached' (ibid.: 198; see also Murphy 1990; Bohannon 1952; Gilbert 1988).

I heard similar stories in Ghana in the 1990s, while researching the history of land claims in Asante in the twentieth century (Berry 2001). As Murphy found in Liberia in the late 1970s, claims to land in Asante were closely linked to family history. Asked how they had obtained plots of land for farming or building, many informants recounted narratives of ancestral migration and settlement, adding stories about their forebears' encounters with people whom they 'met' on the land in question to explain how the ensuing negotiations, transactions and/or conflicts had determined the terms on which they hold land today. In a recent essay on ancestry, land claims and identity in one Asante chiefdom, Stefano Boni describes 'ancestral origin as a constant and strategic process of forging one's ancestry and its deeds rather than the "true" reconstruction of one's genealogical tree ... Ancestry acts as the common canon used to delimit multiple circuits of membership' – in families, communities, 'traditional' polities and contemporary jurisdictions – that bear, in turn, on contemporary claims to many forms of property, including land, land-based assets, moveable goods, heritable estates and specialized knowledge (Boni 2006: 170; Lentz 2013 and Zongo 2005).

Together with the commercialization of farming, colonial practices of indirect rule, and postcolonial struggles over political power and jurisdiction, the economic and political stakes involved in making claims to land and social membership have risen over the course of the twentieth century – not only in rural areas but also in towns and cities throughout Ghana and many other parts of sub-Saharan Africa. As Boni and others have argued, rising competition over land and authority provokes continuing reinvestigation and reinterpretation of the past, often adding to tensions over land access and control rather than resolving them.[21] The ability to influence or prevail in debates over historical precedents and precedence bears directly and significantly on the prices people pay for land and on who gains or losses in land transactions (Mathieu et al. 2003).

Proprietary claims to history also work to empower custodians of 'tradition' and historical expertise. Those who 'know history' can reveal or withhold it from those who do not – a form of power that gains significance in direct proportion to the value that people place on history in the present. As the *griot* reminds us in D.T. Niane's well-known version of the Sundiata epic, 'we teach to the vulgar just as much as we want to teach them, for it is we who keep the keys to the twelve doors of Mali' (Niane 1965: 1). The point is not that *griots* know things that other people do not and hoard their knowledge in order to exact a price for it. After observing several performances of Sundiata in Kela, a Malian village well known for the many families of *griots* who call it home, Jan Jansen explains that 'everyone in Kela, even the little children' knew the story, but only recognized specialists were entitled to speak it in public (Jansen 1999: 305ff). Historical knowledge is valuable not because it is scarce, but because of the way it is managed in particular social contexts.[22]

Anthropologists have written insightfully about the management of secrecy – 'strategies of concealment' and disclosure – as both a manifestation of power and a technique for exercising it.[23] In Mali and parts of Senegambia with ancient traditions of centralized rule, histories of ruling dynasties are carefully guarded by *jali* and other 'official' historians who specialize in the recitation of royal genealogies, accounts of the foundation of kingdoms or states, and stories that recount or prescribe rules and social relationships that express and reinforce the power of ruling elites. In central Africa, Luba traditions assign historical knowledge to members of Mbudye, a secret society whose initiates learn history and acquire authority through a series of rituals that qualify them to re-enact and interpret the history of the ruling dynasty (Roberts and Roberts 1996).

The power of history and secrecy is not limited to societies with centralized states. In Shrines of the Slave Trade, Robert Baum explains that it took him more than 20 years to reconstruct the history of Esulalu-Diola people's involvement with the Atlantic slave trade, partly because the past was mediated through a 'staggering profusion of spirit shrines', each with its own carefully guarded history. Since 'a researcher cannot walk up to perfect strangers and ask them to explain their religion' (Baum 1999: 19–20), getting beyond 'the public justification of religious practice' requires time and experience on the part of both researcher and researched. In the *adae* festivals of Asante – where, once every six weeks, the Asantehene and senior paramount chiefs

---

[21] A term used in Ghana to denote both territories and people associated with particular chiefly jurisdictions, 'Traditional Areas' have no formal legal standing – an ambiguity that invites continuing reinterpretation of the social and spatial boundaries of chiefly jurisdictions, and debate over their historical provenance (Boni 2005, 2006; see also Berry 2001).
[22] Jansen 1999: 305ff. Note the parallel with modern academia, where authority to teach and write history is regulated through carefully managed rituals such as tenure and the PhD.
[23] See, e.g., Fermé 2001; Murphy 1980, 1990; Geschiere 1997; Ashforth, 1996.

invoke the blessings of their ancestors and reaffirm the history and authority of their offices – the most sacred rites are carried out before dawn, behind closed doors and away from the public gaze. Secrecy is not reserved to official agencies of power. On more than one occasion, Asantes spoke of their family's history as 'our secret', explaining that 'history is a secret because it can affect you' (Berry 2001: 147–50; Ashforth 1996; Geschiere 1997; Fermé 2001).

Like consumers of history in other forms (antiquities, traditional clothing, cuisine, wildlife preserves), market agents worry about the reliability of relevant historical information as well as its content. How does a buyer know that an item is old or 'authentically' traditional? The values added to such items depend not only on their content – the particular times, places, events, etc., evoked by or inscribed in a marketable item – but also on the way they are represented to potential buyers. The value of historic objects depends, in part, on processes of interpretation and verification similar to those that engage anyone involved in studying the past. Techniques of representation may differ between commercial markets, academic institutions, courts of law, and community gatherings, but they work and are deployed to a common end. In all of these venues, history's value added depends on the performative skill and reputation of those who purvey or 'produce' it, as well as the particular events or eras that are embodied or represented in contemporary forms. History does not add value unilaterally: it works through interactions between sellers, buyers and often-numerous intermediaries who participate, one way or another, in interpreting the past to those who pay for it in the present.[24] See, for example, the poignant scene in Sembène's film, *Borom Sarret* (1963), in which the cart driver gives all the money he has made during the morning to a street *griot* who is singing the praises of his ancestors.

Whether referring to specific events and eras or to shared understandings of 'tradition,' our knowledge of the past is, by definition, incomplete: there is always the possibility of finding more evidence, reinterpreting its significance or bringing new perspectives to bear that alter people's assessments of the meaning of historical moments or their relevance in the present. Always open to discovery, re-examination and debate, knowledge of the past is never stable, and the values it adds in market transactions are not stable either. We may be able to name the price we paid (or received) for an artefact, an object, a plot of land, a text or a performance, but do we know what it is worth? Much the same question may be asked of all market values, whether they are historically significant or not. A price is a social construct – a momentary convergence between the aims and capacities of buyer(s) and seller(s) – that is subject to change as conditions change, transactors rethink their priorities, or relations among them are altered (Berry 1995). Like Bakhtin's theory of utterance, market value inheres neither in the object sold nor the minds of the

---

[24] Historical associations or content can also *de*value things as well as add value to them. Garments of outmoded fashion that are sold cheaply in thrift shops, or bundled and sold to dealers in Africa by weight are one example; historic buildings torn down to make way for new structures are another. I owe this point to Nathan Connolly, whose work illuminates the way '"historically black" neighborhoods [in the US] tend to be of little value' (Connolly, personal communication).

buyer and seller, but in the space of interaction between them (Barber 1991, Bakhtin 1981).

Like the social meanings of guns and cattle in southern Sudan (Hutchinson 1996), market values are often influenced, at least in part, by the provenance of the thing(s) exchanged. Employing a rhetoric of 'social capital', economists have suggested that the terms of market transactions are influenced by 'trust' – a kind of willing suspension of disbelief that increases the acceptability of certain offers, raising or lowering their price to the advantage of those who are trusted. Individuals or organizations that 'trust' one another may exchange things at lower prices, or be more inclined to do so on credit, than those who distrust one another's motives or willingness to live up to the terms of an agreement. 'Trust' in this sense is a product of history or, more precisely, historical knowledge. Transactors do not need to know one another personally in order to establish trust: it is enough to have reliable knowledge of the other's past. Access to such knowledge and people's assessment of its reliability figure in every market transaction, whether or not they are explicitly acknowledged.

Viewed in these terms, the marketing of personal histories in the form of credit records and reputations (or biographies of market performance) suggests a reading of 'social capital' that does not depend on attachment, affect or shared identity. Instead, social capital may be thought of as a kind of collective biography: knowledge formed by repeated encounters with suppliers, customers and creditors influences the terms of present and future transactions by shaping people's assessments of one another's reliability and allowing them to keep track of accrued obligations. Rather than predetermined norms or structural attributes such as kinship or affinity, social relationships and the knowledge that informs them are produced and continually revalued as people accumulate and evaluate knowledge about one another (Berry 2001: 198–9).[25]

Conclusion: Who Owns the Past?

As increased competition over 'historic' goods intensifies competition over claims to historical knowledge and expertise, history as a form of property may become subject to competing claims of ownership and efforts to exclude

---

[25] My approach to this issue is somewhat different from those of Parker Shipton and David Graeber. In his extensive writings on trust and social payments in western Kenya, Shipton details the particularities of Luo 'fiduciary culture' – shared understandings of obligation and how to manage it – contrasting them with Western ideas about credit and debt (Shipton 2007, 2009). For Graeber, debt is a moral issue: capitalist debt is 'the perversion of a promise ... a promise corrupted by both math and violence' (Graeber 2011: 391). Citing a study of NGO development projects in Egypt, he concludes 'aspects of economic life that had been based on longstanding relations of trust were, through the intrusion of credit bureaus, becoming effectively criminalized'(ibid.: 380). I am less convinced that one can draw an unambiguous line between Western or capitalist on one hand and African or local on the other; more interested in how people embrace some new ideas and practices, while rejecting others, and how their assessments change over time. For an example from western Kenya, see Mutongi 2007.

rival claimants from sharing in its gains. In an essay provocatively titled 'Who owns the past?' Richard Handler suggested that contemporary claims to historical ownership are a manifestation of the 'possessive individualism' of modern culture mapped on to nations and ethnic groups by people who seek to assert or defend claims to power. Debates over whether or not to return cultural treasures from Western museums or private collections to their '"original" settings', he suggests, reflect 'the hegemony of Western culture and the disappearance of alternative modes of living. That putatively diverse national and ethnic groups understand one another well enough to fight about who "owns" the past suggests that all of them have been assimilated into a homogenized global culture of the present' (Handler 1991: 71–2).

Such claims express a proprietary relationship with the past that, *pace* Handler, is not simply a product of global homogenization. Reluctance to speak of another's history, reported by many historians and ethnographers working in different African societies, not only attests to the connections between history and social position, but also raises questions about how secrecy affects the marketing of history itself. If silencing the past allows powerful people and institutions to exercise power by suppressing dissenting accounts, does it also work to create monopoly power in the marketplace – inflating the values of 'historic' objects, sites, information, etc., by limiting their supply?

Such an argument is suggestive, but incomplete. As we've seen, the quantity of history is not finite – past events may be re-presented and reinterpreted indefinitely. To add value to an object or an idea, history must be seen and heard: secret knowledge does not matter if nobody knows it exists. When Asantes told me 'our history is our secret', they did not necessarily mean that they would not reveal it. More than once, assertions of secrecy were followed by detailed accounts of the historical events and practices in question. In the same vein, the *adae* festival – the six-weekly ritual in which chiefs commemorate their ancestors – begins in secret, with pre-dawn rituals held behind closed doors, but ends in a public forum, with chiefs in splendid regalia assembled to receive the greetings and invite the gaze of all who may wish to attend.

If powerful people sometimes suppress knowledge of the past, at other times, declarations or displays of secrecy serve to remind whoever may be listening that the performers have the power to relay or withhold their stories as they choose. Like the publication of historical writing, a declaration of secrecy serves as an assertion of the author's or speaker's proprietorship. By publishing or narrating her story, an author/speaker performs an act of generosity – a gift to her audience that invites further interaction. Readers or listeners become witnesses, potential interlocutors who may respond directly, building or sustaining a relationship with the author, or propose their own interpretations, enriching the stock of historical knowledge and adding to its abundance (cf. Barber 1991).

In a widely cited essay, Jane Guyer and Samuel Eno Belinga (1995) use ethnographic and literary examples from Equatorial Africa to argue that people have long been valued in African economies for their individual attributes – specialized knowledge, skills, even personal idiosyncrasies – as well as for more generic qualities such as labour power, 'loyalty' to patrons, or collective identity. By demonstrating implicitly the conceptual parallels between 'wealth-in-people' and what economists often call 'human capital', while providing vivid descriptions of valued attributes and activities in particular African contexts, Guyer and Eno Belinga's argument broadened debates about what is (and is not) 'exceptional' about economic values in Equatorial African economies.

Their insight may, I think, be taken a step further. Individuals don't just embody expertise – they manage it. The value of knowledge depends not only on its content, but also on the actions of the knower(s) and their interactions with others. Unlike the impersonal exchanges of discrete pieces of information imagined in neoclassical models of the market, historical knowledge is performative, made and valued through interacting processes of representation, persuasion, concealment and disbelief, in which transactors seek to influence one another's calculations, as well as to predict them (see Rose 1994). The value that history adds to market transactions is mediated through knowledge: both knowledge of the historical provenance or attributes of things, and knowledge that parties to any transaction may have of one another's histories of market performance. Since historical knowledge is always incomplete, and open to interpretation, when history figures in the equation, it may be easier to name the price paid for an object or experience than to say just what has been bought or sold. Reflections on the value of history in market transactions, illustrated here with recent examples from African countries, suggest that market value is a matter of performance as well as production – dialogically enacted, partly hidden, never fully determined or knowable. If value, like history, is in part a secret, there's no such thing as a market 'free' of the politics of knowledge.

References

Alexander, J., J. McGregor and T. Ranger (2003). *Violence and memory: one hundred years in the dark forests of Matabeleland*. Oxford: James Currey.

Amanor, K. (2012). 'Global resource grabs, land concentration and the smallholder: two West African Case Studies', *Journal of Peasant Studies*, 39 (3–4): 731–49.

Anderson, D. and A.T. Grove (eds) (1987). *Conservation in Africa: peoples, policies and practices*. Cambridge, UK: Cambridge University Press.

Appadurai, A. (1988). *The social life of things: commodities in cultural perspective*. Cambridge, UK: Cambridge University Press.

Ashforth, A. (1996). 'Of secrecy and the commonplace: witchcraft and power in Soweto', *Social Research*, 63 (4): 1183–233.

Austen, R. (1999). *In search of Sunjata: the Mande oral epic as history, literature and performance*. Bloomington, IN: Indiana University Press.

Bakhtin, M. (1981). *The dialogic imagination*. Austin, TX: University of Texas Press.
Bako-Arifari, N. (1997). 'Démocratie entre formes officielles et dynamiques locales. Dynamiques et formes de pouvoir à Founogo (Bénin)'. Working Paper on African Societies, 6. Berlin: Das Arabische Buch.
Barber, K. (1991). *'I could speak until tomorrow': oríkì, women and the past in a Yoruba town*. Washington, DC: Smithsonian.
Bassett, T. (2003). 'Dangerous pursuits: hunter associations (*donzo ton*) and national politics in Côte d'Ivoire', *Africa*, 73 (1): 1–30.
Bassett, T. and D. Crummey (eds) (1993). *Land in African agrarian systems*. Madison, WI: University of Wisconsin Press.
Bassett, T. and M.-C. Cormier-Salem (eds) (2007). 'Nature as local heritage in Africa: longstanding concerns, new challenges'. *Africa*, 77 (1): 1–17.
Bassett, T., C. Blanc-Pamard and J. Boutrais (2007). 'Constructing locality: the *terroir* approach in West Africa', *Africa*, 77 (1): 104–29.
Baum, R. (1999). *Shrines of the slave trade: Diola religion and society in precolonial Senegal*. New York: Oxford.
Beinart, W. and J. McGregor (eds) (2003). *Social history and African environments*. Oxford: James Currey.
Benjaminsen, T. and C. Lund (eds) (2003). *Securing land rights in Africa*. London: Frank Cass.
Berry, S. (1995). 'Stable prices, unstable values: some thoughts on monetization and the meaning of transactions in West African economies'. In J.I. Guyer (ed.), *Money matters: monetization, value and instability in modern West Africa*. Portsmouth, NH: Heinemann.
—. (1997). 'Tomatoes, land and hearsay: property and history in the time of structural adjustment', *World Development*, 25 (8): 1225–41.
—. (2001). *Chiefs know their boundaries: essays on property, power and the past in Asante, 1896–1996*. Portsmouth, NH: Heinemann.
—. (2002). 'Debating the land question in Africa', *Comparative Studies in Society and History*, 44 (4): 638–68.
Bierschenk, T., J.-P. Chauveau and J.P. Olivier de Sardan (2000). *Courtiers en développement: les villages africaines en quête de projets*. Paris: Karthala.
Bohannon, L. (1952). 'A genealogical charter?' *Africa*, 22 (4): 301–315.
Boni, S. (2005). *Clearing the Ghanaian forest*. Legon, Ghana: Institute of African Studies.
—. (2006). 'Indigenous blood and foreign labour: the "ancestralization" of land rights in Sefwi (Ghana)'. In R. Kuba and C. Lentz (eds), *Land and the politics of belonging in West Africa*. Leiden: Brill.
Bourdieu, P. (1977). *Outline of a theory of practice*. Cambridge, UK: Cambridge University Press.
Chanock, M. (1985). *Law, custom and social change in colonial Zambia and Malawi*. Cambridge, UK: Cambridge University Press.
Chauveau, J.-P. (2000). 'La question foncière en Côte d'Ivoire et le coup d'état', *Politique Africaine*, 78: 94–125.
Claassens, A. and B. Cousins (eds) (2008). *Land, power and custom: controversies*

generated by South Africa's Communal Land Rights Act. Cape Town, SA: Legal Resources Centre.

Colson, E. (1971). 'The impact of the colonial period on the definition of land rights'. In V. Turner (ed.), *Profiles of change: African society and colonial rule,* vol. III of L. Gann and P. Duignan (eds), *Colonialism in Africa.* Cambridge, UK: Cambridge University Press.

Cotula, L., S. Vermeulen, R. Leonard and J. Keeley (2009). *Land grab or development opportunity? Agricultural investment and land deals in Africa.* London: IIED.

Ebron, P. (2002). *Performing Africa.* Princeton, NJ: Princeton University Press.

Fermé, M. (2001). *The underneath of things: violence, history and the everyday in Sierra Leone.* Berkeley and Los Angeles: University of California Press.

Geschiere, P. (1997). *The modernity of witchcraft: politics and the occult in postcolonial Africa.* Charlottesville, VA: University of Virginia Press.

—. (2009). *The perils of belonging: autochthony, citizenship and exclusion in Africa and Europe.* Chicago, IL: University of Chicago Press.

Gilbert, M. (1988). 'The sudden death of a millionaire: conversion and consensus in a Ghanaian kingdom', *Africa,* 58 (3): 291–314.

Giles-Vernick, T. (2002). *Cutting the vines of the past: environmental histories of the Central African rain forest.* Charlottesville, VA: University Press of Virginia.

Graeber, D. (2001). *Toward an anthropological theory of value: the false coin of our dreams.* London: Palgrave Macmillan.

—. (2011). *Debt: the first 5000 years.* London: Melville House.

Gray, L and M. Kevane (2001). 'Evolving tenure rights in southwestern Burkina Faso', *World Development,* 29 (4): 573–87.

Grove, R. (1995). *Green imperialism: colonial expansion, tropical island Edens, and the origins of environmentalism, 1600–1880.* Cambridge, UK: Cambridge University Press.

Guyer, J.I. (ed.) (1995). *Money matters: monetization, value and instability in modern West Africa.* Portsmouth, NH: Heinemann.

—. (2004). *Marginal gains: monetary transactions in Atlantic Africa.* Chicago, IL: University of Chicago Press.

Guyer, J.I. and S.M. Eno Belinga (1995). 'Wealth-in-people as wealth-in-knowledge: accumulation and composition in Equatorial Africa', *Journal of African History,* 36: 91–120.

Hamilton, C. (1998). *Terrific majesty: the powers of Shaka Zulu and the limits of historical invention.* Cambridge, MA: Harvard University Press.

Handler, R. (1991). 'Who owns the past?' In B. Williams (ed.), *The politics of culture.* Washington, DC: Smithsonian.

Hecht, S., K. Morrison and C. Padoch (eds) (2014). *The social life of forests.* Chicago, IL: University of Chicago Press.

Hulme D. and M. Murphree (eds) (2001). *African wildlife and livelihoods: the promise and practice of community conservation.* Cape Town and Portsmouth, NH: D Philip and Heinemann.

Hutchinson, S. (1996). *Nuer dilemmas: coping with money, war and the state.* Madison, WI: University of Wisconsin Press.

Jansen, J. (1999). 'Ethnography of the epic of Sunjata in Kela'. In R.A. Austen (ed.), *In Search of Sunjata: the Mande Epic as History, Literature and Performance.* Bloomington, IN: University of Indiana Press.

Juul, K. and C. Lund (eds) (2002). *Negotiating property in Africa.* Portsmouth, NH: Heinemann.

Kopytoff, I. (1987). *The African frontier: the reproduction of traditional African societies.* Bloomington, IN: Indiana University Press.

Kuba, R and C. Lentz (eds) (2006). *Land and the politics of belonging in West Africa.* Leiden: Brill.

Lentz, C. (2013). *Land, mobility and belonging in West Africa.* Bloomington, IN: Indiana University Press.

Levin, R. (1997). *When the sleeping grass awakens.* Johannesburg, SA: Witwatersrand University Press.

MacGaffey, W. (2013). *Chiefs, priests and praise-singers: history, politics and land ownership in northern Ghana.* Charlottesville, VA and London: University of Virginia Press.

Macgonagle, E. (2006). 'From dungeons to dance parties: contested histories of Ghana's slave forts', *Journal of Contemporary African Studies*, 24 (2): 249–60.

McGregor, J. (2009). *Crossing the Zambezi: the politics of landscape on a southern African frontier.* Woodbridge, UK and Rochester, NY: James Currey; Harare: Weaver.

Mamdani, M. (1996). *Citizen and subject: the legacy of late colonialism in Africa.* Princeton, NJ: Princeton University Press.

Mathieu, P., P. Delville, H. Ouédraogo, M. Zongo, L. Paré et al. (2003). *Making land transactions more secure in western Burkina Faso.* Issue paper 117. London: DFID.

Murphy, W. (1980). 'Secret knowledge as property and power in Kpelle society: elders versus youth', *Africa*, 50 (2): 193–208.

—. (1990). 'Creating the appearance of consensus in Mende political discourse', *American Anthropologist*, 92 (1): 24–41.

Mutongi, K. (2007). *Worries of the heart: widows, family and community in Kenya.* Chicago, IL and London: University of Chicago Press.

Niane, D.T. (1965). *Sundiata: an epic of old Mali*, Trans. G.D. Pickett. London: Longman.

Peters, P. (2004). 'Inequality and conflicts over land in Africa', *Journal of Agrarian Change*, 4 (3): 269–314.

—. (2013). 'Conflicts over land and threats to customary tenure in Africa', *African Affairs*, 112 (449): 543–62.

Renne, E. (2004). 'The production and marketing of *babban riga* in Zaria, Nigeria', *African Economic History*, 32: 103–22.

Roberts, M. and A. Roberts (1996). *Memory: Luba art and the making of history.* New York: Museum for African Art.

Roberts, R. (1990). 'Text and testimony in the Tribunal de première instance,

Dakar, during the early 20th century', *Journal of African History*, 31 (3): 447–63.

Rose, C. (1994). *Property and persuasion: essays on the history, theory and rhetoric of ownership.* Boulder, CO: Westview.

Schoneveld, G.C. (2011). 'Anatomy of large-scale farmland acquisitions in sub-Saharan Africa', Working Paper 85. Bogor, Indonesia: Center for International Forestry Research.

Shipton, P. (2007). *The nature of entrustment: intimacy, exchange and the sacred in Africa.* New Haven, CT: Yale University Press.

—. (2009). *Mortgaging the ancestors: ideologies of attachment in Africa.* New Haven, CT: Yale University Press.

Soares, B. (2005). *Islam and the prayer economy: history and authority in a Malian town.* Ann Arbor, MI: University of Michigan Press.

Sorrenson, M.P.K. (1967). *Land reform in the Kikuyu country.* Nairobi: Oxford University Press.

Steiner, C. (1994). *African art in transit.* Cambridge, UK: Cambridge University Press.

Stiansen, E. and J.I. Guyer (eds) (1999). *Credit, currencies and culture: African financial institutions in historical perspective.* Uppsala: NAI.

Trouillot, M.R. (1995). *Silencing the past: power and the production of history.* Boston, MA: Beacon.

Tsikata, D. and J. Yaro (2011). 'Land market liberalization and transnational commercial land deals in Ghana since the 1990s'. Paper presented at a Conference on Global Land Grabbing, Institute of Development Studies, University of Sussex, UK.

van Beek, W. (1988). 'Functions of sculpture in Dogon religion', *African Arts*, 21 (4): 58–65, 91.

Vernick, T.G. (2002). *Cutting the vines of the past: environmental histories in the Central African rainforest.* Charlottesville, VA: University of Virginia Press.

Witz, L., C. Rasool and G. Minkley (2001). 'Repackaging the past for South African tourism', *Daedalus*, 130 (1): 277–96.

World Bank (2010). *Rising global interest in farmland: can it yield sustainable and equitable benefits?* Washington, DC: World Bank.

Zongo, M. (2005). 'Les prélèvements en milieu rural'. Etude no. 7, Laboratoire de recherche sur les citoyennetés en transformation. Ouagadougou, BF: ACE-RECIT.

12

Cultural Mediation, Colonialism & Politics
Colonial 'Truchement', Postcolonial Translator

Souleymane Bachir Diagne

I admit that it is a good thing to place different civilizations in contact with each other; that it is an excellent thing to blend different worlds; that whatever its own particular genius may be, a civilization that withdraws into itself atrophies; that for civilizations, exchange is oxygen; that the great good fortune of Europe is to have been a crossroads, and that because it was the locus of all ideas, the receptacle of all philosophies, the meeting place of all sentiments, it was the best center for the redistribution of energy. But then I ask the following question: has colonization really placed civilizations in contact? Or, if you prefer, of all the ways of establishing contact, was it the best? I answer no. And I say that between colonization and civilization there is an infinite distance.

(Aimé Césaire, *Discourse on Colonialism* 2001: 11–12)

Every culture wants to be self-sufficient and use this imaginary self-sufficiency in order to shine forth on the others and appropriate their patrimony. Ancient Roman culture, classical French culture, and modern North-American culture are striking examples of this. Here, translation occupies an ambiguous position. On the one hand, it heeds this appropriationary and reductionary injunction, and constitutes itself as one of its agents. This results in ethnocentric translations, or what we may call 'bad' translations. But, on the other hand, the ethical aim of translating is by its very nature opposed to this injunction: The essence of translation is to be an opening, a dialogue, a crossbreeding, a decentering. Translation is 'a putting in touch with,' or it is nothing.

(Antoine Berman, *The Experience of the Foreign* 1992: 4)

Let me start with a scene from a book by anthropologist, historian, novelist, but above all interpreter then translator of West African oral cultures and literatures into French: Amadou Hampâté Bâ (1901–1991) from Mali. The book is entitled *Vie et enseignement de Tierno Bokar le Sage de Bandiagara* (literally: 'The life and teachings of Tierno Bokar, the Sage of Bandiagara') and is the biography of his master and guide in Islamic sciences and spirituality (Tierno means 'master'). The scene in question takes place in 1937, in the Malian town of Mopti under French colonial rule. The *dramatis personae* are the master Tierno Bokar, the French commander of the town, named

Colonial 'Truchement', Postcolonial Translator

Levavasseur, and the official interpreter for the colonial administration whose name is Oumar Sy. As soon as Tierno appears before him commander Levavasseur angrily and impatiently gets directly to the point: 'Tierno', he asks in French of course, 'are you willing to go back to the spiritual practice of which you are one of the masters, namely the 12 beads, so that all is over, yes or no?' (Bâ 1980: 104).

The interpreter then turns towards Tierno and 'translates' for him the question into Fulani language as follows: 'Your cousin Tidjani Aguibou Tall, the chief of Bandiagara, accompanied by other prominent personalities has come to meet you and take you with him to Bandiagara, Are you ready to follow him?'

To which Tierno then answers 'yes', nodding also with his head, a universal human sign that needs no translation and which the commander can easily understand. Then the interpreter adds in French that Tierno was ready to follow his cousin to Bandiagara, and would certainly obey him when asked to reintegrate the Tall family and its spiritual tradition. Later, Levavasseur could write in his administrative report: 'This day, Tierno Bokar Salif Tall and members of his family appeared before me. The marabout Tierno Bokar will resume the practice of the 12 beads and abandon that of the 11 beads. His people have come to fetch him. All is settled, the case is closed.'

What the scene and the interpreter's trick manifest is that the situation in the colony is not the simple, clear face to face between the European imperial authority and its subject. That could only be the case if the same language was shared across the line separating the realm of the dominant and the space of the dominated. But because there is more than one language involved in the relationship of domination, the colonial confrontation is inevitably troubled and the colonial power supposed to be exercised exclusively and unequivocally by the representative of the imperial authority can find itself bent, diverted, diffused, and ultimately turned round: it can literally get lost in translation. So in this chapter, starting with the examination of this particular scene of translation, I want to illustrate how translation in the context of 'imperial encounter' (Mandair 2009: xiii) 'is always complicit with the building, transforming or disrupting of power relations' (Sakai 2006: 72).

But let me first present the context which gives meaning to the different elements that constitute the scene and to expressions such as 'practice of the 12 beads' vs 'practice of the 11 beads'.

The Context

Tierno Bokar is a spiritual guide from the Sufi order named Tijaniyya after its founder Ahmad at-Tijani who was born in Ayn Madi, in Algeria but then lived and taught in Fez, Morocco, dying there in 1815. An important ritual characteristic of his spiritual path is the daily recitation, *11 or 12 times*, of a particular prayer, praising the prophet of Islam and calling upon him God's blessings. The actual prescription was to repeat it 11 times, until a day when the prayer was recited an additional twelfth time so that at-Tijani, who had come late to the session of recitation could join his disciples and be part of it. Subsequently, the practice of '12' was adopted by most of his disciples as the right count but '11' was also kept by some of them as the official, written rule of the Order. The Sufi order of the Tijaniyya spread throughout West Africa during the nineteenth and twentieth centuries through the 'jihad' the holy scholar, warrior Shaykh Umar Tall (d. 1864 in Bandiagara, Mali) but mainly though the teachings of Tijani masters such as Tierno Bokar who belonged to the same Tall family. Shaykh Umat Tall had fought against the French and their local allies before being killed in a battle in 1864. His descendants lost temporal power under colonial rule but retained the spiritual aura of the warrior, and guidance of the order. Eventually the colonial administration found a path of accommodation with the Tijaniyya and the Tall family. Then, in the 1920s, another branch of the Tijaniyya developed in the region formed by the territories of Mauritania, Senegal and Mali. It was led by Shaykh Hamaullah from Mauritania who had adopted with his followers the '11 beads practice', thus starting a controversy with the '12 beads' establishment. The controversy led to a violent political conflict which took an anti-colonial turn as the French administration got involved because of the possible troubles. Shaykh Hamaullah, having always voiced his opposition to the colonial administration, was imprisoned for five years in 1925 then deported to Côte d'Ivoire for another five years. He was briefly liberated and was back in his town of Nioro in 1936 thanks to the political change that happened in France that same year, when the Popular Front came to power. Hamaullah's enemies would still insist that he was preparing a jihad. Eventually he was arrested again in 1940 and in 1942 the Vichy Governor Buisson deported him to Eveaux-les-Bains, France. He died soon after in January 1943 and was buried in Montluçon. His disciples were persecuted by the French colonial administration.

Tierno Bokar had adopted the '11 beads' practice after becoming a disciple of Shaykh Hamaullah whom he met in 1937 at Nioro, a conversion that the Tall family considered a betrayal. The French colonial administration also went after him as it considered the '11 beads' faction an anti-France movement and because it wanted to please the Tijaniyya establishment.

So the scene from his biography presented earlier came just after Tierno had joined the 11 beads movement. It shows that the French administration was wary of the new situation thus created by the rallying of a prestigious and respected member of the Tall family to what they labelled an 'anti-France' dissident branch of the Tijaniyya. The commander had summoned the Sufi master to seek confirmation of the fact of his conversion and probably arrest and deport him after the hearing and his confession. The 'translation' to which he had responded positively had avoided him such a fate. But when it was later discovered that the case was not closed as Levavasseur had been led to believe, retaliation followed and Tierno lived through persecution, house arrest, and hardships of all nature until his death three years later in February 1940.

Translating versus Interpreting

I have described the scene as a dialogue. Commander Levavasseur did think that he was in a dialogue in its simplest form, that he was posing a precise 'yes or no' question to be answered by his interlocutor. He assumed that his words were conveyed to Tierno through the interpreter (meaning that the intermediary just made the words in French pass through him to be expressed in Tierno's tongue at the other end) and that in return the sounds uttered by the Malian Sufi master came back to him in the same way, accompanied by the universal body language of acquiescence that he could decipher. The interpreter should not have had any agency. He was supposed to be a simply intermediary, an instrument to convey words from a language into another language, *salva veritate*, the information remaining unaltered. *Truchement* is an interesting word in French, coming from the Arabic *tarjumān* meaning translator. It has then come to mean 'instrument', or 'means', a channel 'through' which some effect is produced. In that sense the *truchement* is not an agent but a tool. But in this scene agency is claimed by Oumar Sy, the official interpreter. We are presented with an instance of the intermediary playing the colonial power by a false translation.

For the past two decades historians of colonialism have paid great attention to the important actors of a third space, the space of hybridity participating both in the world of the imperium and that of the colonized: intermediaries and other colonial clerks have become categories of great interest in the studies of empires with a focus more particularly on the figure of the interpreter and the question of translation in general in colonial context. Full understanding of the colonial encounter in its complexity supposes an exploration of what Homi Bhabha (Rutherford 1990) has called a 'third space', complicating the face-to-face colonizer–colonized encounter. Taking that into account means questioning the one-sided dimension of interpretation, as an interpreter, a representative *par excellence* of the third space, always, inevitably, exceeds the role of a mere *truchement*.

Great attention has been paid recently to the transactional nature of the colonial system and to the figure of the interpreter as its best manifestation and illustration. Two titles could be thus evoked: African Agency and European Colonialism, Latitudes of Negotiations and Containments, edited by Femi J. Kolapo and Kwabena O. Akurang-Passy (2007) and Intermediaries, Interpreters and Clerks: African Employees in the Making of Colonial Africa, edited by Benjamin Lawrence, Emily Lynn Osborn and Richard L. Roberts (2006). No contribution shows better the transactional nature of colonialism than the article by Tamba Mbayo in African Agency on the Senegalese interpreter Bou El Moghdad Seck. The text is entitled: 'Bou El Moghdad Seck (1826–1880): Interpretation and Mediation of Colonialism in Senegal'. The very title of that article expresses the important notion of 'African agency' under colonial rule as a move from interpretation to mediation or transaction: action through translation.

Coming back to the scene from *Tierno Bokar*, we understand that the decision had been made by the interpreter to save Tierno from himself by deceiving him, in addition to deceiving the French commander: Oumar Sy, as a benevolent deceiver, needed the Sufi master's body language to be directly readable by Levavasseur so that it would conform with with his own 'translation'.

What was the meaning of that decision? What Oumar Sy understood is that the hearing as it was set and the 'yes or no' question as it was asked, failed to take into account the true situation, the reality of the whole affair. He knew Tierno and knew that he could not possibly be the agitator and the trouble-maker that for Levavasseur a 'no' to his question would make him be. He also knew that the master would not answer 'yes' just to avoid trouble. So the Oumar Sy's deceptive 'interpretation' was done in the name of what the *true translation* of the whole situation was. Simply interpreting in this case, that is to say transferring a given uttered meaning from a language to another would have been the real deception. What was then needed was a translation whereby the totality of the meaning would be present, a situation far more complex where 'yes, Tierno is a partisan of the 11 beads movement' and 'no, Tierno could not possibly be an agitator and an "anti-France" trouble-maker' could be both true beyond the binary 'yes or no' to which Levavasseur wants to reduce the hearing. Both Levavasseur and Tierno are agents of simplification, both for totally different reasons would simplify the situation into the predictable consequences of a 'yes or no' answer, the former because he is the power to decide between what is right and what is wrong, the latter because he is committed by his faith to the simple bare truth. The wisdom of the official interpreter is to understand that the truth is not simple and is best realized in translation, that is *transaction*. So he makes the move from the instrumental nature of the *truchement* or the *intermediary* (who transmits information up to the colonial administrator, and conveys instructions down to the colonized administered) to the agency of a *mediator*. In so doing the interpreter aims at moving from interpretation to translation and at the establishment of a true *dialogue*.

Cultural Mediators & Translators

But is such a dialogue possible in colonial context? Antoine Berman has written that there is a contradiction between, on the one hand, the fundamental drive of any given culture – *a fortiori* an imperial one – to appropriate and reduce to itself other cultures and languages and, on the other hand, what he calls 'the ethical aim of translation' which implies 'openness, dialogue, crossbreeding, and decentering'. Translation, he concludes, means 'putting in a relationship, lest it is nothing' (Berman 1992: 4). That is precisely the ultimate goal of interpretation: to 'put in a relationship', to create reciprocity and respect. It must be recalled that Amadou Hampâté Bâ himself started his career as an interpreter at the service of the colonial administration like the one, Oumar Sy, whose trick to save Tierno from punishment he

Colonial 'Truchement', Postcolonial Translator

has reported. In fact, in 1973, Bâ published a novel, *L'étrange destin de Wangrin ou les roueries d'un interprète africain*,[1] which is largely autobiographical as it describes precisely the life of an interpreter who helped the colonial administration establish its rule over the West African territories it controlled in the early twentieth century and who could sometimes use his privileged position to 'manipulate [the] Europeans and even defend other Africans against them' (Austen 2006: 167). Beyond the anecdotes about the interpreters as tricksters, what is important is the way in which they expanded the significance of their position as *écrivains-interprètes* (the official title in French meaning literally 'writer-interpreter') by becoming translators of their cultures and the literature (or rather *orature*) of their own indigenous languages. To use the title of Ralph Austen's article, 'Interpreters Self-Interpreted', they created their autonomous voices by interpreting themselves.

That colonialism understands translation not as relation, transaction and reciprocity, but as a one-directional process of Europeanization has found its best expression in the views of British historian and politician Lord Thomas Macaulay (1800–59) concerning the value of non-European languages and the meaning of educating colonized people. In his famous 'Minute on Indian Education' in 1835 he addressed the question of the best way to employ funds 'for the intellectual improvement of the people of [India]'. Given what was for him a simple fact that 'the dialects commonly spoken among the natives contain neither literary nor scientific information', he argued that it would take huge enrichment if 'any valuable work were to be translated into them'. So, the only possible improvement would come through 'some language not vernacular amongst them'. Then Macaulay asked whether such a language could be Sanskrit or Arabic: such a choice – Sanskrit being the language of Hindu Law and Arabic that of 'Mahometan Law' – would appear to mean an openness to 'cooperation'. This was a purely rhetorical question as he quickly dismissed and ridiculed the very possibility of making such a choice: even the poetry in those tongues is not comparable the least to European languages and as to 'cooperation', why would learners be involved in what is the exclusive privilege of the teachers to 'prescribe' in what language students have to be educated? So, of course, English stands as the language of education and intellectual improvement as 'it stands pre-eminent even among the languages of the West'. Therefore, what Greek and Latin were to Europe, English must be to India. In summary, and given the constraints of 'limited means', Macaulay concludes:

> we must at present do our best to form a class who may be interpreters between us and the millions whom we govern; a class of persons, Indian in blood and colour, but English in taste, in opinions, in morals, and in intellect. To that class we may leave it to refine the vernacular dialects of the country, to enrich those dialects with terms of science borrowed from the Western nomenclature, and to render them by degrees fit vehicles for conveying knowledge to the great mass of the population. (1994: 430)

---

[1] It was translated into English as *The Fortunes of Wangrin* and published in 1999 (Bâ 1999).

Macaulay obviously speaks of translation in terms that are the opposite of Berman's notion of the 'ethics of translation' being 'a putting in touch'. This is because the colonial space rests, by definition, upon the notion of an *imperial language* that defines the meaning of translation simply as *vertical transfer* through interpreters. What the colonial *écrivains-interprètes* tried to achieve by becoming *écrivains* of their own cultures in the imperial language, was to introduce reciprocity, to transform that space into a space of dialogue.

To come back to the case of Amadou Hampâté Bâ, he worked to become a mediator between languages and cultures and to turn the colonial context into a space of translation and reciprocity: when in 1942 he was recruited as a research assistant at the Institut Français d'Afrique Noire (IFAN) thanks to its director, Théodore Monod, he devoted himself mainly to the task of transcribing and translating West African oral literatures into French. The same task had been undertaken by European missionaries, ethnologists and sometimes administrators doing ethnological work, but A.H. Bâ was one of the first and most prominent West African francophone 'interpreters' turned indigenous 'writers': in other words cultural intermediaries who sought to translate their situation of *in between-ness* into literary creation.[2]

Now there are two ways of looking at such an endeavour. One way is to consider that transcription/translation of oral African literature into French only means an assimilation of the local and particular cultures into the imperial and universal language through which it could only truly exist and even simply survive: A.H. Bâ has famously declared that in Africa the death of the elders had the same significance as libraries disappearing in flames, unless the memory of which they were the custodians was safely transferred into the colonial archive. Another way is to read the transcription/translation of *orature* as the gesture of affirming not only the life of the content that is thus transferred into the European language but also that of the indigenous languages from which it was produced. The oral text 'translated' into French is also the presence, virtual of course most of the time and sometimes explicit, of the language from which it was *recreated*. That transcription/translation is co-presence of languages, the indigenous and the European, is marked by the poet Blaise Cendrars who put together in the 1920s an anthology of African oral texts from all over the continent, collected and translated mainly by missionaries and ethnographers. In his very short word of introduction to the volume he wrote that the stories, myths and narratives gathered in the *anthology* pointed towards the 'beauty' and the 'visual power' (*puissance plastique*) of their original languages. He then concluded that the study of the 'primitives' languages and literature was indispensable to the knowledge of the history of the human spirit.

In a certain way, without the dated racialist and evolutionary language of Cendrars, the literary genre of recreation, in written French, of indigenous *orature* illustrates that notion that it constitutes also an authentic praise for

---

[2] Ralph Austen indicates that although Amadou Hampâté Bâ and another colonial clerk from Cameroon, Kuoh Moukouri, 'entered colonial service only in the 1920's', they are the first who were taken by their 'exceptional talents' beyond their level of employment as interpreters and to truly 'write' (2006: 159).

Colonial 'Truchement', Postcolonial Translator

the original African language it is virtually and sometimes actually present in the text produced through 'translation', thus establishing a dialogue between French and itself.[3]

To his reading of Amadou Hampâté Bâ's memoirs, *Amkoullel, l'enfant peul*, Ralph Austen has given the following title: 'From a Colonial to a Postcolonial African Voice: *Amkoullel, l'enfant peul*' (Austen 2000). To consider A.H. Bâ both a colonial and a postcolonial voice at once makes great sense. In the colonial space, of which Aimé Césaire has written that it is not a space of contact, a space where interpretation is uni-linear and can only mean and serve assimilation and Europeanization, A.H. Bâ has played the role of a *'truchement'* and interpreted African cultures and languages into the imperial language. But in so doing he has also naturally expanded the role into dialogue, relation and, ultimately, a postcolonial call for multilingualism and genuine translation.

Conclusion

One should certainly not be naïve about translation. We know that in the global 'Republic of letters', what is translated into what language is the result of decisions that manifest that the world of languages is a world of inequality and domination. The sociological study of translation conducted among others by what we may call the Pierre Bourdieu school, reminds us that, translation happens in a field where certain languages have more weight and prestige than others, and that bilingualism is most of the time not a choice but a necessity for people whose native tongues just do not count much in that field (Casanova 2015).

That being said, it is also true, at the same time, that the response to linguistic domination and imperialism is also translation. Umberto Eco's famous quote: 'the language of Europe is translation' (see Wolf 2014: 224) expresses eloquently the idea that translation is the way of recognizing the simple fact that any language is one among the plurality of human idioms. Eco's saying could certainly be generalized as: 'the universal language is translation'.

Merleau-Ponty has perfectly described the passage from the colonial era to a postcolonial world when he wrote that the time of an 'overarching universal' that Europe had claimed to represent was over and that another kind of universality was to be invented in a world of a plurality of cultures and languages, all equivalent:

> [T]he equipment of our social being can be dismantled and reconstructed by the voyage, as we are able to learn to speak other languages. This provides *a second way*

---

[3] The style of Senegalese author Birago Diop who thus published volumes of 'transcribed/translated' tales from the oral tradition is probably the best illustration of that co-presence of languages in a text. Of course, as Senghor, has noted, his so-called *translations* of orality are in fact written *creations* (Senghor 1961).

to the universal: no longer the *overarching universal* of a strictly objective method, but a sort of *lateral universal* which we acquire through ethnological experience and its incessant testing of the self through the other person and the other person through the self. It is question of constructing a general system of reference in which the point of view of the native, the point of view of the civilized man, and the mistaken views each has of the other can all find a place – that is of constituting a more comprehensive experience which becomes in principle accessible to men of a different time and country. (Merleau-Ponty 1964: 119–20)

As the invitation to learn to speak other languages indicates, caring for universality in a postcolonial world means developing the capacity to be in between languages, to be a translator. I understand a 'lateral universal' to mean translation. Of course, again, that does not mean transparency and the elimination of the untranslatable. On the contrary the untranslatable or the unavoidable misunderstandings or 'mistaken views about each other' are part of this incessant testing, marked by the co-presence of many different views. So 'lateral' universality does not have as its horizon the establishment of a universal grammar, and it does not mean the end game of a final reduction of the plural of the 'chaos-world' to the One and the Same. But it does mean the 'putting in touch' of languages and the creation of reciprocity in the asymmetrical context of linguistic imperialism. The interpreters who became translators understood it to be their task.

References

Austen, R. (2000). 'From a Colonial to a Postcolonial African Voice: *Amkoullel, l'enfant peul*'. *Research in African Literatures*, 31(3): 1–17.

—. (2006). 'Interpreters Self-Interpreted: The Autobiographies of Two Colonial Clerks'. In B. Lawrence, E. Osborn and R. Roberts (eds), *Intermediaries, Interpreters and Clerks: African Employees in the Making of Colonial Africa*. Madison, WI, Wisconsin: University of Wisconsin Press.

Bâ, A.H. (1973). *L'étrange destin de Wangrin ou les rogueries d'un interprète africain*. Paris: Union Générale d'Edition.

—. (1980). *Vie et enseignement de Tierno Bokar le Sage de Bandiagara*. Paris: Seuil.

—. (1999). *The Fortunes of Wangrin*, A. Taylor (trans.). Bloomington, IN: Indiana University Press.

Berman, A. (1992). *The Experience of the Foreign: Culture and Translation in Romantic Germany*. S. Heyvaert (trans.). Albany, NY: SUNY Press.

Casanova, P. (2015). *La langue mondiale: Traduction et domination*, Paris: Seuil.

Cendrars, B. (1921). *Anthologie Nègre*. Paris: Editions de la Sirène.

Césaire, A. (2001). *Discourse on Colonialism*. J. Pinkham (trans.). New York: Monthly Review Press.

Kolapo, F.J. and K.O. Akurang-Passy (eds) (2007). *African Agency and European Colonialism. Latitudes of Negotiations and Containments*. Lanham, MD: University Press of America.

Lawrence, B., E. Osborn and R. Roberts (eds) (2006). *Intermediaries, Interpreters and Clerks: African Employees in the Making of Colonial Africa.* Madison, WI: University of Wisconsin Press.

Macaulay, T. (1994). 'Minute on Indian Education'. In B. Ashcroft, G. Griffith and H. Tiffin (eds), *The Postcolonial Studies Reader.* New York: Routledge.

Merleau-Ponty, M. (1964). 'From Mauss to Levi-Strauss'. In Merleau-Ponty, M., *Signs.* Evanston, IL: Northwestern University Press.

Rutherford, J. (1990). 'The Third Space: Interview with Homi Bhabha'. In J. Rutherford (ed.), *Identity: Community, Culture, Difference.* London: Lawrence and Wishart.

Sakai, Naoki (2006). 'Translation'. *Theory, Culture & Society,* 23(2–3): 71–86.

Senghor, L.S. (1961). 'Préface'. In B. Diop, *Les nouveaux contes d'Amadou Koumba.* Paris: Présence africaine.

Wolf, M. (2014). '"The Language of Europe is Translation": EST Amidst New Europes and Changing Ideas on Translation', *Target: International Journal on Translation Studies,* 26(2): 224–38.

13 'Kos'ona Miran?' Patronage, Prebendalism & Democratic Life in Contemporary Nigeria

Adigun Agbaje

Introduction

In this chapter, I offer a view on the prospects for democracy in Nigeria against a backdrop of Jane Guyer's timeless concern with the dynamics of autonomy, resilience, co-optation and capitulation of micro (marginal, local) processes, structures and actors in their daily interactions and negotiations with the macro (dominant, national). In this regard, I attempt an outline of elements of continuity, change and the suspended – if restive and tense – state between change and continuity, in the role of patronage in the evolving democratic possibilities in Nigeria's Fourth Republic. I do all this in the specific context of Jane Guyer's enduring focus on and contributions to African studies in general and the study of Nigeria in particular. No less important, this chapter also engages with Guyer's intellectual encounters and collaborations with African scholars against the backdrop of her steadfast commitment to, and interest in, life in Nigeria, which has yielded unusual insights evident in her work on the African continent – a continent described by some as characterized by wholesale marginality of entire populations (Guyer 2002: xiii). She has devoted herself to the study of the people and their money, the people in other areas of the economy, the people and energy, the people, their spaces and places (rural and urban), and the people and politics.

I start at the level of the personal. As a student and teacher of political science, I come, along with many others, from a long tradition of adherence to the point, stated recently by Larry Diamond (2013: vii), that:

> The oldest and most enduring story of human political life is this: the strong exploit and abuse the weak. Those who wield political power use it to extract wealth from the powerless ... Historically, force was typically the means by which the wielders of power acquired it and held it. And force remains the ultimate guarantor of power ... Political development can be viewed as a quest to solve three basic problems in the organization and exercise of power. First, how can violence be subdued and contained so that power is acquired and exercised by (largely) peaceful means? Second, how can the abuse of power – the exploitation of the powerless by the powerful – be restrained? And, third, how can the powerless be empowered, so that all members of the collectivity benefit to some fair – if not exactly equal – degree

from the exercise of power, and hence the holders of power are held accountable to the people?

Two sets of intellectual encounters with Jane Guyer, both leading ultimately to the production of edited volumes on Nigeria, contributed to the consolidation of a major re-focusing of aspects of African studies for some of us, signalling an important break with the past. The first relates to the series of meetings (at Stanford University in August 1990 and at the Nigerian Institute of International Affairs, NIIA, Lagos, in January 1991) that led to the production of the well-regarded *Transition Without End* (Diamond, Kirk-Greene and Oyediran 1997). The second comprised the meetings that led to the publication of *Money Struggles and City Life* (Guyer, Denzer and Agbaje 2002). These encounters, taken with the work of others linking political economy and the state with the everyday experience of African peoples, have led to what I consider a better and more nuanced insight into teasing out 'specific resolutions' to 'historically produced' situations 'for both "the people" and the "the state"' (Guyer 1997: 435). Such a nuanced approach thus 'accords greater latitude for manoeuvre' (ibid.) among the people and their institutions and processes on one hand and the state and its institutions and processes on the other, rather than conceiving of all this as 'fixed'.

In the context of the studies that culminated in *Money Struggles and City Life*, Guyer contributed a chapter on personal rule and regional politics in Ibadan under the 1986–99 period of military rule. My objection that local politics was not 'attractive' to me could not persist for long and, over the next couple of years of interaction with the manuscript and meetings at Ibadan (1997) and Evanston (1998), I became fully convinced as to the positive-sum understanding of the study of the everyday life of the people and their state, a most enriching experience in the larger context of the political economy of life in Nigeria.

The perspectives that Guyer brought to bear specifically in her study of local government, chiefs and office holders in rural Ibarapa, Nigeria, and on the general theme of the studies that led to *Transition Without End* (1997) have been seminal and instructive with regard to the wider matters of the quality of democracy and representation in rural Nigeria in the context of political economy and engagement (or failure thereof) of the local populace with 'the corporate sector of society and polity' (Guyer 1997: 424). She has raised issues of theory, method and evidence germane to a nuanced understanding of patronage and democratic possibilities in Nigeria.

Patronage, Prebendalism, & Democratic Possibilities in the Fourth Republic: Insights from the Past & the Present

'Kos'ona Miran' ('No Other Way'), the main title of Guyer's (2002: 115–31) important contribution on continuity and change in rural agriculture (*Money Struggles*) regarding the people's economy and popular responses in the Ibadan region to a harsh economic and political period of currency devaluation in Nigeria (1986–96) under military rule, is evocative when applied to the history of the travails of democracy in that country in the context of the persistence of the underpinning practices of patronage and prebendalism in political and public life over time and across space. As indicated in more detail below, patronage involves a network of flows from state officials down to the people identified as clients. Prebendalism involves manipulation of state offices, resources and symbols for no obvious public good by officials of the state. Between these two, it is acknowledged that there is obviously a sphere of overlap; it is equally generally agreed that, while the criminality in prebendalism is beyond debate, patronage occupies a grey area in acceptable practice, but may in fact be perfectly legal (see below, drawing on Joseph 2013, citing Bratton and van de Walle 1994). The net result for Nigeria has been that:

> the balance of aspirations against undemocratic rule over the period has yielded meaningful democracy for only a couple of years while official and micro-level commitment to a developmental state has not meaningfully transformed the Nigerian economy from one obsessed with consumption, rent-seeking and neo-patrimonial practice to one concerned with production and capacity building for long-term development. (Agbaje 2010: 63, 2004: 203–4)

The rest of this section outlines the elements of this practice as has been observed over time. Perhaps the first major treatment of the private appropriation and subsequent dispensation of state resources by officials of the state at national and sub-national levels in Nigeria for the purpose, among others, of securing loyalty and regime support from among elite and non-elite alike was the seminal work by Richard Joseph (1987) on the travails of democracy in Nigeria's failed Second Republic (1979–1983). The work was recently revisited and reassessed in a recent landmark publication (Adebanwi and Obadare 2013). It has, therefore, been established that the emergence of patron-client relations (not only between the minority that govern and the majority that are governed on one hand but also among and within the various layers and groups that govern and are governed) and prebendalism as major factors in the narrative and understanding of Nigeria's apparently tortuous and unending search for a stable and democratic order, stretch as far back as not only the Second Republic but also the First Republic (see Diamond 1988), and even back to the twilight of colonial rule.

The central argument of this chapter, therefore, is that this long history of the nature and role of patronage, basically defined as the granting of favours by officials of the state in a patron-client relational context involving exchange with the people, as well as prebendal manipulation of state offices and resources for corrupt purposes outside of the purview of the public good, in all their separate manifestations (patrimonial, neo-patrimonial, clientelist and predatory) underscore two things. First, the import of seeking to historicize everyday experience of these elements from above, from below, and in

'Kos'ona Miran?' Patronage, Prebendalism & Democratic Life

their interfaces, underscores popular perceptions of unity of purpose in practice, and elements of continuity and change, only in the details of context and manifestation.

Second, at the level of practice, the Nigerian experience has for long suggested that there may be no escape route from the pathological manner in which patron-client networks, relations and exchanges, as well as prebendalism, have structured the processes and dominant values undergirding everyday engagement in political and public life of elite and non-elite alike, in manners that make democratic possibilities largely unattainable. Recent events, issues and insights in the Fourth Republic appear to suggest that there could be a combination of both episodic and more systematic opportunities for addressing elements of the networks, relations and exchanges extremely toxic to democratic possibilities in the short term and the long run. These include the unrelenting pressure from within, below, and outside the country, episodic interventions from the streets such as those surrounding and emanating from the January 2012 protest and labour strike over the increase in the pump price of fuel oil, the recurring street protests and debates on a 'just price' for sale of petrol to Nigerians (Obadare and Adebanwi 2013: 1–3; Guyer and Denzer 2013: 53–77), as well as matters arising from the 2015 elections. The challenge would then be to begin to focus attention on these escape routes as well as the tactics and strategies for broadening and deepening such pro-democratic ways and means in the face of the demonstrated resilience of anti-democratic forces in the polity. This, I suggest, is critical in understanding the specific challenges that arise from the configurations of the political economy of everyday life in Nigeria, in particular, and Africa, in general. I return to this point towards the end of the chapter.

For now, it needs to be noted that the momentum towards the full enthronement of patron-client relations and prebendalism has been largely organized around or in response to Nigeria's pathological state system and socio-cultural pluralities, and fuelled by burgeoning rent from oil in the first and second decades of independence (1960s-1970s), and especially so from the end of the civil war (1967 to January 1970). In a very important more recent statement, Larry Diamond (2013: vii-xiii, esp. viii-ix), offers an insightful analysis of these two drivers. On the role of the nature of Nigerian elite and society, he builds on Richard Sklar's 1963 seminal work on political parties up to the First Republic to argue that:

> Competitive politics in such a context became a driver of class formation, as rival political elites struggled through elections to enter the emerging dominant class with the transition from colonial rule to independence. Unfortunately, when everything is at stake in an election, when all routes to wealth formation and class attainment pass through political power and the state, it is impossible to conduct competitive elections by democratic rules of the game ... Lacking much in the way of a political program, rival parties and politicians fell back upon ethnic identity as the most reliable way of mobilizing electoral support ... thus the polarization of

politics around ethnic identity was socially constructed and cynically mobilized. (Diamond 2013: viii)

While all this provided the context for the first steps towards the construction of early versions of patron-client relations along ethnic, regional and party lines, the resources with which to fund the supporting networks came in greater abundance in the post-civil war period of oil boom when Nigeria became awash in petro-naira, thanks largely to 'the two great oil price shocks of 1973 and 1979' that ensured that 'staggering new revenues poured into' the country. As Diamond (2013: ix) succinctly puts it, 'these massive oil rents fed the prebendal system the way dry bush fuels a forest fire – except that in this case, the fuel will continue to burn for decades to come'. The implications of this for the lives of the majority of Nigerians have been examined by other scholars (Ezeala-Harrison 1993; Okonta and Douglas 2001; Watts 2004a, 2004b; Ikelegbe 2006).

In the context of this long-lasting 'bush fire', it is important at this stage to briefly outline the conceptual connections between patron-client relations and the varying dimensions of their manifestations and funding practices. To be sure, the meeting point of neo-patrimonial, prebendal and predatory practices is the manner in which they serve to shape the ways and manners in which the people interface with officials of the state for public or private profit or non-profit, and consequences thereof. Richard Joseph himself addresses this matter in a comment that I find useful on how his own work on prebendalism connects to and is separate from the writings of Bratton, van de Walle and Lewis, among others, on patrimonialism and its contemporary version, neo-patrimonialism, patronage and predation. First, Joseph (2013: 266) quotes Bratton and van de Walle (1997) as indicating that:

> in patrimonial political systems, an individual rules by dint of personal prestige and power; ordinary folk are treated as extensions of the 'big man's' household, with no rights or privileges other than those bestowed by the ruler. Authority is entirely personalized, shaped by the ruler's preferences rather than any codified system of laws.

Joseph (ibid.) then clarifies that in the way he uses it in the Nigerian context:

> [T]he term prebend refers to patterns of political behaviour which reflect as their justifying principle that the offices of the existing state may be competed for and then utilized for the benefit of office-holders as well as that of their reference or support group. To a significant extent, the 'state' in such a context is perceived as a congeries of offices susceptible to individual *cum* communal appropriation. The statutory purposes of such offices become a matter of secondary concern, however much that purpose might have been codified in law or other regulations or even periodically cited during competitions to fill them.

Also signposted was the context of the rise of predatory rule as a form of domination in the period from the 1980s to the 1990s under the military regimes of Generals Ibrahim Babangida and Sani Abacha. Perhaps more than any other, these military regimes relied more on despotic rather than infrastructural power to consolidate their rule (on these concepts, see Lucas 1998: 90–113), the net result being, in the words of Lewis as quoted by Joseph (2013: 266–7; see also, Agbiboa 2010):

> a more fundamental change ... the shift from prebendalism, or decentralized patrimonial rule, towards predation, the consolidation of avaricious dictatorship ... State economic tutelage moved from a position of diffuse clientelism under comparatively stable (though weak) institutional auspices to more arbitrary and destabilizing control by a single ruler.

It is further suggested (Joseph 2013: 269, citing van de Walle) that 'prebends and patronage overlap', but that, while 'patronage is often perfectly legal, though it is frowned upon and constitutes a "gray area" of acceptable practice ... prebendalism, on the other hand, invariably entails practices in which important state agents unambiguously subvert the rule of law for personal gain'.

Obviously, the legacy of all this for the Fourth Republic is to be read from footprints of the past etched in the reality of the moment in terms of dominant practices therein in the interactions among the people and the state and its officials. For the Fourth Republic (1999 to date), certain tendencies can be highlighted in terms of this legacy. For instance, a common feature of local life since the first experience of military rule from 1966, and more so since the end of the civil war, has been what Guyer (1997: 424) calls 'a dramatic restriction of corporate collective power at the community level ... a steady diminution of the corporate qualities of local government at the district level ... and a corresponding rise in the absolute and relative prominence of high chieftaincy, private business and parastatal organizations' at the community level, with some of the parastatals having their projects at the local level funded by international financial institutions.

The net result has been continued instability and weakening of local government through meddlesomeness by state and federal government officials even under civil rule, and attendant rise in popular perception of the timidity and developmental as well as democratic irrelevance of local government, 'and the replacement of certain functions by links to office, chieftaincy and private organizations', (Guyer 1997: 441). All this resulted in the need for special skills by local community elites seeking to negotiate their communities' ways through the increasingly complex web of organizational uncertainties and gaps in their search for individual and corporate wellbeing. Thus has been created in the local communities a network of people simultaneously engaging in party political mobilization and ministering to the needs of the local people while also addressing 'the steady stream of other public issues, often at substantial personal expense in money and effort' (ibid.). The fiscal crisis in local government, occasioned by reluctance of people to pay personal and property tax to seemingly non-performing bureaucracies, has further contributed to this trend. Over the years, this has further cemented the foundation for patronage possibilities at the grassroots and especially for chieftaincies, from large urban settings to tiny rural settlements, the result has been that such chieftaincies have over the years attracted into their fold people of means and western education. In such places as the Kano Emirate, it has not been unusual to have within the membership of the Emirate Council former Army Generals, top police officers, retired very senior civil servants, retired professors and top business persons, among others. In 2014, a former Governor of the Central Bank of Nigeria actually became the *Emir*.

In essence, therefore, the roots of the politics of patronage as constructed in the post-civil war era of the 1970s and 1980s drew succour from, and were shaped by, at least three tendencies. The first, as outlined above, related to the decline in capacity of local government as well as in the capacity for corporate local governance by people in local communities, and a parallel rise in the salience of chieftaincies, as well as state and federal officials, often with resources from corporate private organizations, international financial organizations and bilateral and multilateral agencies, as key agents in the delivery of development and developmental agenda in the various communities. The second factor in my estimation has to do with sustained sectionalisation of Nigeria's political landscape, highlighted above, and, as further underscored by Guyer's (1997: 435) understanding and use of the important work by Sara Berry (1985), to the effect that 'as long as sectional loyalties constitute a basis for access to the state, and as long as the state is the major source of resources, the symbols of sectional identity will be an object of investment'.

I draw the third factor again from Guyer's suggestive use of Sandra Barnes' (1986) seminal work on the Mushin community in Lagos, where it is shown that institutional gaps in the context of uncertainties and anxieties arising from rapid changes in the lives of individuals, groups and communities heighten the development of personal allegiances facilitative of patronage. To be sure, no other period in Nigeria's political history has witnessed as much of institutional vacuity and palpable uncertainty as that leading up to and including the Fourth Republic. The hallmark of the period has been a project of de-democratization under which the dominant elements in the ruling elite sought to use 'the promises, imagery and appearances of democratization to de-institutionalize, weaken and cripple democratic processes and structures, while at the same time institutionalizing and invigorating a thoroughgoing system of co-optive rule' (Agbaje 1997: 578). The period has been signposted by a political economy characterized largely 'by a personalization and commodification of politics and society and the politicization of the economy, resulting in the erosion of institutions and the enthronement of mass apathy (politics no longer matters) and alienation (people against politics)' (Agbaje 2002: 21–2).

Against the background of this context, additional insights can be offered on the dynamics of patron-client relations in the period leading up to the Fourth Republic, and in the Republic itself. One abiding observation, supportive of the increasing salience of chieftaincies as noted above, relates to the socio-cultural roots of patronage in the period under review. Against the backdrop of broad theoretical considerations that view social networks as bearers of meaning structures (Futse 2009: 51), studies have focused on how major transformations arising from colonialism and 'the imposition of money economy and capitalism' have changed the socio-cultural bases of patron-client relations, ensuring that patronage no longer works for the overall development of society but largely 'for personal benefit only' (Omobowale 2008: 219). However, such personal benefits are hardly ever generalized, nor are they practically generalizable (in relation to the greater population) in a politically egalitarian way.

On the other hand, as reflected in Yoruba proverbs, patron-client relations have the potential to provide public good in rural and urban life while working to broaden public-mindedness among the elite; at the same time, 'the patron is expected to be a role model' in character (Omobowale 2008: 219; Omobowale and Olutayo 2007, 2010: 453–72; also, Obadare 2007; Kingston 2001: 55–72). This culturally embedded everyday expectation continues to resonate in many of the perspectives and expectations of traditional, including Islamic, societies (Omobowale and Olutayo 2010; Umar 2013: 177–200; Pierce 2006: 887–914), and it now uneasily exists side by side, and in a context of interpenetrations, with the more dominant postcolonial perspectives and expectations. This has yielded interesting realities for Nigeria's Fourth Republic, a central element of which has been the consolidation of a network of patrons and clients at national and regional levels with changeable locations and assignments up and down the rungs of patronage and prebendalism, in and out of formal public offices. Thus, key personalities become highly visible and exert great influence on the political and socio-economic processes, with wide-ranging implications for party and opposition politics as well as the electoral process, among others. In such contexts, the persistence of more-constructive elements of patron-client relations in local communities, albeit in attenuated form, directly or indirectly, cannot be overlooked especially in situations in which the consequences of such relations could mark the difference between elements of local development and non-development in terms of the siting of state projects, as well as injection of state and non-state resources into local economies.

The general picture that emerges from the many excellent studies of this phenomenon in the Fourth Republic and the background leading to it is that of a complex and far-flung network of highly personalized relationships from the national to state and local levels among holders of power not only along but also across party lines as well as along lines of regional, intra-regional, business, friendship and, occasionally, ethnic and religious interests and schisms that often defy party political boundaries, funded at all levels principally by rent from oil and burgeoning corrupt practices (Apter 2005) subscribed to and facilitated by both public and private bureaucracies in a general environment of ineffectuality of oversight and regulatory institutions (cf. Adejumobi 2010; Adebanwi 2012; Adebanwi and Obadare. 2011; Adebanwi 2011; Obadare 2007; Agbaje, 2010; Hoffman, 2010; Agbaje, 2002; Omobowale and

Olutayo 2007; Tade 2011; Omobowale and Olutayo 2010; and the essays in Adebanwi and Obadare 2013, among others).

Presented schematically rather than in the form of narratives that have already been so vividly and excellently rendered in the works cited in this chapter, among others, items in the harvest of consequences for the political terrain in this regard has included the following:

- The 'triumph of crude hegemonic politics over democratic politics' (Agbaje 2010: 78; Agbaje and Adejumobi 2006: 30; Abutudu 2010; Agbaje 2004), leading to a commandist and exclusionary approach to party structure, administration and processes (CDD, 2003: 3) that spills over into the wider political system in form of pressures towards 'centralization, concentration and personalization of political power, the central defining element of modern despotism' (Agbaje and Adejumobi 2006: 30).
- Heightened corruption, including criminal use of money, in party candidate selection processes and the other stages leading to the conduct of elections, the voting process itself, the declaration of results, and litigations arising therefrom (cf. Hoffman 2010: 285–310; Kura 2014: 124–37).
- Institutional recession and the emptying of governmental and policy processes of much of their intrinsic content and meaning through a thoroughgoing strengthening of elements of personal rule at federal, state and local levels.
- Prominence in the political system of local agents of federal and regional patrons whose role as 'middlemen' is to seek to exploit the poverty and increasing levels of inequality in the polity to suborn the poorer segments of the populace through financial and other inducements as well as the selective deployment and corrupt inducement of agents of the state and of trade/artisan and ethnic associations for violence in support of their principals, often determined more by inducement flows and less by principles and, therefore, changeable (Omobowale and Olutayo 2010; Agbaje 2004; Hoffman and Nolte 2013; Hoffman 2010; Pierce 2006; Omobowale 2008; Tade 2011; Obadare 2007; Animasawun 2009; Albert 2007; Nolte 2007; Adebanwi 2005).
- The role of regional power brokers in the strengthening of oppositional politics at the centre to serve as countervailing force to central power brokers and the latter's tendency to seek to loosen the grip of such regional brokers on their regions.
- The potentials for destabilization of politics at national, regional and local levels arising from struggles for patronal supremacy within and among political parties, governments at federal, state and local levels, or in the contexts of struggles for patronal succession arising from death or intra-party purges or schisms (cf. Tade 2011: 108–23).
- Emergence of popular protest and strikes as platform for 'key democratic' claims 'by the Nigerian people on their government' (Guyer and Denzer 2013: 72).

Weapons of the Wealthy

Specifically, the role of the elite in governance deserves a comment or two in at least two areas. Generally, in what has been cryptically reported as the deployment of weapons of the wealthy in certain other parts of the developing world (cf. Kimse 2012: 375–7), the Nigerian ruling elite across the political divide appear to have strengthened their capacity to assume leadership of popular protests and related activities such as strikes with a view to preventing such from escalating to the stage of regime disruption in manners that are not easily or directly discernible. In addition, and in recognition of the relatively volatile, unstable and unpredictable terrain in which they operate, African politicians, including their Nigerian counterparts, have come to rely more and more on spiritual consultations, consequently drawing religious leaders and organizations into their patronage networks (McCauley 2013: 1–21). In Nigeria, this has manifested in an increasingly public and prominent role for leaders of Islamic, Christian and Traditional religious groups in party, political and policy matters.

These have system-wide implications for governance in terms of its structure as well as its moral/legal foundations with reference to poverty, inequality, corruption and rent seeking, among others. Noting that federalism is 'Janus-faced' and a 'double-edged sword', respected student of federalism in Nigeria, Suberu (2013: 79–101, esp. 79), goes on to elaborate that 'depending on historical legacies, socioeconomic contexts, the quality of political leadership, and, especially, the ingenuity of institutional design, federalism can significantly advance, rather than subvert, good governance'. Against the background of this cheering principle, however, Suberu proceeds to

> analyse prebendalism's permeation, degradation, and emasculation of the formal institutions and informal practices of contemporary Nigerian federalism [and] highlight the largely shallow and weak effects on the institutional distortion of ongoing efforts and struggles to reform the country's federalism. (Suberu 2013: 80)

Another noted student of local governance, Vaughan (2013: 227–42) underscores the dynamic interconnections between ethno-regionalism and federalism in Nigeria over time, with Nigeria's practice of federalism widely believed to have worked largely to deepen fissiparous tendencies of ethnic and regional particularism in the putative federal arrangement – even more so in the Fourth Republic (Abutudu 2010: 23–60).

The last set of considerations to be flagged in this section relates to how corruption has been evidence and driver of some of the pathologies that have complicated the search for democracy in the Fourth Republic in the context of clientelist tendencies. Flagging this challenge, Pierce (2006: 887–914, esp. 887–8) notes of Nigeria that:

> Potentially wealthy from its oil revenue, it symbolizes Africa's promise denied. Within Nigeria's litany of woes, its notorious corruption is particularly prominent.

Nigeria regularly tops Transparency International's list of most corrupt countries ... this very notoriety may obscure a more complicated totality: practices almost everyone would term 'corrupt' are rampant, though they are a contingent product of contemporary social structures rather than the result of some kind of African or Nigerian 'dysfunction.' Corruption is a long history of politics, state formation, and economic exploitation, and of a complex interplay between indigenous and foreign understandings of appropriate governmental conduct.

Elements of this corruption include distortions in party and political funding and candidate selection as hinted earlier (Kura 2014: 124–37), primacy of patron-client relations over formal and institutional aspects of politics such as the rule of law, properly structured and effectively functioning party system, institutions and processes for rule-making, rule enforcement, rule interpretation, regulation, oversight, accountability, transparency and, for a credible electoral system (Fagbadebo 2007: 28–37), as well as rent seeking through exploitation of public policy, resources and institutions (Anugwom 2011: 204–16); as reflected in an Indonesian study of a largely undocumented practice in Nigeria as reported in Kristiansen and Ramli (2006: 207–33) in a context of poverty, growing inequality and troubled economy (Yusuf et al. 2014), among others.

Obviously, therefore, the image that ensues from all this is that of a Fourth Republic trapped in a largely undemocratic present with a future circumscribed by the clientelist manner, among other factors, in which the relations and encounters among the state, state officials, socio-economic, ethno-regional, as well as religious and traditional institutions, and the people have been structured over time. However, as indicated earlier, developments before and during the Fourth Republic have highlighted the extent to which pressures for change have persisted. Along with street protests and other forms of popular action, pressures for change have served to signpost the potentials for limiting the reach, efficacy and invincibility of patron-client relations as a factor for undemocratic rule and hindrance to the emergence of a truly democratic order that could ensure the greatest good for the greatest number of people in Nigeria. On the first front, Diamond (2013: xii-xiii) optimistically but accurately notes that 'there are three possible sources of pressure for reform: from within, from below, and from outside the country'. According to him:

despite the pervasiveness of the prebendal logic and culture, at least some Nigerian state officials are disgusted by the country's developmental failures and want to see it exit the cul-de-sac of prebendalism ... Nigerian civil society has long boasted a vibrant array of NGOs, professional associations, interest groups, mass media, think tanks, and intellectual networks that – while not immune from the pressures and entitlements of prebendalism – have long been advocates for accountability, transparency, clean elections, and the rule of law ... Carefully targeted financial and technical assistance can ... strengthen reform elements within the state and civil society and gradually help to give critical mass to a coalition for reform that cuts across ethnic, religious, regional, and other social divides ... In the absence of revolution, reform will be a long, messy, and incremental struggle. But the past few years in Nigeria have shown that progress is possible.

It is also generally acknowledged that a series of events in the Fourth Republic have helped to underscore the possibility of democratic triumph. As indicated earlier, notable ones relate to protests, campaigns and strikes relating to the pump price of oil, including the one of January 2012 that shook the foundations of the Republic and its patronage and prebendal scaffolding (Adebanwi and Obadare 2013: xvii-xviii; Guyer and Denzer 2013: 52–77). These were occasions in which the people stood up to challenge the political-economic processes and institutions that they assumed to be standing between them and the possibilities of personal and collective good life. These incidents and demands in regard of disputations about the 'right and just pump price' of petroleum have been perceived as having the possibility (Guyer and Denzer 2013: 72–3) of being seen:

> as the key democratic claim by the Nigerian people on their government, crossing boundaries of regime type, market conditions, and forefront organizations leading the articulation of the terms. Even more striking than the recurrence of these confrontations is their ubiquity. They do not, in fact, replicate the 'fundamental processes' of Nigerian political sociology in regional, ethnic, or religious terms. On this one theme at least – the fuel price – the people reach far beyond sectarian interests, and may have given up altogether on prebendalism as a source of resources, for them ... But clearly the people have not given up altogether. They protest. They claim their right as citizens to a national good and their access to a key input into their livelihoods. As the dilemma rolls forward over decades, they may be looking now to the large government and corporate organizations, and mid-level office-holders, as the chief suspects.

This provides one source of hope for a future of disrupted large-scale patronage, prebendalism, and democratic nominalism. For now, one recent empirical manifestation of the limits of patronage and prebendalism in electoral democracy has been the period leading to the 2015 elections, and the conduct as well as the pattern of the results of the elections themselves. Generally, the elections were perceived as one of the most contested and most divisive in Nigeria's political history as well as one in which there was extensive and corrupt use of inducements by politicians and their supporters to influence election outcomes. Interestingly, however, the presidential election in March 2015 led to the unprecedented defeat at the polls of incumbent President Goodluck Jonathan of the then ruling People's Democratic Party (PDP) by then opposition candidate and now new President Muhammadu Buhari of the All Progressives Congress (APC), the latter being widely perceived as more disciplined and more charismatic individual and holding more promises of a better and less corrupt future for the country, underscoring the ultimate superiority of the people's will over patronage and other chicaneries of incumbency.

The defeat of the ruling party in Nigeria shows a trend pointing, through the possible complicating haze of electoral malpractices, towards the point that incumbency and control over funds for campaign activities, including dispensation of patronage with a view to influence election outcomes, was not as prominent as perception of party, party candidate, and prior performance and record in office in determining such outcomes. This augurs well for the future of elections conducive to the development of democratic life, practices and ethos in Nigeria.

Conclusion: Prospects for a More Democratic Life

The argument of this chapter has been that, although the dynamics of the political economy of the interactions among and within state officials and the people in Nigeria have tended to weigh in over the years on the side of patronage and prebendal practices toxic to the realization of the country's democratic possibilities, recent developments have shown that these practices are not as unassailable as they have appeared. Indeed, the precariousness of the state of these practices has increasingly been demonstrated by events and outcomes of recent elections in the Republic. In a perceptive comment on this matter of the future of patronage and patrimonialism in determining the fate of democracy in Nigeria, Hoffman and Nolte (2013: 46) comment that,

> while the central state plays a potentially growing role in the provision of local patronage, and although patronage ties challenge the rational and legal structures upholding the institutions of the modern state, the fact that financial investment alone does not guarantee enduring patrimonial ties illustrates that patron-client networks do not exist outside of considerations of political ideology and even morality.

On a final note, it would therefore appear, to appropriate Pratten (2013), that it is in the precariousness of patronage and prebendal politics and in the contradictions in their logics and consequences, coupled with pressures from below and dissension and strategic disagreements among the ruling elite, that Nigeria's democratic possibilities can blossom in the foreseeable future and begin to bear fruits in the interest of its people and their state.

References

Abutudu, M. (2010). 'Federalism, Political Restructuring, and the Lingering National Question'. In S. Adejumobi (ed.), *Governance and Politics in Post-Military Nigeria: Changes and Challenges*. New York: Palgrave Macmillan.

Adebanwi, W. (2005). 'The Carpenter's Revolt: Youth, Violence and the Reinvention of Culture in Nigeria', *Journal of Modern African Studies*, 43(3): 339–65.

—. (2012). *Authority Stealing: Anti-Corruption War and Democratic Politics in*

Post-Military Nigeria. Durham, NC: Carolina Academic Press.

Adebanwi, W. and E. Obadare (2011). 'When Corruption Fights Back: Democracy and Elite Interest in Nigeria's Anti-Corruption War', *Journal of Modern African Studies*, 49(2): 185–213.

—. (2011). 'Introducing Nigeria at 50: The Nation in Narration'. In E. Obadare and W. Adebanwi (eds), *Nigeria at 50: The Nation in Narration*. London: Routledge.

—. (eds) (2013). *Democracy and Prebendal Politics in Nigeria: Critical Interpretations*. New York: Palgrave Macmillan.

Adejumobi, S. (ed.) (2010). *Governance and Politics in Post-Military Nigeria: Changes and Challenges*. New York: Palgrave Macmillan.

Agbaje, A. (1997). 'Party System and Civil Society'. In P. Beckett and C. Young (eds), *Dilemmas of Democracy in Nigeria*. Rochester, NY: Rochester University Press.

—. (2002). 'Personal Rule and Regional Politics: Ibadan under Military Regimes, 1986–1996'. In J.I. Guyer, L. Denzer and A. Agbaje (eds), *Money Struggles and City Life: Devaluation in Ibadan and Other Urban Centres in Southern Nigeria*. Portsmouth, NJ: Heinemann.

—. (2004). 'Nigeria: Prospects for the Fourth Republic'. In E. Gyimah-Boadi (ed.), *Democratic Reform in Africa: The Quality of Progress*. Boulder, CO and London: Lynne Rienner.

—. (2010). 'Whose Catalyst? Party Politics and Democracy in the Fourth Republic: From Theory to Denial'. In Said Adejumobi (ed.), *Governance and Politics in Post-Military Nigeria: Changes and Challenges*. New York: Palgrave Macmillan.

Agbaje, A. and S. Adejumobi (2006). 'Do Votes Count? The Travails of Electoral Politics in Nigeria', *Africa Development*, 31(3): 25–43.

Agbiboa, D. (2010). 'The Corruption-Underdevelopment Nexus in Africa: Which Way Nigeria?' *Journal of Social, Political and Economic Studies*, 35(4): 474–509.

Albert, I. (2007). 'NURTW and the Politics of Motor Parks in Lagos and Ibadan'. In L. Fouchard (ed.), *Gouverner Les villes d'Afrique: État, Gouvernement Local et actuers privés*. Paris: Karthala.

Animasawun, A. (2009). '"Godfatherism" and Nigeria's Fourth Republic: Violence and Political Insecurity in Ibadan'. In C. Boutillier (ed.), *IFRA Conference on Conflict and Violence in Nigeria*. Zaria: IFRA.

Anugwom, E. (2011). 'From Babangida to Obasanjo: The State, Rent-Seeking Behaviour and the Realities of Privatization in Nigeria', *International Journal of Sociology and Anthropology*, 3(7): 204–16.

Apter, D. (2005). *The Pan-African Nation: Oil and the Spectacle of Culture in Nigeria*. Chicago, IL: University of Chicago Press.

Barnes, S. (1986). *Patrons and Power: Creating a Political Community in Metropolitan Lagos*. Bloomington, IN: Indiana University Press.

Berry, S. (1985). *Fathers Work for Their Sons: Accumulation, Mobility, and Class Formation in an Extended Yoruba Community*. Berkeley, CA: University of California Press.

Bratton, M. and N. van de Walle (1994). 'Neopatrimonial Regimes and Political Transitions in Africa', *World Politics*, 46(4): 453–89.
—. (1997). *Democratic Experiments in Africa: Regime Transitions in Comparative Perspective*. New York: Cambridge University Press.
CDD – Centre for Democracy and Development (2003). *CDD Summary Report on Nigeria's 2003 Elections*. Lagos: Centre for Democracy and Development.
Diamond, L. (1988). *Class, Ethnicity and Democracy in Nigeria: The Failure of the First Republic*. Syracuse, NY: Syracuse University Press.
—. (2013). 'Foreword'. In W. Adebanwi and E. Obadare (eds), *Democracy and Prebendalism in Nigeria: Critical Interpretations*. New York: Palgrave Macmillan.
Diamond, L. A. Kirk-Greene and O. Oyediran (eds) (1997). *Transition Without End: Nigerian Politics and Civil Society under Babangida*. Ibadan: Vantage Press.
Ezeala-Harrison, F. (1993). 'Structural Re-Adjustment in Nigeria: Diagnosis of a Severe Dutch Disease Syndrome', *American Journal of Economics and Sociology*, 52(2): 193–208.
Fagbadebo, O. (2007). 'Corruption, Governance and Political Instability in Nigeria', *African Journal of Political Science and International Relations*, 1(2): 28–37.
Futse, J. (2009). 'The Meaning Structure of Social Networks', *Sociological Theory*, 27(1): 51–73.
Guyer, J.I. (1992). 'Representation Without Taxation: An Essay in Democracy in Rural Nigeria', *African Studies Review*, 35(1): 41–79.
—. (1997). 'Local Chiefs and Office Holders in a Rural Area: An Interpretation Based on Ibarapa, Oyo State'. L. Diamond, A. Kirk-Greene and O. Oyediran (eds), *Transition Without End: Nigerian Politics and Civil Society Under Babangida*. Ibadan: Vantage Press.
—. (2002). 'Preface'. In J. Guyer, L. Denzer and A. Agbaje (eds), *Money Struggles and City Life: Devaluation in Ibadan and Other Urban Centres in Southern Nigeria*. Portsmouth, NJ: Heinemann.
Guyer, J.I. and L. Denzer (2013). 'Prebendalism and the People: The Price of Petrol at the Pump'. In Wale Adebanwi and Ebenezer Obadare (eds), *Democracy and Prebendalism in Nigeria: Critical Interpretations*. New York: Palgrave Macmillan.
Guyer, J.I., L. Denzer and A. Agbaje (eds) (2002). *Money Struggles and City Life: Devaluation in Ibadan and Other Urban Centres in Southern Nigeria*. Portsmouth, NJ: Heinemann.
—. (2002). 'Introduction'. In J. Guyer, L. Denzer and A. Agbaje (eds), *Money Struggles and City Life: Devaluation in Ibadan and Other Urban Centres in Southern Nigeria*. Portsmouth, NJ: Heinemann.
Hoffman, L. (2010). 'Fairy Godfathers and Magical Elections: Understanding the 2003 Electoral Crisis in Anambra State, Nigeria', *Journal of Modern African Studies*, 48(2): 285–310.
Hoffman, L. and I. Nolte (2013). 'The Roots of Neopatrimonialism: Opposition Politics and Popular Consent in Southwest Nigeria'. In W. Adebanwi and

E. Obadare (eds), *Democracy and Prebendalism in Nigeria: Critical Interpretations*. New York: Palgrave Macmillan.

Ikelegbe, A. (2006). 'The Economy of Conflict in the Oil Rich Niger Delta Region of Nigeria', *African and Asian Studies*, 5(1): 23–56.

Joseph, R. (1987). *Democracy and Prebendal Politics in Nigeria: The Rise and Fall of the Second Republic*. Cambridge, UK: Cambridge University Press.

—(2013). 'Epilogue: The Logic and Legacy of Prebendalism in Nigeria'. In W. Adebanwi and E. Obadare (eds), *Democracy and Prebendalism in Nigeria: Critical Interpretations*. New York: Palgrave Macmillan.

Kimse, S. (2012). 'Review of *Weapons of the Wealthy: Predatory Regimes and Elite-led Protests in Central Asia*', *Europe-Asia Studies*, 64(2): 375–7.

Kingston, P. (2001). 'Patrons, Clients and Civil Society: A Case Study of Environmental Politics in Postwar Lebanon', *Arab Studies Quarterly*, 23(1): 55–72.

Kristiansen, S. and M. Ramli (2006). 'Buying an Income: The Market for Civil Service Positions in Indonesia', *Contemporary Southeast Asia*, 28(2): 207–33.

Kura, S. (2014). '"Clientele Democracy": Political Party Funding and Candidate Selection in Nigeria', *African Journal of Political Science and International Relations*, 8(5): 124–37.

Lewis, P. (1996). 'From Prebendalism to Predation: The Political Economy of Decline in Nigeria', *Journal of Modern African Studies*, 34(1): 79–103.

Lucas, J. (1998). 'The Tension Between Despotic and Infrastructural Power: The Military and the Political Class in Nigeria, 1985–1993', *Studies in Comparative International Development*, 33(3): 90–113.

McCauley, J. 2013. 'Africa's New Big Man Rule? Pentecostalism and Patronage in Ghana', *African Affairs*, 112(446): 1–21.

Nolte, I. (2007). 'Ethnic Vigilantes and the State: The Oodua People's Congress in Southwestern Nigeria', *International Relations*, 21(2): 217–35.

Obadare, E. (2007). 'Lamidi Adedibu ou L'état Nigérian entre contradiction et sans-traitance', *Politique Africaine*, 106: 110–27.

Obadare, E. and W. Adebanwi (2013). 'Introduction – Democracy and Prebendalism: Emphases, Provocations, and Elongations'. In W. Adebanwi and E. Obadare (eds), *Democracy and Prebendal Politics in Nigeria: Critical Interpretations*. New York: Palgrave Macmillan.

Okonta, I. and O. Douglas (2001). *Where Vultures Feast: Shell, Human Rights, and Oil in the Niger Delta*. London and New York: Verso.

Omobowale, A. (2008). 'Clientelism and Social Structure: An Analysis of Patronage in Yoruba Social Thought', *Afrika Spectrum*, 43(2): 203–24.

Omobowale, A. and A. Olutayo (2007). 'Chief Lamidi Adedibu and Patron Politics in Nigeria', *Journal of Modern African Studies*, 45(3): 425–46.

—. (2010). 'Political Clientelism and Rural Development in South-Western Nigeria', *Africa*, 80(3): 453–72.

Pierce, S. (2006). 'Looking Like a State: Colonialism and the Discourse on Corruption in Northern Nigeria', *Comparative Studies in Society and History*, 48(4): 887–914.

Pratten, D. (2013). 'The Precariousness of Prebendalism'. In W. Adebanwi and E. Obadare (eds), *Democracy and Prebendalism in Nigeria: Critical Interpretations*. New York: Palgrave Macmillan.

Sklar, R. (1983[1963]). *Nigerian Political Parties*. Princeton, NJ: Princeton University Press.

Suberu, R. (2013). 'Prebendal Politics and Federal Governance in Nigeria'. In W. Adebanwi and E. Obadare (eds), *Democracy and Prebendalism in Nigeria: Critical Interpretations*. New York: Palgrave Macmillan.

Tade, O. (2011). 'Dynastic Struggle and the People's Democratic Party in the Post-Adedibu Era in Oyo State, Nigeria', *Ibadan Journal of the Social Sciences*, 9(2): 108–23.

Umar, M. (2013). 'Hausa Traditional Political Culture, Islam and Democracy: Historical Perspectives on Three Political Traditions'. In W. Adebanwi and E. Obadare (eds), *Democracy and Prebendalism in Nigeria: Critical Interpretations*. New York: Palgrave Macmillan.

Vaughan, O. (2013). 'Ethno-Regionalism and the Origins of Federalism in Nigeria'. In W. Adebanwi and E. Obadare (eds), *Democracy and Prebendalism in Nigeria: Critical Interpretations*. New York: Palgrave Macmillan.

Watts, M.J. (2004a). 'Oil as Money: The Devil's Excrement and the Spectacle of Black Gold'. In T. Barnes, J. Peck, E. Sheppard and A. Tickell (eds), *Reading Economic Geography*. Malden, MA: Blackwell.

—. (2004b). 'Resource Curse? Governmentality, Oil and Power in the Niger Delta, Nigeria', *Geopolitics*, 9(1): 50–80.

Yusuf, M., C. Malarvizhi, M. Mazumder and Z. Su (2014). 'Corruption, Poverty, and Economic Growth Relationship in the Nigerian Economy', *The Journal of Developing Areas*, 48(3): 95–107.

AFTERWORD

The Landscapes Beyond the Margins
Agency, Optimization & the Power of the Empirical

Jane I. Guyer

This collection exemplifies the kinds of engagements across disciplines, subjects of study, and areas of the world that are so important to initiate and sustain, once we have recognized the fruitfulness of all the connections that provoke commitment to the intellectual tasks of the twenty-first century, appreciation of originality, and a stamina in our scholarship that can do justice to the commitment, originality and stamina of our colleagues and the world we study. The authors all represent disciplines with which I have tried to work – history, geography, economics, political studies, philosophy and broad subfields within anthropology – in ways that can open up new vistas.

When all the chapters are taken together, the impetus of the collection goes forward into futures: both intellectual and regional. Every chapter opens a new pathway or draws new attention to one already on the map, even though it may have become neglected for a while and needs re-clearing and re-directing. That the authors can find, in my own past work, the clues to some of these pathways, and the encouragement to keep hacking away at the older ones and opening up new ones, is also a source of new cues for me, as to where to go next. The image reminds me of other, previous, experimental maps for thought that derive from Africa: *Paths in the Rainforest*, by Jan Vansina (1990), *Paths Towards a Clearing*, by Michael Jackson (1989), *The African Frontier*, edited by Igor Kopytoff (1987), and the journeys of the epic *Moneblum*, transcribed by Samuel Eno Belinga (1978), on which I drew for the idea of 'wealth-in-people as wealth-in-knowledge' and 'traditions of invention', both of them cited in these chapters. The journey, as exploration and inspiration rather than conquest, is a common orientation in African studies. Its literal nature is expressed in the African arts, as in Amos Tutuola's (1987) book *Pauper, Brawler, Slanderer*, which I used to explore a philosophy of life that incorporates recurrent 'confusion' (Guyer 2015), in a paper cited here by Michael Watts. The journey as a literal trajectory is similar to the intellectual orientation highlighted here by Fred Cooper, that concepts 'launch an enquiry, not ... close off analysis by slotting something definitively into a category'. I used the image of *compagnons de voyage*, travel companions, in ethnographic research in my review of three new books on urban research in Africa (Guyer 2011). For the inclusion of the 'endogenous knowledge' of

Africa in intellectual life, Paulin Hountondji (1994) lays out *'Pistes Pour Une Recherche'*, paths for research. Michael Watts picks up on the journey imagery here for a further purpose, when he infers from my work that we 'keep going', as far as we can, trying to get our own attentiveness and creativity to live up to the creativity of the worlds we pass through and study.

After a short narrative entitled 'Recognition', as on a new journey, I draw out some specific points on which both the editor and the authors indicate that we could meet and 'keep going.' In the second section, I pick out two conceptual themes identified by the editor, Wale Adebanwi, as being present in all the chapters – margins and agency – and add another which is richly manifest here, the power of the empirical, which can invoke Michael's Jackson's 'pathways' again, in his subtitle concept of 'radical empiricism'. In the final section I comment on the groupings of chapters, each of which falls under the common heading for the group but addresses that issue from a different angle, so that the points of convergence and difference provide new insights.

Recognition

Most of the contributors to this volume have already informed and enriched my own work, some of them for several decades. It is to them, and many other named and unnamed people, that I owe the interdisciplinarity and varied intellectual inspirations that they pick up and highlight in my work. These include: my undergraduate colleagues at the London School of Economics in the early 1960s, who came from the former colonial world in the immediate postcolonial era; the people of the African communities where I have worked and lived, across almost 50 years; and the members of the wider networks and groups to which I have belonged since 1977 when I returned to the United States from three years in Cameroon. Many of these people already inhabit my work explicitly, as was indicated in the Preface to *Marginal Gains* (2004). However, even before I was able to work in the active collaborations in Africa to which Adigun Agbaje draws attention, and before this present generation of colleagues, I had learned from a senior generation in Africa. As a young researcher, I met Abbé Théodore Tsala and read Jean-Marc Ela's work in Cameroon, was encouraged by Akin Mabogunje and Bolanle Awe in Nigeria and, a little later, had conversations with Claude Ake, whose *Social Science as Imperialism* (1982) was deeply influential at that time. Indeed, Ake asked me to publish a longer version of my paper of 1992 on Representation Without Taxation as Occasional Monograph No. 3. (1994) in the newly-established Monograph Series of his Centre for Advanced Social Science in Port Harcourt. The idea of wealth-in-people as wealth-in-knowledge, commented on in several of these papers, would never have come to me without my conversations with Samuel Eno Belinga in Yaoundé, and the availability of his own work on Beti epic performances. Many other inspirations and encouragements could be added, some of them as small as a side comment or explanation of a word, by a Nigerian elder, diviner, woman trader, or even a child. It was a song by the

The Landscapes Beyond the Margins

Lumba Brothers – *Sika Asem*, in Twi: *It's a Matter of Money* – that was popular at the time of our conference in Ghana in 1992, that offered the title of our collection on monetary instability in African History, *Money Matters* (1995a). It is quoted directly and acknowledged in the Preface (translation by Takyiwaa Manuh): 'It is money that makes the elder become a child ... It is because of money that I am always travelling ... Because of money all my bright ideas are left unrealized ... It is a matter of money' (1995a: xiii).

Without these past insights, conversations and collaborations I could not have cultivated some of the qualities that the present chapters recognize and develop in new directions. To play further on the imagery of 'cultivation' in a way that resonates with my earliest work on farming and material life, they have repeatedly inhabited the space – like a clearing where we meet and a threshing floor for the harvest – where ideas can be gathered together, turned over, winnowed and redistributed for a new season of work and growth. So their fascinating chapters re-inhabit this gathering-space where we have met before, turning over, sorting and redistributing ideas for another phase of development, bringing together the current intellectual frontiers in our own disciplines and on our own topics, and offering promising new conversations with each other and beyond.

I find particularly compelling that Wale Adebanwi has configured a group of such aspirational scholars, all developing crucial examples and suggestions for 'next steps' in ways that can speak to each other and, together, can place African work more centrally in the complex theoretical world of the twenty-first century. Hence his title, *Beyond the Margins*, and his themes of a 'political economy of life' and 'agency' within contexts of 'social forces', which can draw on intellectual and substantive diversity within the social sciences and humanities, while opening up the potentials for disciplinary mutuality much further, hopefully in a direction towards liberational dynamics (as he puts it). It is this cumulative potential that I pick up first, in the richly provisioned gathering place they have created. Before examining the five groupings of chapters, I bring out the following transverse topics and ideas: (i) the question of margins and marginality in the world, their creation, inhabitation and broader relevance than Africa alone; (ii) agency as a concept and a practice, from African evidence; and (iii) the shared dedication to empirical detail and veracity.

Gathering Transverse Themes Towards a Political Economy of Life

Margins

Adebanwi's centring of 'margins' has proved a provocative focus for the development of conceptual and substantive variety in these papers. It is an old concept, etymologically indicating a border, an edge or a boundary, and noted in *Marginal Gains* to be 'multi-referential and ambiguous' (2004: 25), applicable across the intellectual space between politics and economics. Created by power dynamics, as 'marginality' (in political life), and opening spaces in which gains can be calculated, negotiated and realized (in economics), such margins also have enough plasticity in African experience that 'African populations express little of the discouraged passivity attributed to European peasantries in the past' (2004: 26). I had chosen this as my title precisely because of the opening it offered into a variety of registers, in different disciplines.

The chapters in this volume go much further in developing the concept of the 'margin'. Several of them bring the political dynamics at the macro level into higher profile and richer depiction than I did when I used the term to depict the many small points at which monetary transactions bring together scales of value in which gains are fabricated by the immediate participants. In the Introduction to *Money Matters* (1995b), I did use the concept of the 'currency interface' between Europe and Africa, over several centuries of trade, to indicate the macro-context, but the sheer magnitude of the empirical challenge on trade monies made it intractable at the time. These chapters, however, take the question of the macro-margins down several empirical pathways in highly creative ways. They bring into sharper profile both the political-economic and the intellectual margins on which African life has been lived, and make strong cases for Africa-based work to bring generally relevant contributions to the disciplines, especially as the conjunctures in a globalizing world proliferate.

The limitations of sparsely elegant general theories are more widely recognized than they were in Ake's generation, when such critique was cast mainly in a resistance and activist mode. Ake argued strongly against the teleologism, organic analogy and the positing of the West as the ideal, of the dominant social theory of the development era (see an abbreviated version in Lauer and Anyidoho's (2012) collection *Reclaiming the Human Sciences and Humanities Through African Perspectives*). By now it is even more striking that African work, of the kind that influenced my own thinking, can take us in yet further directions: directions infused by politically critical views but also by a particular intellectual acuity to the world that may find some cognate orientations in the Western critical tradition and in certain questions that are being increasingly raised elsewhere. Célestin Monga's chapter on macroeconomics is particularly original in drawing these to our attention in a discipline that we usually think of as orthodoxly doctrinaire in its disciplinary life, and as aspiring to a general theory that applies everywhere.

I will address the substantive political-economic themes later, to focus first on 'life' at 'margins' in the intellectual sense, as expressed in works that have suffused the context in which we all think and as exemplified further in these papers. So I turn first to African philosophical approaches to the marginalization of Africa-based thought. Paulin Hountondji (1994) made an argument to 'demarginalize' Africa 20 years ago when he launched the concept of 'endogenous knowledge' (knowledge generated from within, and in the plural as *savoirs endogènes*) to replace 'indigenous knowledge' which implies 'native' in all its senses, and in French, may still carry the aura of the legal regime for colonial rule, the *indigènât*. It also resonates with the concept of emergence that we find increasingly in Western social theory, following in the tradition of phenomenology. Hountondji compared the appropriation of sources for scientific thought to the capitalist appropriation of raw materials, and advocated 'demarginalization' for the whole global South as well as for Africa: 'so that the macro-margin would no longer be the margin, but an integral part of a plural ensemble, a center for decision making like all other centers of decision making, an autonomous center of production amongst others, this today is a major task' (1994: 31). By this effort he was indicating not only a re-appropriation of the subject matter but also of the 'cognitive and practical legacy ... to reinsert the 'traditional' within a living tradition turning towards the future' (1994: 31). The chapters in his collection then address technologies, structures of thought (including mathematics and classification), medicines and, finally, modes of transmission of knowledge.

In his recent book, Achille Mbembe (2013, Epilogue) focuses closely on the processes of restitution and reparation (repair) that would restore a collective, rather than racialized, consciousness, and a universal justice, to the world. It has, again, been Hountondji who chased this question down many specific pathways, when he asks 'Rationality, Singular or Plural?' (*une ou plurielle?*) (2007). From the opposite starting point, Michel Callon (2008) reviewed *Marginal Gains* to point out how relevant the construction of such multiple scales and margins in African history could be to the analysis of Western economies themselves, with their own assemblages, constructions, realizations and shifting margins for advantage. Hence, by virtue of its close attention to the creation of micro-margins in practice, he argues that Africa-based thought can enrich thought in general. Conjunctures and margins move to the centre of attention, beyond the boundaries and coherence of systems, and thereby move African philosophy and its possible bridges, to certain themes in twentieth-century European philosophy, into much higher relevance than it has had in the past.

In his book *African Art as Philosophy: Senghor, Bergson and the Idea of Negritude*, Souleymane Bachir Diagne (2007) looks precisely at the recognitions and reworkings that African philosophers have undertaken, drawing on the monotheistic religions and European philosophy. He examines the long history of African and other thinking about conjunctures and emergence as continual processes in a cosmology not of the 'imperialist expansion of civilization', but rather the 'convergence of all cultures towards a civilization of the universal' (ibid.: 162), one that would be a 'unity whose true nature is to be made of additions and contributions rather than subtractions and evictions' (ibid.: 141). This approach to 'additions and contributions' resonates strongly with my own depiction (1997) of the Western Nigerian popular economy as a 'niche economy' where new goods, tools, activities and modes of organization, as the market economy expands, simply add themselves to a receptive dynamic whose practices are already in place and functioning.

It is remarkable how relevant to the present, and to daily life, these older philosophical arguments and concepts can be. Tracing Senghor's thinking back to themes in Teilhard de Chardin, Bergson, the interface with Iqbal and others, Diagne suggests that 'this post-essentialist 'new world' lacking an obsession with alterity ... opens up a humanism of hybridity' (2007: 189). In his chapter here, he identifies 'in-betweenness' as exemplified in the philosophy of major figures in the philosophy of negritude, such as Aimé Césaire, whom he quotes as writing that 'exchange is oxygen' and that Europe's great 'good fortune' was its history as a cultural 'crossroads' rather than any intrinsic genius. He also goes 'beyond' this particular philosophical margin to profile the everyday practices of mediation by African interpreters and writers under colonial administrations. Thus can practices within Africa, on margins, become accessible and relevant to broader theories of conjuncture, which then re-open the European sources from which these thinkers and practitioners also drew points of intersection that sharpened their own choice of words. Here, Diagne raises the question of ontology that has begun to preoccupy anthropology: 'an ontology of vital forces in an emergent cosmology open to human action for the purpose of overcoming forms of alienation and gaining access to the freedom of *homo artifex*' (2007: 187). *Homo artifex* is perhaps best in English translation as 'man the toolmaker', if by 'tools' we can include concepts as well as things. In this spirit, in his more recent book, *L'encre des savants* (2013), he draws on John Mbiti to examine the contributions that 'African time' can make to time more broadly, thus escaping from the universal 'physics' grids to which Monga draws attention. In African thought, he suggests, time is a composition of 'events' and the past is the most important dimension; in a world where events are expected the future is impossible to conceptualize abstractly, and thereby, resolutions amongst differing visions will be created by practice and reflection rather than by formal compromises (2013: 110).

Empirical works have pointed out comparable potential contributions of Africa to current social science. James Ferguson, in his book *Global Shadows* (2006), deplored the relative negligence of Africa in the 1990s scholarship about the new era of globalization. I made a similar point in the Preface to our edited collection (with Adigun Agbaje and LaRay Denzer) *Money Struggles and City Life* (published in 2002 in the United States and 2003 in Nigeria), whose papers explored devaluation and general turbulence, which my co-editors and the authors described in ways that could be linked to a much broader history and a wider geography in the world. In the realm of technology, Clapperton Mavhunga has argued for the importance of African knowledge and skills in *Transient Workspaces. Everyday Innovation in Zimbabwe* (2015). Complex ecological interactions were deeply intuited and acted upon by 'the professoriate of the hunt', in ways that are highly relevant to new understandings of human–environment interaction. Again, the embeddedness of inventiveness comes into sharp focus.

In a more political register, James Ferguson's (2015) book on 'The New Politics of Distribution', entitled *Give a Man a Fish*, based on his research on cash grants to the poor in South Africa, is a crucial empirical source on an increasingly widely proposed 'solution' to the yawning income disparities and precarities of life in the twenty-first century. He introduces new questions such as: what is a 'rightful share ... beyond gift and market?' and provokes us to think of new concepts rather than simply recycle old ones. Interestingly, at the end he picks up the same quotation on the bewildering dilemma into which 'property' has placed contemporary society from Lewis Henry Morgan, writing in 1877, that I cite at the end of *Marginal Gains*. Both of these books originated as the Lewis Henry Morgan Lectures at the University of Rochester, so both reach back to the clues towards new pathways that old and unresolved comments may open up, and to the kind of heterogeneous archive of knowledge on which the chapters also draw, within and beyond Africa. Ferguson suggests, from his own African work, that we need new terms and new conceptualizations that go beyond a 'citizenship on the global level' (2015: 215) that mirrors nation-state ideals and theories. His terms resonate precisely with Diagne's reflection on Senghor's rejection of global uniformity, but in a profoundly important practical and political register for the 'political economy of everyday life' in the present, rather than in the immediate postcolonial, world. We keep going.

All these philosophical and empirical works make strong arguments for the creativity that could be released if Africa were not intellectually marginalized, but rather engaged with, as at a crossroads beyond the margins of bounded intellectual geographies that mark off their own terrain. Seeing the crossroads in higher resolution than the bounded units is part of the Yoruba theory of Esu, the trickster god, the maker of confusion but also of new possibility (see Falola 2013). It is to this idea (Guyer 2015; Salami and Guyer 2015) that Michael Watts refers in his chapter on the very large questions in the world of 'violence and poverty; the temporalities of immediate precarity and deep or structural time, and the doctrines of the religious and the secular in relation to the contradictions and failures of modern secular national development'. These can be clearings in the intellectual landscape, threshing floors for ideas as we try to gather all the germinal possibilities from the harvest.

Oestermann and Geschiere make a similar point about the more general importance of detailed examination of times of crisis, economic shifts and chaotic dynamics, and their domestication through the new medium of Western money, which creates a social life full of tensions, and yet still lived with many of its old practices. That sense of the extreme intellectual limitations of Western approaches that attempt to control the variables under focus, and keep other, less tractable, variables out of the analysis, is clearly noted in most of the political economy chapters here. If many of the parameters of life are set by large structural conditions, neither very closely regulated by others nor controllable by the actors, then their imaginative mediations within the margins and convergences become theoretically central to theories of action and emergence. The centrality of recurrent 'crises' in several chapters speaks strongly to the relevance of the empirical research on the history of African margins to the study of the variety of margins that appear in the world and the challenges they pose to general theory.

This is the point made by Gbemisola Animasawun when he describes the lives of motorcycle taxi riders in Lagos, and develops existing theory of 'systemic marginality', lived within 'collateral or temporal marginality', to exemplify situations not unlike that of the rubber boom in southern Cameroon, and to suggest that within a context of unstable prospects for sustainable livelihoods, which are largely due to policy interventions, these 'marginal men' nevertheless make 'positive contributions to society as a whole'. The ethnographic and experiential feedback about living on margins, into the question of the marginality of the theory that comes from those places, is particularly graphic here in the political-economic and historical-anthropological chapters. Both Fred Cooper and Célestin Monga point out that it is precisely the clumsy inapplicability of Western theory to the actual, present economic 'crossroads' that Africa has become, over long periods of time, that makes it a highly stimulating focus for theoretical development in the current world. Cooper writes: 'In the long run, there has been a vast change in how Africans came to participate in the dynamics of capital accumulation outside the continent', in a process that involved labour regimes in highly varied and shifting ways, from slavery to precarious employment in urban informal sectors and migration, none of which is well captured by existing neatly defined theories. Rather, African history 'revealed the limits of explanatory schemes that presumed that one knew what one meant by the category of "labour"'. This is a serious theoretical shortcoming for the analysis of life in a globalizing context. In a highly original way for Economics itself, Célestin Monga's chapter imports the African experiences and concepts with respect to managing the heterogeneity of relevant value scales to make a more broadly relevant case. He points to the possibility of 'optimization' *across* variables rather than 'maximization' of a *singular prioritized* variable, into current micro and macroeconomics. Households and firms have to consider all the interwoven short- and long-term trajectories, and judge the present forces and options in terms of their realizability. In the philosophy of time that Diagne presents, looking closely to the past, it is highly likely that narratives of experience will play a strong role here.

Other chapters pick up the margins *within* formalities in ways that go beyond my own formulation in the final chapter of *Marginal Gains*, also by keeping the intersection with history and narrative at the forefront of attention. Maxim Bolt examines how Zimbabwean workers 'build personal histories through documentation', using 'a multiplicity of regulatory lenses' that emanate from 'the fragmentary mosaic of multiple formalities'. That the formal sector is much less formally coherent than its designation as such would imply becomes a frontier to keep addressing in its own terms, and a series of margins at which people's own narrative histories create some sort of sense for both practical and meaningful purposes.

In an early contribution to our discussions, Anne-Maria Makhulu drew our attention to the micro-narratives of personhood and aspiration that people at the 'bottom of the socio-economic pyramid' in South Africa create for themselves out of their interface with formal credit institutions. These are interfaces to be compared with the kinds of margins on which the papers have focused. Indeed, she drew attention to particularities in those margins, and the improbability of the outcomes when examined through the lens of any limited rational theoretical or cultural-logical model. It was interesting that she developed the concept of 'deliberate incrementalism' to identify the cumulative process here, rather than assuming either instantaneous, situated, 'decision making' or the kind of teleology towards a foreseeable future against which Ake argued, through not letting go of the continuing relevance of the past. The people's own terms can come to the fore, to keep the pathway to analysis from being closed off into a purported globally applicable category. The future as coherent plan, as distinct from being built from an archive of different legacies applied to current exigencies, is a theme I develop in my collected essays entitled *Legacies, Logics, Logistics* (Guyer 2016). Prediction can be utopian projection, with very little plausible grounding in past experience or practical logistics towards realization. Planning, in and of itself, comes into question here, and could attract even more of the ethnographic scrutiny that our contributors offer.

In the cultural world of expert knowledge composition, there are margins and conjunctures between an ancient smallpox deity and a barely dependable Western medical theory and practice described in Elisha Renne's chapter. The overall formation of margins, and the practices of those who mediate them, are presented as becoming familiar to people, and expressible in the language of illness and the dangers of death. We can begin to see clearly how understanding the mediation of margins in the African world draws both the marginalized theory back into empirical study, and the conceptual language of the marginalized people back into possible analytical enrichment. Pratten works on this as a question of discourse and ritual enactment in eastern Nigerian history. In the Comaroffs' chapter we have a particularly strong link shown between margins in theory, in the world, and as lived with one's own categories of existence. Their detailed exploration of the sheer improbability, and even unacceptability, to the Tswana, of conceptualizing 'commensuration' in the generalized transverse sense that was developed under a monetized modernism, led by religious institutions and infused with particular religious ideas, shows clearly how parochial general theory can be. This can be a segue into the second transverse analytical issue raised by Adebanwi, the questions of agency.

Agency

The Tswana verb for action, *go dira*, is a perfect entry point into the mutual implication of margins and agency, since it cannot be abstracted as labour or autonomy. Rather it 'was an intrinsic dimension of the everyday act of making selves and social ties'. Interestingly, I would argue, our own etymological past would be quite similar. In its Latin etymology, our English concept of 'agency' and the French concept of *'agencement'* (which is translated into English as the widely used Deleuzian concept of 'assemblage'), derive from a verb that indicates almost exactly what the Tswana focus on – 'do, make or drive' – hence requiring both a subject and an object while leaving open the nature of their interaction and any eventual mutual interpenetration. Agency here is not an abstract quality intrinsically embedded in a person, such as power or autonomy as is presumed in individualist theory, even in situations where it is restricted in its arenas of application in the kinds of political economy that create the marginality of some populations. Rather, for the Tswana and as implicated in much of African philosophical work on personhood and ontology, agency is a capacity to mediate a world that is continually being constituted and inhabited in emergent ways, as is, also, the person or subject itself. This is a key attribute of what I called 'traditions of invention' (Guyer 1996), inverting Hobsbawm and Ranger's 'invention of tradition' (1983). It is a quality emphasized in a particularly forceful way by Sara Berry in her chapter, namely the *management* of expertise, particularly historical knowledge, performed in negotiations, which surpasses the process of its composition and embodiment. She, too, makes a broadly applicable theoretical claim based on her Africa-based observations of the uses of history in negotiation.

The question of how to conceptualize agency has arisen forcefully in anthropology in recent years, as the influence of science and technology studies has opened it up, beyond a fundamentally traditional humanist-universalist assumption, to what is termed the ontological turn. '(O)ntological anthropology distances itself from cognitive and interpretative approaches because it shifts the focus from interaction and speech to the objects themselves.' (Sivado 2015: 75). This perspective expands from the proposition that agency refers to people's 'power to originate acts' (see Rapport and Overing 2000), and Kockelman's (2007) argument from linguistic anthropology, that it refers to the flexible capacity to represent the world and the element of accountability for that representation, to the deep question of the place of objects themselves, for example, ritual objects as 'mnemonic devices' that inhabit the mind (Sivado 2015: 93).

The ongoing permeability of interactive agents and objects has become a large challenge for both individualist philosophies and collectivist social theories, but from African philosophy we have earlier examinations of the question of agency, especially since the power of words and objects is so widely evident in oral and artistic cultures. In his book mentioned earlier, on *African Art as Philosophy*, Diagne quotes Senghor from 1975 on the question of ontology: 'Everyone must be mixed in their own way' (2013: 186). Doubtless my own work on 'self-realization' – published in 1993, and in a recent paper on 'enhancement' in Equatorial African aesthetics of life (Guyer 2012), the first of which is quoted in several of the chapters here – was already imbued with these sensibilities, without, however, fully developing the philosophical and theoretical implications for 'the ontological turn'. Where agency itself is most invoked in my own earlier work it is with respect to what Adebanwi refers to as a 'political economy of everyday life' where people aspire to creative interventions that have to do with maintaining and extending liberation of action and workable livelihoods, even in the most mundane of manners and situations, such as making a living in a 'niche economy' (Guyer 1997). People 'act' by drawing on archives of multi-varied experience, their own and the inherited tradition, which provides the resources for the kind of 'innovation' to which Mavhunga (2014) refers. The person as a category is neither

The Landscapes Beyond the Margins

an individual nor an atom in a collectivity, but the product and producer of ongoing permeability on the margins of knowledge.

Africa-based work, however, has never lost the sense of agency as political intervention in the public sphere, as well as depending on an ontology with spiritual and object components. I reviewed Achille Mbembe's first major conceptual work, *Afriques Indociles* (1988), in 1989, where he linked Christian religion, power and the state, and placed to the fore the compelling idea that there is a passionate search for spaces of popular creativity, through indocility. This idea of the creation of space itself as a product of agency was liberational to our thinking, as have been my conversations with Mbembe over the 25 years since then. Without explicitly developing a theory of agency, I and LaRay Denzer depicted the more-politically explicit aspects of agency in the public sphere over 20 years later in our chapter on the petrol price in Nigeria (Guyer and Denzer 2013). The escape-critique-resistant aspects of agency are taken further in Obadare and Willems' (2014) recent collection on *Civic Agency in Africa: Arts of Resistance in the 21st Century*, which Chabal introduces as developing a 'more considered notion of agency [as] the myriad ways ordinary people cope with and undermine the politics of hegemony ... in the informal' through 'a ground up approach' (Chabal 2014: xv).

On the complex question of agency in today's world, the chapters in this volume, taken together, develop all these initiatives further, and open up new avenues for engagement with social theory and with the concept of agency itself, which implies that several of the conceptual problems have already been faced in African work. Most of the authors are explicitly working in conditions they depict as turmoil, chaos, violence, instability, or simply mundane emergent unpredictability and/or failure of any coherent system to actually work in the way it purports to do, even for routine activities, as we see in Bolt's and Renne's chapters. I could list each author's reference to these conditions, for their own case, but will simply allude to it and leave to the reader the observation that, to the degree that rapid change is more widespread in the present world, working on this context for developing an approach to agency, is surely generally relevant. Oestermann and Geschiere develop the concept of 'multiple self-realization' to explore the intimate dynamics of people's response to the chaotic conditions of the rubber boom in Cameroon. Indeed, the varied crises and indocilities of life in Africa have provided a vast range of instances where 'there is no other way' than for people to exert agency of some kind, as Agbaje suggests, extending my own use (Guyer 2002) of a phrase that farmers used to express their concern with how to cope with rapid devaluation of their currency under the 'planning' that was termed 'structural adjustment' and the consequent expense of maintaining their tractors.

Others' chapters move into the more-clearly collective and resistant register. For example Jean and John Comaroff show how struggles to retain one's own terms of valuation and conversion, in the face of invasive colonial hegemonic attempts at 'commensuration', is a crucial mode of cultural and political agency: 'such processes of commensuration and conversion, and above all their enabling currencies, have often been the focus of concern, indeed of struggle, among people caught up on all sides of colonial encounters'. The crucial development here is to identify the particular emergent substantive foci for such agency, which is neither so mundane as to revert to 'coping', nor so insurgent as to be 'resistance', but nevertheless, by sheer intransigent recurrence, will have wide implications both for value systems and for the component ontologies. This is surely relevant beyond Africa, since, as they argue: 'Conversion, after all, was not merely a matter of religious reform. It was the key mechanism of imperialism at large.'

David Pratten's chapter greatly enriches the range of social categories that domination, indocility and turbulent monetary conditions can throw into political arenas, and leads us further into a consideration of *all* the participants, in their local specificity. The case of the leopard murders and the 'women's war' in Eastern Nigeria is so dramatic, and relatively well-documented, that he can do this analysis of the male-female axis of the money economy, the occupational differences, the historical colonial and market conditions, and emergent self-presentation by several groups. The richness of the sources and his own empirical commitment to delving into complex configurations, allows him to insert a new topic, namely debt in relation to violent events. Now that Ifi Amadiume's (1987) work on gender in Africa has been republished (2015), we could possibly extend her insights further in the direction of ontology and agency in the sudden cracks and margins that social earthquakes produce. By bringing in the element of debt as Pratten does, in his interpretation of the murders, and perhaps extending the earthquake imagery to the kind of ongoing social fracking that new credit is producing, we can now make the connection between past pressures and the self-creations of the South African poor as described by Makhulu, showing how they mobilize old terms such as 'I'khothane', derived from the Zulu word *ukukhothana*, meaning to 'lick like a snake', a 'playful or performative competition', for new conditions and actions such as 'ritually destructive acts burning money and expensive commodities'. All this is profoundly relevant to an enriched approach to agency.

In the more directly political and contemporary mode of agency as resistance, Watts takes on the consonances amongst the violent popular movements in the Nigerian national context, and Animasawun shows in empirical detail how the motorcycle taxi riders of Lagos engage with the local state. Agbaje identifies ways in which the actions of the ruling elite create precisely the contradictory cracks into which Adebanwi and Obadare (2013) see that populist efforts can insert a new agency, what Animasawun refers to as 'empowering the poor as active agents'.

It is remarkable how these chapters delve so deeply into the details of particular macro-political movements, picking up the terms and patterns of action that take agency to a whole new level of rich cultural depth and history, in the mode of insurgence, particularly at 'margins' as they open up. As Watts points out, there is a 'co-presence of the contemporary and past social orders'. Although these increasingly political chapters on agency do invoke my own work, they take agency in new directions, further towards what Makhulu refers to as 'the creation of new moral worlds'. If my own work has offered something to this effort, it gives me both gratification and an impetus to work in new domains and to encourage theoretical connections on the subject of agency to be woven between all the chapters in the volume: from ontology and philosophies of agency to resistance and insurgence, and outwards to the sources on which they draw and the situations that provoke what is both theoretically and vernacularly referred to, somewhat opaquely and vaguely, simply as 'action'. There are futures at stake here, and exactly how they are envisaged, in life and in theory, remains on the map towards which these chapters offer directions.

Empirical Evidence about 'Life', Imbued with Agency & Outcomes
The empirical richness of these chapters also goes further than, and in new directions from, the work of my own that the authors invoke. It would be impossible for African work to have general relevance in an intellectual world that Fred Cooper depicts as having 'the capacity ... to write off much of a continent' without inserting compelling empirical material into the broader debates. My own commitment to a version of empiricism has been a mode of learning as much (or more) from the world as from the library. I hope to be surprised into totally new thoughts, as I expressed in a recent lecture and paper (Guyer 2013). This is a quality in my work that Nigel Dodd recently depicted as 'resisting straightforward summary and analysis' (2014: 303). It is particularly interesting to find that this combination of grounded evidence and open thought has been remarked by scholars whose own intellectual temperaments work the data in ways that extend further. Fred Cooper notes my own thinking '*with* categories' rather than '*within* them'. As Michael Watts observes, to address certain situations we need to think *within* a sense of turbulence and indeterminacy, as he concludes: 'How these nonsynchronous contradictions with capitalist modernity express themselves may produce radically different forms of generative politics.' An earlier draft of his contribution observed of my own work that 'she poses questions she readily admits she cannot fully answer, that her arguments often proceed non-linearly, and that trying and failing is one of the transcendent qualities of being born in England shortly before the end of the Second World War (otherwise known as "keep calm, and carry on")'. I have, indeed, continued in that spirit, and find the attentiveness of all these papers to an experiential analytics of disturbance to be opening up that frontier in very creative ways.

These efforts are broadly and variously conceived, although all are empirically attentive. Maxim Bolt attends to the patchworking of the fragments of formal economic life by the workers living across the various borders of political-economic life. Sara Berry 'goes further' into composition, as management practised in many, and multifariously recurrent contexts. Célestin Monga works with mathematical logics that could take certain classic economic analyses and general models in new directions. David Pratten suggests a more careful attention to overlapping political-geographic-historical distributions with respect to particular actions. Elisha Renne, Michael Watts, and Geschiere and Oestermann take up specific event analyses and eras of history, while the next generation of scholars – particularly Makhulu and Animasawun – deal with the popular culture of current life in a way that is generally inclusive of politics, culture and imagination. They all show how rich can be the empirical orientation, in all their several disciplines – anthropology, history, political-historical geography, political science, philosophy and economics – and in ways that can be mutually engaged, not only empirically but also theoretically, as I hope to have shown. Interdisciplinary engagement of the kind that this collection can provoke is essential to a social science that Adebanwi defines as 'liberational' and they exemplify how crucial empirical richness is to that engagement. Otherwise it can turn into a disciplinary battle or mutual incomprehension.

As turmoil and increasingly complex margins proliferate in the world, as large populations have 'no other way' than recourse to their own devices for creating a 'political economy of life', and as ontology, philosophy and economics all search for new traction in what some have found to be an impoverished analytical vocabulary, these chapters can bring Africa more prominently into the debates. The grouping of topics also exemplifies crucially important themes arising elsewhere in the world: I, 'Money Matters: Currency and Fiscal Life Struggles'; II, 'Labour, Social Lives and Precarity'; III, 'Marginality, Disaffection and Bio-Economic Distress'; and IV, 'History, Temporality, Agency and Democratic Life'. As Introduction, we have 'Approaching the Political Economy of Everyday Life', with reference in the text to the *Beyond the Margins* of the volume's subtitle. He has crafted this collection not only as a referent to my own work, but as an invitation to the authors to extend their own rich and detailed work, based in African experience, on themes for which their chapters will continue to be a source 'beyond the margins', and the marginalization, of the continent. Their publications since this collection was crafted will doubtless serve as an inspiration for us to go yet further.

The Mutuality of Experience & Inspiration in the Understanding of Everyday Life

In my greatly appreciative reading of the contributions to this collection, I see them exemplifying, in intellectual terms, some of the characteristics I so admired in the *Niche Economy* (Guyer 1997) of Western Nigeria, which is familiar elsewhere in Africa. Skilled craftsmanship is enacted through its own tools, experience and guild-like organizations, but also through its detailed appreciation of the other skills with which it interacts. In a chapter written more recently, for a geographically wide-ranging collection on economies of 'hope' (Miyazaki and Swedberg 2016), I looked at divination, prayer and other modes of creating companionate connections within West African spiritual and economic life, drawing also on the imagery of poetry (in this case T.S. Eliot's *The Hollow Men*), where it is a shadow that falls between 'the idea and the reality'. In West Africa, I suggest, '[b]etween the idea and the reality fall several possibilities; between the emotion and the response fall a quickening of the intellect, an anticipation of the heart and the expectation of change, rather than the "shadow" of despair or the obligation to the next payment in the financial regimen' (Guyer 2016: 167).

We, too, as scholars, work in this way to bridge the limitations we may see in our own disciplines, with respect to the suddenly emergent complexities of life: whether in the event and its aftermath, or throughout everyday life in the twenty-first century. Amongst our own contributors here, there are scholars whose expertise and life-interests straddle disciplinary and topical boundaries, so that the space 'on the margins' between otherwise formalized 'niches' – intellectual and aesthetic margins of mutual inspiration – is richly florescent and carefully cultivated. They are possibly even more inspirational than the structured and bounded 'fields' of our own disciplines. The chapters in this collection encourage us all to give yet more life to our own 'margins' of thought and experience.

I can conclude with a final graphic example of such aspiration. Célestin Monga, Chief Economist of the African Development Bank at the time of our writing, has contributed the only quantitative, model-building chapter to this collection. Yet he has also recently published an appreciative book on African philosophy and the arts, in deeply empirical and experiential mode, devoted to the tensions of everyday life. It is entitled *Nihilism and Negritude: Ways of Living in Africa* (2016). With the kind of strong personal presence that his own academic discipline hardly ever incorporates as method, Monga is here intimately attentive to pleasures and tortures in political and daily life, particularly in his own country of Cameroon. As he does here, we all connect to the experiential, analytical and inspirational sources 'beyond the margins' of our own disciplines (and, perhaps, also our lives), in ways that can provoke original thinking, creative interaction and shared questions about pathways into the future.

Having learned so much from this kind of process over the years of my career, my own appreciation for these engagements and contributions is profound. I can conclude with a return to the theme of 'hope': that such appreciation for what lies on, and beyond, the conventional margins, will be encouraged by the collection of examples that Adebanwi has drawn together here. Every piece of my own work that is referenced here owes itself to the inspirations of others. May this continue.

References

Ake, C. (1982). *Social Science as Imperialism: A Theory of Political Development*. Ibadan, Nigeria: Ibadan University Press.

Amadiume, I. (2015). *Male Daughters, Female Husbands: Gender and Sex in an African Society*. London: Zed Books.

Callon, M. (2008). 'Il n'y a d'économie qu'aux marges: A propos du livre de Jane Guyer (*Marginal Gains: Monetary Transactions in Atlantic Africa*. Chicago, IL: The University of Chicago Press, 2004)'. *Le Libellio d'Aegis*, 4(2): 1–18.

Chabal, P. (2014). 'Foreword'. In W. Willems and E. Obadare (eds), *Civic Agency in Africa: Arts of Resistance in the 21st Century*. Woodbridge, UK: James Currey.

Diagne, S.B. (2007). *African Art as Philosophy: Senghor, Bergson and the Idea of Negritude*. Calcutta, India: Seagull Books.

—. (2013). *L'encre de savants*. Paris: Présence Africaine.

Dodd, N. (2014). *The Social Life of Money*. Princeton,NJ: Princeton University Press.

Eno Belinga, S.M. (1978). *L'Epopée Camerounaise: Mvet. Moneblum ou L'Homme Bleu*. Yaoundé: author's copyright.

Falola, T. (2013). *Esu: Yoruba God, Power, and the Imaginative Frontiers*. Durham, NC: Carolina Academic Press.

Ferguson, J. (2006). *Global Shadows: Africa in the Neoliberal World Order*. Durham, NC: Duke University Press.

—. (2015). *Give a Man a Fish: Reflections on the New Politics of Distribution*. Durham NC: Duke University Press.

Guyer, J.I. (1989). 'Review of *Afriques indociles: Christianisme, pouvoir et État en société postcoloniale*', *American Ethnologist*, 16: 69.

—. (1993). 'Wealth in People and Self-Realisation in Equatorial Africa', *Man (NS)* 28(2): 243-65.

—. (1994). *Representation Without Taxation: An Essay on Democracy in Rural Nigeria 1952–1990*. Port Harcourt, Lagos: Centre for Advanced Social Science; Lagos: Malthouse Press.

—. (1995a) 'Preface'. In *Money Matters: Instability, Values and Social Payments in the Modern History of West African Communities*. Portsmouth NH: Heinemann; London: James Currey: xi-xiii.

—. (1995b). 'Introduction: The Currency Interface and its Dynamics'. In J.I. Guyer (ed.), *Money Matters: Instability, Values and Social Payments in the Modern History of West African Communities*. Portsmouth NH: Heinemann; London: James Currey: 1–33.

—. (1996). 'Traditions of Invention in Equatorial Africa'. *African Studies Review* 39(3): 1–28.

—. (1997). *An African Niche Economy: Farming to Feed Ibadan*. Edinburgh, UK: University of Edinburgh Press for the International African Institute.

—. (2002). '"Kos'ona miran" (No Other Way): Necessity and Invention in Mechanized Farming' In J.I. Guyer, L. Denzer and A. Agbaje (eds), *Money Struggles and City Life*. Portsmouth, NH: Heinemann: 115–32.

—. (2004). *Marginal Gains: Monetary Transactions in Atlantic Africa*. Chicago IL: University of Chicago Press.

—. (2010). 'Solid Work and Rash Experiments: The Imperative to Comparison in the Agro-Ecology of Africa'. Robert Hunt Lecture, Brandeis University.

—. (2011). 'Describing Urban 'No Man's Land' in Africa'. Review article. *Africa*, 81(3): 474–92.

—. (2012). 'The Burden of Wealth and the Lightness of Life: The Body in Body Decoration in Southern Cameroon'. In C. Panella (ed.), Lives in Motion, Indeed: Interdisciplinary Perspectives on Social Change in Honour of

Danielle de Lame. Tervuren, Belgium: Royal Museum for Central Africa: 351–68.
—. (2013). 'The Quickening of the Unknown: Epistemologies of Surprise in Anthropology', *HAU: Journal of Ethnographic Theory* 3(3): 283–307.
—. (2015). 'Response: One confusion after another: "Slander" in Amos Tutuola's *Pauper, Brawler, Slanderer*', *Social Dynamics* 41(1): 69–72.
—. (2016). 'When and How Does Hope Spring Eternal in Personal and Popular Economics? Thoughts from West Africa to America'. In H. Miyazaki and R. Swedberg (eds), *The Economy of Hope*. Philadelphia, PA: University of Pennsylvania Press.
Guyer, J.I. and L. Denzer (2013). 'Prebendalism and the People: The Price of Petrol at the Pump'. In W. Adebanwi and E. Obadare (eds), *Democracy and Prebendal Politics in Nigeria: Critical Interpretations*. New York: Palgrave Macmillan: 53–77.
Guyer, J.I, L. Denzer and A. Agbaje (eds) (2011). *Money Struggles and City Life*. Portsmouth, NH: Heinemann.
Hobsbawm, E. and T.O. Ranger (1983). *The Invention of Tradition*. Cambridge, UK: Cambridge University Press.
Hountondji, P. (1994). *Les Savoirs Endogènes: Pistes Pour Une Recherche*. Dakar, Senegal: CODESRIA.
—. (2007). *La Rationalité, Une ou Plurielle?* Dakar, Senegal: CODESRIA.
Jackson, M. (1989). *Paths Toward a Clearing: Radical Empiricism and Ethnographic Inquiry*. Bloomington, IN: Indiana University Press.
Kockelman, P. (2007). 'Agency: The Relation between Meaning, Power, and Knowledge', *Current Anthropology* 48(3): 375–401.
Kopytoff, I. (ed.) (1987). *The African Frontier: The Reproduction of Traditional African Societies*. Bloomington, IN: Indiana University Press.
Lauer, H. and K. Anyidoho (2012). Reclaiming the Human Sciences and Humanities Through African Perspectives. Legon, Ghana: Sub-Saharan Publishers.
Marshall, R. (2009). *Political Spiritualities: The Pentecostal Revolution in Nigeria*. Chicago, IL: University of Chicago Press.
Mavhunga, C.C. (2014). *Transient Workspaces: Technologies of Everyday Innovation in Zimbabwe*. Cambridge, MA: MIT Press.
Mbembe, A. (1988). *Afriques Indociles: Christianisme, pouvoir et État en société postcoloniale*. Paris: Karthala.
—. (2013). *Critique de la Raison Nègre*. Paris: La Decouverte.
Monga, C. (2016). *Nihilism and Negritude: Ways of Living in Africa*. Cambridge, MA: Harvard University Press.
Obadare, E. and W. Willems (eds) (2014). *Civic Agency in Africa: Arts of Resistance in the 21st Century*. Woodbridge, UK: James Currey.
Rapport, N. and J. Overing (2000). 'Agent and Agency'. In *Social and Cultural Anthropology: The Key Concepts*. London: Routledge: 1–8.
Salami, K.K. and J.I. Guyer (2015). 'Confusion and Personification in Yoruba Thought and Practice'. *Social Dynamics* 41(1): 1–16.
Sivado, A. (2015). 'The Shape of *Things* to Come? Reflections on the Ontolog-

ical Turn in Anthropology', *Philosophy of the Social Sciences* 45(1): 83–99.
Thompson, E.P. (1971). The Moral Economy of the English Crowd in the Eighteenth Century. *Past and Present* 50: 76–136.
Tutuola, A. (1987). *Pauper, Brawler and Slanderer.* London: Faber.
Vansina, J. (1990). *Paths in the Rainforests: Toward a History of Political Tradition in Equatorial Africa.* Madison, WI: University of Wisconsin Press; London: James Currey.

Index

Abacha, Sani 187, 206, 240, 323
accountability
　corporate 196
　government 188, 194, 199, 328, 344
accumulation 15
　capital/capitalist 92, 109, 138, 140, 342
　indigenous processes of 42, 44, 46, 52, 62, 108
　primitive 147
　of wealth 144, 150, 195, 222, 233
Adeloye, Adelola 266, 268–70, 277–8
African economies
　marginality in global economy 1–2, 4, 6–9, 17–18, 20, 288n3, 348
　volatility/crises in 6, 83, 126, 138, 140, 204, 245, 253, 341
　see also household economy; marginal gains: macroeconomics of; Nigeria's oil-based economy; palm-oil economy; political economy, everyday life perspective; Southern Tswana political economy
African pastoralism 60–61, 63 *see also* cattle
African Pentecostalism 14, 201, 207
African political/economic elites 24, 138, 142–4, 147–50, 182, 299
　Nigerian 182, 189, 191–5, 320–21, 323–5, 327, 330, 346
　South African 221
　Southern Tswana 60, 65
Africanism 4, 6, 25–6, 135–7
Afro-pessimism 1, 12, 188
Agamben, Giogior 18, 20
agency 5–7, 9, 11–12, 23, 44, 48, 247–8, 336–7, 343–7
　and 'composition' of different forms of knowledge 8, 15–16, 22, 92–3, 99, 106, 110, 340, 343
　and entrepreneurship 4, 8–9, 94, 100, 139, 216, 229, 233, 242, 252
　and notion of multiple self-realization 16, 92–3, 99, 102, 105–6, 110, 344–5
　see also political economy, everyday life perspective
Ake, Claude 10, 336
Akerlof, GA 124–5
Algeria 145, 204, 309
Angola 94, 117, 143n11
anthropology 3, 23, 26, 122–3, 135–6, 140, 335, 340
　economic 4, 6–7, 16, 108, 115–16, 118–20, 125, 127–8,
　linguistic 344
　social 128, 166, 288, 299, 308
　urban 137
apartheid 149, 165
　anti-apartheid struggle 230, 232
Asante 292n8, 298–300, 302
Atlantic Africa
　analysis of monetary transactions in 12, 14, 72, 232, 338
　convergence of economies in 11, 15, 72–3
Atlantic slave trade 17–18, 72, 84, 140–43&n11, 179, 295, 299
　anti-slavery/abolitionist movement 38, 143–5
　relations of dependence within 143&n13, 144
authoritarianism, 191–3, 195, 240
　see also militarization; Nigeria's Fourth Republic: rise of authoritarian leviathan in

Bâ, Hampâté Amadou 23, 308, 312, 314–5
Bakhtin, M 296, 300–301
Barchiesi, F 149, 160, 220
Bassett, Tom 292n7, 296–7&n20

Bayart, J-F 109, 180
Bechuanaland 52–3, 59, 61
Beck, RB 45&n3, 47, 49–51, 55n13, 57
Belinga, Samuel Eno 23, 302–3, 335–6
Berman, Antoine 308, 312, 314
Biafran civil war of 179, 191–4
bio-politics 3, 9, 10, 22, 267&n1
   colonial attitudes to 22
   health and illness 21–2, 267
   and goal of optimization of life 22
Bloch, M 40–41, 86, 107n39, 211
Bokar, Tierno 308–10, 312
Boko Haram 7
   affiliation with global jihadist networks/Islamic State 179, 184, 202–4&n15, 205, 209
   comparison with MEND 179–80, 201–2, 208–9
   emergence/Salafist origins of 180, 182–3, 202, 204
   establishment of caliphate 179, 184, 195
Boko Haram insurgency 20, 180–81&n1, 186n4, 187, 189, 207–9, 211
   abduction of Chibok girls 183&pic, 205
   Abuja attacks 182, 184, 186, 203
   Bauchi uprising 203
   mortality and displacement figures 187, 203
   sectarian differences within 204–5&n16
   see also Islamist Nigeria
Botswana 66, 117, 251
'bottom of the pyramid' capitalism 216, 218, 222, 228, 231, 233–4, 342
   and extension of micro-finance 216, 223–4, 231
bourgeoisie 65, 109, 138, 191, 194, 220
bovine capital *see* cattle as currency
Brazil 94, 250
brideprice *see* bridewealth
bridewealth 16, 43, 64, 84, 86–8, 99, 108&n41
Britain/UK 93, 157, 160, 164
British colonialism 14, 22, 35, 48, 83–4, 100, 144–5, 146, 148
   indirect rule under 73, 267, 298
British Nonconformist Protestants 14, 35, 38, 51 *see also* Christian Nonconformist political economy; colonial evangelism
Buhari, Muhammadu 187, 329

Burchell, WJ 44–5, 48, 50
Butler, Judith 1, 5, 13, 17–19

Calabar Province, Nigeria 74, 76–7, 79, 81, 245
   Annang society 15, 72–3, 75, 83, 86–7
   see also man-leopard murders
Cameroon 183, 200, 243, 336, 349
   Bamiléké 107, 109&n43
   Beti group 109&n43, 110, 336
   gerontocratic structure of society in 16, 99–101
   Maka villages 93, 108, 111
   see also ivory trade: in Cameroon; rubber boom, German Kamerun
Campbell, J 44–5&n4, 46–7, 56
Cape Colony 45n3, 47, 49, 52, 55, 59, 62&n27
Cape Town 224–6, 228, 230–31
capitalism 14, 40, 43, 54, 65
   economic-institutional reality of 3–4, 7
   exploitative side of 54
   and growth of inequality 221–3
   industrial 41, 222
   racialized 149, 170
   see also global capitalism; labour: capitalist
capitalist modes of production 10, 41, 44, 58, 92
   classical/neoclassical 120, 124, 129, 296, 303
   Fordist/post-Fordist 151, 219–20, 233
   Keynesian/neo-Keynesian 122, 124, 129
   see also macroeconomic modelling
Castells, Manuel 2, 249
casualization *see* informalization
cattle
   as currency/wealth 14, 36, 42–3, 45–6, 52, 54–5, 58, 61–3, 65–6
   social and symbolic value of 42, 44–5, 48, 59–60, 62–5, 301
   see also Southern Tswana political economy: impact of rinderpest pandemic on
Césaire, Aimé 308, 315, 340
Chabal, Patrick 241, 248–9, 251, 345
Chad 117, 183, 204, 257
China 117, 119, 148, 232, 242
Christian Nonconformist political economy 35, 41, 53–5, 57

Index

charity as means of redistribution 41
and concept of moral economy 39, 41, 55–7, 64, 231
currencies of conversion/salvation in 14–15, 35–6, 38–40, 66
introduction of money/coinage 36, 45, 47, 51, 55–7, 64
involvement of missionaries in 38, 40–2, 47–54, 60
see also commodification: role of missionaries in
citizenship 22, 109, 149, 152, 202, 209, 287, 341
acquisition of 172
exclusionary notions of 148–9
industrial 210
insurgent 211
and national identity 294
rights 195
civil society 7, 40
activism 194, 247, 256–7*pic*, 328–9
class 191
black/African middle 20, 60, 233
coalitions/pacts 148, 180–81, 189–94, 328
conflict 188, 191, 204
inequalities 44
relations 10, 150–51, 189, 202
salaried 73, 79, 81–2, 88, 193, 220
see also bourgeoisie; working class
clientelism 180, 320, 323, 327–8 *see also* patronage
colonial conflict
anti-colonial resistance 35, 94, 97, 107, 137–8, 190, 209, 309–10, 346
in Nigeria 14, 72, 190, 206, 209
see also violence: colonial; Women's War (1929)
colonial economy 22, 65
and corrupting force of colonial market 39, 48, 53, 59
dependence on human labour 21–2, 37, 40, 46, 48, 59–60, 73, 82, 137, 144–5
relations of exploitation/appropriation in 15, 22, 24, 37, 48, 66, 95–6, 142–4, 232, 294
see also commensuration: in colonial economy; currency, colonial; rubber boom, German Kamerun; taxation, colonial systems of; Women's War (1929)

colonial evangelism 35–6, 42, 47–51, 53, 56–8, 60–61, 63, 65
'New System' Calvinism of 38, 65
impact on Southern Tswana 36, 42, 49, 59, 65
see also Christian Nonconformist political economy
colonial imagination 53, 146
colonialism 35, 220
African agency under 311–12
French 23, 92, 94, 96, 102, 106, 108n41, 110, 144–8, 310
modern 14, 24, 37
see also British colonialism; currency, colonial
colonization *see* colonialism
commensuration
in colonial economy 14, 35–7, 39, 60–61
currency as mechanism of 20, 35–7, 40
in Southern Tswana economy 14, 36, 60–66, 343–6
commodification 14, 36, 43, 54, 57
of African land 55
impact on health 53
of labour 55, 63–5, 136, 142, 144
of politics and society 14, 324
role of missionaries in 39, 50–52, 54–5, 57–8
see also commensuration
commoditization 86, 93, 107
of sex 55, 107n39, 110&n45
see also monetization
communalism 191–2
Congo Basin 16, 99
Congo colonies 16, 92–7, 102, 105, 107, 144
corruption 75, 125, 188, 196, 198, 201–2, 209, 320, 325–9 *see also under* colonial economy
Côte d'Ivoire 202, 249, 310
donzow hunters of 292n7, 296–7&n20
cultural capital 64, 225
cultural imperialism 57
and assimilation/Europeanization 302, 313–15
linguistic 312, 314–16, 339
currency, colonial 14, 47, 56
beads/buttons as 45&n3&4, 46–7, 50, 54–5, 57, 66
British 73, 77–8, 82

commodity theory of 39
and exchange rate fluctuations/
   instability 15, 64, 73, 75–7, 80–83,
   85, 87
historical evolution in Africa 13, 16,
   338
implications of instability for Africans
   13–15, 79
see also cattle: as currency/wealth;
   Christian Nonconformist political
   economy: currencies of conversion/
   salvation

debt 3, 10, 15, 60, 63, 84–5, 87–9
   bondage and pawning 142
   Native Courts and 74, 86
   and relations of trust 86, 100–101,
      292–3, 301&n25
   see also indebtedness
debt imperium, post-apartheid South
   Africa 5, 221–4
   debtor/creditor relations 20, 219–20,
      227–9, 230–31
   evictions of homeowners 230–31
   formal/informal lending institutions
      220, 229
   and Guyer's theory of deliberate
      incrementalism 40, 218, 228,
      230–32, 343
   impact of financialization on 218,
      222–4, 229, 234
   insurance racket and 40, 227–31, 234
   role of SA Reserve Bank in 223–4
   SaveAct programme 217–8&*pics*
   see also 'bottom of the pyramid'
      capitalism
deliberate incrementalism *see under*
   debt imperium, post-apartheid South
   Africa
democracy 3, 6, 22, 24, 148, 180, 250
   liberal 7
   transition to *see* democratization
   violent 199–200, 240
democratic life *see* democracy
Democratic Republic of Congo 116–7
democratization 63, 287
   in Nigeria 179–80, 190, 194–5
   in South Africa 216, 219, 221, 224,
      232–3
   see also Nigeria's Fourth Republic:
      search for democracy in
Desai, A 223, 229–30

development 1, 3, 10, 53, 117, 138n4,
   189–90, 219, 223, 226, 301n25
   capitalist 142, 147, 193
   challenges to 10, 128
   discordant 251
   economists/theorists 118–19
   failures of 20, 179, 187–8, 197–200,
      204, 208, 253, 320, 324–5, 328
   'Third World' 216, 251
   see also economic growth;
      underdevelopment
Diamond, Larry 318, 320–21, 328
dispossession 20, 61, 222, 228–9
   neoliberal 20, 199
   see also under Nigeria
Dominick, Hans 101–102

economic formalization 118–19, 129, 151
economic growth 9, 116, 119–20
   institutional factors 117
   natural resources and 116–17
   see also macroeconomics
elites/elitism 11, 148–9, 152, 189 *see also*
   African political elites
endogenous knowledge/endogeneity 117,
   121, 335, 338
Equatorial Africa 14–15, 92, 106, 144,
   302–3, 344
ethno-regionalism 192–3, 327
everydayness *see* political economy in
   Africa: everyday life perspective
exclusion *see* marginality/
   marginalization

Fashola, Raji 239, 253, 256, 258–9&*pic*
Fayemi, Kayode 248, 253
Federation of Informal Workers
   Organizations of Nigeria (FIWON) 256
finance capital 39, 194, 216, 222–3
First World War 76, 78
formal economic sector 2, 13, 149, 157,
   161
formal employment 151–2, 157
   linkages between informal and 115,
      158, 160–61
   place of documents in 158–9, 166–7
Foucault, Michel 3, 10, 267
France 145–8, 150, 222, 310 *see also*
   colonialism: French

Gabon 94, 117, 119
Galtung, Johan 248, 251

Index 357

Gbomo, Jomo 184, 205
gender relations 7, 75, 88–9
German Kamerun 92–110; *see also* violence, colonial
Germany 94, 97
  Hamburg 97–8, 103
  Reichstag (Berlin) 96–8
  see also rubber boom, German Kamerun
Ghana 242, 244, 251, 257, 298–9n21, 337
global capitalism 4, 7, 10, 18, 66, 138
  'bottom of the pyramid' argument 139n6, 216
  see also 'bottom of the pyramid' capitalism
global economic relations 17
  debt and 20, 221
  disparities 141
  interface with local processes 4, 6–10, 12, 16, 18, 20, 45, 138, 221–3
global economy 1–2, 9, 72
  financial crisis/recession 115, 119, 123–5, 138, 218, 221
  effectiveness of fiscal policies in 129
  see also African economies
Gold Coast 94, 145
Graeber, D 45–6, 288, 292, 301
Griqualand West 61
  Griqua community 44, 56, 58
Grootplaas farm, South Africa 157–9*pic*, 160–61, 164, 166–8*pic*, 169 *see also* migrant labour, border farms of South Africa
Gutkind, Peter 9, 241

Hage, Ghassan 1n2, 4
Hahnel, Robin 11, 25n15
Harms, RW 94, 99, 101
Hart, K 38–9
Harvey, D 222, 229
Hoffman, D 201, 209, 250, 330
Hountondji, Paulin 336, 338–9
household 135–6
  health 266
  impact of migrant labour system on 232–3
  labour 142
household economy 16, 51, 75, 119–20, 122–3, 126–7, 342
  and indebtedness 218–20, 228–9, 231, 233

Hull Matthew 19, 159, 170
human capital 116, 120–21, 126, 303
human production as source of value 19, 21, 38, 41–2
Human Rights Watch 161, 163, 198
Hull, Matthew S 19, 159, 166, 170

Ijaw, Niger Delta 185, 205
  Federated Niger Delta Ijaw Communities (FNDIC) 205
  Ijaw Youth Congress (IYC) 205–7
imperial domination *see* imperialism
imperialism 12, 66, 143–4, 309, 346
  conversion as key mechanism of 66, 346
  economic 36, 47, 52, 56, 101, 127, 288n3
  humane 41
  see also cultural imperialism
indebtedness 10, 30, 61
  and concept of credit apartheid 20, 218–21
  see also household economy: and indebtedness
inequality 250, 253, 315
  among Southern Tswana 44
  deepening/growing 151, 220–3, 233, 288n3, 326–8
informal sector/informality 2, 4, 7, 11, 139n5, 158–9, 210, 216, 218
  continuities with formal economy 4n4, 115, 152, 231, 233
  money lending institutions/credit schemes 220, 231
  role of 'big men' in 16, 92, 99–101, 103–5n34, 138–9
  savings clubs 229
  urban 138–9&n5, 242, 244, 247–8, 260, 342
  see also labour: informal
informal settlements 219, 225–6
informalization 21, 194, 240, 252
injustice 195, 220, 250
insurgence/insurgency 181, 346–7
  see also Boko Haram insurgency; Movement for the Emancipation of the Niger Delta
International Labour Organization (ILO) 144–5
  Decent Work Agenda 149–50
International Monetary Fund (IMF) 188, 198

Islamist Nigeria 209
   changing face of 199, 202–5
   hegemony of Sufi brotherhoods 183, 200, 204
   implementation of shari'a law 179–80, 182–3, 199–202, 204
   Islamic Movement for Nigeria (IMN) 182, 201
   opportunities for *yan boko* in 199, 209
   see also Boko Haram
ivory trade 16, 44–5, 48–9, 51–3, 58,
   in Cameroon 94–5, 99–100, 104–5

Jackson, Michael 5, 26, 335–6
James, Deborah 218, 220, 228
joblessness/job shedding *see* unemployment
Jonathan, Goodluck 184, 187, 189n8, 329
Joseph, Richard 251, 320, 322–3

kinship 11, 136, 142, 199, 301
   access to land through 147
   see also money: impact on kinship networks and exchanges
kos'ona miran see under rural economy
Kumar, Ajay 243–5
Kupolati, Chief GO 274–5&*pic*

labour 3, 10
   agricultural/farm 87, 145, 161
   capitalist 17–18, 136, 141
   child 41, 126, 151
   exchange value 41–2, 136
   forced/coerced 73, 93, 105–6, 141, 144–5, 163
   history 17, 59, 136–7, 140–41
   informal 11, 138–9
   interface of precarity and freedom with 6, 17–19, 140–42, 144–5, 148, 150, 152
   linking livelihood and dignity with 18, 26, 149–50
   mobilization 138, 140n7, 144–5, 149
   wage 18, 41, 46, 55, 59–3, 137–40, 144–5, 152, 160, 188, 232–3
   women's 75, 77, 137, 145
   see also Atlantic Slave Trade; colonial economy: dependence on human labour; informal sector/informality; proletarianization; vulnerability of human life

labour migration *see* migrant labour
labour organization/movement 137–8, 140, 148–9, 232
   minimum wage 137, 148, 161, 165
   protests/strikes 140, 151, 190, 321, 326–7, 329
   recognition/rights and 137, 146, 148
labour power 37, 42, 136, 142, 148, 150n19, 210, 303
Lagos, Nigeria
   Lagos State Transport Management Authority (LASTMA) 255, 257–8, 260
   transport crisis in 244–5&*pic*, 246, 253–5
   see also okada riders, Lagos
land/property rights
   impact of monetization on 85–6, 287
   and land claims 22, 206, 293–4, 298–9
land reform 219, 293
land seizure/expropriation 144, 220
land tenure 293–4
   Kenya's Swynnerton Plan 293&n14
   traditional systems 22, 293–4
lateral universality, concept of 23, 315–16, 339
Lazzarato, M 220, 223–4
League of Nations 144–5
Lefebvre, H 180–81
liberalization, financial/market 20, 163, 219, 229–30, 291n5
Liberia 142, 145, 242, 297–8
livelihood/s 5–6, 18, 149, 161–2, 195, 216, 255, 329
   informal strategies 158, 170
   rural 20, 170, 180
   sustainable 8, 261, 342, 344
   urban 20–21, 180, 243, 246, 248, 252, 257, 260
   women as means of 15
   see also labour
Livingstone, David 38, 45n4, 49, 51, 58
London Missionary Society (LMS) 38, 47n6, 49, 56
Lubeck, P 199, 202, 204
Lugard, Sir Frederick 77–8

macroeconomic modelling 116–21, 122–5, 128–9, 296, 303
   dynamic stochastic general equilibrium (DSGE) 122

Index

limitations/failure of 124–6, 128
and move to post-macroeconomics 116, 118, 123–4, 126
see also capitalist modes of production
macroeconomics 118
and endogenization of productivity 16, 116–17, 121
and issues of aggregation 120–3
and microeconomic heterogeneity 5, 7, 16–17, 24, 86, 118–23, 127–8, 342
see also marginal gains: macroeconomics of
Mali 150, 295, 299, 308
Sufi Order of Tijaniyya 23, 309–12
Malinvaud, E 126, 128
man-leopard murders (1943–48) 15, 72, 83, 88, 346
motives behind 84–5&*tab*, 86–8
Manchuelle, François 141, 148
Mandé hunters *see* Côte d'Ivoire: *donzow* hunters of
manilla currency 72–89; *see also* palm-oil economy
marginal gains
Guyer's concept of 12, 15, 92&n1, 216, 218, 232, 234, 288n3
macroeconomics of 115, 119, 122
marginal men *see okada* riders, Lagos
marginality/marginalization 22–3, 180, 189, 191, 201, 209–11, 294, 318, 337–8, 341–4
and concept of demarginalization 338–9
contingent 249–50
exploitation of 19, 249, 257–8, 318
of migrant farmworkers 158, 172
of youth 20, 180–81, 187, 200–1, 204–8, 251
systemic/hegemonic 249–50, 341
urban 21, 231, 239–40, 244, 248, 252, 257, 260–61
margins *see* marginality/marginalization
market value 19, 110, 231, 297, 300–301
see also production of history, market value of
markets 1–3, 5, 7, 40–1, 48, 56
domestic/local 11, 54–5, 58, 60–1, 64–5, 79, 108, 110
export 11, 180, 191
free/neoliberal 23, 39, 48–9, 145

global 7–8, 12, 20, 93, 160, 216, 220
Marx, Karl 21, 43, 47, 152
Capital 146–7
Marxist theory 1, 9, 11, 39, 42, 136–7, 142
post-Marxist arguments 36, 107n39
Maurer, Bill 6, 13, 20
Mbembe, Achille 9, 339, 345
McGovern, Mike 180, 195, 201–2
Mehretu, A 244, 249–51
Merleau-Ponty, M 315–6
Methodism 38–9, 41, 57
Wesleyan Methodist Missionary Society (WMMS) 49, 56
see also British Nonconformist Protestants
migrant labour 3, 17, 52, 59–60, 149, 151, 223, 232–3, 251, 293, 298, 342
migrant labour, border farms of South Africa 5, 163, 347
paternalist approach to 161, 164
permanent 60, 164, 169, 171–2
recruitment of 167–8&*pic*, 169–71
relations with police and border garrisons 162–3, 166, 170–71
seasonal 160, 162, 164–5, 167, 169–72
state institutional neglect of 160–62, 164
working/living conditions 157, 160–61, 164–5
migrant labour, navigation of formality in 18, 160–61, 163, 165, 168
role of documentation/paperwork 19, 157–9, 162, 164–7, 169–73, 342
see also Grootplaas farm, South Africa; Zimbabwean migrant workers in South Africa
migration 22, 140, 151
and concept of 'willing migrants' 18, 141, 143, 145, 147
role of *Mouride confrérie* in 150&n19
rural-urban 210, 224–5, 241–2, 253
see also migrant labour
militarization 191–3, 198, 206
demilitarization 205
Mkandawire, Thandika 1, 16, 116, 124
modernism 36, 46, 60, 65, 184, 343
modernity 7, 36, 41, 202, 211, 347
aporias of 19, 179, 198
Moffat, Mary 49–51, 55
Moffat, Robert 49–50, 55

Molema, Silas 42, 60, 62
monetization 57, 85–6, 108, 232
   and commoditization 93, 107n39, 110
   demonetization 73, 77, 79
money 7, 13–14, 12, 35, 39–40
   and African notions of worth 41, 46&n5, 47–8, 50, 54–5, 63–5
   and everyday fiscal life struggles 6, 11–15, 21–3, 25–6
   impact on kinship networks and exchanges 100, 107&n39, 108–10
   and undermining of traditional autonomy 63–5
   see also bridewealth; currency; Atlantic Africa: monetary transactions in; palm-oil economy; wealth
money as capital *see* finance capital
motorcycle taxis in African cities 241–2
   conflict with local government 242–4
   impact on everyday economy 243
   see also okada riders, Lagos
Movement for the Emancipation of the Niger Delta (MEND) 179–81, 186–7, 189, 201–2, 205–6, 208–9, 211
   attacks on oil infrastructure 184–5&*pic*
   counter-insurgency 185–6
   displacement/deaths caused by 186
   sectarian tendencies within 207
   see also Ijaw, Niger Delta

nationalism 179, 190, 198
   Irish Fenian 208, 210
   Italian Risorgimento 208, 210
Nattrass, N 160, 219
neoliberalism 1, 5–6, 8, 23, 199, 210, 248, 281
   and concept of economic inclusion 216, 218, 228
   in post-apartheid South Africa 20–21, 219, 224, 229, 231–2
   see also liberalization, financial/market; Structural Adjustment Programmes
neo-patrimonialism 1, 189, 320, 322 *see also* patrimonialism
niche economy 10, 137, 139, 234, 339, 344, 348 *see also* livelihood/s: sustainable; socioeconomic valuation and rationality
Niger Delta region 20, 72, 180, 184, 196, 199, 247
   environmental degradation in 5, 199, 205, 210
   ethnic vigilante groups in 206–9
   Kaiama declaration 205–6
   Maiduguri 182, 203
   multi-ethnic federalism of 72n2, 179, 188–90, 192–4, 196–7, 199, 205–6, 322, 327
   Niger Delta Avengers 187
   Niger Delta Development Commission (NDDC) 197
   politics of resource control in 179, 181, 184, 197, 201, 207–8
   Report of the Technical Committee of the Niger Delta (RTCND) 185
   Warri region 205–7
   see also Movement for the Emancipation of the Niger Delta insurgency
Nigeria 5–6, 19–20, 319
   developmental failures of 179–80, 187–8&n6
   First Republic of 190–91, 320–21
   Ibadan 17, 239, 274, 278, 319–20
   military rule in 191–2, 195, 198, 201, 240, 322–3
   National Union of Road Transport Workers 253
   politics of appropriation/dispossession in 193, 195–6, 198–9, 202
   Second Republic of 253, 320
   State Security Services (SSS) 184
   see also Atlantic Africa; Biafran civil war; Niger Delta region; Lagos, Nigeria; Yorubaland
Nigeria's Fourth Republic 193, 246, 323–5, 325–6
   People's Democratic Party (PDP) 194, 199, 258n6, 329
   rise of authoritarian leviathan in 187, 189, 192, 199, 201–2, 204
   search for democracy in 24–5, 199–201, 245, 250, 253, 318–21, 323–4, 327–30
   sectionalisation of political landscape 199, 324
   see also prebendalism in contemporary Nigeria
Nigeria's oil-based economy
   conflict/violence over unequal access to resources 180–1, 184–9, 193,

Index

196–7, 206–9
impact of currency devaluation on 240n1, 320, 345
politics of fiscal federalism in 179, 187–8, 193–4, 197
provisioning/protection pacts/coalitions in 180, 187–96, 198
state capture/centralization of oil rents 180, 188, 193, 195, 197, 200, 322, 325, 327–8
see also marginality/marginalization: of youth; patronage; prebendalism in contemporary Nigeria

objectification of value 14, 35–6, 43, 46, 54
okada riders, Lagos 5, 241*pic*, 257–61, 341
alliance with middle class 244, 256
Amalgamated Commercial Motorcycle Owners and Riders Association of Nigeria (ACCOMORAN) 21, 244, 246, 248
banning/restriction of 21, 239, 243–8, 254, 256–7, 259–60
clashes/conflict with state 246–8, 251–2, 256–7&*pic*, 258–260, 346
electoral value of 247–8, 250, 253, 258–9&*pic*, 261
everyday interactions of 255–6
see also resilience/persistence in African political economies: struggle/survival strategies of urban poor

palm-oil economy 74, 180
as determined by manilla/shilling exchange rate 14–15, 72–3, 77–8&*tab*, 79–81&*tab*, 83, 86–9
gendered aspect of 75–7, 79, 88–9, 346
impact of wartime economy on 82–3, 88
Manilla Currency (Amendment) Ordinance 82
Parry, J 40–41, 86, 107n39
patrimonialism 181, 194–5, 198, 308, 320, 322–3, 330
see also neo-patrimonialism
patronage 44, 64, 168, 187, 194, 198, 204, 253, 318–19, 326, 329
patron-client networks 24, 42–3, 52, 138, 150, 320–25, 327–8, 330
see also prebendalism in contemporary Nigeria; predatory economic order
Peel, Michael 247, 256
Petersen, Erich Robert 104–5
Philip, John 38, 45–6, 48, 51, 58
Pigozzi, BW 244, 249–51
Piketty, Thomas 221–2
Pithouse, R, 223, 229–30
Plaatje, Sol 46, 53
political economy, everyday life perspective 3–6, 8–10, 13, 17–19, 21, 25–6, 339
imagination/creativity in 5, 7–8, 12, 37, 66, 181, 341, 344
and health/disease 9–10, 19, 21–22, 267, 281
plight of young people in 17–18, 20, 180–81, 241
see also bio-politics; agency; rural econom; Nigeria's oil-based economy; resilience/persistence in African political economies
political violence 138, 162, 182–3, 189, 191
inter-ethnic 188–9, 191–2, 207, 209, 249
role of dispossession and *ressentiment* in 180–81, 193–6, 198, 199, 202
state/police 199, 201, 203–4, 242, 246–7, 250
see also Boko Haram insurgency; democracy: violent; Movement for the Emancipation of the Niger Delta; violence, relationship between poverty and
politics of governance 3, 7, 117, 267
centralization 180, 189, 192–3, 195, 197, 242, 326
decentralization 180, 199, 287, 323
politics of governance, local level 17, 242
centralization/decentralization 63, 207, 323
politics of life *see* bio-politics
Portugal/Portuguese 73, 143, 145
poverty alleviation 245, 248, 250, 260–61
power
implementation in economic life 2, 16, 44, 60, 62, 66
kinship from order of 181, 187, 189–90, 199

political 13, 63, 180, 191–2
power relations
  asymmetrical/unequal 19, 23, 63, 136, 142, 150–51, 170, 173, 309, 318–19
  colonial 23–4, 144, 152, 309
  externalization of 143
  see also gender relations
prebendalism in contemporary Nigeria 24, 194, 318–23, 325, 327–30 *see also* patronage
precariat 152, 210, 233
precarity 5–6
  and African originality 17, 25
  of everyday life in Nigeria 20, 179–81, 195, 201, 210–11
  existential 180, 208
  politics of 195, 201, 210–11
  temporal and spatial dimensions of 19, 21–2, 166–7, 179
  as reverse of stabilization 148–9
  of migrant/undocumented workers 140–41, 149–50, 152, 158–9, 162, 164, 166–7
  see also labour: interface of precarity and freedom with
predation *see* predatory economic order
predatory economic order 23, 26, 138, 180–81, 189, 227, 231, 320, 322–3
production of history, market value of 22–3, 287–8, 292–3
  antiquities/art works 288–9, 292, 295, 300
  competition over 301–302
  cultural activities 289–90
  historical knowledge 291, 294, 296–7, 301, 344
  historical sites/tourism/eco-tourism 290–91, 295–6
  power of secrecy 297–300, 302
  processes of interpretation/verification 300
proletarianization 10, 137–8, 146–7, 149
  of Southern Tswana 53, 59
property rights *see* land/property rights

Qatar 117, 119

Radcliff, Benjamin 1, 7
resilience/persistence in African political economies 2, 4, 7–9, 12, 23–4, 239, 318, 321

struggle/survival strategies of urban poor 21, 239–41, 243–4, 248–52, 255–6, 261, 341–2
see also household economy; rural economy
Richards, K 242, 254
rixdollar 47, 52, 56
Rohrbach, Paul 109–10n45
rubber boom, German Kamerun 15, 99, 101–2, 105–10, 342, 345
  dual trade forms (free/coercive) 16, 93–4, 97, 102–3, 105
  involvement of young men and elders in 16, 92–3, 97, 99–104&n34, 105
  trade monopolies in 94, 96–7
  role of intermediary traders/'trust' system 98, 100–106, 107n40
  Süd-Expedition 102, 105–6
  trade-back system 101, 103–4n34
  see also violence, colonial: German Kamerun
rubber trade, concessionary system 93
  Batanga-Firmen 94–6, 98–103, 107
  Gesellschaft Süd-Kamerun (GSK) 16, 94–7&n14, 98–102n29, 103–7
  Nieuwe Afrikaansche Handels-Vennootschap (NAHV) 95–6, 99
  Société Anonyme Belge pour le Commerce du Haut-Congo (SAB) 95–6, 99
rule of law 231, 323, 328
rural economy 7, 64, 319
  and concept of *kos'ona miran* (no other way) 5–6, 8, 24, 319
  and financial self-help schemes 218
  and rural-urban relationships 10–11, 17, 59, 137
  see also livelihoods: rural
Rwanda 239, 243, 249

sacred hunger, concept of 41, 54
scientific validity of economic methods 115, 118, 123, 125
Schapera, I 42–3, 52, 58, 63
Scheunemann, Hauptmann Peter 102–4
Sechele, Tswana chief 48, 51, 55
Second World War 87, 145, 148, 189–90, 249, 267, 347
Seekings, J 160, 219
Sembène, Ousmane 290, 300
Senegal 150&n19, 310–11, 315n3
Senghor, LS 315n3, 339, 341, 344

Index

separatism 181, 191–2
sexual violence 51, 183–4
Shekau, Abubakar 183, 203
Shell 185, 205–6
Shiller RJ 124–5
Sierra Leone 94, 206, 208–9&n19, 297
   Kuranko of 5
Simmel 39–40, 46, 57
Slater, D 187–90&n10, 192, 194
smallpox outbreaks, Ekiti, Nigeria 266
   colonial conceptualization of smallpox 266–7, 281
   colonial vaccination/prevention measures 268, 271–8&*pic*
   connection between measles and smallpox 279–80
   involvement of *olorisa* in 270–71, 274–5, 280
   Iye-Ekiti outbreak 267, 271, 274–6
   local resistance to colonial practices 274–6, 277–8, 281
   Sopona practices 268–70, 274, 276
   traditional beliefs about Sopona 22, 266–7, 273–4&n16, 276, 278–80
   Vaccination Ordinance 276–7, 281
Smith, Adam 38, 42, 127
Smith, Andrew 44, 47, 52
socioeconomic valuation and rationality 3, 7–8, 13, 15, 128, 194, 219, 339
   alternative forms of 6–8, 16, 93
   and bio-sociality 9, 21–2
   and Eurocentric perceptions of irrationality 6–7, 12, 125–6
   and human life/people 4–6, 10, 13–14, 302
   impact of historicity on 22–4, 288, 293
   interplay of church and business in 38–40
   and modalities of valuelessness 13
   role of currency/money in 16, 57–8, 89
   and formatting/composing of social relationships 3–4, 17, 42, 118, 136–7, 292–3
   see also production of history, market value of; wealth: in people, Guyer's concept of
Sokothi, Gugulethu (Gugs) 224–31
Sommers, LM 244, 249–51
South Africa, post-apartheid 6,
   African National Congress (ANC) in 225–6
   Democratic Alliance (DA) 226
   Department of Home Affairs 171–3
   Department of Labour 160–61
   legacy of racial Fordism in 219–20
   HIV/AIDS in 221, 231, 234
   Limpopo Province 157, 160–61, 166, 170
   protests against material deprivation in 219
   state distributional regime in 219
   xenophobia in 162, 226
   see also debt imperium, post-apartheid South Africa; migrant labour, border farms of South Africa; neoliberalism: in post-apartheid South Africa; Southern Tswana people
Southeast Asia 93, 189–90, 192
Southern Tswana political economy 14, 43
   agriculture and 58, 62
   impact of civilizing mission on 45, 48, 53–4, 65
   impact of diamond mining on 53, 56, 58–9
   impact of rinderpest pandemic on 61–2, 64
   notions of wealth/value 41–4, 46–7, 54–5
   role of trade/barter in 45–9, 51–2, 54–5, 57–8
   see also cattle; commensuration: in Southern Tswana economy
Sprigg, Sir Gordon 59, 61
Standing, G 210, 233
state territorialities 9, 11, 181, 193, 196, 207, 209
   traditional notions of 20
stockwealth *see* cattle: as currency/wealth
Structural Adjustment Programmes (SAP) 18, 149, 151, 240, 243, 293 *see also* neoliberalism
Sudan 117, 249, 301
Sy, Oumar 309, 311–12

taxation, colonial systems of 15, 63, 73, 76–7, 80, 89, 94, 102
   riots against 74–5, 79–80
   role of warrant chiefs 73, 75
   see also Women's War (1929)

The Economist 2&n3, 248
Tlhaping territory 44–5&n4, 49, 53, 55, 58
Tom, Ateke 207–8
traditional authority/rule 142–4, 182, 195, 289, 294n16, 299
   customary 199–200
   Tswana 51, 53, 62–3
traditional/sociocultural beliefs 251, 298
   about health 22, 266–7, 269, 276, 278–9n20, 280–81
translation
   cultural challenges of 309
   ethics of 308, 312, 314
   as form of anti-colonial resistance 309, 311–13
   Lord Macaulay's views on 313–14
   and mediation practices of interpreters, 311–13, 340
   of oral African literature 23, 308, 314–15
   and 'third space' of hybridity 23–4, 311, 340
   see also cultural imperialism: linguistic
Trouillot, Michel-Rolph 23–4, 293n11, 294, 297–8

underdevelopment 10, 12
unemployment 251
   Nigeria 187, 210, 243, 252
   South Africa 218–21, 224–7, 229
United Nations (UN) 182, 208
United States 148, 150–51, 157, 250
Unsworth, Barry 35, 41
urban renewal, need for 21, 253, 260
urbanization 11, 241, 248, 252, 255, 259

violence, colonial 62, 143, 145
   German Kamerun 16, 73, 92–5, 98, 101–3, 105–7, 110
   see also Women's War (1929)
violence, relationship between poverty and 17, 19–20, 75, 179, 181, 200–201, 257, 346 *see also* man-leopard murders; *okada* riders, Lagos: clashes/conflict with state
violence, structural 194, 248
von Hayek, Friedrich 16, 115
vulnerability of human life 1, 188n6, 216, 231

immigrants/displaced people 141, 150, 158, 162, 172
workers 19–20n12, 137, 139, 244, 249–50

wealth
   cultural constructions of 36, 41–2
   medieval European church on 40
   in people, Guyer's concept of 10–11, 14, 16, 36, 54, 93, 136, 228–9, 231, 303, 335–6
   Wesley on 39
   see also accumulation: of wealth
wealth in kine *see* cattle: as currency/wealth
Weber, M 40, 194
Wesley, John 38
   'mammon of unrighteousness' 39, 41, 54
West Africa 17, 35, 94, 143, 310
   currency of 73, 77–8, 80, 82
   oral tradition of 23, 308, 314
Wheelan, N 208, 210
Williams, Rev. H 61–4
Women's War (1929) 15, 72–4, 84, 88, 346
   causes of 75–7, 80–81
   commissions of enquiry into 75–6, 80
   mass violence during 74–5
Wookey, AJ 52–3, 58
working class 137, 139,
   black/African 59, 137, 233–4, 246
   colonial version of 146–7, 152
   and non-working class 149
   see also proletarianization
World Bank 16, 187–8, 198, 244
World War II *see* Second World War

xenophobia *see under* South Africa, post-apartheid

Yoruba/Yorubaland 10, 22, 268n2, 270
Yusuf, Mohamed 182–3, 202–4n16, 205

Zambia 18, 148–9
Zenker, Georg August 104, 106
Zimbabwe 162, 226, 340
Zimbabwean migrant workers in South Africa 19, 157–8, 160, 162–3, 166–9
   documentation of 171–3, 342